"The topic of this book is as important and timely as its contributions are expert and original. As the phenomenon of mass migration has come to increased prominence on the agenda of global public policy, so too the efforts made by states to control their borders, restrict immigration and engage in cross-border law–enforcement and surveillance have raised important questions about the negative effects on human rights protection of cooperative activities by states at a regional and global level. This book It offers an impressive and authoritative tour d'horizon of the key legal aspects, and as such is essential reading for policy makers, practitioners, academics and students working on the topic."

— *Ralph Wilde, Faculty of Laws, University College London, UK*

HUMAN RIGHTS AND THE DARK SIDE OF GLOBALISATION

This edited volume examines the continued viability of international human rights law in the context of growing transnational law enforcement. With states increasingly making use of global governance modes, core exercises of public authority, such as migration control, surveillance, detention and policing, are increasingly conducted extraterritorially, outsourced to foreign governments or delegated to non-state actors.

New forms of cooperation raise difficult questions about divided, shared and joint responsibility under international human rights law. At the same time, some governments engage in transnational law enforcement exactly to avoid such responsibilities, creatively seeking to navigate the complex, overlapping and sometimes unclear bodies of international law. As such, this volume argues that this area represents a particular dark side of globalisation, requiring both scholars and practitioners to revisit basic assumptions and legal strategies.

The volume will be of great interest to students, scholars and practitioners of international relations, human rights and public international law.

Thomas Gammeltoft-Hansen is Research Director at the Raoul Wallenberg Institute on Human Rights and Humanitarian Law in Lund, Honorary Professor of Law at Aarhus and member of the Danish Refugee Appeals Board.

Jens Vedsted-Hansen is Professor at the School of Law, Aarhus University, Denmark.

Routledge Studies in Human Rights

Series Editors: Mark Gibney, *UNC Asheville, USA,*
Thomas Gammeltoft-Hansen, *The Raoul Wallenberg Institute on Human Rights and Humanitarian Law, Sweden* and
Bonny Ibhawoh, *McMaster University, Canada*

www.routledge.com/series/RSIHR

The Routledge Human Rights series publishes high quality and cross-disciplinary scholarship on topics of key importance in human rights today. In a world where human rights are both celebrated and contested, this series is committed to create stronger links between disciplines and explore new methodological and theoretical approaches in human rights research. Aimed towards both scholars and human rights professionals, the series strives to provide both critical analysis and policy-oriented research in an accessible form. The series welcomes work on specific human rights issues as well as on cross-cutting themes and institutional perspectives.

HUMAN RIGHTS AND THE DARK SIDE OF GLOBALISATION

Transnational law enforcement and migration control

Edited by
Thomas Gammeltoft-Hansen
and Jens Vedsted-Hansen

 Routledge
Taylor & Francis Group

LONDON AND NEW YORK

First published 2017
by Routledge
2 Park Square, Milton Park, Abingdon, Oxon OX14 4RN

and by Routledge
711 Third Avenue, New York, NY 10017

Routledge is an imprint of the Taylor & Francis Group, an informa business

British Library Cataloguing in Publication Data
A catalogue record for this book is available from the British Library

Library of Congress Cataloging in Publication Data
Names: Gammeltoft-Hansen, Thomas, editor. | Vedsted-Hansen, Jens, editor.
Title: Human rights and the dark side of globalisation: transnational law
enforcement and migration control / edited by Thomas Gammeltoft-
Hansen and Jens Vedsted-Hansen.
Description: Abingdon; New York, NY: Routledge, 2016. |
Series: Routledge studies in human rights | Includes bibliographical references
and index.
Identifiers: LCCN 2016037868| ISBN 9781138222236 (hardback) |
ISBN 9781138222243 (pbk.) | ISBN 9781315408262 (ebook)
Subjects: LCSH: Human rights and international law. | Law enforcement –
International cooperation. | Exterritoriality. | Emigration and immigration –
Government policy.
Classification: LCC K3240 .H8544 2016 | DDC 341.4/8 – dc23
LC record available at https://lccn.loc.gov/2016037868

ISBN: 978-1-138-22223-6 (hbk)
ISBN: 978-1-138-22224-3 (pbk)
ISBN: 978-1-315-40826-2 (ebk)

Typeset in Bembo and Stone Sans
by Florence Production Ltd, Stoodleigh, Devon, UK

CONTENTS

CONTRIBUTORS

André Nollkaemper is Professor of Public International Law at the Faculty of Law at the University of Amsterdam and President of the European Society of International Law.

Birgit Feldtmann is Associate Professor at the Department of Law at University of Southern Denmark.

Douglas Guilfoyle is Associate Professor at the Faculty of Law at Monash University.

Efthymios Papastavridis is Adjunct Lecturer at the Democritus University of Thrace and Postdoctoral Researcher at the University of Oxford.

Elspeth Guild is Jean Monnet Professor ad personam at Queen Mary, University of London, and is Associate Senior Research Fellow at the Centre for European Policy Studies.

Fabiane Baxewanos is Research Fellow at the Department of Constitutional and Administrative Law at University of Vienna.

Jens Vedsted-Hansen is Professor at the School of Law, Aarhus University, and member of the Danish Refugee Appeals Board

Julian M. Lehmann is Research Associate at the Global Public Policy Institute, Berlin.

Maïté Fernandez is a lecturer and a PhD candidate at the Research Centre on Human Rights and Humanitarian Law of Panthéon-Assas University, Paris.

Mark Gibney is the Raoul Wallenberg Visiting Professor of Human Rights and Humanitarian Law at Lund University and the Raoul Wallenberg Institute.

Marko Milanovic is Associate Professor in Law at the University of Nottingham and member of the Executive Board of the European Society of International Law.

Melanie Fink is Ph.D. researcher at Leiden University and the University of Vienna.

Niels W. Frenzen is Clinical Professor of Law at the School of Law, University of Southern California, and is Director of the USC Law Immigration Clinic.

Nikolas Feith Tan is PhD researcher at Aarhus University and the Danish Institute for Human Rights.

Peter Vedel Kessing is Senior Researcher at the Danish Institute for Human Rights and member of the Danish Refugee Appeals Board.

Thomas Gammeltoft-Hansen is Research Director at the Raoul Wallenberg Institute for Human Rights and Humanitarian Law at Lund University and member of the Danish Refugee Appeals Board.

PREFACE

The core idea for this volume emerged at the workshop 'Human Rights and the Dark Side of Globalisation: Transnational Law Enforcement and Migration Control' held at the Danish Institute for Human Rights in December 2013. The discussions during this workshop were extraordinarily stimulating and several core insights were developed during the discussions that helped frame both the overall volume and subsequent editions of each chapter. In addition to the contributors to this volume, we are indebted to Daniel Augenstein, John Cerone, Cathryn Costello, Francois Crepeau, Gregor Noll, Sten Schaumburg-Müller, Isabelle Swerissen, Seline Trevisanut, Arne Vandenbogaerde, Wouter Vandenhoule and Ralph Wilde who all made valuable contributions at the workshop.

We would further like to thank Nikolas Feith Tan for taking on a substantive role in the editing process. Jytte Mønster, Helle Hjorth Christiansen and Lucy Seton-Watson have provided professional assistance in preparing the final manuscript. Last, but not least, Nicola Parkin, Emily Ross and Lydia de Cruz have provided impeccable editorial support.

Funding for this project has generously been provided by the Danish Council for Independent Research as well as 'Beyond Territoriality: Globalisation and Transnational Human Rights Obligations (GLOTHRO)' funded by the European Science Foundation.

This volume reflects the law as it stood, to the best of the authors' knowledge, on 1 May 2016. These areas of law are, however, still developing. Readers are advised to pay attention to more recent legislation and case law.

Thomas Gammeltoft-Hansen and Jens Vedsted-Hansen
Aarhus University, 7 June 2016

INTRODUCTION

Human rights in an age of international cooperation

Thomas Gammeltoft-Hansen and
Jens Vedsted-Hansen

I.1 Introduction

Our present era is characterised by an unprecedented degree of international cooperation, largely couched in the language of international law. Over the past century states have spun a web of bilateral and multilateral treaty law[1] and empowered international organisations and adjudicatory institutions, ceding and pooling sovereignty on issues hitherto strictly reserved for the domestic sphere.[2] The evolving system of human rights protection is a prime example. New norms and institutions have emerged to advance human rights protection, and several existing adjudicatory and supervisory mechanisms have been expanded and strengthened in recent decades.[3] States have willingly submitted themselves to this complex range of treaty norms, with treaty monitoring bodies and regional courts constantly developing and nuancing their interpretation.

Yet international cooperation has also facilitated new patterns of state governance that challenge the liberal world vision and undermine the effectiveness of human rights. Digital surveillance, offshore detention camps, drone attacks, rendition flights, extraterritorial migration control, anti-piracy operations and private military contractors are but a few examples. If there is one unifying factor between these different cases, it is that none of them seem to easily fit the traditional dictum that a state's executive power is to be exercised by its own officials within its territory.[4] This in turn raises tough questions about the reach and applicability of international human rights norms that, for all their universal aspirations, remain deeply vested in the Westphalian notion of state sovereignty.

For some time, these instances of what might collectively be termed *transnational law enforcement*[5] have been viewed as aberrations or exceptions, effectively creating 'legal black holes'.[6] This metaphor is misleading, however. First of all, there is nothing to suggest that these practices are isolated or exceptional. The number of situations where states are exercising their sovereign powers transnationally, jointly, or through private intermediaries has been steadily increasing.[7] As international cooperation and use of private contractors have developed, states are increasingly willing to outsource or internationalise core law enforcement issues, such as migration control, that would have been unthinkable just a few years ago. Technology has similarly opened new avenues, allowing states to share data, conduct mass surveillance, and initiate remote attacks.[8] Knowledge is shared in international networks of police and security professionals, and policies developed in one context often serve as inspiration in other areas.[9] Second, more often than not, these practices are themselves facilitated by bilateral or multilateral agreements. Rather, transnational law enforcement may be seen as a by-product of the international law of cooperation through which states seek to reassert regulatory capacity and control in areas where domestic action is either seen as insufficient or legally constrained, or both.[10]

The starting premise for this volume is that transnational law enforcement has become a systematic feature in today's world. For the reasons explained above, it is not likely to subside or disappear. The critical question to which this volume is addressed then becomes how can and should international human rights law respond to these new governance practices? Some responses have emerged already. A growing body of case law on extraterritorial application of human rights has developed and there is no shortage of scholarly doctrine to fill in the gaps.[11] Yet, contrary to what might be expected, this has not provided legal closure. Transnational law enforcement practices have instead continuously been refined and tweaked, often in direct response to legal injunctions. As we will argue, policy in these areas is characterised by 'creative legal thinking' on the part of states, and this requires human rights lawyers to think differently about how to approach this topic.

New forms of cooperation in turn raise additional difficult questions about divided, shared and joint responsibility under international human rights law, as well as the inter-operation of different legal regimes. Under what circumstances do states incur human rights responsibility when engaging in international cooperation on law enforcement? When assisting or aiding other states, or acting through international agencies and organisations? When enlisting the help of private companies? And how does international human rights law relate to other legal regimes, such as the law of the sea, international humanitarian law and the law on state responsibility? These questions are likely to represent the next frontier for adjudicators and hence require more scholarly attention. Moreover, the existing literature on these issues is fragmented in terms of addressing different aspects of transnational law enforcement in isolation. The present collection thus takes the reality of state practice as its starting point in bringing together different perspectives and issue areas related to transnational law enforcement. In doing so, we hope to paint the bigger picture and draw out common suggestions and answers.

To this end, the present chapter proceeds in three sections. In Section I.2 we argue that the drive towards transnational law enforcement is not only a response to new challenges and security threats, but also, and importantly, a reaction to the obligations imposed by international human rights law, which are perceived by states to prevent more effective responses. By geographically shifting or outsourcing law enforcement, sponsoring states believe that they can insulate themselves from legal liability. In that sense, transnational law enforcement may be described as 'the dark side of globalisation', aimed at reasserting state sovereignty and challenging the traditional, more liberal, view of the international law of cooperation.

How these practices impact human rights protection is the focus of Section I.3. Although human rights bodies have tried to respond, if often belatedly, to several of the challenges brought about by transnational law enforcement, legal clarity is still lacking in some areas. In addition, the constant developments in law enforcement practices raise a number of additional legal questions and practical challenges that have still to be answered. The dynamic development in this area demonstrates the normative game of cat-and-mouse played out between international human rights law and the policy practices of states.[12] Section I.4 outlines the structure of the remaining volume and summarises the main argument of each individual chapter.

I.2 Human rights and the dark side of globalisation

It is often assumed that economic and political globalisations tend to significantly reduce or modify the actual exercise of state sovereignty. On the one hand, states are faced with increasingly uncontrollable flows of capital, information and people. On the other hand, states have handed over more and more power and regulatory competences to international organisations and institutions, submitting themselves to a constantly expanding set of international legal commitments.[13]

There is a flipside to this dynamic, however. An often-overlooked aspect of this debate is the extent to which states, and especially more resourceful states, are themselves making increasing use of the possibilities afforded by processes linked to globalisation.[14] International cooperation itself has enabled de-territorialised and networked projections of power. For these states a variety of key interests are at stake, which may prompt attempts to regain control or exercise sovereign or *quasi-sovereign* executive powers in response to those globalisation processes that are undeniably challenging traditional state authority. At the same time, the more re-sourceful states are in possession of the political, economic and military potential necessary for the vindication of attributes of sovereign control and perhaps even global influence on certain policy matters. State sovereignty and governance is not simply being challenged by globalisation, it also appears to be fundamentally reconfiguring. Looking at the field of law enforcement today, exercises of public authority such as policing, surveillance, detention and migration control have each undergone certain transformations in terms of both the location and mode of their operation. Three common trends can be observed in the current exercise of transnational law enforcement today.

First, a common trend has been the use of extraterritorial locations – often referred to as *extraterritorialisation* or *jurisdiction shopping*.[15] Since the 1990s states have attempted to interdict migrants on the high seas, arguing that this nullified any right to claim asylum as a matter of international refugee law, since the asylum-seekers would never reach their territories.[16] Offshore law enforcement and detention has similarly been used to disclaim sovereign obligations in relation to domestic due process guarantees or international human rights. This may involve the concomitant commercialisation of sovereignty by the territorial state, as in the case of Guantanamo Bay, where a bilateral agreement is drawn up 'renting' parts of Cuban territory to the United States.[17] Less explicitly, Australia's agreements with Papua New Guinea and Nauru, effectively lease territory for the purposes of immigration detention.[18] At the multilateral level, such extraterritorialisation may involve more complex arrangements between multiple states, as in the case of the Central Intelligence Agency (CIA) rendition programme and international cooperation on data surveillance.[19]

A second form of international cooperation entails more hands-on involvement of partnering states, allowing sponsoring states to *outsource* certain law enforcement tasks. The United States has been known to send terrorist suspects to partner states in order to effect interrogations with techniques that would clearly be unlawful in the sponsoring state under both domestic and international law. In both the Pacific and in the Americas, deals have similarly been struck to involve third-state authorities in efforts to combat international crime, and in particular drug smuggling and piracy, thereby circumventing the obvious constraints posed by international law when intercepting suspected vessels on the high seas or carrying out raids inside the territory of another state. It may equally involve joint or concerted actions.[20] The use of ship-riders (bringing on board authorities of a territorial or neighbouring state) has thus become increasingly popular in the area of both migration control and efforts to stop drug smuggling.[21] Similarly, countries such as Denmark have routinely involved British soldiers when undertaking military patrols in Iraq in the attempt to avoid triggering any direct human rights obligations when taking persons into custody. Much the same is happening as part of European Union's border cooperation, where authorities of twenty-five member states are simultaneously empowered to enforce migration control along the Greek–Turkish border, yet Greek authorities embedded in all patrols in order to avoid any extraterritorial obligations in regard to asylum-seekers by the contributing states.

Third, states may implement transnational law enforcement by delegating authority to non-state actors. *Privatisation* of law enforcement functions is most commonly associated with private military companies, who have come to play an increasing role in international military operations and in anti-piracy operations.[22] But privatisation is equally rife in other areas of law enforcement.[23] Not least in migration management, where commercial actors today are involved in everything from visa processing to running offshore detention centres, carrying out extraterritorial border control and forced removals.[24] Similarly, several governments require commercial actors, such as internet providers and Google, to submit data and cooperate in regard to the interception of digital communication.[25] Law enforcement may equally be implemented through *international agencies and organisations*. As Fernandez outlines in this volume, European Union's border agency, Frontex, not only serves to coordinate the joint operations between the individual member states, it has also been authorised to deploy its own immigration officers to third countries, as well as to 'initiate and carry out joint operations'.[26] Relatedly, international organisations may also take on roles traditionally reserved for states. Thus in his chapter in this volume, Lehmann discusses the outsourcing of refugee protection by states to the UN refugee agency, United Nations High Commissioner for Refugees (UNHCR), as a form of 'protection elsewhere'.[27]

From an operational viewpoint the development of transnational law enforcement is often seen as direct response to new global threats.[28] Asymmetric warfare has prompted drone strikes, prolonged international policing missions are a consequence of the last decades' military interventions, home-grown terrorism necessitates surveillance, international anti-piracy operations protect the global shipping system and the threat from uncontrolled migration has led states to extend migration control around the world.[29] As Guilfoyle argues in his chapter in this volume, we may be seeing the emergence of a *transnational security state*. A process driven by professional networks of security and police practitioners, who in the face of new threats and various difficulties in mounting countermeasures have shifted from a hierarchical to a more networked logic, in which international governance forums become the primary forum for handling both individual and collective challenges.[30]

The allure of transnational law enforcement, however, may also partly stem from the way that such practices allow states to minimise or wholly circumvent correlate human rights obligations. By moving law enforcement outside their territorial jurisdiction, the applicability of both domestic and international human rights law is cast into doubt. In the case of international cooperation, outsourcing states further seek to engage the sovereignty of another country. Rather than arguing for a primarily territorial application of international human rights law – a claim that has been substantially challenged by recent jurisprudence – the logic of practices such as joint patrolling, ship-riders and other forms of third-country involvement is thus to activate the jurisdiction of a competing duty holder. The argument being that where actions are taken that solely or significantly involve the territory and/or personnel of another state, the sponsoring state itself is thereby relieved from any legal liability for the consequences.[31]

Moreover, transnational law enforcement entails a geographical distancing of what is often some of the more unpalatable aspects of state governance. Human rights victims – be they refugees, foreigners subjected to surveillance or the relatives of civilians killed during drone strikes – remain far away from the public eye of the sponsoring state. In the vast majority of cases, victims are unable to access any of the domestic remedies ordinarily available when human rights violations occur within the acting state's territorial jurisdiction, and it can be equally difficult to establish effective oversight.[32] Last, but not least, the potential of new technologies, such as drone strikes and digital surveillance can be difficult to fully understand and regulate, creating what has been called the 'fog of technology'.[33]

The difficulty of ensuring remedies and oversight, and of international human rights law to properly capture these practices, could of course be argued to be a mere side-effect of transnational law enforcement. International cooperation on these matters would likely occur whether or not this was the case. Yet it is hard to escape the sense that in several cases policies seem designed specifically to eclipse domestic or international legal constraints. States have repeatedly raised concerns that human rights obligations have become a straitjacket standing in the way of designing effective responses to immigration, terrorism and international security threats, and both courts and treaty monitoring bodies have been accused of 'judicial activism' when trying to ensure the continued effectiveness of international human rights law in these situations.[34] Some states have been quite open about their motivation to avoid or shift human rights responsibility when engaging in transnational law enforcement.[35] Similarly, in some areas law enforcement practices have clearly evolved in response to developments in legal interpretation, shifting maritime operations from the high seas to third-country territorial waters, or more actively involving foreign authorities and private contractors.

Common to many of the practices described in this volume is that states exhibit a degree of 'creative legal thinking'[36] to act at the fringes of international human rights law. Such policies tend to work in between the normative structures established by international human rights treaties, exploiting interpretative uncertainties, overlapping legal regimes, reverting on soft law standards or establishing novel categories and concepts on the basis of domestic or other parts of international law. This is not just a result of new governance patterns, but also of international law itself. As H. L. A. Hart famously noted, international obligations are by definition 'open-textured'.[37] Progressive developments in the form of soft law, adjudication and treaty codification are often assumed to remedy this problem by further clarifying interpretation. As international law has developed, however, this may equally work in reverse. The multiplication of legal regimes, overlapping jurisdictions and diffusion of authority also provides for more conflict and confusion at the normative level.[38] This in turn opens up an increased room for political manoeuvring in relation to international human rights law, where states are able to apply a pick-and-choose approach across different legal regimes, standards, and adjudicatory avenues.

These policies often seem to stand in stark contrast to the repeated rhetorical support to the relevant legal regimes by the very same governments. Importantly, however, such creative legal thinking is not tantamount to a rejection of international law as such – far from it. In most cases, shifting law enforcement to the high seas or foreign territory to avoid incurring correlate legal obligations *inter alia* presumes that such norms do actually, under ordinary circumstances, affect state action.[39] If governments felt they could simply disrespect international human rights law 'at home', then there would be little need to engage in cumbersome and often costly schemes to shift interrogations, detentions and migration control elsewhere. Yet it suggests that states may be developing a much more instrumental relationship to international law than traditionally assumed.[40]

The way that governments appear to respond to the duties imposed by international human rights law in this area may perhaps best be likened to the kind of strategies pursued by self-interested individuals and corporations to circumvent national tax laws.[41] Just as the Panama Papers have helped cast light on and document the extent of offshore practices as a structural element of the world economy today, increased international cooperation affords states with a wider transnational playing field. States applying a more 'managerial' logic in regard to their human rights obligations may thus seek to creatively navigate international law by strategically engaging in extraterritorialisation, international cooperation and privatisation.

In this light, transnational law enforcement may be thought to represent a kind of dark side to globalisation, through which states seek to reassert their sovereign authority in response to both global challenges and legal and political constraints. These policies all exploit areas where the applicability or division of legal norms is contested or institutional invisibility or distancing hamper the legal process. None of this conforms to the largely positive picture of the international law of cooperation painted by Wolfgang Friedmann and most liberal theories of international law.[42] Yet transnational law enforcement is not simply a sign of international law's inherent fungibility.[43] On the contrary, it could be seen as a reaction to the impositions and advances made by international human rights law and institutions in the first place. More important, international human rights law does not necessarily remain static in the process, and legal interpretation has equally developed to rein in these practices.

1.3 Implications for the international human rights regime

That states would someday reach out and do outside their territories what is prohibited inside them could hardly have been foreseen by the drafters to the current human rights treaties.[44] The major achievement of the human rights movement was to introduce to international law a set of norms that did not simply concern the *horizontal* relationship between states, but a *vertical* obligation between each state and its subjects and others within its territory and jurisdiction.[45] As Matthew Craven points out:

> The general problem . . . is that the international human rights project, far from being one that is essentially antithetical to the inter-state order, is one that relies upon a relatively sharp demarcation between respective realms of power and responsibility. Human rights obligations typically require not merely that states abstain from certain courses of action, but also act with 'due diligence' to protect individuals from others, and to progressively fulfil rights in certain circumstances. In order for these obligations to be in any way meaningful, some distinction has to be maintained between those contexts in which a state may reasonably be said to assume those responsibilities and those in which it does not.[46]

Even so, international human rights law has made substantial inroads to extend protection where states act extraterritorially. Several transnational law enforcement practices have, even if sometimes very belatedly, been successfully challenged, forcing states to abandon or substantially adjust their policies. Since 2001, when the European Court of Human Rights held that any extension of Convention rights beyond the territory required special justification,[47] subsequent jurisprudence has done nothing but systematically expand those exceptions. Today, there is a broad case law to extend human rights responsibility extraterritorially in a wide range of instances relevant to transnational law enforcement.[48] It is thus well-established that a state may exercise jurisdiction for human rights purposes as a result of military occupation and international policing operations,[49] where vessels are boarded or persons brought on board government vessels in international or foreign waters,[50] where individuals are apprehended or kidnapped in a third country,[51] or detained inside military bases, embassies or other facilities of the extraterritorially acting country.[52] Scholarship has equally assisted to clarify interpretation, not least as regards more specific issues and problems on which the authoritative solutions may have appeared inconsistent or untenable.[53]

Dynamic developments may equally be observed in specialised regimes, such as international refugee law. Most obligations under the 1951 Convention Relating to the Status of Refugees are explicitly reserved for refugees already within the territory of the asylum state. Yet for a few core rights, most notably the principle of *non-refoulement*, no geographical application is defined. This has led early scholars to insist on a similar territorial limitation,[54] an interpretation sustained by the United States Supreme Court ruling in *Sale*, thereby allowing the US Coastguard to continue its interdiction programme against Haitian refugees because the interceptions took place in international waters.[55] Over time, however, the dominant interpretation has developed to include not only application at the border, but also situations where states exercise extraterritorial jurisdiction on par with general human rights treaties.[56]

Last, but not least, attempts to write off human rights obligations through bilateral agreements or references to other regimes under international law have largely been struck down, at least in Europe. In *Al-Saadoon and Mufdhi*[57] the United Kingdom argued that a bilateral agreement with Iraq required it to transfer two detainees to the Iraqi authorities, regardless of any obligations under the European Convention of Human Rights. The Court replied that

> a Contracting Party is responsible under Article 1 of the Convention for all acts and omissions of its organs regardless of whether the act or omission in question was a consequence of domestic law or of the necessity to comply with international legal obligations.[58]

In *Hirsi*, concerning Italy's responsibility for migrants interdicted in international waters and returned to Libya, the Court similarly held that 'Italy cannot circumvent its "jurisdiction" under the Convention by describing the events at issue as rescue operations on the high seas'.[59]

Despite these positive contributions, interpretative uncertainties still persist in the context of transnational activities with crucial impact on various aspects of human rights protection. As pointed out by Marko Milanovic in this volume, adjudicators have struggled to find a coherent and suitable approach in many cases, and the existing jurisprudence on jurisdiction thus remains arbitrary and inchoate in several areas.[60] Compounding this problem, the European Court of Human Rights has insisted on preserving precedent regardless of the substantial interpretative developments, and thus consistently presented new rulings as being fully in line with past case law. As a result, we have yet to see *the* authoritative case on extraterritorial jurisdiction, and several contributors to this volume suggest that it is better to more fundamentally rethink the way this issue is approached.[61]

More importantly, judicial and other developments in the interpretation of this area may themselves drive and enable policy developments in this area in a more unfortunate way. Rather than simply accepting legal developments, states have instead opted to continuously adapt and modify their policies in an attempt to ensure their viability vis-à-vis international human rights law. This problem is compounded by the fact that adjudication of alleged human rights violations by definition takes place *ex post*, and hence the actual conduct of states may have evolved in the meantime. In many cases, the findings of monitoring bodies may thus be somewhat outdated already at the time of the pronouncement of their decisions or conclusions. In order to remain effective, human rights doctrine must become pre-emptive. Akin to Oliver Wendell Holmes' famous jurisprudential doctrine,[62] a *bad state theory* may be a necessary starting point for moving beyond the cat-and-mouse game between politics and law in this field and think about how to better address the way states act and respond to these aspects of international human rights law.

First and foremost, current developments are raising new and complex legal questions. So far the majority of cases involving extraterritorial human rights obligations have been directed against a single state. As Baxewanos asks in relation to the posting of immigration liaison officers, what happens when two or more states are acting jointly or in concert, as is increasingly the case? Even accepting a broader notion of extraterritorial obligations, jurisdiction is often approached as an all-or-nothing proposition.[63] Yet recent case law has accepted that jurisdiction may be 'divided and tailored',[64] and we need a better understanding of shared jurisdiction in order to hold states responsible for many forms of joint or collective law enforcement. And what about situations where the involvement of the transnationally acting state will not, under any meaningful reading, amount to jurisdiction? The principle of complicity is the subject of increasing scholarly interest and activity,[65] but has yet to find application in international human rights law. Likewise, there is little in the existing jurisprudence to take account of situations where states enact transnational law enforcement through commercial actors.[66]

Addressing these questions, human rights lawyers might look to general international law. It is a well-established principle that two or more states responsible for the same internationally wrongful act can both be held individually liable on the basis of their own conduct and international obligations.[67] The law on state responsibility similarly provides a possible road map for thinking about how other forms of responsibility, such as 'aiding and assisting' and attribution of conduct both in relations between states and in relation to non-state actors might meaningfully be applied in a human rights context.[68]

Such an approach may help break the mould in human rights scholarship doctrine. Since *Bankovic*, many human rights lawyers have vigorously defended the position that human rights jurisdiction and jurisdiction in public international law have nothing but the name in common: the latter is a question of legal entitlement, the former turns exclusively on the degree of *de facto* power exercised.[69] This position is understandable insomuch as a state's human rights obligations do not hinge on the permissibility of its actions.[70] Yet the two need not be mutually exclusive. Several cases affirm that human rights jurisdiction may flow from both *de facto* and *de jure* control,[71] and the interaction between public international law and human rights law has often been positive.[72] In *Al-Skeini*, the European Court of Human Rights thus held that the United Kingdom had jurisdiction in Iraq by virtue of the public powers it exercised by maintaining security in southeast Iraq.[73] As argued elsewhere, such an approach may serve as a particularly important basis from which to establish extraterritorial jurisdiction in cases where law enforcement cooperation is based on bilateral agreements or international mandates;[74] paraphrasing Scheinin, ought empowerment not create responsibility as well?

Similarly, a number of recent cases suggest that human rights jurisdiction may be established even when there is no evidence of ongoing direct or indirect control, but instead based on the extraterritorial *effects* of the rights-violating conduct.[75] This principle has similarly been expressed in other areas of public international law.[76] Yet for some reason this basis for jurisdiction has not been seriously pursued in human rights scholarship. In his chapter, Kessing demonstrates how such an approach may provide a stronger basis for ensuring state responsibility for contentious practices such as drone strikes and digital surveillance.[77]

A final set of challenges relate to the factual implications of transnational law enforcement, such as standing, evidence and access. Even when human rights norms are held to be applicable as a matter of principle to extraterritorial activities, this does not necessarily imply that their concrete applicability and their actual application are readily made subject to effective scrutiny by human rights monitoring bodies, whether domestic or international. In certain situations it is unclear who can and will be the *victims of human rights violations* in the context of transnational law enforcement. Precisely because this is about law enforcement, target persons affected by the executive measures carried out extraterritorially may be rather unlikely to identify themselves as victims of possible violations that occur in connection with, for example, irregular border crossing where they may be under the instruction by human smugglers to say nothing about the logistic manner in which they attempted to cross the borders and enter the territory.[78]

A related procedural hurdle to overcome is to provide the necessary *evidence of operative measures* taken by law enforcement agents in order to obtain a review of alleged human rights violations. This is often far more complicated than what is the case in more traditional law enforcement scenarios within the territory of the state prescribing and normally conducting enforcement measures. This may effectively render many transnational law enforcement operations invisible as far as scrutiny of human rights compliance is concerned. In situations where states are acting by proxy in terms of formally or *de facto* delegating law enforcement powers to non-state actors or third-state authorities, that may effectively create an evidentiary smokescreen institutionalised.[79]

An obvious example of evidentiary uncertainty, likely to render traditional perceptions of territorially based protection obligations and monitoring mechanisms more or less illusory, relates to the use of digital surveillance technology. We know that *interception of electronic communications* is a widely used transnational law enforcement measure, yet outsiders are unable to properly document how much data is being intercepted and how extensive and systematic these practices are.[80] Comparing with the approach taken by the European Court of Human Rights in previous cases concerning secret surveillance operations such as *Klass*,[81] *Liberty*[82] and *Weber and Saravia*,[83] it is clearly more difficult to establish the facts necessary to conduct judicial review of the human rights compatibility of the mass surveillance programmes run by the National Security Agency (NSA) or its European counterparts. And even where it is possible to initiate judicial review, the absence of any openly available legal basis for such surveillance programmes in many affected countries will significantly enhance the evidentiary problems. Last, but not least, the human rights challenges in this area are likely to be exacerbated by certain state representatives' resort to *plausible denial* of the existence of interception programmes, as well as the reasonable suspicion that such programmes have been conducted with tacit approval within the intelligence community.

In sum, it is crucial to make the principles of jurisdiction and state responsibility reflect the realities of current transnational law enforcement. This is not merely a matter of abstract interpretation of the relevant human rights treaties. Equally important, the effectiveness of human rights law require us to think about how victims and human rights advocates can tackle problems of access, evidence and standing. Failing that, we will be left with a *de facto* impunity for human rights violations, which is hard to reconcile with the basic tenets of human rights law, inasmuch as it essentially leaves executive powers able to act in any manner whatsoever without any real possibility of being held responsible by monitoring bodies at either the domestic or the international level.

I.4 Structure of the volume

The volume charts its course in three parts. Part I takes as its point of departure the current state of play in two key normative frameworks relevant to transnational law enforcement: the extraterritorial application of human rights law and the law on shared responsibility. In the opening chapter, André Nollkaemper sets out what he calls 'a relational understanding' of human rights responsibility. Drawing on both the law on state responsibility (including notions of 'derived responsibility', 'responsibility in connection with the acts of others' and 'complicity') as well as moral theory and legal philosophy, he argues that a broader understanding of shared responsibility is needed to reflect the growing number of situations where states engage in interdependent rather than independent courses of action. Such responsibility may be based on interdependence at different levels – obligations, conduct and outcomes – and involve different degrees of liability depending on the factual nature of cooperation in a given area.

In the following chapter, Marko Milanovic revisits the magic word 'jurisdiction', which remains the operative legal concept across most (but not all) human rights treaties. Laying bare the varied and often conflicting jurisprudence in regard to this single word, he provides an accessible primer to the various strands of existing jurisprudence, and outlines current and possible future challenges and the directions that the jurisprudence might take. Using armed conflict and extraterritorial electronic surveillance as cases, he argues that the jurisprudence on the extraterritorial application of human rights treaties would rest on more secure and principled foundations if it were to adopt a distinction between the negative obligation of states to respect human rights (which should be territorially unlimited) and the positive obligation to secure or ensure human rights (which would depend on territorial control).

Part II focuses on transnational law enforcement and security operations. Peter Vedel Kessing discusses the United States' use of armed drones in other states, for example Pakistan, Yemen and Somalia. Many commentators have argued that such strikes do not give rise to extraterritorial jurisdiction as a matter of international human rights law, since the responsible state in these situations neither exercises effective control over territory or over individuals. Yet as acts planned, controlled and carried out from a state's – that is the United States' – own territory, it is argued that drone strikes may be dealt with under the doctrine of extraterritorial *effect* of international human rights law. Locating this doctrine as a matter of both public international law and human rights case law, Kessing shows the wider potential of this approach for ensuring liability in a range of situations where acts carried out from the state's own territory lead to human rights violations within the territory of another state.

In the following chapter, Mark Gibney turns his analysis on to the international law implications of the revelations regarding NSA surveillance. With a particular focus on the right to privacy, this contribution examines US practice in light of the enormous growth of surveillance in the post-9/11 period. Gibney argues that the NSA surveillance programme directly challenges three essential principles of international law: sovereignty, jurisdiction and territory. The chapter concludes with the claim that NSA spying not only represents the 'darkest' side of globalisation, but also a perverted version of globalisation.

Moving to the maritime environment, Douglas Guilfoyle traces the rise of what he terms *the transnational security state*. In an era where it is common to talk of transnational threats and challenges, it seems increasingly apparent that territorial borders no longer provide meaningful security protection to states and their populations. The old assumption that power could be accumulated within exclusive territorial borders to preserve security against symmetrical actors has broken down in the world of transnational threats posed by asymmetrical non-state actors seen as challenging a state's autonomy: be they transnational terrorists, transnational criminals or other transnational actors (such as migrants). Taking migrant interdiction as his case, Guilfoyle shows how states are increasingly projecting their power into previously 'non-sovereign' spaces, such as the high seas, or the sovereign territory of other states. According to Guilfoyle, this is a process facilitated largely by transgovernmental networks of mid-level decision-makers, such as ad hoc working groups and technical experts, and that in this process issues about human rights responsibilities – in this context a fairly straightforward matter from a doctrinal standpoint – tend to be ignored or deconstructed.

The underlying question of Birgit Feldtmann's chapter is how the problem of piracy in the Horn of Africa region has been met by the international community and which legal challenges have been identified and addressed in this context. Based on an analysis of the legal framework for counter-piracy operations in international law, she depicts the co-relation between international law, domestic law and human rights law by an example taken from the Danish experience, the question of detention of suspected pirates on naval vessels and of subsequent legal control of such detention. This leads her to raising the question of which state(s) are able and willing to initiate criminal proceedings against the detained suspected pirates.

The final chapter in this part, by Efthymios Papastavridis, focuses on the obligation to perform rescue at sea by European authorities. In several reported incidents of migrants drowning in the Mediterranean authorities have clearly failed to act in order to rescue the migrants. This chapter discusses the broader responsibility for violations of international law, including both the law of the sea and human rights law, arising from such incidents in the Mediterranean Sea, and how this responsibility is distributed among different kinds of states and international organisations, such as NATO and the European Union.

Part III focuses on the increasing bilateral and multilateral cooperation in regard to migration control and refugee protection. Fabiane Baxewanos examines the case of immigration liaison officers (ILOs) as an example of the increasing extra-territorialisation of migration control. In her chapter, Baxewanos highlights the network of ILOs and the carrier sanctions scheme in operation under EU law, with an emphasis on how private actors are used to carry out migration control. The contribution argues that, extraterritoriality notwithstanding, states retain substantial means of influence triggering obligations under human rights and refugee law.

In his analysis of state responsibility in the context of migration control, Nikolas Feith Tan focuses on international cooperation with particular reference to the deterrence model employed by Australia, a state with a broad array of transnational law enforcement arrangements with nearby countries of origin and transit. The chapter defines such arrangements, designed to prevent access to asylum, as cooperative non-entrée, positing that these extraterritorial cooperation arrangements challenge the reach of human rights and refugee law. Tan considers two avenues to meet this challenge, namely extraterritorial human rights jurisdiction and complicity under the law of state responsibility. Despite the extraterritorial and transnational character of its cooperative non-entrée regime, it is concluded that Australia is not beyond the reach of international law.

Moving to more complicated forms of multilateral cooperation, Maïté Fernandez examines the international responsibility of member states during joint operations coordinated by the EU border agency, Frontex. Using a multiple responsibilities analysis, this chapter applies the concept of attribution as a matter of international law to Frontex-coordinated operations, and assesses the consequences for the allocation of international responsibilities under international human rights law. Fernandez finally suggests a framing of accountability aligned to the practical involvement and influence of actors within such operations.

Closely related, Melanie Fink, examines the difficulty in allocating responsibility for alleged human rights violations where two or more states are jointly engaged in transnational law enforcement, and the more general challenge to deal with multi-actor situations in the law of international responsibility. Taking as a case the Frontex-coordinated joint border control operations of the EU member states, she analyses third-party responsibility under international law and its relationship with functionally similar rules under the European Convention on Human Rights. She concludes that in several respects human rights law is more far-reaching in terms of the limits placed on third parties, even though the 'jurisdiction' requirement in many human rights treaties may render those limits less suitable in an extraterritorial context.

Niels Frenzen examines the first sea operation coordinated by Frontex, Joint Operation 'Hera', against the background of Spain's readmission agreements with multiple West African countries. Comparing with the efforts of Italy to stem migration by sea from North Africa, it is argued that the latter have not yielded the same results as Spain's migration control successes in West Africa. The practices of migration control that occurred in the context of Operation 'Hera', such as pre-departure arrests, maritime controls and pushbacks, are being analysed in the light of the European Court of Human Rights' 2012 judgement in *Hirsi Jamaa and Others* v. *Italy*, and Frenzen concludes that this judgement calls into question the legality of many of the control practices that unfolded during the 'Hera' Operation, including the practices engaged in by Spain and Frontex to intercept and turn back migrant boats off the West African coast. Raising broader questions of responsibility in regard to transnational migration control, Elspeth Guild asks whether EU border controls indirectly contribute to the rising number of migrant deaths in the Mediterranean. With a focus on old and new border control technologies, the chapter finds two main frameworks around border control in the European Union.

The first is the traditional approach of passports, visas and checks carried out by border guards at the external frontiers. The second is the use of biometric identifiers, electronic checks and satellite images at external frontiers. Guild argues that the rise of 'smarter' technologies against the relatively low numbers of irregular migrants is disproportionate to the issue of EU border controls.

The final chapter, by Julian Lehmann, focuses on transnational obligations in regard to refugee protection. Lehmann interrogates policies of 'protection elsewhere' through the prism of UNHCR. Lehmann documents how the rise of outsourcing practices has extended to actors other than states, including the UN refugee agency, now responsible for refugee status determination and the running of camps in various, mostly developing, countries. The contribution argues for a return to the 1951 Refugee Convention in assessing the legality of these 'protection elsewhere' measures, which provides compelling reasons against non-state actors affording refugee protection.

Notes

1   The UN Treaty Collection currently counts more than 158,000 treaties and subsequent actions. More than 6,000 multilateral treaties have been signed since the beginning of the twentieth century. Available online at http://treaties.un.org. Martti Koskenniemi, *From Apology to Utopia* (Cambridge: Cambridge University Press, 2006): 7; Charlotte Ku, *Global Governance and the Changing Face of International Law* (Yale University, CT: The Academic Council of the United Nations System, 2001).

2   Karen J. Alter, *The New Terrain of International Law: Courts, Politics, Rights* (Princeton, NJ: Princeton University Press, 2014); J. H. H. Weiler *et al.*, 'Special Issue: Changing Paradigms in International Law', *European Journal of International Law* 20 (2009): 21–109; Georges Abi-Saab, Laurence Boisson de Chazournes and Vera Gowlland-Debbas, *The international legal system in quest of equity and universality = L'ordre juridique international, un système en quête d'équité et universalité: liber amicorum Georges Abi-Saab* (The Hague: Kluwer Law International, 2001).

3   For example, the proliferation of individual communication mechanisms at UN treaty level.

4   *Case of the SS Lotus*. 7 September 1927. Permanent Court of International Justice. PCIJ Series A – No. 10, p 18. See also H. J. Morgenthau, 'The Problem of Sovereignty Reconsidered', *Columbia Law Review* 48 no. 3 (1948): 344.

5   We use the term transnational law enforcement to denote a broad range of activities through which law enforcement activities are carried out either by or on behalf of States beyond their borders. Some confusion in terms of terminology exists here, with some scholars preferring the terms *extraterritorial* or *offshore* activities. The term *transnational* was chosen to bring attention to the continuous link between the law enforcement activities themselves and the State acting transnationally. Further, we distinguish between the actual enforcement measures under examination and the establishment of legal liability under international human rights law, which may be based on different modes of responsibility, including extraterritorial jurisdiction, joint responsibility and responsibility for aiding and assisting. Cf. Mark Gibney, 'On Terminology: Extraterritorial Obligations', in *Global Justice, State Duties: The Extraterritorial Scope of Economic, Social and Cultural Rights in International Law*, eds M. Langford *et al.* (Cambridge: Cambridge University Press, 2013): 34, 38–42.

6   J. Steyn, 'Guantanamo Bay: The Legal Black Hole'. *The International and Comparative Law Quarterly* 53 no. 1 (2004): 1–15; Ronen Palan, *The Offshore World: Sovereign Markets, Virtual Places, and Nomad Millionaires* (Ithaca: Cornell University Press, 2003).

7 Sigrun Skogly and Mark Gibney, 'Transnational Human Rights Obligations'. *Human Rights Quarterly* 24 no. 3 (2002): 781–798; P. Alston, (ed.), *Non-State Actors and Human Rights* (Oxford: Oxford University Press, 2005); P. R. Verkuil, *Outsourcing Sovereignty: Why Privatisation of Government Functions Threatens Democracy and What We Can Do About it* (Cambridge: Cambridge University Press, 2007); André Nollkaemper and Dov Jacobs, 'Shared Responsibility in International Law: A Conceptual Framework', *Michigan Journal of International Law* 34 no. 2 (2013): 362.

8 Vedel Kessing, Milanovic and Gibney, this volume.

9 Guilfoyle, this volume.

10 S. Sakellaropoulos, 'Towards a Declining State? The Rise of the Headquarters State', *Science & Society* 71 no. 1 (2007): 7–32; W. Friedmann, *The Changing Structure of International Law* (London: Stevens & Sons, 1964); C. Leben, 'Symposium: The Changing Structure of International Law Revisited: By Way of Introduction', *European Journal of International Law* 8 no. 3 (1997): 399–408.

11 For major works in this area see Marko Milanovic, *Extraterritorial Application of Human Rights Treaties: Law, Principles, and Policy* (Oxford: Oxford University Press, 2011 and 2013); Mark Gibney and Sigrun Skogly, (eds), *Universal Human Rights and Extraterritorial Obligations* (Philadelphia, PA: University of Pennsylvania Press, 2010); Sigrun Skogly, *Beyond National Borders: States' Human Rights Obligations in International Cooperation* (Antwerp: Intersentia, 2006); Fons Coomans and Menno T. Kamminga, (eds), *Extra-territorial Application of Human Rights Treaties* (Antwerp: Intersentia, 2004).

12 Thomas Gammeltoft-Hansen (2013), 'International Refugee Law and Refugee Policy: The Case of Deterrence Policies', *Journal of Refugee Studies* 27 no. 4 (2014): 574–595.

13 J. A. Camilleri and J. Falk, *End of Sovereignty?: The Politics of a Shrinking and Fragmenting World* (Aldershot: Edward Elgar Publishing, 1992); Serge Sur, 'The State between Fragmentation and Globalization', *European Journal of International Law* 8 no. 3 (1997): 421–435; Susan Strange, *The Retreat of the State: The Diffusion of Power in the World Economy* (Cambridge: Cambridge University Press, 1996); Saskia Sassen, *Losing Control: Sovereignty in an Age of Globalisation* (New York: Columbia University Press, 1995); Gunther Teubner (ed.), *Global Law Without a State* (Dartmouth: Aldershot, 1997); L. Henkin, 'That "S" Word: Sovereignty, and Globalisation, and Human Rights, Et Cetera', *Fordham Law Review* 68 no. 1 (1999): 1–14; C. Clapham, 'Sovereignty and the Third World State', *Political Studies* 47 no. 3 (1999): 522.

14 Wouter Werner and Jaap De Wilde, 'The Endurance of Sovereignty', *European Journal of International Relations* 7 no. 3 (2001): 283–313; N. Walker, (ed.), *Sovereignty in Transition* (Oxford: Hart Publishing, 2003); R. Adler-Nissen and T. Gammeltoft-Hansen, (eds), *Sovereignty Games: Instrumentalizing State Sovereignty in Europe and Beyond* (New York: Palgrave Macmillan US, 2008).

15 Ronen Palan, 'Tax Havens and the Commercialization of State Sovereignty', *International Organization* 56 no. 1 (2002): 151–176.

16 Frenzen, this volume. See more generally Thomas Gammeltoft-Hansen, *Access to Asylum: International Refugee Law and the Globalisation of Migration Control* (Cambridge: Cambridge University Press, 2011).

17 Steyn, 'Guantanamo Bay', 1–15.

18 Regional Resettlement Arrangement between Australia and Papua New Guinea, 19 July 2013; Memorandum of Understanding between the Republic of Nauru and the Commonwealth of Australia, relating to the Transfer to and Assessment of Persons in Nauru, and Related Issues, 3 August 2013.

19 Gibney, this volume.

20 Feldtmann, this volume.

21 Guilfoyle, this volume.

22 Peter W. Singer, *Corporate Warriors: The Rise of the Privatized Military Industry* (Ithaca: Cornell University Press, 2003); S. Chesterman and C. Lehnardt, (eds), *From Mercenaries to Markets* (Oxford: Oxford University Press, 2007); Carsten Hoppe, 'Passing the Buck:

State Responsibility for Private Military Companies', *European Journal of International Law* 19 no. 5 (2008): 989–1014.

23   Alston, (ed.), *Non-State Actors*; Verkuil, *Outsourcing Sovereignty*.

24   Baxewanos, this volume. See more generally Thomas Gammeltoft-Hansen, 'Private Security and the Migration Control Industry', in *Routledge Handbook of Private Security*, ed. Rita Abrahamsen and Ann Leander (London: Routledge, 2015).

25   Gibney, this volume.

26   Regulation (EU) 1168/2011, (EC), amending Council Regulation (EC) 2007/2004, arts. 1, 3(b), establishing a European Agency for the Management of Operational Cooperation at the External Borders of the Member States of the European Union, 2004 O.J. (L349/1). Fernandez, this volume.

27   Lehmann, this volume.

28   Wilde, this volume; Didier Bigo, 'When Two Become One: Internal and External Securitisations in Europe', in *International Relations and the Politics of European Integration: Power, Security and Community*, ed. M. Kelstrup and M. C. Williams (London: Routledge, 2000): 171–205.

29   Guild, this volume.

30   Guilfoyle, this volume. On the transnationalisation of policing and security networks and the role of professionals see more generally Didier Bigo, *Polices en réseaux: L'expérience européenne* (Paris: Presses de Sciences Po, 1996); Didier Bigo, 'The Globalisation of (In)Security', *Traces* 3 (2003); Nadia Gerspacher and Benoît Dupont, 'The Nodal Structure of International Police Cooperation: An Exploration of Transnational Security Networks', *Global Governance* 13 no. 3 (2007): 347–364; Anna Leander and Tanja Aalberts, 'Introduction: The Co Constitution of Legal Expertise and International Security', *Leiden Journal of International Law* 26 no. 4 (2013): 783–792; D. Kennedy, 'Challenging Expert Rule: The Politics of Global Governance', *Sydney Law Review* 27 no. 1 (2005): 5.

31   Thomas Gammeltoft-Hansen and James C. Hathaway, 'Non-Refoulement in a World of Cooperative Deterrence', *Columbia Journal of Transnational Law* 53 no. 2 (2015): 244.

32   See further Section II.

33   Duncan Hollis, 'The Fog of Technology and International Law', *Opinio Juris*, 15 May 2015. For a contrary perspective, arguing that e.g. drone technology presents new possibilities for estimating the risk of civilian casualties and hence lift the 'fog of war', see Frederik Rosén, 'Extremely Stealthy and Incredibly Close: Drones, Control and Legal Responsibility', *Journal of Conflict and Security Law* 19 no. 1 (2013): 113–131.

34   Jonas Christoffersen and Mikael Rask Madsen, *The European Court of Human Rights between Law and Politics* (Oxford: Oxford University Press, 2011); J. S. Watson, *Theory and Reality in the International Protection of Human Rights* (New York: Transnational Publishers, 1999).

35   See e.g. UK Home Office, New Vision for Refugees, (7 March 2003).

36   Thomas Gammeltoft-Hansen, ' "Creative Legal thinking" and the Evolution of International Refugee Law', *Lakimies* 112 no. 1 (2013): 99.

37   H. L. A. Hart, *The Concept of Law* (Oxford: Clarendon Press, 1961): 121–144; Brian Bix, 'H. L. A. Hart and the "Open Texture" of Language', *Law and Philosophy* 10 no. 1 (1991): 51–72.

38   Andreas Fischer-Lescano and Gunther Teubner, 'Regime-Collisions: The Vain Search for Legal Unity in the Fragmentation of Global Law', *Michigan Journal of International Law* 25 no. 4 (2004): 999–1046; Martti Koskenniemi, 'The Fate of Public International Law: Between Technique and Politics', *Modern Law Review* 70 no. 1 (2007): 1–30; Margaret Young, (ed.), *Regime Interaction in International Law: Facing Fragmentation* (Cambridge: Cambridge University Press, 2012); Alter, *The New Terrain of International Law*.

39   See Wilde, this volume.

40   Tanja Aalberts and Thomas Gammeltoft-Hansen, (eds), *The Changing Practices of International Law* (Forthcoming 2016).

41 Itamar Mann, 'Dialectic of Transnationalism: Unauthorised Migration and Human Rights, 1993–2013', *Harvard International Law Journal* 54 no. 2 (2013): 366; Thomas Gammeltoft-Hansen, 'International Refugee Law and Refugee Policy'.

42 Friedmann, *The Changing Structure of International Law*; Leben, 'Symposium'.

43 Koskenniemi, *From Apology to Utopia*.

44 L. Henkin, 'Notes from the President', *American Society of International Law Newsletter* (Sept.–Oct. 1993): 1. See further *Legal Consequences of the Construction of a Wall in the Occupied Palestinian Territory*, Advisory Opinion, ICJ 131, 9 July 2004, par. 109.

45 H. Steiner, 'International Protection of Human Rights', in *International Law*, ed. M. D. Evans, 2nd edn (Oxford: Oxford University Press, 2006): 769; Skogly and Gibney, 'Transnational Human Rights Obligations', 782.

46 M. Craven, 'Human Rights in the Realm of Order: Sanctions and Extraterritoriality', in *Extraterritorial Application of Human Rights Treaties*, ed. F. Coomans and M. T. Kamminga (Antwerp: Intersentia, 2004): 255.

47 *Bankovic and Others v. Belgium and Others*. European Court of Human Rights. Appl. No. 5207/99. 12 December 2001, par. 61.

48 For a general overview of this area, see Milanovic, this volume.

49 *Isaak and Others v. Turkey*. European Court of Human Rights. Appl. No. 44587/98. 28 September 2006 (admissibility); *Solomou v. Turkey*. European Court of Human Rights. Appl. No. 36832/97. 24 June 2008 (merits); *Al-Skeini and Others v. United Kingdom*. European Court of Human Rights. Appl. No. 55721/07. 7 July 2011.

50 *J.H.A v. Spain*. Committee Against Torture. CAT/C/41/D/323/2007. 21 November 2008; *Medvedyev and Others v. France*. European Court of Human Rights. Appl. No. 3394/03. 29 March 2010; *Hirsi Jamaa and Others v. Italy*. European Court of Human Rights. Appl. No. 27765/09. 23 February 2012.

51 *Lopez Burgos v. Uruguay*. Human Rights Committee. UN Doc. A/36/40. 6 June 1979; *Lilian Celiberti de Casariego v. Uruguay*. Human Rights Committee. UN Doc. CCPR/C/OP/1. 29 July 1981; *Reinette v. France*. European Court of Human Rights. Appl. No. 14009/88. 2 October 1989; *Ramirez Sánchez v. France*. European Commission of Human Rights. Appl. No. 28780/95. 24 June 1996; *Ocalan v. Turkey*. European Court of Human Rights. Appl. No. 46221/99. 12 March 2003; *El-Masri v. The Former Yugoslav Republic of Macedonia*. European Court of Human Rights, Appl. No. 39630/09. 13 December 2012.

52 *W.M. v. Denmark*. European Commission of Human Rights. Appl. No. 17393/90. 14 October 1992; *Al-Skeini and others v. Secretary of State for Defence*. House of Lords. UKHL 26. 13 June 2006; *J.H.A v. Spain*. Committee Against Torture. CAT/C/41/D/ 323/2007. 21 November 2008.

53 The literature on extraterritorial human rights obligations alone is extensive. Some important contributions include, Theodor Meron, 'Extraterritoriality of Human Rights Treaties', *American Journal of International Law* 89 (1995): 78–82; Mark Gibney, Katarina Tomaševski and Jens Vedsted-Hansen, 'Transnational State Responsibility for Violations of Human Rights', *Harvard Human Rights Journal* 12 (1999): 267–295; F. Coomans and M. T. Kamminga, (eds), *Extraterritorial Application of Human Rights Treaties*; Ralph Wilde, 'Legal "Black Hole"?: Extraterritorial State Action and International Treaty Law on Civil and Political Rights', *Michigan Journal of International Law* 26 no. 3 (2005): 739–806; Gibney and Skogly, (eds), *Universal Human Rights and Extraterritorial Obligations*; Marko Milanovic, *Extraterritorial Application of Human Rights Treaties Principles, and Policy*; Malcolm Langford et al., (eds), *Global Justice, State Duties: The Extraterritorial Scope of Economic, Social and Cultural Rights in International Law* (Cambridge: Cambridge University Press, 2013).

54 N. Robinson, *Convention Relating to the Status of Refugees: Its History, Contents and Interpretation: A Commentary* (New York: Institute for Jewish Affairs, World Jewish Congress, 1953): 163; A. Grahl-Madsen, *Commentary on the Refugee Convention 1951 Articles 2–11, 13–37* (Geneva: Division of International Protection of the United Nations High Commissioner for Refugees, 1963 (republished 1997)).

55 *Sale, Acting Cmmr, Immigration and Naturalisation Service v. Haitian Center Council.* United States Supreme Court. 113 S.Ct. 2549, 509 US 155.
56 UNHCR, 'Advisory Opinion on the Extraterritorial Application of Non-Refoulement Obligations under the 1951 Convention relating to the Status of Refugees and its 1967 Protocol', 26 January 2007. For an overview of scholarly positions, see Gammeltoft-Hansen, *Access to Asylum*, 44ff. This has equally been confirmed by case law, see notably *Haitian Center for Human Rights v. United States* ('*US Interdiction of Haitians on the High Seas*'), Inter-American Commission of Human Rights. Case 10.675. 13 March 1997; *Plaintiff M61 and Plaintiff M69 v. Commonwealth of Australia* [2010] HCA 41, 11 November 2010; *Hirsi Jamaa and Others v. Italy.* European Court of Human Rights. Appl. No. 27765/09. 23 February 2012. In a separate opinion to the latter case, Judge Pinto de Albuquerque even observed that 'the United States Supreme Court's interpretation contradicts the literal and ordinary meaning of Article 33 of the UN Refugee Convention and departs from the common rules of treaty interpretation'. (para. 66, separate opinion).
57 *Al-Saadoon and Mufdhi v. United Kingdom.* European Court of Human Rights. Appl. No. 61498/08. 2 March 2010.
58 Ibid., par. 128.
59 *Hirsi Jamaa and Others v. Italy.* European Court of Human Rights. Appl. No. 27765/09. 23 February 2012, par. 79. See further Papastavridis, this volume.
60 Milanovic, this volume.
61 See in particular the chapters by Milanovic, and Kessing, this volume.
62 Oliver Wendell Holmes Jr, 'The Path of the Law', *Harvard Law Review* 10 (1897): 457–461.
63 *Bankovic*, par. 71; *Hess v. the United Kingdom*, European Commission of Human Rights, Appl. No. 6231/73. 28 May 1975, Decisions & Reports vol. 2, p. 72.
64 *Al-Skeini*, par. 137; *Hirsi*, par. 74.
65 See for example, Helmut Philipp Aust, *Complicity and the Law of State Responsibility* (Cambridge: Cambridge University Press, 2011).
66 As a possible example, see *Stocke v. Germany.* European Court of Human Rights. Series A, No. 199. 19 March 1991.
67 *Certain Phosphate Lands in Nauru (Nauru v. Australia), Preliminary Objections.* International Court of Justice, 26 June 1992; *East Timor (Portugal v. Australia).* International Court of Justice. ICJ Reports 1995. 30 June 1995; *Corfu Channel Case.* International Court of Justice. ICJ Reports 1949. 9 April 1949. See further International Law Commission, *Articles on the Responsibility of States for Internationally Wrongful Acts*, art. 47, UN Doc. A/56/10; GAOR, 56th Sess., Supp. No. 10 (2001); André Nollkaemper and Dov Jacobs, *State responsibility: An Appraisal of the State of the Art* (Cambridge: Cambridge University Press, 2014); James Crawford, *State Responsibility: The General Part* (Cambridge: Cambridge University Press, 2013): 325:28, 333:34.
68 See in particular the chapters by Nollkaemper, Fink, and Tan in this volume. See further *Articles on the Responsibility*, arts. 5, 8 and 16; Marko Milanovic, 'State Responsibility for Genocide: A Follow-Up', *European Journal of International Law* 18 no. 4 (2007): 669–694; Aust, *Complicity and the Law of State responsibility*.
69 Milanovic, *Extraterritorial Application of Human Rights Treaties*, 199–207; Martin Scheinin, 'Extraterritorial Effect of the International Covenant on Civil and Political Rights', in *Extraterritorial Application of Human Rights Treaties*, ed. Fons Coomans and Menno T. Kamminga (Antwerp: Intersentia, 2004): 78.
70 Or as Scheinin puts it, 'facticity creates normativity', ibid., 75–76. This was clearly established by the Human Rights Committee in *Lopez Burgos*, pointing out that extraterritorial jurisdiction may be triggered solely based on the degree of factual control or authority asserted over the individual in question, *Lopez Burgos v. Uruguay.* Human Rights Committee. UN Doc. A/36/40. 6 June 1979, par. 12.3 as well as the separate opinion by Christian Tomuschat.

71 See e.g. *Armando Alejandre Jr. and Others v. Cuba* ('*Brothers to the Rescue*'). Inter-American Commission for Human Rights. Case 11.589. 29 September 1999; *Medvedyev*, par. 61; and *Hirsi*, par. 80.

72 Loukis Loucaides, 'Determining the Extraterritorial Effect of the European Convention: Facts, Jurisprudence and the *Bankovic* Case', *European Human Rights Law Review* 4 (2006): 393–394; Hugh King, 'The Extraterritorial Human Rights Obligations of States', *Human Rights Law Review* 9 no. 4 (2009): 521–556.

73 *Al-Skeini*, par. 135.

74 Gammeltoft-Hansen and Hathaway, 'Non-Refoulement in a World of Cooperative Deterrence', 32ff. See further Papastavridis, this volume.

75 *Georgia Andreou v. Turkey*. European Court of Human Rights. Appl. No. 45653/99. 3 June 2008 (admissibility); *Solomou v. Turkey*. European Court of Human Rights. Appl. No. 36832/97. 18 May 1999 (admissibility); *Isaak and Others v. Turkey*. European Court of Human Rights. Appl. No. 44587/98. 28 September 2006 (admissibility); *Pad and Others v. Turkey*. European Court of Human Rights. Appl. No. 60167/00. 28 June 2007.

76 *Trail Smelter Arbitral Decision (United States v. Canada)*. Trail Smelter Arbitral Tribunal. Reports of International Arbitral Awards 3 1938. 1941, p. 1965. For a more contemporary affirmation of this principle see further *Legality of the Threat or Use of Nuclear Weapons, Advisory Opinion*. International Court of Justice. 8 July 1996, par. 29.

77 Kessing, this volume.

78 For a concrete illustration, see the 'left-to-die' boat incident in Papastavridis, this volume. For a more general treatment of this issue in the context of transnational migration control, see Gammeltoft-Hansen, *Access to Asylum*, ch. 6.

79 For illustration, even within the formal framework of an international human rights monitoring body, see *J.H.A. v. Spain*, Committee Against Torture, CAT/C/41/D/323/2007, 21 November 2008, concerning the detention of twenty-three Indian immigrants detained in Mauritania under Spanish control. The detention followed their transfer from the cargo vessel *Marine I* upon the arrival of a Spanish maritime vessel due to a distress call from *Marine I*. The Committee considered that the alleged victims were subject to Spanish jurisdiction insofar as the complaint forming the subject of the communication was concerned, but held the communication inadmissible due to the complainant's lack of competence to act on behalf of the alleged victims, cf. paras 8.2 and 8.3 of the Committee Decision.

80 See Gibney, this volume.

81 *Klass and Others v. Germany*, European Court of Human Rights, Appl. No. 5029/71. 6 September 1978.

82 *Liberty and Others v. United Kingdom*, European Court of Human Rights, Appl. No. 58243/00. 1 July 2008.

83 *Weber and Saravia v. Germany*, European Court of Human Rights, Appl. No. 54934/00. 29 June 2006.

Bibliography

Aalberts, Tanja, and Thomas Gammeltoft-Hansen, (eds). *The Changing Practices of International Law*. Forthcoming 2016.

Abi-Saab, Georges, Laurence Boisson de Chazournes and Vera Gowlland-Debbas. *The international legal system in quest of equity and universality = L'ordre juridique international, un système en quête d'équité et universalité: liber amicorum Georges Abi-Saab*. The Hague: Kluwer Law International, 2001.

Adler-Nissen, Rebbeca, and Thomas Gammeltoft-Hansen, (eds). *Sovereignty Games: Instrumentalizing State Sovereignty in Europe and Beyond*. New York: Palgrave Macmillan US, 2008.

Alston, Philip, (ed.). *Non-State Actors and Human Rights*. Oxford: Oxford University Press, 2005.

Alter, Karen J. *The New Terrain of International Law: Courts, Politics, Rights*. Princeton, NJ: Princeton University Press, 2014.

Aust, Helmut Philipp. *Complicity and the Law of State Responsibility*. Cambridge: Cambridge University Press, 2011.

Bigo, Didier. *Polices en réseaux: L'expérience européenne*. Paris: Presses de Sciences Po, 1996.

Bigo, Didier. 'When Two Become One: Internal and External Securitisations in Europe'. In *International relations theory and the politics of European integration: Power, security and community*, ed. M. Kelstrup and M. C. Williams, 171–205. London: Routledge, 2000.

Bigo, Didier. 'The Globalisation of (In)Security'. *Traces* 3 (2003).

Bix, Brian. 'H. L. A. Hart and the "Open Texture" of Language'. *Law and Philosophy* 10 no. 1 (1991): 51–72.

Camilleri, Joseph A., and Jim Falk. *The End of Sovereignty?: The Politics of a Shrinking and Fragmenting World*. Aldershot: Edward Elgar Publishing, 1992.

Chesterman, Simon, and Chia Lehnardt, (eds). *From Mercenaries to Market*. Oxford: Oxford University Press, 2007.

Christoffersen, Jonas, and Mikael Rask Madsen. *The European Court of Human Rights between Law and Politics*. Oxford: Oxford University Press, 2011.

Clapham, Christopher. 'Sovereignty and the Third World State'. *Political Studies* 47 no. 3 (1999): 522–537.

Coomans, Fons, and Menno T. Kamminga, (eds). *Extraterritorial Application of Human Rights Treaties*. Antwerp: Intersentia, 2004.

Craven, Matthew. 'Human Rights in the Realm of Order: Sanctions and Extraterritoriality'. In *Extraterritorial Application of Human Rights Treaties*, ed. F. Coomans and M. T. Kamminga, 233–257. Antwerp: Intersentia, 2004.

Crawford, James. *State Responsibility: The General Part*. Cambridge: Cambridge University Press, 2013.

Fischer-Lescano, Andreas, and Gunther Teubner. 'Regime-Collisions: The Vain Search for Legal Unity in the Fragmentation of Global Law'. *Michigan Journal of International Law* 25 no. 4 (2004): 999–1046.

Friedmann, Wolfgang. *The Changing Structure of International Law*. London: Stevens & Sons, 1964.

Gammeltoft-Hansen, Thomas. *Access to Asylum: International Refugee Law and the Globalisation of Migration Control*. Cambridge: Cambridge University Press, 2011.

Gammeltoft-Hansen, Thomas. '"Creative Legal Thinking" and the Evolution of International Refugee Law'. *Lakimies* 112 no. 1 (2013): 99–103.

Gammeltoft-Hansen, Thomas. 'International Refugee Law and Refugee Policy: The Case of Deterrence Policies'. *Journal of Refugee Studies* 27 no. 4 (2014): 574–595.

Gammeltoft-Hansen, Thomas. 'Private Security and the Migration Control Industry'. In *Routledge Handbook of Private Security Studies*, eds R. Abrahamsen and A. Leander, 207–216. London: Routledge, 2015.

Gammeltoft-Hansen, Thomas, and James C. Hathaway. 'Non-Refoulement in a World of Cooperative Deterrence'. *Columbia Journal of Transnational Law* 53 no. 2 (2015): 235–284.

Gerspacher, Nadia, and Benoît Dupont. 'The Nodal Structure of International Police Cooperation: An Exploration of Transnational Security Networks'. *Global Governance* 13 no. 3 (2007): 347–364.

Gibney, Mark. 'On terminology: Extraterritorial Obligations'. In *Global Justice, State Duties: The Extraterritorial Scope of Economic, Social and Cultural Rights in International Law*, eds

M. Langford, W. Vanderhoule, M. Scheinin and W. van Genugten, 32–47. Cambridge: Cambridge University Press, 2013.

Gibney, Mark, and Sigrun Skogly, (eds). *Universal Human Rights and Extraterritorial Obligations*. Philadelphia, PA: University of Pennsylvania Press, 2010.

Gibney, Mark, Katarina Tomaševski and Jens Vedsted-Hansen. 'Transnational State Responsibility for Violations of Human Rights'. *Harvard Human Rights Journal* 12 (1999): 267–295.

Grahl-Madsen, Atle. *Commentary on the Refugee Convention 1951 Articles 2–11, 13–37*. Geneva: Division of International Protection of the United Nations High Commissioner for Refugees, 1963, republished 1997.

Hart, Herbert Lionel Adolphus. *The Concept of Law*. Oxford: Clarendon Press, 1961.

Henkin, Louis. 'Notes from the President'. *American Society of International Law Newsletter*, Sept.–Oct. 1993.

Henkin, Louis. 'That "S" Word: Sovereignty, and Globalisation, and Human Rights, Et Cetera'. *Fordham Law Review* 68 no. 1 (1999): 1–14.

Hollis, Duncan. 'The Fog of Technology and International Law'. *Opinio Juris*, 15 May 2015.

Hoppe, Carsten. 'Passing the Buck: State Responsibility for Private Military Companies'. *European Journal of International Law* 19 no. 5 (2008): 989–1014.

Kennedy, David. 'Challenging Expert Rule: The Politics of Global Governance'. *Sydney Law Review* 27 no. 1 (2005): 5–28.

King, Hugh. 'The Extraterritorial Human Rights Obligations of States'. *Human Rights Law Review* 9 no. 4 (2009): 521–556.

Koskenniemi, Martti. *From Apology to Utopia*, (2nd edn). Cambridge: Cambridge University Press, 2006.

Koskenniemi, Martti. 'The Fate of Public International Law: Between Technique and Politics'. *The Modern Law Review* 70 no. 1 (2007): 1–30.

Ku, Charlotte. *Global Governance and the Changing Face of International Law*. Yale University, CT: The Academic Council of the United Nations System, 2001.

Langford, Malcolm, Wouter Vandenhole, Martin Scheinin and Willem van Genugten, (eds). *Global Justice, State Duties: The Extraterritorial Scope of Economic, Social and Cultural Rights in International Law*. Cambridge: Cambridge University Press, 2013.

Leander, Anna, and Tanja Aalberts. 'Introduction: The Co-Constitution of Legal Expertise and International Security'. *Leiden Journal of International Law* 26 no. 4 (2013): 783–792.

Leben, Charles. 'Symposium: The Changing Structure of International Law Revisited: By Way of Introduction'. *European Journal of International Law* 8 no. 3 (1997): 399–408.

Loucaides, Loukis. 'Determining the Extraterritorial Effect of the European Convention: Facts, Jurisprudence and the *Bankovic* Case'. *European Human Rights Law Review* 4 (2006) 391–407.

Mann, Itamar. 'Dialectic of Transnationalism: Unauthorised Migration and Human Rights, 1993–2013'. *Harvard International Law Journal* 54 no. 2 (2013): 315–391.

Meron, Theodor. 'Extraterritoriality of Human Rights Treaties'. *American Journal of International Law* 89 (1995): 78–82.

Milanovic, Marko. 'State Responsibility for Genocide: A Follow-Up'. *European Journal of International Law* 18 no. 4 (2007): 669–694.

Milanovic, Marko. *Extraterritorial Application of Human Rights Treaties: Law, Principles, and Policy*. Oxford: Oxford University Press, 2011 and 2013.

Morgenthau, Hans J. 'The Problem of Sovereignty Reconsidered'. *Columbia Law Review* 48 no. 3 (1948): 341–365.

Nollkaemper, André, and Dov Jacobs. 'Shared Responsibility in International Law: A Conceptual Framework'. *Michigan Journal of International Law* 34 no. 2 (2013): 359–438.

Nollkaemper, André, and Dov Jacobs. *State Responsibility: An Appraisal of the State of the Art*. Cambridge: Cambridge University Press, 2014.

Palan, Ronen. 'Tax Havens and the Commercialization of State Sovereignty'. *International Organization* 56 no. 1 (2002): 151–176.

Palan, Ronen. *The Offshore World: Sovereign Markets, Virtual Places, and Nomad Millionaires*. Ithaca, NY: Cornell University Press, 2003.

Robinson, Nehemiah. *Convention Relating to the Status of Refugees: Its History, Contents and Interpretation: A Commentary*. New York: Institute of Jewish Affairs, World Jewish Congress, 1953.

Rosén, Frederik. 'Extremely Stealthy and Incredibly Close: Drones, Control and Legal Responsibility'. *Journal of Conflict and Security Law* 19 no. 1 (2013): 113–131.

Sakellaropoulos, Spyros. 'Towards a Declining State? The Rise of the Headquarters State'. *Science & Society* 71 no. 1 (2007): 7–32.

Sassen, Saskia. *Losing Control?: Sovereignty in an Age of Globalisation*. New York: Columbia University Press, 1995.

Scheinin, Martin. 'Extraterritorial Effect of the International Covenant on Civil and Political Rights'. In *Extraterritorial Application of Human Rights Treaties*, eds F. Coomans and M. T. Kamminga, 73–82. Antwerp: Intersentia, 2004.

Singer, Peter W. *Corporate Warriors: The Rise of the Privatized Military Industry*. Ithaca, NY: Cornell University Press, 2003.

Skogly, Sigrun. *Beyond National Borders: States' Human Rights Obligations in International Cooperation*. Antwerp: Intersentia, 2006.

Skogly, Sigrun, and Mark Gibney. 'Transnational Human Rights Obligations'. *Human Rights Quarterly* 24 no. 3 (2002): 781–798.

Steiner, Henry J. 'International Protection of Human Rights'. In *International Law*, ed. M. D. Evans, 753–782. 2nd edition. Oxford: Oxford University Press, 2006.

Steyn, Johan. 'Guantanamo Bay: The Legal Black Hole'. *The International and Comparative Law Quarterly* 53 no. 1 (2004) 1–15.

Strange, Susan. *The Retreat of the State. The Diffusion of Power in the World Economy*. Cambridge: Cambridge University Press, 1996.

Sur, Serge. 'The State between Fragmentation and Globalization'. *European Journal of International Law* 8 no. 3 (1997): 421–434.

Teubner, Gunther, (ed.). *Global Law Without a State*. Dartmouth: Aldershot, 1997.

Verkuil, Paul R. *Outsourcing Sovereignty: Why Privatization of Government Functions Threatens Democracy and What We Can Do About it*. Cambridge: Cambridge University Press, 2007.

Walker, Neil, (ed.). *Sovereignty in Transition*. Oxford: Hart Publishing, 2003.

Watson, J. Shand. *Theory and Reality in the International Protection of Human Rights*. New York: Transnational Publishers, 1999.

Weiler, Joseph, H. H. *et al.* 'Special Issue: Changing Paradigms in International Law'. *European Journal of International Law* 20 (2009): 21–109.

Wendell Holmes, Oliver, Jr. 'The Path of the Law'. *Harvard Law Review* 10 (1897): 457–461.

Werner, Wouter, and Jaap De Wilde. 'The Endurance of Sovereignty'. *European Journal of International Relations* 7 no. 3 (2001): 283–313.

Wilde, Ralph. 'Legal "Black Hole"?: Extraterritorial State Action and International Treaty Law on Civil and Political Rights'. *Michigan Journal of International Law* 26 no. 3 (2005): 739–806.

Young, Margaret, (ed.) *Regime Interaction in International Law: Facing Fragmentation*. Cambridge: Cambridge University Press, 2012.

PART I

General issues pertaining to human rights and transnational law enforcement

1

SHARED RESPONSIBILITY FOR HUMAN RIGHTS VIOLATIONS

A relational account

André Nollkaemper[1]

1.1 Introduction

The premise of this paper is that when international cooperation for the purposes of transnational law enforcement conflicts with human rights, such cooperation may engage the shared responsibility of the multiple states and/or international organisations involved. Shared responsibility means that the responsibility of a multiplicity of actors for human rights violations is distributed separately among more than one of the actors, rather than to just a single actor.[2] An example is the constellation of facts reviewed by the European Court of Human Rights in *El-Masri v. Macedonia*.[3] The Court held Macedonia responsible for its violation, during the extraordinary rendition of El-Masri, of his rights. However, there was little doubt that Macedonia was not responsible *alone* for the mistreatment of El-Masri by CIA (Central Intelligence Agency) agents, and that the responsibility was thus shared by both Macedonia and the United States.[4] Other examples of situations where shared responsibility may be engaged as a result of transnational law enforcement include migration policy,[5] anti-piracy operations,[6] antiterrorism operations abroad[7] and 'border management' by Frontex.[8]

While the premise that in such cases responsibility is shared may seem uncontroversial, the question of why it is justifiable to distribute responsibility among multiple actors in some cases, but not in others, has not received much attention. Clearly, multiple actors contribute to a particular outcome in a great many cases. Take the example of the EU naval operation to intercept migrant smugglers off the coast of Libya. If during such an operation a suspected smuggler was detained and his vessel destroyed, even if later it were to appear that there were no grounds for doing so, a great many actors could be said to have contributed to the outcome. These would include the individual agents who arrested the suspected smuggler and destroyed his property, the members of the crew of the vessel that carried out the operation, the EU institutions that approved the operation, the UN Security Council and its members that granted the mandate,[9] etc. Would responsibility be distributed among all of these actors, or only some of them?

The general conditions in terms of attribution, breach and the resulting obligations of reparation that provide an answer at the level of positive international law have been articulated.[10] But these principles provide a patchwork of grounds of shared responsibility that seem to have been developed in a rather ad hoc manner, mostly in response to a particular type of incident. Neither separately nor in combination do they provide a coherent answer to the questions of when, and in particular why, responsibility is or is not to be shared. This lack of a clear conceptual basis has practical relevance, especially when established principles do not lead to clear outcomes, and there is a need for guidance as to which direction, and for what reasons, rules may need to be interpreted or developed.[11]

In this chapter I will argue that a justification for sharing responsibility for 'cooperative human rights violations' lies in the relations between actors, and more particularly in the fact that because of these relations, actors may realise results that they could not have achieved alone. I therefore argue that in order to understand whether or not shared responsibility is justified, and what the consequences thereof would be, we have to supplement the traditional account of international responsibility as *independent* responsibility with a *relational* account of international responsibility.

The relational account of international responsibility that will be articulated in this chapter is essentially a conceptual clarification of what the situations in which we can speak of shared responsibility have in common. It does not seek to replace the well-established principles of responsibility articulated by the International Law Commission (ILC). Rather, it provides a conceptual angle that underlies such principles and allows us to systematise practices that can qualify as shared responsibility and those that do not.

I will first discuss the drawbacks of the prevailing paradigm of independent (or 'individual') responsibility (Section 1.2). I will then discuss what it means to speak of international responsibility in relational terms (Section 1.3) before explaining how the relations between actors can translate into shared responsibility, and how this can to some extent mitigate the drawbacks of the paradigm of independent responsibility (Section 1.4). Finally, I will discuss how a relational account of responsibility can provide a conceptual basis for allocating the obligation to provide reparation for cooperative human rights violations (Section 1.5). Section 1.6 concludes.

1.2 Limitations of an individualistic account of international responsibility

The potential contribution of a relational account of international responsibility in the context of human rights violations can be demonstrated by contrasting it with the prevailing account, which understands responsibility in individual, or independent, terms.[12] In this latter account, actors are only responsible for their *own* wrong, irrespective of their connection to other actors.[13] While in many cases this principle leads to satisfactory outcomes, in certain cases of concerted action the principle of independent responsibility may leave victims empty-handed.

The dominant paradigm of individual responsibility rests essentially on two grounds. The first ground is of a methodological nature. For the purposes of determinations of responsibility, the relevant units of analysis would be individual actors rather than collectivities of actors. This ground is premised on methodological individualism: in the final analysis all conduct is explained by the actions of individuals.[14] This approach is commonly applied to justify individual criminal responsibility.[15] Given the centrality of the sovereign state as the dominant agent in international law, this perspective can also be applied to justify the focus on individual states as agents that cause harmful effects. The second ground underlying the paradigm of individual responsibility is of a normative nature. Just as international criminal law rejects the concepts of collective responsibility or guilt by association, instead relying on the principle of individual autonomy to limit responsibility to individuals only for their actual conduct, it would be normatively problematic to require states to be responsible for conduct other than their own.[16]

This idea of independent responsibility is reflected in the Articles on the Responsibility of States for Internationally Wrongful Acts (ARSIWA). The idea that individual states commit individual wrongful acts (expressed in Article 1: 'every internationally wrongful act of a state entails the international responsibility of that State') underlies the ARSIWA as a whole.[17] In view of the possibility that a state might be responsible not only for its own acts but also for the acts of others, Special Rapporteur Ago suggested opting for a broader opening Article, providing that 'every international wrongful act by a State gives rise to international responsibility', without specifying that this responsibility would necessarily attach to the state that had committed the wrongful act in question.[18] However, the ILC was of the opinion that the situations in which responsibility was attributed to a state other than the state that committed the internationally wrongful act were so exceptional that they should not influence the basic principle in Article 1,[19] and that following Ago's proposal would detract from the principle's basic force.[20] Thus state responsibility for the state's *own* wrongful conduct came to be the basic rule underlying the ARSIWA.

In the relatively scarce case law, international courts have based themselves on this principle of independent responsibility. The International Court of Justice (ICJ) focused on independent wrongdoing in *Corfu Channel*[21] and Certain Phosphate Lands in Nauru.[22] Likewise, the European Court of Human Rights considered the responsibility of Belgium and Greece independently in *M.S.S. v. Belgium and Greece*.[23] The Tribunal in the *Eurotunnel* case also preferred to approach international responsibility for common conduct through the lens of independent responsibility.[24]

While these examples show that independent responsibility can be helpful to solve situations of concerted action, reducing complex relationships to the responsibility of individual states may not always result in satisfactory outcomes. In combination with the procedural limitations of dispute settlement,[25] the conceptual tools of individual responsibility of states have led courts to condense complex cooperative schemes to binary categories, which may not do justice to the multiparty context.[26]

One particular reason why it is problematic to apply the principle of independent responsibility in situations where states act in concert is that in such situations responsibility may be diffused. Contributions may be spread over multiple actors, and for outsiders the respective contributions and responsibilities may be difficult to penetrate. The diffusion of responsibility in cases of concerted action is a manifestation of the so-called 'problem of many hands'.[27] Assigning responsibility becomes more difficult when more persons – 'many hands' – were involved in a process that caused harm. This is captured well in Mark Bovens' observation that '[a]s the responsibility for any given instance of conduct is scattered among more people, the discrete responsibility of every individual diminishes proportionately'.[28]

The diffusion of responsibility, which can arise in cases of cooperation in transnational law enforcement, can be problematic for two main reasons. One reason is that diffusion can undermine the assignment and performance of obligations and thereby the achievement of objectives. It is a plausible proposition that if no one can be meaningfully called to account after the event, 'no one need feel responsible beforehand'.[29] If obligations to achieve a particular result are spread over a multitude of actors so that it is not clear who has to do what, this may reduce the possibility that individual actors perform obligations and that the interests that the law seeks to protect are actually protected. Thus it can be said that in military actions by 'coalitions of the willing',[30] or in collaborations of the North Atlantic Treaty Organisation, the European Union, and member states,[31] the very multitude of actors may make it unclear who has to do what, with the effect that individual actors have less incentive to ensure that all obligations are performed than if actors were to act individually.

A second drawback of diffusion of responsibility is that this can hamper justice for victims.[32] The position of victims tends to be weaker in situations of concerted action since it may be difficult for injured parties to determine which actors were involved and what roles were played by such actors in a particular concerted action. This is especially so in the case where information is spread over many actors and such information is of an informal nature – for instance in the case of partnerships between international institutions and private parties,[33] or in the context of transborder police cooperation.[34]

In the light of these drawbacks of the principle of independent responsibility, we need to consider whether an alternative basis can be articulated that would better reflect that in situations of concerted action, states and international institutions do not act alone, and which would be able to avoid these shortcomings.

1.3 A relational account of international responsibility

A useful starting point for a concept of responsibility that is not grounded in individual action but rather in the relations between actors, and which is better attuned to the practices of cooperative action in the context of transnational law enforcement, is Article 1 of the Articles on the Responsibility of International Organisations (ARIO). This Article stipulates that the ARIO apply not only to the responsibility of an international organisation for its own wrongful conduct, but rather to 'the international responsibility of an international organisation for *an* internationally wrongful act'.[35] This concept of responsibility thus refers to a responsibility of international organisations and states that derives not only from their *own* wrongful conduct, but also for wrongful acts brought about by a cooperative action of which they were a part. Given the possibility that international organisations would contribute to the wrongful acts of member states, or vice versa,[36] the ILC found the suggestion of basing the entire law of international responsibility on individual responsibility to be unpersuasive and opted for a construction that it had rejected in relation to the responsibility of states. In this sense, the ARIO as a whole are based on a 'relational account' of international responsibility.

We can unpack the concept of 'relational responsibility' by distinguishing between two constitutive elements: interdependence of conduct (Section 1.3.1) and interdependence of outcomes (Section 1.3.2).

1.3.1 Interdependent conduct

The first constitutive element of relational responsibility is that the conduct of the actors who are involved in a concerted action is interdependent. Such interdependence arises when the conduct of one state or international institution is conditional on and/or conducive to acts or omissions of other actors who are part of the concerted action. The observation by Lucas that 'often our actions are concerted to form one coherent whole, and the action is described in terms of that whole, not of its individual constituents',[37] captures the idea well. If cooperative conduct in transnational law enforcement cannot be reduced to conduct of individual participating actors, responsibility needs to connect to the relationship between the individual actors. Individualising responsibility may miss the point.

Relational responsibility, then, does not refer to parallel individual wrongdoing, but involves interactions between actors who in combination cause harm.[38] Miller observes in relation to moral responsibility that

> there are instances of morally significant joint actions in which the individual contributory actions are not directly causally necessary (or causally sufficient) for the outcome, but in which the individual contributory actions are indirectly (via interdependence with the actions of other agents) causally necessary for the outcome; in these cases the participating agents can be ascribed collective moral responsibility.[39]

This observation is also relevant to legal responsibility. The extraordinary rendition practice illustrates the point: the contributions by the dozens of states that assisted the United States in extraordinary renditions would not have been sufficient in themselves to cause the outcome in terms of human rights violations. But in combination with the conduct of US agents, they were necessary for the result to occur, and on that basis both the assisting states and the United States can be held responsible.[40] We can thus speak of relational responsibility when multiple actors act together or contribute to each other's acts.[41]

The relatively well-established forms of such concerted action in the law of international responsibility, such as complicity,[42] direction and control,[43] and circumvention of responsibility,[44] are all characterised by the fact that the conduct of one actor influences or is influenced by the acts of other actors. Beyond these terms that appear in the ARSIWA and the ARIO, there are different terms that capture similar phenomena, such as contribution, collusion, connivance and condoning.[45] Common to such concepts is that multiple actors interact and that the conduct of each of the individual actors is dependent on, or contributes to, the actions of another.

The proper unit of analysis then is not the individual actor that influences or is influenced by another actor, but rather the relationship, or the collectivity of actors who participate in the concerted action. It is that relationship that influences the action of individual participants.[46] For instance, the collectivity can slice up tasks and thereby affect the role of individual actors in the collective action.[47] May's comment on social groups can be transposed to joint action in transnational law enforcement; he noted that social groups should be analysed as 'individuals in relationships' and that whereas groups themselves do not exist in their own right, the individuals who compose groups are often not understandable 'as acting in isolation from one another'.[48] The conduct of individual actors can, in these situations, be understood only in the context of purposes shared by them all; it is the common purpose that makes such conduct intelligible.[49]

The degree to which the conduct of actors is indeed interdependent and, accordingly, the normative justifiability of holding an individual actor responsible in connection with the acts of others, varies from case to case. The connection between actors is strong in cases where the actors act through a common organ, as in *Eurotunnel*[50] or the *Nauru* case.[51] In joint police operations the impact might be weaker, but may still be strong enough to hold one state responsible in connection with the conduct of another actor.[52] In cases where states have agreed to common obligations but do not act together, it may be that only the individual conduct is the proper unit of analysis.

1.3.2 Interdependent outcomes

The flipside of interdependence of conduct is that concerted action in the field of transnational law enforcement can achieve results that could not be achieved by actors alone. Concerted actions 'enable their members to perform actions that they could not have performed on their own'.[53] Erskine notes in this context that 'agents who come together, even in an informal association, to work towards a shared goal are able to achieve things by cooperating that they would not be able to achieve independently'.[54] Again, the extraordinary rendition saga is a good example. The conduct of states such as Macedonia and Poland was influenced by the conduct of the United States, and in turn influenced the subsequent conduct of the United States.[55] Together they realised results that they could not have alone.

The implication is that if the harm is caused by multiple actors acting in a particular relationship, we may not be able to say that the conduct of individual states or international organisations is the direct and exclusive cause of the harm. In that sense, the phrase that 'a State is responsible only for its *own* conduct' (as the ICJ put it in the *Genocide* case),[56] is misleading when the harm only occurs because of the involvement of other actors. The Court emphasised that there should be a sufficiently close connection 'between the conduct of a State's organs and its international responsibility'.[57] There certainly needs to be such a connection; however, there may well be other actors positioned between the conduct of a state's organs and the eventual harm.

One example, based on an insightful chapter by Pierre D'Argent, is the situation where state A abducted a person in state B, and state B was instrumental in aiding or assisting that abduction. In that case, state B committed a separate wrongful act of aiding or assisting. Yet that wrong was also a cause of the illegal abduction committed by state A. The aid or assistance was necessary for the abduction to occur. In that case the eventual harm was the result of both the acts of both states. Neither of the two states could have produced the outcome alone.[58]

When two or more actors contribute to a particular harmful outcome, the eventual harm (such as a violation of human rights) can be indivisible. That is, it cannot, without loss of meaning, be divided between the individual contributing actors. Multiple contributions are causally linked to the harmful outcome, but none of such contributions is by itself sufficient to produce the harmful outcome.[59] Rather, the harm may be an indivisible totality that results from the addition of various contributions and the interaction between them. Whether or not this is indeed the case needs to be assessed on a case-by-case basis; I will return to this in Section 1.5 in the context of reparation.

It may be argued that since human rights are by definition held against particular states, which each owe individual obligations towards individuals under their jurisdiction, an eventual human rights violation can always be traced back to individual states rather than to 'collective actors'. In cases where the harmful outcome is a human rights violation, the harmful outcome would then necessarily lead to individual actors rather than to 'relationships'. However, that argument could be critiqued on three grounds. First, even if we were to accept an exclusive relationship between an individual duty and an individual rights holder, under established principles of international responsibility it would still be possible that other states would incur derivative responsibility for their contributions to a human rights violation by the duty holder, for instance based on complicity. Second, and related to this, there is a strong argument that in certain situations the protection of individual rights is not only a matter for individual states, but rests on a collectivity of states. This holds in particular for extraterritorial obligations. It is precisely the difficulty of disentangling this collectivity that would justify shared-over individual responsibility.[60] Third, it is possible to distinguish between the specific human rights violation consisting of a singular breach by one actor vis-à-vis an individual, on the one hand, and a 'global harm' that consists of a cumulation of acts of multiple actors vis à vis that individual. In the context of extraordinary rendition, where one state illegally arrests and then hands over an individual to another state, which then illegally detains and tortures that person, we can identify both two separate wrongs, on the one hand, and a larger, 'global' wrong that results from two separate wrongs, on the other.[61]

For the above reasons, we can indeed identify situations where states and/or international institutions can achieve results by acting in concert that they could not achieve alone. If so, the proper unit of analysis in understanding responsibility is not the individual actor, but rather the relationship between the actors contributing to the harm.

1.4 Relations between actors as a basis of shared responsibility

If individual conduct and outcomes are explained in terms of the relations between actors in causing the harm, it follows that in principle responsibility for such harm should not be allocated to individual actors, but rather to all actors involved in such a relationship. In this section I will first develop this proposition in general terms (Section 1.4.1) before identifying several dimensions in which this proposition needs to be contextualised (Section 1.4.2) and discussing how shared responsibility can address the drawbacks of individual responsibility (Section 1.4.3).

1.4.1 In general

The basic proposition is that when the conduct of individual actors can be understood only 'in the context of purposes shared by them all', and when all actors contribute to the eventual harm, in principle 'responsibility for the actions taken all together is ascribed to each and all of those taking part'.[62] The fact that two or more actors who contributed to the harm stand in a relevant relationship to each other, and together achieve a result that could not have been achieved by them alone, justifies allocating responsibility to each of them – and thus to share responsibility.[63] As May observes, the concept of shared responsibility focuses attention 'on the interaction of one with the other, rather than on acts of isolated agents'.[64]

Shared responsibility thus is not simply the aggregation of two or more individual responsibilities. The responsibility of separate actors is connected by the interdependence of conduct and by their respective links to the same harmful outcome. The prototypical example of the concept of shared responsibility is a situation where multiple actors contribute to each other's acts and thereby to the eventual outcome.[65]

It can be said that in such cases shared responsibility is a collective responsibility. This ties in with the idea that when people are doing things together, there is an assumption that they 'constitute some sort of collectivity who are collectively responsible'.[66] However, such responsibility should not be understood as a *non-distributive* collective responsibility that only rests on the collectivity as such.[67] If the responsibility were to rest on a collectivity as such, it would no longer be shared.[68] A defining feature of shared responsibility is that the responsibility of two or more actors for their contribution to a particular outcome is *distributed between them separately*, rather than resting on them collectively.[69] Somewhat counterintuitively, because the term may suggest otherwise, shared responsibility, by definition, is thus a responsibility that rests on individual actors for their contribution to a harm.

This distributive understanding of shared responsibility thus presumes that when multiple actors together contribute to a harmful outcome, the responsibility of each of them should be understood in non-exclusive terms. Assignment of responsibility to one actor does not exclude the other. Such a non-exclusive concept has been defended on theoretical terms. Lucas observes that responsibility is not a material object – 'I can be held responsible for an action you did, without your being thereby any the less responsible for it too'.[70] It is also recognised in the ARSIWA and the ARIO,[71] though in exceptional cases (such as coercion), responsibility can in fact become exclusive.[72]

1.4.2 The need for differentiation

The images of cooperation and concerted action in pursuit of common objectives that underlie the need for shared responsibility, as well as the notion of shared responsibility itself, can easily be misleading. They may be taken to suggest that in cases where actors engage in a concerted action, they will do so on a level of equality and that they will all share equally in the responsibility. That, however, is not necessarily the case. Concerted action can hide differences between actors, which are relevant to their eventual shared responsibility. In this sense, shared responsibility is not a one-dimensional concept, but reflects a variety of types of relations between the relevant actors, and hides a variety of ways in which responsibility can be shared.

In particular, we need to differentiate along three dimensions. First, states participating in cooperation for purposes of transnational law enforcement may have separate interests and aims. For instance, in a coalition that seeks to respond to mass atrocities, some actors may seek protection of the population, while others may seek regime change.[73] In cooperation aiming to control the influx of refugees, some participating actors may seek to identify persons with or without legitimate entitlement to refugee status, whereas others may prefer to close the border entirely. Such differences may be legally relevant, to the extent that shared responsibility may presume shared knowledge and, in some readings, even shared intentions relating to the eventual wrong.[74]

Second, there may be significant power distinctions between parties. Concerted action will often be seen as an example of what Slaughter calls 'collaborative power'.[75] Actors exercise power 'with' others, rather than 'over others'. As Slaughter explains, 'power with' is 'the power of many to do together what no one can do alone'.[76] However, the fact that states engage in the exercise of collaborative power does not exclude the possibility that within a group of actors, some states exercise (soft) power *over* others.[77] Such power relations may be relevant for the eventual assigning of responsibility, for instance, as they 'allow some to blame others'.[78] Differences in power relations within a group of actors that engages in a concerted action will influence and shape the modalities of sharing between the relevant actors. At one extreme, it may mean that one actor is subjected to the power of another to such an extent that its autonomy, and thereby the basis for assignment of responsibility, is lost.[79]

Third, whether and how relations between multiple actors will be legally relevant depends very much on the types of actors who are involved in the concerted action resulting in a particular human rights violation. It is quite common that a state is held responsible in conjunction with acts of non-state actors. However, relations between actors who are bound by international obligations are significantly more relevant than relations with non-state actors who are not similarly bound by international obligations, such as rebel movements[80] or private military corporations, the conduct of which cannot be attributed to a state.[81]

The role of non-state actors can still be relevant in relation to the contents and scope of responsibility of actors who *are* subject to international obligations.[82] For instance, in the *Nicaragua* case, the ICJ found that the acts of the *contras* could not be treated as acts carried out by the United States.[83] While the Court did note that 'the *contras* remain responsible for their acts',[84] the use of the term 'responsible' probably should not be qualified in terms of international law. However, the question may be raised whether, if the Court had come to a liability phase, any responsibility of the *contras* for their own acts would, as concurrent causes, be relevant in that they might limit the degree to which the United States could have been held liable to compensate for specific injuries committed by the *contras*. Such a determination would have to be based on causation between the violations attributed to the United States, on the one hand, and the specific harm, on the other. In that causal relationship, the responsibility of the *contras* at least as a factual matter seems to be an intervening variable. It may be recalled that according to the ILC, international law may require a reduction in reparation for concurrent causes when 'an identifiable element of injury can properly be allocated to one of several concurrently operating causes alone'.[85]

However, even though acts of non-state actors may be relevant as a concurrent cause for the sake of mitigating the obligation to compensate, the Court could not determine responsibility of the *contras* as a matter of international law. When such actors are not bound by international law, their responsibility in international law will not be engaged. Even when they are bound by international law (e.g. armed opposition groups), it is not generally accepted that their responsibility in international law can be engaged.[86]

The general point, therefore, is that while at a general conceptual level we can speak of a relational account of international responsibility that provides a conceptual basis for shared responsibility, the legal relevance of such relations for shared responsibility depends very much on the context – on the nature of the actors involved, on the nature of their mutual relations, and on their aims.

1.4.3 Potential advantages of shared responsibility

Leaving aside the diversity in relationships between relevant actors, as a general proposition, shared responsibility could address some of the pitfalls of diffusion of responsibility identified in Section 1.2. On the one hand, assigning responsibility to all may prevent diffusion of responsibility undermining the incentives for performance of obligations. On the other hand, assigning responsibility to all can protect the position of injured parties. In situations of concerted action, it may be difficult for injured parties to determine which actors played what role in a particular concerted action. If responsibility is assigned to multiple parties, the danger of buck-passing is reduced.

Moreover, shared responsibility provides a better basis for remedial measures. In situations where outcomes are the result of relationships between actors, individual actors may not be able to alter the course of action. It is true that a single responsible party may be able to provide compensation. However, this may not provide a solution if, due to jurisdictional limitations, a party that would be able to provide compensation is out of reach. Reliance on a single paying party also does not help to ensure a return to legality of all parties. Shared responsibility would impose obligations of cessation on all parties, and thereby lead to superior outcomes.

An example that illustrates the potential benefits of shared responsibility is the decision of the European Court of Human Rights in *Behrami*. The Court attributed all acts and omissions relating to the failed demining operations in Kosovo exclusively to the United Nations, and not to its member states, without considering the possibility of a more nuanced solution in which responsibility would be shared.[87] Such exclusive responsibility of a single actor undermines the incentives of the contributing states to perform their obligations. It also impedes the access of victims to relief, particularly when the responsible entity is the United Nations, which will enjoy immunity before national courts and which does not provide alternative remedies. Moreover, such independent responsibility sits uneasily with the essential function of international responsibility: ensuring a return to legality and that the actors who acted in breach of international law will comply with their obligations.[88]

An additional advantage of translating the relations that constitute concerted action into shared responsibility rather than independent responsibility is that it may be unfair to hold a single party responsible for all injury, when in fact that actor could only cause the injury through the involvement of others. Reducing situations of shared responsibility to individual responsibility may create an accountability gap that increases the costs for the injured parties and raises questions of fairness among the responsible parties. In the *East Timor* case, Judge Weeramantry, dissenting from the majority judgement, noted that '[e]ven if the responsibility of Indonesia is the prime source, from which Australia's responsibility derives as a consequence, Australia cannot divert responsibility from itself by pointing to that primary responsibility'.[89] Likewise, while in the *Nauru* case Australia's own role in regard to the treaty was therefore sufficient for its (independent) responsibility, this does not necessarily mean that between the three parties it would have been fair to place all responsibility on Australia.[90]

In conclusion, it can be stated that the concept of shared responsibility allows for distribution of responsibility among all the actors who engage in a particular concerted action, rather than to only one of them, and that doing so can avoid at least to some extent the drawbacks of the principle of independent responsibility as discussed in Section 1.2.

1.5 Implications for reparation

The litmus test for the usefulness of the relational account of responsibility in relation to cooperative action in transnational law enforcement is the question of whether it can help us to answer not only the question of whether there should be a shared responsibility in the first place, but also how responsibility should be allocated among multiple actors engaged in the cooperative action. In other words, does the concept of relational responsibility provide a useful conceptual basis for the application of the principles on reparation articulated by the ILC in situations of shared responsibility? And what do the variations in relations, for instance in terms of power, matter for the purposes of reparation?[91]

Exploring how the obligation to provide reparation is to be applied in situations of multiple wrongdoers cannot be a matter of a mechanical application of firmly established principles of positive law. While the principles on reparation articulated by the ILC as such seem clear and relatively uncontested, how they apply in situations of shared responsibility is a matter of considerable uncertainty.[92] The lack of practice makes it almost impossible to determine the state of customary law in this field. Rather than seeking to pinpoint the 'state of the law', in this section I will explore different ways in which principles on reparation can be understood as a reflection and articulation of a relational account of responsibility.

While various typologies can be defended, in this Article I explore a threefold distinction that may help us to understand how the obligation to provide reparation may be connected to the relational nature of wrongdoing in cases of transnational law enforcement. I will thus identify three different types of relations between actors who, in cooperative action, engage in human rights violations and that each underpin a particular allocation of the obligation to provide reparation: situations of shared responsibility arising out of concurrent human rights violations (Section 1.5.1);

shared responsibility arising out of separate wrongs that cumulatively result in the violation of human rights (Section 1.5.2); and shared responsibility arising out of a single human rights violation (Section 1.5.3). It will appear that the distinctions between these situations are not sharp, and that each of them can be construed in a way that distributes the obligation to provide reparation to all participating actors.

1.5.1 Concurrent responsibility

In the first situation, multiple actors engaging in concerted transnational law enforcement commit separate wrongful acts resulting in particular human rights violations. The conduct of the states may have been interdependent and together they may have realised outcomes that they could not have achieved alone. In this sense, the conduct of the states can be understood in terms of a relational account of responsibility. But they committed separate wrongs for which they can be held individually responsible. The consequence will be that they are independently under an obligation to terminate the wrong and to provide reparation. An example is a situation where one state intercepts migrants at sea and sends the migrants back to a country of origin where they are subject to illegal detention or torture. Another example is the involvement of states in the US rendition policy, whereby states assisted the United States (thereby committing a separate wrong) in the illegal detention or torture of persons suspected of terrorism, triggering the responsibility of the United States. In the logic of the ILC Articles, Article 16 of the ARSIWA stipulates that the aiding state is not responsible for the wrongful act of the United States, but only for the aiding or assisting.[93] In such a situation, two different wrongful acts, for which two different states bear responsibility, contributed to the human rights violations.

In such cases, we can stick to the fundamental principle according to which each entity has to provide reparation for the injury caused by its own wrongful act, but not for the injury caused by another wrongdoer. This solution is thus identical to the application of the principle of independent responsibility discussed in Section 1.2.

However, this approach does not work if it is not possible to disentangle contributions and to divide the harm. In the example given above, if the state that intercepts migrants at sea and sends them onward to a state where the migrants are subjected to torture, both states actually contributed to the torture and it is difficult to divide that harm. While there are separate wrongs, there appears to be one eventual human rights violation to which both actors contributed. The principle of independent responsibility (in which each actor is responsible for its own wrong) can only provide a basis for reparation for that eventual injury if the separate wrongs can separately causally be connected to the injury. Whether that is possible depends on the circumstances of the case, the particular concept of causation that is employed, and the available evidence. But given the contested nature of causation, this perspective provides a feeble basis for allocating the obligation to provide reparation to all the actors involved.

1.5.2 Cumulative responsibility

In the second situation, conduct by one actor contributes to a particular injury but is by itself insufficient to produce the human rights violation. This construction ties in with the emphasis that I placed above on the fact that in situations of concerted action, actors may realise objectives that they cannot achieve alone. In such a situation, the different causes (the wrongs of separate actors) are 'cumulative': each of them is causally linked to the injury, but none of them is by itself sufficient to produce the harmful outcome as it occurred.[94] Thus in the example given above, the interception of migrants and the torture could be seen as 'cumulative' causes of the eventual human rights violation. The interception and handing over could be seen as wrongful aid or assistance in the commission of torture, without which torture would not have been possible.[95]

In such a situation there are several ways in which the obligation to provide reparation can reflect the relational nature of responsibility. A first solution is to apply a principle of proportionality. This was suggested by the ILC in its Commentary to Article 44 as adopted on the first reading in 1996. The ILC said:

> Innumerable elements, of which actions of third parties . . . are just a few, may contribute to a damage as concomitant causes. In such cases . . . to hold the author State liable for full compensation would be neither equitable nor in conformity with a proper application of the causal link criterion. The solution should be the payment of damages in proportion to the amount of injury presumably to be attributed to the wrongful act and its effects, the amount to be awarded being determined on the basis of the criteria of normality and predictability.[96]

This solution presumes that it will be possible to single out elements of harm that can be properly allocated to one of the contributing actors alone.[97] However, as indicated above, it will not always be easy to disentangle the contributions.

A second solution is to identify one cause as the most important one, and to consider this to be the 'adequate cause'.[98] Many would say that in the case of extraordinary renditions, where the eventual illegal detention or torture is carried out by the United States, it would be the conduct of the United States rather than that of the aiding state that is the adequate cause. If so, the United States, being responsible for the most important cause, would alone bear the obligation to make full reparation vis-à-vis the injured party. This construction thus transforms the relationship between multiple wrongdoing actors in effect into a single responsible state, or at least into a single state that has to provide reparation. The other states would still bear responsibility for their own acts, but would not have to provide reparation for the eventual wrong. It may be said that this solution is easier for the victims, who only have to litigate against one state. However, it is also true that when procedures against the principal wrongdoer are not readily available (this was certainly the case in relation to extraordinary renditions), this outcome may leave victims worse off. More fundamentally, it may be said that this does not properly reflect the relational nature of the responsibility, as it would disconnect the contributing states from the eventual injury. However, it also should be said that such a solution does not exclude a possible right of recourse against the other wrongdoers – which may be based on the relationship between the wrongdoers.[99]

The third approach is to consider all contributions as equal on the ground that the injury would not have occurred without all of the contributions. This approach would lead to full responsibility of all wrongdoers for the injury. It presumes that no single wrongful act is more important than another. The implication then is that all participating states have to bear the obligation to make reparation. The practical consequence is that the injured party would be free to decide to present its full reparation claim to any one of the states. This construction was supported by Special Rapporteur Crawford, who wrote that once it is shown that the harm suffered has been caused by the wrongful act of a state, the state must make reparation therefor. This obligation is not affected by any role of concurrent causes.[100]

This approach resembles the notion of joint and several responsibility. It would be joint in the sense that the parties take responsibility for each other's wrongful conduct vis-à-vis third parties; it would be several in that they can be severally (i.e. separately) sued for the full amount by the injured parties.[101]

However, this is clearly only one aspect of a fully fledged principle of joint and several responsibility as it operates in national legal systems. For instance, in general international law there is no provision for recourse between wrongdoers. Hence it may be misleading and also unnecessary to refer to this outcome as an example of joint and several responsibility.[102]

1.5.3 Joint responsibility for a single wrongful act

In addition to situations in which relations between actors can be classified as concurrent responsibility or cumulative responsibility (with different consequences for reparation), there is a third set of relations that has distinct consequences for the obligation to provide reparation. In this third category, all responsible states and/or international organisations acting together commit one wrong, rather than multiple wrongs. So, rather than seeing the relationship as a combination of discrete acts that are each wrongful (Section 1.5.1), or as a cumulation of separate wrongs that together cause harm (Section 1.5.2), the emphasis here is on the fact that there is a single, joint operation, resulting in a single harmful outcome.

The question of when a harm caused by a joint operation can be considered as a single wrongful act is not easily answered. In the work of the ILC and related scholarship there appear to be three main strands of thought. The first is that the qualification of a single wrongful act is appropriate when cooperation between the actors is particularly close. The ARSIWA Commentary refers to situations where 'two or more States . . . combine in carrying out together an internationally wrongful act in circumstances where they may be regarded as acting jointly in respect of the entire operation'.[103] Crawford also referred to special rules of responsibility for 'common adventures'. He noted that whereıtwo persons jointly engage in a common adventure causing loss to another, it is usually held that the victim can recover its total losses against either of the participants, on the common sense ground that the victim should not be required to prove which particular elements of damage were attributable to each of them.[104] The idea is that in the case of a single operation, the conduct in such an operation will be attributable to all the states or organisations involved, and will be internationally wrongful for each of them.[105]

A second situation in which one can speak of a single wrongful act arises if two or more states or international institutions act through a common organ.[106] This is the situation that arose in the *Nauru* case and in *Eurotunnel*.[107] In *Nauru*, Judge Shahabuddeen wrote in his separate opinion that 'where States act through a common organ, each State is separately answerable for the wrongful act of the common organ'.[108]

The third situation in which we can speak of a single wrongful act involves situations where conduct is attributed to one state or international institution and responsibility is attributed to another state ıor international organisation. The basis for such attribution of responsibility may be direction and control and, in the context of international institutions, circumvention.[109] Since direction and control and circumvention are not themselves wrongful, the ground for attribution eventually has to be a single wrongful act to which they contributed.

Given the lack of practice, in particular on the first and third construction, the scholarship on the notion of the single wrongful act is fairly unsettled. This also holds for the consequences in terms of reparation: are all the actors who participated in such a wrongful act similarly obliged to provide full reparation? The question was considered, but not answered, in the *Nauru* case. Australia raised the question of whether the liability of the three states that were part of the Administering Authority would be 'joint and several', so that any one of the three would be liable to make full reparation for damage flowing from any breach of the obligations of the Administering Authority, and not merely a one-third or some other proportionate share. The Court reserved this question – and noted that it was independent of the question of whether Australia could be sued alone – for the merits, and answered it in the affirmative.[110] However, it would seem that in such cases the normal rule is that each state participating in the single wrongful act is separately responsible, and that neither this responsibility, nor the resulting obligation to provide reparation, is diminished or reduced by the fact that some other state (or states) is also responsible for the same conduct.[111] The principle is also confirmed (rather implicitly, as the Article is actually concerned with invocation rather than reparation) by Article 47 of the ARSIWA: when there is a wrongful act for which several states are responsible, the responsibility of each of them can be invoked for the purpose of claiming reparation.[112]

This outcome, whereby each participating state is to provide full reparation, is identical to the outcome of the situation that was described in Section 1.5.2 in terms of cumulative responsibility. In this respect, the question of whether a situation where states acted jointly 'in respect of the entire operation' is to be characterised as a single wrongful act or as a situation of cumulative responsibility is largely a theoretical one; in both cases full reparation could be claimed from any of the wrongdoers.[113]

Like the third scenario in Section 1.5.2, the outcome resembles, in some respects, a situation of 'joint and several liability'. However, here the result is reached simply by operation of the principle of independent responsibility in a situation of multiple wrongdoers that commit a single wrongful act. Similar to what was noted in Section 1.5.2, here also it would be too simple to equate this situation with joint and several liability, if only because of the lack of an arrangement for recourse between the wrongdoing actors.

Precisely this question of allocation of responsibility between the wrongdoing actors remains unresolved. Assuming that indeed it will not be possible to apportion responsibility based on causation, allocation will depend on the nature of the relations between the actors. In particular, a ground for allocation may be found in the fact that one state exercises a larger degree of power and control in a particular relationship.[114] For instance, it can be argued that the influence of each responsible subject on the wrongful act itself would have to be taken into account. In this context, it may be speculated that in the *Nauru* case, given that Australia played a dominant role in the administration of Nauru, its share in reparation may well have been different from that of the other states.[115] Any such grounds of differentiation only operate between the responsible parties and could not be applied to an injured party in order to limit the reparation due to that party.

However, this question of internal differentiation is largely theoretical. While Article 47(2) of the ARSIWA stipulates that the principle enunciated in Paragraph 1 is without prejudice to the allocation of reparation between the responsible parties, neither the principle nor the Commentary provide the beginning of an analysis on how this allocation should proceed. The absence of both institutional mechanisms and normative grounds for recourse between the parties is a key reason why it is problematic to speak in international law of a principle of joint and several responsibility – even though, in the situations sketched, the outcome whereby an injured state can claim full reparation from each of the actors participating in the wrong leads to the same substantive outcome.

1.6 Conclusion

A relational account of responsibility, based on both interdependence of conduct and interdependence of outcomes, provides a justification for shared rather than individual responsibility. If multiple actors interact and thereby achieve results that they could not have achieved alone, assigning responsibility to all the actors who contributed to the harmful outcome, rather than to only one of them, can better serve the aims of the law of responsibility.

In the context of transnational law enforcement, where cooperative action may lead to human rights violations, a relational account of responsibility may capture various types of cooperation in relation to, for instance, extraterritorial migration control, anti-piracy operations, and extraordinary rendition. Sharing of responsibility would provide a proper match for the cooperative nature of the conduct. It would ensure that incentives remain in place for all actors to comply with their obligations, and would provide the best protection to injured parties.

How in such situations reparation is to be allocated between multiple parties remains, as a matter of positive law, an issue of some uncertainty. However, the three situations discussed in Section 1.5 demonstrate that the relational nature of responsibility can underlie and justify an obligation to provide reparation for all parties involved. While the first construction (essentially based on independent responsibility combined with causation) is likely to present significant difficulties, both the second construction (based on cumulative wrongs, and allocation of reparation to all actors involved) and the third construction (based on the notion of a single wrongful act) can lead to a determination that all the states that contributed to the harmful outcome are obliged to provide full reparation, leaving it to them to allocate reparation between themselves.

That the absence of proper procedures and substantive grounds for recourse between responsible states would lead to an outcome where one responsible state would have to pay full reparation may be objectionable and unjust. However, it could be countered that the failure to provide for such arrangements cannot be advanced to deny relief to the injured parties, and that precisely this consequence may serve as an incentive for responsible parties to provide for proper arrangements.

The state of positive law on shared responsibility remains relatively uncertain, due, in particular, to the fact that only a few cases have been decided. However, the above overview has indicated that the conceptual building blocks are available for interpreting and developing the law in a way that matches the cooperative structure of policies for transnational law enforcement.

Notes

1 The research leading to this chapter has received funding from the European Research Council under the European Union's Seventh Framework Programme (FP7/2007–2013)/ERC grant agreement no 249499, as part of the research project on Shared responsibility in International Law (SHARES), carried out at the Amsterdam Centre for International Law (ACIL) of the University of Amsterdam.

2 André Nollkaemper and Dov Jacobs, 'Shared responsibility in International Law: A Conceptual Framework' *Michigan Journal of International Law* 34 (2013): 359–438 at 368.

3 *El-Masri v. the Former Yugoslav Republic of Macedonia*, App. no. 39630/09 (European Court of Human Rights, 13 December 2012).

4 There is substantial evidence of the wrongful conduct of US agents: see e.g. Council of Europe, Committee on Legal Affairs and Human Rights, *Alleged secret detentions and unlawful inter-state transfers involving Council of Europe member states* (2006) (Dick Marty report I); Council of Europe, Committee on Legal Affairs and Human Rights, *Secret Detentions and Illegal Transfers of Detainees Involving Council of Europe Member States: second report* (2007) (Dick Marty report II); European Union, *Report of the Temporary Committee on the alleged use of European countries by the CIA for the transportation and illegal detention of prisoners* (30 January 2007) (Fava inquiry); Amrit Singh, *Globalizing Torture: CIA Secret Detention and Extraordinary Rendition* (New York: Open Society Foundations,

2013) 6 et seq; Amnesty International, 'Open Secret: Mounting Evidence of Europe's Complicity in Rendition and Secret Detention' (London: Amnesty International Publications, 2010), EUR 01/023/2010; Amnesty International, 'Breaking the Conspiracy of Silence: USA's European "Partners in Crime" Must Act After Senate Torture Report' (London: Amnesty International Publications, 2015).

5 See e.g. Thomas Gammeltoft-Hansen and Ninna Nyberg Sørensen, (ed.), *The Migration Industry and the Commercialisation of International Migration* (London: Routledge, 2012).

6 See generally Robin Geiss and Anna Petrig, *Piracy and Armed Robbery at Sea. The Legal Framework for Counter-Piracy Operations in Somalia and the Gulf of Aden* (Oxford: Oxford University Press, 2011).

7 Helen Duffy, *The 'War on Terror' and the Framework of International Law*, 2nd edn (Cambridge: Cambridge University Press, 2015).

8 E. Papastavridis, ' "Fortress Europe" and Frontex: Within or Without International Law?' *Nordic Journal of International Law* 79 no. 1 (2010): 75–111.

9 UN Security Council Resolution 2240 (2015).

10 See André Nollkaemper and Ilias Plakokefalos, (ed.), *Principles of Shared Responsibility in International Law: An Appraisal of the State of the Art* (Cambridge: Cambridge University Press, 2014).

11 André Nollkaemper and Ilias Plakokefalos, 'Conclusions: Beyond the ILC Legacy', in *Principles of Shared Responsibility in International Law: An Appraisal of the State of the Art*, ed. André Nollkaemper and Ilias Plakokefalos (Cambridge: Cambridge University Press, 2014), 342–464 at 349.

12 The terms 'individual' and 'independent' are closely related and are often used interchangeably. Strictly speaking, the former term relates to the fact that the responsibility of an actor is based on its individual wrongdoing, rather than on the wrongdoing in connection with another actor, whereas the latter term relates to the fact that the responsibility of an actor is not dependent on the responsibility of another actor. Generally speaking, the terms will cover the same set of situations.

13 See Commentary to Articles on the Responsibility of States for Internationally Wrongful Acts, ILC *Yearbook* 2001/II(2) (ARSIWA Commentary), commentary to Article 47, para. 8.

14 Kenneth J. Arrow, 'Methodological Individualism and Social Knowledge' *American Economic Review* 84 no. 2 (1994): 1; Steven Lukes, 'Methodological Individualism Reconsidered' *British Journal of Sociology* 19 no. 2 (1968): 119; John W. N. Watkins, 'The Principle of Methodological Individualism' *British Journal for the Philosophy of Science* 3 no. 10 (1952): 186.

15 E.g. Harmen van der Wilt, 'Joint Criminal Enterprise. Possibilities and Limitations' *Journal of International Criminal Justice* 5 (2007): 91–108.

16 Compare *Application of Convention on Prevention and Punishment of Crime of Genocide (Bosn. & Herz. v. Serb. & Montenegro)*, Judgment, 2007 ICJ 43, ¶ 406 (Feb. 26) (critiquing on this ground the overall test as a basis for attribution of conduct).

17 Articles 16–18 of the ARSIWA (n 12) to some extent form an exception.

18 ILC, 'Second Report on State responsibility by Special Rapporteur Roberto Ago' (1970) UN Doc. A/CN.4/233, paras 29–30.

19 ILC, 'Third Report on State responsibility by Special Rapporteur Roberto Ago' (1971) UN Doc. A/CN.4/246 and Add.1–3, para. 47.

20 ILC, 'Report of the International Law Commission on the work of its twenty-fifth session' (7 May–13 July 1973) UN Doc. A/9010/Rev.1, 176, para. 11.

21 *Corfu Channel Case (United Kingdom v. Albania)* (Judgment) [1949] ICJ Rep. 244.

22 *Certain Phosphate Lands in Nauru (Nauru v. Australia)* (Preliminary Objections, Judgment) [1992] ICJ Rep. 240.

23 *M.S.S. v. Belgium and Greece* [GC] App no. 30696/09 (European Court of Human Rights 21 January 2011).

24 *Eurotunnel Arbitration (The Channel Tunnel Group Ltd & France-Manche S.A. v. United Kingdom & France)*, Partial Award, 30 January 2007, para. 187.

25   See the Themed Section: Procedural Aspects of Shared responsibility in International Adjudication (2013) 4(2) *J Int. Disp. Settlement*, 277 et seq.

26   *Corfu Channel* (n 20); *Military and Paramilitary Activities in and against Nicaragua (Nicaragua v. United States of America)*, Judgment, ICJ Reports 1986, 14; *Nauru* (n 21); *East Timor (Portugal v. Australia)*, Judgment, ICJ Reports 1995, 90; and *Legality of Use of Force (Serbia and Montenegro v. United Kingdom)*, Provisional Measures, Order of 2 June 1999, ICJ Reports 1999, 826.

27   Dennis F. Thompson, 'Moral responsibility of Public Officials: The Problem of Many Hands' *The American Political Science Review* 74 (1980): 905.

28   Mark Bovens, *The Quest for Responsibility: Accountability and Citizenship in Complex Organisations* (Cambridge: Cambridge University Press, 1998), 46.

29   Bovens, *The Quest for Responsibility* (n 27) 49. See also Andrew Linklater, *The Problem of Harm in World Politics: Theoretical Investigations* (Cambridge: Cambridge University Press, 2011), 57, 225; Michael A. Wallach, Nathan Kogan and Daryl J. Bem, 'Group influence on individual risk taking' *Journal of Abnormal & Social Psychology* 65 (1962): 75; Michael A. Wallach, Nathan Kogan and Daryl J. Bem, 'Diffusion of responsibility and level of risk taking in groups' *Journal of Abnormal & Social Psychology* 68 (1964): 263.

30   Matteo Tondini, 'Shared Responsibility in Coalitions of the Willing', in *The Practice of Shared Responsibility*, eds André Nollkaemper and Ilias Plakokefalos (Cambridge: Cambridge Univerity Press, 2016, forthcoming).

31   Martin Zwanenburg, 'Shared Responsibility in NATO-led Operations', in *The Practice of Shared Responsibility*, eds André Nollkaemper and Ilias Plakokefalos (Cambridge: Cambridge University Press, 2016, forthcoming).

32   Ibo van de Poel *et al.*, 'The Problem of Many Hands: Climate Change as an Example' *Science and Engineering Ethics* 64 (2004) 49; Bovens, *The Quest for Responsibility* (n 27) 49.

33   L. Boisson de Chazournes, 'United in Joy and Sorrow: Some Considerations on Responsibility Issues Under Partnerships among International Financial Institutions', in *Responsibility of International Organizations – Essays in Memory of Sir Ian Brownlie*, ed. M. Ragazzi (The Hague: Martinus Nijhoff Publishers, 2013), 211–224.

34   Saskia Hufnagel, *Policing Cooperation Across Borders: Comparative Perspectives on Law Enforcement within the EU and Australia* (Farnham: Ashgate Publishing, 2013).

35   Articles on the Responsibility of International Organisations (ARIO), with commentaries, ILC Report on the work of its sixty-third session, UNGAOR 66th Sess., Supp. No. 10, UN Doc. A/66/10 (2011) (ARIO), 4 (emphasis added).

36   See ARIO (n 34), Arts. 14–17.

37   John R. Lucas, *Responsibility* (Oxford: Oxford University Press, 1995), 75.

38   Larry May, *Sharing Responsibility* (Chicago: University of Chicago Press, 1996), 36. Compare also French, distinguishing between an 'aggregate collectivity' – 'merely a collection of people' – and a 'conglomerate collectivity' – 'an organisation of individuals such that its identity is not exhausted by the conjunction of the identities of the persons in the organisation'. Peter A. French, *Collective and Corporate responsibility* (New York: Columbia University Press, 1984), 46–47; see also 5, 32.

39   May, *Sharing Responsibility* (n 37), 76.

40   See generally Helen Duffy, 'Detention and Interrogation Abroad: The "Extraordinary Rendition' Programme", in *The Practice of Shared responsibility*, eds André Nollkaemper and Ilias Plakokefalos (Cambridge: Cambridge University Press, 2016, forthcoming).

41   May, *Sharing responsibility* (n 37), 36–38.

42   ARSIWA (n 12), Article 16; ARIO (n 34), Arts. 14 and 58.

43   ARSIWA (n 11), Article 17; ARIO (n 34), Arts. 15 and 59.

44   ARIO (n 34), Arts. 17 and 61.

45   See Chaira Lepora and Robert E. Goodin, *On Complicity and Compromise* (Oxford: Oxford University Press, 2013), 36ff.

46   May, *Sharing Responsibility* (n 37) 7–8.

47 May, *Sharing Responsibility* (n 37).
48 Larry May, *The Morality of Groups: Collective Responsibility, Group-Based Harm and Corporate Rights* (Notre Dame: University of Notre Dame Press, 1987), 9.
49 Lucas, *Responsibility*, (n 36) 75.
50 *Eurotunnel* case (n 23).
51 *Nauru* case (n 21).
52 Hufnagel, *Policing Cooperation Across Borders* (n 33).
53 May, *The Morality of Groups* (n 47) 26.
54 Toni Erskine, ' "Coalitions of the Willing" and the Shared Responsibility to Protect', in *Distribution of Responsibilities in International Law*, eds André Nollkaemper and Dov Jacobs (Cambridge: Cambridge University Press, 2015), 227 at 256.
55 *El-Masri* (n 2).
56 *Genocide* case (n 15), para. 406.
57 *Genocide* case (n 15), para. 406.
58 Pierre d'Argent, 'Reparation, Cessation, Assurances and Guarantees of Non-Repetition', in *Principles of Shared responsibility in International Law: An Appraisal of the State of the Art*, eds André Nollkaemper and Ilias Plakokefalos (Cambridge: Cambridge University Press, 2014), 209–251 at 225.
59 Brigitte Bollecker-Stern, *Le Préjudice dans la Théorie de la Responsabilité Internationale* (Paris: Pedone, 1973), 267; d'Argent *Reparation* (n 57) at 228.
60 Malcolm Langford *et al.*, *Global Justice, State Duties: The Extraterritorial Scope of Economic, Social and Cultural Rights in International Law* (Cambridge: Cambridge University Press, 2014).
61 D'Argent, 'Reparation' (n 57) at 225.
62 Lucas, *Responsibility*, 75.
63 Seumas Miller, 'Collective Responsibility' *Public Affairs Quarterly* 15 no. 1 (2001): 65.
64 May, *Sharing Responsibility*, 38.
65 May, *Sharing Responsibility*, 36–38.
66 Lucas, *Responsibility*, 75, 76.
67 Joel Feinberg, 'Collective Responsibility' *Journal of Philosophy* 65 no. 21 (1968): 687.
68 May, *Sharing Responsibility*, 116. A major reason why, in the present state of international relations, exclusive collective responsibility in cases of cooperative action is not an attractive option is that the organisational structures remain too weak and the power of states too strong.
69 May, *Sharing Responsibility*, 116.
70 Lucas, *Responsibility*, 75. Also, Zimmerman notes that 'surely more than one person can be responsible for the same outcome'; see Michael J. Zimmerman, 'Sharing Responsibility' *American Philosophical Quarterly* 22 no. 2 (1985): 115.
71 See e.g. Article 19 of the ARIO (n 34), stating that '[t]his chapter is without prejudice to the international responsibility of the State or international organisation which commits the act in question, or of any other State or international organisation'; see similarly Article 63.
72 The coerced state could 'plead force majeure as a circumstance precluding the wrongfulness of its conduct, therefore possibly leaving the coercing state as the only responsible entity for that act'; see ARSIWA Commentary (n 12) 65.
73 See e.g. on multiple aims of actors in relation to the responsibility to protect Spencer Zifcak, 'The Responsibility to Protect after Libya and Syria' *Melbourne Journal of International Law* 13 no. 1 (2012): 1.
74 In particular in relation to aid and assistance, see ARSIWA Commentary (n 12), commentary to Article 16, para. 5.
75 Anne-Marie Slaughter, 'A New Theory for the Foreign Policy Frontier: Collaborative Power' *The Atlantic*, available at www.theatlantic.com/international/archive/2011/11/a-new-theory-for-the-foreign-policy-frontier-collaborative-power/249260/.
76 Slaughter, 'New Theory' (n 74).

77 Joseph S. Nye, *Soft Power: The Means to Success in World Politics* (New York: Public Affairs, 2005).

78 Anthony Lang, 'Shared Political Responsibility', in *Distribution of Responsibilities in International Law*, eds André Nollkaemper and Dov Jacobs (Cambridge: Cambridge University Press, 2015): 62 at 68 (discussing M. Smiley, *Moral Responsibility and the Boundaries of Community: Power and Accountability from a Pragmatic Point of View* (Chicago: University of Chicago Press, 1992)).

79 Thus in the case of coercion, only the coercing state would be responsible, even though it may well be argued that even a coerced state has a degree of freedom that would justify the consideration of its international responsibility; see James D. Fry, 'Coercion, Causation, and the Fictional Elements of Indirect State Responsibility' *Vanderbilt Journal of Transnational Law* 40 (2007), 611, 639. See also Christian Dominicé, 'Attribution of Conduct to Multiple States and the Implication of a State in the Act of Another State', in *The Law of International Responsibility*, eds James Crawford *et al.* (2010): 281, 284–288.

80 Veronika Bilkova, 'Armed Opposition Groups and Shared responsibility' *Netherlands International Law Review* 62 (2015): 69–89.

81 Sorcha MacLeod, 'Private Security Companies and Shared responsibility: The Turn to Multistakeholder Standard-Setting and Monitoring through Self-Regulation-Plus' *Netherlands International Law Review* 62 (2015): 199–140.

82 André Nollkaemper, 'Issues of Shared Responsibility before the International Court of Justice', in *Evolving Principles of International Law, Studies in Honour of Karel C. Wellens*, eds Ehun Rieter and Henri de Waele (Leiden-Boston: Martinus Nijhoff Publishers, 2012), 199–237, at 231.

83 *Nicaragua case* (n 25), para. 115.

84 *Nicaragua case* (n 26), para. 116.

85 Commentaries to the ARSIWA (n 12), Commentary to Article 31.

86 See generally Jean d'Aspremont *et al.*, 'Sharing Responsibility Between Non-State Actors and States in International Law: Introduction' *Netherlands International Law Review* 62 (2015): 49–67.

87 *Behrami v. France*, App nos. 71412/01 & 78166/01, Admissibility Decision (European Court of Human Rights 2007).

88 For a discussion of the relationship between the rule of law and state responsibility, see Ian Brownlie, *The Rule of Law in International Affairs: International Law at the Fiftieth Anniversary of the United Nations* (The Hague: Martinus Nijhoff Publishers, 1998), 79.

89 See *East Timor (Port. v. Austl.)*, Judgment, 1995 ICJ 90, 172 (June 30) (dissenting opinion of Judge Weeramantry).

90 Roberto Ago wrote on this point that if the Court were to decide that Australia was to shoulder the responsibility in full it could only do so on an extremely questionable basis; see Dissenting Opinion of Judge Ago in *Certain Phosphate Lands in Nauru (Nauru v. Australia)* [1992] ICJ Rep 1992, 326–328.

91 See also May, 1996 (n 37) at 85 (noting that groups can be collectively responsible but that this does not answer the question of who should have the greatest share of responsibility within the group).

92 André Nollkaemper and Ilias Plakokefalos, 'Conclusions: Beyond the ILC Legacy' (n 10) 351.

93 ARSIWA Commentary (n 12), para. 10; Helmut Philipp Aust, *Complicity and the Law of State Responsibility* (Cambridge: Cambridge University Press, 2011), 487; see also Vladyslav Lanovoy, 'Complicity in an Internationally Wrongful Act', in *Principles of Shared Responsibility in International Law: An Appraisal of the State of the Art*, eds André Nollkaemper and Ilias Plakokefalos (Cambridge: Cambridge University Press, 2014), 135–169 at 144–145.

94 D'Argent, *Reparation* (n 57) at 224.

95 ARSIWA Commentary (n 12), para. 10 (note that the Commentary also suggests that 'in cases where that internationally wrongful act would clearly have occurred in any

event, the responsibility of the assisting State will not extend to compensating for the act itself (ibid., at 66, para. 1).
96 Yearbook ILC 1993, vol. II (Part Two), Commentary to Article 8, p. 70, para. 13.
97 ILC, Third Report of Special Rapporteur Crawford, para. 35
98 Andrea Gattini, 'Breach of International Obligations', in *Principles of Shared Responsibility in International Law: An Appraisal of the State of the Art*, eds André Nollkaemper and Ilias Plakokefalos (Cambridge: Cambridge University Press, 2014), 25 at 28; d'Argent *Reparation* (n 57) 230.
99 ARSIWA (n 12), Article 47(2).
100 See Crawford, 'Third Report on State responsibility', UN Doc. A/CN.4/507/Add.4, paras 34–37. This approach is also supported by d'Argent *Reparation* (n 57) 231.
101 See James Crawford, 'Third Report on State Responsibility' (n 99), para. 272.
102 ARSIWA Commentary (n 12) 124, para. 3: 'analogies [with 'joint and several responsibility' or 'solidary responsibility' in domestic law] must be applied with care'. See also Ian Brownlie, *System of the Law of Nations: State Responsibility, Part I* (Oxford: Clarendon Press, 1983), 189–192; Crawford, 'Third Report on State Responsibility' (n 99) para. 263 et seq.
103 ARSIWA Commentary (n 12), Commentary to Article 47, para. 2.
104 Crawford, 'Third Report' (n 99), para. 276.
105 ARSIWA Commentary (n 12), Commentary to Article 47, para. 3.
106 ARSIWA Commentary (n 12), Commentary to Article 47, para. 2. See also *Eurotunnel* (n 23), para. 317.
107 *Nauru* case (n 21); *Eurotunnel* case (n 23).
108 *Nauru* case (n 21), Separate opinion of Judge Shahabuddeen.
109 Arts. 17–18 of the ARSIWA (n 12); Arts. 15–16, and 59–60 of the ARIO (n 34).
110 *Nauru* case (n 21), para. 57.
111 ARSIWA Commentary (n 12), Commentary to Article 47, para. 1.
112 See also the discussion in A. M. H. Vermeer-Künzli, 'Invocation of responsibility', in *Principles of Shared responsibility in International Law: An Appraisal of the State of the Art*, eds André Nollkaemper and Ilias Plakokefalos, (Cambridge: Cambridge University Press, 2014), 252–284 at 254.
113 Similarly, d'Argent, *Reparation* (n 57) 245.
114 See section 4.2 and generally André Nollkaemper, 'Power and responsibility', in *A Lackland Law? Territory, Effectiveness and Jurisdiction in International Law*, ed. Alfredo Di Stefano (Turin: G. Giappichelli Editore, 2015), 19–44.
115 *Nauru* case (n 21), para. 56 (referring to 'characteristics of the Mandate and Trusteeship Systems outlined above and, in particular, the special role played by Australia in the administration of the Territory').

Bibliography

Amnesty International. *Open Secret: Mounting Evidence of Europe's Complicity in Rendition and Secret Detention*. London: Amnesty International Publications, 2010.

Amnesty International. *Breaking the Conspiracy of Silence: USA's European "Partners in Crime" Must Act After Senate Torture Report*. London: Amnesty International Publications, 2015.

Arrow, Kenneth J. 'Methodological Individualism and Social Knowledge'. *American Economic Review* 84 no. 2 (1994): 1–9.

Aust, Helmut Philipp. *Complicity and the Law of State Responsibility*. Cambridge: Cambridge University Press, 2011.

Bilkova, Veronika. 'Armed Opposition Groups and Shared Responsibility'. *Netherlands International Law Review* 62 (2015): 69–89.

Bollecker-Stern, Brigitte. *Le Préjudice dans la Théorie de la Responsabilité Internationale*. Paris: Pedone, 1973.

Bovens, Mark. *The Quest for Responsibility: Accountability and Citizenship in Complex Organizations*. Cambridge: Cambridge University Press, 1998.

Brownlie, Ian. *System of the Law of Nations: State Responsibility: Part I*. Oxford: Clarendon Press, 1983.

Brownlie, Ian. *The Rule of Law in International Affairs: International Law at the Fiftieth Anniversary of the United Nations*. The Hague: Martinus Nijhoff Publishers, 1998.

Crawford, James. 'Third Report on State Responsibility, by Mr. James Crawford, Special Rapporteur'. Document A/CN.4/507 and Add. 1–4, 52nd Session, 15 March–4 August 2000. New York: United Nations International Law Commission.

D'Argent, Pierre. 'Reparation, Cessation, Assurances and Guarantees of Non-Repetition'. In *Principles of Shared Responsibility in International Law: An Appraisal of the State of the Art*, edited by André Nollkaemper and Ilias Plakokefalos, 209–251. Cambridge: Cambridge University Press, 2014.

D'Aspremont, Jean, André Nollkaemper, Ilias Plakokefalos and Cedric Ryngaert. 'Sharing Responsibility Between Non-State Actors and States in International Law: Introduction'. *Netherlands International Law Review* 62 (2015): 49–67.

De Chazournes, Laurence Boisson. 'United in Joy and Sorrow: Some Considerations on Responsibility Issues Under Partnerships among International Financial Institutions'. In *Responsibility of International Organizations – Essays in Memory of Sir Ian Brownlie*, edited by Maurizio Ragazzi, 211–224. The Hague: Martinus Nijhoff Publishers, 2013.

Dominicé, Christian. 'Attribution of Conduct to Multiple States and the Implication of a State in the Act of Another State', in James Crawford *et al.* (eds.), *The Law of International Responsibility* (2010): 281, 284–88.

Duffy, Helen. *The 'War on Terror' and the Framework of International Law*, (2nd edn). Cambridge: Cambridge University Press, 2015.

Duffy, Helen. 'Detention and Interrogation Abroad: The "Extraordinary Rendition" Programme'. In *The Practice of Shared Responsibility*, edited by André Nollkaemper and Ilias Plakokefalos. Cambridge: Cambridge University Press, 2016, forthcoming.

Erskine, Toni. '"Coalitions of the Willing" and the Shared Responsibility to Protect'. In *Distribution of Responsibilities in International Law*, edited by André Nollkaemper and Dov Jacobs, 256–227. Cambridge: Cambridge University Press, 2015.

Feinberg, Joel. 'Collective Responsibility'. *Journal of Philosophy* 65 no. 21 (1968): 674–688.

French, Peter A. *Collective and Corporate Responsibility*. New York: Columbia University Press, 1984.

Fry, James D. 'Coercion, Causation, and the Fictional Elements of Indirect State Responsibility'. *Vanderbildt Journal of Transnational Law* 40 (2007): 611–639.

Gammeltoft-Hansen, Thomas, and Ninna Nyberg Sørensen. *The Migration Industry and the Commercialization of International Migration*. London: Routledge, 2012.

Gattini, Andrea. 'Breach of International Obligations'. In *Principles of Shared Responsibility in International Law: An Appraisal of the State of the Art*, edited by André Nollkaemper and Ilias Plakokefalos, 25–59. Cambridge: Cambridge University Press, 2014.

Geiss, Robin, and Anna Petrig. *Piracy and Armed Robbery at Sea: The Legal Framework for Counter-Piracy Operations in Somalia and the Gulf of Aden*. Oxford: Oxford University Press, 2011.

Hufnagel, Saskia. *Policing Cooperation Across Borders: Comparative Perspectives on Law Enforcement within the EU and Australia*. Farnham: Ashgate Publishing, 2013.

Lang, Anthony. 'Shared Political Responsibility'. In *Distribution of Responsibilities in International Law*, edited by André Nollkaemper and Dov Jacobs, 62–68. Cambridge: Cambridge University Press, 2015.

Langford, Malcolm, Wouter Vandenhole, Martin Scheinin and Willem van Genugten. *Global Justice, State Duties: The Extraterritorial Scope of Economic, Social and Cultural Rights in International Law*. Cambridge: Cambridge University Press, 2014.

Lanovoy, Vladyslav. 'Complicity in an Internationally Wrongful Act'. In *Principles of Shared Responsibility in International Law: An Appraisal of the State of the Art*, edited by André Nollkaemper and Ilias Plakokefalos, 135–169. Cambridge: Cambridge University Press, 2014.

Lepora, Chaira, and Robert E. Goodin. *On Complicity and Compromise*. Oxford: Oxford University Press, 2013.

Linklater, Andrew. *The Problem of Harm in World Politics: Theoretical Investigations*. Cambridge: Cambridge University Press, 2011.

Lucas, John R. *Responsibility*. Oxford: Oxford University Press, 1995.

Lukes, Steven. 'Methodological Individualism Reconsidered'. *British Journal of Sociology* 19 no. 2 (1968): 119–129.

MacLeod, Sorcha. 'Private Security Companies and Shared Responsibility: The Turn to Multistakeholder Standard-Setting and Monitoring through Self-Regulation-Plus'. *Netherlands International Law Review* 62 (2015): 199–140.

May, Larry. *The Morality of Groups: Collective Responsibility, Group-Based Harm and Corporate Rights*. Notre Dame: University of Notre Dame Press, 1987.

May, Larry. *Sharing Responsibility*. Chicago: University of Chicago Press, 1996.

Miller, Seumas. 'Collective Responsibility'. *Public Affairs Quarterly* 15 no. 1 (2001): 65–82.

Nollkaemper, André. 'Issues of Shared Responsibility before the International Court of Justice'. In *Evolving Principles of International Law: Studies in Honour of Karel C. Wellens*, edited by Ehud Rieter and Henri de Waele, 199–237. Leiden-Boston: Martinus Nijhoff Publishers, 2012.

Nollkaemper, André. 'Procedural Aspects of Shared Responsibility in International Adjudication'. *Journal of International Dispute Settlement* 4 no. 2 (2013): 277–294.

Nollkaemper, André. 'Power and Responsibility'. In *A Lackland Law? Territory, Effectiveness and Jurisdiction in International Law*, edited by Alfredo Di Stefano, 19–44. Turin: G. Giappichelli Editore, 2015.

Nollkaemper, André, and Dov Jacobs. 'Shared Responsibility in International Law: A Conceptual Framework'. *Michigan Journal of International Law* 34 (2013): 359–438.

Nollkaemper, André, and Ilias Plakokefalos. *Principles of Shared Responsibility in International Law: An Appraisal of the State of the Art*. Cambridge: Cambridge University Press, 2014.

Nye, Joseph S. *Soft Power: The Means to Success in World Politics*. New York: Public Affairs, 2005.

Papastavridis, Efthymios. 'Fortress Europe and FRONTEX: Within or Without International Law?'. *Nordic Journal of International Law* 79 no. 1 (2010): 75–111.

Singh, Amrit. *Globalizing Torture: CIA Secret Detention and Extraordinary Rendition*. New York: Open Society Foundations, 2013.

Thompson, Dennis F. 'Moral Responsibility of Public Officials: The Problem of Many Hands'. *The American Political Science Review* 74 no. 4 (1980): 905–915.

Tondini, Matteo. 'Shared Responsibility in Coalitions of the Willing'. In *The Practice of Shared Responsibility*, edited by André Nollkaemper and Ilias Plakokefalos. Cambridge: Cambridge University Press, 2016, forthcoming.

Van de Poel, Ibo *et al*. 'The Problem of Many Hands: Climate Change as an Example'. *Science and Engineering Ethics* 64 (2004): 18–49.

Van der Wilt, Harmen. 'Joint Criminal Enterprise Possibilities and Limitations'. *Journal of International Criminal Justice* 5 (2007): 91–108.

Wallach, Michael A., Nathan Kogan, and Daryl J. Bem. 'Group influence on individual risk taking'. *Journal of Abnormal & Social Psychology* 65 (1962): 75–86.

Wallach, Michael A., Nathan Kogan, and Daryl J. Bem. 'Diffusion of responsibility and level of risk taking in groups'. *Journal of Abnormal & Social Psychology* 68 (1964): 263–274.

Watkins, John W. N. 'The Principle of Methodological Individualism'. *British Journal for the Philosophy of Science* 3 no. 10 (1952): 186–189.

Zifcak, Spencer. 'The Responsibility to Protect after Libya and Syria'. *Melbourne Journal of International Law* 13 no. 1 (2012).

Zimmerman, Michael J. 'Sharing Responsibility'. *American Philosophical Quarterly* 22 no. 2 (1985): 115–122.

Zwanenburg, Martin. 'Shared Responsibility in NATO-led Operations'. In *The Practice of Shared Responsibility*, edited by André Nollkaemper and Ilias Plakokefalos. Cambridge: Cambridge University Press, 2016, forthcoming.

2

EXTRATERRITORIALITY AND HUMAN RIGHTS

Prospects and challenges

Marko Milanovic

2.1 Introduction

The territorial scope of application of human rights treaties is undoubtedly one of the most current and complex topics of contemporary public international law. The scope of many human rights treaties is at least partly determined by how we interpret their (often significantly different) jurisdiction clauses, which set out threshold criteria for the emergence of state obligations. For example, Article 2(1) of the International Covenant on Civil and Political Rights (ICCPR) provides that '[e]ach State Party to the present Covenant undertakes to respect and to ensure to all individuals within its territory and subject to its jurisdiction the rights recognised in the present Covenant', Article 1 of the European Convention on Human Rights stipulates that the 'High Contracting Parties shall secure to everyone within their jurisdiction the rights and freedoms defined in Section I of this Convention', while under Article 2(1) of the UN Convention against Torture (CAT) '[e]ach State Party shall take effective legislative, administrative, judicial or other measures to prevent acts of torture in any territory under its jurisdiction'.

Even a casual look at these provisions will reveal some important differences. For instance, while under the ICCPR and the European Convention on Human Rights it is the *individual* who is subject to or within the state's jurisdiction, under the CAT it is the *territory* that must be under the state's jurisdiction. The ICCPR also seems to set out a conjunctive requirement that for the treaty to apply, the individual must be *both* within the state's territory (to which the European Convention on Human Rights does not at all refer) *and* subject to its jurisdiction, although the Human Rights Committee has chosen to interpret this text as requiring states to ensure the human rights of all individuals within their territories *and* all individuals subject to their jurisdiction.[1] The ICCPR also explicitly distinguishes between the obligations to respect and to ensure human rights, while the European Convention on Human Rights speaks of the obligation to respect in the heading of Article 1, but only of the obligation to secure in the actual text.[2]

Despite these differences, the magic word in all three texts is (state) 'jurisdiction', which is the main operative legal concept, although it must be said that some important treaties do not use it, primarily those dealing with socioeconomic rights.[3] The interpretation of this single word has provoked many controversies, a rich, varied and often conflicting jurisprudence (especially on the part of the European Court of Human Rights) and a veritable mountain of scholarship.[4] The purpose of this chapter is not to add a pebble to this mountain by presenting a novel theory on the extraterritorial application of human rights treaties; rather, I wish to provide an accessible primer to the various strands of existing jurisprudence and to outline current and possible future challenges, as well as the directions that the jurisprudence might take. I will focus in that regard on the extraterritorial applicability of human rights in armed conflict, electronic extraterritorial surveillance conducted by the United States National Security Agency (NSA) and its allies, such as the British Government Communications Headquarters (GCHQ), and various scenarios of shared responsibility.[5]

My argument is that existing case law suffers from numerous gaps and inconsistencies with regard to questions of both state jurisdiction and state responsibility. In respect of the former, it is difficult to predict with confidence how the European Court in particular will address some of the most complex challenges before it. That said, in my view the jurisprudence on the extraterritorial application of human rights treaties would rest on more secure and principled foundations if it were to adopt a distinction between the negative obligation of states to respect human rights (which should be territorially unlimited) and the positive obligation to secure or ensure human rights (which would depend on territorial control). Such an approach would be conceptually coherent, and would achieve a better balance between the considerations of universality of human rights (which favour an expansive approach towards extraterritorial application) and considerations of effectiveness (which favour a more restrictive approach). It would, for example, allow for relatively simple and predictable solutions to threshold questions of applicability with regard to various scenarios of extraterritorial surveillance. Questions of shared responsibility, on the other hand, are genuinely difficult; not simply because the existing human rights jurisprudence is insufficiently developed, but also because of the lack of clarity in the wider responsibility framework of general international law. Overcoming these difficulties would require, at the very least, a higher degree of conceptual precision than that currently employed by human rights bodies, which need to explain more fully and clearly how and why they approach specific questions of state responsibility.

2.2 The story thus far: three models of extraterritorial application

2.2.1 In general

This section will provide a brief outline of the (often conflicting and confusing) case law on the meaning of the concept of state jurisdiction in human rights treaties.

I will examine the spatial model of jurisdiction (which conceptualises it as effective overall control of an area), the personal model of jurisdiction as authority and control over individuals, and a third model which distinguishes between the positive and negative obligations of states under human rights treaties.

The European Court has produced by far the most case law on extraterritorial application, both in quantity and in variety. The jurisprudence of the Human Rights Committee, on the other hand, is not as conflicting or contradictory, even if it is less varied. The Committee has also tended to be more generous towards applicants than the European Court. Unless I am mistaken, there is not a single case in which the Committee rejected the communication of a person who made an arguable claim that his or her rights were violated extraterritorially, on the grounds that this person was not subject to the jurisdiction of the relevant state.[6] The same is generally true of other UN treaty bodies, as well as the institutions of the inter-American system.

2.2.2 The spatial model

The spatial model of jurisdiction as *de facto* effective control over areas is the least controversial. The European Court famously articulated it in the *Loizidou* case dealing with Northern Cyprus,[7] the Human Rights Committee similarly applied it to, e.g. the occupation by Israel of the Palestinian territories,[8] and the International Court of Justice (ICJ) likewise found the ICCPR to apply during occupation in the *Wall*[9] and *Congo v. Uganda* cases.[10] Under this model, an individual who is located in a territory under a state's *control* (but not necessarily its *sovereignty*) has human rights vis-à-vis that state. This approach makes intuitive sense: if a state exercises control over the territory of another state that in many respects replicates the extent of control that it has over its own territory, then it is only appropriate for it to have human rights obligations towards the territory's inhabitants. As the European Court held in *Loizidou*, what matters is the *fact* of such control, regardless of whether it was obtained lawfully or unlawfully (i.e. in violation of the territorial state's sovereignty).

While control is a matter of fact, the required degree of control, i.e. what makes control over territory *effective*, may in some situations pose difficult problems.[11] That said, the main benefit of this conception of jurisdiction is its clarity. There will always be borderline cases,[12] but the test itself is still workable and provides some limits on states' obligations. Yet the test's benefit is also its drawback, since the spatial model may be *too* limiting. There are many situations in which a state is factually perfectly capable of violating the rights of individuals *without* controlling the actual area. For example, the whole point of using drones for targeted killing is that the state does *not* need to have troops on the ground. Similarly, the 'enhanced interrogation' of high-value Al-Qaeda detainees after 9/11 was conducted at the Central Intelligence Agency (CIA) black sites in third states, such as Lithuania and Poland, where US agents were using facilities provided to them by the territorial state.[13] The more such cases keep popping up (and there have been plenty), the more morally arbitrary it seems to condition the state's obligations on territorial control when such control is entirely irrelevant to the substance of the violation, and consequently the more unsatisfactory and unappealing the spatial model becomes. And thus we come to the alternative, a personal conception of jurisdiction as control over *individuals*, rather than spaces.

2.2.3 The personal model

The idea that the word 'jurisdiction' in human rights treaties denotes authority and control exercised by states over individuals, rather than over territories or areas, also has a long pedigree. It was first set out by the European Commission in one of the early interstate cases between Cyprus and Turkey,[14] but its biggest proponent has been the Human Rights Committee. In *Lopez-Burgos*, a case dealing with an abduction by Uruguayan agents of an individual on Argentine territory, the Committee held that:

> The reference in Article 1 of the Optional Protocol to 'individuals subject to its jurisdiction' does not affect the above conclusion because the reference in that article is not to the place where the violation occurred, *but rather to the relationship between the individual and the state in relation to a violation of any of the rights set forth in the Covenant, wherever they occurred*. . . . Article 2 (1) of the Covenant places an obligation upon a State Party to respect and to ensure rights 'to all individuals within its territory and subject to its jurisdiction', but does not imply that the State Party concerned cannot be held accountable for violations of rights under the Covenant which its agents commit upon the territory of another State, whether with the acquiescence of the Government of that State or in opposition to it. . . . In line with this, *it would be unconscionable* to so interpret the responsibility under Article 2 of the Covenant as to permit a State Party to perpetrate violations of the Covenant on the territory of another State, *which violations it could not perpetrate on its own territory*.[15] (emphasis mine)

Note how the Committee is essentially making an appeal to the universality of human rights in order to justify the personal model. It has reiterated this approach in General Comment No. 31, when it held that:

> A State Party must respect and ensure the rights laid down in the Covenant to anyone within the power or effective control of that State Party, even if not situated within the territory of the State Party . . . regardless of the circumstances in which such power or effective control was obtained.[16]

So articulated, the principle is broad enough to make any human rights lawyer happy. But the benefit is, once again, also a drawback, since it seems impossible to limit this principle in a non-arbitrary way. If depriving an individual of liberty would constitute 'authority and control' or 'power and effective control' over that person, why would depriving that person of life not also qualify as authority, power and control?[17] Is there any meaningful difference between detaining a person and then killing them, and just killing them outright, be that by a missile fired from a drone, in a commando raid by troops on the ground as with the killing of Osama bin Laden by US forces in Pakistan, or simply by poison in their soup?[18] And if killing an individual is an exercise of power over them, as it surely must be, why would not the same apply to destroying their property, or reading their emails?

In other words, applying the personal model consequentially would lead to human rights treaties governing *any* extraterritorial state action. While that may not overly concern the Human Rights Committee (yet), it was precisely this kind of fear – of possible overreach, lack of institutional competence and all sorts of practical and political difficulties on the merits – that in the immediate wake of 9/11 led the European Court to render its *Bankovic* inadmissibility decision, which dealt with the destruction of a TV station in central Belgrade in a North Atlantic Treaty Organisation (NATO) airstrike during the 1999 Kosovo intervention.[19] The *Bankovic* Court not only held that the victims of aerial bombardment were not within the jurisdiction of the NATO states (since without troops on the ground, the NATO states lacked effective control over the actual area despite controlling its airspace), but did so on methodologically dubious grounds while studiously ignoring the personal model of jurisdiction. It moreover explicitly held that the extraterritorial application of the European Convention on Human Rights can only be *exceptional* and is an all-or-nothing proposition: Convention rights could not be divided and tailored to suit the circumstances of the particular extraterritorial act in question.[20] The reference to the exceptional nature of extraterritorial application was not to the simple and incontestable fact that states will generally far more frequently be on their own territory than outside it, but was meant to send a message that the Court will only rarely be prepared to accept claims originating in an extraterritorial context.[21]

Rarely has an admissibility decision produced so much controversy as *Bankovic*. As the criticism of *Bankovic* mounted,[22] as its arbitrariness was increasingly exposed in a succession of smaller cases,[23] and as the composition of the Court itself changed, the Court decided to systematically revisit the question of extraterritorial application in the *Al-Skeini* case. It took the opportunity to repair some of the damage done by the often-arbitrary distinctions drawn in its own conflicting case law, as well as by the British courts which had tried faithfully to apply it.[24]

The Court reaffirmed the validity both of the spatial model[25] and of the personal model,[26] concluding with regard to the latter that:

> It is clear that, whenever the state through its agents exercises control and authority over an individual, and thus jurisdiction, the state is under an obligation under Article 1 to secure to that individual the rights and freedoms under Section 1 of the Convention that are relevant to the situation of that individual. In this sense, therefore, the Convention rights can be 'divided and tailored' (compare *Bankovic*, cited above, § 75).[27]

The Court thus not only defined 'jurisdiction' as state 'control and authority over an individual', but it also partly overruled (or, in its words, 'compared') *Bankovic* by allowing for the dividing and tailoring of Convention rights, as opposed to the all-or-nothing *Bankovic* approach. But the Court was still aware that if it defined jurisdiction in such terms the Convention would apply *everywhere*. Again, there is no normatively sound, non-arbitrary way of concluding, for instance, that physical custody qualifies as 'control and authority', while killing (or the ability to kill) does not. Indeed, the Court held that the five applicants killed by British troops on patrol in Basra were within the United Kingdom's jurisdiction precisely because killing *was* authority and control.[28] The Court hence felt compelled to find a limiting principle, and found one in the concept of 'public powers' that it imported from the *Bankovic* analysis of the spatial model of jurisdiction: the killing of the applicants was thus an exercise of UK jurisdiction, but only because due to the occupation of Iraq and relevant resolutions of the Security Council, the United Kingdom 'assumed authority and responsibility for the maintenance of security in South East Iraq'.[29]

In sum, *Al-Skeini* was a major attempt by the Court at fixing *Bankovic*, in which it was partly successful. But it would still not go all the way. It in fact preserved the result of *Bankovic* and by using the nebulous concept of 'public powers' managed to avoid the application of the European Convention on Human Rights to foreign military interventions *simpliciter*, as, e.g. recently in Libya. The use of drones in areas not under a state's control would likewise be outside the scope of the Convention per *Al-Skeini* and *Bankovic*. The uncertainties of *Al-Skeini* similarly left the door open for the United Kingdom to argue that it is confined to the specific facts of Iraq, and that the Convention largely does not apply to UK activities in Afghanistan.[30] The lines drawn by the judgement are better than those in *Bankovic*, but they remain arbitrary and uncertain. *Al-Skeini* will certainly not be the last word on the matter.[31]

2.2.4 A third model: positive and negative obligations

Just as the spatial model can *in extremis* collapse into the personal one, the more the area subject to jurisdiction shrinks in size, so does the personal model ultimately collapse, and the extraterritorial application of human rights treaties becomes limitless. The European Court's attempt to prop it up through the 'public powers' concept may work for a while, but will increasingly be exposed as unstable.

I have hence argued in favour of a third model which would be based on the distinction between the overarching positive obligation of states to secure or ensure human rights (which extends even to preventing human rights violations by third parties) and the negative obligation of states to respect human rights (which only requires states to refrain from interfering with the rights of individuals without sufficient justification).[32] Under this model, 'jurisdiction' would primarily mean effective overall control over areas, and the overarching positive obligation would be predicated on a state having such control over an area, because in the overwhelming majority of situations the state actually *needs* such control in order to be able to comply with this obligation.

On the other hand, the negative obligation to respect human rights would be territorially unlimited and not subject to any jurisdiction threshold, because any such threshold that was non-arbitrary would collapse anyway. Textually this would flow from Article 1 European Convention on Human Rights referring only to the obligation to *secure*, while Article 2(1) ICCPR could reasonably be read as attaching the jurisdiction threshold only to the obligation to *ensure*, but not the obligation to respect. Alternatively, negative obligations could still be subject to the jurisdictional threshold under the personal model, but as we have seen, this threshold actually collapses and the end result would be the same. The rationale for not limiting negative obligations is that states are *always* perfectly able to comply with them, since they remain in full control of their own organs and agents.[33]

The moral logic of universality is thus brought to its ultimate conclusion, while jurisdiction still serves as a limiting factor for (most of) the normally far more onerous positive obligations. I am not arguing that this model is perfect,[34] but I do claim that it is clear, predictable, precludes the vast majority of arbitrary outcomes and provides a relatively stable balance between considerations of universality and effectiveness. Similarly, while I argue that this is how human rights treaties *should be* interpreted, I am not claiming that this is what human rights bodies or courts are already doing. Rather, I am saying that this model presents an equilibrium towards which the spatial and personal conceptions of jurisdiction will naturally tend to gravitate.

Having canvassed the jurisprudence and the possible conceptual approaches to the extraterritorial application of human rights treaties, I wish to take a look at three challenges that human rights courts and bodies will have to address in the near future: the application of human rights treaties to extraterritorial armed conflicts, to extraterritorial surveillance and in the context of the involvement of multiple state actors in complex or compound human rights violations.

2.3 Challenges: armed conflict

The most obvious cases in which the issue of extraterritorial application arises and will continue to arise are those of armed conflict, whether international or non-international, which is cross-border in nature from the perspective of the relevant state. Indeed, as we have seen, much of the jurisprudence regarding extraterritorial application was born out of situations of armed conflict, be that the Northern Cyprus line of cases, *Bankovic* or *Al-Skeini*. That said, the question of extraterritorial application goes well beyond situations of armed conflict, even if it is particularly acute therein.

If we only take a look at the docket of the European Court, we will observe a number of recent or pending cases dealing with extraterritorial armed conflicts. First, the Grand Chamber has already held in the case of *Hassan v. United Kingdom*,[35] dealing with the detention of an Iraqi individual by British troops and his subsequent detention on the premises of a US military base, and his later death in unclear circumstances, in which it reaffirmed that custody *ipso facto* constitutes authority and control, and thus jurisdiction, over an individual.[36] Second, judgment is pending in another Grand Chamber case concerning Iraq, *Jaloud v. The Netherlands*,[37] dealing with the procedural obligation to investigate a killing by Dutch troops manning a checkpoint. Third, the Grand Chamber will soon hold hearings in the interstate case *Georgia v. Russia (No. 2)*,[38] concerning the 2008 conflict between the two states and alleged human rights violations by Russian or Russian-controlled forces on the territory of Georgia. Fourth, almost as soon as the 2014 Crimea crisis erupted, Ukraine filed another interstate case against Russia, in which the Court immediately ordered interim measures of protection.[39] It will obviously take a number of years before that case is heard, and it may ultimately even be withdrawn as a part of an eventual larger political deal between the two states. But the message here is nonetheless clear: it is not only individual applicants who are aggressively pushing extraterritorial application arguments against states, but the states are also doing so against each other.

Similarly, several important cases on extraterritorial application have been decided by domestic courts, especially by UK courts under the Human Rights Act 1998. For instance, the High Court recently decided *Serdar Mohammed v. Ministry of Defence*, in which it held that the detention of captured Taliban fighters by British troops in Afghanistan was covered by the Convention, and that if it lasted beyond 96 hours it was contrary to Article 5 European Convention on Human Rights.[40] The case will undoubtedly be appealed. Even so, it is emblematic of the failure of the principal legal strategy of the UK government: denial that the European Convention on Human Rights applies extraterritorially to Afghanistan. Even after having lost *Al-Skeini* in the European Court, the UK government chose to read *Al-Skeini* as confined to the specific facts of Iraq with no relevance to Afghanistan, an argument that British domestic courts have found or will likely find unpersuasive.[41]

British domestic courts also decided two very interesting cases (both confusingly called *Smith*) that were practically *Al-Skeini* in reverse.[42] They concerned the right to life of the United Kingdom's own soldiers vis-à-vis the United Kingdom regarding the failure of the UK authorities to supply them with proper equipment, such as body armour, for their deployment in Iraq. The UK Supreme Court found all UK soldiers to be within the jurisdiction of the United Kingdom under the personal model, and therefore also to be subject to the United Kingdom's authority and control. A similar case, *Pritchard v. United Kingdom*, was pending before the European Court but was settled after the UK Supreme Court's second *Smith* decision.[43] It seems inevitable that further such cases will be brought before domestic and international courts against the United Kingdom and other states, challenging hitherto judicially untouchable procurement and operational decisions in military deployments, as well as potentially under other substantive rights beyond the right to life.

In addition to the threshold question of extraterritorial application, armed conflict situations inevitably involve the substantive question of the interaction between human rights law and international humanitarian law (IHL). This is an issue of great complexity that most human rights bodies have yet to grapple with systematically. The approach of the European Court in particular has been characterised by much avoidance of IHL. Similarly, a further issue not limited to armed conflict, but crucial for the interplay between human rights and IHL, is the availability of *derogations* from human rights treaties in an extraterritorial context. According to the dicta of some of the judges of the highest UK courts, such derogations would not be available, since an extraterritorial public emergency could not threaten the life of the derogating nation as required by the text of the derogation clauses, such as Article 15 European Convention on Human Rights.[44] In other words, no matter how bad the insurgency in Iraq was during the UK forces' presence in that state, that situation did not threaten the life of the United Kingdom itself.

The better view, however, is that extraterritorial derogations should be available by reference to the effects the emergency has on the life of the affected local population. In particular, the more expansive the territorial scope of application of human rights treaties becomes, the more arbitrarily derogation seems to be limited strictly to the derogating state's territory – even though derogations can be a useful tool in providing sufficient clarity and flexibility in extraordinary and frequently very difficult situations, such as the conflicts in Iraq and Afghanistan.[45] The European Court and other human rights bodies have yet to provide authoritative guidance on this issue, but it seems inevitable that they will soon have to do so.[46]

2.4 Challenges: extraterritorial surveillance

2.4.1 In general

The 2013 revelations by Edward Snowden of the scope and magnitude of electronic surveillance programmes run by the NSA and GCHQ have provoked intense and ongoing public debate regarding the proper limits of such intelligence activities. The political fallout of the Snowden disclosures has undoubtedly been very significant. They revealed the sheer technological capacity of the NSA and other signals intelligence agencies to collect personal data on a vast scale and to subvert and intercept communication over the internet.

It is inevitable that human rights language and forums will be used in challenging the legality of electronic surveillance programmes, as is already being done by privacy activists.[47] Special rapporteurs of the UN Human Rights Council have started examining the impact of counterterrorism measures on the right to privacy.[48] Litigation already is or soon will be pending, either before domestic courts in states where human rights treaties are directly applicable, or before international judicial and quasi-judicial bodies. Indeed, one case before the European Court of Human Rights dealing with GCHQ interception of external communications has already been communicated to the UK government, with the Court moving at (for it) an almost unprecedented speed in dealing with the case.[49]

Crucially, human rights language has also been used at a purely inter-governmental level. Prompted by allegations of US spying on their leaders, in October 2013 Brazil and Germany submitted a draft resolution entitled 'the right to privacy in the digital age' to the Third Committee of the UN General Assembly.[50] After some revision and the usual diplomatic wrangling, this was adopted without a vote by the Assembly itself.[51]

On any assessment, the Assembly's resolution on the right to privacy in the digital age represents a major development. It locates the issue of electronic surveillance firmly within the framework of international human rights law. It directly invokes Article 12 of the Universal Declaration of Human Rights and Article 17 ICCPR. In the preamble, the Assembly expresses its deep concern

> at the negative impact that surveillance and/or interception of communications, *including extraterritorial surveillance and/or interception of communications*, as well as the collection of personal data, in particular when carried out on a mass scale, may have on the exercise and enjoyment of human rights (emphasis added).

Nor is the resolution the last word on the matter from within the UN system. As requested by the resolution, in June 2014 the Office of the High Commissioner for Human Rights produced a major report on privacy in the digital age,[52] while in September 2014 a panel discussion was held on the topic at the twenty-seventh regular session of the Human Rights Council, in which many states, experts and NGOs took part.[53] It is to be expected that electronic surveillance will be on the agenda of UN bodies for many years to come.

I will leave aside the substantive compatibility of surveillance programmes with the human rights to privacy, and focus on the preliminary, threshold question of whether human rights treaties even apply to *extraterritorial* surveillance activities. Do I, for example, have the right to privacy under the ICCPR vis-à-vis the United States if the NSA collects and reads my emails while I am sitting in the United Kingdom? This will obviously be the first question that various human rights institutions will have to answer, and it is also very much one of first impression.

I would argue that the third model of extraterritorial application – which distinguishes between positive and negative obligations – is the only one which provides easy, clear answers to whether human rights treaties apply to foreign surveillance. If the negative obligation to respect the right to privacy is territorially unlimited, then *any* interference with this right in *any* place in the world would implicate the ICCPR or the European Convention on Human Rights. This is not to say that such interferences, whether through a mass surveillance programme or a targeted one, would necessarily be *illegal*. Rather, any such interference would need to be substantively *justified* within the analytical framework of human rights treaties (in other words, is the interference prescribed by law; does it serve a legitimate aim; is it proportionate to that aim). No threshold question of jurisdiction would arise and, just as with purely internal surveillance, the analysis would need to be one on the merits.[54]

The third model may provide a clear answer on the threshold question of applicability, but it is also one which is very broad and immediately leads to examination of the merits, which carries with it its own uncertainties. This is precisely why the third model may not be appealing to those actors, be they governments, secret services, courts, or what have you, who would want to *avoid* the difficulties of a merits analysis or the constraints of human rights treaties altogether. Let us thus also look at how this question would be addressed within the spatial and personal models of jurisdiction.

2.4.2 Spatial model: individual in an area under the state's control

The application of the spatial model would be straightforward in principle. If an individual is located in an area under the state's control and the individual's privacy is interfered with by the agents of the state, human rights treaties would clearly apply. Thus if Angela Merkel was in New York City visiting the United Nations and a CIA agent searched her hotel room,[55] physically tampered with her phone or computer, or intercepted her communications remotely,[56] she would be subject to US jurisdiction under the spatial model and her privacy would be protected by the ICCPR. (This does not mean that the surveillance would necessarily be unlawful, but it would have to be justified in order to be lawful.) Note also that for the spatial model, it is *control* over territory alone rather than *title* that matters: the result of this inquiry would be the same if Angela was visiting Iraq while it was under US occupation and the CIA was doing its business there.

When in control of territory, states also have the positive obligation to secure or ensure human rights, and to protect individuals within their jurisdiction from human rights violations by third parties.[57] In the surveillance context, this obligation would have two main components. First, states would need to regulate private companies operating in areas under control that collect, store, process or have access to personal data. This would include, but not necessarily be limited to, basic standards on data protection. Second, states would need to exercise due diligence and undertake all effective measures reasonably available to them to prevent interferences with privacy by third parties. If, for example, France knew that a third state was intercepting the communications of individuals living in France on a massive scale, and if such interferences were objectively unjustified under the framework of human rights law, France would need to implement such technological and other measures that are at its disposal to obstruct these interferences – for instance, mandating the use of encryption when transmitting personal data.[58]

2.4.3 Spatial model: interference in an area under the state's control

New technologies can today frequently lead to a disconnect between the location of the *individual* and the location of the *interference* with the individual's privacy.[59]

For example, while sitting in her office in Berlin, Angela Merkel can send an email to someone in Australia, but the communication itself can be routed through a server in the United Kingdom and intercepted there by GCHQ. Thus although Angela is located in Germany, the actual interference with her privacy took place in the United Kingdom.

The question is how to determine state jurisdiction in situations in which the interference was carried out in an area under a state's control, but the individual is not in any such area. Should we look at such cases under the spatial model (on the basis of the location of the interference) or under the personal model (by seeing whether the interception as such qualifies as an exercise of authority and control over the individual)?

At both a textual and conceptual level, I am sceptical that the spatial model could be applied on the basis of the location of the interference alone. If the inquiry is whether the individual is within or subject to a state's jurisdiction, and if 'jurisdiction' means an area under the state's effective control, it is hard to see why the location of the interference should matter.[60] But our *intuitions*, on the other hand, do seem to favour the application of human rights treaties in such circumstances. For example, I normally live and work in the United Kingdom, but I travel relatively frequently. If the UK police were to search my flat in Nottingham or to hack into my office computer while I was out of the country, *surely* the ICCPR and the European Convention on Human Rights would apply and my privacy rights would be engaged. If they were to seize my UK bank account while I was outside the United Kingdom, *surely* my property rights under Protocol No. 1 to the European Convention on Human Rights would be engaged. And so forth.

There have been plenty of cases before the European Court or the Human Rights Committee with such an extraterritorial element, in which everyone, including the respondent state, simply took for granted that the treaty applied.[61] Nobody ever doubted, for instance, that Article 6 European Convention on Human Rights fair trial rights applied to a person who was tried *in absentia* but who *absconded to another state's territory* while the trial went on.[62] The Court similarly found Article 6 to apply to civil proceedings brought in Italy by claimants living in Serbia for damages arising from the destruction of the same Belgrade TV station that was at issue in *Bankovic.*[63] Indeed, it would seem manifestly arbitrary for the Convention not to apply. If that is so, then why should privacy rights be any different? The question is *what theory* covers these kinds of situations.

The first option is to treat such situations under the spatial model, but as I have explained above that is problematic, since the focus of that model is on the location of the individual rather than on the location of the interference. The second is to examine them under the personal model. But if we accept, for example, that I am an individual under the 'authority and control' of the United Kingdom when UK agents search my flat in Nottingham even when I am outside the United Kingdom, I do not see how we could deny that I would also be under the authority and control of the United Kingdom if UK agents surreptitiously searched my flat in Belgrade. Similarly, if the European Convention on Human

Rights would apply to a search of my desktop computer in the United Kingdom even while I am in Serbia, then, because in performing this search the United Kingdom is exercising authority and control over me, I do not see why the European Convention on Human Rights would not apply to a similar search of my laptop by UK agents operating in Serbia, whether lawfully or unlawfully. In other words, the location of both the individual and the interference seems irrelevant under the logic of the personal model. A third option was adopted in the Office of the United Nations High Commissioner for Human Rights report on privacy in the digital age, which relies on state control *over telecommunications infrastructure*.[64] This option to an extent disregards the focus of Article 2(1) ICCPR on the *individual* as the object of jurisdiction, and it is also questionable in light of scenarios in which states do not need to control or penetrate infrastructure in order to conduct surveillance (by tampering with or hacking a smartphone directly, for example).

My own preferred solution to such cases is, hence, the third model of jurisdiction, which distinguishes between positive and negative obligations. The reason why human rights treaties would apply to these scenarios is because they should apply to *all* potential violations of negative obligations, including, for example, the negative obligation to refrain from interfering with privacy, regardless of the technological means employed.

Whatever theory one chooses, surveillance programmes in which the interference with privacy takes place within an area under the state's control even though the individual is not located in this area may be more open to challenge than those programmes in which both the interference and the individual are outside areas controlled by the state. For example, GCHQ's massive Tempora programme taps transatlantic fibre-optic cables as they pass *through the United Kingdom* or its territorial sea, and obtains enormous amounts of data.[65] The interference hence takes place within the United Kingdom, even though the person whose communication is intercepted is located outside it. And even if the interception of communication or the collection of personal data does *not* take place in an area under the state's control, its subsequent storage, processing and use – all of which would constitute separate, fresh interferences with privacy – may well take place within such an area.

Notably, at least two surveillance/data collection cases before the European Court dealt with situations in which the interference was territorial but the individual was outside any area under the state's control. In the first case, *Weber and Saravia v. Germany*,[66] the applicants lived in Uruguay while their communication was allegedly intercepted in Germany. Germany actually even objected that the case was outside its jurisdiction under *Bankovic*,[67] but the Court avoided the matter and dismissed the case as manifestly ill-founded on the merits.[68] In the second case, *Liberty and Others v. the United Kingdom*,[69] two of the applicants were Irish organisations communicating with a British one, whose communication was allegedly intercepted in the United Kingdom. Neither the UK government nor the Court *proprio motu* considered that an Article 1 jurisdiction issue arose with respect to the

Irish applicants: in other words, they both assumed that the European Convention on Human Rights applied. The Court went on to find a violation of Article 8.

2.4.4 Personal model

The most problematic situation of surveillance is one where both the individual and the interference with their privacy are located in an area outside the state's control, and we look at such cases through the personal model of jurisdiction. We have seen how the case law of the European Court and the Human Rights Committee defines such jurisdiction in similar terms, as 'authority and control' or 'power and effective control' over individuals. The question is what exactly qualifies as such: authority, power or control, and how these criteria would apply to overseas surveillance. Consider the following scenarios, all of which, for the sake of the argument, take place in Berlin:

1   A CIA agent grabs Angela Merkel, disables her escort (assume he is some kind of judo master), and then physically searches her for items in her possession.
2   A CIA agent breaks into and searches Angela's apartment, and plants cameras and listening devices.
3   A CIA agent manages to get Angela's phone when she is not looking and furtively plants a tracking device in it.
4   A CIA agent breaks into Angela's office and hacks into her computer, uploading a virus and downloading sensitive data.
5   A CIA agent observes and listens to Angela, using a high-resolution camera/directed mike.
6   A CIA agent observes and monitors Angela's residence from the outside, using a high-resolution camera/directed mike, without necessarily observing Angela herself.
7   A CIA agent hacks Angela's phone or computer remotely.
8   A CIA agent intercepts Angela's calls, texts or emails midstream.
9   A CIA agent is able to collect information about who Angela calls, when, for how long (telephony metadata) or whom and when she emails (internet metadata).
10   The NSA obtains Angela's personal information from its partners in GCHQ, and proceeds to store and process that information.

Which of these situations qualify as an exercise of authority, power or control over Angela? All, some or none? As I explained before, the personal model of jurisdiction is prone to collapse (and that may be either a bug or a feature, depending on your point of view). It is very difficult to draw lines that are not arbitrary.

Of these ten scenarios, only (1) involves the exercise of physical power against Angela herself in the sense of an agent handling her bodily. Scenarios (2)–(4) all involve the exercise of physical power, but against Angela's property rather than her person. Scenarios (5) and (6) are physical but non-corporeal, as it were. Scenarios (7)–(10) are entirely virtual or digital.[70]

I personally see no legitimate way of drawing lines here. Scenario (1) surely must qualify as an exercise of power, authority or control over Angela, who is held and searched against her will by a state agent. But if (1) equals jurisdiction, then why not (2)–(4), and so on. In particular, if virtual methods can in principle accomplish the exact same result as physical ones, then there seems to be no valid reason to treat them differently and insist on some kind of direct corporeal intervention.[71] Therefore, unless one is willing to knowingly draw lines that are arbitrary, which by their very nature invite evasion and abuse, for instance by requiring such direct physical intervention or by using a nebulous and undefined criterion such as the *Bankovic/Al-Skeini* concept of 'public powers', the personal model would again seem to collapse, so that all cases of overseas surveillance by a state would be within the state's jurisdiction. The end result would ultimately be no different than if we applied my third model from the outset, dispensing with any jurisdictional inquiry with regard to possible violations of states' negative obligations.

In sum, I would submit that human rights treaties apply to most, if not all, foreign surveillance activities. This would certainly be the case under the third model of jurisdiction, and would equally be true of the personal model, if applied consistently and coherently. But the European Court may well decide to draw an arbitrary line somewhere, especially because whatever it decides in the context of extraterritorial privacy violations will necessarily have ramifications for other controversial issues, such as targeted killings (e.g. there seems to be no way of saying that reading Angela's email is an exercise of power, authority and control over her, but that killing her is not). Even though I have argued what the Court *should* do, it is impossible to predict what the Court *will* in fact do, except to say that it is more likely to find interferences with privacy that occur within a territory controlled by the state (e.g. the GCHQ Tempora programme) to be covered by the Convention. The Human Rights Committee's track record, on the other hand, suggests that it will be more generous than the European Court, even if its views may prove to have less of an impact. Indeed, already when it considered the US fourth periodic report in March 2014, the Committee expressed serious concerns about the NSA's surveillance programmes, noting in particular that the United States should:

> take all necessary measures to ensure that its surveillance activities, *both within and outside the United States*, conform to its obligations under the Covenant, including Article 17; in particular, measures should be taken to ensure that any interference with the right to privacy complies with the principles of legality, proportionality and necessity *regardless of the nationality or location* of individuals whose communications are under direct surveillance.[72] (emphasis added)

The Committee here undoubtedly endorsed the extraterritorial application of the Covenant to foreign surveillance, albeit without explaining under exactly what theory the Covenant would do so.

2.5 Challenges: shared responsibility

The last challenge I wish to address is that posed by having a multiplicity of actors involved in the same, complex, extraterritorial human rights violations. Take so-called extraordinary rendition as but one example. Such renditions involve at least two states: the state on whose territory the individual is located, and the state acquiring custody over the individual. But they can also involve more, for example a third state that is providing intelligence or other information while knowing that there is a serious risk that this could be used for rendition,[73] or a state that knowingly allows rendition flights to refuel on its territory, or pass through its airspace.[74] Each state in this scenario may have a share in the responsibility for the overarching wrongful conduct, or be responsible for some of its components.

Similarly, the involvement of multiple actors is now commonplace in military operations. Consider only the multinational deployments in Iraq or Afghanistan. Thus, for example, Danish troops can detain an individual on Afghan territory, move them to a base run by the United States, and later transfer them to Afghan custody, or can provide security to Afghan police officers who are actually doing the arresting. To complicate matters further, military operations are frequently conducted under the umbrella of an international organisation, as, for example, with regard to the 1999 NATO bombing of Serbia that was at issue in *Bankovic.*

Surveillance and intelligence-gathering also provide ample opportunity for various complicity scenarios.[75] One example is if a state engages in the surveillance of its own population and then provides the information it collected to a third party. The Five Eyes states (Australia, Canada, New Zealand, the United Kingdom and the United States) share with one another both signals intelligence and the data they collect, although the specifics are of course unclear. In terms of the applicability threshold of human rights treaties, the individuals concerned could be within the jurisdiction of the collecting/sending state, but not necessarily under the jurisdiction of the receiving state, at least not under the spatial model. Similarly, UK intelligence agencies could feed information and questions for the interrogation of an individual in Pakistani custody, or they could provide intelligence to US authorities for the purpose of executing a drone strike.[76]

Examples such as these introduce legal and factual complexities that I am not able to explore further in this chapter, other than by saying that such scenarios can implicate both the secondary rules of state responsibility (and the responsibility of international organisations) under general international law[77] and specific primary rules of international human rights law, often in combination with jurisdictional threshold issues and the problem that not all states are parties to the same treaties. Existing case law is not developed enough to provide for easy answers. Even when they do the right thing, human rights bodies may fail to do so with sufficient doctrinal rigour and conceptual clarity. For example, in the *El-Masri* case, which concerned the rendition of an individual from Macedonia to US custody,[78] the European Court apparently found Macedonia responsible not only for its own conduct in enabling the applicant's transfer to US authorities, but also for his subsequent detention and treatment at the hands of the United States. As André Nollkaemper aptly put it, '[w]hile the fact that the Court does not feel compelled to follow the ILC s conceptual straitjacket is in many respects refreshing, its own line is at times somewhat inconsistent and confusing'.[79] The general international responsibility framework laid down by the International Law Commission (ILC) may or may not be fully satisfactory, but the Court's terminological and conceptual imprecision also makes it difficult to see what exactly it is being replaced with.

My own position, which I will only articulate but not defend fully here, would be based on the same general idea as my extraterritorial application model, which distinguishes between positive and negative obligations while simultaneously sticking to the ILC's set of secondary rules. I would argue that states not only have a territorially unlimited negative obligation not to directly violate the rights of any given individual, but also a territorially unlimited, primary negative obligation to refrain from assisting third (state or private) parties in violating human rights, by analogy to the non-refoulement rule as set out in cases such as *Soering* or *Judge*.[80] By contrast, the positive obligation to protect individuals and prevent the violation of their rights by third parties would only arise if the individuals in question were in an area under the state's effective control, or otherwise subject to its jurisdiction. Thus, for example, if the United Kingdom knew that by providing intelligence to the United States it would enable the United States to unlawfully kill an individual in Pakistan, the United Kingdom would have an obligation under both the European Convention on Human Rights and the ICCPR not to provide this information, even though the individual was in Pakistan and not subject to any direct control by the United Kingdom. Similarly, the United Kingdom would have an obligation to refuse access to its airspace and facilities to a US flight carrying an unlawfully rendered person. But if that flight entered UK airspace or landed in UK-controlled territory, a stronger, positive obligation would arise that would require the United Kingdom to take all reasonable steps to secure custody over the rendered person and prevent further violation of his rights.

This model would stem not from the secondary rules of state responsibility, but from the primary rules implicit in human rights treaties, specifically the state obligation to respect and secure or ensure human rights. This approach is admittedly broad, but it is also clear, easy to apply, and consonant with the moral logic of the universality of human rights.[81]

2.6 Conclusion

There can be little doubt that international and domestic courts, as well as other human rights institutions, have enough on their plate when it comes to the extraterritorial application of human rights treaties. The possible scenarios of extra-territorial application are so many, so varied and potentially so complex and so intertwined with other issues that developing a principled and conceptually coherent approach is difficult at best. Difficult, but not impossible. The trend in recent years has certainly been towards a more expansive approach to extraterritoriality, with the normative pull of universality being hard to resist. But as I have argued elsewhere, that normative pull needs to be tempered with considerations of effectiveness if it is to become workable in reality. This requires providing states with sufficient flexibility in the substance of their human rights obligations, and with sufficient allowance made for the often extraordinary circumstances in which they find themselves, as well as doctrinal and conceptual clarity.[82]

As things stand, it seems more likely than not that courts will gravitate towards a model in which at least the negative obligations of states are for all intents and purposes territorially unlimited. How could it be, after all, that international human rights law has nothing to say with regard to the cross-border surveillance of billions of people? How could human rights fall silent in armed conflict?

But if the trend is there, there is still nothing *inevitable* about it. The fulfilment of the promise of extraterritorial application still requires time and a favourable political environment that will enable a series of sensible accommodations between courts, governments and activists. In particular, activists should realise that premature or overly aggressive strategies can ultimately prove to be counterproductive, while governments should stop blindly arguing against the extraterritorial application as such and focus more on the merits of the substantive rights at issue. In any event, there are many more exciting extraterritorial cases yet to come.

Notes

1   See Human Rights Committee, General Comment No. 31, UN Doc. CCPR/C/21/ Rev.1/Add.13 (2004), para. 10.

2   On positive obligations in the European Convention on Human Rights and the ICCPR, see generally P. van Dijk *et al.*, (eds), *Theory and Practice of the European Convention on Human Rights*, 4th edn (Antwerp: Intersentia, 2006), at 13; M. Nowak, *U.N. Covenant on Civil and Political Rights: CCPR Commentary*, 2nd edn (Kehl: Engel, 2005), at 37–41. I will return to the distinction between positive and negative obligations below.

3   For example, the International Covenant on Economic, Social and Cultural Rights (ICESCR) has no clause dedicated to its territorial scope of application; its Article 2(1) obliges each state party to undertake 'to take steps, individually and through international assistance and cooperation, especially economic and technical, to the maximum of its available resources, with a view to achieving progressively the full realisation of the rights recognised in the present Covenant by all appropriate means, including particularly the adoption of legislative measures'. The absence of any express reference to territorial application allows for a number of possible interpretations regarding the scope of the ICESCR – on one end of the spectrum as being strictly limited to the state's own territory, on the other as being territorially unlimited (especially having regard to the mention of 'international assistance and cooperation'), or somewhere in between as incorporating a jurisdiction criterion *sub silentio*. The concept of jurisdiction does make one appearance in the ICESCR in its Article 14, which provides that: '[e]ach State Party to the present Covenant which, at the time of becoming a Party, has not been able to secure in its metropolitan territory or other territories under its jurisdiction compulsory primary education, free of charge, undertakes, within two years, to work out and adopt a detailed plan of action for the progressive implementation, within a reasonable number of years, to be fixed in the plan, of the principle of compulsory education free of charge

for all'. The territorial scope of application of treaties on socioeconomic rights has been the subject of little jurisprudence, but has provoked significant scholarly inquiry. See *Maastricht Principles on Extraterritorial Obligations of States in the Area of Economic, Social and Cultural Rights* (Heidelberg: ETO Consortium, 2012), at www.etoconsortium.org/ en/library/maastricht-principles/; O. de Schutter *et al.*, 'Commentary to the Maastricht Principles' *Human Rights Quarterly* 34 (2012), 1084; M. Langford *et al.*, (eds), *Global Justice, State Duties: The Extraterritorial Scope of Economic, Social, and Cultural Rights in International Law* (Cambridge: Cambridge University Press, 2012); S. Skogly, *Beyond National Borders: States' Human Rights Obligations in International Cooperation* (Antwerp: Intersentia, 2006).

4   For book-length treatments, see F. Coomans and M. T. Kamminga, (eds), *Extraterritorial Application of Human Rights Treaties* (Antwerp: Intersentia, 2004); M. Gibney and S. Skogly, *Universal Human Rights and Extraterritorial Obligations* (Philadelphia: University of Pennsylvania Press, 2010); M. Gondek, *The Reach of Human Rights in a Globalising World: Extraterritorial Application of Human Rights Treaties* (Antwerp: Intersentia, 2009); M. Milanovic, *Extraterritorial Application of Human Rights Treaties: Law, Principles, and Policy* (Oxford: Oxford University Press, 2011); K. Da Costa, *The Extraterritorial Application of Selected Human Rights Treaties* (Leiden: Nijhoff, 2012). Among dozens of scholarly articles, see esp. J. Cerone, 'Jurisdiction and Power: The Intersection of Human Rights Law and the Law of Non-International Armed Conflict in an Extraterritorial Context' *Israel Law Review* 40 no. 2 (2007), 72; R. Wilde, 'Triggering State Obligations Extraterritorially: The Spatial Test in Certain Human Rights Treaties' *Israel Law Review* 40 (2007), 503.

5   Parts of the discussion that follows draw heavily on M. Milanovic, 'Human Rights Treaties and Foreign Surveillance: Privacy in the Digital Age' *Harvard International Law Journal* 56 no. 1 (2015): 81–146.

6   The Committee's generosity can be explained, in my view, by the fact that it does not necessarily need to live with the consequences of an expansive approach in the same way as the Strasbourg Court, where the stakes are higher because of the greater robustness of the regime and the binding nature of the Court's decisions.

7   *Loizidou* v. *Turkey*, App. No. 15318/89, Judgment (preliminary objections), 23 February 1995, para. 62: 'Bearing in mind the object and purpose of the Convention, the responsibility of a Contracting Party may also arise when as a consequence of military action – whether lawful or unlawful – it exercises effective control of an area outside its national territory. The obligation to secure, in such an area, the rights and freedoms set out in the Convention, derives from the fact of such control whether it be exercised directly, through its armed forces, or through a subordinate local administration.'

8   See Concluding Observations of the Human Rights Committee: Israel, UN Doc. CCPR/C/79/Add.93, 18 August 1998, para. 10: 'the Covenant must be held applicable to the occupied territories and those areas . . . where Israel exercises effective control'. See also Concluding Observations of the Committee on Economic, Social and Cultural Rights: Israel, UN Doc. E/C.12/1/Add.27, 4 December 1998, para. 8: 'The Committee is of the view that the State's obligations under the Covenant, apply to all territories and populations under its effective control'; Concluding Observations of the Committee on the Rights of the Child: Israel, UN Doc. CRC/C/15/Add.195, 4 October 2002, paras 2, 5, 57–58; Conclusions and Recommendations: United Kingdom of Great Britain and Northern Ireland, UN Doc. CAT/C/CR/33/3, 10 December 2004, para. 4(b).

9   International Court of Justice, *Legal Consequences of the Construction of a Wall in the Occupied Palestinian Territory*, Advisory Opinion, ICJ Reports 2004 (The Hague: International Court of Justice, 2004), p. 136, paras 109–111.

10   International Court of Justice, *Armed Activities on the Territory of the Congo (Democratic Republic of the Congo* v. *Uganda)*, Judgment, ICJ Reports (The Hague: International Court of Justice, 2005), p. 168, paras 179, 216–217.

11   For extended discussions of the spatial model, see, e.g., Wilde, 'Triggering State Obligations Extraterritorially'; Milanovic, *Extraterritorial Application of Human Rights Treaties*, at 135ff.

12   Cf. *Ilascu and others* v. *Moldova and Russia* [GC], App. No. 48787/99, 8 July 2004, paras 382–394 (speaking of a 'decisive influence' of Russia over a separatist part of Moldova as sufficing for jurisdiction), and its sequel, *Catan and Others* v. *Moldova and Russia* [GC], App. Nos. 43370/04, 8252/05 and 18454/06, 19 October 2012.

13   The European Court recently decided two cases regarding human rights abuses in the CIA 'black sites' in Poland, but obviously from the perspective of the *territorial* state, rather than the state that directly committed the abuse – see *Al Nashiri* v. *Poland*, App. No. 28761/11, 24 July 2014; *Abu Zubaydah* v. *Poland*, App. No. 7511/13, 24 July 2014. See also *El-Masri* v. *Macedonia* [GC], App. No. 39630/09, 13 December 2012.

14   *Cyprus* v. *Turkey* (dec.), App. Nos. 6780/74 and 6950/75, 26 May 1975, at 136, para. 8.

15   *Lopez-Burgos* v. *Uruguay* (1981) 68 ILR 29, Communication No. R.12/52, UN Doc. Supp. No. 40 (A/36/40) at 176 (1981), paras 12.2–12.3.

16   General Comment No. 31 (see note 1 above), para. 10. For similar decisions from the Inter-American system, see *Saldaño* v. *Argentina*, Report No. 38/99, Annual Report of the IACHR 1998, esp. paras 15–23; *Coard et al.* v. *United States*, Case No. 10.951, Report No. 109/99, Annual Report of the IACHR 1999, para. 37; *Armando Alejandre Jr and Others* v. *Cuba* ('Brothers to the Rescue'), Case No. 11.589, Report No. 86/99, 29 September 1999, para. 23; Decision on Request for Precautionary Measures (Detainees at Guantánamo Bay), 12 March 2002, 41 ILM 532 (2002).

17   One potential argument for saying that physical custody qualifies as authority and control over an individual, whereas killing them does not, is that custody allows for a broader spectrum of possible violations of an individual's rights, i.e. that the control exercised over the individual is more comprehensive. But while it is undeniably true that custody enables the state to do many different things to the individual (other than just killing them outright), why should such control be necessary for the individual to have human rights vis-à-vis that state? Compare, in that regard, the US Supreme Court's consideration of the meaning of the word 'seizure' in the Fourth Amendment to the Constitution, which it does *not* limit only to establishing custody over that individual, but extends also to the use of lethal force: see *Tennessee* v. *Garner*, 471 U. S. 1, 7 (1985) ('While it is not always clear just when minimal police interference becomes a seizure. . . there can be no question that apprehension by the use of deadly force is a seizure subject to the reasonableness requirement of the Fourth Amendment'.) The Court was unanimous on this point: 'For purposes of Fourth Amendment analysis, I agree with the Court that Officer Hymon "seized" Garner by shooting him'. 471 U. S. 1, 25 (O'Connor, J., joined by Burger, C. J., and Rehnquist, J., dissenting).

18   Compare the case of Alexander Litvinenko, a former Russian spy killed in London in November 2006 by radioactive poisoning, ostensibly at the hands of Russian agents. His widow filed an application against Russia before the European Court, which is still pending. See 'Strasbourg Court Sets Deadline for Russia on Litvinenko Case', Ria Novosti, 15 December 2010, at http://en.ria.ru/world/20101215/161786652.html.

19   *Bankovic and Others* v. *Belgium and Others* [GC] (dec.), App. No. 52207/99, 12 December 2001.

20   Ibid., para. 75.

21   See Wilde, 'Triggering State Obligations Extraterritorially', at 670.

22   See, e.g., E. Roxstrom, M. Gibney and T. Einarsen, 'The NATO Bombing Case (*Bankovic et al. v. Belgium et al.*) and the Limits of Western Human Rights Protection' *Boston University International Law Journal* 23 (2005), 55; R. Lawson, 'Life after Bankovic: On the Extraterritorial Application of the European Convention on Human Rights', in *Extraterritorial Application of Human Rights Treaties*, eds F. Coomans and M. T. Kamminga (Antwerp: Intersentia, 2004), at 83; O. De Schutter, 'Globalisation and Jurisdiction: Lessons from the European Convention on Human Rights' *Baltic Yearbook*

of International Law 6 (2006), 183; A. Orakhelashvili, 'Restrictive Interpretation of Human Rights Treaties in the Recent Jurisprudence of the European Court of Human Rights' *European Journal of International Law* 14 no. 3 (2003), 529.

23 See, e.g., *Issa* v. *Turkey*, App. No. 31821/96, 16 November 2004; *Isaak and Others* v. *Turkey* (dec.), App. No. 44587/98, 28 September 2006; *Pad and Others* v. *Turkey* (dec.), App. No. 60167/00, 28 June 2007.

24 *Al-Skeini and others* v. *United Kingdom* [GC], App. No. 55721/07, 7 July 2011 (hereinafter *Al-Skeini*). Notably, of the seventeen judges who sat on the *Al-Skeini* Grand Chamber, only three sat on the *Bankovic* Grand Chamber – Costa, Rozakis and Casadevall. Whereas Judge Costa, presiding over the *Al-Skeini* Grand Chamber, had also presided over the 2004 *Issa* Chamber, which openly contradicted *Bankovic* while directly invoking the language of the Human Rights Committee in *Lopez-Burgos*. See *Issa*, ibid., para. 71.

25 As 'effective control over an area': *Al-Skeini*, paras 138–140.

26 As 'state agent authority': ibid., paras 133–137.

27 Ibid., para. 137.

28 Ibid., para. 149.

29 Ibid., paras 135, 149–150.

30 See Communication from the United Kingdom concerning the case of Al-Skeini against United Kingdom to the Committee of Ministers, DH–DD (2012) 438, 2 May 2012, at https://wcd.coe.int/com.instranet.InstraServlet?command=com.instranet.CmdBlob Get&InstranetImage=2082643&SecMode=1&DocId=1885434&Usage=2 ('The UK considers that the Al-Skeini judgment is set in the factual circumstances of UK's past operations in Iraq and that it has no implications for its current operations elsewhere, including in Afghanistan'.)

31 For a detailed analysis of *Al-Skeini*, see M. Milanovic, '*Al-Skeini* and *Al-Jedda* in Strasbourg' *European Journal of International Law* 23 no. 1 (2012), 121.

32 See Milanovic, *Extraterritorial Application of Human Rights Treaties*, at 209–222.

33 See also B. Van Schaack, 'The United States' Position on the Extraterritorial Application of Human Rights Obligations: Now is the Time for Change' *International Law Studies* 90 (2014), 20, at 49–52.

34 See M. Milanovic, 'Reply to Shany, Lowe and Papanicolopulu', *EJIL: Talk!*, 5 December 2011, at www.ejiltalk.org/reply-to-shany-lowe-and-papanicolopulu/. See also Y. Shany, 'Taking Universality Seriously: A Functional Approach to Extra-territoriality in International Human Rights Law' *The Law & Ethics of Human Rights* 7 no. 1 (2013), 47.

35 *Hassan* v. *United Kingdom* [GC], App. No. 29750/09, 16 September 2014.

36 Ibid., paras 75–80.

37 App. No. 47708/08.

38 App. No. 38263/08.

39 *Ukraine* v. *Russia*, App. No. 20958/14.

40 *Serdar Mohammed* v. *Ministry of Defence* [2014] EWHC 1369 (QB).

41 See note 30 above.

42 *Smith* v. *Secretary of State for Defence* [2010] UKSC 29; *Smith* v. *Ministry of Defence* [2013] UKSC 41.

43 *Pritchard* v. *United Kingdom* (dec.), App. No. 1573/11, 18 March 2014.

44 See, e.g., *Smith* v. *Ministry of Defence* [2013] UKSC 41, paras 59–60. See also the contribution by Ralph Wilde to this volume.

45 See further M. Milanovic, 'Extraterritorial Derogations from Human Rights Treaties in Armed Conflict,' in N. Bhuta (ed.), *The Frontiers of Human Rights: Extraterritoriality and its Challenges*, Oxford: Oxford University Press, 2016: 55.

46 See also *Serdar Mohammed* (note 40 above), paras 155–156.

47 See International Principles on the Application of Human Rights to Communications Surveillance, 10 July 2013, at https://en.necessaryandproportionate.org/text (a set of thirteen principles drawn from human rights law that would apply to both domestic

and extraterritorial surveillance, drafted by numerous civil society organisations in comprehensive process led by Privacy International, Access, and the Electronic Frontier Foundation).

48 See Report of the Special Rapporteur on the Promotion and Protection of Human Rights and Fundamental Freedoms while Countering Terrorism, Martin Scheinin, UN Doc. A/HRC/13/37, 28 December 2009; Report of the Special Rapporteur on the Promotion and Protection of Human Rights and Fundamental Freedoms while Countering Terrorism, Martin Scheinin, UN Doc. A/HRC/14/46, 17 May 2010; Report of the Special Rapporteur on the Promotion and Protection of the Right to Freedom of Opinion and Expression, Frank La Rue, UN Doc. A/HRC/23/40, 17 April 2013; Report of the Special Rapporteur on the Promotion and Protection of Human Rights and Fundamental Freedoms while Countering Terrorism, Ben Emmerson, UN Doc. A/69/397, 23 September 2014.

49 *Big Brother Watch and Others* v. *United Kingdom*, App. No. 58170/13, lodged on 4 September 2013, communicated on 9 January 2014. Similarly, a domestic UK case was filed before the Investigatory Powers Tribunal by Privacy International, at www.privacyinternational.org/press-releases/privacy-international-files-legal-challenge-against-uk-government-over-mass.

50 'Exclusive: Germany, Brazil Turn to UN to Restrain American Spies', *The Cable*, 24 October 2013, at http://thecable.foreignpolicy.com/posts/2013/10/24/exclusive_germany_brazil_turn_to_un_to_restrain_american_spies. The draft itself is available as UN Doc. A/C.3/68/L.45, 1 November 2013.

51 UN Doc. A/RES/68/167, 18 December 2013.

52 Privacy in the digital age: report of the OHCHR, UN Doc. A/HRC/27/37, 30 June 2014. The report, as well as a number of contributions from different stakeholders, can be found at www.ohchr.org/EN/Issues/DigitalAge/Pages/DigitalAgeIndex.aspx.

53 See 'Human Rights Council holds panel discussion on the right to privacy in the digital age', OHCHR press release, 12 September 2014, at www.ohchr.org/en/NewsEvents/Pages/DisplayNews.aspx?NewsID=15017&LangID=E.

54 For a fuller argument, see Milanovic, 'Human Rights Treaties and Foreign Surveillance'.

55 It has been reported that GCHQ's programme 'Royal Concierge' is able to automatically identify and track potential hotel reservations for diplomats, so as to leave enough time to make the necessary technical preparations if person in question is a valuable surveillance target so that the hotel room, its phone lines and network can be bugged. See L. Poitras, M. Rosenbach and H. Stark, ' "Royal Concierge": GCHQ Monitors Hotel Reservations to Track Diplomats', *Spiegel Online International*, 17 November 2013, at www.spiegel.de/international/europe/gchq-monitors-hotel-reservations-to-track-diplomats-a-933914.html.

56 See, e.g., 'GCHQ Intercepted Foreign Politicians' Communications at G20 Summits', *The Guardian*, 17 June 2013, at www.theguardian.com/uk/2013/jun/16/gchq-intercepted-communications-g20-summits ('Foreign politicians and officials who took part in two G20 summit meetings in London in 2009 had their computers monitored and their phone calls intercepted on the instructions of their British government hosts, according to documents seen by the Guardian. Some delegates were tricked into using internet cafes which had been set up by British intelligence agencies to read their email traffic'.)

57 Cf. op. para. 4 of the Right to Privacy in a Digital Age resolution (note 51 above).

58 See also A. Peters, 'Surveillance without Borders: The Unlawfulness of the NSA Panopticon, Part II', *EJIL: Talk!*, 4 November 2013, at www.ejiltalk.org/surveillance-without-borders-the-unlawfulness-of-the-nsa-panopticon-part-ii/.

59 See also C. Nast, 'Interference-Based Jurisdiction Over Violations of the Right to Privacy', *EJIL: Talk!*, 21 November 2013, at www.ejiltalk.org/interference-based-jurisdiction-over-violations-of-the-right-to-privacy/.

60 See Milanovic, *Extraterritorial Application of Human Rights Treaties*, pp. 7–8.

61   See, e.g., *Ibrahima Gueye et al.* v. *France*, Communication No. 196/1985, UN Doc.
     CCPR/C/35/D/196/1985 (1989) (Article 26 ICCPR applied to former French Army
     servicemen of Senegalese nationality residing in Senegal, whose French pensions were
     reduced solely on grounds of nationality); *Bosphorus Hava Yollan Turizm ve Ticaret Anonim
     şirketi* v. *Ireland* [GC], App. No. 45036/98, 30 June 2005 (Convention applies to the
     impounding of an aircraft in Ireland that was leased by a company incorporated in
     Turkey); *Mullai and Others* v. *Albania*, App. No. 9074/07, 23 March 2010 (property
     rights under the Convention regarding a building permit dispute in Albania, even though
     some of the applicants were not physically located in Albania); *Vrbica* v. *Croatia*, App.
     No. 32540/05, 1 April 2010 (applicant's fair trial rights were engaged regarding the
     recognition and enforcement of a judgment by a Montenegrin court in Croatia, even
     though he never lived in Croatia).
62   See *Sejdovic* v. *Italy* [GC], App. No. 56581/00, 1 March 2006.
63   See, e.g., *Markovic and Others* v. *Italy* [GC], App. No. 1398/03, 14 December 2006,
     paras 49–56.
64   OHCHR Report (note 52 above), para. 34.
65   See 'GCHQ Taps Fibre-Optic Cables for Secret Access to World's Communications',
     The Guardian, 21 June 2013, at www.theguardian.com/uk/2013/jun/21/gchq-cables-
     secret-world-communications-nsa.
66   *Weber and Saravia* v. *Germany* (dec.), App. No. 54934/00, 29 June 2006.
67   Ibid., para. 66.
68   Ibid., para. 72.
69   *Liberty and Others* v. *the United Kingdom*, App. No. 58243/00, 1 July 2008.
70   Note that all of these methods are physical in a wider sense. The transmitting and
     sensation of images via photons, or of sounds via vibrations of particles in the air, or
     of information via electrons are physical phenomena, no less than the interaction
     between the atoms of the CIA agent's hands and those of Angela's body.
71   Similarly, see P. Margulies, 'The NSA in Global Perspective: Surveillance, Human
     Rights, and International Counterterrorism' *Fordham Law Review* 82 no. 5 (2014), 2,
     137 (arguing for a concept of virtual control).
72   Concluding Observations on the Fourth Report of the United States of America, UN
     Doc. CCPR/C/USA/CO/4, 23 April 2014, para. 22.
73   Consider, for example, news reports that a British agency supplied certain financial
     information about a British national to Iranian authorities, with Iranian agents
     subsequently kidnapping that individual in Dubai: see 'British-Iranian Man's Kidnap
     in Dubai: Wife Blames UK', *BBC News*, 24 February 2014, at www.bbc.co.uk/
     news/uk-26272281.
74   Consider, for example, the use of the Diego Garcia facility, which is part of a British
     overseas territory, by US authorities for rendition purposes: See 'Revealed: Senate
     Report Contains New Details on CIA Black Sites', *Al-Jazeera America*, 9 April 2014,
     at http://america.aljazeera.com/articles/2014/4/9/senate-cia-torture.html (claiming that
     a classified US Senate report finds that the CIA operated a fully fledged 'black site' on
     Diego Garcia, and that it did so with the 'full cooperation' of the UK government,
     despite its public protestations to the contrary); 'The Use of Diego Garcia by the United
     States', Report of the Foreign Affairs Committee, House of Commons, HC 377, 19
     June 2014, at www.publications.parliament.uk/pa/cm201415/cmselect/cmfaff/377/
     377.pdf.
75   See, e.g., J. Ball, 'US and UK Struck Secret Deal to Allow NSA to "Unmask" Britons'
     Personal Data', *The Guardian*, 20 November 2013, at www.theguardian.com/world/
     2013/nov/20/us-uk-secret-deal-surveillance-personal-data (reporting on the UK
     allowing the United States to 'unmask' the personal data of UK residents that was
     collected by the NSA but was previously subject to minimisation procedures);
     E. MacAskill, J. Ball and K. Murphy, 'Revealed: Australian Spy Agency Offered
     to Share Data About Ordinary Citizens', *The Guardian*, 2 December 2013, at
     www.theguardian.com/world/2013/dec/02/revealed-australian-spy-agency-offered-

to-share-data-about-ordinary-citizens (reporting on Australia sharing unminimised personal data of ordinary Australians with the NSA); G. Weston, G. Greenwald and R. Gallagher, 'New Snowden Docs Show US Spied during G20 in Toronto', *CBC News*, 27 November 2013, at www.cbc.ca/news/politics/new-snowden-docs-show-u-s-spied-during-g20-in-toronto-1.2442448 (reporting on Canada allowing the United States to conduct surveillance operations on its territory during a G20 summit in Toronto).

76   See, e.g., J. Stratford QC and T. Johnston, Advice in the Matter of State Surveillance, commissioned by the UK All Party Parliamentary Group on Drones, January 2014, at www.brickcourt.co.uk/news-attachments/APPG_Final_%282%29.pdf.

77   See, e.g., Article 16 of the ILC Articles on State Responsibility; H. Aust, *Complicity and the Law of State Responsibility* (Cambridge: Cambridge University Press, 2011); J. Crawford, *State Responsibility: The General Part* (Cambridge: Cambridge University Press, 2013), at 325ff.

78   *El-Masri* v. *the former Yugoslav Republic of Macedonia* [GC], App. No. 39630/09, 13 December 2012.

79   A. Nollkaemper, 'The European Court of Human Rights Finds Macedonia Responsible in Connection with Torture by the CIA, but on What Basis?', *EJIL: Talk!*, 24 December 2012, at www.ejiltalk.org/the-ecthr-finds-macedonia-responsible-in-connection-with-torture-by-the-cia-but-on-what-basis/.

80   See *Soering* v. *United Kingdom*, App. No. 14038/88, 7 July 1989; *Judge* v. *Canada*, Communication No. 829/1998, UN Doc. CCPR/C/78/D/829/1998 (2003).

81   For a more detailed discussion of the various shared responsibility issues, see André Nollkaemper's contribution to this volume.

82   See further Milanovic, *Extraterritorial Application of Human Rights Treaties*, at 106ff.

Bibliography

Aust, H. *Complicity and the Law of State Responsibility*. Cambridge: Cambridge University Press, 2011.

Cerone, J. 'Jurisdiction and Power: The Intersection of Human Rights Law and the Law of Non-International Armed Conflict in an Extraterritorial Context'. *Israel Law Review* 40 no. 2 (2007): 72–128.

Coomans, F., and M. T. Kamminga, (eds). *Extraterritorial Application of Human Rights Treaties*. Antwerp: Intersentia, 2004.

Crawford, J. *State Responsibility: The General Part*. Cambridge: Cambridge University Press, 2013.

Da Costa, K. *The Extraterritorial Application of Selected Human Rights Treaties*. Leiden: Nijhoff, 2012.

De Schutter, O. 'Globalisation and Jurisdiction: Lessons from the European Convention on Human Rights'. *Baltic Yearbook of International Law* 6 (2006).

De Schutter, O., A. Khalfan, M. Orellana, M. Salomon and I. Seiderman. 'Commentary to the Maastricht Principles on Extraterritorial Obligations of States in the Area of Economic, Social and Cultural Rights'. *Human Rights Quarterly* 34 (2012): 1084–1169.

Gibney, M., and S. Skogly. *Universal Human Rights and Extraterritorial Obligations*. Philadelphia: University of Pennsylvania Press, 2010.

Gondek, M. *The Reach of Human Rights in a Globalising World: Extraterritorial Application of Human Rights Treaties*. Antwerp: Intersentia, 2009.

House of Commons Foreign Affairs Committee. 'The Use of Diego Garcia by the United States'. Report by the Foreign Affairs Committee, House of Commons, HC 377. London: House of Commons, 19 June 2014. www.publications.parliament.uk/pa/cm201415/cmselect/cmfaff/377/377.pdf.

Langford, M., W. Vandenhole, M. Scheinin and W. van Genugten, (eds). *Global Justice, State Duties: The Extraterritorial Scope of Economic, Social, and Cultural Rights in International Law*. Cambridge: Cambridge University Press, 2012.

Lawson, R. 'Life after Bankovic: On the Extraterritorial Application of the European Convention on Human Rights'. In *Extraterritorial Application of Human Rights Treaties*, edited by F. Coomans and M. T. Kamminga. Antwerp: Intersentia, 2004: 83–123.

Margulies, P. 'The NSA in Global Perspective: Surveillance, Human Rights, and International Counterterrorism'. *Fordham Law Review* 82 no. 5 (2014): 2137–2167.

Milanovic, M. *Extraterritorial Application of Human Rights Treaties: Law, Principles, and Policy*. Oxford: Oxford University Press, 2011.

Milanovic, M. '*Al-Skeini* and *Al-Jedda* in Strasbourg'. *European Journal of International Law* 23 no. 1 (2012): 121–139.

Milanovic, M. 'Human Rights Treaties and Foreign Surveillance: Privacy in the Digital Age'. *Harvard International Law Journal* 56 no. 1 (2015): 81–146.

Milanovic, M. 'Extraterritorial Derogations from Human Rights Treaties in Armed Conflict,' in N. Bhuta (ed.), *The Frontiers of Human Rights: Extraterritoriality and its Challenges*, Oxford: Oxford University Press, 2016: 55.

Nast, C. 'Interference-Based Jurisdiction Over Violations of the Right to Privacy'. *EJIL: Talk!*, 21 November 2013, at www.ejiltalk.org/interference-based-jurisdiction-over-violations-of-the-right-to-privacy/.

Nollkaemper, A. 'The European Court of Human Rights Finds Macedonia Responsible in Connection with Torture by the CIA, but on What Basis?' *EJIL: Talk!*, 24 December 2012, at www.ejiltalk.org/the-ecthr-finds-macedonia-responsible-in-connection-with-torture-by-the-cia-but-on-what-basis/.

Nowak, M. *U.N. Covenant on Civil and Political Rights: CCPR Commentary* (2nd edn). Kehl: Engel, 2005.

Orakhelashvili, A. 'Restrictive Interpretation of Human Rights Treaties in the Recent Jurisprudence of the European Court of Human Rights'. *European Journal of International Law* 14 no. 3 (2003): 529–568.

Peters, A. 'Surveillance without Borders: The Unlawfulness of the NSA Panopticon, Part II'. *EJIL: Talk!*, 4 November 2013, at www.ejiltalk.org/surveillance-without-borders-the-unlawfulness-of-the-nsa-panopticon-part-ii/.

Roxstrom, E., M. Gibney and T. Einarsen. 'The NATO Bombing Case (*Bankovic et al. v. Belgium et al.*) and the Limits of Western Human Rights Protection'. *Boston University International Law Journal* 23 (2005): 55–136.

Shany, Y. 'Taking Universality Seriously: A Functional Approach to Extraterritoriality in International Human Rights Law'. *Law & Ethics of Human Rights* 7 no. 1 (2013): 47–71.

Skogly, S. *Beyond National Borders: States' Human Rights Obligations in International Cooperation*. Antwerp: Intersentia, 2006.

Van Dijk, P., Y. Arai and G. J. H. van Hoof, (eds). *Theory and Practice of the European Convention on Human Rights*, (4th edn). Antwerp: Intersentia, 2006.

Van Schaack, B. 'The United States' Position on the Extraterritorial Application of Human Rights Obligations: Now is the Time for Change'. *International Law Studies* 90 (2014): 20 65.

Wilde, R. 'Triggering State Obligations Extraterritorially: The Spatial Test in Certain Human Rights Treaties'. *Israel Law Review* 40 (2007): 503–526.

PART II

Law enforcement and security operations

3

TRANSNATIONAL OPERATIONS CARRIED OUT FROM A STATE'S OWN TERRITORY

Armed drones and the extraterritorial effect of international human rights conventions

Peter Vedel Kessing

3.1 Introduction

With the emergence of new technologies it is becoming easier for states to carry out law enforcement operations and military operations on other states' territories from their own territory (hereinafter 'transnational operations'). 'Boots on the ground' are redundant. States do not have to be physically present in another state to monitor, spy and ultimately kill people in that state. This may easily be done from a state's own territory via the internet, a satellite or drones. A prominent example is the United States' targeted killing of individuals with armed drones, in Pakistan, Yemen and Somalia, for example. Armed drones are fully controlled and operated via satellite, primarily by the Central Intelligence Agency (CIA), from US territory.[1] Another example is the United States' extraterritorial electronic surveillance and interception of communication in a number of states, including France and Germany.

At a general level, it seems unacceptable and unconscionable for a state to carry out activities on another state's territory that it cannot carry out at home. Additionally, it would undermine the territorial sovereignty of states, which is a fundamental cornerstone of international law according to which states on their own territory exercise jurisdiction over persons and things to the exclusion of the jurisdiction of other states.[2] Similarly, human rights bodies and the International Court of Justice (ICJ) have emphasised that states should not be allowed to perpetrate human rights violations on another state's territory that it could not perpetrate on its own territory.[3]

From a human rights perspective, the challenge is that new technology often leads to a disconnect between the location of the victim of a human rights violation and location of the perpetrator of the violation: the individual suffering a possible human rights violation resides in one state (the territorial state), and the act leading to the violation is decided, controlled and carried out by another state from its territory (the responsible state).

International human rights responsibility traditionally presupposes a relation of control between the perpetrator-state and the victim. The victim is protected by human rights to the extent that the perpetrator-state exercises effective control over the victim, or effective control over the territory where the victim is located. In transnational operations carried out from a state's own territory – for example, US drone strikes – such a link is absent, or at least, not evident.

Commentators have suggested three ways to bring drone strikes and other transnational operations performed from a state's own territory under the control of human rights: through the extraterritorial application of international human rights conventions; through the extraterritorial application of customary international human rights law (IHRL); and through the positive human rights obligations of the territorial state. None of these approaches are successful. The consequence is that states may commit human rights violations abroad that they cannot commit at home. Potentially, a state may ask another state to monitor, intercept and ultimately target and kill individuals on its territory, with the consequence that none of the two states are accountable under IHRL, and the affected individuals are deprived of their human rights protection.

I propose an alternative, or rather, additional approach to holding states accountable for transnational behaviour carried out from their own territory – the extraterritorial effects doctrine. According to this doctrine states are responsible if their territory is used to harm other states. The effects doctrine is well-known and accepted in international law, and by international human rights bodies.

Section 3.2 briefly explores the three ways IHRL is claimed to apply to drone strikes and other transnational operations carried out from a state's own territory, and assesses the extent to which they can ensure that such operations are controlled by IHRL.

Section 3.3 examines the extraterritorial effects doctrine and its potential for bringing transnational operations within the reach and control of IHRL. It demonstrates that the extraterritorial effects doctrine is well-established in other branches of public international law, for example, with regard to international environmental and international trade law. A state is responsible under international law if an act carried out on its territory has a direct negative consequence on the territory of another state, for example, with respect to cross-border pollution. Furthermore, it explores how human rights bodies, particularly the European Court of Human Rights (ECtHR), have used the extraterritorial effects doctrine. The doctrine has been used and referred to in a number of cases, however, only in a rather general and superficial way. Hence, individuals are less effectively protected from the extraterritorial effects of state conduct under IHRL than they are under international environmental or international trade law.[4]

Section 3.4 concludes and urges human rights bodies to explore and develop the extraterritorial effects doctrine to bring transnational state behaviour under the control of IHRL.

3.2 Transnational operations, the extraterritorial application of IHRL and the obligations of the territorial state

3.2.1 Drones and the extraterritorial application of international human rights conventions

The first way IHRL may apply to transnational operations carried out from a state's own territory is through the extraterritorial application of IHRL.[5]

The ECtHR has indicated that a state's jurisdictional competence under Article 1 in the European Convention on Human Rights (ECtHR) is primarily territorial. However, the Court has recognised two principal exceptions to this principle: when a state party exercises 'effective control of an area' on the territory of another state,[6] or exercises 'authority and control over individuals' on another state's territory.[7] However, the question is whether a state is exercising 'authority and control' over an individual, when it targets and kills an individual on another state's territory with an armed drone.

In the famous *Bankovic* case of 2001, the ECtHR found that the North Atlantic Treaty Organisation (NATO) airstrikes were insufficient to establish a jurisdictional link between the Serbian victims and the NATO member states.[8] Airstrikes – and arguably, transnational drone strikes – do not amount to exercising effective 'authority and control' over the targeted individuals so as to bring them under the ECtHR jurisdiction of the targeting state or states.[9]

Recent case law from the ECtHR may demonstrate a change in the position of the Court.

Two newer Chamber decisions may indicate that the shooting of an individual may, in itself, amount to exercising effective control over that individual. In the 2007 *Pad* case the Court found that the European Convention on Human Rights was applicable to a state party's killing of individuals from helicopters, on another state's territory (in the border areas between the targeting state, Turkey, and the territorial state, Iran).[10] Likewise, in the 2006 *Isaak* case, the European Convention on Human Rights was found to be applicable to the killing of an individual with firearms, in a neutral UN buffer zone.[11] In this regard, it is noteworthy that in the *Hirsi Jama* case of 2012, the ECtHR stated that an instantaneous extraterritorial act such as the bombing of individuals in the *Bankovic* case does not establish effective control over an area.[12] The Court did not rule out that an instantaneous extraterritorial act – like a drone attack – could establish 'authority and control' over individuals. This possible new position of the Court would seem to be in line with the position of The Inter-American Commission on Human Rights. In the *Armando Alejandre* case, the Commission found that the Cuban Air Force exercised 'power and authority' over the deceased when they shot down two small, unarmed, civilian aircraft in international airspace, killing four people.[13]

The ECtHR indicated furthermore in the *Al-Skeini* case of 2011 that the European Convention on Human Rights – in addition to situations where a state exercises effective control over area or individuals – might also be applicable to extraterritorial acts when a state exercises 'public authority' over another state's territory with the 'consent, invitation or acquiescence of the Government of that territory'.[14] It could be claimed that a state that controls and operates a drone programme or a surveillance programme on another state's territory (the territorial state) with its knowledge and consent is exercising executive 'public authority' normally exercised by the residing state, and that this is enough to establish jurisdiction under Article 1 ECtHR. However, it must be noted that in *Al-Skeini* the Court emphasised that the circumstances – and presumably the jurisdiction – were of an exceptional character.

The UN Human Rights Committee (UN HRC) has laid down that the International Covenant on Civil and Political Rights (ICCPR) is applicable to anyone within the 'power or effective control' of a state party acting outside its territory, regardless of the circumstances in which such power or effective control was obtained.[15] This 'effective control' requirement seems to imply that the ICCPR is not applicable to extraterritorial drone or surveillance operations, where the responsible state may hardly be said to exercise effective control over the victims. Nevertheless, in its concluding observations on the fourth periodic report on the United States in April 2014, the Committee said that the United States 'should ensure that any use of armed drones complies fully with its obligations under Article 6 [the right to life] of the Covenant'; and in relation to surveillance, that the United States 'should take all necessary measures to ensure that its surveillance activities, both within and outside the United States, conform to its obligations under the Covenant, including Article 17 [the right to private and family life]'.[16] Since the HRC provides no reasoning for its concluding observations, the legal rationale and justification for its position on the extraterritorial application of the ICCPR is unclear and, hence, difficult to assess.

To sum up, opinions and case law from human rights bodies demonstrate that human rights conventions are applicable when states act outside their territory, exercising 'effective control' over areas (the spatial model of jurisdiction) or individuals (the personal model of jurisdiction). Nevertheless, the extent of control required to establish 'effective control' is unclear and contested. There is no consensus among human rights bodies, and case law and opinions are often unclear and confusing. It is difficult to claim that the 'effective control' requirement is met when states undertake transnational operations in other states from their own territory, via drones, satellites, the internet and so on. Such operations will often – if not always – be stand-alone operations of an instantaneous character, where the responsible state has not exercised any prior form of control over the affected individual(s).

3.2.2 Extraterritorial application of customary IHRL

The second way IHRL has been claimed to regulate transnational law enforcement operations carried out from a state's own territory is by means of customary international law, or as a general principle of law (cf. Article 38 of the Statute of the ICJ).

It is argued that human rights norms that have the status of customary international law or general principles of law are not limited to situations occurring 'within the jurisdiction' of states as human rights conventions. On the contrary, customary international human rights norms must be respected and protected by states wherever they act.[17] For example, the duty to respect life has turned into customary international law, and therefore, a state's duty to respect the right to life (as opposed to its duty to ensure that right) follows its agents, wherever they operate. Authoritative sources support this view. Two UN Special Rapporteurs have claimed that the right to life is customary international law, and applicable to extraterritorial killings:

> The right to life [has status] as a general principle of international law and a customary norm. This means that, irrespective of the applicability of treaty provisions recognizing the right to life, States are bound to ensure the realization of the right to life when they use force, whether inside or outside their borders.[18]

Likewise, the ICRC has stated:

> A legal issue that could be posed in this scenario [extraterritorial targeted killings with armed drones] is the extraterritorial applicability of human rights law based on the fact that the state using force abroad lacks effective control over the person (or territory) for the purposes of establishing jurisdiction under the relevant human rights treaty. *It is submitted that customary human rights law prohibits the arbitrary deprivation of life* and that law enforcement standards likewise belong to the corpus of customary human rights law.[19] (Italics added)

Similar arguments have been put forward by researchers, for example, in a report to the European Parliament:

> The international law prohibition on murder and extrajudicial killings does not depend on the applicability of particular human rights treaties, but can safely be regarded as part of customary law, and even as a general principle of law binding upon all States at all times and in all places.[20]

Even though a number of legal experts argue that customary international law and general principles of law bind states when they are acting on other states' territories, this is contested by states, and there is no uniform, widespread state practice or *opinio juris* supporting the position.

3.2.3 The territorial state's human rights obligations

The final way IHRL is argued to be relevant to drone strikes and other transnational operations carried out from a state's own territory is by way of the IHRL obligations of the territorial state.[21]

Whereas Sections 3.2.1 and 3.2.2 discussed the responsible state's extraterritorial human rights obligations, this section deals with the territorial state's human rights obligations, and whether it can somehow influence the conduct of the responsible state.

In a situation where the territorial state invites, consents to or accepts that the responsible state will carry out transnational operations on its territory, for example a drone attack, the territorial state may be held responsible for a human rights violation.

Pursuant to Article 16 in the International Law Commission's (ILC's) Articles on State responsibility, a state is responsible for 'aid or assistance' to another state's breach of IHRL. However, the threshold set by the ILC is high. The 'assistance must be given with a view to facilitating the commission of a wrongful act [e.g. a human rights violation], and must actually do so'.[22] The ECtHR seems to operate with a lower threshold for complicity; in a number of cases it has laid down that a state is responsible for acts performed by foreign officials on its territory with the acquiescence or connivance of its authorities.

In the *Husayn* (*Abu Zubaydah*) case of 2014, Poland was found responsible for the torture and illegal detention carried out by US officials in a secret detention place (CIA black site) in Poland. The Court stated that 'Poland, for all practical purposes, had facilitated the whole process [CIA black site in Poland], created the conditions for it to happen and made no attempt to prevent it from occurring'. Accordingly, on account of its 'acquiescence and connivance' to and with the United States' detention and treatment of suspected terrorists on Polish territory, Poland was held responsible for violating the European Convention on Human Rights.

Even in a situation where the territorial state has not consented to or accept the transnational act of the state responsible – and therefore, cannot be accused of complicity ('aid or assistance') – it may be held indirectly responsible. The territorial state is under the positive due diligence obligation to prevent the responsible state from violating human rights obligations on its territory. This principle is supported *inter alia* by the ECtHR's decision in the 2012 *Catan* case concerning violations of the ECtHR in the separatist Moldavian Republic of Transdniestria (under decisive Russian influence and control) established on Moldovan territory. The Court stated that the territorial state must do its utmost, employing all possible legal and diplomatic means to make the responsible state guarantee and respect human rights, for example the right to life and privacy, of individuals on its territory.[23] The approach to holding states responsible for transnational operations under IHRL is weakened by the fact that it places the responsible state under no direct obligation.

To sum up, commentators have suggested three approaches to bringing drone attacks and other transnational operations carried out from a state's own territory under the control of IHRL: extraterritorial application of human rights conventions; extraterritorial application of customary IHRL; and through the human rights obligations of the territorial state.

None of these approaches can successfully ensure that transnational operations are effectively regulated and controlled by IHRL. There is a need to search for alternative ways to hold states accountable.

3.3 Transnational operations carried out from a state's own territory and the extraterritorial effect of IHRL

3.3.1 Are transnational operations carried out from a state's own territory extraterritorial conduct?

The discussion in Section 3.2, above, was founded on the premise that an extraterritorial act has been committed when a state targets an individual in another state's territory via satellite, from its own territory, with an armed drone, or monitors and intercepts communication in another state. However, human rights bodies distinguish between the extraterritorial application and the extraterritorial effect of human rights conventions.

While the extraterritorial application of IHRL relates to acts that a state (the responsible state) performs outside its own territory, on the territory of another state (the territorial state), possibly leading to a human rights violation, for example, targeting individuals from a military aircraft, or capturing and detaining an individual; the extraterritorial effect of IHRL concerns acts that a state controls and carries out on its own territory, leading to a human rights violation on the territory of another state.

The foregoing distinction is clearly described in the ECtHR Factsheet on 'Extraterritorial jurisdiction of states party to the European Convention on Human Rights'.[24] The Factsheet distinguishes between a state's acts occurring outside its own territory, and a state's act on its own territory producing effects in another state.

The question is whether transnational drone operations and other transnational operations performed from a state's own territory should be considered an act occurring on another state's territory (extraterritorial application), or an act carried out on the responsible state's own territory producing effects in another state – the territorial state (extraterritorial effect).

The case law from the ECtHR on the extraterritorial *application* of the convention – as discussed in Section 3.2.1 – deals with conduct that is exclusively decided, controlled, carried out and occurring in another state's territory. The specific act leading to the (possible) human rights violation, for example, the decision to target, arrest or search an individual in the territorial state, is decided on and carried out by state agents from the responsible state, who are present on the territory of the territorial state.

The case law from the ECtHR on the extraterritorial *effect* of the European Convention on Human Rights – as discussed in Section 3.3.3. – concerns conduct that occurs exclusively on the responsible state's territory and that has a direct and immediate wrongful effect on another state's territory (i.e. in the territorial state), for example, the passing of legislation or executive measures.

Drone strikes and other transnational operations decided, controlled and carried out from a state's own territory share the same characteristics as the cases the ECtHR has decided under the extraterritorial effects doctrine, and consequently should be dealt with under this doctrine.

Furthermore the extraterritorial effects doctrine is well-known and accepted in public international law.

3.3.2 The extraterritorial effects doctrine in public (and private) international law

IHRL forms part of public international law, and consequently should be interpreted and understood against the background of public international law.[25] It has consistently been stressed by the ECtHR that the European Convention on Human Rights should be interpreted in 'harmony with other rules of public international law, of which it forms part'.[26] In situations of doubt, public international law informs the interpretation and understanding of IHRL.

A well-established principle in public international law is that a state must ensure that its territory is not used to harm other states. This principle was laid down in international security law as early as in 1949 by the ICJ in the *Corfu Channel* case. Two British destroyers hit sea mines in Albanian waters in the Corfu straits in 1946, damaging them, and killing naval personnel. The ICJ ordered Albania to pay compensation to the United Kingdom and recognised:

> Every State's obligation not to allow knowingly its territory to be used for acts contrary to the rights of other States.[27]

A state is obligated to use all the means at its disposal to ensure that activities in its territory – and presumably also in any area under its jurisdiction – do not conflict with the rights of other states. This 'no harm' principle is also established in the UN Declaration on Friendly Relations and Co-operation among states:

> Every State has the duty to refrain from organizing, instigating, assisting or participating in acts of civil strife or terrorist acts in another State or acquiescing in organized activities within its territory directed towards the commission of such acts, when the acts referred to in the present paragraph involve a threat or use of force.[28]

A similar principle is recognised in public international law related to cross-border pollution. In the old *Trail Smelter Arbitration* case of 1906, a private mining company bought a zinc and lead smelter plant in Canada near the Columbia river flowing between Canada and the United States. In the following decades, the sulphur released from the plant polluted the neighbouring US state of Washington. Both states agreed to let a Mixed Arbitral Tribunal settle the conflict. The Tribunal found that:

> Under the principles of international law, as well as the law of the United States, no state has the right to use or permit the use of its territory in such a manner as to cause injury by fumes in or to the territory of another or the properties or persons therein, when the case is of serious consequence and the injury is established by clear and convincing evidence.[29]

Similarly, in the *Advisory Opinion on the Legality of Nuclear Weapons* of 1996, and more recently in the *Pulp Mills* case of 2010, the ICJ established that 'there is a general obligation on States to ensure that activities within their territory respect the environment of other States'.[30]

The effects doctrine is also recognised in soft law documents, for example, in the UN Stockholm Declaration (1972), and Rio Declarations (1992) on the protection of the environment (soft law).[31]

The final example of public international law acknowledging the extraterritorial effects doctrine is international financial law. World Trade Organisation (WTO) member states may not adopt subsidies – that is, financial contribution from a public body to private companies – that have adverse effects on the interest of other member states, for example, injuring the producer companies of other WTO member states, regardless of whether the injury occurs in the subsidising state, the state of the affected producer or in a third state.[32]

The founding principle behind the effect doctrine – that a state cannot use its territory to the direct detriment of other states – is also recognised in international private law related to the transnational conduct of private individuals and companies. States may assert jurisdiction over private conduct occurring in another state if that conduct has an effect on their territory.

Jurisdiction based on offences that merely produce effects in their territory has been claimed by various states as diverse as Singapore, Indonesia, Zimbabwe, Iraq, Russia, France, the United Kingdom, Mexico, Canada, the United States, Japan, Israel and Thailand.[33]

The scope of the effects principle is controversial, particularly regarding the proposition that a purely economic effect would suffice.[34] Accordingly, a somewhat modified effects doctrine – a so-called targeting model – has been proposed, pursuant to which a state may only assert jurisdiction if the activity was intended to have effects within the territory of the state.[35]

In any event it may safely be concluded that the extraterritorial effects doctrine is well-known and recognised in public and private international law. However, within IHRL the extraterritorial effects doctrine is still in its infancy.

3.3.3 The use of the extraterritorial effects doctrine by human rights bodies

There are several cases from the ECtHR where the Court has referred to the extraterritorial effects doctrine but the Court has never discussed the effects doctrine in a more comprehensive and in-depth way. The Court has stated that states may be accountable for legislative and executive measures taken within their territory that directly interfere with the Convention rights of persons in another state.[36]

Most cases concern the extraterritorial effect of *legislative measures*. The ECtHR has found that State A may be responsible under the European Convention on Human Rights if it adopts legislation that negatively affects individuals in State B. In the *Kovacic* case of 2003 it became impossible for the applicants – several Croatian citizens living in Croatia – to withdraw currency from a Slovenian bank in Croatia, owing to a legislative amendment adopted by the Slovenian National Assembly. The Court observed:

> The Court first acknowledges that, as the Croatian Government and the applicants have submitted, the responsibility of the High Contracting Parties may be engaged by acts of their authorities that produce effects outside their own territory. The Court reiterates that the Slovenian National Assembly introduced legislation addressing the issue of foreign-currency savings deposited with branches of Slovenian banks outside Slovenian territory . . . The applicants' position as regards their foreign-currency savings deposited with the Zagreb Main Branch was and continues to be affected by that legislative measure. This being so, the Court finds that the acts of the Slovenian authorities continue to produce effects, albeit outside Slovenian territory, such that Slovenia's responsibility under the Convention could be engaged.[37]

Another line of case law in which the ECtHR has referred to the extraterritorial effects doctrine concerns *executive measures*. The first and classic example is the *Soering* case of 1989, where the ECtHR found the United Kingdom responsible for violating Article 3 for extraditing the applicant to a real risk of ill-treatment in the United States (prolonged stay on a death row). The Court explained that:

> [. . .] Liability was incurred by the extraditing Contracting State [UK] by reason of its having taken *action which has as a direct consequence* the exposure of an individual to proscribed ill-treatment.[38] (Italics added)

However, as the Court also noted in the *Bankovic* case, discussed above in Section 3.2.1, the liability in extradition and expulsion cases is incurred 'by an action of the respondent state concerning a person while he or she is on its territory, clearly within its jurisdiction, and such cases do not concern the actual exercise of a State's competence or jurisdiction abroad'.[39]

The question remains whether the extraterritorial effects doctrine may be applied in situations where there is no link whatsoever between the responsible state and the victim. In the case of a drone strike, for example, the victim might not be a citizen of the responsible state, and might never have been present in its territory.

In the *Andreou* case, the ECtHR dealt with a situation in which Turkish soldiers in the northern part of Cyprus – controlled by Turkey – opened fire during a demonstration and killed a woman, Ms. *Andreou* – in the southern part of Cyprus controlled by Cyprus. The Turkish government argued that the woman was not under the jurisdiction of Turkey since she was killed in the southern part of Cyprus, and Turkey exercised control over neither that territory nor the deceased woman. In the judgement, the Court first describes the case law on the extraterritorial application of the European Convention on Human Rights – namely spatial and personal control – and then turns to the effect doctrine. It states:

> The Court reiterates that, in exceptional circumstances, the acts of Contracting States which produce effects outside their territory and over which they exercise no control or authority may amount to the exercise by them of jurisdiction within the meaning of Article 1 of the Convention.

The Court continues:

> In these circumstances, even though the applicant sustained her injuries in territory over which Turkey exercised no control [Cyprus], the *opening of fire on the crowd from close range*, which was the *direct and immediate cause* of those injuries, was such that the applicant must be regarded as 'within [the] jurisdiction' of Turkey within the meaning of Article 1 and that the responsibility of the respondent State under the Convention is in consequence engaged.[40] (Italics added)

The requisite jurisdictional link may be established in situations where there is a 'direct and immediate causality' between the act the responsible state performs in its territory and the human rights effect on the territory of another state, and apparently, also in situations where there is no link whatsoever between the victim and the responsible state (Turkey). *Mutatis mutandis*, with regard to drones it could be argued that an extraterritorial targeted killing with an armed drone fully controlled and operated from the responsible state's territory similarly has the 'direct consequence' that an individual in the territory of the territorial state is killed, possibly violating the right to life. Owing to the responsible state's effective territorial control over the drone, there is a difference between drones and airstrikes.

Although a drone is certainly not fired from 'close range', there is a 'direct and immediate' causality between the act the responsible state carries out in its territory – namely the operation and control of an armed drone via satellite – and the killing of an individual in the territorial state's territory. Also, from a practical point of view, it would hardly make sense if Denmark were bound by right-to-life obligations if a Danish police officer in the Danish city of Helsingør were to shoot a Swedish citizen in the Swedish city of Helsingborg (two cities in Denmark and Sweden that are very close to each other) with a police rifle, but not bound by right-to-life obligations if the Danish police were to target the Swedish citizen with an armed drone.

The extraterritorial effects doctrine has also been recognised by the UN HRC in relation to the ICCPR, albeit not explicitly. In its concluding observations in a state report from Iran, the Committee stated that a state violates the right to security of a person under Article 9 of the ICCPR if it, from its own territory, purports to exercise jurisdiction over a person outside its territory by issuing a fatwa or similar death sentence authorising the killing of the victim.[41]

The 2014 recommendation from the UN HRC, discussed in Section 3.2.1, that the United States should ensure that extraterritorial drone attacks and surveillance operations comply with the ICCPR, may also be explained under the extraterritorial effects doctrine.

Finally, the extraterritorial effects doctrine has at least been indirectly accepted by the Court of Justice in the European Union.[42]

In *Zaoui*, the applicants sought compensation for the loss of a family member killed by a Hamas bomb in Israel.[43] The applicants claimed that the EU Commission had granted funds to education programmes and projects in Palestinian territories that incited hatred and terrorism, and led to an attack by a Palestinian terrorist. The Court stated that there must be:

> A *direct link of cause and effect* between the wrongful act of the institution concerned and the harm pleaded, a causal link in respect of which applicants bear the burden of proof. (Emphasis added).

As no such direct link was established the Court dismissed the case, but it was not disputed by the Court that the EU could be responsible for the extraterritorial effect of EU policies.

3.3.4 How to delimit the extraterritorial effects doctrine?

Assuming that the extraterritorial effects doctrine may be applied in situations where there is no prior link or connection between the victim of the extraterritorial act and the responsible state in terms of citizenship or residence, it is evident that the doctrine must be delimited.

Marko Milanovic argued that 'in every case one can draw some kind of causal link between the territorial act (e.g. the decision to bomb Serbia in 1999 made by NATO governments in their own territories) and the extraterritorial consequences (e.g. the bombing itself)'.[44]

There are various ways of delimiting the extraterritorial effects doctrine.

The ECtHR requires a 'direct and immediate' causal link between the act carried out by the responsible state on its territory and the human rights effect on another state's territory. The Court of Justice in the European Union has applied an almost identical test ('direct link of cause and effect').

With regard to drones and electronic surveillance and interception, it may be evident that there is a 'direct and immediate' link between the act carried out in the responsible state and the human rights effect in the territorial state; however, in other types of transnational operations carried out from a state's own territory, it may be more difficult to establish.

The ECtHR has rejected several cases because the link between the act and the extraterritorial effect was too remote and distant.

In *Ben El Mahi v Denmark*, a case concerning the Muhammad cartoons, the required jurisdictional link was not established, as there was no 'direct and immediate causality' between the act carried out in Denmark and the Moroccan applicants living in Morocco.[45] The applicants complained that, as Muslims, they had been discriminated against by Denmark, since Denmark had permitted the publication of offensive caricatures of the Prophet Muhammad in a private newspaper. The Court found the complaint inadmissible, observing that:

[. . .] the applicants are a Moroccan national resident in Morocco and two Moroccan associations which are based in Morocco and operate in that country. The Court considers that there is no jurisdictional link between any of the applicants and the relevant member State, namely Denmark, or that they can come within the jurisdiction of Denmark on account of any extraterritorial act.

In *Bankovic* the Court rejected the applicants' final argument that the impugned act – the bombing – was, in fact, the extraterritorial effect of the responsible state's prior decision to interfere in the conflict in Kosovo and to launch the missile strike in Belgrade (jus ad bello). A decision that was made on the territory of the respondent state. The jurisdictional link between the responsible state and the victim of the bombing was too distant or weak. In other words, there was no 'direct and immediate causality' between the decision and the violation of the European Convention on Human Rights.

As described previously, the Court of Justice in the European Union found that the link between funds provided by the EU Commission and a terror attack in Palestine was too remote and distant.

In 2011, a large group of researchers and human rights experts adopted *The Maastricht Principles on Extraterritorial Obligations in the Area of Economic, Social and Cultural Rights*.[46] In the *Principles* it is argued that states have obligations to respect, protect and fulfil economic, social and cultural rights in situations where 'State acts or omissions bring about foreseeable effects on the enjoyment of economic, social and cultural rights, whether within or outside its territory'. 'Foreseeable effects' seems to be a very narrow delimitation of the extraterritorial effects doctrine, with the consequence that in a number of situations states may be responsible for the extraterritorial effects of measures taken in their territory.

In private international law, a state may assert jurisdiction if private conduct in another state has effects – or if it is the intention it shall have effects – on the state asserting jurisdiction. This standard seems to be a lower standard than that applied under the human rights effects doctrine (direct and immediate causality).

3.4 Conclusion

The emergence of new technologies will make it easier for states to carry out transnational law enforcement and military operations from their own territory, as evidenced by armed drones and extraterritorial electronic surveillance. As a result, it must be expected that there will be an increase in transnational operations performed from a state's own territory in the coming years. At the same time, there is broad consensus among monitoring and human rights bodies, including the ICJ, that states should not be allowed to perpetrate human rights violations in the territory of another state that it could not perpetrate on its own territory.

Consequently, there is a need to discuss whether and how IHRL can regulate such extraterritorial behaviour. So far, the focus has been on three ways or approaches: the extraterritorial application of human rights conventions; the extraterritorial application of customary human rights law; and through the human rights responsibility of the residing state. None of these three approaches can effectively ensure that transnational operations from a state's own territory are controlled by IHRL in line with the universality requirement in IHRL. Such operations are often stand-alone operations of an instantaneous character, where the responsible state did not exercise any prior physical (or mental) control over the affected individual. It has been convincingly argued that the clearest and most principled approach would be if states were responsible for the human rights violations they commit (negative human rights obligations), regardless of whether the violation occurred in the responsible state's own territory, or in territory of another state.[47] However, there are no indications that human rights monitoring bodies will adopt such a cause and effects doctrine any time soon, or that it would be accepted by states.

The extraterritorial effects doctrine may remedy the situation. Transnational operations carried out from a state's own territory, such as drone and surveillance operations, are fully decided, controlled and carried out from the responsible state's own territory, and there is a 'direct and immediate causality' between the behaviour of the responsible state and the interference with an individual's human rights in the territorial state.

The effects doctrine is well-established in other areas of international law, and arguably in customary international law. States are not allowed to use their territory to harm other states, and must prevent non-state actors from using their territory to do so. Furthermore, the effects doctrine has at least implicitly been acknowledged by human rights monitoring bodies, and by the Court of Justice in the European Union. However, human rights monitoring bodies have only dealt with the extraterritorial effects doctrine in a very superficial and unsystematic way. The ECtHR has referred to the effects doctrine in a number of judgements, but never made a thorough and in-depth analysis of the content, scope and delimitation of the doctrine, in contrast to the extraterritorial application doctrine, which has been explored and developed by the Court in a large number of judgements, starting with the *Bankovic* case in 2001.[48]

It is remarkable that human rights bodies, at the least the ECtHR, has indicated a high threshold for establishing responsibility under the extraterritorial effects doctrine requiring 'direct and immediate causality'. A threshold that arguably is higher than in other areas of international law. Consequently, it appears that individuals are less effectively protected from the extraterritorial effects of state conduct under IHRL than they are under other areas of international law, such as international environmental or trade law.[49]

Under international human rights conventions, a state should be held accountable for killing individuals in violation of the right to life, or for intercepting telecommunication in violation of the right to privacy, regardless of whether it is done on the state's own territory or on another state's territory.

The extraterritorial effects doctrine may prove to be a useful, indeed necessary, new instrument for holding states responsible under IHRL when they are carrying out transnational operations from their own territories, an instrument that should be further explored and elaborated by human rights monitoring bodies.

Notes

1 For example, see Peter Vedel Kessing, 'The Extraterritorial Use of Armed Drones and International Human Rights Law: Different Views on Legality in the US and Europe?', in *Europe and the Americas*, eds Erik A. Andersen and Eva Maria Lassen (Leiden: Brill, 2015).

2 Andrew Clapham, *Brierly's Law of Nations*, 7th edn (Oxford: Oxford University Press, 2012), 168.

3 See quote from the European Court of Human Rights, *Issa a.o. v. Turkey*, 16 November 2004, para. 71. See the UN Human Rights Committee for an almost identical statement in *Lopez Burgos v. Uruguay*, Communication no. 52/1979, 29 July 1981, para. 12.3; and *Celiberti de Casariego v. Uruguay*, 56/1979, para. 10.3. Similarly, the International Court of Justice (ICJ) has stated that 'it would seem natural that States parties to the Covenant [The International Covenant on Civil and Political Rights (ICCPR)] should be bound to comply with its provisions when exercising jurisdiction outside their national territory'.

4 For a similar conclusion, see Lorand Bartels, 'The EU's Human Rights Obligations in Relation to Policies with Extraterritorial Effects', *European Journal of International Law* 25 no. 4 (2015).

5 For example, see Nils Melzer, 'Human Rights Implications of the Usage of Drones and Unmanned Robots in Warfare', European Parliament, Directorate General for External Policies, Policy Department Study (Brussels, 2013), 18; Alex Conte, 'Human Rights Beyond Borders: A New Era in Human Rights Accountability for Transnational Counter-Terrorism Operations?', *Journal of Conflict and Security Law* 18 no. 2 (2013); David Kretzmer, 'Targeted Killing of Suspected Terrorists: Extra-Judicial Executions or Legitimate Means of Defence?', *European Journal of International Law* 16 no. 2 (2005):

183–185; Stuart Casey-Maslen, 'Pandora's box? Drone strikes under jus ad bellum, jus in bello, and international human rights law', *International Review of the Red Cross* 94 no. 886 (2012): 1–29.

6   See the line of cases concerning Turkish control over Northern Cyprus referred to in e.g. *Al-Skeini and Others v. The United Kingdom*, 7 July 2011 (Grand Chamber), paras 138–140.

7   See *Al-Skeini*, op. cit., para. 136. For a thorough analysis of the case law from the ECtHR, see Marko Milanovic, *Extraterritorial Application of Human Rights Treaties: Law, Principles, and Policy* (Oxford: Oxford University Press, 2011).

8   ECtHR, *Bankovic and Others v. Belgium and 16 other contracting States*, 12 December 2001 (Grand Chamber).

9   The court further discussed and denied a *cause and effect* notion of jurisdiction as argued by the claimants. The responsibility for a human rights violation does not in itself lead to 'jurisdiction' in ECHR.

10 ECtHR, *Pad v. Turkey*, 28 June 2007. However, it was not disputed in the case that the victims were within the ECHR jurisdiction of Turkey the targeting State. See para. 54: 'In the instant case, it was not disputed by the parties that the victims of the alleged events came within the jurisdiction of Turkey. While the applicants attached great importance to the prior establishment of the exercise by Turkey of extraterritorial jurisdiction with a view to proving their allegations on the merits, the Court considers that it is not required to determine the exact location of the impugned events, given that the Government had already admitted that the fire discharged from the helicopters had caused the killing of the applicants' relatives, who had been suspected of being terrorists'.

11 ECtHR, *Isaak v. Turkey*, 28 September 2006. The Court concluded: '. . . [E]ven if the acts complained of took place in the neutral UN buffer zone, the Court considers that the deceased was under the authority and/or effective control of the respondent State through its agents. It concludes, accordingly, that the matters complained of in the present application fall within the "jurisdiction" of Turkey within the meaning of Article 1 of the Convention and therefore entail the respondent State's responsibility under the Convention'.

12 ECtHR, *Hirsi Jama and Others v. Italy*, 23 February 2012, para. 73: 'Since the wording of Article 1 does not accommodate such an approach to "jurisdiction"'.

13 *Armando Alejandre v. Cuba ('Brothers to the Rescue')*, IACHR Report No. 86/99, Case No. 11.589, 29 September 1999, para. 25.

14 ECtHR, *Al-Skeini and Others v. The United Kingdom*, 7 July 2011 (Grand Chamber), para. 135.

15 UN Human Rights Committee General Comment No. 15 (1986) and General Comment No. 31, para. 10.

16 The UN Human Rights Committee, *Concluding observations on the fourth periodic report of the United States of America*, CCPR/C/USA/CO/4, 23 April 2014, paras 9 and 22 respectively.

17 For example, see Anthony E. Cassimatis, 'International Humanitarian Law, International Human Rights Law, and Fragmentation of International Law', *International & Comparative Law Quarterly* 56 no. 3 (2007): 623–639. Likewise John Cerone, 'Human Rights on the Battlefield', in *Human Rights in Turmoil: Facing Threats, Consolidating Achievements*, eds Stéphanie Lagoutte, Hans-Otto Sano and Peter Scharff Smith (Leiden: Martinus Nijhoff Publishers, 2007), 97–132.

18 Un Special Rapporteur on extrajudicial, summary and arbitrary executions, A/68/382, 13 September 2013, para. 43; and UN Special Rapporteur on counter-terrorism and human rights, A/68/389, 18 September 2013, para. 60.

19 ICRC, International Humanitarian Law and the challenges of contemporary armed conflicts, Geneva 2011, 31IC/11/5.1.2, p. 22.

20 Nils Melzer, *Human Rights Implications*, 18. Likewise, Kretzmer, 'Targeted Killing of Suspected Terrorists', 183–185 supra note 5.

21 For a proponent of this view, see John C. Dehn, 'Targeted Killing, Human Rights and Ungoverned Spaces: Considering Territorial State Human Rights Obligations', *Harvard International Law Journal* 54 (2012): 84–91.

22 See International Law Commission, Commentary to the Articles on the Responsibility of States for Internationally Wrongful Acts, A/56/10, 2001, 66.

23 ECtHR, *Catan and Others v. Moldova and Russia*, 19 October 2012, para. 110. Likewise ECtHR, *Ilascu and Others v. Moldova and Russia*, 8 July 2004.

24 Factsheet is compiled by the ECtHR on various themes based on the Court's case law, available at: www.echr.coe.int/Pages/home.aspx?p=press/factsheets&c=#n134789085 5564_pointer (accessed February 2015).

25 Also, see Article 31 in the Vienna Convention on the Law of Treaties.

26 For example, see ECtHR, *Bankovic v. Belgium and Others*, 12 December 2001, paras 55–58. On the relation between IHRL and public international law, see, for example, James C. Hathaway and Thomas Gammeltoft-Hansen, 'Non-Refoulement in a World of Cooperative Deterrence', *Columbia Journal of Transnational Law* 53 no. 2 (2015): 235–284.

27 *Corfu Channel (United Kingdom v. Albania)*, Merits, Judgment, ICJ Reports 1949, p. 22.

28 UN Assembly, Declaration on principles of international law friendly relations and cooperation among states in accordance with the Charter of the United Nations, RA Res. 2625 (XXV), 24 October 1970, principle 1.

29 Ad Hoc International Arbitral Tribunal 11 March 1942, *Trail Smelter Arbitration (United States v Canada)*. 33 AJIL, 182 and (1941) AJIL, 684.

30 ICJ, *Advisory Opinion on the Legality of Nuclear Weapons*, 1996, para. 29.

31 See principle 21 in the Stockholm declaration and principle 2 in the Rio Declaration: 'States have, in accordance with the Charter of the United Nations and the principles of international law, the sovereign right to exploit their own resources pursuant to their own environmental policies, and the responsibility to ensure that activities within their jurisdiction or control do not cause damage to the environment of other States or of areas beyond the limits of national jurisdiction'.

32 See Articles 5 and 6 of the *WTO Agreement on Subsidies and Countervailing Measures* and Bartels, 'The EU's Human Rights Obligations', 1072 supra note 4.

33 For a description of and reference to the various domestic laws, see Danielle Ireland-Piper, 'Prosecutions of Extraterritorial Criminal Conduct and the Abuse of Rights Doctrine', *Utrecht Law Review* 9 (2013): 71–72.

34 For example, see supra note 37, 78.

35 See supra note 38, 816. Also, see the discussion on delimitation in section D below.

36 See Maarten den Heijer, *Europe and Extraterritorial Asylum* (Oxford: Hart Publishing, 2012).

37 ECtHR, *Kovacic and others v Slovenia*, 9 October 2003.

38 ECtHR, *Soering v. Germany*, 7 July 1989, para. 91.

39 ECtHR, *Bankovic and Others v Belgium and Others*, 12 December 2001, para. 68.

40 ECtHR, *Andreau v. Turkey*, 3 June 2008.

41 UN HRC, Concluding observations, Islamic Republic of Iran 1992, para. 256.

42 For example, see Bartels, 'The EU's Human Rights Obligations' supra note 4.

43 CJEU, *Zaoui*, Case C-288/03.

44 Marko Milanovic, Foreign Surveillance and Human Rights, Part 4: Do Human Rights Treaties Apply to Extraterritorial Interferences with Privacy, *EJIL: Talk!*, 28 November 2013, available at: www.ejiltalk.org/foreign-surveillance-and-human-rights-part-4-do-human-rights-treaties-apply-to-extraterritorial-interferences-with-privacy/.

45 ECtHR, *Ben El Mahi and Others v Denmark*, 11 December 2006.

46 The principles are available at: www.etoconsortium.org/nc/en/library/maastricht-principles/?tx_drblob_pi1%5BdownloadUid%5D=23 (Last accessed February 2015).

47 Marko Milanovic, '*Extraterritorial Application of Human Rights Treaties: Law, Principles, and Policy*', 18.

48   See section 2.A. for further cases from the ECtHR concerning the extraterritorial application doctrine.
49   For a similar conclusion, see Bartels, 'The EU's Human Rights Obligations'.

Bibliography

Bartels, Lorand. 'The EU's Human Rights Obligations in Relation to Policies with Extraterritorial Effects'. *European Journal of International Law* 25 no. 4 (2015): 1071–1091.

Casey-Maslen, Stuart. 'Pandora's box? Drone strikes under jus ad bellum, jus in bello, and international human rights law'. *International Review of the Red Cross* 94 no. 886 (2012): 1–29.

Cassimatis, Anthony E. 'International Humanitarian Law, International Human Rights Law, and Fragmentation of International Law'. *International & Comparative Law Quarterly* 56 no. 3 (2007): 623–639.

Cerone, John. 'Human Rights on the Battlefield'. In *Human Rights in Turmoil: Facing Threats, Consolidating Achievements*, edited by Stéphanie Lagoutte, Hans-Otto Sano and Peter Scharff Smith, 97–132. Leiden: Martinus Nijhoff Publishers, 2007.

Clapham, Andrew. *Brierly's Law of Nations* (7th edn). Oxford: Oxford University Press, 2012.

Conte, Alex. 'Human Rights Beyond Borders: A New Era in Human Rights Accountability for Transnational Counter-Terrorism Operations?'. *Journal of Conflict and Security Law* 18 no. 2 (2013): 233–258.

Dehn, John C. 'Targeted Killing, Human Rights and Ungoverned Spaces: Considering Territorial State Human Rights Obligations'. *Harvard International Law Journal* 54 (2012): 84–91.

den Heijer, Maarten. *Europe and Extraterritorial Asylum*, Oxford: Hart Publishing, 2012.

Hathaway, James C., and Thomas Gammeltoft-Hansen. 'Non-Refoulement in a World of Cooperative Deterrence'. *Columbia Journal of Transnational Law* 53 no. 2 (2015): 235–284.

Ireland-Piper, Danielle. 'Prosecutions of Extraterritorial Criminal Conduct and the Abuse of Rights Doctrine'. *Utrecht Law Review* 9 no. 4 (2013): 68–89.

Kessing, Peter Vedel. 'The Extraterritorial Use of Armed Drones and International Human Rights Law: Different Views on Legality in the US and Europe?'. In *Europe and the Americas*, edited by Erik A. Andersen and Eva Maria Lassen, 360–392. Leiden: Brill, 2015.

Kretzmer, David. 'Targeted Killing of Suspected Terrorists: Extra-Judicial Executions or Legitimate Means of Defence?'. *European Journal of International Law* 16 no. 2 (2005): 171–212.

Melzer, Nils. 'Human Rights Implications of the Usage of Drones and Unmanned Robots in Warfare'. European Parliament, Directorate General for External Policies, Policy Department Study (Brussels, 2013): 18.

Milanovic, Marko. *Extraterritorial Application of Human Rights Treaties: Law, Principles, and Policy*. Oxford: Oxford University Press, 2011.

Milanovic, Marko. 'Foreign Surveillance and Human Rights, Part 4: Do Human Rights Treaties Apply to Extraterritorial Interferences with Privacy'. *EJIL: Talk!*, 28 November 2013, at www.ejiltalk.org/foreign-surveillance-and-human-rights-part-4-do-human-rights-treaties-apply-to-extraterritorial-interferences-with-privacy/.

4

NSA SURVEILLANCE AND ITS MEANING FOR INTERNATIONAL HUMAN RIGHTS LAW

Mark Gibney

Seemingly every month or so, there is some new revelation regarding National Security Agency (NSA) surveillance. I might have added the adjective 'shocking', but by now there is almost nothing in this realm that would surprise anyone. Without attempting to be exhaustive, at the time of this writing, some of the things that are known about such practices are these. The NSA has conducted a massive metadata surveillance programme that catalogues every single phone call and email sent or received by US citizens; the agency has wiretapped the offices of dozens of foreign leaders, including some of those 'friendly' to the United States, most notably Chancellor Angela Merkel of Germany; tracking chips have been clandestinely inserted into computers during the manufacturing process; and finally, devices have been installed on mobile phone apps – including every child's favourite game, *Angry Birds* – in order to gather certain personal information.[1]

Amid the public outcry, what has been ignored is the enormous implications of NSA spying on international law, which is the focus of the present chapter. However, because the NSA is a federal US agency, I will provide an overview of domestic US law in this area, particularly the Fourth Amendment rights of those being spied upon – assuming, of course, that such rights even exist. Perhaps what is most pertinent for present purposes is the ready distinction that has oftentimes been made between 'domestic' and 'foreign' surveillance, with the former receiving at least some form of constitutional protection while the latter, apparently, does not, although it is important to note that the line between these two has started to blur considerably.

The analysis of NSA spying is broken down into two parts. The first involves wiretapping under Section 702 of the Foreign Intelligence Surveillance Act (FISA) Amendments of 2008, which allows the US government to target communications of non-US persons 'reasonably believed' to be outside the United States. The second part will be the bulk collection of telephone metadata that the US government has grounded on Section 215 of the USA Patriot Act of 2001, which allows the US government to obtain any tangible record from a third party if it is deemed 'relevant' to international terrorism, counter-espionage or foreign intelligence investigation. These tangible records include: business records, phone provider records, apartment rental records, driver's licences, library records, book sale records, gun sale records, tax returns, educational records and medical records. The Obama administration has interpreted this to allow for the collection of information on when telephone calls have been made, the number these calls have been made to and also the length of the conversation – but it has strenuously argued that the NSA does not listen to the content of these monitored calls without following agency procedure. Edward Snowden has provided a much different rendition of NSA practice. In an interview with journalists Glenn Greenwald and Laura Poitras, he explained how he and other NSA analysts had the ability to listen to anyone's conversations at any time: 'I, sitting at my desk, could wiretap anyone, from you or your accountant, to a federal judge or even the president, if he had a personal email.'[2]

Responding to an American public that was discomfited, if not outraged, by the very real prospect that it was being spied upon, the US Congress passed a law in early June 2015 – the USA Freedom Act – that six months from the date of the passage of the bill ends the NSA metadata collection programme under Section 215, although government officials would still have access to such information, but only upon a more particularised showing of possible terrorist connections. However, in a nod to modern technology, what was added in the new legislation was the ability to gain access to mobile phone records. Interestingly enough, and perhaps consistent with its name, what the USA Freedom Act left untouched were the spying operations against foreign nationals under Section 702, although President Obama had already enacted some slight modifications to this programme in January 2014 on the basis of the recommendations of a review group he had convened.[3]

Section 4.1 is devoted to privacy as a human right. Section 4.2 examines US practice, with a particular focus on the enormous growth of surveillance in the post-9/11 period. Section 4.3 returns to international human rights law. The argument I set forth is that NSA spying directly challenges three essential principles of international law: sovereignty, jurisdiction and territory. As I say in my concluding remarks, NSA spying not only represents the 'darkest' side of globalisation, but a perverted version of globalisation as well.

4.1 The human right to privacy

> No one shall be subjected to arbitrary interference with his privacy, family, home or correspondence, nor to attacks upon his honour and reputation. Everyone has the right to the protection of the law against such interference or attacks. (UDHR, Article 12)

> No one shall be subjected to arbitrary or unlawful interference with his privacy, family, home or correspondence, nor to unlawful attacks on his honour and reputation. (ICCPR, Article 17(1))

> Surveillance, whether electronic or otherwise, interceptions of telephonic, telegraphic and other forms of communication, wiretapping and recording of conversations should be prohibited. (Human Rights Committee, General Comment 16: Article 17 (Right to Privacy))

To begin with, it is important to briefly examine privacy, which is a firmly established right under international human rights law.[4] At its core, the right to privacy serves to protect individual autonomy. Without privacy, a person's beliefs, views, creeds, habits, feelings and so on can be exposed and exploited by others, especially by the state itself.[5] Related to this, the right to privacy is vital to the protection of other human rights, as recognised by the UN High Commissioner for Human Rights in the report 'The Right to Privacy in the Digital Age':

> While the mandate for the present report focused on the right to privacy, it should be underscored that other rights also may be affected by mass surveillance, the interception of digital communications and the collection of personal data. These include the rights to freedom of opinion and expression, and to seek, receive and impart information; to freedom of peaceable assembly and association; and to family life – rights all linked closely with the right to privacy and, increasingly, exercised through digital media. (par. 14)[6]

The final point relates to the enormous damage that occurs when the right to privacy is violated – or is merely thought to be violated. It is now established that the telephone calls of ordinary citizens in Spain and Portugal were wiretapped by the NSA.[7] I suspect that few people were aware of this at the time. However, in all likelihood, not only the entire citizenry in these two countries – but also people in other states as well – are now on notice that their conversations might well be tapped and their email messages read. What this also means is that these people, and others, will speak differently (or not at all); they will communicate differently (or not at all); and perhaps they will come to think differently as well.[8] All of this arises from the violation of the human right to privacy.

As a party to the International Covenant on Civil and Political Rights (ICCPR), the United States has acted in apparent violation of Article 17. One possible defence the United States might invoke relates to the 'within its territory and subject to its jurisdiction' language in Article 2(1).[9] Thus the US government might argue that its obligations under the ICCPR only apply within the territorial boundaries of the United States, but nowhere beyond this.[10] However, in *Lopez Burgos*, the Human Rights Committee (HRC) addressed this very same argument in a case involving an extraterritorial abduction.[11] The applicant, a Uruguayan national, claimed that Uruguayan agents had kidnapped her husband and secretly detained him in Argentina. The Uruguay government not only denied these allegations, but it also argued that the claim should be dismissed because the ICCPR does not apply to actions taken by a state outside its own territorial jurisdiction.

The HRC soundly rejected this position, holding that the territorial and jurisdiction language of Article 2 simply imposes a mandate on the state parties to uphold the provisions of the Covenant within its own territory, but that it says nothing that would permit states to perpetuate violations on the territory of another state. The Committee went on to hold that

> 'it would be unconscionable to so interpret responsibility under Article 2 of the Covenant to permit a state party to perpetuate violations of the Covenant on the territory of another state, which violation it could not perpetrate on its own territory' (para. 12.3).

Thus according to this interpretation, the United States should not be able to claim that it only has a responsibility to protect the privacy rights of those who are within the territorial borders of the United States. And what this also shows is that 'jurisdiction' is by no means synonymous with 'territory', a point we will return to.

4.2 United States domestic law

> The right of the people to be secure in their persons, houses, papers, and effects, against unreasonable searches and seizures, shall not be violated, and no warrants shall issue, but upon probable cause, supported by oath or affirmation, and particularly describing the place to be searched, and the persons or things to be seized. (Fourth Amendment, US Constitution)

Although the right to privacy is not specifically mentioned in the US Constitution, the Supreme Court has found such a right in various provisions or 'penumbras' of the Bill of Rights and the Fourteenth Amendment.[12] In terms of government surveillance activities in particular, in *Katz* v. *United States* (1967)[13] the Court ruled that the Fourth Amendment's warrant requirement based upon probable cause applied to a wiretap that was affixed to a telephone booth where the criminal suspect had placed illegal bets and wages. The Court ruled that absent the required warrant, the evidence obtained from these wiretaps was inadmissible. However, and for whatever reason, the Court also raised the issue of the possibility of a different result in cases involving 'national security'.[14] This issue, whether the Fourth Amendment applies in equal force – or applies at all – in cases involving US national security interests, remains unresolved to this day.

The same kind of possible domestic/international distinction was also referenced in *United States* v. *US District Court* (1972).[15] This case involved a warrantless wiretap used during an investigation of the bombing of a Central Intelligence Agency facility in Ann Arbor, Michigan. The Supreme Court ruled that without a warrant the wiretap was illegal and the evidence obtained from it excludable. However, as in *Katz*, the Court seemed to suggest that there might be a distinction in the law between terrorist activities performed by 'domestic organisations' as opposed to those carried out by a 'foreign power', the idea being that the strictures of the Fourth Amendment would apply in the former case but not the latter.

In 1975, the US Senate Foreign Relations Committee held hearings chaired by Senator Frank Church which uncovered a wide array of abuses by US security officials, including warrantless surveillance practices, both domestically and internationally. One of the policy responses to this was the passage of the 1978 FISA, which mandated that a warrant be obtained by the executive prior to *all* wiretapping, foreign and domestic alike.[16] To accomplish this, the Act created the Foreign Intelligence Surveillance Court (FISC), made up of eleven sitting federal judges selected by the Chief Justice of the Supreme Court.

Several aspects of the FISC are deserving of mention. The first is that the FISC operates in secret, and even the identity of the judges sitting on the Court is not made public. What is also noteworthy is the government's success in obtaining warrants from the FISC. By no means atypically, in 2012 the executive was successful in 1,855 of the 1,856 warrant requests that it filed. One explanation for such results is that FISA does not operate under the same probable cause standard that is applicable in criminal law, but something considerably lower. The final thing to note is that in its 37 years in existence, the US Supreme Court has never passed judgement on the constitutionality of FISA itself, nor on the composition or operations of FISC.

4.2.1 Wiretapping: post September 11, 2001

The September 11 attacks on the United States brought a fundamental change to US surveillance practices. The Bush administration responded immediately by issuing a private executive order instituting what was called the Terrorist Surveillance Program (TSP). As mentioned above, prior to this, the executive was required to obtain a warrant for all wiretaps. Under TSP, the warrant requirement was limited to communications that were solely domestic or those involving US nationals in foreign lands. According to later congressional testimony by the then Attorney-General Alberto Gonzalez, these changes to FISA in late 2001 were made under the authority of the Authorisation for the Use of Military Force[17] as well as the president's commander-in-chief powers, which, according to Gonzalez, superseded any contrary actions and policies that Congress might enact.[18] After four years of operations and hundreds, if not thousands, of warrantless wiretaps, the TSP was unveiled to public scrutiny by the *New York Times* in December 2005.[19]

Despite such publicity, there was no change in practice, and in January 2007 the Attorney-General was able to obtain a blanket order from an FISC judge authorising existing TSP wiretapping. Congress responded by providing the administration this same power, first through the Protect America Act on 5 August 2007,[20] followed several months later by passage of the FISA Amendments Act of 2008.[21] The latter was set to expire in 2012, but was renewed at that time until 2017.

Although the 2008 legislation was termed as being an amendment to the 1978 FISA statute, the new legislation differed from its predecessor in a number of important ways. As Owen Fiss has noted,[22] perhaps the most fundamental change is that while the earlier FISA statute and TSP were specifically founded on the principle of fighting international terrorism, the 2008 FISA statute was much broader than this. Its stated goal was obtaining 'foreign intelligence' – perhaps as a way of combating international terrorism, but perhaps not exclusively this. In addition, what the government now has to show is that gathering foreign intelligence is a significant, as opposed to a primary, purpose of the wiretap.

In terms of procedure, the 2008 FISA amendments continued to mandate warrants where the target is located in the United States, citizens and non-nationals alike. In these cases, in addition to meeting the significant purpose standard, what must also be established is that there is a reason to believe that the target is an agent or employer of a foreign power. The same standard applies to wiretaps on US citizens or permanent resident aliens who are outside the United States. On the other hand, a US citizen communicating with a foreign national in another country can be wiretapped so long as s/he is only the 'incidental' rather than the 'main' target.[23]

Unlike the 1978 FISA, the 2008 amendments treat foreign nationals located outside the United States differently than US citizens. As in the original statute, there is no need to obtain authorisation of any kind from a FISA judge when the wiretap does not require access to facilities located in the United States – which is to say that no one on the call or email is within the United States and the call/email is never routed through the United States. However, when the tap aimed at foreigners abroad requires access to facilities located in the United States, permission of a FISA judge is still required, but what the executive has to prove is considerably less than under the old FISA standard. Fiss describes the effects of some of these changes:

> Although the government must state that a significant purpose of the tap is to gather foreign intelligence, little more is required. The government need not have reason to suspect that the targets of the tap are agents or employees of a foreign power, only that they are foreigners and that they are located outside the United States.[24]

The 2008 Act also allows for the issuance of 'blanket' authorisations, which could be as broad (and as meaningless) as 'Al-Qaeda sympathisers'. Related to this, unlike the previous legal standard, Section 1881a does not require the government to specify the nature and location of each of the particular facilities or places at which electronic surveillance will occur. In addition, as a result of changes to the law, the 2008 Act reduced the ability of a FISA judge to challenge the factual predicates of the government's application for a warrant, and finally, the warrant request must now be handled within a thirty-day period.

There are at least two important questions raised by the application of Section 702. The first is whether foreign nationals outside the territorial boundaries of the

United States have any Fourth Amendment protection. The leading case in this area is *Verdugo-Urquidez* (1990) where the issue involved the legality of a warrant-less search conducted by agents of the US Drug Enforcement Agency in Mexico of the home of a Mexican national who had been arrested and was awaiting trial in the United States.[25] The defendant sought to exclude the evidence obtained from the warrantless search. However, the Supreme Court held that Fourth Amendment protections only applied to 'the governed', and that notwithstanding the defendant's previous trips to the United States or his present status as a prisoner in a federal penitentiary, he was not a part of 'the governed'. In a puzzling concurring opinion, Justice Kennedy argued that due to logistical considerations, it would be unreasonable to expect federal agents to obtain a warrant when conducting a foreign search against foreign nationals. However, Kennedy went on to say that a warrant would be required in any search of the abode of a US citizen anywhere in the world that was carried out by American agents, although these same logistical problems would certainly still be present. Finally, in a vigorous dissent, Justice Brennan argued that the defendant became one of 'the governed' the moment the United States began to apply its criminal laws against him.[26] The broader point is that notwithstanding the global enforcement of American criminal law, the US Supreme Court continues to give the Constitution a decidedly territorial interpretation.[27]

The second issue is that even if foreign nationals do have Fourth Amendment protection, what remedy would they have for violations of those rights in the present context? For one thing, the 'exclusionary rule' is applicable only to evidence that the government seeks to have admitted in a criminal proceeding. If, however, there is no trial, there is no evidence to exclude.

Another possible cause of action would be to pursue what is referred to as a *Bivens*-style remedy, named after the US Supreme Court opinion that ruled that federal agents (although not the US government itself) could be sued for civil damages for particularly egregious constitutional violations.[28] Yet what remains unclear is whether *Bivens* is applicable to extraterritorial violations. In addition, how could governmental action that is (literally) directed against everyone be viewed as 'egregious'? Finally, as Denise Gilman has shown, the reality is that this avenue for relief has been greatly overblown.[29]

4.2.2 Metadata operations

Thus far we have limited our discussion to NSA wiretap surveillance. However, the most stunning of all Snowden's revelations was that the NSA has engaged in a massive metadata collection programme that collects information on every phone call and every email made by US citizens. Some of this is information that the US government has demanded – and received – from private internet providers and phone companies. However, a large portion of this data has been collected by the NSA itself.[30]

The repeated response of the Obama administration has been that 'no one is listening to your calls', although Snowden has suggested that any clear division between monitoring and listening is not nearly as ironclad as President Obama's assurances would suggest. And these remarks must also be viewed against a background of improper government denials. Perhaps the worst example of this occurred in a Senate hearing in March 2013 when James Clapper, the director of national intelligence, was asked whether 'the NSA collect[s] any type of data at all on millions or hundreds of millions of Americans'. To which Clapper replied: 'No, sir. . . . not wittingly'. However, a few months later, following the public revelations of the NSA's metadata programme, Clapper maintained that his answer before the Senate panel was not a lie, but that he had responded in the 'least untruthful manner'.

In the first legal test case, the FISC upheld the constitutionality of the meta-data programme, holding that the controlling precedent is the Supreme Court's decision in *Smith* v. *Maryland* 1979,[31] which involved a pen register installed by the police. In *Smith*, law-enforcement officials failed to obtain a warrant for the pen register, which is a device for recording the outgoing numbers dialled from a telephone but not the content of the call. The Supreme Court declined to apply the Fourth Amendment, concluding that 'a person has no legitimate expectation of privacy in information he voluntarily turns over to third parties'.[32] Thus according to its ruling, the FISC views the NSA metadata programme as *Smith* writ large (very large)

> where one individual does not have a Fourth Amendment interest, grouping together a large number of similarly-situated individuals cannot result in a Fourth Amendment interest springing into existence *ex nihilo*.[33]

ACLU v. *Clapper* (2013),[34] the first federal court to address the issue of the constitutionality of the NSA metadata collection programme, agreed with the FISC's analysis, noting in the same kind of vein that the 'collection of breathtaking amounts of information unprotected by the Fourth Amendment does not transform the sweep into a Fourth Amendment search'.[35] However, in May 2015, the Second Circuit Court of Appeals overturned this decision, holding that there was no evidence that Congress had authorised anything even remotely approaching the all-encompassing (and, apparently, never-ending) NSA metadata programme.[36]

This is consistent with the ruling by the district court for the District of Columbia in *Klayman* v. *Obama* (2013).[37] In its holding, the district court thoroughly rejected the idea that *Smith* – decided decades earlier based on vastly different technology than what exists today and affecting only one individual – was in any way applicable to the NSA's massive metadata collection. Instead Judge Leon relied heavily on the Supreme Court's 2012 ruling in *United States* v. *Jones*,[38] which ruled that a GPS device placed on an automobile of a suspected drug-dealer for nearly a month constituted a 'search' that was governed by the Fourth Amendment. The court in *Klayman* weighed three competing interests. The first was each individual's right to privacy; the second was the government's interest in preventing terrorist attacks; and finally, the efficacy of the methods employed by the government to achieve this end. Challenging the government's assertion that metadata was responsible for averting fifty-four terrorist attacks, Judge Leon concluded that there was, at most, one incident where this might have occurred, a finding that is consistent with other studies.[39]

4.3 International law

Our discussion thus far has focused primarily on US law and practice, although what should be obvious is that NSA surveillance activities have few, if any, territorial boundaries or limitations. Moreover, while American citizens have, for the most part, 'only' been subjected to the NSA metadata collection programme, violations of privacy rights against foreign nationals have routinely and systematically gone beyond this. In that way, not only have a host of foreign leaders been subject to wiretapping, but millions of foreign nationals have had their phone calls and emails monitored by the US government.

Unfortunately, besides finding that the United States is acting in a lawless fashion, there has been almost no discussion of the larger implications of NSA spying. As I explain here, NSA surveillance practices challenge three of the most important principles in all of international law: sovereignty, jurisdiction and territory.

4.3.1 Sovereignty

It is almost a truism that sovereignty serves as a linchpin of the international system. Under this principle, each country is a sovereign entity that other states are required not to interfere with. Historically, states enjoyed sovereignty almost as a matter of default. In that way, even some of the most brutal and corrupt regimes could hide from the scrutiny of the international community under the cover of state sovereignty. However, this principle has evolved in the past decade or so, led in large part by the Responsibility to Protect initiative, so that sovereignty is something that states now have to earn – and they do this by protecting their own citizens.[40]

NSA spying calls into question two important aspects of state sovereignty. The first involves this principle of non-interference, and the question is how to square this with the massive levels of NSA spying which have already taken place and which, in all likelihood, are still being carried out. The point, quite simply, is that spying on the political leadership of another country and conducting surveillance activities against the citizens of that state constitute clear infringements on the sovereign integrity of this other country. The (weak) reply has been that 'all' states engage in some kind of spying – as if the act of spying were an essential component of state sovereignty itself. It is by no means clear whether this is true or not, and what also has to be pointed out is that this (conveniently) ignores the fact that some states, most notably the United States, are in a vastly preferred situation in terms of their ability to spy than other countries would be. Still, it is internally inconsistent to venerate the principle of non-interference while, at the same time, states feel quite free to violate this principle with impunity.

The second aspect of state sovereignty that is directly challenged by NSA spying practices involves the principle that a state has an obligation to protect its citizens from human rights violations, or else may lose at least some element of its sovereignty. One thing that is now eminently clear is that a number of states left their citizens vulnerable to NSA surveillance practices. More than that, there is substantial evidence that certain states, including the United Kingdom and Australia, enlisted the NSA to spy on their own citizens.[41] And to go beyond the surveillance practices themselves, what also has been deeply disturbing has been the muted response by most, if not all, states and their apparent unwillingness to invoke legal mechanisms to challenge US practices.

4.3.2 Jurisdiction

NSA spying also challenges our understanding of 'jurisdiction', a term that is used in a number of international and regional human rights treaties.[42] To use a concrete example, one of the Snowden revelations was that the NSA monitored some 60 million phone calls by ordinary Spanish citizens in early 2013.[43] The issue, then, is whether Spanish citizens were thereby brought within the 'jurisdiction' of the United States. In Europe, where the issue of 'jurisdiction' has spawned an enormous amount of interest and scrutiny going back to the European Court of Human Rights ruling in *Bankovic* v. *Belgium*,[44] there has been a decided tendency to limit notions of 'jurisdiction' in an extraterritorial context to security situations, whether this involves soldiers killing foreign nationals (on the ground, not from the air),[45] arrests of suspected terrorists[46] or situations involving a formal military occupation.[47]

However, what this approach ignores – purposely or otherwise – is that there are many ways in which a state can exercise 'jurisdiction' over citizens in another state.[48] NSA spying serves as a perfect example of this. Moreover, what this example also shows is that a person can be within a state's jurisdiction and not even be aware of this. And perhaps more controversially, states can exercise 'jurisdiction' over others even while they are not (actually) exercising jurisdiction, as in the case where individuals believe (erroneously) that their emails or phone calls are being monitored and intercepted, prompting them to act much differently than they had before.

4.3.3 Territory

The final principle of international law directly challenged by NSA spying is the notion of territory itself. Much of international law is founded on the basis of territory. States can always act lawfully within their own territory, while they need permission to act on the territory of another state. What must also be said about the notion of territory is that, with rare exception, its boundaries (literally) are fixed and have already been determined. In that way, it has been commonplace to speak with almost absolute certainty that some event did (or did not) occur within the 'territory' of a particular state.

Yet what does 'territory' mean in an age when an email can be sent to a colleague who is literally across the hall and which appears on this person's computer almost instantly – but which had been routed through one or more other countries? Or consider a mobile phone call that traverses the airspace of several states as it is beamed up to a satellite and then sent back to Earth. What (and where) is the meaning of 'territory' in all this?

Related to this, one of the most unique aspects of surveillance practices is that there will be times when there is a disjuncture between where a victim is physically located and where the human rights violation takes place. Consider an email that is sent to a person in another country (or to a person in the same country but where the transmission is routed through another state) and intercepted by agents of this other state(s). The person whose privacy rights have been violated is situated in one state, but those committing the violation – and arguably the human rights violation itself – are in another country.

There are two other aspects of the 'territory' that challenge our understanding of that term that need to be mentioned. The first is the temporal connection with the state. To say that something is 'within' a state's territory is a way of recognising and honouring a particular kind of attachment to that state. However, consider an email that is written by someone in Tanzania and sent to a colleague in Brazil – but which is routed through the United States. The point is that the notion of something being 'within the territory' of a state has never before been measured in nanoseconds.

Related to this, because of the dominance of US-based internet carriers, virtually every email that is sent in the world will pass through the United States, for whatever brief period of time. Thus all (or nearly all) emails will be 'within the territory' of the United States. However, 'territory' has never been something so thoroughly dominated by just one state. The larger point is that 'territory' in the context of NSA surveillance bears little connection to the ordinary meaning of that term under international law.

In sum, NSA spying directly challenges three core principles (at a minimum) of international law. One involves the sovereign integrity of states, a principle that is difficult to square with practices where the electronic communications of an entire citizenry are being monitored by a foreign power and where, in at least several instances, the political leadership of a (purportedly) sovereign state has been systematically spied upon. The second principle is jurisdiction, which generally has been limited to some kind of effective control over foreign territory or over an individual. Yet what we see in the present context is that one state can exercise 'jurisdiction' over an entire foreign population – and it can do so without ever entering on to the territory of this other country. The third principle involves territory. NSA spying activities certainly do not change or alter existing national borders. But what these practices do challenge is our conceptualisation of how and why territory plays such a central role under international law.

4.4 Conclusion

In a book devoted to the dark side of globalisation, I would maintain that the 'darkest' side of all is NSA surveillance. I say this for several reasons. One is simply the number of people who have been brought within the NSA's dragnet. A conservative estimate would be that hundreds of millions of people have had their emails/phone calls either monitored or listened to. In 2012, former NSA analyst William Binney calculated that the agency had collected some 20 *trillion* transactions about US citizens with other US citizens alone. But because of the nature of spying, these (breathtaking) numbers are only estimates.

Yet it is not only the number of people who are affected (or think they have been affected), but the nature of what is being spied on: our communications with others, whether it be loved ones, friends, colleagues – or even our enemies. Because of this worldwide surveillance, two instruments that were thought to bring people (and even peoples) together – the phone and the internet – are instead discovered to be instruments of government intrusion and oppression.

The last comment relates to globalisation itself. This term has always been depicted as something that all states, and most people in these states, have been influenced by and, in many instances, benefited from. Yet what is unique (let us hope) about NSA spying practices is its astounding one-sidedness. I cannot hope to improve on Glenn Greenwald's depiction of the 'one-way mirror' that the United States has established for itself, which in so many ways is the antithesis of true globalisation. I conclude, therefore, with his extended and trenchant remarks:

> Ultimately, beyond diplomatic manipulation and economic gain, a system of ubiquitous spying allows the United States to maintain its grip on the world. When the United States is able to know everything that everyone is doing, saying, thinking and planning – its own citizens, foreign populations, international corporations, other government leaders – its power over those factions is maximised. That's doubly true if the government operates at ever greater levels of secrecy. The secrecy creates a one-way mirror: the US government sees what everyone else in the world does, including its own population, while no one sees its own actions. It is the ultimate imbalance, permitting the most dangerous of all human conditions: the exercise of limitless power with no transparency or accountability.[49]

Notes

1   An overview of some NSA practices can be found in Scott Shane, 'No Morsel Too Minuscule for All-Consuming NSA', *New York Times*, 2 November 2013, 1. See also, James Bamford, 'They Know Much More Than You Think', *New York Review of Books*, 15 August 2013, available at: www.nybooks.com/articles/archives/2013/aug/15/nsa-they-know-much-more-you-think/; James Bamford, 'Why NSA Surveillance is Worse Than You've Ever Imagined', *Reuters*, 11 May 2015, available at: http://blogs.reuters.com/great-debate/2015/05/11/if-youre-not-outraged-about-the-nsa-surveillance-heres-why-you-should-be/.

2   Glenn Greenwald, *No Place to Hide: Edward Snowden, the NSA, and the US Surveillence State* (New York: Metropolitan Books, 2004), 157.

3   US President's Review Group on Intelligence and Communications Technologies, Office of the Director of National Intelligence, 'Liberty and Security in a Changing World'. Report by Office of the Director of National Intelligence (Washington, DC: White House, December 2013), available at: www.whitehouse.gov/sites/default/files/docs/2013-12-12_rg_final_report.pdf.

4   Several months after the Snowden revelations, the UN General Assembly overwhelmingly passed a resolution reaffirming the (human) right to privacy. UN General Assembly, *The right to privacy in the digital age*, A/RES/68/167, 68th Sess., 18 December 2013.

5   In the elegant words of the Court of Justice of the European Union, in the case of Digital Rights Ireland:

> To establish the existence of an interference with the fundamental right to privacy, it does not matter whether the information on the private lives concerned is sensitive or whether the persons concerned have been inconvenienced in any way . . .
>
> (para. 33, CJEU, Grand Chamber, 8 April 2014)

6   Human Rights Council, 'The Right to Privacy in the Digital Age'. Report by the United Nations High Commissioner for Human Rights, A/HRC/27/37 (Geneva: Office of the UN High Commissioner for Human Rights, 30 June 2014).

7   Andrés Cala, 'Spain Protests, but not too much, over NSA spying (1 video)', *Christian Science Monitor*, 28 October 2013, available at: www.csmonitor.com/World/Europe/2013/1028/Spain-protests-but-not-too-much-over-NSA-spying-video.

8   As explained by the European Court of Human Rights:

> Telephone, facsimile and email communications are covered by the notions of 'private life' and 'correspondence' within the meaning of Article 8. . . The Court recalls its findings in previous cases to the effect that the mere existence of legislation which allows a system for the secret monitoring of communications entails a threat of surveillance for all those to whom the legislation may be applied. This threat necessarily strikes at freedom of communication between users of the telecommunications services and thereby amounts in itself to an interference with the exercise of the applicants' rights under Article 8, irrespective of any measures actually taken against them. . . . (par. 56)
>
> (Case of *Liberty and Others* v. *United Kingdom*, Appl. No.
> 58243/00, 1 July 2008)

9   International Covenant on Civil and Political Rights, adopted and opened for signature, ratification and accession by General Assembly resolution 2200A (XXI) of 16 December 1966, entry into force 23 March 1976, in accordance with Article 49. Article 2(1) reads:

> Each State Party to the present Covenant undertakes to respect and to ensure to all individuals within its territory and subject to its jurisdiction the rights recognised in the present Covenant, without distinction of any kind, such as race, colour, sex, language, religion, political or other opinion, national or social origin, property, birth or other status.

10 Marko Milanovic has documented how problematic the US government position on this issue has been. Marko Milanovic, 'Human Rights Treaties and Foreign Surveillance: Privacy in the Digital Age' *Harvard International Law Journal* 56 no. 1 (2015), 81–146.

11 *Sergia Euben Lopez Burgos* v. *Uruguay*, Communication No. 12/52 (5 June 1979) UN Doc. Supp. No. 40 (A/36/40) (1981).

12 See e.g., *Griswold* v. *Connecticut*, 381 U.S. 479 (1965) (striking down state statute that prohibited the sale of birth control devices); *Roe* v. *Wade*, 410 U.S. 113 (1973) (striking

down Texas statute that proscribed abortion); *Lawrence v. Texas*, 539 U.S. 558 (2003) (striking down Texas sodomy law).

13 *Katz v. United States*, 389 U.S. 347 (1967).

14 'Whether safeguards other than prior authorisation by a magistrate would satisfy the Fourth Amendment in a situation involving the national security is a question not presented by this case'. Ibid. at 358 note 23.

15 *United States v. US District Court (Keith)*, 407 U.S. 297 (1972).

16 Foreign Intelligence Surveillance Act of 1978, Pub. L. No. 95–511, 92 Stat. 1783 (codified as amended in scattered sections of 8, 18 and 50 U.S.C.).

17 Authorisation for the Use of Military Force, Pub. L. No. 107–140 codified at 115 Stat. 224, passed as S.J. Res. 23 September 14, 2001.

18 Wartime Executive Power and the National Security Agency's Surveillance Authority: Hearing Before the Senate Committee on the Judiciary, 109th Cong. 10–15 (2006).

19 James Risen and Eric Lichtblau, 'Bush Lets US Spy on Callers Without Courts', *New York Times*, 16 December 2005, available at: www.nytimes.com/2005/12/16/politics/bush-lets-us-spy-on-callers-without-courts.html.

20 Protect America Act of 2007, Pub. L. No. 110–153, 121 Stat. 552 (codified at 50 U.S.C. Sec. 1801, 1803, 1805 (2021)).

21 FISA Amendment Acts of 2008, Pub. L. No. 110–261, 122 Stat. 2436 (codified at 50 U.S.C. Sec. 1881a (2012)).

22 See, generally, Owen Fiss, 'Even in a Time of Terror' *Yale Law & Policy Review* 31 (2012), 1–31.

23 Greenwald, *No Place to Hide*, 127.

24 Fiss, 'Even in a Time of Terror', 17.

25 *United States v. Verdugo-Urquidez*, 494 U.S. 259 (1990).

26 See generally, Mark Gibney, 'Policing the World: The Long Reach of US Law and the Short Arm of the Constitution' *Connecticut Journal of International Law* 6 (1990), 103–126.

27 See generally, Kal Raustiala, 'The Geography of Justice' *Fordham Law Review* 73 (2005), 2501–2560; Kal Raustiala, *Does the Constitution Follow the Flag? The Evolution of Territoriality in American Law* (New York: Oxford University Press, 2009).

28 *Bivens v. Six Unknown Named Agents of Federal Bureau of Narcotics*, 403 US 388 (1971).

29 Denise Gilman, 'Calling the United States' Bluff: How Sovereign Immunity Undermines the United States' Claim to an Effective Domestic Human Rights System' *Georgetown Law Journal* 95 (2007), 591–652.

30 See generally, Bamford, 'They Know Much More Than You Think'.

31 *Smith v. Maryland*, 442 U.S. 735 (1979).

32 Ibid., 743–744.

33 *In re* Application of the Federal Bureau of Investigation for an Order Requiring the Production of Tangible Things from [Redacted], No. BR 13–109, at 6 (FISA Ct. 2013), available at: www.uscourts.gov/uscourts/courts/fisc/br13–09-primary-order.pdf.

34 *ACLU v. Clapper*, 959 F. Supp. 2d 724 (S.D.N.Y. 2013).

35 Ibid., 752.

36 *ACLU v. Clapper*, Docket no. 14–42-cv (2d Cir. 2015).

37 *Klayman v. Obama*, No. 13–0881, 2013 WL 6598728 (D.D.C. December 2013).

38 *United States v. Jones*, 132 S. Ct. 945 (2012).

39 See generally, Bailey Cahall, Peter Bergen, David Sterman and Emily Schneider, 'Do the NSA's Bulk Surveillance Programs Stop Terrorists?' (Washington, DC: New America, January 2014), available at: www.newamerica.net/publications/policy/do_nsas_bulk_surveillance_programs_stop_terrorists.

40 See generally, International Commission on Intervention and State Sovereignty, 'The Responsibility to Protect' (Ottawa, Ontario: International Development Research Centre, 2001).

41 Greenwald, *No Place to Hide*, 122.

42 For example, Article 1 of the European Convention provides: 'The High Contracting Parties shall secure to everyone within their jurisdiction the rights and freedoms. . . of this Convention'.
43 Cala, 'Spain Protests'.
44 *Bankovic et al.* v. *Belgium et al.*, Appl. No. 52207/99 European Court of Human Rights (2001), 41 I.L.M. 517.
45 *Issa* v. *Turkey*, Appl. No. 31821/96, European Court of Human Rights (2005).
46 *Ocalan* v. *Turkey*, Appl. No. 46221/99, European Court of Human Rights (2000).
47 *Al-Skeini* v. *United Kingdom*, Appl. No. 55721/07 European Court of Human Rights (2011).
48 For an in-depth analysis of jurisdictional issues in this respect, see Marko Milanovic's chapter in this volume, 'Extraterritoriality and human rights: prospects and challenges'.
49 Greenwald, *No Place to Hide*, 169.

Bibliography

Bamford, James. 'They Know Much More Than You Think'. *New York Review of Books*, 15 August 2013, available at: www.nybooks.com/articles/archives/2013/aug/15/nsa-they-know-much-more-you-think/ (accessed September 24, 2016).

Cahall, Bailey, Peter Bergen, David Sterman and Emily Schneider. 'Do the NSA's Bulk Surveillance Programs Stop Terrorists?'. Washington, DC: New America, January 2014, available at: www.newamerica.net/publications/policy/do_nsas_bulk_surveillance_programs_stop_terrorists. (accessed September 24, 2016).

Fiss, Owen. 'Even in a Time of Terror'. *Yale Law & Policy Review* 31 (2012): 1–31.

Gibney, Mark. 'Policing the World: The Long Reach of US Law and the Short Arm of the Constitution'. *Connecticut Journal of International Law* 6 (1990): 103–126.

Gilman, Denise. 'Calling the United States' Bluff: How Sovereign Immunity Undermines the United States' Claim to an Effective Domestic Human Rights System'. *Georgetown Law Journal* 95 (2007): 591–652.

Greenwald, Glenn. *No Place to Hide: Edward Snowden, the NSA, and the US Surveillance State.* New York: Metropolitan Books, 2014.

Human Rights Council. 'The Right to Privacy in the Digital Age'. Report by the Office of the United Nations High Commissioner for Human Rights. A/HRC/27/37. Geneva: Office of the UN High Commissioner for Human Rights, 30 June 2014.

International Commission on Intervention and State Sovereignty. 'The Responsibility to Protect'. Ottawa, Ontario: International Development Research Centre, 2001.

Milanovic, Marko. 'Human Rights Treaties and Foreign Surveillance: Privacy in the Digital Age'. *Harvard International Law Journal* 56 no. 1 (2015): 81–146.

Raustiala, Kal. 'The Geography of Justice'. *Fordham Law Review* 73 (2005): 2501–2560.

Raustiala, Kal. *Does the Constitution Follow the Flag? The Evolution of Territoriality in American Law.* Oxford: Oxford University Press, 2009.

US President's Review Group on Intelligence and Communications Technologies. 'Liberty and Security in a Changing World'. Report by Office of the Director of National Intelligence. Washington, DC: US Government White House, December 2013, available at: www.whitehouse.gov/sites/default/files/docs/2013-12-12_rg_final_report.pdf. (accessed September 24, 2016).

5

JURISDICTION AT SEA

Migrant interdiction and the transnational security state

Douglas Guilfoyle

5.1 Introduction

The presently observable reality of maritime migrant interdiction is open to a range of readings.[1] The main theme I wish to explore is whether maritime migrant interdiction operations signal the rise of a transnational security state.[2] This chapter contends that examining maritime migrant interdiction evidences four basic propositions: first, that in response to transnational security threats the state itself is becoming increasingly transnational; second, that the resulting permeability of sovereignty and jurisdiction is most apparent when we examine action by states on the high seas or within the maritime zones of other states; third, that the application of human rights law to high seas operations is, if doctrinally straightforward, fragmented in practice; and fourth, that the fragmentation of human rights tells us something about the way international relations are increasingly conducted, and the risks those processes create for real human beings.

I can best elucidate what I mean by 'transnational security state' through an example. Guy Goodwin-Gill has said of the EU response to maritime migration that in such activities, we can see states

> operating . . . in a physical domain where borders, as we commonly understand them, simply do not exist – at sea, on the high seas or even in the contiguous zone or territorial waters of other states, in fact, at notional or virtual borders reconstituted on the basis of national and regional interest. . . . [states can] project a non-territorial conception of national interests into a common or even a contested space . . . the fact that migrants and those in search of refuge may be obliged to cross the seas offers new opportunities for states now to project power and influence.[3]

The tools used may also be transnational in a specific sense. Humphreys suggests that a key characteristic of transnational law is that it is not law between equals: as noted in this chapter, a variety of legal responses to transnational threats involve treating 'partner' states as subservient, lesser sovereign states.[4] This may be the case particularly when the mechanism chosen is an ostensibly non-legal and non-binding memorandum of understanding, but it is equally apparent in some treaties concluded between ostensibly juridically equal sovereign states.

Goodwin-Gill's observation also draws our attention to a very important idea. Migrant smuggling is seen as a transnational threat to states (indeed, as a form of transnational organised crime). That threat has itself created a new opportunity for states to project power. Once we take this idea seriously, we can begin to unravel a number of assumptions that permeate the maritime security debate generally, and migrant interdiction operations in particular.

In an era when it is common to speak of transnational threats and challenges, it seems increasingly apparent that territorial borders no longer provide meaningful security protection to states and their populations. The old assumption that power could be accumulated within exclusive territorial borders (i.e. as a state) to preserve security against symmetrical actors (other states) has broken down in the world of transnational threats posed by asymmetrical, non-state actors seen as challenging a state's autonomy, be they transnational terrorists, transnational criminals or other transnational actors (such as migrants).[5] The territorial state exists in a borderless, deterritorialised world at the mercy of transnational forces. Thus the state that responds to transnational security threats appears vulnerable.

The foregoing vision of state security risks our falling into the 'territorial trap' of assuming that states are 'fixed units of sovereign space'[6] rather than potentially more porous or protean configurations of power and authority. In the final analysis, no matter how 'real' they may seem, states are simply 'juridical abstractions'.[7] Even in our lived experience, state power and authority seldom coincide neatly with territorial boundaries. This point is obvious to anyone, who has ever had their passport checked by a French official in London before boarding the Eurostar, or by a US official at Montreal airport, before boarding a plane. At a more abstract level, international lawyers, like international relations scholars, have tended to assume the centrality of the geographic or territorial state, even while debating its continued relevance in the face of economic globalisation,[8] mass migration or increasing transnational or post-national governance.[9]

This obscures the extent to which the state itself has become transnational in its responses to (what are constructed as) security threats to its autonomy and interests. This is the 'transnational security state' in which I am interested, here: the state capable of projecting its power beyond its own borders into previously 'non-sovereign' spaces (such as the high seas), and even into the sovereign or jurisdictional spaces of other states (such as a territorial sea or contiguous zone). Its projections of power may be undertaken in response to threats to either its own autonomy (matters seen as impinging on a state's ability to make and implement its own 'internal' policy choices) or to shared interests (a more diffuse category

including such 'external' or 'common' matters as global trade or weapons proliferation).

However, there is a further layer I would like to add. The transnational security
state seldom acts alone. Sometimes it does, as in the United States' efforts to
externalise its customs border into foreign ports through the Container Security
Initiative.[10] Increasingly, though, in response to maritime security threats (be they
migrants, pirates or traffickers engaged in proliferation of weapons of mass
destruction), states respond through what Klabbers terms 'transgovernmentalism':
the 'effective, goal-oriented management of international issues' by 'informal networks of decision makers'.[11] This also draws our attention to what I will call, in
my conclusion, 'the internal or decision-maker-oriented view' of the transnational
security state. That is, although the security state may seem monolithic from without,
it is composed of real people performing real jobs, whether as naval or customs
officers, migration control agents or government lawyers.

A key question for transgovernmentalism is the extent to which it is regarded
as either a legally regulated activity or simply as 'not law' (and therefore not an
activity subject to judicial supervision).[12] I suggest that although it is doctrinally
straightforward to assume that the rule of law applies to all maritime interdiction
operations, in practice the rule of law finds easier purchase when the threat is seen
as one to *common interests*, rather than to core questions of state *autonomy*. Where
a threat is constructed as impinging on a state's ability to make and implement its
own policy choices (such as on questions of migration), it is a threat to autonomy.
In turn, threats to autonomy are easier to classify as existential threats that should
be addressed with exceptional measures.[13] Threats to shared or common interests,
such as the threat that piracy poses to the interests of all states in maritime trade,
are harder to parlay into existential threats. Therefore, they are more susceptible
to a 'business as usual' application of the law to transgovernmental cooperation or
multinational operations.[14]

The key test for the analytical usefulness of this approach lies in examining the
projection of sovereignty into the high seas in maritime interdiction operations,
and the exercise of various forms of concurrent jurisdiction in other maritime zones.
Superficially, the idea of sovereign power being asserted over the high seas is a
contradiction. Sovereignty is commonly described with respect to a defined
territory,[15] and by definition, the high seas are a space not subject to sovereign
claims or territorial occupation.[16] Nonetheless, even the classical doctrine of the
law of the sea allows for overlapping or concurrent exercise of jurisdiction in this
non-sovereign space, and, as we will see, the duty of rescue of mariners (or migrants)
in distress may itself become a potent tool for power projection. The second question
concerns how this plays out in practice: how do multinational migrant interdiction
operations work as examples of transgovernmentalism? With regard to this, I
particularly wish to examine the ship-rider model in EU Frontex operations. Third,
returning to the 'internal view' noted above, we may ask whether the transnational
security state is quite as monolithic as I might be taken to suggest. Although
I consider the idea useful, what it may draw most attention to is the lack of a

centralised strategy on some issues, and the potential for intermediate-level decision-makers to have more influence on outcomes than they might be comfortable admitting.[17] What may seem to be the outcome of a deliberate legal strategy to create jurisdictional 'black holes' may in part be the result of modern methods of international cooperation. If intergovernmental activity is increasingly conducted by ad hoc working groups at the level of technical assistance carried out under memoranda of understanding,[18] it may simply have a natural tendency to fragment at the level of legal compliance, with human rights questions simply falling through the cracks.

5.2 The law of the sea and problems of sovereignty, jurisdiction and territoriality

5.2.1 Introduction

The practice of maritime interdiction brings into sharp relief the concept of jurisdiction in general public international law, and its porous nature. Jurisdiction may be understood in a number of ways, or as having a number of aspects. It is certainly correct to say that jurisdiction has 'more than one *ordinary* meaning' in public international law.[19] It may describe what states may do (their juridical authority under the law of prescriptive and enforcement jurisdiction), what they must or should do (as a question of human rights),[20] and the actual exercise of executive authority or public power (legal or not). This understanding loosely correlates with Allott's conception of the triple constitution of any society or legal order. That is, any society has a three-dimensional constitution consisting of a legal constitution, an ideal constitution (i.e. a society's shared higher ideals) and a real constitution (i.e. the actual distribution of power in lived experience).[21] Each of these dimensions interacts with, and shapes, the other two in a dynamic constitutive process. Similarly, our discussion of jurisdiction cannot simply be compartmentalised, it needs to be considered in the round. In this chapter I focus more on what the real practice of high seas migrant interdiction tells us about the underlying structures of power involved, and less on what the legal constitution governing ocean space tells us should be done in concrete cases (though this will be a significant part of the discussion). Put more simply, without the distraction of territoriality, high seas maritime interdiction operations become a test case for certain questions concerning sovereignty and jurisdiction. Focusing on activity in maritime space allows us to more readily see that sovereignty and jurisdiction are not contingent on territory, but on the exercise of power. Looking to the high seas – and indeed, multilateral operations in the territorial sea – also allows us to see situations in which multiple sovereignties may simultaneously (co)exist in the same space. Collectively, these questions may reveal the outlines of a transnational security state in the making. However, we must begin with certain questions of doctrine.

5.2.2 The legal constitution of the high seas

The high seas are a unique jurisdictional space. By definition we know it only by what it is not. That is, classically, it was the space beyond the territorial sea of all states, and was beyond being subjected to claims of sovereignty.[22] Doctrinally, the concept is now somewhat more porous. The regime of the high seas has a certain limited, residual application in the *sui generis* exclusive economic zone,[23] a zone where the rights and interests of coastal states are balanced against the rights and interests of all other states in freedom of navigation.[24]

The starting point with respect to authority on the high seas is the jurisdiction of flag states over vessels which have their nationality. Ships are special jurisdictional objects attached to their state of nationality: they are not considered 'floating territory' in modern international law (if indeed they ever were).[25] A flagged vessel is said to fall under the exclusive jurisdiction of each flag state over vessels enjoying its nationality.[26] In practice, this jurisdiction is not very exclusive. For example, it does not exclude other states from attaching consequences to the actions of their nationals aboard a foreign flag vessel.[27] Nor does it exclude one state from transferring jurisdiction over the events occurring on board to another state. This is most evident in the field of drug interdiction. It is not uncommon for a flag state to waive its jurisdiction over a vessel intercepted by another state (typically by the United States, but recent cases have involved France and the United Kingdom), and allow the prosecution of narcotics smuggling offences discovered aboard under the law of the interdicting state.[28] Such jurisdiction swapping is expressly permitted under a number of international treaties, and has been successfully challenged on human rights grounds only when no such treaty was already in place (on the theory that the defendant had no notice that they might be subject to the laws of an intercepting state).[29] There are also certain universal exceptions to the principle of exclusive flag state jurisdiction, codified under the UN Convention on the Law of the Sea, a number of which allow the assertion of jurisdiction by an intercepting state over offences discovered aboard (most notably in the case of piracy and unauthorised broadcasting).[30]

On close analysis, 'exclusive jurisdiction' is simply a general immunity from interference by the government vessels of other states.[31] This general rule is subject to certain exceptions codified in Law of the Sea Convention (UNCLOS) (as noted above) or by waiver under treaty (as in drug interdiction arrangements). Also, it is not generally doubted that at least some forms of intervention against a foreign flag vessel on the high seas may be authorised simply by the express consent of the flag state.[32] Thus there is no true rule of 'one ship, one law', as is sometimes suggested.[33]

This brings into relief the difficult question of stateless vessels, or as UNCLOS puts it, vessels 'without nationality' – those with no claim to the nationality of any state.[34] If only nationality protects vessels from interference, then a stateless vessel is indeed a very vulnerable creature of law. Two difficulties arise when considering the legal status of stateless vessels. The first is the extent to which enforcement jurisdiction may be justified over stateless vessels encountered by government vessels on the high seas. One view, taken in (at least some) Anglo-American jurisprudence, is that such vessels may be subjected to the authority of any state, because they enjoy the protection of none.[35] The other view is that some further jurisdictional nexus between the acts of the vessel (or the persons aboard) and the intercepting state is required to justify such an extension of jurisdiction.[36] The second difficulty is determining whether or not a vessel is in fact stateless. Although it is commonly thought that if a vessel is not formally registered in any state and carries no papers, it is stateless, this is not necessarily the case. It has long been observed that some states do not require small craft (or pleasure craft) under a certain length or weight to register, and instead, such craft may enjoy nationality based on the nationality of their owner.[37] This position is actually reflected in the UN Convention on the Law of the Sea, which accepts that a vessel may have nationality either by registration or by some other right to fly a flag.[38] Strict application of this principle could make it almost impossible to determine in practice whether or not a small vessel enjoys a nationality.[39]

Bringing this general framework to bear on the small vessels typically used in irregular maritime migration, we might expect that either: (a) a general multilateral treaty modelled on drug interdiction treaties to allow such operations on the high seas (which includes the exclusive economic zone for such purposes[40]) would need to be concluded; or, otherwise, (b) the ambiguities in the law applicable to stateless vessels would prove an insuperable obstacle. This has not been the case.[41] In practice, the duty of rescue is likely to provide all the authority required for the interception of such small craft – at least when engaged in migrant smuggling – irrespective of any ambiguity regarding to their legal status. This is because such craft are typically unsafely overloaded with people. States may characterise such vessels as 'vessels in distress', where the circumstances are such as 'to produce, on the mind of a skilful mariner, a well-grounded apprehension of the loss of the vessel and cargo or of the lives of the crew'.[42] A state is under the obligation 'to render assistance to any person found at sea in danger of being lost', and therefore a presumption that such overloaded vessels are inherently in distress may give rise to a duty of 'compulsory' rescue.[43] This potentially self-serving characterisation opens the door to potentially serious abuses of rights: the misuse of the duty of rescue as a power of interception.

The most egregious case of the foregoing is Australia's 'Operation Sovereign Borders'. This has involved, in part, the interception on the high seas of overcrowded migrant vessels, and either towing them back to the limit of Indonesian territorial waters, or removing persons from such boats, placing them in special life boats and releasing these at the edge of Indonesia's territorial waters.[44] Not only do such operations involve no effective opportunity to assess whether those intercepted may have international protection claims, but they do not comply with even the letter of the law concerning rescue at sea. The obligation to rescue at sea is *only* discharged when rescued persons are delivered to a place of safety. There is no serious debate that such a place of safety is a port, not a lifeboat cast adrift.[45]

The Italian approach to unilateral migrant interdiction in the Mediterranean is illustrated by the *Hirsi* case before the European Court of Human Rights, in which Italy was forced to give a legal explanation of its actions.[46] *Hirsi* involved the high seas rescue of a group of Somali and Eritrean migrants who were transferred to Italian warships and then returned to Tripoli.[47] As in such cases elsewhere (e.g. Australia's Operation Sovereign Borders or US practices in the Caribbean), the duty of rescue was used as a *de facto* means of interdicting migrants. No consideration was given to non-refoulement obligations.[48] Italy's position was that it did not owe extraterritorial Convention obligations to the intercepted migrants because they had not come under its authority and control, a position that was not upheld by the European Court of Human Rights.

Moreno-Lax in particular has drawn attention to the rhetorical division asserted here and in other cases[49] between rescue at sea and law enforcement at sea.[50] Rescue is presented as an involuntary act resulting from compliance with a duty, as opposed to a voluntary assertion of jurisdiction for law-enforcement or migration control purposes. In *Hirsi*, Italy pleaded that rescue did not involve an assertion of jurisdiction sufficient to prompt protective human rights obligations. Italy claimed before the ECHR it had neither any intent to assert law-enforcement jurisdiction nor had it exercised a sufficient degree of coercion to establish extraterritorial, *de facto* 'authority and control' over the individuals affected.[51] The Court found that the *de jure* control Italy exercised aboard its warship was decisive. Moreno-Lax regards this as potentially reducing the threshold of control that needs to be demonstrated for Convention rights to be invoked.[52] It is difficult to imagine that the Court would have ever reached a different conclusion. Yet Italy sought to argue – one would think paradoxically – that having rescued persons in an extremely vulnerable position, it owed them no human rights obligations. In contrast, Italy has not disputed (and has implicitly conceded) that it has human rights obligations to captured pirates.[53]

5.2.3 The transnational security state and multilateral migrant interdiction

Introduction

The questions considered so far have touched on the theme of the transnational security and the transnational state in a number of ways.[54] I have examined, at least in passing, how unilateral acts of rescue may become a means of projecting state power into the high seas. In certain cases the duty of rescue has clearly been transformed into a powerful tool for external border management. However, this is not the only manner in which the transnational state may operate in the maritime domain. As foreshadowed, there is the important possibility of creating areas of concurrent jurisdiction. Drug interdiction practices (discussed above) demonstrate that this is a well-accepted doctrinal possibility. The further question is whether some of the tools developed in the drug interdiction context may be turned into tools for use in migrant interdiction operations. One of these tools in particular – the ship-rider model – may, where adopted, further the fragmentation of applicable human rights law and state responsibility in this field, at least as matters of lived experience. That is, they may create a degree of ambiguity as to which state is responsible for what. This may allow states and international organisations to hide behind each other, each claiming that some other entity is responsible for human rights compliance. Whether the legal views that states appear to adopt when justifying such operations are convincing is not to the point; the question is whether they are superficially plausible enough to support such operations being launched in the first place. How such doctrinally incoherent policies come to be adopted in the name of transnational security is further considered in this chapter's conclusions. First, I propose to examine the use of the ship-riders model as a general tool of maritime law enforcement, and in the counter-migration context.

The ship-rider model

The general practice of migrant interdiction at sea is examined in other chapters of this volume, and is treated extensively in other literature. One of the legal mechanisms sometimes used in such contexts is that of ship-riders, particularly in the Rapid Border Intervention Team operations coordinated by the EU border agency, Frontex (as discussed below). The ship-rider mechanism is another means by which sovereignty may be exercised as a matter of convenience.

Ship-riders first emerged in US narcotics interdiction practice.[55] The essential idea is simple: if State A wishes to patrol an area of the high seas for vessels suspected of smuggling drugs, and it knows many of the vessels it encounters will be registered with State B, would it not be convenient to have a law enforcement official from State B embarked on a patrol vessel of State A? Such an official could authorise boardings, or could, indeed, conduct them. Such an embarked official might even exercise powers of arrest and evidence gathering, pending determination as to which state (if any) would prosecute any crimes discovered. In practice, however, the actual deployment of ship-riders may raise any number of logistical problems, and therefore occurs infrequently.[56] Instead, many ship-rider arrangements contain provisions allowing for the exercise of ship-riders' powers, even in the absence of any actually embarked ship-rider. This may happen in general (i.e. the ostensible authority of an absent ship-rider is delegated to the patrolling state by treaty), or under self-assessed 'exceptional' circumstances.[57] The idea of a ship-riding policeman effectively becomes something of a fig leaf covering the exercise of other sovereign powers conferred or delegated under a treaty.[58] Thus ship-rider agreements are capable as being seen as a technique of transnational law, in the sense of law that may place one sovereign in a role subservient to another.[59]

Ship-rider arrangements typically have at least four critical features (though not all ship-rider arrangements necessarily provide for all these elements). First, by definition such arrangements must provide for the placement of a foreign law enforcement official aboard the patrolling government's vessel. Second, as noted, in the absence of such an emplaced official, ship-rider arrangements may grant prospective authority to the patrolling state to intervene with regard to its treaty-partner's flag vessels on the high seas, or authorise pursuit into the territorial sea of the partner state, to maintain contact with a suspicious vessel[60] (some treaties potentially allow the intervening state to arrest a pursued vessel in a partner state's territorial sea). Third, such treaties may provide for the allocation of state responsibility with regard to the conduct of such operations. Fourth, these treaties usually provide that the final 'disposition' of the case, suspects, vessel and property on board rest with the flag state. Nonetheless, they usually provide for the interdicting state to exercise jurisdiction, if the flag state permits it to do so (discussed as jurisdictional transfers above).

Ship-rider arrangements as a tool of migrant interdiction

For the present purposes, I will confine my discussion to the use of RABITs (Rapid Border Intervention Teams) in the context of operations coordinated by the EU external border agency, Frontex.[61] These may seem a particularly pertinent example of ship-rider-type operations: they typically involve experts from one EU jurisdiction aboard the vessel of another EU member state, where the latter lacks the capacity or specialist expertise to deal with a sudden influx of migrants by sea.

RABIT scenarios take three basic forms. First, multiple states may be involved in a migrant interdiction operation that occurs on the high seas. For example, Spain might provide a platform for operations (a Coast Guard vessel or similar), although some of the personnel conducting the operation might be drawn from other EU states. Second, such a platform may operate in the territorial seas with the coastal state's consent (with or without multiple EU states being involved in the operation). Third, a foreign vessel may operate in the territorial sea of a state of departure with a ship-rider from the coastal state embarked. All these mechanisms appear to have been employed in EU operations off Senegal, or RABIT taskforces despatched to the Canary Islands. However, on close inspection, such operations lack many of the vital features of those pioneered in US practice, problematic as that practice may be in some respects.[62] Frontex Operation *Hera* was directed at the interdiction of migrants leaving Senegal and Mauritania for the Canary Islands. Usually, the procedure in such operations is to try to either intercept migrant vessels in the territorial sea of the state and return them to shore (which requires some form of delegated authority from the coastal state), or, alternatively, to shadow them on the high seas. In the latter case, a migrant vessel may be followed until either a 'safety of life at sea' event occurs, and those aboard need to be rescued, or the vessel passes into the contiguous zone of the Canary Islands. As I have noted elsewhere, Operation *Hera* features:

- 'interceptions in the territorial sea and contiguous zone of the states of departure ostensibly occurring under technical agreements or MOUs concluded below the level of treaty law between Spain and Senegal/Mauritania';

- 'the deployment of personnel/resources from other EU member states to assist these operations under EU Frontex auspices';
- 'a degree of legal uncertainty surrounding the precise basis for that Frontex participation given that it is not a party to the relevant technical agreements';
- 'the participation of coastal state law-enforcement officials ("ship-riders") who apparently direct and control the return of intercepted vessels to shore'.[63]

Operation *Hera* also features the classic high-seas maritime interdiction of migrant vessels, usually on the basis that they are dangerously overcrowded, and those aboard are in need of rescue.

A number of difficulties arise with regard to the legal basis of activities such as Operation *Hera*.[64] These operations are not conducted directly by the EU border agency Frontex. Rather, that organisation provides a facilitating or coordinating role. It claims that such operations as it coordinates have a legal basis in arrangements reached between the state providing the platform (usually Spain) and the coastal state. The literature notes that whether such agreements provide adequate legal authority for operations involving third parties, particularly perhaps third party law enforcement or government personnel, is open to doubt.[65]

There have been recent efforts to make Frontex operations more human-rights-focused from their outset. The 2014 Frontex regulations, and their fate in the face of the contemporary maritime migration crisis in the Mediterranean, is discussed below.

Human rights and multilateral migrant interdiction operations

It is sometimes claimed that operations in the territorial sea of a coastal state such as Senegal do not engage the non-refoulement obligations of a patrolling state such as Spain. As Klein points out, such an argument might be made on the narrow and legalistic basis that such obligations apply only once an individual has left the territory of a state where he or she faces persecution, and while an individual remains within Senegal's territorial sea, arguably, any such obligation is owed only by the territorial state.[66] There are a number of obvious problems with this proposition, some of which Klein notes. The first is it presumes that such persons face no persecution within the coastal state, or are its nationals (and therefore not covered by the Refugee Convention while they remain in its territory). On either basis the Refugee Convention would no longer apply. Second, it assumes that the fact that State A is operating in a law enforcement capacity in State B's territorial jurisdiction with State B's consent means that State A lacks the power to comply with its human rights obligations. A similar argument was made regarding the transfer of Iraqi detainees from British custody to the Iraqi territorial government, in cases such as *Al Saadoon* and *Al Skeini*.[67] This line of European case law (discussed further below) confirms that the mere fact of operating extraterritorially – even within the territorial jurisdiction of another state – does not mean that one's human rights obligations do not exist when a person comes under your effective control.

From the point of view of states, this result is somewhere between 'inconvenient' and 'catastrophic'. It would be far more convenient to not owe extraterritorially intercepted persons human rights obligations. Human rights may be difficult to implement at sea, and disembarking irregular migrants ashore to conduct status determinations and assess any international protection claims is usually politically unpopular and fraught with policy complications (such as the prospect of having to resettle unwanted migrants who cannot, for whatever reason, be deported). Thus it is common to speak of a conflict between human rights law and the law of maritime interdiction operations. Klein correctly suggests that the question is not one of conflict between branches of public international law. She concludes that it is not 'that international human rights law, including refugee law, should [necessarily] trump the law of the sea', but that once an interdicting 'state crosses the threshold of effective control in relation to the vessels or individuals concerned, human rights obligations should apply'.[68] One can only agree, stressing that in fact, in such cases human rights *do* apply. Klein calls for a 'harmonisation' approach based on exercising state power at sea in a manner that respects the effective control threshold found in human rights law.[69]

At first sight, it seems odd that Klein calls the above-described approach one of 'harmonisation'. 'Harmonisation' suggests a blending of standards, or even their levelling down. The first question is whether the standards are engaged (here, the threshold of effective control is relevant), and, second, how, as a matter of practicality, such standards (once engaged) may be complied with.[70] This is less a question of harmonisation of divergent legal standards than the systemic reintegration at the operational level of legal obligations that have been fragmented at the policy level.[71] As Moreno-Lax argues, the fragmentation of law in this field is less a question of diverging standards requiring harmonising, and more one of a deliberately (or at least wilfully blindly) adopted politico-legal strategy.[72] Somewhat more charitably, Klein suggests that the problem for states (and the officials tasked with implementing policy) is the divergence of policy goals involved:

> Rather than providing protection to individuals who may be fleeing from persecution or otherwise seeking a better life elsewhere, states have been primarily concerned with controlling who may enter their territory and become part of that state's community.[73]

Klein reasonably suggests that integrating human rights law into maritime interception strategies might be more readily achieved if there was greater acceptance of a common, underlying rationale by both bodies of law for such operations: for example, saving lives.[74] However, this seems a remote prospect, for reasons outlined below in relation to EU practice, and further discussed in Section 5.4.

At one level, the European Union appears to have got the message implicit in cases such as *Hirsi*: that human rights planning needs to be built into maritime migrant interdiction/rescue operations from the outset (though one should note that the EU is not, presently, a party to the European Convention on Human

Rights, or bound by decisions of the European Court of Human Rights). In 2014, the European Parliament approved a new Frontex Maritime Guidelines Regulation.[75] This applies to all Frontex-coordinated maritime border surveillance operations, and subjects them to a broad understanding of the non-refoulement principle.[76] The Regulation describes detailed search and rescue and disembarkation obligations for participating law-enforcement vessels,[77] emphasising that the duty of rescue must be carried out 'in accordance with international law and respect for fundamental rights'.[78] The approach taken by the Regulation is clearly to be welcomed, particularly in specifying a clear default rule: that absent other arrangements being reached the state hosting the Frontex operation must receive rescued persons who need to be disembarked.[79] However, it is difficult to find any case where the Regulation has been applied in practice, possibly precisely because states are keen to avoid any such obligations of disembarkation.[80]

Perhaps unsurprisingly, the Frontex regulations have not been the principal mechanism invoked in response to the present surge in Mediterranean migrant smuggling. Instead, the European Council established 'EUNAVFOR MED' in 2015. The mission of EUNAVFOR MED is

> disruption of the business model of human smuggling and trafficking networks in the Southern Central Mediterranean . . . [through] systematic efforts to identify, capture and dispose of vessels and assets used or suspected of being used by smugglers or traffickers, in accordance with applicable international law, including UNCLOS and any UN Security Council resolution.[81]

The preamble of the Council Decision establishing EUNAVFOR MED refers to the need to 'prevent "human tragedies"' and 'more people from dying at sea', and asserts that the operation will be carried out in a manner respecting the Refugee Convention and the principle of non-refoulement.[82] Its preamble further refers to the 'obligation to assist persons in distress at sea and to deliver survivors to a place of safety', and states that EUNAVFOR MED vessels 'will be ready and equipped to perform' rescue duties.[83] Although worthy insofar as it goes, the placement of these ostensible commitments in the preamble, their absence from the mission statement and the lack of any supporting detail are revealing. The Council Decision outlines a mission to destroy migrant smuggling boats, rather than deploy a major rescue at sea operation with well-thought-out procedures for disembarkation and the humane treatment of rescued persons.[84] In fairness one should note that as of December 2015 EUNAVFOR MED had rescued over 3,000 people.[85]

A similar approach is found in UN Security Council resolution 2240, which was intended to give further legal support to counter-migration operations in the Mediterranean. The resolution certainly reminds states of their existing human rights and refugee law obligations.[86] However, the only substantive powers created, or obligations imposed, under the resolution concern rights of search and seizure over vessels on the high seas suspected of involvement in smuggling migrants.[87]

Sadly, the overall picture of multilateral migrant interdiction operations is not one that considers human rights before 'thinking policy'.[88]

5.3 Jurisdiction and power on the high seas: The problem of territorial thinking in a non-terrestrial space

Reflection on the general law governing maritime interdiction operations suggests a number of things about jurisdiction and sovereignty. We have seen that the allocation of authority in maritime spaces is seldom, if ever, exclusive, and mechanisms such as ship-rider agreements may create further situations where jurisdictional competence may overlap. This pliability may be manipulated to serve a number of policy ends. Before considering these questions, we should also place the duty of rescue in a broader context. Both high-seas rescue and questions of transnational maritime law enforcement cooperation raise questions of the role of territoriality in our thinking about these issues as legal problems.

The duty of rescue has some features in common with a human right. It is a non-reciprocal protective duty owed by a state under international law, not to another state but to an individual.[89] However, unlike human rights (classically understood), the duty of rescue applies horizontally: one individual is indirectly obligated to go to the rescue of another. The obligation is *not* placed directly on the individual by international law; it is for flag states to impose this duty on the masters of their government vessels and other vessels of their nationality.[90] Thus under the duty of rescue, flag states are bound to ensure the conduct of both private and public actors, and these duties are owed irrespective of the nationality of those who benefit from its enforcement. It is, in the final resort, a duty that devolves on states, owed to individuals irrespective of nationality. In this sense it is not strictly a human right, any more than the protective rules of international humanitarian law.

On land, territoriality is a useful mechanism for allocating primary responsibility for the fulfilment of such protective obligations, however characterised. Other states may have a role in human rights protection (or violation), but the starting point will always be that the territorial state – absent exceptional circumstances – has certain duties to those under its territorial jurisdiction. The responsibility of the territorial state is an intuitive and easy case. However, presumptions about territoriality and its consequences clearly have no application at sea. State responsibility for a situation of distress will immediately devolve on the coastal state responsible for the maritime area in which the situation of distress occurs, and also on the flag state of any passing vessel obligated to go to the rescue of the distressed vessel.[91] The flag state of the vessel in distress also has certain responsibilities, principally to ensure that the vessel was seaworthy in the first place, though to some extent this responsibility may also fall to any port states visited by the vessel.[92] These duties are concurrent, and bind various actors. As we have seen, none of them preclude the act of rescue becoming a tool of power, rather than the involuntary fulfilment of a duty.

In addition, the law of the high seas in general, and the ship-rider model in particular, demonstrates that two sovereignties may exist in the same space at the same time. This proposition causes courts a degree of concern and difficulty. Galina Cornelisse has discussed the problems of the reification of territory and the conflation of sovereignty and territory.[93] Difficulties with such reified thinking are apparent in the general case law on transnational law enforcement cooperation. Extraterritorial police cooperation *always* involves the exercise of enforcement jurisdiction by the state agents sent abroad to operate in another state's territory. Yet in cases such as *R v Hape* it was held that the Canadian Charter of Rights and Freedoms did not apply to the conduct of Canadian officials present in the Turks and Caicos. The Supreme Court of Canada reasoned that to give extraterritorial effect to the requirement that Canadian officials cannot conduct certain types of searches without a warrant would be to impose requirements of Canadian law on the Turks and Caicos, in violation of the latter's sovereignty.[94] This is nonsensical. There is no principled reason that a domestic law restraint on the actions of an executive agent should not apply abroad. If the law says 'do not do X unless you satisfy condition Y', then that is an obligation which may be obeyed anywhere. If that domestic law prohibition is not well-adapted to extraterritorial operations, then the problem is not one of foreign sovereignty, but of a law that was not drafted with transnational law enforcement cooperation in mind.

Such essentially territorial conceptions of jurisdiction are dangerous because they risk creating situations of executive authority without legal responsibility. The state has historically been a complex of public authority, rights (i.e. those of citizens) and territory.[95] When public authority is exercised beyond territory, respect for rights, especially those of non-citizens, is clearly at risk. That is, any presumption against extraterritorial application[96] – even in cases where state agents act extraterritorially – has the risk of turning operations on ships on the high seas into operations in non-places or, perhaps, to borrow Marc Augé's term, 'non-relational spaces'. Augé uses the idea of non-relational spaces to describe or denote places such as airports where we do not relate to the environment around us as we would to our ordinary environment. These are places without history, locality or interpersonal connections.[97] Such a lack of interpersonal connection is dangerous, if it allows state agents to not relate to the people they encounter as persons enjoying the protection of law.[98] Hannah Arendt reminds us that, whatever their position in normative theory, in our lived experience *humans* are generally not the bearers of rights – *citizens* are.[99] To be reduced to the status of being merely human – to be unclothed by citizenship, and left protected by only 'the abstract nakedness of being human'[100] – is to be made exceptionally vulnerable. Against this backdrop, the person in distress at sea is in a classic position of bare humanity unprotected by citizenship. There is no territorial state to hold accountable for their treatment. This situation of extreme vulnerability is generally said to have given rise to the practice, customary since time immemorial, of seafarers rescuing those in distress.[101] However, as we have seen, that duty is not necessarily the comfort it might be to the persons actually rescued, when it is used as means of interdiction.

5.4 Conclusions: the contours of the transnational security state

This chapter has sought to illustrate two broad perspectives. The central argument has been about what we see if we consider the transnational security state from the outside. The other, secondary, largely implicit, theme has been the internal view of decision-makers within the transnational security state. First, looking in from the outside, this chapter has sought to contest the sovereignty-in-decline account of the modern state as one fundamentally challenged by transnational forces. Transnational challenges such as irregular maritime migration have actually provided new opportunities for deterritorialised power projection, not only on the high seas, but also in maritime zones otherwise under the jurisdiction of another state. Such interpenetration of jurisdictions and the concurrent exercise of power is not alien to international law; international law actively supports it. This ability to act transnationally is only furthered by transgovernmentalism: the formation of horizontal networks of decision-makers connecting governments. Such instrumental networks have the virtue of efficiency. They support practical, solutions-oriented operations that do not require the conclusion of new treaties. Furthermore, at the policy level transgovernmental operations conducted outside ordinary oversight mechanisms may lead to fragmentation on issues such as human rights. Faced with the messy business of attempting to find effective mechanisms for implementing human rights obligations in these operations, decision-makers appear to prefer to find legal constructs in which human rights either do not apply, or (more usually) apply to some other state only. Usually, the strategy does not involve denying that human rights obligations exist, but simply asserting that someone else is responsible for ensuring compliance.

However, this approach appears to result in such operations being carried out in a state of cognitive dissonance. The applicable law is not unfamiliar. Nor is the possibility that more than one state might be responsible for wrongful conduct.[102] That state responsibility might involve a form of joint and separate liability for certain acts is scarcely a revolutionary proposition.[103] Indeed, that responsibility might arise simply for providing the platform – the flag vessel – involved in maritime interdiction operations carried out by agents of other states or international organisations could not possibly be surprising. An elementary principle of international law is that one must not allow activities that harm the rights and interests of other states or, indeed, their nationals, to be conducted within one's jurisdiction.[104] Furthermore, the idea that, simply because an operation is carried out under the mandate of an international organisation, the consequence must be that only that international organisation is liable for any wrongs committed has received very little judicial support, other than in *Behrami* and *Saramati*.[105] *Behrami* was widely regarded in the academic literature as wrongly decided at the time, and was (unusually) directly criticised by the International Law Commission.[106] It has not been followed in subsequent national human rights jurisprudence, at least not in the United Kingdom.[107] The inability of a state to construct a one hundred per cent bullet-proof liability shield with respect to operations involving extraterritorial detention of foreign nationals should not be shocking. Nonetheless, legal theories are constantly put forward by governments as to why such legal obligations do not apply, usually on the *a priori* assumption that such an application would be absurd, impractical or destroy the ability to conduct transnational law enforcement cooperation (or extraterritorial combat operations).

I do not suggest that individual government lawyers see their role as merely facilitating the effective conduct of foreign operations in the national interest. I have personally spent a great deal of time interacting with government legal advisers, and am usually enormously impressed by their diligence and sincere commitment to the law, often in the face of difficult policy and operational environments. However, it is apparent that as a group, bureaucracies may tend to gravitate towards legal theories that pose the fewest problems for them, irrespective of how thinly substantiated those theories appear to be, based on available legal information. The dangers of such groupthink in government are well-known.[108]

Part of the problem identified here, the tendency for human rights considerations to fall through the cracks in maritime interdiction operations, may also be fostered by the way in which much modern international cooperation is conducted. We no longer live in an age when states are keen to conclude new, major multilateral treaties, or to found new international organisations.[109] Intergovernmental activity is increasingly conducted by ad hoc working groups and at the level of technical assistance carried out under memoranda of understanding.[110] Such a 'technical' and operational focus may make it easier to inadvertently take a compartmentalised view of the applicable law. Regardless, agreements concluded below the level of law may engage legal obligations, and actions carried out under them may have legal consequences.

From the point of view of the government official attempting to implement policy, a number of tensions are at play. There may be strong institutional incentives to minutely parse the applicability of obligations, and thus to further fragment their implementation at the operational level (though at the doctrinal level the only question is the relevant threshold of applicability). Certainly, there may appear to be a practice of creating strategic ambiguity and hiding behind other actors when possible. More sympathetically, it is likely that government legal advisers are often caught between the confused imperatives of finding 'practical solutions' (requiring no complex implementation mechanisms or, worse, legislative changes in domestic law), and having to answer to increasingly absolutist human rights mechanisms, activists and courts. Bafflingly, the response often appears to be reactive, rather than demonstrating a strategic attempt to head off such difficulties beforehand.[111] One Foreign Office official quipped of the response to Somali piracy that 'before you go looking for pirates, it's a good idea to be clear about who will be assuming jurisdiction'.[112] That was very obviously not the case in early counter-piracy operations. It may simply be that in many situations the political imperative is to deploy first and engage in consideration of human rights consequences second. Alternatively, it may sometimes be that the required inter-agency coordination within a government (or between governments) seems too difficult to implement until events force decision-makers' hands. However, as I have argued elsewhere, counter-piracy operations have been marked by a (perhaps surprisingly) high level of commitment to the application of human rights law, compared with certain other extraterritorial operations, even if those human rights compliance mechanisms were reactively and sometimes hurriedly assembled.[113]

Whether we look at such matters from an external or an internal perspective, there remain clear incentives for states to create deterritorialised spaces, non-places in which responsibility may be disclaimed.[114] To this end, ships at sea are convenient. International and national law is *always* applicable aboard ships, yet they often seem to remain something mysteriously other. Although human rights are increasingly acknowledged to apply beyond territory in law, the ship at sea remains a challenging space to police in practice. Human rights obligations are difficult for courts to supervise in an entirely isolated and self-contained environment far from metropolitan territory. A ship at sea may serve as a non-place owing to the practical difficulty of providing (or policing compliance with) the right to access to a remedy and the duties of enquiry and reporting. This may hollow out rights, leaving them formally applicable but avoided, in practice. The present, disgraceful, media blackout perpetuated by the Australian government regarding 'Operation Sovereign Borders' is merely the most egregiously obvious example of how this may work.

Notes

1   Elsewhere I have argued one can see counter-migration policies as generally poorly designed to achieve their stated purpose (preventing migration) but well designed as a labour-market tool that creates an effectively right-less labour pool of irregular migrants: Douglas Guilfoyle, 'Transnational Criminal Law as a Governance Strategy in the Global Labour Market: Criminalizing Globalization From Below', *Refugee Survey Quarterly* 29 no. 1 (2010), 185; compare: Anna Triandafyllidou and Maurizio Ambrosini, 'Irregular Immigration Control in Italy and Greece: Strong Fencing and Weak Gate-Keeping Serving the Labour Market', *European Journal of Migration and Law* 13 (2011), 251–273.

2   The concept of the transnational security state developed here draws strongly on research done for Douglas Guilfoyle, 'Transnational Crime and the Rule of Law at Sea: Responses to Maritime Migration and Piracy Compared', in '*Boat Refugees' and Migrants at Sea*, eds Efthymios Papastavridis and Violeta Moreno-Lax (Leiden: Brill, forthcoming).

3   Guy S. Goodwin-Gill, 'The Right to Seek Asylum: Interception at Sea and the Principle of *Non-Refoulement*', *International Journal of Refugee Law* 23 (2011), 443, 447.

4   Stephen Humphreys, *Theatre of the Rule of Law: Transnational Legal Intervention in Theory and Practice* (Cambridge: Cambridge University Press, 2010), 10.

5   Hartmut Behr, 'Political Territoriality and Deterritorialization', *Area* 39 (2007), 113–114.

6   John Agnew, 'Territorial Trap: The Geographical Assumptions of International Relations Theory', *Review of International Political Economy* 1 (1994), 53–80; compare Hartmut Behr, 'Deterritorialisation and the Transformation of Statehood: The Paradox of Globalisation', *Geopolitics* 13 (2008), 359–382.

7 James Crawford and Simon Olleson, 'The Character and Forms of International Responsibility', in *International Law*, 4th edn, ed. Malcolm D. Evans (Oxford: Oxford University Press, 2014), 453.

8 E.g. Shah M. Tarzi, 'Multinational Corporations and American Foreign Policy: Radical, Sovereignty-at-Bay, and State-Centric Approaches', *International Studies* 28 (1991), 366–368.

9 E.g. Nico Krisch, *Beyond Constitutionalism: The Pluralist Structure of Postnational Law* (Oxford: Oxford University Press, 2010), chapter 1.

10 Jessica Romero, 'Prevention of Maritime Terrorism: The Container Security Initiative', *Chicago Journal of International Law* 4 no. 2 (2003), 597; Yi-Chih Yang, 'Impact of the Container Security Initiative on Taiwan's Shipping Industry', *Maritime Policy and Management* 37 (2010), 699–722.

11 Jan Klabbers, *An Introduction to International Institutional Law*, 2nd edn (Cambridge: Cambridge University Press, 2009), 311.

12 Klabbers, *An Introduction to International Institutional Law*.

13 For a critique of this kind of approach to securitisation theory see Andrew W. Neal, 'Securitization and Risk at the EU Border: The Origins of Frontex', *Journal of Common Market Studies* 47 (2009), 352 (preferring the notion of a 'governmentality of unease' driven by networks of security professionals often working outside public view).

14 Oren Gross and Fionnuala Ni Aolain, *Law in Times of Crisis: Emergency Powers in Theory and Practice* (Cambridge: Cambridge University Press, 2006), 384–385; and Douglas Guilfoyle, 'Counter-Piracy Law Enforcement and Human Rights', *International & Comparative Law Quarterly* 59 (2010), 141–169.

15 E.g. Behr, 'Deterritorialisation', 361–362.

16 Article 89, UNCLOS.

17 See generally: David Kennedy, 'Challenging Expert Rule: The Politics of Global Governance', *Sydney Law Review* 27 (2005), 5–28.

18 Kennedy, 'Challenging Expert Rule'; for an example consider Douglas Guilfoyle, 'Prosecuting Pirates: The Contact Group on Piracy off the Coast of Somalia, Governance and International Law', *Global Policy* 4 (2013), 73–79.

19 Marko Milanovic, *Extraterritorial Application of Human Rights Treaties: Law, Principles, and Policy* (Oxford: Oxford University Press, 2011), 30.

20 My position is not to deny that 'jurisdiction' in human rights law may have – in part – a meaning autonomous from the 'general' meaning of jurisdiction as some advocate: see James C. Hathaway and Thomas Gammeltoft-Hansen, 'Non-Refoulement in a World of Cooperative Deterrence', *Columbia Journal of Transnational Law* 53 no. 2 (2015), 235–284 (arguing in Part III that the concept of 'public powers' jurisdiction in European Court of Human Rights jurisprudence goes beyond ordinary understandings of 'jurisdiction'). My contention is that jurisdiction is a multifaceted concept with multiple authentic meanings which cannot be wholly divorced from one another.

21 Philip Allott, *The Health of Nations: Society and Law Beyond the State* (Cambridge: Cambridge University Press, 2002), 79–80, 290.

22 See further: Douglas Guilfoyle, 'The High Seas', in *The Oxford Handbook of the Law of the Sea*, eds Donald Rothwell et al. (Oxford: Oxford University Press, 2015), 203–225; Articles 86 and 89, UNCLOS.

23 Article 56(2), UNCLOS.

24 Article 58, UNCLOS; and on balancing such interests in practice see now: *The M/V 'Virginia G' Case* (Panama/Guinea-Bissau), International Tribunal for the Law of the Sea, 14 April 2014, especially at paras 209–224.

25 The highest it has been put in the modern period is that flagged vessels may be *assimilated* to territory for certain purposes: *Lotus Case* (1927) PCIJ Ser. A No. 104.

26 Articles 92(1) and 94, UNCLOS.

27 Article 117, UNCLOS; Douglas Guilfoyle, *Shipping Interdiction and the Law of the Sea* (Cambridge: Cambridge University Press, 2009), 101.

28 Guilfoyle, *Shipping Interdiction*, 89–94; Efthymios Papastavridis, *The Interception of Vessels on the High Seas* (London: Bloomsbury, 2013), 227–236; Douglas Guilfoyle, '*Medvedyev and Others v. France*, European Court of Human Rights', *International Journal of Marine and Coastal Law* 25 (2010), 437.

29 *Medvedyev v. France*, Appl. No. 3394/03, ECtI IR, 10 July 2008, paras 57–63; upheld in the Grand Chamber judgment of 29 March 2010, paras 82–103. See further Tullio Treves, 'Human Rights and the Law of the Sea', *Berkeley Journal of International Law* 28 (2010), 1–14; Efthymios Papastavridis, 'European Court of Human Rights *Medvedyev et al. v. France*', *International and Comparative Law Quarterly* 59 (2010), 867–882.

30 Article 110, UNCLOS. On enforcement jurisdiction see Article 105 (piracy) and Article 109(4) (unauthorised broadcasting).

31 Guilfoyle, 'The High Seas', 209–210.

32 *Medvedyev v. France*, Appl. No. 3394/03, ECtHR, Grand Chamber, 29 March 2010, paras 96–97.

33 Robin Geiss and Anna Petrig, *Piracy and Armed Robbery at Sea: The Legal Framework for Counter-Piracy Operations in Somalia and the Gulf of Aden* (Oxford: Oxford University Press, 2011), 91.

34 E.g. Article 110(1)(d).

35 *Molvan v. Attorney General for Palestine* (1948) AC 351 at 369; (Privy Council) (1948) 15 ILR 115, 124.

36 Robin R. Churchill and Alan V. Lowe, *The Law of the Sea*, 3rd edn (Manchester: Manchester University Press, 1999), 214.

37 Daniel P. O'Connell, *The International Law of the Sea*, vol. 2, ed. Ivan A. Shearer (Oxford: Clarendon Press, 1984), 753. See various exceptions in national legislation such as: s. 1(1)(d), Merchant Shipping Act 1995 (UK); s. 13, Shipping Registration Act 1981 (Australia); 46 USC § 12102(b) and 12303(a); compare s. 47(a), Canada Shipping Act 2001.

38 Article 91(1), UNCLOS.

39 One possible way around this is presumptive flag state jurisdiction, that is, asking the master to identify a 'flag' state and seeking that state's permission to interdict. See Guilfoyle, *Shipping Interdiction*, 96.

40 Article 58(2), UNCLOS. See further Guilfoyle, 'The High Seas', 212–214.

41 While there is a multilateral instrument on intercepting irregular migrants at sea through a flag state consent mechanism, it is effectively unused in practice: Articles 7–9, Protocol against the Smuggling of Migrants by Land, Sea and Air, Supplementing the United Nations Convention against Transnational Organized Crime 2000, 2241 UNTS 507 (entered into force 28 January 2004 with 141 parties as at 18 December 2014).

42 *The New York* (1818) 3 Wheat. 59, 68; and compare *The Rebecca* (1929) 4 RIAA 444, 447–448.

43 Guilfoyle, *Shipping Interdiction*, 195.

44 See: Senate Standing Committees on Foreign Affairs Defence and Trade (Australia), Report: Breaches of Indonesian territorial waters, 27 March 2014, www.aph.gov.au/Parliamentary_Business/Committees/Senate/Foreign_Affairs_Defence_and_Trade/Breach_of_Indonesian_Territorial_Waters/Report/index.

45 Violeta Moreno-Lax, 'Seeking Asylum in the Mediterranean: Against a Fragmentary Reading of EU Member States' Obligations Accruing at Sea', *International Journal of Refugee Law* 23 (2011), 192–193.

46 *Hirsi Jamaa and Others v. Italy*, Application No 27765/09, European Court of Human Rights, 23 February 2012.

47 *Hirsi*, paras 9–10.

48 Violations were found under Article 3 of the ECHR (non-refoulement); Article 13 (failure to provide access to a remedy with automatic suspensive effect); and under Article 4 of Protocol 4 (on collective expulsions).

49 Moreno-Lax, 'Seeking Asylum in the Mediterranean'.

50 Violeta Moreno-Lax, '*Hirsi Jamaa and Others v. Italy* or the Strasbourg Court versus Extraterritorial Migration Control?', *Human Rights Law Review* 12 (2012), 579–582.
51 Moreno-Lax, '*Hirsi Jamaa*', 580–581; discussing *Medvedyev* and *Al-Skeini*.
52 Moreno-Lax, '*Hirsi Jamaa*', 582.
53 See further: Guilfoyle, 'Transnational Criminal Law as a Governance Strategy'; Guilfoyle, 'Counter-Piracy Law Enforcement and Human Rights', 164.
54 On 'transnationality' as the basic state of contemporary international law, see Douglas Guilfoyle, 'Reading *The City and the City* as an International Lawyer: Reflections on Territoriality, Jurisdiction and Transnationality', *London Review of International Law* 4 (2016, forthcoming), 195–207.
55 See Kathy-Ann Brown, *The Shiprider Model: An Analysis of the US Proposed Agreement Concerning Maritime Counter-Drug Operations in its Wider Legal Context* (Bridgetown: Faculty of Law, University of the West Indies, 1997); Guilfoyle, *Shipping Interdiction*, 72, 89–93; Papastavridis, *The Interception of Vessels*, 221–222, 229–236; Geiss and Petrig, *Piracy and Armed Robbery at Sea*, 85–95.
56 Guilfoyle, *Shipping Interdiction*, 91.
57 Guilfoyle, *Shipping Interdiction*, 93–94.
58 E.g. Natalie Klein, *Maritime Security and the Law of the Sea* (Oxford: Oxford University Press, 2011), 188.
59 See discussion above at note 4.
60 Ibid. Of many possible examples see: Articles 6, 9 and 10, Agreement between the USA and Nicaragua Concerning Cooperation to Suppress Illicit Traffic by Sea and Air, 2001, KAV 5964.
61 Frontex has its legal basis in: Council Regulation (EC) No 2007/2004 of 26 October 2004 establishing a European Agency for the Management of Operational Cooperation at the External Borders of the Member states of the European Union (25 November 2004) OJ L 349/1; as amended by Regulation (EC) No 863/2007 (31 July 2007) OJ L 199/30 and Regulation (EU) No 1168/2011 (22 November 2011) OJ L 304/1. It is these amendments which established the RABIT mechanism.
62 Principally in the US position that the Refugee Convention has no extraterritorial application in such cases: e.g. *Sale v. Haitian Centres Council*, 509 US Reports 155 (1992).
63 Guilfoyle, 'Transnational crime and the rule of law at sea'.
64 See generally: Papastavridis, *The Interception of Vessels*, 286–290; Moreno-Lax, 'Seeking Asylum in the Mediterranean'.
65 Papastavridis, *The Interception of Vessels*, 286–290.
66 See Natalie Klein, 'A Case for Harmonizing Laws on Maritime Interceptions of Irregular Migrants', *International and Comparative Law Quarterly* 63 (2014), 787–814.
67 *Al-Saadoon and Mufdhi v. United Kingdom*, European Court of Human Rights, Application no. 61498/08, 2 March 2010; *Al-Skeini and Others v. United Kingdom*, Application no. 55721/07, European Court of Human Rights, 7 July 2011. See generally: Milanovic, *Extraterritorial Application of Human Rights Treaties*, 131–135, 151–152.
68 Ibid.
69 Klein, 'A Case for Harmonizing Laws', 809.
70 See, e.g., Guilfoyle, 'Counter-Piracy Law Enforcement and Human Rights'.
71 Moreno-Lax, 'Seeking Asylum in the Mediterranean'.
72 Moreno-Lax, 'Seeking Asylum in the Mediterranean'.
73 Klein, 'A Case for Harmonizing Laws', 813.
74 Klein, 'A Case for Harmonizing Laws', 813.
75 See: Regulation No 656/2014 of the European Parliament and of the Council establishing rules for the surveillance of the external sea borders in the context of operational cooperation coordinated by the European Agency for the Management of Operational Cooperation at the External Borders of the Member states of the European Union, (2014) OJ L 189/93 ('Frontex Regulation 2014').
76 Ibid., Articles 1 and 4.
77 Ibid., Articles 9 and 10.

78 Ibid., Article 9(1).

79 Ibid., Articles 9 and 10.

80 Barnes notes the need for a rule on disembarkation without which the duty of rescue remains incomplete: Richard Barnes, 'Refugee Law at Sea', *International and Comparative Law Quarterly* 53 no. 1 (2004), 44–77.

81 Council Decision (CFSP) 2015/778 of 18 May 2015 on a European Union military operation in the Southern Central Mediterranean (EUNAVFOR MED) (2015) OJ L 122/31, Article 1.

82 Ibid., recitals 1–2.

83 Ibid., recital 6.

84 See, e.g., Julian Lehmann, 'The Use of Force Against People Smugglers: Conflicts with Refugee Law and Human Rights Law', *EJIL: Talk!*, 22 June 2015, www.ejiltalk.org/the-use-of-force-against-people-smugglers-conflicts-with-refugee-law-and-human-rights-law/.

85 European External Action Service, 'EUNAVFOR MED Op SOPHIA: Six Monthly Report 22 June–31 December 2015', 28 January 2016, https://wikileaks.org/eu-military-refugees/EEAS/EEAS-2016–126.pdf, 9 and 15.

86 UN Doc S/RES/2240 (2015), preamble, paras 12–13.

87 Ibid., paras 7–8. See further discussion in Guilfoyle, 'Transnational Crime and the Rule of Law at Sea'.

88 Goodwin-Gill, 'The Right to Seek Asylum', 455.

89 See generally Human Rights Committee, General Comment 24, UN Doc. CCPR/C/21/Rev.1/Add.6 (1994); and Robert McCorquodale, 'The Individual and the International Legal System', in *International Law*, 4th edn, ed. Malcolm D. Evans (Oxford: Oxford University Press, 2014), 284–291.

90 Article 98(1), UNCLOS.

91 See generally Papastavridis, *The Interception of Vessels*, 296–300; Moreno-Lax, 'Seeking Asylum in the Mediterranean', 194–200.

92 See generally Churchill and Lowe, *The Law of the Sea*, 264–272.

93 Galina, Cornelisse, *Immigration Detention and Human Rights: Rethinking Territorial Sovereignty* (Netherlands: Brill, 2010), 317ff.

94 *R v. Hape* (2007) 46 ILM 815.

95 Saskia Sassen, *Territory, Authority, Rights: From Medieval to Global Assemblages* (Princeton, NJ: Princeton University Press, 2008).

96 In using the term 'presumption' here I mean an implicit bias in legal reasoning, as opposed to a formal constitutional doctrine which may exist in some legal systems (e.g. in the United States).

97 Marc Augé, *Non-Places: Introduction to an Anthropology of Supermodernity*, trans John Howe (New York: Verso, 1995), 77–78, 101.

98 See e.g. Chapters 2 and 9.

99 Serena Parekh, 'Resisting Dull and Torpid Assent: Returning to the Debate over the Foundations of Human Rights', *Human Rights Quarterly* 29 (2007), 754; Alison Kesby, *The Right to Have Rights: Citizenship, Humanity, and International Law* (Oxford: Oxford University Press, 2012), 3.

100 Hannah Arendt, *The Origins of Totalitarianism* (Cleveland, OH: World Publishing, 1958), 299.

101 E.g. Barnes, 'Refugee Law at Sea', 47 citing Emer de Vattell, *The Law of Nations*, trans J. Chitty (1834), 170.

102 Goodwin-Gill, 'The Right to Seek Asylum', 447.

103 Article 47(1), 'Articles on Responsibility of states for Internationally Wrongful Acts', (2001) *Yearbook of the International Law Commission*, Vol. II(2), 124.

104 *Corfu Channel*, Merits, Judgment, ICJ Reports 1949, 4 at 22–23; *Pulp Mills on the River Uruguay (Argentina v. Uruguay)*, Judgment, ICJ Reports 2010 at para. 101.

105 *Behrami v. France* and *Saramati v. France, Germany and Norway* (2007) 45 EHRR SE10 (2008) 133 ILR 1; paras 128ff and 151.

106   See generally Marko Milanovic and Tatjana Papic, 'As Bad as it Gets: The European Court's *Behrami* and *Saramati* Decision and General International Law', *International & Comparative Law Quarterly* 58 (2009), 267–296; and International Law Commission, 'Report of the 61st Session', UN Doc A/64/10 (2009), 67 and note 102.

107   *Serdar Mohammed v. Ministry of Defence* (2014) EWHC 1369; and Marko Milanovic, 'High Court Rules that the UK Lacks IHL Detention Authority in Afghanistan', *EJIL: Talk!*, 3 May 2014, www.ejiltalk.org/high-court-rules-that-the-uk-lacks-ihl-detention-authority-in-afghanistan/.

108   The term 'groupthink' is usually attributed to Irving L. Janis, *Victims of Groupthink: A Psychological Study of Foreign-Policy Decisions and Fiascoes* (Boston, MA: Houghton Mifflin, 1972).

109   Though reports of the death of treaties may be exaggerated: Joel P. Trachtman, 'Reports of the Death of Treaty Are Premature, But Customary International Law May Have Outlived Its Usefulness', *AJIL Unbound*, 29 April 2014, www.asil.org/blogs/reports-death-treaty-are-premature-customary-international-law-may-have-outlived; Duncan Hollis, 'The End of Treaties? The End of History?', *Opinio Juris*, 29 April 2014, http://opiniojuris.org/2014/04/29/end-treaties-end-history/.

110   E.g.: Kennedy, 'Challenging Expert Rule'; Klabbers, *An Introduction to International Institutional Law*, 311; and by way of concrete example, Guilfoyle, 'Prosecuting Pirates'.

111   Goodwin-Gill, 'The Right to Seek Asylum', 455.

112   K. Westcott, 'Pirates in the dock', BBC News, 21 May 2009, http://news.bbc.co.uk/1/hi/world/africa/8059345.stm.

113   Guilfoyle, 'Counter-Piracy Law Enforcement and Human Rights'.

114   Although, intriguingly, the language of law is almost always used to do so, even if spoken in a register of 'disavowal and differentiation': Fleur Johns, *Non-Legality in International Law: Unruly Law* (Cambridge: Cambridge University Press, 2013), 69.

Bibliography

Agnew, John. 'Territorial Trap: The Geographical Assumptions of International Relations Theory'. *Review of International Political Economy* 1 (1994): 53–80.

Allott, Philip. *The Health of Nations: Society and Law Beyond the State*. Cambridge: Cambridge University Press, 2002.

Arendt, Hannah. *The Origins of Totalitarianism*. Cleveland, OH: World Publishing, 1958.

Augé, Marc. *Non-Places: Introduction to an Anthropology of Supermodernity*. Translated by John Howe. New York: Verso, 1995.

Barnes, Richard. 'Refugee Law at Sea'. *International and Comparative Law Quarterly* 53 no. 1 (2004): 47–77.

Behr, Hartmut. 'Political Territoriality and De-Territorialization'. *Area* 39 (2007): 112–115.

Behr, Hartmut. 'Deterritorialisation and the Transformation of Statehood: The Paradox of Globalisation'. *Geopolitics* 13 (2008): 359–382.

Brown, Kathy-Ann. *The Shiprider Model: An Analysis of the US Proposed Agreement Concerning Maritime Counter-Drug Operations in its Wider Legal Context*. Bridgetown: Faculty of Law, University of the West Indies, 1997.

Churchill, Robin R., and Alan V. Lowe. *The Law of the Sea*, (3rd edn). Manchester: Manchester University Press, 1999.

Cornelisse, Galina. *Immigration Detention and Human Rights: Rethinking Territorial Sovereignty*. Netherlands: Brill (2010): 317ff.

Crawford, James, and Simon Olleson. 'The Character and Forms of International Responsibility'. In *International Law*, (4th edn), edited by Malcolm D. Evans, 443–476. Oxford: Oxford University Press, 2014.

Geiss, Robin, and Anna Petrig. *Piracy and Armed Robbery at Sea: The Legal Framework for Counter-Piracy Operations in Somalia and the Gulf of Aden*. Oxford: Oxford University Press, 2011.

Goodwin-Gill, Guy S. 'The Right to Seek Asylum: Interception at Sea and the Principle of *Non-Refoulement*'. *International Journal of Refugee Law* 23 (2011): 443–457.

Gross, Oren, and Fionnuala Ni Aolain. *Law in Times of Crisis: Emergency Powers in Theory and Practice*. Cambridge: Cambridge University Press, 2006.

Guilfoyle, Douglas. *Shipping Interdiction and the Law of the Sea*. Cambridge: Cambridge University Press, 2009.

Guilfoyle, Douglas. 'Counter-Piracy Law Enforcement and Human Rights'. *International & Comparative Law Quarterly* 59 (2010): 141–169.

Guilfoyle, Douglas. '*Medvedyev and Others v. France*, European Court of Human Rights'. *International Journal of Marine and Coastal Law* 25 (2010): 437–442.

Guilfoyle, Douglas. 'Transnational Criminal Law as a Governance Strategy in the Global Labour Market: Criminalizing Globalization From Below'. *Refugee Survey Quarterly* 29 no. 1 (2010).

Guilfoyle, Douglas. 'Prosecuting Pirates: The Contact Group on Piracy off the Coast of Somalia, Governance and International Law'. *Global Policy* 4 (2013): 73–79.

Guilfoyle, Douglas. 'The High Seas'. In *The Oxford Handbook of the Law of the Sea*, edited by Donald Rothwell, Alex Oude Elferink, Karen Scott and Tim Stephens, 203–225. Oxford: Oxford University Press, 2015.

Guilfoyle, Douglas. 'Reading *The City and the City* as an International Lawyer: Reflections on Territoriality, Jurisdiction and Transnationality'. *London Review of International Law* 4 (2016): 195–207.

Guilfoyle, Douglas. 'Transnational Crime and the Rule of Law at Sea: Responses to Maritime Migration and Piracy Compared'. In *'Boat Refugees' and Migrants at Sea*, edited by Efthymios Papastavridis and Violeta Moreno-Lax. Leiden: Brill, forthcoming.

Hathaway, James C., and Thomas Gammeltoft-Hansen. 'Non-Refoulement in a World of Cooperative Deterrence'. *Columbia Journal of Transnational Law* 53 no. 2 (2015): 235–284.

Hollis, Duncan. 'The End of Treaties? The End of History?'. *Opinio Juris*, 29 April 2014, http://opiniojuris.org/2014/04/29/end-treaties-end-history/.

Humphreys, Stephen. *Theatre of the Rule of Law: Transnational Legal Intervention in Theory and Practice*. Cambridge: Cambridge University Press, 2010.

Janis, Irving L. *Victims of Groupthink: A Psychological Study of Foreign-Policy Decisions and Fiascoes*. Boston, MA: Houghton Mifflin, 1972.

Johns, Fleur. *Non-Legality in International Law: Unruly Law*. Cambridge: Cambridge University Press, 2013.

Kennedy, David. 'Challenging Expert Rule: The Politics of Global Governance'. *Sydney Law Review* 27 (2005): 5–28.

Kesby, Alison. *The Right to Have Rights: Citizenship, Humanity, and International Law*. Oxford: Oxford University Press, 2012.

Klabbers, Jan. *An Introduction to International Institutional Law*, (2nd edn). Cambridge: Cambridge University Press, 2009.

Klein, Natalie. *Maritime Security and the Law of the Sea*. Oxford: Oxford University Press, 2011.

Klein, Natalie. 'A Case for Harmonizing Laws on Maritime Interceptions of Irregular Migrants'. *International and Comparative Law Quarterly* 63 (2014): 787–814.

Krisch, Nico. *Beyond Constitutionalism: The Pluralist Structure of Postnational Law*. Oxford: Oxford University Press, 2010.

Lehmann, Julian. 'The Use of Force Against People Smugglers: Conflicts with Refugee Law and Human Rights Law'. *EJIL: Talk!*, 22 June 2015, www.ejiltalk.org/the-use-of-force-against-people-smugglers-conflicts-with-refugee-law-and-human-rights-law/.

McCorquodale, Robert. 'The Individual and the International Legal System'. In *International Law*, (4th edn), edited by Malcolm D. Evans. Oxford: Oxford University Press, 2014.

Milanovic, Marko. *Extraterritorial Application of Human Rights Treaties: Law, Principles, and Policy*. Oxford: Oxford University Press, 2011.

Milanovic, Marko. 'High Court Rules that the UK Lacks IHL Detention Authority in Afghanistan'. *EJIL: Talk!*, 3 May 2014, www.ejiltalk.org/high-court-rules-that-the-uk-lacks-ihl-detention-authority-in-afghanistan.

Milanovic, Marko, and Tatjana Papic. 'As Bad as it Gets: The European Court's *Behrami and Saramati* Decision and General International Law'. *International & Comparative Law Quarterly* 58 (2009): 267–296.

Moreno-Lax, Violeta. 'Seeking Asylum in the Mediterranean: Against a Fragmentary Reading of EU Member States' Obligations Accruing at Sea'. *International Journal of Refugee Law* 23 (2011): 174–220.

Moreno-Lax, Violeta. '*Hirsi Jamaa and Others v. Italy* or the Strasbourg Court versus Extraterritorial Migration Control?'. *Human Rights Law Review* 12 (2012): 574–598.

Neal, Andrew W. 'Securitization and Risk at the EU Border: The Origins of FRONTEX'. *Journal of Common Market Studies* 47 (2009): 333–356.

O'Connell, Daniel P. *The International Law of the Sea*, (vol. 2), edited by Ivan A. Shearer. Oxford: Clarendon Press, 1984.

Papastavridis, Efthymios. 'European Court of Human Rights *Medvedyev* et al. *v. France*'. *International and Comparative Law Quarterly* 59 (2010): 867–882.

Papastavridis, Efthymios. *The Interception of Vessels on the High Seas*. London: Bloomsbury, 2013.

Parekh, Serena. 'Resisting Dull and Torpid Assent: Returning to the Debate over the Foundations of Human Rights'. *Human Rights Quarterly* 29 (2007): 754–778.

Romero, Jessica. 'Prevention of Maritime Terrorism: The Container Security Initiative'. *Chicago Journal of International Law* 4 no. 2 (2003).

Sassen, Saskia. *Territory, Authority, Rights: From Medieval to Global Assemblages*. Princeton, NJ. Princeton University Press, 2008.

Tarzi, Shah M. 'Multinational Corporations and American Foreign Policy: Radical, Sovereignty-at-Bay, and State-Centric Approaches'. *International Studies* 28 (1991): 359–371.

Trachtman, Joel P. 'Reports of the Death of Treaty Are Premature, But Customary International Law May Have Outlived Its Usefulness'. *AJIL Unbound*, 29 April 2014, www.asil.org/blogs/reports-death-treaty-are-premature-customary-international-law-may-have-outlived.

Treves, Tullio. 'Human Rights and the Law of the Sea'. *Berkeley Journal of International Law* 28 (2010): 1–14.

Triandafyllidou, Anna, and Maurizio Ambrosini. 'Irregular Immigration Control in Italy and Greece: Strong Fencing and Weak Gate-Keeping Serving the Labour Market'. *European Journal of Migration and Law* 13 (2011): 251–273.

Yang, Yi-Chih. 'Impact of the Container Security Initiative on Taiwan's Shipping Industry'. *Maritime Policy and Management* 37 (2010): 699–722.

6

COUNTER-PIRACY

Navigating the cloudy waters of international law, domestic law and human rights

Birgit Feldtmann

> We may be dealing with a seventeenth Century crime,
> but we need to bring twenty-first Century solutions to bear.
> (US Secretary of State Hillary Clinton in connection with
> the pirate attack on the Mærsk *Alabama* in Spring 2009[1])

6.1 Introduction

In May 2010, various media reported that a Russian naval vessel had seized a group of Somali pirates after they allegedly had tried to attack a Russian-owned vessel. According to the reports, the pirates were, due to a 'lack of legal basis', 'released' from custody in a small boat without means of navigation, some 300 nautical miles (about 600 km) from shore. After the incident, Russian officials declared that they expected the pirates were lost at sea.[2] In this context, a Russian military official was quoted as asking: 'Why should we feed a group of pirates?'[3] The Russian president at that time, Dmitry Medvedev, called for 'international authorities' who could deal with similar situations in the future, and he concluded: 'But until then we have to treat them like our ancestors did in the old days – and you do understand well, what I mean.'[4]

As far as we know, the above-mentioned incident is a far-from-typical example of counter-piracy law enforcement in the Horn of Africa region; however, it suggests the existence of a number of issues, two of which are at the core of this chapter: first, it suggests that a sufficient legal framework (or what could be called 'law enforcement tools') for countering piracy may be lacking; second, it suggests that the presumed lack of legal framework may lead to practices that raise serious human rights concerns.

The underlying question in this chapter is how the problem of piracy in the Horn of Africa region has been met by the international community, and which legal challenges have been identified and consequently addressed in due course. More to the point, this chapter spotlights the correlation between the legal framework for counter-piracy operations in international law, relevant domestic legislation (e.g. domestic criminal law and criminal procedure) and human rights issues.

This chapter begins with a brief analysis of the legal framework for counter-piracy operations in international law. This relates to the first question raised by the Russian example mentioned above, concerning whether there is a lack of sufficient legal framework for countering piracy. Against this background the correlation between international law, domestic law and human rights issues is illustrated with an example taken from the Danish experience. The example concerns the *M/V Torm Kansas* case, which raises the question of detention of suspected pirates on naval vessels and the question of subsequent legal control in connection with the deprivation of liberty. The case also raises other questions, in particular, the question of who (which state) is able and willing to initiate criminal proceedings against the detained suspected pirates. This second aspect will be only briefly touched upon. This part of the chapter refers to the second question raised by the above-mentioned Russian example; the interplay among counter-piracy, domestic law and human rights. This chapter concludes with some considerations of the question of 'lessons learned' from counter-piracy efforts in the region of the Horn of Africa.

6.2 The legal framework for counter-piracy law enforcement[5]

In the early days of counter-piracy efforts in the Horn of Africa region, one of the questions raised concerned the general legal regime for the navies' counter-piracy operations: may counter-piracy operations be categorised as conducted in an armed conflict setting and therefore as conducted under humanitarian law?[6] The answer to this question is clearly 'no': piracy is unlawful activity, and counter-piracy is a question of law enforcement at sea. The general legal framework for counter-piracy activities is set out by international law, with the Law of the Sea Convention (UNCLOS)[7] forming the core set of regulation, and restricted by human rights.

6.2.1 The definition of piracy by UNCLOS

International law considers piracy an unlawful act, and expects all states to cooperate in the 'repression of piracy on the high seas' (UNCLOS Article 100). The concept of piracy in international law is defined in UNCLOS Article 101:

Piracy consists of any of the following acts:

(a) Any illegal acts of violence or detention, or any act of depredation, committed for private ends by the crew or the passengers of a private ship or a private aircraft, and directed:

(i) on the high seas, against another ship or aircraft, or against persons or property on board such ship or aircraft;

(ii) against a ship, aircraft, persons or property in a place outside the jurisdiction of any State.

(b) Any act of voluntary participation in the operation of a ship or of an aircraft with knowledge of facts making it a pirate ship or aircraft.

(c) Any act of inciting or of intentionally facilitating an act described in subparagraph (a) or (b).

UNCLOS's definition of piracy includes four central elements: first, piracy consists of a number of illegal acts (violence, detention or acts of deprivation) committed against a ship and its crew/passengers. The wording of Article 101, with its use of the plural (e.g. 'illegal *acts* of violence') and singular (e.g. 'any *act* of depredation') raises the question of whether *one* of those acts is sufficient to define an act of piracy, or whether more than one act has to be committed to meet the definition. Furthermore, the question of which legal system defines the illegality of such an act has been raised.[8] These questions are of academic interest only; there is no doubt that the attacks committed against vessels in the Horn of Africa region fall under the definition of piracy.

The definition of piracy in Article 101 includes a geographic limitation. Piracy is committed 'on the high sea' or 'outside the jurisdiction of any State'. This means that the acts in question must be committed *outside* the territorial sea (12 nautical miles).[9] Also, in this context acts committed in the exclusive economic zone (EEZ)[10] are interpreted as being within UNCLOS's definition of piracy, as the specific regime of the EEZ is connected only to the management, exploitation and such of natural resources, and not connected to the question of piracy.[11] Acts against vessels *in* territorial waters fall outside the UNCLOS definition of piracy. Such acts are covered by other international legislation (see Section 6.2.3, below) and are usually referred to as 'armed robbery at sea', 'armed robbery against ships'[12] or in similar terminology. The use of language concerning acts *similar to piracy but committed in territorial waters* is inconsistent, for example, the relevant Security Council resolutions apply varied terminology and the implications, intended or unintended, of the varied terminology remain uncertain.[13] However, in the context of the general legal framework for counter-piracy activities, it is sensible to use consistent language by referring to acts covered by UNCLOS Article 101 as 'piracy', and to similar acts in territorial waters as 'armed robbery at sea'.[14]

Another central element of the definition of piracy is the so-called 'two-ship-requirement'. Acts of piracy are committed by one private vessel against another. Internal attacks, for example, conducted by terrorists posing as passengers of a vessel, as occurred in the *Achille Lauro* incident in 1985, are not within the scope of UNCLOS's definition of piracy, but are covered by the Convention for the suppression of unlawful acts against the safety of maritime navigation (SUA Convention see below, Section 6.2.3).[15]

Finally, the vessel from which an act of piracy is initiated has to be a 'private ship', and UNCLOS stipulates that the acts must be 'committed for private ends'. The interpretation of this requirement has sparked a legal debate in which it is argued that the wording 'for private ends' excludes all acts committed for political reasons, and therefore acts of terrorism cannot be piracy.[16] This seems to be the position of the International Maritime Organisation (IMO).[17] Another position is that the interpretation of 'private ends' should distinguish between acts sanctioned by state authorities (e.g. not for private ends) and acts not sanctioned by a state (e.g. for private ends). According to this reasoning, the correct dichotomy in connection with the 'for private ends' criterion is 'private/public' and not 'private/political'.[18] In the context of Somali piracy, the pirates usually launch their attacks from smaller vessels (so-called 'skiffs') with the aim of hijacking a vessel and its crew for the purposes of exacting a substantial ransom, and today it is not seriously challenged that those attacks against vessels do indeed fall under the definition of piracy in Article 101, as long as the attacks are conducted outside territorial waters.[19]

6.2.2 Counter-piracy law enforcement powers granted by UNCLOS

UNCLOS provides states with a substantial range of counter-piracy law enforcement powers in situations where there is the suspicion of piracy. UNCLOS Article 110 (1)(a) grants the right to visit foreign-flagged vessels in order to verify an initial suspicion of piracy, the threshold for the enforcement of this power being 'reasonable grounds for suspecting' that a vessel is engaging in piracy. The right to visit granted by Article 110 is an exception to the general regime on the high seas, where state vessels are not allowed to interfere with foreign vessels.[20] When a 'suspicion remains after the documents have been checked', the investigating state vessel has the right to 'proceed to a further examination on board the ship', UNCLOS Article 110(2). The wording in Article 110(2) indicates that the powers given by UNCLOS extend proportionally, while the initial suspicion is gradually sustained.[21] If the initial suspicion is proved to be unfounded, no further actions may be taken and compensation for any loss or damage must be provided (UNCLOS Article 110(3)).

The powers granted by UNCLOS Article 110 aim to confirm that the vessel in question is a 'pirate ship' in accordance with UNCLOS Article 103. A 'pirate ship' is either a vessel intended to be used for acts of piracy as defined in Article 101, or a vessel that has been used for such acts, and which is still under the control of the persons who have committed those acts.[22]

If the suspicion that a vessel is a 'pirate ship' is confirmed, further powers granted by Article 105 may be enforced. According to this provision, any state may seize a 'pirate ship', arrest the suspected pirates and seize the property on board. Consequently, any naval vessel that meets pirates on the high seas (including the EEZ) has the right to take the necessary action concerning pirate equipment (such as weapons, ladders, GPS, mobile phones etc.) and arresting the suspected pirates. Concerning the disposal of pirate equipment (including the sinking of pirate ships), Article 105 grants the courts of the seizing state to decide what to do with pirate equipment and ships.[23]

Article 105 does not raise the question of the use of (lethal) force in counter-piracy operations. In fact, the question of the use of force is not directly addressed anywhere by UNCLOS, but it is argued that UNCLOS implicitly permits the use of force under law enforcement activities, as a last resort.[24] This opinion was supported by the International Tribunal for the Law of the Sea in *The M/V 'Saiga'* (*No. 2*) *Case*, where the tribunal noted that the use of force must 'be avoided as far as possible', but also accepted that under certain circumstances, the use of force may be 'unavoidable', and consequently justifiable. If force is used, the court requires that 'it must not go beyond what is reasonable and necessary in the circumstances', and that 'Considerations of humanity must apply'.[25] Guilfoyle points out that the use of force is also supported by the *UN Basic principles on the Use of Force and Firearms by Law Enforcement Officials*, which permits the use of firearms in cases of self-defence or the defence of others, and to prevent 'the perpetration of a particularly serious crime involving a grave threat to life'.[26] He argues that under certain circumstances, lethal force as a first resort (e.g. without first firing warning shots) when conducting counter-piracy operations may be unavoidable, for example, when attempting to free hostages.[27] Situations where the use of lethal force seems to be the only alternative may occur in counter-piracy situations,[28] but it should be kept in mind that this should remain an exception. The starting point is that usually, the use of force should be a last resort, applied only after other, less intrusive, means have failed. In any case, the principle of proportionality must be obeyed when using force in a counter-piracy context.[29]

In addition to the above-mentioned counter-piracy measures, Article 105 also raises the question of criminal proceedings against suspected pirates:

> The courts of the State which carried out the seizure may decide upon the penalties to be imposed.

This means that the state, having seized the suspected pirates, has the right to exercise criminal jurisdiction in connection with piracy. It is argued that UNCLOS Article 101 in conjunction with Article 105 enables *any* state, not only the seizing state, to implement universal jurisdiction for piracy.[30] This question is rather crucial in the context of Somali piracy, because several navies engaging in counter-piracy operations have, after the initial seizure of the suspected pirates, transferred suspected pirates for prosecution to countries in the region, for example Kenya or the Seychelles. This transferral is often conducted without any nexus between the piracy incident or the seizure of the suspected pirates and the receiving/prosecuting state.[31] If the wording in Article 105 excludes others than the seizing state from initiating criminal proceedings against pirates, the practice of transferring suspected pirates would conflict with international law. The legal debate concerning this question raises a number of points and legal arguments, starting with the position that Article 105 contains a 'limited universality principle' (meaning that only the seizing state is competent to exercise universal jurisdiction), to the argument that the provision only provides a 'conflict-of-law rule', and to the argument that the concept expressed in Article 105 only reaffirms that prosecution is based on domestic criminal law, to name only a few positions in the debate.[32] The understanding that Article 105 *does not* grant the seizing state the *exclusive* right to prosecute is most convincing, and also in line with state practice. The opposite position is not in accordance with the general intention of the provisions on piracy, granting all states counter-piracy law enforcement powers, and universal jurisdiction[33] over suspected pirates. Furthermore, an exclusive right to prosecute by the seizing state would also conflict with other regulations in international law (e.g. the SUA Convention), for example, granting the right to exercise domestic jurisdiction, based on the flag state principle.[34]

Article 105 does not express a general obligation of the seizing, nor any other state, to prosecute suspected pirates. The wording in Article 105 ('may') is too weak to establish any specific obligation to subject suspected pirates to criminal proceedings. Also, Article 105, in conjunction with the general obligation to repress piracy as stated in Article 100 (which uses the imperative 'shall'), establishes no explicit general obligation to either subject suspected pirates to domestic criminal proceedings or to extradite a suspected pirate to criminal proceedings in a receiving country.[35]

6.2.3 Other international legislation with relevance for counter-piracy law enforcement

The counter-piracy provisions of UNCLOS are supplemented by other international legislation, such as the SUA Convention and the Hostage Convention.[36] The Hostage Convention may be relevant, due to the modus operandi of Somali pirates;[37] however, in the context of the Somali problem of piracy, the relevance of the Hostage Convention is limited and adds little to the range of powers enforced, beside other reasons, owing to the fact that Somalia is not a party to the Hostage Convention.[38]

The drafting of the SUA Convention may be seen in connection with the above-mentioned *Achille Lauro* incident, which revealed some gaps and limitations in UNCLOS's provisions.[39] The SUA Convention was inspired by the United Nations General Assembly's considerations concerning terrorism and terrorist attacks against ships.[40] This does not mean that the provisions of the SUA Convention are limited to acts of terrorism.[41]

The SUA Convention does not focus on the problem of piracy, nor does it deal directly with piracy in the sense that UNCLOS does; it deals in more general terms with unlawful attacks against vessels and maritime navigation. Article 5 of the SUA Convention obliges the contracting states to criminalise certain specific acts against ships and their crews/passengers as defined in Article 3. Those acts may be acts of piracy as defined in UNCLOS Article 101, but also include internal attacks on board a single vessel, or acts committed in territorial waters, as long as the attacked vessel navigated, or intended to navigate, beyond a single state's territorial waters.[42]

Parties to the SUA Convention are obliged to ensure the legal basis for criminal proceedings of those acts in their own legal system by criminalising certain acts and establishing domestic criminal jurisdiction if they are committed against a ship sailing under the state's flag, if the acts are committed in the state's territorial waters, or if the act is committed by a citizen of the state (Article 6(1)). Furthermore, the SUA Convention permits – but does not oblige – states to have jurisdiction in a number of other situations (Article 6(2)), for example, if a national of that state is 'seized, threatened, injured or killed' in the unlawful attack.[43]

The master of a vessel on which a person suspected of having committed illegal acts – as defined in the convention's Article 3 – is present 'may deliver' him[44] to a contracting state, for example, to the nearest port state (Article 8(1)).

The intention of the SUA Convention is clearly for attacks against ships to not only be criminalised on paper, but for such acts to actually be prosecuted in domestic courts if a suspected perpetrator is found in a contracting state. This intention is codified as an 'extradite or prosecute obligation' in the SUA Convention; however, the implications of this obligation are not quite clear, and strongly debated.[45] One of the main questions in the debate is whether Article 10 (in conjunction with Article 6(4)) simply obliges states to prosecute, or whether the obligation to prosecute is only activated if another state requests extradition, and the state in which the suspect is present is refusing to extradite.[46] Geiss and Petrig interpret the relevant provisions in the SUA Convention as following the so-called 'Hague Model',[47] which means that the obligation to prosecute is not dependent on an extradition request by another state and the subsequent denial by the state in which the suspect is present.[48] They further argue that such an obligation to prosecute is also established in situations where a suspect is not present on shore, but on board one of the state's warships.[49] This understanding of the SUA Convention provision on the 'extradite or prosecute obligation' is challenged in the legal debate, and furthermore, state practice in connection with the Somali piracy problem clearly indicates that many states engaging in counter-piracy do not accept the concept of a general obligation to prosecute.[50]

6.2.4 The extension of the law enforcement of powers by UN Security Council Resolutions

In the specific case of the problem of Somali piracy, the general international legal framework for counter-piracy law enforcement is supplemented by a number of specific UN Security Council resolutions. One example is the question of disposal of pirate ships and equipment without a court order.[51] However, in the context of this chapter, another aspect should be briefly mentioned, concerning the geographical scope of the enforcement of counter-piracy measures.

A number of UN Security Council resolutions authorise, to a certain extent and under certain preconditions, counter-piracy law enforcement (and law enforcement against 'armed robbery at sea'[52]) within Somalia's territorial sea, airspace and land territory.[53] The relevant resolutions refer to the use of 'all necessary means'.[54] This wording raises the question of whether this may be interpreted as an extension of powers, for example concerning the question of the use of (military) force beyond the general law enforcement regime of UNCLOS.[55] Geiss/Petrig assume that the answer to this question depends on the Security Council resolution in question: SC Res. 1846 (2008) (which grants counter-piracy law enforcement measures in Somalia's territorial sea) does not broaden the scope of powers, because at the same time, the resolution clearly emphasises that the powers granted are to be conducted 'in a manner consistent with such action permitted on the high seas with respect to piracy under relevant international law'.[56] Concerning SC Res. 1851 (2008) (which permits counter-piracy law enforcement measures 'in Somalia', e.g. also on land territory[57]), Geiss/Petrig argue that the Security Council is indeed widening the scope of powers beyond UNCLOS's regime to include military force, without specifying what that means in practical terms.[58] They argue that this resolution does not mean that the Security Council has declared international humanitarian law applicable to the context of Somali piracy; counter-piracy operations on the high seas and on Somali land and sea territory is law enforcement, based on, and limited by, human rights law.[59]

6.2.5 Conclusion of the legal framework for counter-piracy law enforcement

The legal framework for counter-piracy law enforcement granted to states may seem somewhat fragmented, and certain aspects may be disputed in the legal debate, but the general conclusion is that it is essentially robust. States are generally granted the right to enforce a substantial range of powers against suspected pirates and their equipment, including the appropriate use of force. Some of the gaps that are present under the UNCLOS regime have been addressed in connection with Somali piracy; the geographical scope of counter-piracy operations is not necessarily limited to the high seas, and the difference between piracy and 'armed robbery at sea' is therefore less relevant. The conclusion is that counter-piracy law enforcement may include a variety of actions, including the arrest of suspected pirates and the prosecution in domestic courts. This means that the above-mentioned assumption, that the international legal framework is insufficient, cannot be verified. International law provides a decent framework for counter-piracy efforts. But the question of a sufficient framework of international law does not exist in isolation; the framework needs to be used and implemented in domestic settings, for example, in connection with the question of criminal proceedings against suspected pirates. There is no international system to deal with suspected pirates, therefore criminal proceedings depend on the state's willingness to use the power to prosecute granted by international law in their domestic legal systems.

The use of the powers granted by international law is not without limitations. It is limited by the framework of human rights. The implications of human rights in counter-piracy law enforcement raise a number of complex questions at different levels,[60] not all of which may be addressed in this chapter. The question of human rights and counter-piracy has been an important focus of many states engaging in counter-piracy. However, certain challenges do remain, and the following example from a Danish experience of counter-piracy efforts may shed light on the correlation among international law, domestic law, actual practices and human rights.

6.3 Counter-piracy in action, domestic law and human rights

As discussed above, the general framework for counter-piracy activities is granted in international law. However, the navies participating in counter-piracy operations are also subject to other regulations, such as the specific mandate of the operation at hand,[61] and domestic legislation and procedures. Therefore, in the context of counter-piracy law enforcement, a central question is *whether* and *how* the 'law enforcement tools' provided by international law are reflected in domestic law. One example is the question of criminal jurisdiction. As mentioned above, states are granted by UNCLOS Article 105 that their domestic courts 'may decide upon the penalties to be imposed'. However, to be able to initiate criminal proceedings in domestic courts, national law must both criminalise the acts in question and grant jurisdiction for piracy cases. And if there is domestic jurisdiction in a piracy case, the state in question must also be willing to use its jurisdiction in that specific case.[62] Another example is the question of arrest; UNCLOS Article 105 states that every state engaging in counter-piracy 'may seize a pirate ship . . . and arrest the persons'. However, the specific legal framework for arrest, including the question of legal control, must be addressed by national legislation, which leads to the question of how (if at all) the question of arrest/detention of suspected pirates on naval vessels is regulated by domestic law. Furthermore, the question of detention and associated guarantees is also crucial from the standpoint of human rights. How are human rights guarantees connected to the deprivation of liberty dealt with in connection with counter-piracy operations? To a certain extent, these two questions are linked, as will be illustrated by the *M/V Torm Kansas* case, below. The underlying assumption in this context is that insufficient domestic legislation could – in certain situations – result in practical solutions that do not necessarily secure human rights guarantees in an entirely satisfactory way.

6.3.1 The facts of the M/V Torm Kansas case

On 9 November 2013 the Danish naval vessel *Esbern Snare*, participating in NATO's counter-piracy Operation Ocean Shield,[63] received a distress call from the Danish merchant vessel *M/V Torm Kansas* at 17.01, local time. The *M/V Torm Kansas* was under attack by a group of pirates in a skiff; however, the attack was unsuccessful, because the pirates in the skiff were unable to board the vessel, as they were repulsed by on-board security after an exchange of gunfire. The *Esbern Snare* searched the surrounding area, and came across a whaler and a skiff. On 10 November all nine persons who were aboard the whaler were taken on board the *Esbern Snare* under the suspicion of being involved in the attack on the *M/V Torm Kansas*, and on a Chinese vessel (*M/V Zhongji No. 1.*) a few days earlier. The whaler and the skiff were taken into Danish custody and various items were secured as evidence.[64] The Danish prosecution service was informed of the suspicions on the same day. On 22 November the Danish prosecution service decided that there was a Danish case, and the individuals were charged for violating section 183a and section 21 of the Danish Criminal Code (attempt to attack a vessel). On 23 November the prosecution brought the question of detention on board the *Esbern Snare* to the local court in Copenhagen, as part of the procedure for legal control in absentia, and a request for pre-trial detention according to section 762, paragraph 1, no. 1 and no. 3 of the Danish Procedural Code was submitted. The local court in Copenhagen confirmed the detention, and the defence subsequently appealed the decision in the Eastern High Court. On 28 November 2013 the Danish prosecution service decided that they would not prosecute in Denmark, as it was not expected that an initiation of court proceedings would result in a guilty verdict (section 721, 1, no. 2 of the Danish Procedural Code).[65] The group of defendants was formally released from Danish custody in the Seychelles, and handed over to the authorities of the Seychelles with the aim of initiating criminal proceedings there.[66] The verdict in the case in the Seychelles was delivered in March 2015, with a convictions on all charges, including the attack on the *M/V Torm Kansas*.

6.3.2 Questions raised by the handling of the M/V Torm Kansas case

The Danish authorities' handling of the *M/V Torm Kansas* case is interesting from at least three perspectives.[67] First, as mentioned, the case in Denmark was abandoned on the basis of the assessment that court proceedings would not result in a guilty verdict, section 721, 1, no. 2 of the Danish Procedural Code. This means that the case was dismissed owing to the assessment that the evidence was insufficient to obtain a conviction.[68] A crucial element of criminal proceedings is that criminal cases may be continued only if there is sufficient evidence. What is interesting in this context is that on the one hand, the Danish authorities assessed the evidence as insufficient to support criminal proceedings in Denmark, but on the other hand, seemed to consider the evidence sufficient to support the transfer of the suspects to the Seychelles authorities, with the aim of initiating criminal proceedings there. The suspected pirates were subsequently prosecuted, and found guilty by the Supreme Court of the Seychelles in March 2015. To a large extent, the verdict was based on the evidence collected by the Danish navy and by witness statements of Danish naval officers.[69] This raises the question of why the case was not prosecuted in Denmark: was the dismissal of the case in Denmark really due to insufficient evidence, or were other considerations influencing the handling of the case, for example, the desire to avoid bringing suspected Somali pirates to court in Denmark.[70] Another interpretation of the handling of the case could be that the Danish authorities conducted some kind of 'forum shopping', for example, transferring the case to a legal system were it might be easier to obtain a conviction. However, in the handling of the case by the legal system of the Seychelles there is no suggestion that the threshold for a conviction is lower there than it would have been in Denmark, or that procedural standards in the Seychelles could not be compared with those in Denmark.[71] All in all, the question of why the case could not be prosecuted in Denmark and could be prosecuted in the Seychelles remains.

The second perspective on the *M/V Torm Kansas* case concerns the question of transferring the suspected pirates to the law enforcement authorities of the Seychelles after 'releasing' them from Danish custody.[72] What exactly was the legal nature of this transfer? Was it a form of extradition? Extradition usually requires a state requesting the extradition, and is conducted under certain procedures with associated safeguards. In the case of counter-piracy in the Horn of Africa region, the initiative for the transfer often comes from the seizing state, meaning that the state which initially conducted the counter-piracy operation and detained the suspected pirates. Furthermore, there is often no legal procedure or legal remedy associated with the transfer.[73] The practice of transferring suspected pirates from naval vessels of one state to the law enforcement agencies of another state raises the question of the legal basis for such transfers. This question is the subject of quite a substantial legal debate in which the legality of those transfers is questioned.[74] Others argue that international law 'neither endorses nor prohibits such transfers',[75] and that there is no clear and absolute prohibition of these practices.[76] However, it is also argued that the non-refoulement principle sets an absolute limit on the practice of transfer, in the sense that transfer to a country is prohibited if there is a risk that the transferred person would be subjected to human rights violations in the aftermath of the transferral.[77] The exact scope of the non-refoulement principle depends on the specific situation and legal basis; in the context of counter-piracy and transferal, the human rights at stake are mainly the prohibition of torture, and inhuman and degrading treatment and punishment, and the right to life.[78]

The third question raised by the *M/V Torm Kansas* case is that of detention on naval vessels, and the question of legal control; this is the topic of the following sections. The question of legal control may be considered from both an international and a national perspective.

6.3.3 An international perspective on the question of legal control in connection with detention on naval vessels

To a certain extent, the question of legal control is connected to the reasons for the detention on naval vessels and the connected legal basis for deprivation of liberty. It may be argued that initial short-term seizure is covered by the law enforcement powers under UNCLOS, in particular, Article 105.[79] Once the initial suspicion is confirmed and the first evidence is collected, the detention of suspected pirates on naval vessels usually suits at least one of two purposes: detention is continued with view to transferring/extraditing the suspect to another legal system for prosecution, or with view to criminal proceedings in the own legal system. When keeping suspected pirates on board naval vessels against their will, their right to liberty comes into play, and their deprivation of liberty falls within the scope of Article 5 ECHR (European Court of Human Rights) and Article 9 ICCPR (International Covenant on Civil and Political Rights).[80] In this connection it should be mentioned that states engaging in counter-piracy seem to tend to avoid 'classical terminology', meaning, they avoid technical criminal justice terminology used in domestic legislation, such as 'arrest' and 'pre-trial detention'.[81] This use of language may lead to the conclusion that in these situations, human rights obligations are not relevant. However, avoiding certain terminology does not result in the avoidance of associated human rights obligations. The crucial point is the nature of a measure, not what the acting state terms it. Another issue raised with view to the application of the ECHR and the ICCPR is the question of the extraterritorial application of human rights. In connection with this, Geiss/Petrig not only argue that the question of the extraterritorial application of human rights in connection with counter-piracy is 'challenging', but also clearly conclude that human rights obligations of the flag state are applicable when detaining suspected pirates on board naval vessels.[82] In this context, it is argued that there is an overlap between 'effective control' and 'authority and control' criteria, when talking about the extraterritorial application of human rights associated with detention outside the acting state's own territory, hereunder for example in connection with detention on naval vessels.[83] The position that human rights apply in connection with detention outside the detaining state's own territory is supported by various international/regional bodies, such as the Committee against Torture and the ECHR.[84]

The central human rights issue raised in connection with the *M/V Torm Kansas* case is the question of legal control associated with the detention of suspected pirates on naval vessels. The question of legal control in connection with the deprivation of liberty is raised under both Article 5(3) ECHR and Article 9(4) ICCPR, in this chapter the focus is on the guarantee of the ECHR. The suspected pirates were taken on board the *Esbern Snare* on 10 November and the Danish prosecution service was informed on the same day, and subsequently started its preliminary investigation, which led to the conclusion on 22 November that there was a Danish case. The proceedings concerning the lawfulness of the detention at the local court in Copenhagen were conducted on 23 November. This means that the detention on board the *Esbern Snare* was 'for the purpose of bringing him before the competent legal authority on reasonable suspicion of having committed an offence', and therefore falls under Article 5(1)(c) ECHR. The decisive criterion is the purpose of the detention at the time when it was initiated and executed, it is therefore not relevant if criminal proceedings subsequently will be conducted in the detaining state, in another state or are finally dismissed.[85] This means that the detaining state, here, Denmark, is bound by the requirement of Article 5(3): 'Everyone arrested or detained in accordance with the provisions of paragraph 1(c) of this Article shall be brought promptly before a judge or other officer authorised by law to exercise judicial power. . . .' In the *M/V Torm Kansas* case, the question of detention was first brought to a Danish court after 12 days. This raises the question of whether this was in accordance with the promptness requirement of Article 5(3) ECHR. It has been argued that when assessing the promptness requirement in the context of counter-piracy, the specific challenges connected with law enforcement at sea must be considered.[86]

The general approach of the ECHR towards the promptness requirement may be described as rather strict; the provision 'leaves little flexibility in interpretation, otherwise there would be a serious weakening of a procedural guarantee to the detriment of the individual and the risk of impairing the very essence of the right protected by this provision'.[87] However, the Court does not apply a clear time frame, but emphasises that the promptness requirement must be assessed in light of the special features of each case. In some cases, a period of two days between arrest and judicial control was accepted, and the court seems to consider periods in excess of four days as a violation.[88] However, these interpretations of the promptness requirement may be reconsidered in light of the specific circumstances of a given case; in several cases, the Court has accepted that specific circumstances connected with law enforcement and subsequent arrests at sea could lead to longer periods (up to 16 days) between arrest and legal control, and did not violate Article 5(3).[89] However, newer case law of the court indicates that the court on the one hand accepts that there in connection with counter-piracy could be situations of 'wholly exceptional circumstances' in temporal and geographical terms leading to the acceptance of a longer time frame than usual. The court does, on the other hand, not accept the wish to get extra time for further investigation or to consider the case as a valid argument to prolong the time frame.[90] With regard to the *M/V Torm Kansas* case, it is difficult to argue that there were exceptional circumstances that demanded a larger time frame to fulfil the requirement for legal control, as the Danish procedural rules allow for a court hearing in absentia (section 762, paragraph. 1, no. 1 and no. 3 of the Danish Procedural Code). This means that there was no need to bring the suspected pirates ashore/to Denmark to proceed with the court hearing on their detention. To emphasise the main argument, the ECHR accepts a broader understanding of the promptness requirement based on 'wholly exceptional circumstances', but it does not accept delay that is due to a lack of planning and preparation, or due to an insufficient domestic legal framework. This means that it seems quite unlikely that the ECHR would accept the handling of the *M/V Torm Kansas* case with view to the promptness requirement of Article 5(3).

6.3.4 A national perspective on the question of legal control in connection with detention on naval vessels

The question of legal control should also be viewed from a domestic perspective. In the Danish legal system, section 71, subsection 3 of the Danish constitution ('grundlov') demands that:

Any person who is taken into custody shall be brought before a judge within twenty-four hours. When the person taken into custody cannot be released immediately, the judge shall decide, in an order to be given as soon as possible and at the latest within three days, stating the grounds, whether the person taken into custody shall be committed to prison; and in cases in which he can be released on bail, the judge shall also determine the nature and amount of such bail.

This means that the Danish constitution works with a time frame of twenty-four hours for legal control associated with detention. The time frame given in the Danish constitution is reflected in the procedural rules (section 760 of the Danish Procedural Code). Under certain circumstances, the twenty-four-hour time frame may be prolonged up to three days.[91] As mentioned above, in the *M/V Torm Kansas* case the suspected pirates were taken aboard a naval vessel on 10 November, and on 23 November the proceedings concerning the lawfulness of their detention were conducted at the local court in Copenhagen, according to the rules for pre-trial detention decisions in absentia. Under those proceedings the local court in Copenhagen ruled to continue the detention of the suspected pirates; this decision was appealed by the defence. Under the appeal proceedings the prosecution service argued that the twenty-four-hour time frame should be calculated from the time that the prosecution service decided that there was a Danish case, that is, from 22 November. The Eastern High Court rejected the argument, and concluded that the twenty-four hours must be calculated from the actual beginning of the detention, and that the international rules on counter-piracy do not suggest a prolonged time frame. The court further concluded that the violation of the time frame by 12 days was a 'substantial violation of a fundamental rule-of-law guarantee', and must incur 'severe criticism of the prosecution service'.[92] This wording indicates the Eastern High Court's view of the seriousness of the violation of the handling of the detention. It is also worth mentioning that the question of whether or not the rules concerning the time frame could be applied to detention on board naval vessels was not raised.

The decision of the Eastern High Court was delivered on 10 December 2013, the suspected pirates having already been transferred to the Seychelles at that time. However, the matter was not finished in the Danish legal system. As a consequence of the ruling of the Eastern High Court, in October 2014 the Prosecutor General issued a decision on the question of compensation for unlawful detention, and granted each of the unlawfully detained suspected pirates compensation of DKK 19,600.[93] This was according to usual procedure in Denmark, where the Prosecutor General deals with the question of compensation following unlawful detention. The specific amount was determined according to the principles set out in the guidelines for compensation.[94] So, at a first glance, the decision by the Prosecutor General seems very straightforward, but there are two interesting points: first, the decision does not mention the fact that, before the Eastern High Court delivered its decision, the suspected pirates were transferred to the law enforcement authorities of the Seychelles. This fact was also not mentioned in the court's decision. Here, it is only mentioned that on 28 November the prosecution service decided to close the case in Denmark, and that the suspects were 'released' that same day.[95] As we know, this is a partial truth. Second, the question of compensation was decided under section 1018h of the Danish Procedural Code, the general rule on compensation in Danish law. This is interesting, as there is another legal basis for compensation that could have been applied in this case: section 1018a, which specifically regulates compensation in cases where the person in question had been detained under the suspicion of a criminal offence, and the case is ended under section 721 of the Danish Procedural Code, a provision used when the criminal case cannot proceed. As mentioned above, section 721 was used as the legal basis for ending criminal proceedings in Denmark in the *M/V Torm Kansas* case, which leads to the question of why section 1018a was not used when granting compensation.

6.3.5 How to address the challenges of counter-piracy

As discussed above, the handling of the question of detention and legal control by the Danish authorities raises a number of issues. What is interesting in this context is that the question of legal control in connection with detention on Danish naval vessels under counter-piracy operations had been raised previously. On 2 January 2009 the Danish naval vessel *Absalon* seized a group of five persons suspected of having attacked a vessel under the flag of the Dutch Antilles. The suspected pirates were transferred to the Dutch authorities on 10 February 2009, and subsequently subjected to criminal proceedings in Rotterdam. The court in Rotterdam qualified the detention on board the Danish naval vessel as pre-trial detention by the seizing state (Denmark) on behalf of the ultimately prosecuting state (the Netherlands), and severely criticised the detention of the suspected pirates on board the Danish vessel for 40 days without any form of legal controls, stating that this violated Article 5(3) ECHR.[96]

The question of lack of legal control when detaining suspected pirates on board Danish naval vessels was thus already raised in 2009/2010. However, it seems that this question was not subsequently addressed in Denmark. This is surprising, as other states, including states with close ties to Denmark, have tried to address the challenges connected with counter-piracy, and to adapt domestic legislation and procedures with a view to creating a sufficient legal framework to meet the issues at stake. One example is Norway, which in June 2013 adopted a set of specific rules for criminal procedures regarding cases of piracy ('Forskrift om behandling av saker om straff for personer mistenkt for piratvirksomhet i Det indiske hav').[97] The aim of this new legislation is to ensure adequate provision for the apprehension, detention and transfer of suspected pirates. Other states, including Italy, France and the Netherlands, have tried to address the challenges in question, for example the question of legal control connected with detention on naval vessels, by introducing the option of court hearings/legal controls via video link or other means of communication. The question of the protection of human rights, detention and legal control was also raised in Working Group 2 (WG2) on legal issues of the Contact Group on Piracy off the Coast of Somalia, which was headed by Denmark and a 'non-paper' describing some of the issues at hand, and possible solutions initiated by various states, was prepared and distributed.[98] This means that inspiration was easily accessible; however, it seems that the Danish approach was not to carefully prepare for the challenges at hand with sufficient procedures or legislation. On the contrary, it seems that the Danish approach was to address the issues at hand in due course and with a more pragmatic approach. As the *M/V Torm Kansas* case illustrates, this approach leads, at least to a certain extent, to questionable results.

6.4 Conclusions and lessons learned

The problem of Somali piracy has tested the legal regime for counter-piracy law enforcement. Many issues have been addressed in due course, and a number of legal questions were clarified. One of the myths connected to the legal side of counter-piracy has been that the legal framework is insufficient, and sometimes this assumption has been used to justify questionable practices.[99]

This chapter is challenging the assumption that sufficient legal basis for effective counter-piracy is lacking in international law. The international legal framework for counter-piracy operations may not be perfect and is somewhat fragmented, and some questions may remain, but the legal framework as a whole is essentially robust, and provides a good basis for law enforcement at sea. It provides states with a solid basis for dealing with suspected pirates within domestic systems of criminal justice, if states wish to do so. This means that the major legal challenges identified in connection with dealing with suspected pirates are not necessarily rooted in international law, but in domestic law, for example in connection with the lack of sufficient domestic rules on jurisdiction in cases of piracy, or on the legal control of detention on naval vessels. The lack of sufficient domestic regulations and procedures, and subsequent practices that could be labelled 'pragmatic', may raise serious human rights concerns. The *M/V Torm Kansas* case shows this quite clearly.

The *M/V Torm Kansas* case seems to cloud the general picture for counter-piracy law enforcement to a certain extent; it would be wrong to conclude that human rights issues in general have been neglected in connection with counter-piracy at the international, or even at the national level. Human rights have actually been a significant focus in connection with the legal debate concerning counter-piracy, for example in the work of (WG2), on legal issues of the Contact Group on Piracy off the Coast of Somalia, which was headed by Denmark.[100] Therefore, it is not entirely understandable why the remaining practices that raise human rights concerns have not been sufficiently addressed by all states engaging in counter-piracy. Also, the question of legal control in connection with detention on naval vessels has been on the agenda of WG2,[101] but the participating states were unable to find common ground. From a Danish perspective, at least in the aftermath of the 'Dutch case' of 2009/2010,[102] it is evident that the question of legal control when detentioning on board naval vessels is one to which Denmark needs to pay further attention. Against this background it is surprising that the issue was still not properly addressed in 2013, when the *M/V Torm Kansas* case was handled by the Danish authorities. And there was inspiration enough: other states had taken action on the matters in question, and created rules and procedures to avoid violating human rights in connection with detention on naval vessels.

It may be argued that the *M/V Torm Kansas* case also shows that the back-up system seems to work when things are handled wrongly. The Eastern High Court did not hesitate to protect the rights of the suspected pirates, and severely criticised the conduct of the Danish prosecution service. Subsequently, the Prosecutor General did grant each of the suspected pirates DKK 19,600 in financial compensation for unlawful detention, according to the rules of Danish procedural law. This 'payment to pirates' got quite some media attention in Denmark,[103] but from a legal perspective it was the only legitimate way to respond to the unlawful detention.

To date, the lesson learned from counter-piracy is that it is crucial for the states engaged in the fight against piracy to do their homework, meaning that they must consider the legal challenges connected to counter-piracy law enforcement, and create a domestic legal framework and procedures to adequately address the issues at hand. This is not only crucial for the effectiveness of counter-piracy operations, but also for protecting individual rights. By addressing the challenges at hand, it should be possible to establish a workable balance among international law, domestic law and human rights.

Notes

1 From Andrew J. Shapiro (31 March 2010), 'Counter-Piracy Policy: Delivering Judicial Consequences': www.state.gov/t/pm/rls/rm/139326.htm (last visited 10 May 2016).

2 See BBC news (11 May 2010), 'Freed Somali pirates "probably died" – Russian source': http://news.bbc.co.uk/2/hi/africa/8675978.stm; *Jyllandsposten* (11 May 2010), 'Pirater blev løsladt og døde': http://jp.dk/udland/article2065530.ece (last visited 10 May 2016). However, *Somalilandpress* questions the Russian report on the incident, and suggests that the pirates in question may have been executed by Russian forces, *Somalilandpress* (12 May 2010), 'SOMALIA: Russia executed all Somali pirates' – spokesman: www.somalilandpress.com/somalia-russia-executed-all-somali-pirates-spokesman/ (all last visited 10 May 2016).

3 Quote from *Jyllandsposten* (11 May 2010), 'Pirater blev løsladt og døde': http://jp.dk/udland/article2065530.ece (last visited 10 May 2016).

4 Quote from *Jyllandsposten* (11 May 2010), 'Pirater blev løsladt og døde': http://jp.dk/udland/article2065530.ece (last visited 10 May 2016).

5 The considerations of the legal framework for Counter-piracy presented here are based on Birgit Feldtmann, 'Fighting Maritime Piracy: On Possible Actions and Consequences', in *Economic Analysis of International Law: Contributions to the XIIIth Travemünde Symposium on the Economic Analysis of Law* (March 29–31, 2012), eds Thomas Eger, Stefan Oeter and Stefan Voigt, 173–198 (Tubingen: Mohr Siebeck, 2014), 177 ff.

6 This debate has been partly connected to the wording of some Security Council resolutions referring to both international humanitarian law and human rights, for example SC Res. 1851 (2008), para. 6: 'that any measures undertaken pursuant to the authority of this paragraph shall be undertaken consistent with applicable international

humanitarian and human rights law', see Robin Geiss and Anna Petrig, *Piracy and Armed Robbery at Sea: The Legal Framework for Counter-Piracy Operations in Somalia and the Gulf of Aden* (Oxford: Oxford University Press, 2011), 131 ff.

7   United Nations Convention on the Law of the Sea (1982).
8   Douglas Guilfoyle, 'Treaty Jurisdiction over Pirates: A Compilation of Legal Texts with Introductory Notes', report prepared for Contact Group on Piracy off the Coast of Somalia, 26–27 August 2009 (New York: Contact Group on Piracy off the Coast of Somalia, 2009), 3; Geiss and Petrig, *Piracy and Armed Robbery at Sea*, 60.
9   On the concept of the territorial sea, see article 86 ff. Also see Churchill, Robin R., and Alan Vaughan Lowe, *The Law of the Sea*, 3rd edn (Manchester: Manchester University Press, 1999), 71 ff.
10   On the concept of the EEZ see article 55 ff. Also see Churchill and Lowe, *The Law of the Sea*, 160 ff.
11   See Feldtmann, 'Fighting Maritime Piracy', 178.
12   See Martin Murphy, 'Piracy and UNCLOS: Does International Law Help Regional States Combat Piracy?', in *Violence at Sea: Piracy in the Age of Global Terrorism*, ed. Peter Lehr, 155–182 (London: Routledge, 2007), 155, 64; and Douglas Guilfoyle, 'Counter-piracy Law Enforcement and Human Rights', *International and Comparative Law Quarterly* 59 (2010), 144.
13   See Geiss and Petrig, *Piracy and Armed Robbery at Sea*, 72 ff.
14   Geiss and Petrig, *Piracy and Armed Robbery at Sea*, 75.
15   Geiss and Petrig, *Piracy and Armed Robbery at Sea*, 62, and Douglas Guilfoyle, 'The Legal Challenges in Fighting Piracy', in *The International Response to Somali Piracy: Challenges and Opportunities*, eds Bib van Ginkel and Frans-Paul van der Putten 127–152 (Leiden: Brill, 2010), 128.
16   On this debate, see Geiss and Petrig, *Piracy and Armed Robbery at Sea*, 61 with further references.
17   IMO Doc. LEG 98/8 2011, para. 14.
18   Guilfoyle, 'Counter-piracy Law Enforcement', 143.
19   Birgit Feldtmann, 'Er strafferet et effektivt middel i kampen mod sørøveri? Et dansk indblik i strafferetlige udfordringer på baggrund af kapringen af *CEC Future* [Is criminal law an effective tool in the fight against piracy? A Danish insight into criminal law challenges based on the hijacking of the *CEC Future*]', in *Liber amicarum et amicorum Karin Cornils: Glimt af nordisk straffrätt og straffeprosessrett*, eds Thomas Elholm, *Vagn Greve*, Petter Asp, Ragnheidur Bragadottir, Dan Frände and Asbjørn Strandbakken, 101–120 (Copenhagen: Djøf, 2010), 103 ff.; and Guilfoyle, 'Counter-piracy Law Enforcement', 142 ff. Also see *Report of the Secretary-General on the situation with respect to piracy and armed robbery at sea off the coast of Somalia* to the Security Council (21 October 2013), S/2013/623, para. 60, which stresses: 'Somalia-based piracy is a criminal activity that has transnational aspects and that is driven by the quest for illicit profit'.
20   See Geiss and Petrig, *Piracy and Armed Robbery at Sea*, 55 ff. and article 110 (1) UNCLOS.
21   Geiss and Petrig, *Piracy and Armed Robbery at Sea*, 56.
23   Geiss and Petrig, *Piracy and Armed Robbery at Sea*, 59 and Guilfoyle, 'Treaty Jurisdiction over Pirates', 5.
23   Douglas Guilfoyle, 'Prosecuting Somali Pirates: A Critical Evaluation of the Options', *Journal of International Criminal Justice* 10 (2012), 775 f. On the question whether only the courts of the seizing state or indeed also other courts are granted powers by article 105, see below.
24   Geiss and Petrig, *Piracy and Armed Robbery at Sea*, 68 f.
25   International Tribunal for the Law of the Sea, *The M/V 'Saiga' (No. 2) Case, Saint Vincent and the Grenadines v. Guinea*, Judgment of 1 July 1991, para. 155.
26   Article 9 United Nations Basic Principles on the Use of Force and Firearms by Law Enforcement Officials, UN Doc. A/CONF.144/28/Rev.1, 7 September 1990.

27 Guilfoyle, 'Prosecuting Somali Pirates', 773 f.
28 See Murdoch, Andrew, and Douglas Guilfoyle, 'Capture and Disruption Operations: The Use of Force in Counter-Piracy off Somalia', in *Modern Piracy: Legal Challenges and Responses*, ed. Douglas Guilfoyle, 147–171 (Cheltenham: Elgar, 2013), 152 with reference to the Maersk *Alabama* hostage rescue incident.
29 This position is illustrated in the previously-mentioned *The M/V 'Saiga' (No. 2) Case*, in which the court describes a number of measures which should be used before turning to the use of force: International Tribunal for the Law of the Sea, *The M/V 'Saiga' (No. 2) Case, Saint Vincent and the Grenadines v. Guinea*, Judgment of 1 July 1991, para. 156. Also see Birgit Feldtmann, 'Må man skyde en pirat? Et indblik i den retlige ramme for statslige aktørers magtanvendelse [Can you shoot a pirate? A glimpse into the legal framework for state actors' use of force]', in *Festskrift til Nis Jul Clausen*, eds Nina Dietz Legind, Bent Ole Gram Mortensen, Hans Viggo Godsk Pedersen and Karsten Engsig Sørensen, 123–137 (Copenhagen: Djøf, 2013), 132 ff.
30 Birgit Feldtmann and Kristina Maria Siig. 'Dine, mine og vore pirater: Et indblik i juridiske (og andre) problemstillinger i forbindelse med bekæmpelse af pirateri i internationale farvande [Your, my and our pirates: An insight into the legal (and other) issues relating to the fight against piracy in international waters]', in *Juridiske Emner ved Syddansk Universitet 2009*, ed. Hans Viggo Godsk Pedersen, 68–82. (Odense: Syddansk Universitet, 2009), 71; Maggie Gardener, 'Piracy Prosecutions in National Courts', *Journal of International Criminal Justice* 10 (2012), 803 ff.
31 See Gardner, 'Piracy Prosecutions in National Courts', 801 f.; Geiss and Petrig, *Piracy and Armed Robbery at Sea*, 197 ff. and below 3.1.
32 On this debate see Gardner, 'Piracy Prosecutions in National Courts', 803 ff., Geiss and Petrig, *Piracy and Armed Robbery at Sea*, 148 ff. and Eugene Kontorovich, 'The Penalties for Piracy: A Discussion Paper' (Broomfield, CO: Oceans Beyond Piracy, 2012), available at: http://oceansbeyondpiracy.org/sites/default/files/obp_penalties_for_piracy_final.pdf, 4 ff.
33 On the concept of universal jurisdiction over piracy see Eugene Kontorovich, 'The Piracy Analogy: Modern Universal Jurisdictions Hollow Foundation', *Harvard International Law Journal* 45 (2004), 188 ff.
34 See Gardner, 'Piracy Prosecutions in National Courts', 803 ff. and Geiss and Petrig, *Piracy and Armed Robbery at Sea*, 148 ff. with further arguments for this position.
35 Birgit Feldtmann, 'Should We Rule Out Criminal Law as a Means of Fighting Maritime Piracy? An Essay on the Challenges and Possibilities of Prosecuting Somali Pirates', in *Festskrift til Per Ole Träskman*, eds Ulrika Anderson, Christoffer Wong and Helén Örnemark Hansen, 179–188 (Stockholm: Norstedts Juridik, 2011), 184; and Geiss and Petrig, *Piracy and Armed Robbery at Sea*, 151 f.
36 International Convention against the Taking of Hostages (1979).
37 See Feldtmann, 'Er strafferet et effektivt middel', 107 f.
38 See Geiss and Petrig, *Piracy and Armed Robbery at Sea*, 162 and Guilfoyle, 'Treaty Jurisdiction over Pirates', 27 f.
39 Geiss and Petrig, *Piracy and Armed Robbery at Sea*, 42.
40 See UN General Assembly, A/RES/40/61 (9 December 1985), para. 13, which 'Requests the International Maritime Organisation to study the problem of terrorism aboard or against ships with a view to making recommendations on appropriate measures': www.un.org/documents/ga/res/40/a40r061.htm (last visited 10 May 2016).
41 Guilfoyle, 'Treaty Jurisdiction over Pirates', 12.
42 Concerning the geographical scope of the SUA Convention see article 4 (1).
43 See SUA Conventions article 6 (2) no. 2 and Feldtmann, 'Er strafferet et effektivt middel', 106 f.
44 It seems justifiable to limit oneself to use the male form only when referring to pirates, as we have not seen female Somali pirates.
45 See Guilfoyle, 'Treaty Jurisdiction over Pirates', 14 ff; Geiss and Petrig, *Piracy and Armed Robbery at Sea*, 163 f.

46 See Guilfoyle, 'Treaty Jurisdiction over Pirates', 14 ff.
47 See Geiss and Petrig, *Piracy and Armed Robbery at Sea*, 163 f. (and footnote 691) with further references.
48 Geiss and Petrig, *Piracy and Armed Robbery at Sea*, 163.
49 Geiss and Petrig, *Piracy and Armed Robbery at Sea*, 163 f.
50 For example see Guilfoyle, 'Prosecuting Somali Pirates', 774 f.; Feldtmann, 'Should We Rule Out Criminal Law', 185 ff.
51 SC Res. 1851 (16 December 2008), para. 2; also see SC res. 1846 (2 December 2008), para. 6; Guilfoyle, 'Prosecuting Somali Pirates', 775 f.
52 On the concept of 'armed robbery at sea' and the distinction to piracy in UNCLOS's sense see above 3.1.
53 SC Res. 1846 (2 December 2008), para. 10 (b), SC Res. 1851 (16 December 2008), para. 6; and SC res. 1897 (30 November 2009) para. 7; all periodically re-enacted. Also see Yoshifumi Tanaka, *The International Law of the Sea* (Cambridge: Cambridge University Press, 2012), 360 f.
54 SC Res. 1846 (2 December 2008), para. 10 (b) and SC Res. 1851 (16 December 2008), para. 6.
55 Geiss and Petrig, *Piracy and Armed Robbery at Sea*, 76.
56 Geiss and Petrig, *Piracy and Armed Robbery at Sea*, 76 f.
57 SC Res. 1851 (16 December 2008), para. 6.
58 Geiss and Petrig, *Piracy and Armed Robbery at Sea*, 83.
59 This question was raised because SC Res. 1851 (16 December 2008) in para. 6 refers to both international humanitarian law and human rights: 'that any measures undertaken pursuant to the authority of this paragraph shall be undertaken consistent with applicable international humanitarian and human rights law'. See Geiss and Petrig, *Piracy and Armed Robbery at Sea*, 131 ff.
60 See Geiss and Petrig, *Piracy and Armed Robbery at Sea*, 101 ff.
61 See Feldtmann, 'Fighting Maritime Piracy', 192 ff.
62 On the question of prosecution of piracy cases, see Guilfoyle, 'Prosecuting Somali Pirates', 767 ff. and Feldtmann, 'Fighting Maritime Piracy', 187 ff.
63 On Operation Ocean Shield: www.mc.nato.int/ops/Pages/OOS.aspx (last visited 10 May 2016).
64 This account of the facts is based on a Judgment by the Supreme Court of the Seychelles, Criminal Side: CO 73/2013, of 13 March 2015.
65 The account of the events is based on decision S3462001-SF of 10 December 2013 of the Eastern High Court ('Østre Landret') and the decision of the Prosecutor General ('Rigsadvokaten') of 2 October 2014, RA-2014–521–2801 (the author has access to both documents).
66 Værnfælles Forsvarskommando, ESBERN SNARE overdrager formodede pirater til Seychellerne, 1 December 2013: http://forsvaret.dk/MST/Nyt%20og%20Presse/pirateri/Pages/ESBERNSNAREoverdragerformodedepiratertilSeychellerne.aspx (last visited 10 May 2016).
67 The *M/V Torm Kansas* case also raises the question of the treatment of juveniles suspected of piracy, as two of the pirates were under the age of 18 at the time of the piracy attacks in question. The issue of child pirates raises a number of legal questions; however, these are beyond the scope of this chapter.
68 On section 721, 1, no. 2 of the Danish Procedural Code, see Birgit Feldtmann, 'Zwangloses Strafverfahren? Verfahrensbeendigungen aus Gründen der Opportunität durch die Anklagebehörde in Dänemark aus deutscher Sicht [Informal criminal proceedings? Dismissal of criminal cases due to the "opportunity principle" by the prosecution service in Denmark from the German perspective]' (Bremen: Bremen University, 2002): Available at: http://suche.suub.uni-bremen.dremote_access.php?http%3A%2F%2Fnbn-resolving.de%2Furn%3Anbn%3Ade%3Agbv%3A46-00105197-18, 65.
69 See Judgment by the Supreme Court of the Seychelles, Criminal Side: CO 73/2013, of 13 March 2015.

70 See Feldtmann, 'Fighting Maritime Piracy', 191 (note 98).
71 See Judgment by the Supreme Court of the Seychelles, Criminal Side: CO 73/2013, of 13 March 2015.
72 Anna Petrig, *Human Rights and Law Enforcement at Sea: Arrest, Detention and Transfer of Piracy Suspects* (Leiden: Brill, 2014), 315 ff.
73 Håkan Friman and Jens Lindborg, 'Initiating Criminal Proceedings with Military Force: Some Legal Aspects of Policing Somali Pirates by Navies', in *Modern Piracy: Legal Challenges and Responses*, ed. Douglas Guilfoyle, 173–201 (Cheltenham: Elgar, 2013), 192 f.; Geiss and Petrig, *Piracy and Armed Robbery at Sea*, 192 ff.
74 See Geiss and Petrig, *Piracy and Armed Robbery at Sea*, 186 ff. and Friman and Lindborg, 'Initiating Criminal Proceedings, 192 f.
75 Geiss and Petrig, *Piracy and Armed Robbery at Sea*, 220.
76 Petrig, *Human Rights and Law Enforcement at Sea*, 315 ff.
77 See Geiss and Petrig, *Piracy and Armed Robbery at Sea*, 207 ff.; Guilfoyle, 'Counter-piracy Law Enforcement', 153 ff.
78 See article 3 UNCAT (Convention against Torture and Other Cruel, Inhuman or Degrading Treatment or Punishment, 1984), Article 6 and 7 ICCPR (International Covenant on Civil and Political Rights, 1966), and Article 3 ECHR (European Convention on Human Rights, 1950). Also see Geiss and Petrig, *Piracy and Armed Robbery at Sea*, 207 ff.
79 Petrig, *Human Rights and Law Enforcement at Sea*, 197 f.
80 See Petrig, *Human Rights and Law Enforcement at Sea*, 156 ff. Here, the considerations are focused on the requirements of the ECHR (European Convention on Human Rights, 1950), as those also extensively cover the requirements set in ICCPR (International Covenant on Civil and Political Rights, 1966).
81 See Geiss and Petrig, *Piracy and Armed Robbery at Sea*, 111 f.
82 Geiss and Petrig, *Piracy and Armed Robbery at Sea*, 103 and 104 ff.
83 Guilfoyle, 'Counter-piracy Law Enforcement', 153. f
84 See Guilfoyle, 'Counter-piracy Law Enforcement', 153 f., with further references.
85 See Petrig, *Human Rights and Law Enforcement at Sea*, 200.
86 See Petrig, *Human Rights and Law Enforcement at Sea*, 266, 271.
87 *McKay v the United Kingdom* App no 543/03 (3 October 2006) para. 33.
88 See Petrig, *Human Rights and Law Enforcement at Sea*, 272.
89 See Petrig, *Human Rights and Law Enforcement at Sea*, 272, with further references.
90 See Press release by Registrar of the Court; ECHR 361 (2014), 04 December 2014. Also see *Samatar et autres c. France* App nos 17110/10 and 17301/10 (4 December 2014) and *Hassan et autres c. France* Requêtes nos 46695/10 et 54588/10 (4 December 2014).
91 See section 760, paragraph 2, 4 and 5 of the Danish Procedural Code.
92 Decision S3462001-SF of 10 December 2013 of the Eastern High Court (the author has access to the decision).
93 Decision of the Prosecutor General ('Rigsadvokaten') of 2 October 2014, RA-2014–521–2801 (the author has access to the document).
94 See *Rigsadvokatens Meddelelse*, January 2013.
95 See Decision S3462001-SF of 10 December 2013 of the Eastern High Court (the author has access to the decision).
96 ECLI:NL:RBROT:2010:BM8116, Rechtsbank Rotterdam 17–06–2010: http:// uitspraken.rechtspraak.nl/inziendocument?id=ECLI:NL:RBROT:2010:BM8116&keyword=ECLI%3aNL%3aRBROT%3a2010%3aBM8116+Rechtbank+Rotterdam+17-06-2010 (last visited 10 May 2016). Also see Petrig, *Human Rights and Law Enforcement at Sea*, 203 f.
97 Norwegian criminal procedure regarding piracy in the Indian Ocean: www.lovdata.no/ cgi-wift/wiftldrens?/app/gratis/www/docroot/for/sf/jd/xd-20130614–0622.html (last visited 10 May 2016).

98 See CGPCS WG2: 'Non-paper': Human Rights Considerations in Relation to Detention of Suspected Pirates – Case studies based on discussions and presentations at WG2 April 2013 (the author has access to the non-paper).
99 See above 1.
100 On the work of the WG2, see Ulrik Trolle Smed, 'Small States in the CGPCS: Denmark, Working Group 2, and the End of the Debate on an International Piracy Court'. Working Paper of the CGPCS Lessons Learned Project. New York: Contact Group on Piracy off the Coast of Somalia. 2015, available at www.lessonsfrompiracy. net/analysis/.
101 See CGPCS WG2: 'Non-paper': Human Rights Considerations in Relation to Detention of Suspected Pirates – Case studies based on discussions and presentations in WG2 April 2013 (the author has access to the non-paper).
102 See footnote 97.
103 For example, see *Politiken* (8 December 2014), Formodede pirater får erstatning af den danske stat: http://politiken.dk/indland/ECE2478282/formodede-pirater-faar-erstatn ing-af-den-danske-stat/ (last visited 10 May 2016).

Bibliography

Churchill, Robin R., and Alan Vaughan Lowe. *The Law of the Sea*. (3rd edn). Manchester: Manchester University Press, 1999.

Feldtmann, Birgit. 'Zwangloses Strafverfahren?Verfahrensbeendigungen aus Gründen der Opportunität durch die Anklagebehörde in Dänemark aus deutscher Sicht [Informal criminal proceedings? Dismissal of criminal cases Process termination due to for reasons of the "opportunity principle" expediency by the prosecution service in Denmark from the German perspective]'. Bremen: Bremen University, 2002. Available at: http://suche. suub.uni-bremen.de/remote_access.php?http%3A%2F%2Fnbn-resolving.de%2Furn%3 Anbn%3Ade%3Agbv%3A46-00105197-18

Feldtmann, Birgit. 'Er strafferet et effektivt middel i kampen mod sørøveri? Et dansk indblik i strafferetlige udfordringer på baggrund af kapringen af *CEC Future* [Is criminal law an effective tool in the fight against piracy? A Danish insight into criminal law challenges based on the hijacking of the *CEC Future*]'. In *Liber amicorum et amicorum Karin Cornils: Glimt af nordisk straffrätt og straffeprosessrett*, edited by Thomas Elholm, Vagn Greve, Petter Asp, Ragnheidur Bragadottir, Dan Frände and Asbjørn Strandbakken, 101–120. Copenhagen: Djøf, 2010.

Feldtmann, Birgit. 'Should We Rule Out Criminal Law as a Means of Fighting Maritime Piracy? An Essay on the Challenges and Possibilities of Prosecuting Somali Pirates'. In *Festskrift till Per Ole Träskman*, edited by Ulrika Anderson, Christoffer Wong and Helén Örnemark Hansen, 179–188. Stockholm: Norstedts Juridik, 2011.

Feldtmann, Birgit. 'Må man skyde en pirat? Et indblik i den retlige ramme for statslige aktørers magtanvendelse [Can you shoot a pirate?: A glimpse into the legal framework for state actors' use of force]'. In *Festskrift til Nis Jul Clausen*, edited by Nina Dietz Legind, Bent Ole Gram Mortensen, Hans Viggo Godsk Pedersen and Karsten Engsig Sørensen, 123–137. Copenhagen: Djøf, 2013.

Feldtmann, Birgit. 'Fighting Maritime Piracy: On Possible Actions and Consequences'. In *Economic Analysis of International Law: Contributions to the XIIIth Travemünde Symposium on the Economic Analysis of Law (March 29–31, 2012)*, edited by Thomas Eger, Stefan Oeter, and Stefan Voigt, 173–198. Tubingen: Mohr Siebeck, 2014.

Feldtmann, Birgit, and Kristina Maria Siig. 'Dine, mine og vore pirater: Et indblik i juridiske (og andre) problemstillinger i forbindelse med bekæmpelse af pirateri i internationale farvande [Your, my and our pirates: An insight into the legal (and other) issues relating to the fight against piracy in international waters]'. In *Juridiske Emner ved Syddansk Universitet 2009*, edited by Hans Viggo Godsk Pedersen, 68–82. Odense: Syddansk Universitet, 2009.

Friman, Håkan, and Jens Lindborg. 'Initiating Criminal Proceedings with Military Force: Some Legal Aspects of Policing Somali Pirates by Navies'. In *Modern Piracy: Legal Challenges and Responses*, edited by Douglas Guilfoyle, 173–201. Cheltenham: Elgar, 2013.

Gardener, Maggie. 'Piracy Prosecutions in National Courts'. *Journal of International Criminal Justice* 10 (2012): 797–821.

Geiss, Robin, and Anna Petrig. *Piracy and Armed Robbery at Sea: The Legal Framework for Counter-Piracy Operations in Somalia and the Gulf of Aden*. Oxford: Oxford University Press, 2011.

Guilfoyle, Douglas. 'Treaty Jurisdiction over Pirates: A Compilation of Legal Texts with Introductory Notes'. Report prepared for Contact Group on Piracy off the Coast of Somalia, 26–27 August 2009. New York: Contact Group on Piracy off the Coast of Somalia, 2009.

Guilfoyle, Douglas. 'Counter-piracy Law Enforcement and Human Rights'. *International and Comparative Law Quarterly* 59 (2010): 141–169.

Guilfoyle, Douglas. 'The Legal Challenges in Fighting Piracy'. In *The International Response to Somali Piracy: Challenges and Opportunities*, edited by Bib van Ginkel and Frans-Paul van der Putten, 127–152. Leiden: Brill, 2010.

Guilfoyle, Douglas. 'Prosecuting Somali Pirates: A Critical Evaluation of the Options'. *Journal of International Criminal Justice* 10 (2012): 767–796.

Kontorovich, Eugene. 'The Piracy Analogy: Modern Universal Jurisdictions Hollow Foundation'. *Harvard International Law Journal* 45 (2004): 183–236.

Kontorovich, Eugene. 'The Penalties for Piracy: A Discussion Paper'. Broomfield, CO: Oceans Beyond Piracy, 2012. Available at: http://oceansbeyondpiracy.org/sites/default/files/obp_penalties_for_piracy_final.pdf.

Murdoch, Andrew, and Douglas Guilfoyle. 'Capture and Disruption Operations: The Use of Force in Counter-Piracy off Somalia'. In *Modern Piracy: Legal Challenges and Responses*, edited by Douglas Guilfoyle, 147–171. Cheltenham: Elgar, 2013.

Murphy, Martin. 'Piracy and UNCLOS: Does International Law Help Regional States Combat Piracy?'. In *Violence at Sea: Piracy in the Age of Global Terrorism*, edited by Peter Lehr, 155–182. London: Routledge, 2007.

Petrig, Anna. *Human Rights and Law Enforcement at Sea: Arrest, Detention and Transfer of Piracy Suspects*. Leiden: Brill, 2014.

Shapiro, Andrew J. 'Counter-Piracy Policy: Delivering Judicial Consequences', 2010. Available at: www.state.gov/t/pm/rls/rm/139326.htm (accessed on 10 May 2016).

Smed, Ulrik Trolle. 'Small States in the CGPCS: Denmark, Working Group 2, and the End of the Debate on an International Piracy Court'. Working Paper of the CGPCS Lessons Learned Project. New York: Contact Group on Piracy off the Coast of Somalia. 2015. Available at: www.lessonsfrompiracy.net/analysis/.

Tanaka, Yoshifumi. *The International Law of the Sea*. Cambridge: Cambridge University Press, 2012.

UN Security Council. *Report of the Secretary-General on the situation with respect to piracy and armed robbery at sea off the coast of Somalia* (21 October 2013), S/2013/623.

7

RESCUING MIGRANTS AT SEA AND THE LAW OF INTERNATIONAL RESPONSIBILITY

*Efthymios Papastavridis**

7.1 Introduction

In the first two months of 2016 alone, 410 people died or went missing in the Mediterranean sea, according to the UN Office of the High Commissioner for Refugees (UNHCR).[1] In 2015, 3,772 people perished in these waters.[2] Since the sinking of a boat with 500 people off the coast of Lampedusa on 3 October 2013,[3] the death toll has not stopped; rather, it has steadily increased. These tragic deadly sea incidents mark the significance and urgency of the problem of migration by sea. Indeed, thousands of people are currently undertaking very perilous journeys and putting their lives in serious danger in order to flee from their country of origin. They flee by whatever means are possible, including overcrowded, unseaworthy vessels which are often at risk of sinking. Indeed, many of them do sink. The result is that thousands of lives are lost every year.

The challenges in the Mediterranean are mirrored in other regions. For example, according to an October 2014 UNHCR report on the situation in Yemen,

> there has been a sharp increase this year [2014] in the number of migrants and asylum-seekers losing their lives in attempts to get to Yemen, mainly from the Horn of Africa, with more deaths at sea in 2014 than in the last three years combined . . . bring the yearly tally for 2014 to 215, exceeding the combined total for 2011, 2012 and 2013 of 179.[4]

Equally serious is the problem in the Asia–Pacific region. While there is no 'boat crisis' on the scale seen in Indochina in the 1970s and 1980s, the maritime migration movements remain considerable.[5] States and the international community have not remained idle, but their response has been tailored more to averting the 'threat' posed by maritime migration to their 'territorial integrity' than to saving these people's lives. Among the 'non-arrival' policies employed to this end,[6] a primary role is attributed to interception, which has attained even more vigour recently in light of the relevant practice of Australia[7] and of various European states individually[8] or under the coordination of the EU (Frontex).[9] It is worrisome that the need to save the lives of the contemporary 'boat people' is underestimated. Even in the aftermath of the shocking death of more than 700 people in mid-April 2015, the European Union's response has not been comprehensive and satisfactory. What was decided on was confined to increasing the resources and operational area of the existing Frontex-coordinated operations in the region,[10] as well as launching EUNAVFOR MED, later renamed Operation Sophia. This is an EU naval operation designed primarily to counteract smuggling of migrants in the central Mediterranean, and only incidentally to save lives at sea.[11] To these initiatives may be added the deployment of the standing naval forces of NATO in the Aegean sea in order to fight the smuggling of migrants and refugees to Greece. These were planned to be fully operational on 30 March 2016.[12]

In addition to this unfortunate inaction by the relevant stakeholders on the policy level, there are also certain gaps in the legal framework. Suffice to note that while there is a clear duty on the part of the shipmaster to provide assistance in case of vessels or persons in distress at sea, there is no equally clear obligation on the part of the flag states or the coastal state to accept the rescued persons in their territory.[13] Unwillingness on the part of the coastal states to allow disembarkation, in conjunction with costs incurred through uncertainty and delay, which fall entirely on the ship-owner, put the masters of the rescuing vessels in a difficult predicament. As a consequence, many ships have ignored distress calls, leading to significant loss of life.[14]

It is beyond the compass of the present chapter to address all issues relating to the phenomenon of the contemporary 'boat people'. This phenomenon raises a host of perplexing legal questions, including questions concerning the international law of the sea, international refugee and human rights law and immigration law.[15] Rather, this chapter will focus on questions of international responsibility arising from rescue operations at sea, in particular from non-rescue at sea. It will endeavour to address whether states (whether as flag or as coastal states) as well as the international organisations involved in such operations incur any responsibility for violation of the rules of international law, when they fail to save lives at sea.

Accordingly, reference will be made, first, to the obligations of states and international organisations in respect of rescue operations, in particular to the pertinent rules under the law of the sea as well as to the right of life as enshrined in the applicable human rights treaties and customary international law. Then the focus will shift to the secondary rules of international responsibility and their application in the context of the present inquiry. In order to facilitate the assessment of potential responsibility in cases of non-rescue of migrants at sea, we will use the widely debated 'left to die incident' of March 2011, in which sixty-one people were left to die off the coast of Libya.[16] In this incident, allegations were made that warships taking part in NATO's Operation Unified Protector had intentionally ignored the distress signals of the people on the boat. The incident was further examined by Ms Tineke Strik, a member of the parliamentary assembly of the Council of Europe, who issued a report in 2012.[17] Even though Ms Strik acknowledged that without full information on this matter it is difficult to draw conclusions about the responsibility of the states involved as well as that of NATO, it was clear to her that there was a failure by many states, including NATO, to react to the distress signals.[18]

This is not to say that there has been no other similar incident bringing about international responsibility issues; rather, this is the only recent incident that has been officially examined and can thus be of assistance in the present discussion.[19]

7.2 The legal regime of rescue at sea

7.2.1 The law of the sea framework

The duty to assist persons in distress at sea is a long-established rule of customary international law. It extends both to other vessels and coastal states in the vicinity; all persons, including irregular maritime migrants, remain protected. The duty to rescue has been codified in the UN Convention on the Law of the Sea (LOSC).[20] LOSC prescribes relevant duties for both the flag and the coastal states. First, with regard to flag states, Article 98(1) of LOSC provides that:

> Every State shall require the master of a ship flying its flag, in so far as he can do so without serious danger to the ship, the crew, or the passengers . . . to render assistance to any person found at sea in danger of being lost . . . and to proceed to the rescue of persons in distress, if informed of their need for assistance, in so far as such action may be reasonably be expected of him.

The first pertinent question in this context is what qualifies as 'distress'. At the outset, distress is not defined by LOSC; however, the term 'distress phase' is defined in paragraph 1.3.13 of the annex of the 1979 International Convention on Maritime Search and Rescue (the SAR Convention) as 'a situation wherein there is a reasonable certainty that a person, a vessel or other craft is threatened by *grave and imminent danger* and requires immediate assistance'. Further clarifications have been provided in relevant jurisprudence. For example, in the *Eleanor* case it was held that distress must entail urgency, but that 'there need not be immediate physical necessity'.[21] In the words of the US Supreme Court, the test of distress is that the circumstances would produce in 'the mind of a skilful mariner, a well-grounded apprehension of the loss of the vessel and cargo or of the lives of the crew'.[22]

In the EU context, the 2010 European Council decision, which was subsequently annulled by the Court of Justice of the European Union, indicated that the existence of a situation of distress should not be determined exclusively on the basis of an actual request for assistance. A number of objective factors, such as the seaworthiness of the vessel, the number of passengers on board, the availability of supplies, the presence of qualified crew and navigation equipment, the prevailing weather and sea conditions, as well as the presence of particularly vulnerable, injured or deceased persons, should be taken into account.[23] Interestingly, Regulation 656/2014 on Frontex operations at sea reiterates these factors.[24]

The next question, and the more important for the present purposes – that is, for determining when states would be responsible for failing to save lives at sea – is the content and nature of the obligations under the LOSC. Reading Article 98(1) of LOSC at face value, it is apparent that the responsibility to rescue and provide assistance rests initially with the master of the rescuing ship, and entails the duty to deliver the rescued people to a place of safety. The obligation incumbent upon the shipmaster is without qualification, and no distinction must be made according to the legal status of the persons to be rescued.[25] The only exception is the extent to which it would be unreasonable to render assistance. Accordingly, if the vessel is too far away, the rescue vessel is ill-equipped to render assistance, or other vessels are more readily available to render assistance, then the master may not be required to render assistance.

With respect to the obligations of the flag state, every flag state must require the master of a ship, whether a state or a private ship flying the state's flag, to proceed with all possible speed to the rescue of persons in distress, when informed of their need for assistance. This obligation on the part of the flag state is essentially an obligation of result, in the sense that the flag state has to achieve a certain result, i.e. to provide for the duty in question in its domestic legislation. Article 98(1) is non-self-executing, and requires implementing legislation to acquire the force of law.[26] Besides this, there is no other obligation of result, such as an obligation to guarantee that the people in distress will be saved.[27]

In addition, the flag state is under a 'due diligence' obligation to monitor whether the masters of vessels flying its flag discharge these duties.[28] The due diligence obligations of flag states were discussed at length in the International Tribunal for the Law of the Sea (ITLOS) advisory opinion of 2 April 2015 on the request by the Sub-Regional Fisheries Commission, in which the Tribunal acknowledged that the flag states are under such obligations in relation to illegal, unregulated and unreported fishing (IUU fishing) within the exclusive economic zone of third states.[29] It can tenably be supported that these duties apply *mutatis mutandis* in relation to the rescue obligations of the flag states under Article 98(1) of LOSC. Such duties involve an obligation not only to adopt appropriate national 'rules and measures', but also to exercise 'a certain level of vigilance in their enforcement', including exercising 'administrative control' over relevant 'public and private operators'.[30]

In the case of public vessels, such as warships or coastguard vessels, it would be easier to establish responsibility on the part of the flag state for any omission to discharge this duty of due diligence, since the flag state retains full command and control of these vessels and thus is cognizant of all their actions. In the case of private vessels, while not directly responsible for the actions of a master who neglects his duty, the flag state may nonetheless incur international responsibility for not acting with due diligence, in not inquiring into such incidents. Yet the question that may reasonably be posed is *how* the flag state is supposed to know about these incidents. This is possible insofar as the shipmaster observes the duty to record any reason for failing to render assistance. Indeed, according to Chapter V, Regulation 33 of the 1974 Safety of Life at Sea Convention (SOLAS),[31] which complements the LOSC, the shipmaster is required 'to enter in the log-book the reason for failing to proceed to the assistance of the persons in distress ... [and] to inform the appropriate search and rescue service accordingly'.[32] This registration would allow the flag state to inquire into whether the master did discharge his or her duties, and if not, to impose penalties according to its domestic legislation.

With regard to coastal states, Article 98(2) of LOSC stipulates:

> Every coastal State shall promote the establishment, operation and mainten-
> ance of an adequate and effective search and rescue service regarding safety
> on and over the sea and, where circumstances so require, by way of mutual
> regional arrangements cooperate with neighbouring States for this purpose.

On the face of this provision, it is evident that LOSC postulates a general obligation on the part of coastal states to maintain search and rescue services, as well as a general obligation of cooperation with other states to this end.

The search and rescue regime under LOSC is complemented by the SOLAS Convention and the SAR Convention on maritime search and rescue.[33] The SAR Convention aims to create an international system for coordinating rescue operations and for guaranteeing their efficiency and safety. Contracting states are obliged to provide SAR services in the area under their responsibility, and they are invited to regulate and coordinate operations and rescue services in the maritime zone designated in the agreement.[34]

In May 2004, in the wake of the infamous *Tampa* incident[35] and the initiatives that it fuelled,[36] the SAR and SOLAS Conventions were amended to impose additional obligations upon the state parties, including an obligation on states to 'cooperate and coordinate' to ensure that ships' masters are allowed to disembark rescued persons to a place of safety.[37] As recognised by the International Maritime Organisation (IMO) Maritime Safety Committee, the aim of the amendments is to ensure that a place of safety is provided within a reasonable time. The primary responsibility to provide a place of safety or to ensure that a place of safety is provided rests with the government responsible for the SAR region in which the survivors were recovered.[38]

The term 'place of safety' is defined neither by the SOLAS nor by the SAR Convention. The 2004 IMO Guidelines on the Treatment of Persons rescued at Sea define a 'place of safety' as any place 'where the survivors' safety of life is no longer threatened and where their basic human needs (such as food, shelter and medical needs) can be met.'[39] While these guidelines are not themselves binding, they provide an important means for interpreting the obligations set forth in LOSC,

SOLAS and the SAR Conventions, since they may be considered as subsequent practice under Article 31(3)(a) of the Vienna Convention on the Law of Treaties (1969).[40]

In light of the foregoing, the obligations of the coastal states are as follows. First, there is an obligation to '*promote* the establishment, operation and maintenance of *adequate and effective* search and rescue services' (emphasis added).[41] The coastal state is thus bound by an obligation of result to establish search and rescue services, but also by an obligation of due diligence, pursuant to which it has to make sure that *adequate and effective* SAR services are maintained in its SAR zone (emphasis added).

Second, in case of a distress situation, the coastal state is under a two-fold obligation: on the one hand, it 'shall, so far as possible, provide adequate means of locating and rescuing such persons'[42] and shall coordinate search and rescue activities, and on the other, it shall cooperate with other states to this end.[43] As regards the former obligation, it is submitted that the coastal states have to discharge 'best efforts obligations', to use James Crawford's terminology,[44] namely to deploy all adequate measures so as to provide rescue services. This means that if the persons in distress are not saved notwithstanding these 'best efforts', the coastal state concerned does not automatically or *ipso jure* incur responsibility.

Finally, in case the rescue operation is successful, the coastal state is under an additional obligation to ensure cooperation and coordination, such that the rescuing ship's master is allowed to disembark the rescued persons at a place of safety.[45] This obligation to ensure that a place of safety is provided is an obligation of result, in the sense that the responsible coastal state is required to guarantee this outcome.[46]

However, this obligation does not explicitly stipulate that the state responsible for the SAR zone is obliged to disembark the survivors in its own territory. In other words, the formal treaty law does not oblige a coastal state to allow disembarkation on its own territory when it has not been possible to do so elsewhere. This has been criticised as the major shortcoming of the treaty regime.[47] As a matter of policy, this has as a consequence that the vessels rescuing migrants at sea do not have clear and foreseeable guidelines as to where they are supposed to disembark these persons, as this would depend on ad hoc cooperation rendered by the competent coastal states. This amounts to a very significant impediment or disincentive for the main 'users' of the oceans – the private mariners[48] – to discharge their traditional humanitarian duty.

7.2.2 Human rights law

Obligations upon states concerning persons in distress at sea may also arise not only from the law of the sea, but also from international human rights law. In the context of rescue at sea, the human right of most immediate concern is the right to life, enshrined, among other rights, in Article 2 of the European Convention on Human Rights (ECHR)[49] and Article 6 of the International Covenant on Civil and Political Rights (ICCPR).[50] As held by the European Court of Human Rights

(ECHR) in *Osman v. United Kingdom* (1999), Article 2 requires states not only to refrain from causing death, but also to take positive measures to protect the lives of individuals within their jurisdiction.[51]

Thus both flag and coastal states involved in rescue operations have to take all necessary measures to protect the lives of individuals in distress, provided, of course, that they are within their jurisdiction. Extraterritorial jurisdiction has been established for activities occurring on the high seas in a number of cases,[52] yet as noted by several authors to this volume, the exact scope of human rights treaties in relation to various situations of extraterritorial action remains contested.[53] In the present milieu, it is questioned whether the master of the vessel rescuing migrants on the high seas or the coastal state that coordinates the rescue operation are bound by human rights obligations even when these acts take place outside their territory. In other words, at which point are the persons in distress considered as subject to the jurisdiction of the states concerned?

Having in mind the prerequisite of authority and control as discussed in both international case law and theory, the following comments are in order. First, as regards flag states, it is beyond doubt that persons brought on board would come under the jurisdiction of the flag state of the rescuing state vessel.[54] Human rights jurisdiction has also been established in cases where migrants do not come on board the rescuing vessel but a certain interference with the navigation of their vessel takes place by a state vessel, like a coastguard vessel, in the context of immigration control.[55] Arguably, from the moment that the coastguard vessel exercises such '*de facto* control' over the navigation of a vessel carrying migrants, the latter persons come within the respective flag state's extraterritorial jurisdiction.

On the contrary, when rescue operations are conducted by private vessels, the situation is different. In such cases, a jurisdictional link between the rescued persons and the flag state can only be established where the master is given specific instructions by the competent authorities of the flag state as to how they should proceed with the persons concerned, and where action is taken accordingly. In that case, arguably, the master becomes a *de facto* organ of the flag state under Article 8 of Articles on Responsibility of states for Internationally Wrongful Acts (ARSIWA), through which the flag state exercises jurisdiction over these persons.[56]

Second, as regards the coastal States, it is debatable whether the coastal state that receives a distress call in relation to boats within its SAR zone and is aware of their location exercises control over these persons such that the latter come within its jurisdiction. On the one hand, it is difficult to speak of a *de jure* control exercised by the coastal state *a priori* over vessels and persons within its search and rescue zone, because it is not a maritime zone, in which coastal states exercise *ipso jure* sovereignty. Their jurisdictional reach extends only to the simple fact that according to Article 98(2) of LOSC and the SAR Convention they have to 'promote the establishment, operation and maintenance of an adequate and effective search and rescue service' therein. Consequently, there is no warrant for the assertion that the coastal state exercises *a priori* and *ipso facto* jurisdiction over all vessels and persons found in its search and rescue zone.

On the other hand, a different conclusion may be drawn in cases of distress calls that are received and acknowledged by the rescue coordination centre of the coastal state. In these cases, arguably, the coastal state that is responsible for the SAR zone and has received the distress call exerts a certain functional jurisdiction over the persons in distress within this zone under the law of the sea. Indeed, according to the SOLAS Convention, governments are responsible for ensuring 'that necessary arrangements are made for distress communication and coordination in their area of responsibility and for the rescue of persons in distress at sea around its coasts'.[57]

Do these arrangements, or more generally do the search and rescue services that the coastal state is called to perform vis-à-vis the persons in distress, bring these persons within its 'jurisdiction' in terms of, for instance, Article 1 of the European Convention on Human Rights? The two-model approach, which has been generally acknowledged as the basis for extraterritorial jurisdiction, seems *prima facie* not to serve well in the present context. Both the *spatial model* (as *de facto* effective control over a foreign territory) and the *personal model* (as authority and control exercised by states over individuals) appear not to be applicable here.[58] However, on a closer reading, there is room for the argument that due to the functional jurisdiction and its due diligence obligations that the coastal state is called to perform in relation to people in distress in its SAR zone, the coastal state does exercise a certain degree of 'spatial control' over this area. This degree of control suffices to bring about the positive obligation to ensure the right to life of these people spotted therein.[59] A prerequisite for the establishment of jurisdiction in this regard, and thereby for such due diligence obligation to ensure the right to life, is knowledge of the location of the people in distress.[60]

That said, it is one thing that the coastal state is under the obligation to ensure the right to life in this regard, and another to argue that any failure to do so would entail the coastal state's responsibility. This would depend in each and every case on whether the coastal state exerted its 'best efforts' to ensure the right to life and on whether it met its procedural obligations, such as investigating the deaths of the persons concerned.

7.2.3 Obligations of international organisations

Having discussed the obligations of states in relation to the rescue of persons at sea under the law of the sea, the question arises whether international organisations are also bound by the same obligations and human rights law. International organisations involved in rescue operations include the European Union through its agency (Frontex) and, arguably, NATO. The latter organisation's responsibility was one of the core findings of Ms Tineke Strik's PACE (Parliamentary Assembly of the Council of Europe) report concerning the incident of April/May 2011.

Accordingly, are the European Union and NATO under any obligations in this regard? In general, the issue of primary obligations of international organisations seems straightforward, but, in reality, it is not. Notably, the Commentary of the

Articles on the Responsibility of International Organisations (ARIO) makes only a cursory reference to the content of these obligations as follows:

> As in the case of State responsibility, the term 'international obligation' means an obligation under international law 'regardless of the origin' of the obligation concerned [. . .] this is intended to convey that the international obligation 'may be established by a customary rule of international law, by a treaty or by a general principle applicable within the international legal order'.[61]

While 'international obligations' established by a treaty are clear, the same is not the case with respect to obligations under customary international law. Are international organisations *qua* subjects of international law bound by the totality of the rules of customary law, on an equal footing with states? It is the view of the present author that, due to the 'principle of speciality',[62] international organisations are bound only by the rules of customary law that are applicable to the exercise of their powers. This view finds cogent support in the case law of the European Court of Justice, which has repeatedly confirmed that the European Union, including the Communities, must, as subject of international law, respect international law (both treaty and customary) in the exercise of its powers.[63]

2.c (i) The European Union

As far as the European Union and its obligations under the law of the sea are concerned, as a matter of treaty law the European Union is not party to LOSC in respect of Part VII on the high seas. By virtue of Article 4(3) of Annex XI of LOSC, 'an international organisation shall exercise the rights and perform the obligations which its Member States which are Parties would otherwise have under this Convention, *on matters relating to which competence has been transferred to it by those Member States*' (emphasis added). The EU member states never transferred competence to the Union in respect of rescue at sea.[64]

As regards customary international law, the European Union is bound by the relevant customary rules, even though it is not a 'state of registry' of vessels such as to have an obligation to provide for the master's duty to assist persons in distress at sea. This is due to the fact that it has competence pursuant to Article 77(2)(d) of the Treaty on the Functioning of the European Union to adopt 'any measure necessary for the gradual establishment of an integrated management system for external borders'; more importantly, it is also due to the fact that, in the exercise of this competence, it is about to adopt a regulation establishing rules governing, among other things, rescue at sea.[65] Indeed, in the preamble of Regulation 656/2014, it is stated that:

> When coordinating border surveillance operations at sea, the Agency should fulfil its tasks in full compliance with the relevant Union law, including the

Charter of Fundamental Rights of the European Union and relevant international law, in particular as referred to in Recital (4)[.]

Recital 4 includes:

the United Nations Convention on the Law of the Sea, the International Convention for the Safety of Life at Sea, the International Convention on Maritime Search and Rescue . . .[66]

The European Union may not be party to the above conventions; nevertheless, when engaged in joint border operations at sea, both Frontex and EU member states are obliged to respect these treaties as a matter of EU law.

In addition, Frontex is bound by the EU Charter of Fundamental Rights (EUCFR).[67] This is equally acknowledged in the above-mentioned recital of the Regulation. Moreover, Article 51(1) of the EUCFR makes clear that the 'provisions of the Charter are addressed to the institutions, bodies, offices and agencies of the Union with due regard for the principle of subsidiarity and to the Member States only when they are implementing Union law'. Thus the EUCFR applies whenever the European Union and its member states act, not only within the territorial borders of the Union, but also beyond them, provided that they are 'implementing Union law', as in the case of Frontex-coordinated operations.

2. c (ii) NATO

Turning to NATO, the analysis is rather different, at least as regards situations such as the alleged non-rescue of migrants off the coast of Libya in April 2011, where NATO was concurrently engaged in its Operation Unified Protector.[68]

NATO is not a party to the LOSC and SOLAS Conventions and hence is not directly bound by the provisions regarding rescue at sea contained therein. As a subject of international law, NATO must respect customary international law in the exercise of its powers. In contrast to the European Union, however, rescuing people at sea is not evidently part of NATO's powers, either explicitly or implicitly.

Moreover, it is not clear that NATO is bound by the right to life in respect of people in distress at sea. While NATO is, in principle, bound by the fundamental provisions of humanitarian law and human rights law, including the right to life, in the course of its operations, it is doubtful whether safeguarding lives on the high seas is part of the NATO mandate, at least with respect to Operation Unified Protector.

In reality, when warships come under NATO command, it does not mean that NATO (as an organisation) assumes all of the obligations that a state has. It acquires operational control over the ships only for a certain mandated task, in this case the protection of civilians in Libya and the enforcement of a no-fly zone, as was set forth by Security Council Resolutions 1970/2011 and 1973/2011. Safeguarding lives at sea was not part of NATO's mandate in accordance with the said resolutions, and consequently it fell outside the remit of the normative framework of this operation. This operation notwithstanding, however, we cannot exclude the possibility that in future NATO may be authorised to conduct rescue operations; in that case, it will inevitably be subject to the relevant legal framework. This may be the case with the planned NATO deployment in the Aegean sea. Such an assertion would however depend on the mandate and the operation plan of the operation.

7.3 International responsibility arising from rescue at sea

Having discussed the international obligations applicable to rescue at sea, it is time to scrutinise the responsibility of flag and coastal states, as well as international organisations. Following the structure of Article 2 of the ARSIWA or Article 4 of ARIO, I will examine both the element of the attribution of wrongful acts to states and organisations, and the element of breach of the relevant obligations.

Starting with states and the rules for the attribution of conduct, Articles 4–11 of the ARSIWA set forth the conditions under which conduct is attributed to the state for the purposes of determining its international responsibility.[69] In the present milieu, the conduct that is, in principle, attributable to a state would be either the non-rescue of persons in distress on the part of the flag state or the non-coordination of the rescue operation and the non-provision of a place of safety on the part of the coastal state. Assuming that such conduct has occurred, the existence of a wrongful act would be contingent upon the attribution of the conduct in question to the state concerned.

With regard to the element of breach of international obligations, 'there is a breach of an international obligation when conduct attributed to a State as a subject of international law amounts to a failure by that State to comply with an international obligation incumbent upon it. . . .'[70] Nonetheless, as the International Law Commission explains:

> [i]n determining whether given conduct attributable to a state constitutes a breach of its international obligations, the principal focus will be on the primary obligation concerned. It is this which has to be interpreted and applied to the situation, determining thereby the substance of the conduct required, the standard to be observed, the result to be achieved, etc.[71]

In the present case, the primary obligations of states under LOSC, the relevant IMO conventions and customary international law have been adequately determined and construed in the previous section. Therefore, the inquiry that follows will focus on whether the attribution of the conduct in question to either the flag or the coastal state establishes an internationally wrongful act, and thus the international responsibility of these states.

7.3.1 The international responsibility of the flag state

As regards the flag state and the requisite element of attribution, the fact that a vessel flying the flag of a particular state has failed to render assistance to persons in distress at sea could be attributable to the latter state in a number of cases. On the one hand, if the vessel in question is a warship or other duly designated state vessel, the master, with whom the pertinent duty lies, is a *de jure* organ of a state, and thus his or her conduct is attributable to the flag state pursuant to Article 4 of ARSIWA.[72] This does not mean however that in each and every case this omission would entail the responsibility of the flag state, as this omission must also amount to a violation of Article 98(1) of LOSC and, additionally, of the concomitant due diligence obligation of the flag state, as well as a violation of the right to life under human rights law. On the other hand, if the vessel in question is private, the attribution to the flag state is not so obvious, in the sense that the master of the vessel is not a *de jure* organ of the state. However, there are other rules of attribution that might be applicable here.

Pursuant to Article 5 of ARSIWA:

> [t]he conduct of a person or entity which is not an organ of the State under Article 4, but which is empowered by the law of that State to exercise elements of the governmental authority shall be considered an act of the State under international law, provided the person or entity is acting in that capacity in the particular instance.

Hypothetically, should the flag state have explicitly authorised the master of the vessel to exercise 'elements of governmental authority' in this regard, then the conduct of the non-rescue of migrants could be attributed to the state. Indeed, flag states often empower masters with certain public powers, such as the power to arrest on board the vessel.[73] However, it is the view of the author that such delegation of authority cannot exist in respect of rescue at sea. And the reason is not that the criterion of 'empowerment by law' is not met. Quite to the contrary, flag states do provide in their domestic legislation for the duty of the master to perform search and rescue activities; this is not a prerogative of the flag states, but, as said, their obligation pursuant to Article 98(1) of LOSC. The reason is simply that there is no delegation of 'elements of governmental authority'. According to the International Law Commission:

> [t]he justification for attributing to the State under international law the conduct of 'parastatal' entities lies in the fact that the internal law of the State has conferred on the entity in question the exercise of certain elements of the governmental authority. If it is to be regarded as an act of the State for purposes of international responsibility, *the conduct of an entity must accordingly concern governmental activity* and not other private or commercial activity in which the entity may engage. (Emphasis added)[74]

Evidently, rendering assistance to persons in distress at sea falls short of qualifying as 'governmental activity'; rather, it is a traditional maritime and 'humanitarian' duty par excellence, which, under international law, falls upon the master of any vessel to discharge. Accordingly, the conduct of private vessels should not, in principle, be attributed to the flag state according to Article 5 of ARSIWA.

However, under Article 8 of ARSIWA:

> the conduct of a person or group of persons shall be considered an act of a State under international law if the person or group of persons is in fact acting on the instructions of, or under the direction or control of, that State in carrying out the conduct.[75]

On the face of this provision, it can tenably be argued that should the flag state instruct the master of the vessel flying its flag to turn a blind eye to persons in distress at sea, and should the master comply with this instruction, this omission would be attributable to the flag state.

On the other hand, even if the conduct of the master of the private vessel is considered to be attributable to the flag state, this does not *ipso facto* entail that the latter incurs international responsibility. The conduct in question must also give rise to a breach of the relevant international obligation, pursuant to Article 2 of ASR (Articles on State Responsibility). Accordingly, it might be the case that the vessel in question did not proceed to the rescue of the persons in distress because it was unable or considered it unnecessary, yet it informed the rescue authorities pursuant to the relevant regulations.[76] This would not amount to a breach of the obligations of the flag state.

In any case, the flag states involved may incur responsibility not for the failure to assist the persons at sea, but for not exercising the due diligence obligation provided for in Articles 98(1) of LOSC and the SOLAS Convention. Thus if there is a pattern of incidents of private vessels ignoring people in distress without registering 'in the log-book the reason for failing to proceed to the assistance of the persons in distress' or informing 'the appropriate search and rescue service accordingly' and the flag state remains idle, then there are good reasons to assert that the flag state has breached its due diligence obligations under the LOSC and SOLAS Conventions.

As regards the responsibility for violations of human rights law, it is contended that exceptionally, and only in the case that the flag states had been informed about the boat in distress and had instructed their vessels not to render assistance, would the persons have been within the 'jurisdiction' of the flag states. In such a case, the master may be considered as a '*de facto* organ' under Article 8 of ARSIWA, and thus the failure to render assistance can be attributed to the flag state. In that case, responsibility on the part of the flag state for the violation of the right to life might consequently have arisen. Nevertheless, it is not usual practice for commercial shipping to inform flag-state authorities about such matters, nor for flag-state authorities to instruct private vessels to ignore the obligation to render assistance.

At this juncture, it is instructive to consider the left-to-die incident of March 2011. According to the available information, the boat in distress was initially assisted by a military helicopter (there were reports that it was Italian);[77] it had encountered two fishing boats, one flying an Italian flag and the other a Tunisian flag, neither of which rendered assistance.[78] In addition, three warships were allegedly in the vicinity: the Spanish frigate *Méndez Núñez* (11 miles away), the Italian *ITS Borsini* (37 miles away)[79] and a French vessel.[80] None of them assisted the boat people.

In applying the rules on state responsibility, we can make a number of assertions. First of all, as regards the military helicopter, its presence and the initial assistance provided to the persons in distress brought about the result that these persons were under the *personal* control, and hence under the jurisdiction of the state of registry of the helicopter. The omission to provide any further assistance was clearly attributed to that state, and constituted a breach of the positive obligation set forth by the right to life under Article 2 of the European Convention on Human Rights and Article 6 of ICCPR. In addition, the state of registry of the helicopter may also incur responsibility for the lack of cooperation with other naval and aerial assets in the region so as to provide the assistance required to the persons in distress.

Second, with respect to the other military vessels, it seems difficult to sustain the argument that the flag states of the *Méndez Núñez* and the *ITS Borsini* had exercised any kind of 'control' over the persons on the boat so as to fulfil the relevant human rights obligations. A distress call to all vessels in a wide area does not establish 'jurisdiction' on the part of all flag states over the persons concerned. Nor can it be said that the non-assistance as such infringed the applicable rules of the law of the sea. The only obligation of the flag states concerned was to discharge *ex post* their duty of due diligence, as analysed above, which, however, presupposes awareness of the incident and of the reasons for the failure to assist. In view of the location of these two warships and their parallel mandate under Operation Unified Protector in Libya – but more importantly, the lack of definite know-ledge as to whether they did indeed receive the distress signal – it is difficult to make such a claim.

However, the situation is different in relation to the other, probably French, military vessel. Allegedly, this vessel had visual contact with the 'boat people'; it was aware of the situation, namely that people (including children) had already died; nonetheless, it did not provide assistance.[81] Arguably, the visual contact and the awareness of the situation triggered its obligation to provide assistance in accordance with the law of the sea; the failure to do so and the lack of any reporting to the responsible rescue coordination centre – as well as, allegedly, the lack of any act in due diligence by the flag state of the warship – may bring about the latter's responsibility for not abiding by the pertinent rules under the law of the sea.

As with any human rights violation, first, it must be established that the 'boat people' were under the jurisdiction of the (unknown) flag state of the military vessel. This would require the extension of the 'personal control' model, to the extent that any such encounter would bring about the 'positive obligation' to ensure the right to life in keeping with the *Osman v. UK* case law of the European Court of Human Rights.[82] Even though this argument might appear far-fetched in other contexts and not in accordance, for example, with the premise that positive obligations require certain control over a specific territory,[83] it is submitted that due to the nature of the high seas as an area over which only the flag state may exercise jurisdiction under international law,[84] it is inevitable that this jurisdiction would extend to such distress situations. This is also the raison d'être of Article 98(1) of LOSC, which explicitly calls for the assertion of such jurisdiction on the high seas on the part of the flag states. In other words, the jurisdiction that flag states are called to exercise on the high seas – including the jurisdiction to exercise due diligence control over their vessels – also informs the extent of their 'jurisdictional reach' in the same area for the purposes of the application of human rights treaties.

Consequently, it is the view of the author that in the context of the present inquiry, the 'boat people' in distress may have come within the jurisdiction of the flag state of the warship, which was aware of their situation and had the due diligence obligation, or a 'best efforts' obligation, to secure their lives. Needless to say, because a warship is a state organ, any failure to assist the boat people is directly attributed to the flag state and may amount to a breach of Article 2 of ECHR or Article 6 of ICCPR.

Third, as to the responsibility of the flag states of the private vessels which, allegedly, failed to render assistance, it is submitted that the omission as such cannot be attributed to the respective states – *in casu*, Italy, Tunisia and Cyprus – and thus that no responsibility for a violation of the right to life can be incurred. Only the lack of due diligence *ex post facto* by the said states may give rise to their responsibility for the violation of Article 98(1) of LOSC and the SOLAS Convention.

7.3.2 The international responsibility of coastal states

Similar to the above, in respect of their duties under the law of the sea and/or international human rights law, responsibility on the part of the coastal states will arise if the conduct in question is attributed to them and constitutes a breach of their primary obligations.

Under the law of the sea, the primary obligation of the coastal states under both treaty and customary law is to have in place a certain coordinating mechanism for search and rescue operations in their areas of responsibility (SAR zones), and to activate it at the moment they receive a distress call from a vessel within this area. Coastal states are obliged to take all measures necessary in order to coordinate the operation for the rescue of the persons in distress – that is, they are under an obligation of conduct – and, in addition, they are called upon to cooperate with other neighbouring countries. For state parties to the SOLAS and SAR Conventions, there is the additional obligation, since July 2006, to ensure that a 'place of safety' is furnished for the persons rescued at sea.

In this context, the question of attribution presents fewer problems than in the case of flag states. The conduct that might lead to an internationally wrongful act will always be attributed to the coastal states pursuant to Article 4 of the ARSIWA, since the administrators of the rescue coordination centres are *de jure* organs of the latter states. Establishing a breach of the primary obligations set out above, and thus of an internationally wrongful act, is subject to an individual assessment in each case.

To take the example of the incident of April/May 2011, the coastal state that was mainly involved was Italy. According to the PACE report, the Rome Maritime Rescue Coordination Centre (MRCC) was notified by Father Zerai about the boat on 27 March, and it immediately undertook several steps to coordinate the rescue. First, it tried to contact the boat. From the audio records, it is clear that the conversation was interrupted before any substantial exchange could take place. It also sent out a number of messages, using various networks and satellites, to make sure they reached a maximum number of vessels in the area. In addition, it launched a DISTRESS call on the Inmarsat–C Gateway Enhanced Group Call (EGC), which was addressed to all ships transiting in the Sicily Channel. Finally, it informed Malta MRCC by phone, and later by fax, as well as the NATO headquarters allied command in Naples and Frontex. It is also noteworthy that Rome MRCC kept sending this distress message every four hours, for ten days.[85]

Nevertheless, Italy never initiated a search and rescue operation as such. The explanation given to Ms Strik was that they did not have available resources, and that they did not consider themselves as the responsible authority because the boat was not located in the Italian SAR zone.[86]

With regard to Italy's responsibility, the first remark to be made is that the boat in distress was not within Italy's SAR zone. Thus Italy was not *prima facie* under all of the aforementioned obligations. Nevertheless, the 2004 IMO Guidelines on the Treatment of Persons Rescued at Sea set out that:

> when appropriate, the first RCC contacted should immediately begin efforts to transfer the case to the RCC responsible for the region in which the assistance is being rendered . . . The first RCC, however, is responsible for coordinating the case until the responsible RCC or other competent authority assumes responsibility.[87]

As mentioned above, though non-binding, these guidelines are generally recognised as an important means for interpretation. According to the guidelines, Italy should thus have acted as the responsible coastal state, because Libya, which was the responsible RCC *ratione loci*, was unable to assume responsibility. In actual fact, Italy never informed the Libyan RCC. However, as reported by Ms Strik:

> the Rome MRCC has confirmed to me that Tripoli MRCC at the relevant time did not respond to attempts by the Rome MRCC to communicate or to have an exchange of information.[88]

Accordingly, can it be concluded that Italy was in breach of these obligations? On the one hand, Italy did take all necessary measures to inform not only all the vessels in the vicinity, but also the Maltese RCC, as well as international organisations (NATO, EU Frontex) engaged in activities in the area of the incident. Thus it tried to coordinate the rescue of the persons concerned, and it did cooperate with other states. On the other hand, Italy did not launch a search and rescue operation on the scene as such. However, as stated by the Italian authorities, they did not have any search and rescue units available to dispatch, while, erroneously, they did not consider themselves as the responsible RCC. This, in the author's view, was the most significant failure of Italy in this case; namely, that it considered itself not responsible and it did not undertake any further measures. However, taking into account that the IMO guidelines are not binding *per se*, and that the relevant obligations are obligations of conduct *par excellence* and not of result, it is hard to hold Italy responsible in this regard. To hold otherwise would also require that we read obligations of result into Article 98 of LOSC and the SAR Convention, which would not find support in the relevant state practice.[89]

A similar conclusion may be drawn insofar as human rights law is concerned. Even if the persons had come under its jurisdiction, Italy had, to a large extent, abided by its positive obligations concerning the right to life. It did take all the measures available under the circumstances to notify all the relevant stakeholders (vessels, states, international organisations) and to cooperate in the rescue of these persons. In addition, it lacked the necessary resources, i.e. available search and rescue units, to send on the scene. Hence, even though the omission is attributable to Italy, Italy should not be held in violation of the right to life (Article 2 European Convention on Human Rights).

In conclusion, the international responsibility of coastal states for breaches of obligations under the law of the sea and under human rights law would usually arise when they fail to effectively coordinate the rescue operation and to cooperate with each other for the provision of a temporary place of safety. Therefore, the establishment of the responsibility of the states concerned depends on the individual assessment of each case.

7.3.3 The responsibility of international organisations

International organisations, in particular the European Union and, allegedly, NATO, may be involved in rescue operations. In the previous section, the relevant obligations of these international organisations were discussed. In this part, the question to address is whether the European Union or NATO incur responsibility in cases where they or their member states fail to rescue people at sea, or when they fail to disembark the rescued persons in a 'place of safety'.

3. c (i) The European Union

To begin with, in respect of the European Union, it is evident that responsibility questions would only arise in cases of Frontex-coordinated operations. According to Article 9 of the Regulation 656/2014:

> Member States shall observe their obligation to render assistance to any vessel or person in distress at sea and during a sea operation, they shall ensure that their participating units comply with that obligation, in accordance with international law and in respect of fundamental rights [. . .] For the purpose of dealing with search and rescue situations that may occur during a sea operation, the operational plan shall contain, in accordance with relevant international law including that on search and rescue . . .

Accordingly, it rests primarily with the member states to adhere to the relevant obligations in the course of Frontex operations. However, Frontex has the responsibility to include in the 'operation plan', which it draws up in cooperation with the member states,[90] all the specific rules of engagement. It is thus questioned whether any failure in this regard may also be attributable to Frontex.

Without dwelling upon the controversial question of attribution of responsibility to international organisations,[91] it is the view of the present author that the conduct of the member states in this regard cannot be attributed to the European Union. In particular, the participating units and the rescue coordination centre of the host member state cannot qualify as 'organs' or 'agents' of the European Union within the meaning of Article 6 of ARIO.[92] Furthermore, the European Union falls short of asserting effective control over the conduct of the member states in this respect, as required under Article 7 of ARIO.[93]

Does this mean that the European Union cannot be held responsible for the violation of the applicable human rights law? On the contrary, the European Union may incur 'indirect responsibility' or responsibility for the acts of its member states under Article 14 of ARIO, namely for aiding or assisting the wrongful conduct of the member states. In addition, the European Union may incur 'parallel' responsibility for not preventing the international wrongful act. As regards the former, Article 14 provides that:

> An international organisation which aids or assists a State or another international organisation in the commission of an internationally wrongful act by the State or the latter organisation is internationally responsible for doing so if: (a) the former organisation does so with knowledge of the circumstances of the internationally wrongful act; and (b) the act would be internationally wrongful if committed by that organisation.[94]

Frontex does aid and assist states, in that it not only draws up the 'operation plan', but significantly facilitates the actual action of the participating units by sending the relevant assets of member states to be placed under the disposal of the host member states, as well as by coordinating the joint operations, including the rescue operations. Thus, arguably, the conduct of the participating units in the course of the operations is actively facilitated by Frontex, as these units would not be in this particular location without Frontex's coordination. As to the requirement of 'knowledge' under Article 14 of ARIO, it is asserted that through the establishment of the International Coordination Centre, Frontex does acquire 'knowledge' of the particular circumstances of a non-rescue incident.[95] It follows that there are sound reasons to hold the European Union responsible for 'aiding and assisting' in this regard.

With respect to the latter option of 'parallel' responsibility, it is certain that the European Union is under the obligation to safeguard, first and foremost, the right to life.[96] Moreover, Frontex is supposed to 'ensure the operational implementation of all the organisational aspects, including the presence of a staff member of the Agency during the joint operations and pilot projects referred to in this Article';[97] thus it is presumed to have 'knowledge' of the conduct of the rescue operations. Accordingly, should any violation of these rules occur that Frontex could have prevented, its responsibility for the violation of the obligation to prevent may arise.

3. c (ii) NATO

Moving on to NATO, it has been previously submitted that this organisation, at least in the context of Operation Unified Protector, was not under any obligation in question. In any case, assuming, for the sake of argument, that NATO had been under these obligations, would it have incurred responsibility for the failure to save the lives of 'boat people' in 2011?

To hold NATO responsible for the omission to render assistance to the boat in distress would require finding that the omission amounted to a breach of an international obligation by NATO as such, and was attributable to NATO itself and not to its member states. In the present case, the key question is whether the decision to leave the 'boat people' without assistance was made by the NATO commander or by the commanding officer of the warship concerned. If the former, then the conduct would be attributable to NATO; if the latter, to the flag state. In principle, this would depend on the rules of engagement of Operation Unified Protector, which set forth the operational procedures to be followed by the warships in the context of the operation, and additionally on whether the operational command in such cases would rest with NATO or with the contributing member state. Such information, however, is not generally available to the public, and as stated above, NATO has refuted any involvement in the incident.

However, to the author's knowledge, NATO's position concerning rescue at sea is that the member states alone, not NATO, are responsible, even though the warships may be under NATO's command. Member states alone are also responsible for the actions *ex post facto*. A NATO commander cannot give any order concerning the rendering of assistance or its aftermath. This is also the view of individual member states – namely, that NATO has no formal responsibility or any role in rendering assistance, which remains the responsibility of individual states.[98]

With regard to human rights law in particular, it has been argued that NATO cannot be responsible for any violation of the right to life, since it is not bound by such an obligation with regard to the 'boat people' in question. This means that it falls upon the flag states of the vessels participating in the operation to render assistance to the persons concerned, as well as to protect their right to life. It is well worth mentioning here that these flag states could invoke the justification that they were under NATO command and, hypothetically, that their warships were not able to render assistance to the persons in distress due to their mandate. However, according to the recent judgement of the European Court of Human Rights in the case of *Jaloud v. The Netherlands*, since the participating states retain the 'full command and control' of their units in the course of multinational operations, they are not absolved from their obligations under international law[99] – in the present case, from their obligation to notify and cooperate with other states and assets in this regard.

This notwithstanding, these states could claim that they were acting under a Chapter VII Resolution and thus, by virtue of Article 103 of the UN Charter, their obligations under the LOSC and SOLAS Conventions were superseded.[100] A counter-argument to this would be that the right to life is such a fundamental right, attaining the status of a peremptory norm, that it cannot be superseded by a SC Resolution under Chapter VII, since *jus cogens* sets limits to the powers of the Security Council.[101] Alternatively, it could be argued that, in the light of the *Al-Jedda v. UK* case, there ought to be a different interpretation of the relevant resolutions.[102]

In conclusion, NATO was under no obligation to rescue persons on the high seas, and thus it could not incur any responsibility under international law. This, however, does not exonerate its member states from their individual responsibility, *qua* flag states, in this regard. As remarked above, these comments are without prejudice to NATO's upcoming involvement in the Aegean sea and its potential responsibility.

7.4 Conclusion

The recent incidents in the Mediterranean, including the 'left to die' boat incident, reveal the inadequacies, the lack of resources, or even the inertia on the part of a number of actors – states, international organisations, private mariners – in rescuing people in distress at sea. Indeed, many opportunities for saving the lives of persons in the above-mentioned incident were lost. Of course, this incident is just the tip of the iceberg, since an incredible number of silent tragedies occur every year in the Mediterranean. Nevertheless, the main efforts of the states concerned are directed towards securing their borders rather than saving people's lives. Even in the aftermath of the more recent death of more than 700 people in the central Mediterranean in April 2015, states and the international community do not seem ready to seriously address this scourge.[103]

The present inquiry focused on the issue of responsibility on the part of both states and international organisations that may arise from the failure to save lives at sea and from not safeguarding a 'place of safety' for disembarkation. For international responsibility to arise, there has to be conduct that is attributable to a state or an international organisation, and this conduct must amount to a breach of an obligation of that state or of that organisation. Accordingly, prior to the discussion of any responsibility in this regard, the primary obligations incumbent upon the flag or the coastal states, as well as upon the international organisations involved in rescue operations, had to be ascertained.

The relevant primary obligations were indeed succinctly presented and discussed, including obligations under the law of the sea and international human rights law. Special reference was made to the respective obligations of international organisations, which, according to the present author, are not identical to those of states. Having identified these obligations, the responsibility, first, of the flag states, second, of the coastal states involved in such operations as well as, finally, the potential responsibility of the European Union or NATO was assessed against the background of the relevant rules of international responsibility. The element of attribution of the conduct to the state or international organisation and the element of breach of the primary obligations were discussed in each case. The discussion was not made only on a theoretical level, but also in relation to the real 'left to die' incident.

As has become apparent from the discussion of the responsibility questions in cases of non-rescue at sea, many 'stakeholders' – namely states, both flag and coastal states, and international organisations and in particular the European Union – 'share' the international responsibility for not meeting their obligations in this regard. That the legal framework is not perfectly adequate is no excuse for this inertia on the part of all relevant 'stakeholders'. It is sad, but true, that the 'dark side of globalisation' is manifesting itself in the seas and along the coasts of the Mediterranean.

Notes

* This chapter is an updated and revised version of Efthymios Papastavridis, 'Rescuing Migrants at Sea: The Responsibility of States under International Law', in *Protection des Migrants et des Réfugiés au XXIe Siècle: Aspects de Droit* [Migration and Refugee Protection in the Twenty-first century: International Aspects], eds Guy Goodwin-Gill and Philippe Weckel (Leiden: Nijhoff for The Hague Academy of International Law, 2015). The author would like to thank Dr Thomas Gammeltoft-Hansen for his invaluable comments on a previous draft of this chapter.

1 See at http://data.unhcr.org/mediterranean/regional.php (accessed 5 March 2016).

2 See at http://missingmigrants.iom.int/sites/default/files/Mediterranean_Update_29_January_2016_0.pdf (accessed 9 February 2016).

3 It is reported that 'the boat – that had sailed from Misrata in Libya – carried mainly migrants from Eritrea, Somalia and Ghana. After a journey of two days, the vessel began taking on water when its motor stopped working. Some passengers set fire to a piece of material to try to attract the attention of passing ships. However, the fire spread to the rest of the boat, creating a panic. As the migrants all moved to one side, the boat capsized. . .Although an emergency response involving the Italian Coastguard resulted in the rescue of 155 survivors, the total number of dead was reported as more than 360'. Jasmine Coppens, 'The Lampedusa Disaster: How to Prevent Further Loss of Life at sea?', *International Journal on Marine Navigation and Safety of Sea Transportation* 7 no.4 (2013), 589.

4   See UNHCR, '2014 becomes the deadliest year at sea off Yemen', News Stories, 17 October 2014, available at www.unhcr.org/544103b06.html.

5   Reportedly, in 2012 Australia received 17,202 asylum seekers by boat, its highest annual number. See Janet Phillips and Harriet Spinks, 'Boat arrivals in Australia since 1976', Parliamentary Library Background note, updated 23 July 2013 (Canberra, ACT: Parliament of Australia, 2011), 22; as cited in Jane McAdam, 'Australia and Asylum Seekers', *International Journal of Refugee Law* 25 no. 3 (2013), 445.

6   The usual measures employed in order to tackle this problem, besides interception, are *inter alia* pre-inspection, visa requirements, carrier sanctions, 'safe third country' concepts, security zones, and international zones; see Guy S. Goodwin-Gill and Jane McAdam, *The Refugee in International Law*, 3rd edn (Oxford: Oxford University Press, 2007), 374.

7   In September 2013, the newly elected conservative government in Australia committed to a policy of pushing back boats carrying 'unauthorised maritime arrivals'. See e.g. on Operation Sovereign Borders, The Liberal Party of Australia, 'The Coalition's Operation Sovereign Borders Policy' (July 2013), available at www. liberal.org.au/our plan/immigration. For commentary on recent Australian policy, see Mary Crock, 'Shadow Plays, Shifting Sands and International Refugee Law: Convergences in the Asia–Pacific', *International and Comparative Law Quarterly* 63 no. 2 (2014), 247–280.

8   From time to time, European states such as Italy or Spain have engaged in interception at sea. Most famous have been the 'pushback' operations conducted by Italy in cooperation with Libya in the central Mediterranean sea; see *inter alia* Mariagiulia Giuffré, 'State Responsibility Beyond Borders: What Legal Basis for Italy's Push-backs to Libya?', *International Journal of Refugee Law* 24 no. 4 (2012), 692–734.

9   Frontex was established in 2004 to help EU member states in implementing Union legislation on the surveillance of EU borders, including maritime borders, and to coordinate their operational cooperation. See Council Regulation (EC) No 2007/2004 of 26 October 2004 establishing a European Agency for the Management of Operational Cooperation at the External Borders of the Member States of the European Union as amended by Regulation (EU) No 1168/2011 of the European Parliament and of the Council of 25 October 2011, OJ L 304 of 22.11.2011 (henceforth 2011 Regulation). For further information see http://frontex.europa.eu/ (last accessed 6 March 2016). On the surveillance operations of Frontex, see Efthymios Papastavridis, 'Fortress Europe and FRONTEX: Within or Without International Law?', *Nordic Journal of International Law* 79 no. 1 (2010), 75.

10 See Conclusions of the Special Meeting of the EU Council of 23 April 2015, available at www.consilium.europa.eu/en/meetings/european-council/2015/04/23/; also http://frontex.europa.eu/news/frontex-expands-its-joint-operation-triton-udpbHP.

11 See further information, at www.eeas.europa.eu/csdp/missions-and-operations/eunav for-med/pdf/factsheet_eunavfor_med_en.pdf (accessed 29 January 2016).

12 See Statement by the NATO Secretary-General on NATO support to assist with the refugee and migrant crisis (25 February 2016), available at www.nato.int/cps/en/natohq/opinions_128372.htm.

13 In the words of James Pugash, 'the master of the ship is obliged to rescue those in peril on the sea, but no state is bound to accept those rescued': see James Z. Pugash, 'The Dilemma of the Sea Refugee: Rescue Without Refuge', *Harvard Journal of International Law* 18 no. 3 (1977), 578.

14 See Ernst Willheim, '*MV Tampa*: The Australian Response', *International Journal of Refugee Law* 15 no. 2 (2003), 168.

15 On these issues see particularly the chapters by Douglas Guilfoyle, Fabiane Baxewanos, Niels Frenzen, and Maïté Fernandez in this volume.

16 On Sunday, 8 May 2011, the British newspaper *The Guardian* reported the story of a boat carrying 72 persons, among them asylum seekers, women and children, which left Tripoli (Libya) for the Italian island of Lampedusa at the end of March 2011. After

sixteen days at sea, the boat was washed up on the Libyan shore with only eleven survivors. See 'Aircraft Carrier Left Us to Die, Say Migrants', *The Guardian*, 8 May 2011.

17 See the report by the Parliamentary Assembly of the Council of Europe, 'Lives Lost in the Mediterranean sea: Who Is Responsible?' (Strasbourg: PACE Committee on Migration, Refugees and Displaced Persons, March 2012), available at assembly.coe.int/CommitteeDocs/2012/20120329 mig RPT.EN.pdf.

18 PACE, 'Lives Lost', para. 148.

19 PACE, 'Lives Lost'.

20 See United Nations Convention on the Law of the sea, 1833 *UNTS* 397, entered into force 16 November 1994; as at 7 January 2015, LOSC has 167 parties, including the EC, available at www.un.org/Depts/los/reference_files/chronological_lists_of_ratifications.htm#The United Nations Convention on the Law of the sea (accessed 5 March 2016).

21 The *Eleanor* case (1809) 165 English Reports p. 1,068. See also Richard Barnes, 'The International Law of the Sea and Migration Control', in *Extraterritorial Immigration Control: Legal Challenges*, eds Bernard Ryan and Valsamis Mitsilegas, 103–150 (Leiden: Nijhoff, 2010), 135.

22 See *The New York* (1818) 3 Wheaton 59 at 68; compare *The Rebecca* (1929) 4 Reports of International Arbitral Awards 444 at 447–448.

23 Council Decision of 26 April 2010 supplementing the Schengen Borders Code as regards the surveillance of the sea external borders in the context of operational cooperation coordinated by the European Agency for the Management of Operational Cooperation at the External Borders of the Member States of the European Union (2010/252/EU), (2010) OJ L 111/20, para. 1.3, Part II, Annex. The Decision was annulled by the Court of Justice of the EU; see ECJ, *European Parliament v. Council of the European Union*, 5 September 2012, Case C-355/10 (2012), adopted.

24 See Article 9 (f) of Regulation (EU) No 656/2014 of the European Parliament and of the Council of 15 May 2014, establishing rules for the surveillance of the external sea borders in the context of operational cooperation coordinated by the European Agency for the Management of Operational Cooperation at the External Borders of the Member States of the European Union (2014) OJ L 189/93.

25 See e.g. Article 11 of the 1910 International Convention for the Unification of Certain Rules Relating to Assistance and Salvage at sea.

26 For example, Barnes reports that 'in the UK the master has a duty, upon receiving a distress signal, to proceed to their assistance, unless he is unable. . .Failure to do so is a criminal offence'; see Richard Barnes, 'Refugee Law at Sea', *International and Comparative Law Quarterly* 53 no. 1 (2004), 50 (note 12).

27 The classification of obligations, for example between obligations of result and obligations of conduct in international law, can be traced back to Roberto Ago's term as a Special Rapporteur of the International Law Commission. On the topic of state responsibility, see Sixth Report on State Responsibility by Mr Ago, Special Rapporteur, *Yearbook of the International Law Commission* (vol II, Part One 1967) 4, 20. See also Jean Combacau, 'Obligations de résultat et obligations de comportement: Quelques questions et pas de réponse [Obligations of result and obligations of conduct: Some question, no answers]', in *Le droit international: unité et diversité*, ed. Paul Reuter, 181–204 (Pedone 1981), 181.

28 See generally on the obligations of flag states Yoshinobu Takei, 'Assessing Flag State Performance in Legal Terms: Clarifications of the Margin of Discretion', *International Journal of Marine and Coastal Law* 28 no. 1 (2013), 97–133.

29 ITLOS, Request for an Advisory Opinion submitted by the Sub-Regional Fisheries Commission (SRFC), Case No. 21 Advisory Opinion of 2 April 2015; at paras 16–141.

30 ICJ, *Pulp Mills on the River Uruguay (Argentina v. Uruguay)*, Judgment, ICJ Reports 2010, para. 197.

31 See International Convention for the Safety of Life at Sea, adopted 1 November 1974, entered into force 25 May 1980 (1,184 *UNTS* No. 278); as at 11 February 2016 SOLAS had 162 contracting States, available at www.imo.org/About/Conventions/StatusOf Conventions/Pages/Default.aspx (accessed 5 March 2016).

32 SOLAS, Chapter V, Regulation 33 (1).

33 See International Convention on Maritime Search and Rescue, adopted 27 April 1979, entered into force 22 June 1985, (1,405 *UNTS* No. 23,489); as at 11 February 2016 SAR Convention had 106 contracting States, available at www.imo.org/ About/Conventions/StatusOfConventions/Pages/Default.aspx (accessed 5 March 2016) (henceforth SAR Convention).

34 See also SOLAS Chapter V, Regulation 7; and also Seline Trevisanut, 'Search and Rescue Operations in the Mediterranean: Factor of Cooperation or Conflict?', *The International Journal of Marine and Coastal Law* 25 (2010), 524.

35 In August 2001, in response to an Australian-coordinated search and rescue operation, the Norwegian *MV Tampa* rescued 433 asylum seekers from a sinking Indonesian flagged vessel 75 nautical miles off the Australian coast. When the *Tampa* began heading towards the Australian port of Christmas Island, the Australian authorities intercepted the vessel before entering; see the relevant discussion in Chantal Marie-Jeanne Bostock, 'The International Legal Obligation Owed to the Asylum Seekers on the *M. V. Tampa*', *International Journal of Refugee Law* 14 nos 2 and 3 (2002), 279.

36 See *inter alia* IMO Assembly Resolution on the Review of Safety Measures and Procedures for the Treatment of Persons Rescued at Sea, 22nd session, Agenda Item No. 8, IMO Assembly Res. A.920(22), November 2001 and UNHCR, 'Note on International Protection', 53rd session, UN doc.A/AC.96/965 (11 Sept. 2002).

37 Amendments to SOLAS Chapter V, Regulation 33: IMO, MSC Res 153 (78), MSC Doc. 78/26.add.1, Annex 5 (20 May 2004). The amendments entered into force 1 January 2006. They are binding upon all parties to the SOLAS and SAR Conventions, except Malta, which opted out and thus is not bound; see IMO, Status of multilateral Conventions and instruments in respect of which the International Maritime Organisation or its Secretary-General performs depositary or other functions, at p. 42, available at www.imo.org/About/Conventions/StatusOfConventions/Documents/ Status%20-%202014.pdf. (accessed 9 February 2016)

38 See Article 4.1–1 of SOLAS and the Annex of SAR, paragraph 3.1.9.

39 Resolution MSC. 167(78), adopted 20 May 2004; available at http://docs.imo.org.

40 See Article 31 (3) (b) of Vienna Convention on the Law of Treaties (1969) (opened for signature 23 May 1969), 1155 UNTS 331 (henceforth VCLT). See also Hazel Fox, 'Article 31(3)(A) and (B) of the Vienna Convention and the "Kasikili/ Sedudu Island" case', in *Treaty Interpretation and the Vienna Convention on the Law of Treaties: 30 Years on*, eds Malgosia Fitzmaurice *et al.*, 59–74 (Leiden: Nijhoff, 2010), 59.

41 See Article 98 (2), UNCLOS and SOLAS, Chapter V, Regulation 7.

42 SOLAS Convention, Chapter V, Regulation 7.

43 See SAR, Annex I, Chapter 3.

44 As summarised by Crawford, 'obligations of result involve in some measures a guarantee of the outcome, whereas obligations of conduct are in the nature of best efforts obligations, obligations to do all in one's power to achieve a result, but without ultimate commitment'; see James Crawford, Second Report on State Responsibility, at para. 67. See also relevant comments in Pierre-Marie Dupuy, 'Reviewing the Difficulties of Codification: On Ago's Classification of Obligations of Means and Obligations of Result in Relation to State Responsibility', *European Journal of International Law* 10 no. 2 (1999), 379.

45 Amendments to SOLAS Chapter V, Regulation 33: IMO, MSC Res 153 (78), MSC Doc. 78/26.add.1, Annex 5 (20 May 2004), paragraph 3.1.9 of the rules annexed to the Search and Rescue Convention 1979.

46 See Crawford, Second Report on State Responsibility (note 44 above).

47 See further discussion in Efthymios Papastavridis, 'We Saved them, Now What? The Unresolved Question of Disembarkation of Rescued Persons at Sea', in *La Contribution de la Convention des Nations Unies sur le Droit de la Mer à la Bonne gouvernance des mers et des oceans* [*The contribution of the United Nations Convention on the Law of the Sea to Good Governance of the Oceans and Seas*], ed. Jose M. Sobrino Heradia, 587–606 (Naples: Editoriale Scientifica, 2014), 615–635.

48 On the term 'users of the seas' see Emmanuel Roucounas, 'Effectiveness of International Law for the Users of the Seas', in *Cursos Euromediterráneos Bancaja de Derecho Internacional*, Vol. 8, ed., Jorge Cardona Llorens, 855–922 (Valencia, 2009).

49 'Everyone's right to life shall be protected by law. No one shall be deprived of his life intentionally save in the execution of a sentence of a court following his conviction of a crime for which this penalty is provided by law'. See Article 2 of the European Convention for the Protection of Human Rights and Fundamental Freedoms, 4 November 1950, 213 *UNTS* 221.

50 'Every human being has the inherent right to life. This right shall be protected by law. No one shall be arbitrarily deprived of his life': see Article 6 of the International Covenant on Civil and Political Rights, 19 December 1966, 999 *UNTS* 171.

51 See *Osman v. United Kingdom* Application No. 87/1997/871/1083, Grand Chamber Judgment of 28 October 1998, 29 *EHRR* 245. See also on the positive obligation dimension of this right *Furdík v. Slovakia* (Admissibility decision), Application no. 42994/05, 2 December 2008 and *Kemaloglu v. Turkey*, Application no. 19986/06, 10 April 2012.

52 See *inter alia Hirsi Jamaa ao v. Italy* App. no 27765/09 (European Court of Human Rights, Grand Chamber Judgment of 23 February 2012) and *Medvedyev et al. v. France*, judgment of 29 March 2010 (Grand Chamber, Application No. 3394/03). See also Committee against Torture, *J.H.A. v. Spain* (Comm. no. 323/2007) Decision of 21 November 2008.

53 See specifically Efthymios Papastavridis, 'European Convention on Human Rights and the Law of the Sea: the Strasbourg Court in Unchartered Waters?', in *The Interpretation and Application of the European Convention of Human Rights: Legal and Practical Implications*, eds Malgosia Fitzmaurice and Panos Merkouris, 117–146 (Leiden: Nijhoff, 2013), 117. See more generally the introductory chapter as well as the chapter by Marko Milanovic in this volume; Marko Milanovic, *Extraterritorial Application of Human Rights Treaties: Law, Principles and Policy* (Oxford: Oxford University Press, 2011) and Michal Gondek, *The Reach of Human Rights in a Globalising World: Extraterritorial Application of Human Rights Treaties* (Antwerp: Intersentia, 2009).

54 See *Hirsi Jamaa ao v. Italy*, case, para. 81 and *Medvedyev et al. v. France*, para. 67.

55 For cases of interception of vessels and the right to life see European Court of Human Rights, *Xhavara and Others v. Italy and Albania* (Application No 39473/98), Admissibility Decision of 11 January 2001; Judgment of 3 May 2009 as well as UN Committee against Torture, *Sonko v. Spain* (Comm. No. 368/2010), Decision of 20 February 2012.

56 See Article 8 of ILC Articles on Responsibility of States for Internationally Wrongful Acts, UN General Assembly Official Records; 56th Session, Supp. No. 10 at UN. Doc A/56/10; at 31 (henceforth ARSIWA). http://untreaty.un.org/ilc/texts/instruments/english/commentaries/9_6_2001.pdf. See also on persons acting on state 'instructions', James Crawford, *State Responsibility: The General Part* (Cambridge: Cambridge University Press, 2014), 144–146.

57 SOLAS, Chapter V, Regulation 7.

58 See Marko Milanovic, '*Extraterritoriality and Human Rights: Prospects and Challenges*', in the present volume and the relevant case law therein. See also Thomas Gammeltoft-Hansen and James Hathaway, 'Non-Refoulement in a World of Cooperative Deterrence', *Columbia Journal of Transnational Law* 53 no. 2 (2015), 257–271.

59 On the distinction between positive and negative obligations as a third model of extraterritorial obligation see Milanovic, *Extraterritorial Application of Human Rights Treaties*, 209–222.

60 See also the remarks of Seline Trevisanut, 'Is There a Right to be Rescued at Sea? A Constructive View', *QIL (Questions of International Law)* 4 (2014), 3–15.

61 See ARIO Commentary, at p. 31.

62 This means that, unlike states, which have a general competence to act, 'an international organisation can only act where it has been entrusted by the states with the power to act'; see ICJ, *Legality of the Use by a State of Nuclear Weapons in Armed Conflict* (Request by the World Health Organisation), ICJ Reports (1996), at 78–89, para. 25.

63 See *inter alia:* Case C-286/90 *Poulsen and Diva Navigation* (1992) ECR I-6019, paras 9–10; Case C-162/96 *Racke* (1998) ECR I-3655, paras 45–46; Case C-366/10, *The Air Association of America*, Judgment of December 2011, para. 101. See also Alessandra Giannelli, 'Customary International Law in the European Union', in *International Law as Law of the European Union*, eds Enzo Cannizzaro *et al.*, 93–110 (Leiden: Brill, 2012), 93.

64 See declarations of the contracting parties to the LOSC at www.un.org/Depts/los/convention_agreements/convention_declarations.htm.

65 As the ICJ very famously stated in the *Reparations case*, '[u]nder international law the organisation must be deemed to have those powers which, though not expressly provided in the charter, are conferred upon it by necessary implication as being essential to the performance of its duties'; ICJ Reports, 1949, 174, at 182.

66 See Regulation 656/2014 (note 32 above).

67 Charter of Fundamental Rights of the European Union (2010) OJ C83/389.

68 On 22 March 2011, NATO responded to the UN's call to prevent the supply of 'arms and related materials' to Libya by agreeing to launch an operation to enforce the arms embargo against the country. 'The next day [. . .] Nato maritime assets stopped and searched any vessel they suspected of carrying arms, related materials or mercenaries to or from Libya. In support of UNSCR 1973, Nato then agreed to enforce the UN-mandated no-fly zone over Libya on 24 March 2011. The Alliance took sole command and control of the international military effort for Libya on 31 March 2011'. The Operation ended on 1 November 2011, available at www.nato.int/cps/en/natolive/topics_71652.htm.

69 See *ASR Commentary*, at 38. On the issue of attribution see *inter alia* Luigi Condorelli and Claus Kress, 'The Rules of Attribution: General Considerations', in *The Law of International Responsibility*, eds James Crawford *et al.*, 221–236 (Oxford: Oxford University Press, 2010), 221.

70 *ASR Commentary*, 54.

71 *ASR Commentary*, 54.

72 On the question of responsibility of flag states for acts or omissions of their state vessels, see Patricia Mallia, *Migrant Smuggling by Sea: Combating a Current Threat to Maritime Security Through the Creation of a Cooperative Framework* (Leiden: Nijhoff, 2010), 105.

73 See e.g. Section 105 of the UK Merchant Shipping Act, 1995: 'The master of any United Kingdom ship may cause any person on board the ship to be put under restraint if and for so long as it appears to him necessary or expedient in the interest of safety or for the preservation of good order or discipline on board the ship'; available at www.legislation.gov.uk/ukpga/1995/21/section/105

74 ARSIWA Commentary, at 43.

75 See ASR Commentary, at 47. On '*de facto* organs' of States see also *Application of the Convention on the Prevention and Punishment of the Crime of Genocide (Bosnia and Herzegovina v. Serbia and Montenegro)*, Judgment, 26 February 2007, para. 404 *et seq.*

76 See Regulation 33, Chapter V of the SOLAS Convention.

77 See PACE, 'Lives Lost', para. 28.

78 PACE, 'Lives Lost', paras 36–38.

79 PACE, 'Lives Lost', para. 8.

80 PACE, 'Lives Lost', paras 85–57.

81 PACE, 'Lives Lost', paras 41–43.

82 See note 55 above and accompanying text.

83 See Milanovic, *Extraterritorial Application of Human Rights Treaties*.
84 See Article 92 of LOSC. On the nature of the high seas, see Efthymios Papastavridis, 'The Right of Visit on the High Seas in a Theoretical Perspective: *Mare Liberum v. Mare Clausum* Revisited', *Leiden Journal of International Law* 24 (2011), 52–53.
85 PACE, 'Lives Lost', paras 56–61.
86 PACE, 'Lives Lost', para. 69.
87 Resolution MSC. 167(78), adopted 20 May 2004, para. 6.7, available at www.imo.org/OurWork/Facilitation/IllegalMigrants/Documents/MSC.167(78).pdf
88 PACE, 'Lives Lost', para. 66.
89 See in this regard Efthymios Papastavridis, *The Interception of Vessels on the High Seas: Contemporary Challenges to the Legal Order of the Oceans* (Oxford: Hart, 2013), 294–300.
90 See Art. 3 (a) of the 2011 Regulation.
91 See generally on attribution of conduct Francesco Messineo, 'Attribution of Conduct', in *Principles of Shared Responsibility in International Law: An Appraisal of the State of the Art*, eds André Nollkaemper and Ilias Plakokefalos, 60–97 (Cambridge: Cambridge University Press, 2014). In relation especially to the EU, see Pieter Jan Kuiper and Esa Paasivirta, 'EU International Responsibility and its Attribution: From the Inside Looking Out', in *The International Responsibility of the European Union*, eds Malcolm Evans and Panos Koutrakos, 35–71 (Oxford: Hart, 2013), 35.
92 According to Article 6 of ARIO, 'the conduct of an organ or agent of an international organisation in the performance of functions of that organ or agent shall be considered an act of that organisation under international law, whatever position the organ or agent holds in respect of the organisation'.
93 Article 7 enunciates that '[t]he conduct of an organ of a State or an organ or agent of an international organisation that is placed at the disposal of another international organisation shall be considered under international law an act of the latter organisation if the organisation exercises effective control over that conduct'.
94 See ARIO Commentary at 36–37; also August Reinisch, 'Aid or Assistance and Direction and Control between States and International Organizations in the Commission of Internationally Wrongful Acts', *International Organizations Law Review* 7 no. 1 (2010), 63–77.
95 See e.g. Article 9 (2) (b) of the Draft Regulation.
96 See Article 2 of the Charter of Fundamental Rights of the European Union.
97 See 3 (a) (3) of the 2011 Regulation.
98 Information provided under conditions of anonymity by a legal adviser of a NATO member state which participated in Operation Unified Protector.
99 European Court of Human Rights, *The Case of Jaloud v. The Netherlands* (Application no. 47708/08), Grand Chamber, Judgment of 20 November 2014 para. 143. See also short commentary of the case, available at www.ejiltalk.org/jaloud-v-netherlands-new-directions-in-extra-territorial-military-operations/ (accessed 9 February 2016).
100 Article 103 of the UN Charter reads as follows: 'in the event of a conflict between the obligations of the Members of the United Nations under the present Charter and their obligations under any other international agreement, their obligations under the present Charter shall prevail'. See also Christine Chinkin, 'Jus Cogens, Article 103 of the UN Charter and Other Hierarchical Techniques of Conflict Solution', *Finnish Yearbook of International Law* 17 (2006), 63.
101 Judge Lauterpacht in his Separate Opinion in the *Genocide* case between Bosnia-Herzegovina and FRY referred to *jus cogens* and Security Council resolutions maintaining that 'the relief which Article 103 may give to the Security Council in case of one of its decisions and an operative treaty cannot – as a matter of simply hierarchy of norms – extend to a conflict between a Security Council resolution and *jus cogens*': Separate Opinion (1993) ICJ Rep, p. 440.
102 Acts *contra juris gestionis* are beyond the powers of an institution, *in casu* the Security Council and therefore the provisions of the UN Charter on the latter's powers have to be interpreted and executed in a way that is compatible with peremptory norms.

See also the European Convention on Human Rights, *Al-Jedda v. UK* case, App. No. 27021/08, (Grand Chamber) Judgment of 7 July 2011, para. 102.
103   On the reactions to the EU Council Conclusions see *inter alia* Cathryn Costello and Mariagiulia Giuffré, 'Drowning Refugees, Migrants, and Shame at Sea: The EU's Response'. Blog in two parts, 27 April 2015. Oxford: Oxford Human Rights Hub, 2015. Available at http://ohrh.law.ox.ac.uk/drowning-refugees-migrants-and-shame-at-sea-the-eus-response-part-i/ and http://ohrh.law.ox.ac.uk/drowning-refugees-migrants-and-shame-at-sea-the-eu-response-part-ii/.

Bibliography

Barnes, Richard. 'Refugee Law at Sea'. *International and Comparative Law Quarterly* 53 no. 1 (2004): 47–77.

Barnes, Richard. 'The International Law of the Sea and Migration Control'. In *Extraterritorial Immigration Control: Legal Challenges*, edited by Bernard Ryan and Valsamis Mitsilegas, 103–150. Leiden: Nijhoff, 2010.

Bostock, Chantal Marie-Jeanne. 'The International Legal Obligations owed to the Asylum Seekers on the *MV Tampa*'. *International Journal of Refugee Law* 14 nos 2 and 3 (2002): 279–301.

Chinkin, Christine. 'Jus Cogens, Article 103 of the UN Charter and Other Hierarchical Techniques of Conflict Solution'. *The Finnish Yearbook of International Law* 17 (2006): 63–82.

Combacau, Jean. 'Obligations de résultat et obligations de comportement: Quelques questions et pas de réponse [Obligations of result and obligations of conduct: Some questions, no answers]'. In *Le droit international: unité et diversité*, edited by Paul Reuter, 181–204. Paris: Pedone, 1981.

Condorelli, Luigi, and Claus Kress. 'The Rules of Attribution: General Considerations'. In *The Law of International Responsibility*, edited by James Crawford, Alain Pellet and Simon Olleson, 221–236. Oxford: Oxford University Press, 2010.

Coppens, Jasmine. 'The Lampedusa Disaster: How to Prevent Further Loss of Life at Sea?'. *The International Journal on Marine Navigation and Safety of Sea Transportation* 7 no. 4 (2013): 589–598.

Costello, Cathryn, and Mariagiulia Giuffré. 'Drowning Refugees, Migrants, and Shame at Sea: The EU's Response'. Blog in two parts, 27 April 2015. Oxford: Oxford Human Rights Hub, 2015. Available at http://ohrh.law.ox.ac.uk/drowning-refugees-migrants-and-shame-at-sea-the-eus-response-part-i/ and http://ohrh.law.ox.ac.uk/drowning-refugees-migrants-and-shame-at-sea-the-eu-response-part-ii/.

Crawford, James. *State Responsibility: The General Part*. Cambridge: Cambridge University Press, 2014.

Crock, Mary. 'Shadow Plays, Shifting Sands and International Refugee Law: Convergences in the Asia–Pacific'. *International and Comparative Law Quarterly* 63 no. 2 (2014): 247–280.

Dupuy, Pierre-Marie. 'Reviewing the Difficulties of Codification: On Ago's Classification of Obligations of Means and Obligations of Result in Relation to State Responsibility'. *European Journal of International Law* 10 no. 2 (1999): 371–385.

Fox, Hazel. 'Article 31(3)(A) and (B) of the Vienna Convention and the "Kasikili/Sedudu Island" case'. In *Treaty Interpretation and the Vienna Convention on the Law of Treaties: 30 Years on*, edited by Malgosia Fitzmaurice, Olufemi Elias and Panos Merkouris, 59–74. Leiden: Nijhoff, 2010.

Gammeltoft-Hansen, Thomas, and James Hathaway. 'Non-Refoulement in a World of Cooperative Deterrence'. *Columbia Journal of Transnational Law* 53 no. 2 (2015): 235–284.

Giannelli, Alessandra. 'Customary International Law in the European Union'. In *International Law as Law of the European Union*, edited by Enzo Cannizzaro, Paola Plachetti and Ramses A. Wessels, 93–110. Leiden: Brill, 2012.

Giuffré, Mariagiulia. 'State Responsibility Beyond Borders: What Legal Basis for Italy's Push-backs to Libya?'. *International Journal of Refugee Law* 24 no. 4 (2012): 692–734.

Gondek, Michal. *The Reach of Human Rights in a Globalising World: Extraterritorial Application of Human Rights Treaties*. Antwerp: Intersentia, 2009.

Goodwin-Gill, Guy S., and Jane McAdam. *The Refugee in International Law* (3rd edn). Oxford: Oxford University Press, 2007.

Goodwin-Gill, Guy S., and Philippe Weckel. *Protection des Migrants et des Réfugiés au XXie Siècle: Aspects de Droit* [*Migration and Refugee Protection in the Twenty-First Century: International Aspects*]. Leiden: Nijhoff for The Hague Academy of International Law, 2015.

Kuiper, Pieter Jan, and Esa Paasivirta. 'EU International Responsibility and its Attribution: From the Inside Looking out'. In *The International Responsibility of the European Union: European and International Perspectives*, edited by Malcolm Evans and Panos Koutrakos, 35–71. Oxford: Hart, 2013.

McAdam, Jane. 'Australia and Asylum Seekers'. *International Journal of Refugee Law* 25 no. 3 (2013): 435–438.

Mallia, Patricia. *Migrant Smuggling by Sea: Combating a Current Threat to Maritime Security Through the Creation of a Cooperative Framework*. Leiden: Nijhoff, 2010.

Messineo, Francesco. 'Attribution of Conduct'. In *Principles of Shared Responsibility in International Law: An Appraisal of the State of the Art*, edited by André Nollkaemper and Ilias Plakokefalos, 60–97. Cambridge: Cambridge University Press, 2014.

Milanovic, Marko. *Extraterritorial Application of Human Rights Treaties: Law, Principles, and Policy*. Oxford: Oxford University Press, 2011.

PACE (Parliamentary Assembly of the Council of Europe). 'Lives Lost in the Mediterranean Sea: Who Is Responsible?'. Report by PACE Committee on Migration, Refugees and Displaced Persons. Strasbourg: Parliamentary Assembly of the Council of Europe (PACE), March 2012.

Papastavridis, Efthymios. '"Fortress Europe" and FRONTEX: Within or Without International Law?'. *Nordic Journal of International Law* 79 no. 1 (2010): 75–111.

Papastavridis, Efthymios. 'The Right of Visit on the High Seas in a Theoretical Perspective: *Mare Liberum* versus *Mare Clausum* Revisited'. *Leiden Journal of International Law* 24 no. 1 (2011): 45–69.

Papastavridis, Efthymios. 'European Convention on Human Rights and the Law of the Sea: The Strasbourg Court in Unchartered Waters?'. In *The Interpretation and Application of the European Convention of Human Rights: Legal and Practical Implications*, edited by Malgosia Fitzmaurice and Panos Merkouris, 117–146. Leiden: Nijhoff, 2013.

Papastavridis, Efthymios. *The Interception of Vessels on the High Seas: Contemporary Challenges to the Legal Order of the Oceans*. Oxford: Hart, 2013.

Papastavridis, Efthymios. 'We Saved them. Now What?: The Unresolved Question of Disembarkation of Rescued Persons at Sea'. In *La Contribution de la Convention des Nations Unies sur le Droit de la Mer à la Bonne Gouvernance des Mers et des Oceans* [*The Contribution of the United Nations Convention on the Law of the Sea to Good Governance of the Oceans and Seas*], edited by Jose M. Sobrino Heradia, 587–606. Naples: Editoriale Scientifica, 2014.

Phillips, Janet, and Harriet Spinks. 'Boat arrivals in Australia since 1976'. Parliamentary Library Background Note. Canberra, ACT: Parliament of Australia, 2011.

Pugash, James Z. 'The Dilemma of the Sea Refugee: Rescue Without Refuge'. *Harvard Journal of International Law* 18 no. 3 (1977): 577–604.

Reinisch, August. 'Aid or Assistance and Direction and Control between States and International Organizations in the Commission of Internationally Wrongful Acts'. *International Organizations Law Review* 7 no. 1 (2010): 63–77.

Roucounas, Emmanuel. 'Effectiveness of International Law for the Users of the Seas'. In *Cursos Euromediterráneos Bancaja de Derecho Internacional*, Vol. 8, edited by Jorge Cardona Llorens, 855–922. Valencia, 2009.

Takei, Yoshinobu. 'Assessing Flag State Performance in Legal Terms: Clarifications of the Margin of Discretion'. *The International Journal of Marine and Coastal Law* 28 no. 1 (2013): 97–133.

Trevisanut, Seline. 'Search and Rescue Operations in the Mediterranean: Factor of Cooperation or Conflict?'. *The International Journal of Marine and Coastal Law* 25 (2010): 523–542.

Trevisanut, Seline. 'Is There a Right to be Rescued at Sea? A Constructive View'. *QIL (Questions of International Law)* 4 (2014): 3–15.

Willheim, Ernst. '*MV Tampa*: The Australian Response'. *International Journal of Refugee Law* 15 no. 2 (2003): 159–191.

PART III

Migration control and access to asylum

8

RELINKING POWER AND RESPONSIBILITY IN EXTRATERRITORIAL IMMIGRATION CONTROL

The case of immigration liaison officers[1]

Fabiane Baxewanos

8.1 Introduction

Do a state's human rights obligations extend beyond its territory? Do they apply to the conduct of private persons? If so, how can the state be held responsible for potential violations? The present chapter addresses these questions in the context of EU immigration control. It introduces the case of immigration liaison officers (ILOs) as a prime example of the increasing extraterritorialisation and privatisation of immigration control, which is often deplored on the grounds that it produces 'legal black holes'. This chapter argues, against this common perception, that despite these trends, states generally retain substantial means of influence that trigger obligations under human rights and refugee law. By drawing on three different legal concepts, the chapter defends the basic idea that states cannot offshore and delegate immigration control without keeping a corresponding level of legal responsibility.

The extraterritorialisation of EU immigration control and its human rights implications have been the subject of intense academic debate in recent years. Interception on the high seas, Frontex-coordinated operations and other non-entrée mechanisms at the European Union's external borders have been widely analysed in both the legal and political science literature. However, some of the more subtle forms of extraterritorial immigration control have received surprisingly little attention. Instead of just preventing entry into the European Union, these forms aim to take effect at an earlier point, that being, preventing migrants' departure to the European Union in the first place.

The case of ILOs is a notable example here. Although their actions may be less spectacular than pushback operations at the European Union's sea borders, they may have even more serious implications for persons seeking international protection. As systematic controls at the point of departure, ILOs effectively shift the EU border to third states territories, and thereby may block the way to protection. Furthermore, as they are tasked with checking private carriers' compliance with carrier sanction legislation, they contribute to the effective privatisation of immigration control. Therefore, although their actions raise important human rights concerns, these actions are generally not accompanied by appropriate legal safeguards. As ILOs are usually not vested with explicit operational powers (but instead assume an 'advisory' role), their obligations to intercepted persons often remain unclear. Therefore, posting states regularly deny responsibility arising from their potential misconduct, producing what has been generally referred to as 'legal black holes'.[2] The present chapter challenges this idea. It argues that, despite trends to offshore and outsource immigration control, states generally retain substantial powers over their agents and intermediaries. The use of ILOs is a prime example of how privatisation and delegation have in no way diminished states influence but, quite to the contrary, given rise to close supervisory powers that usually trigger corresponding human rights obligations.

Efforts to identify the above-described obligations have been complicated by the fact that ILOs operate in a complex, multilevel legal system, at the intersection of the public/private and European/national spheres. Therefore, the main goal of this chapter is to shed light on the practices of ILOs, and to relate this practice to legal means of establishing the posting state's responsibility. To this end, the chapter will first briefly introduce the case of ILOs in the European Union. It goes on to present the main arguments that support an extraterritorial application of human rights obligations, exploring both the concepts of jurisdiction and positive obligations. The third part addresses the question of state responsibility for internationally wrongful acts. Drawing on the Articles on State Responsibility, it argues that a state – under certain conditions that are regularly fulfilled when it uses ILOs – may be held responsible for violations of its international obligations, even if they are committed by private or third-state actors. Put simply, this chapter defends the basic idea that state control cannot be exercised without a corresponding level of responsibility, be it for actions within or beyond a state's territory.

8.2 The case of ILOs in the European Union

8.2.1 State practice and EU legislation

Among EU member states there is a long tradition of posting ILOs to airports, border crossings or foreign immigration authorities, with the United Kingdom, the Netherlands and France currently operating the largest networks.[3] ILOs are used to reduce the number of undocumented migrants arriving in the European Union, either by checking passengers' identities, or by offering training and advice, for example, instructing private airlines on how to spot forged travel documents.[4] They are also used to gather information on irregular migration routes and to facilitate the return of rejected persons, and for intergovernmental information exchange.[5] For example, in the United Kingdom, full-blown immigration checks are carried out within demarcated zones at the ports of the French cities of Calais, Dunkirk and Boulogne. Pursuant to an agreement with France, UK immigration law directly applies in these zones.[6] A similarly intense system of pre-clearance, including interviews, was carried out at Prague Airport.[7] In most other cases ILOs play a more indirect role, merely *assisting* carriers to decide whether or not to allow a person's embarkation.[8] For example, the ILOs that form part of the United Kingdom's Risk and Liaison Overseas Network (RALON) train and advise airline staff.[9] In these cases, states have generally been careful to stress that ILOs act solely in an advisory capacity.[10]

The question of ILOs has also received some attention at the EU level, its first manifestation being the adoption of a Joint Action in 1996 that provided a common framework for member state initiatives concerning liaison officers.[11] Subsequently, several initiatives were launched to achieve greater harmonisation on the issue.[12] These had only limited success, as the member states failed to agree on the definition of the role and the tasks of ILOs.[13] Therefore, not until 2004 did the European Council pass Regulation No. 377/2004 on the creation of a network of ILOs posted at international airports around the world. This provides the first EU legal basis for ILOs, and defines them as member state representatives that are posted abroad to liaise with the host country's authorities in order to prevent and combat irregular immigration, return undocumented immigrants and manage legal migration.[14] Two years later, in April 2006, the Council published the Draft Common Manual for ILOs, which provides operational guidelines, useful information and best practices.[15] Strikingly, despite the ILOs' broad mandate and the implications for persons seeking international protection, neither the Regulation nor the Draft Common Manual includes a reference to member states' obligations under international refugee law.

8.2.2 Making the system work: carrier sanctions

An EU-wide system of financial penalties for private carriers that transport inadequately documented persons ('carrier sanctions') complements and facilitates the work of ILOs. The fines imposed by the United Kingdom, for example, amount to up to £2,000 per transported person. Additionally, the carrier is charged with all related costs that may arise before such a person's return may be effectuated (e.g. accommodation costs).[16] The EU legal basis for carrier sanctions is Article 26 of the 1990 Schengen Implementation Convention,[17] later supplemented by the Carriers' Liability Directive.[18] According to this latter document, member states are required to introduce a minimum penalty of EUR 3,000 per transported person, and the carrier's obligation to return those whose entry is refused, or otherwise bear all costs of onward transportation.

In contrast to the EU's legal provisions on ILOs cited above, Article 26 of the Schengen Convention does mention international refugee law. It notes that in implementing its rules member states are 'subject to the obligations resulting from [. . .] the Geneva Convention relating to the Status of Refugees'. The vagueness of this reference leaves member states with a significant degree of leeway concerning how to reconcile potentially contradictory obligations under Article 26 of the Schengen Convention on the one hand, and international refugee law on the other. Notably, the Directive allows, but does not require, the suspension of penalties in refugee-related cases.[19] Different interpretations of such conflicting obligations have resulted in a highly varied implementation, with some member states waiving carrier sanctions if the transported person is later granted (some form of) protection, and others fining carriers regardless of the individual's protection status.[20] Even in the first case carriers must pay the fine upfront, and are only reimbursed if the person is granted protection. This decision generally takes at least several months, during which carriers bear the financial cost. Moreover, even if some countries exempt carriers from liability when transporting refugees, it seems that carriers are usually unaware of this exemption.[21] In any case, they bear a significant financial risk when transporting insufficiently documented persons. Therefore carriers are very likely to rely on the embarkation advice offered by ILOs. Not listening to them may prove very costly.

In the context of the United Kingdom, a study conducted in 2008 confirms that private airlines tend to prioritise the avoidance of fines and rapid processing over their passengers' potential protection needs. They are 'keen to avoid long delays, endless security checks and suspicious questioning for fear of antagonising passengers'.[22] Instead, they make 'speedy judgments about the validity of a passenger's documents and the likelihood of incurring a fine upon arrival'. As they are frequently unable to communicate with the passengers, and under heavy time pressure, they rely on 'gut feeling' and 'body language' to decide whether a person should be allowed to board. Under these circumstances, the UK Home Office's recommendation that carriers confronted with asylum claims contact the *United Nations High Commissioner for Refugees* (UNHCR) or a UK representative for advice and guidance on how best to proceed is likely to be ignored. In the Netherlands, although there is a similar obligation to contact the national immigration authorities, there is no evidence that this procedure is effectively implemented.[23]

8.2.3 Undermining refugee protection?

This constellation has been heavily criticised by human rights advocates.[24] It is frequently noted that the combined use of visa requirements, carrier sanctions and ILOs seriously affects the ability of refugees to seek international protection.[25] Obligating carriers to verify travel documents has been described as effectively privatising refugee protection, and 'turn[ing] all the world's major airlines into *de facto* pre-frontier border guards rejecting thousands of travellers each year'.[26] UNHCR criticises such policies as shifting the responsibility for protection to actors that are:

(a) unauthorized to make asylum determinations on behalf of States (b) thoroughly untrained in the nuances and procedures of refugee and asylum principles, and (c) motivated by economic rather than humanitarian considerations.[27]

Although it is impossible to determine exactly how many refugees are turned away at the European Union's borders every year, it may be assumed that they are 'particularly likely to be rejected as they naturally tend to lack full documentation and are unlikely to have been granted a visa'.[28] This was also acknowledged by a Council of Europe/UNHCR round table held in 2002, where it was stated that '[i]t is impossible to be precise about the number of refugees who are denied escape due to stringent checks by transport companies', and estimated that their 'number is [. . .] on the rise, [. . .] not least since transport companies have been assisted by Governmental liaison officers in verifying travel documents'.[29]

Particularly problematic are ILO-led exit controls in countries that are known to systematically violate international human rights law and so-called 'refugee-producing countries'. For instance, the United Kingdom keeps posting ILOs in countries such as Sri Lanka, Ethiopia, the DRC and Sudan, despite the fact that their nationals continue to receive refugee status in the United Kingdom in large numbers. By preventing them from getting on a plane or a ship and instead returning them to the hands of the state authorities, the United Kingdom risks exposing them to the very persons they are trying to escape, violating the principle of non-refoulement.[30] If applied globally and systematically, offshoring and outsourcing immigration control to actors who incur no (direct) responsibility under international refugee law threatens to thoroughly undermine the very concept of refugee protection.[31] The last two sections of this chapter discuss the question that logically follows from such an interim conclusion: what are the legal ways to challenge such developments, and how can we re-establish the link between a state's control and its responsibility?[32]

8.3 Relinking control and responsibility I: applying human rights extraterritorially

Two main legal avenues exist to challenge widespread claims of extraterritorial immigration control being beyond states' human rights obligations: first, the classic concept of jurisdiction as 'effective control', and second, the concept of positive obligations that promises to address some of the older jurisdiction paradigm's shortcomings.

8.3.1 The concept of jurisdiction

The European Court of Human Rights, the Committee Against Torture, the Human Rights Council (HRC) and the International Court of Justice (ICJ) all agree on the fundamental tenet that human rights treaties cannot be interpreted in a way that permits a contracting state to violate treaty obligations on the territory of another state that it could not violate on its own territory.[33] However, there has been considerable controversy over the details of this general statement. Ultimately, it all seems to come down to the interpretation of the concept of 'jurisdiction'. Accepting that human rights may, in principle, be applied extra-territorially does not mean that a state is necessarily responsible for all human rights infringements that may vaguely relate to its actions. Therefore, in the context of immigration control, it is often argued that a state's human rights obligations depend on where it acts. To this end, judicial bodies distinguish among obligations incurred within the country, in international zones and in the territory of another state, suggesting a lesser degree of obligation the further the state moves away from its own territory.[34]

Although this is a more nuanced way to identify a state's protection obligations than supporting a sweeping extraterritorial application, it blurs the element of *factual* control exercised by the state in a specific situation. This 'three-spheres model' is based on the presumption that a state exercises less control on the high seas and on the territory of another state than on its own territory. However, what if a state has full control over an individual on another state's territory (e.g. at consulates and airports)? The above model may lead to gaps in these situations. Therefore, it is submitted here that it is not the *location* of state action, but the specific *level of control* a state exercises that should serve as a starting point for defining state obligations. The concept of jurisdiction should not be understood in territorial terms, but in substantive ones. This is not primarily a question of *where*, but of *how* the state acts.

The foregoing understanding, increasingly supported by international case law, is only the most recent result of what has been a long and controversial debate. As early as 1927, the Permanent Court of International Justice (PCIJ) – the predecessor of the ICJ – addressed the question of jurisdiction in the *Lotus* case. The Court's view in the 1920s was that jurisdiction was defined in purely territorial terms; a state could not exercise jurisdiction outside its territory unless permitted by an international treaty, or by customary international law.[35] Since then, jurisdiction has received much attention by international judicial bodies, and the case law of the European Court of Human Rights, in particular, provides 'an excellent laboratory'[36] for its development, resulting in today's most common interpretation: 'jurisdiction as effective control'.[37]

International courts and supervisory bodies have largely followed the European Court of Human Rights' approach. In their respective interpretations of the International Covenant on Civil and Political Rights (ICCPR) and the Convention against Torture (CAT), both the HRC and the Committee Against Torture held that these treaties were applicable to all persons under the *effective control* of a state party, even if not situated within its territory.[38] Article 33(1) of the Refugee Convention, although lacking a supervisory mechanism that could deliver such an authoritative interpretation, has also been interpreted in light of the 'effective control' requirement by the UNHCR's Executive Committee and many refugee scholars, on the grounds that its non-refoulement provision is largely comparable to the one in international human rights law.[39]

Despite their success, discussions on extraterritorial jurisdiction are always riddled with difficult threshold questions. When are human rights obligations actually triggered? How intense must the relationship between the state and individual be, to justify holding the state accountable? The whole concept caused much confusion. One reason for this may be that jurisdiction in general international law means something quite different than jurisdiction in human rights law. Whereas the first serves mainly as a delineator to allocate competence and to clarify the question whether or not a state is entitled to act, the second is used to define a state's obligations to an individual. Therefore, in the second context, the concrete sovereign relationship between the state and the individual is of interest, and not whether a state is legally competent to act.[40] But not even *within* the human rights field – or, for that matter, the European Court of Human Rights' own case law – was the concept clear. Although the Court had long established that a state exercises jurisdiction over its entire territory, and declaring parts of it 'international zones' does nothing to alter this,[41] situations of extraterritorial state conduct have in no way been treated consistently. Confronted with cases concerning, *inter alia*, military occupation, extraterritorial detention facilities or the NATO (North Atlantic Treaty Organisation) bombings during the Yugoslavian war, the Court reached several different conclusions concerning when the jurisdictional threshold is actually reached. Nevertheless, more recent decisions reveal a certain trend of moving away from the previous, territorially based understanding of jurisdiction,[42] towards a more personally based one.[43] It is no longer solely 'effective control' over a certain territory, but also '*de facto* control' over a particular person, which may trigger jurisdiction.[44]

In sum, this points to a more functional,[45] normative and flexible[46] understanding of jurisdiction, where the decisive criterion is whether a state has sufficient influence over a person's ability to enjoy his or her rights. In this sense, jurisdiction is freed of its restrictive, territorial corset, and essentially becomes synonymous with a particularly intense relationship between the state and the individual.[47]

This shift has of course major practical implications. It may bring a whole range of situations, such as immigration control at consulates, international airports, extraterritorial border posts, ships on the high seas or other international and transit zones, under the purview of a state's human rights obligations. This is exactly what several scholars, and national and international judicial bodies have suggested.[48] According to Judge Albuquerque in the *Hirsi* case, immigration control is always intense enough to trigger jurisdiction, whether it applies territorially or extra-territorially, directly by state officials or indirectly by private persons acting on their advice.[49] In this understanding, a state that uses ILOs to prevent inadequately documented persons from boarding a plane exercises a sufficient degree of control to trigger jurisdiction and, as a consequence, its obligation to prevent refoulement.[50]

However, embracing such a wider notion of jurisdiction does not solve all problems related to this concept. We still face important conceptual difficulties, as the definition of 'effective control', in particular with regard to persons, remains elusive.[51] As den Heijer has suggested, although it is conceivable that a state effectively controls 'an inert object, such as a strip of land', it is hard to imagine how a state 'effectively controls a human being – which has the tendency to engage in all sorts of activities of its own accord'.[52] Furthermore, the concept of jurisdiction may be ill-suited to capturing the more implicit forms of how states may interfere with an individual's rights. It seems likely to fail in situations where a state does not exercise direct control, but engages in more subtle forms of influence, for instance, where its ILOs simply 'advise' private carriers to reject certain persons. Assuming that human rights are triggered only once a person is under the state's, effective – that is, direct, immediate, physical – control would significantly reduce their effectiveness. Therefore, the criterion of 'effective control' has often been perceived as setting too high a threshold, which, in turn, has prompted international courts and scholars to look for alternative ways to hold states accountable.[53]

8.3.2 Positive obligations

The concepts of 'positive obligations' or 'due diligence' may be the most prominent examples in this regard. They are particularly relevant if one agrees that, despite the growing delegation and privatisation of control functions, this has in no way diminished the state's influence but, quite to the contrary, given rise to close managerial powers created by a mixture of legal regulation, financial penalties and direct control.[54]

Concrete means of influence arguably justify the states' corresponding obligation to take positive action. In past cases, the European Court of Human Rights found such obligations with regard to persons who had an especially intense relationship with the state, even if they were not under its 'effective control'. In *Isaak*, for example, the Court held that Turkey violated its obligations to a Greek Cypriot who was beaten to death in the UN buffer zone in Cyprus by Turkish-Cypriot forces, because it 'failed to take preventive measures to protect the victim's life'.[55] In *Ilascu*, concerning the detention of Moldovan nationals by the Russian-controlled Transdniestrian police, Russia was found to have violated its obligations under the convention because it failed to 'put an end to the applicants' situation'.[56] In both cases, the contracting states were under an obligation to take positive action, irrespective of the absence of effective territorial control, or the direct involvement of their state agents.

The reasoning just described is useful in cases of offshored and privatised immigration control. States could be required to take adequate steps to ensure that privatised controls do not violate the principle of non-refoulement, for example, by establishing monitoring and complaints mechanisms. Moreover, states could be obligated to provide human rights training to private carriers, instead of merely instructing them to detect forged documents.[57] More generally, states could be required to take adequate measures to prevent third parties from violating human rights extraterritorially, if they have the legal or political means to do so. The Committee on Economic, Social and Cultural Rights (CESCR) takes what may be the broadest view in this regard, stating that a state incurs obligations to an individual whenever it is able to positively influence this person's human rights situation.[58]

Although the doctrine of positive obligations conflicts with some central notions of international law, in particular the principle of sovereignty and the rule of non-intervention, it seems to enjoy growing support among scholars.[59] Lawson, for instance, broadly acknowledges the responsibility of a state under the European Convention on Human Rights, 'if it has encouraged individuals to engage in acts contrary to human rights'.[60] Moreover, both the European Convention on Human Rights, in *Soering*,[61] and the ICJ, in its *Wall Opinion*,[62] adhere to the doctrine that a state must refrain from any act that may facilitate human rights violations by other actors, even if it does not exercise effective control in that particular situation. Consequently, in the context of immigration control, a state is arguably required to take all reasonable steps to prevent human rights violations, such as establishing monitoring procedures, providing training or facilitating access to complaints mechanisms. This obligation may also arise in extraterritorial situations, as it is not derived from 'the oversimplified shorthand of effective factual control over the individual, but rather from the power or capability of the state to positively influence a person's human rights situation'.[63] In sum, legal doctrine and case law do indeed allow for the interpretation that:

> ... it is not the fact that the affected person has been directly affected or placed under the effective control of a state, but rather the relationship of the state with a particular set of circumstances being of such a unique nature, that is decisive in triggering a state's positive obligations.[64]

However, it is also clear that the contours of this concept depend entirely on the particular circumstances of the case. It is very difficult to more precisely define what the concept of positive obligations actually entails.[65] Its substance is, by nature, highly case-specific and existing case law has not yet come up with a more systematic framework. Therefore, the entire concept remains very open to contestation.[66]

8.4 Relinking control and responsibility II: state responsibility

So far, we have been concerned only with the question of 'linking' or, in other words, the scope of the *application* of human rights. Although this is a necessary precondition for the question of human rights *responsibility*, it is also a separate question. Den Heijer emphasises that the questions of determining applicable law and of allocating responsibility should be kept conceptually distinct.[67]

The principal regime for identifying responsibility under international law is the law of state responsibility, as codified in the Articles on State Responsibility (ASR). The final version of the Articles was adopted by the ILC in 2001, after decades of difficult negotiation. They seek to formulate international legal norms on the responsibility of states for internationally wrongful acts, by way of codification and progressive development.[68] As so-called 'secondary rules', they are triggered only once an international obligation has been violated. Thus a 'primary rule' must be violated by the state in question before the ASR's rules are applicable. For the purposes of this discussion, this is the principle of non-refoulement, as stipulated in Article 33(1) of the Refugee Convention, and complemented by Article 3 European Convention on Human Rights, Article 7 ICCPR and Article 3 CAT.

With a view to the issues of interest here – the outsourcing of immigration control to private and third-state actors – two provisions of the ASR are particularly relevant: first, Article 8 ASR, which stipulates that the conduct of a person shall be considered an act of a state if this person 'is in fact acting on the instructions of, or under the direction or control of, that State'. Therefore, under certain circumstances, a state remains responsible, even if it outsources immigration control to private actors. The second provision of interest is Article 16 ASR, which comes into play in cases where a state outsources control functions to third-state actors. It stipulates that a state is internationally responsible if it:

> . . . aids or assists another State in the commission of an internationally wrong-ful act' under the conditions that it has (a) knowledge of the circumstances of the internationally wrongful act and (b) the act would be internationally wrongful if committed by that same state.

The consequence of these two articles is that violations of non-refoulement committed by private carriers or third-state border guards acting under the state's authority may trigger its responsibility.[69] Although it is subsidiary to the territorial state's 'principal responsibility',[70] in practice this 'subsidiary responsibility' of the outsourcing and delegating state is often crucially important to prevent protection gaps, particularly in cases where immigration control is offshored to countries with low human rights standards.[71]

Other articles that seem pertinent at first glance, such as Article 5 (conduct of persons that exercise elements of governmental authority) and Article 6 (conduct of third-state organs placed under a state's disposal) ASR fail to take into account the informal and ad hoc nature of many immigration control arrangements. In many cases, such arrangements with private actors or third states do not have an explicit basis in national law, or involve the structural integration of staff into another state's administration (as these two provisions require[72]) but originate from informal, administrative decisions. In contrast, the ways in which Article 8 and Article 16 ASR are formulated cover such informal arrangements, with the former focusing on *factual* control, and the latter including any form of aid or assistance, without requiring it to have an explicit, interstate contractual basis.[73] With regard to the first scenario (outsourcing control to private actors), I argue that certain forms of cooperation between EU member states and private carriers fulfil the requirements of Article 8 ASR.[74] Owing to carrier sanction legislation, close governmental supervision via ILOs and state-sponsored training, in many cases private carriers act on the instructions of, or under the direction or control of the state. The United Kingdom may serve as a particularly illustrative example:[75] First, it uses a particularly stringent regime of carrier sanctions, which in itself may amount to *de facto* 'control' or 'direction', as the financial risk imposed on carriers is likely to determine the outcome of their boarding decisions. Second, it has installed a twenty-four-hour hotline to provide on-the-spot advice for carriers, which means that, upon request, UK officials will appear in person to verify documentation, and occasionally also to conduct in-depth interviews with persons suspected of using false documents. The direct influence of the state is obvious in these cases. Third, the UK government provides training for private carriers, covering predominantly security-related questions, such as documentation verification and forgery detection.[76] This also demonstrates the United Kingdom's significant influence on how immigration checks are carried out. Fourth, the United Kingdom provides surveillance equipment, including carbon dioxide detectors, X-ray scanners and heartbeat monitors, free of charge to private carriers, because when transporting inadequately documented persons, fines are waived only if carriers can show that they have taken all reasonable measures to prevent irregular migrants from boarding, so effectively, they are obligated to use this equipment. Failure to do so may have serious consequences for the carriers, in particular, reduced access to UK airports.[77] Again, the state's control function is evident.

The case of the Dutch ILO network further supports the claim that carriers often act under the control of the state in the sense of Article 8 ASR. A study on carrier sanctions in the Netherlands shows that in 3,500 cases in which ILOs provided advice to private airlines in 2004, this advice was followed in ninety-nine per cent of the cases.[78] Rather than merely 'advising' carriers, the Dutch ILOs – their task facilitated by carrier sanctions – effectively made the decisions themselves.

In the second previously mentioned scenario (delegating control to third-state actors), essentially the same logic applies: where a state substantially and knowingly supports a human rights violation by another state's actors, it incurs responsibility under international law. The situation is somewhat different from the first scenario, as, unlike private carriers, the third state incurs responsibility under international law itself. However, this does not relieve the outsourcing state of its own international obligations. Article 16, as the ASR's complicity rule, precisely establishes this link between two states' actions.[79] Although the aiding state's contribution needs to reach a certain threshold, the provision of material aid, for example, is covered according to the ILC's commentary.[80] Therefore, providing advice, sponsoring police training, funding detention centres or providing surveillance equipment to third states is, in principle, suited to meet this criterion. When such forms of aid facilitate the commission of an internationally wrongful act – such as refoulement – and the complicit state has knowledge of the circumstances of this act, it is internationally responsible. By 'imposing responsibility for complicity', Article 16 may be described as a valuable 'cure for [. . .] international law's traditional bilateralism',[81] through which states seek to trade sovereign functions and concomitant human rights obligations.

What needs to be proven in the specific case are the two requirements of (a) knowledge/intent, that is, the necessary subjective element, and (b) the nexus between the assistance and the internationally wrongful act, that is, causation. Although the latter criterion seems to have been less problematic – the very general formulation of Article 16 has generally favoured a broad reading[82] – and must be resolved with a view to the specific circumstances of the case,[83] the former was subject to much controversy in the early ILC discussions and beyond.[84] Although this is not the place to give a full account of the various positions, let me just share the conclusion reached by Aust:[85] the intent requirement should, in principle, be upheld as a criterion for establishing responsibility; however, it must be modified, especially with regard to serious breaches of peremptory rules under international law. Therefore, different primary rules could entail different standards of intent.[86]

To conclude this section, I would like to take up den Heijer's point concerning the ASR's potentially diminishing relevance, owing to the increasingly expansionist concept of jurisdiction.[87] His argument runs as follows: As recent case law departs from traditional international law concepts of jurisdiction, the concept is reframed in a way that encompasses a state's responsibility for human rights violations (whereas before it only described an entitlement to act). In this sense, if a state has jurisdiction, it also has the responsibility to protect human rights: jurisdiction necessarily entails responsibility. The gap that could previously develop between a state's entitlement to act (jurisdiction in the traditional sense) and its human rights responsibility becomes conceptually impossible. Therefore, we no longer need a tool (state responsibility) to close this gap. It is argued that a wider notion of jurisdiction that carries responsibility within its very meaning has rendered the regime of state responsibility obsolete. However, this conclusion is not uncontested. Aust, also addressing the relationship between human rights law and the law of state responsibility,[88] comes to a more nuanced conclusion. He considers human rights law as complementing and reinforcing, rather than diminishing the role of – in his case, Article 16 of – the ASR. In this sense, the provisions for non-refoulement are 'seen as *leges speciales* to the general rule of complicity',[89] and positive obligations as 'viable functional alternatives to Article 16 ASR'.[90] Although Aust thereby acknowledges that the law of state responsibility and human rights law may have a partially overlapping function, this is interpreted as in no way reducing the importance of a general rule of complicity. Instead, Article 16, representing the 'normative environment in which more specialised rules need to be seen', is argued to provide important guidance, a 'yardstick of "no return beyond this point"'.[91] Furthermore, the language of Article 16 may be useful not only for international lawyers, but also for less traditional actors in international law. An international rule that 'no longer tolerate[s] complicit State behaviour' could be a powerful tool for an emerging civil society.[92]

An increasing convergence of human rights law and the law of state responsibility is even less plausible with regard to the concept of positive obligations. In the

Genocide Case,[93] the ICJ carved out two fundamental differences between positive obligations (which it calls the 'obligation to prevent') and the law of complicity: first, complicity always requires some form of positive action, whereas the obligation to prevent may result from the mere failure to act. In the words of the Court, 'while complicity results from commission, violation of the obligation to prevent results from omission'.[94] Second, complicity requires the organs of the state to have full knowledge of the facts, whereas for the obligation to prevent to apply, awareness of serious danger is sufficient. The subjective element required to establish complicity is stricter than the one required to establish positive obligations. In general, positive obligations seem to be the regime setting the higher threshold. In the words of Gattini, '[i]t usually takes more to incur responsibility for an omission than is the case with respect to complicity'.[95]

We now come to the final difficulty of determining whether the intensity of the state–individual relationship that establishes responsibility under the ASR equals the intensity that is necessary to trigger responsibility in the human rights sense. If so, then den Heijer's argument seems valid. If not, that is, if jurisdiction/ positive obligations require a higher threshold than state responsibility, it seems that we are better off keeping the distinction between the two regimes.

8.5 Conclusion

When assessing the human rights compatibility of immigration controls, international bodies and scholars often start by accepting the fundamental right of states to control their borders.[96] Regulating who enters and leaves their territory is widely accepted as one of the most fundamental prerogatives of the sovereign state.[97] However, in the exercise of this sovereign right, states are bound by obligations under international law, of which the principle of non-refoulement forms an integral part.[98] Compliance with what a holistic interpretation of this principle suggests, namely that 'escape from persecution, admission to the country of asylum, procedural access to qualification procedures and enjoyment of status constitute inseparable components of the same continuum' that all should be guaranteed,[99] is far from current reality. It is very difficult to see how current control procedures, often operated extraterritorially and by private or third-state actors, may fulfil obligations such as effectively examining asylum applications, while providing access to procedural safeguards and acknowledging, where applicable, refugee status by competent and accountable authorities. But even under its most restrictive reading, as the mere prohibition to send back refugees to places of persecution, the principle of non-refoulement is fundamentally challenged today.[100]

This chapter looked at one current form of immigration control that is particularly problematic in this regard: posting ILOs to foreign airports around the world. Their basic function is to detect document fraud, not protection needs. In fulfilling this function, they regularly prevent persons from leaving their countries of origin, and thereby shift the (administrative) border closer and closer to the point of departure. Used systematically, their existence threatens to deprive non-refoulement of its practical meaning.[101] However, examining the relevant non-refoulement provisions – Article 33(1) Refugee Convention, Article 3 European Convention on Human Rights, Article 7 ICCPR, Article 3 CAT – and recent developments in relevant case law suggests that wherever states have a sufficiently intense relationship with a person seeking protection, and the factual capacity to protect this person's rights, they are required to ensure protection. This renders unlawful any measure that undermines refugees' ability to leave their country of origin.[102] Furthermore, international law was found to provide some important mechanisms to respond to such unlawful practices. In particular, the concepts of extraterritorial jurisdiction, positive obligations and state responsibility discussed in this chapter are potentially powerful tools. If used appropriately, they can go a long way in ensuring that extraterritorial immigration control does not go unchecked, and that the territorial scope of a state's obligations is congruent with the locus of its activities.[103]

The greater challenge may lie not in reformulating the norms that provide for the international protection of refugees, but in overcoming the barriers to putting them into effect. What we face is not so much a problem of the relevant law, but of its enforceability in practice. First, efforts to bring relevant cases before courts face major *practical obstacles*. Most notably, extraterritorialising controls dramatically reduces their visibility, especially when it comes to less spectacular practices, such as exit controls by ILOs. Indeed, very little is known about their actions. The biannual reports of the EU network of ILO work are classified, on the grounds that they contain 'sensitive data'.[104] Even less is known about the actions of entirely privatised immigration control as, by definition, there are no public reporting mechanisms.[105] Finally, the further abroad controls are taken, the more difficult it becomes to access those who have been rejected, thus preventing refugee lawyers and NGOs from gathering victim-based evidence about what actually happens at or before the border.

In addition to a fundamental lack of available information, a number of *procedural obstacles* seriously hamper the justiciability of rights, such as courts' admissibility thresholds, lack of procedural safeguards, lack of information regarding possible legal remedies, refugees' limited financial resources and lack of legal aid.[106] This situation perfectly explains why there is so little case law on the question of immigration control, and why the role of the courts in the protection of refugees has been very limited so far. As den Heijer notes, the situation 'creates a problematic dynamic whereby the lack of access to judicial review obstructs progressive norm-setting and the concomitant institutionalisation of human rights protection'.[107]

In the absence of robust case law, it is therefore all the more important to work towards practical solutions for the protection of refugees.[108] One of the first goals should be ensuring greater transparency of extraterritorial immigration control. This will require the engagement of a broad coalition of actors. It will be necessary to actively involve national parliaments, UN bodies and civil society to prevent states from continuing to hide their actions in extraterritorial spheres, where human rights obligations are notoriously obscured, and powerful norms of international law often remain unapplied. Only concerted action will be effective in ensuring refugees' right to protection and, as a first step, their fundamental 'right to have rights'.[109]

Notes

1 This chapter is based on a paper presented at a workshop within the research programme on Globalisation and Transnational Human Rights Obligations (GLOTHRO) on 'Human Rights and the Dark Side of Globalisation: Transnational Law Enforcement and Migration Control', Copenhagen, 9–10 December 2013.

2 See, e.g., Tom de Boer, 'Closing Legal Black Holes: The Role of Extraterritorial Jurisdiction in Refugee Rights Protection', *Journal of Refugee Studies* 28 no. 1 (2015), 118–134.

3 The United Kingdom's network currently consists of 50 permanent locations, with extended powers in other countries in the regions, in total covering 120 countries. See the website of the UK Border Agency, www.ukba.homeoffice.gov.uk/business-sponsors/transportindustry/rlon/howrloncanhelp/ accessed 19 November 2014. The Dutch network posts ILOs in 13 countries, covering 56 countries in total. See European Council on Refugees and Exiles, 'Defending Refugees' Access to Protection in Europe' (Brussels: European Council on Refugees and Exiles, 2007), 30; see also Council of the European Union, *Draft Common Manual for Immigration Liaisons Officers Posted Abroad by the Member States of the European Union*, 8418/06, 25 April 2006; Refugee Council, 'Remote Controls: How UK Border Controls are Endangering the Lives of Refugees' (London: Refugee Council, 2008), 35; Areti Sianni, 'Interception Practices in Europe and Their Implications', *Refugee Survey Quarterly* 21 no. 28 (2003); Andrew Brouwer and Judith Kumin, 'Interception and Asylum: When Migration Control and Human Rights Collide', *Refuge* 21 no. 4 (2003), 10.

4 See International Air Transport Association, 'A Code of Conduct for Immigration Liaison Officers' (Montreal, Quebec: IATA Control Authorities Working Group, October 2002).

5 See International Air Transport Association, 'A Code of Conduct for Immigration Liaison Officers'; European Council on Refugees and Exiles, 'Defending Refugees' Access', 32; Refugee Council, 'Remote Controls', 36.

6 Thomas Gammeltoft-Hansen, *Access to Asylum: International Refugee Law and the Globalisation of Migration Control* (Cambridge: Cambridge University Press, 2011), 125–126; for details see Refugee Council, 'Remote Controls', 39–41; Sianni, 'Interception Practices', 28.

7 As this scheme explicitly aimed at reducing the number of Czech nationals of Roma ethnic origin, it was eventually challenged before UK courts for being (a) discriminatory and (b) in contradiction with the Refugee Convention. The House of Lords agreed with the first point; the Refugee Convention, however, was found to be inapplicable on the grounds that the applicants were still in their country of origin. For details see Guy Goodwin-Gill, Submission on behalf of UNHCR to the Court of Appeal considering the Roma Rights Case. C1/2002/2183/QBACF. See also Maarten den Heijer, *Europe and Extraterritorial Asylum* (Oxford: Hart, 2012), 125–132; Refugee Council, 'Remote Controls', 37–38.

8 This is the case for Australia, Canada, the Netherlands and the United Kingdom, where ILOs offer pre-boarding recommendations to private carriers instead of issuing refusals themselves. Den Heijer, *Europe and Extraterritorial Asylum*, 178, note 53.

9 Eleanor T. Nicholson, 'Cutting Off the Flow: Extraterritorial Controls to Prevent Migration' (Berkeley, CA: University of California, Chief Justice Earl Warren Institute on Law and Social Policy, Berkeley Law School, 2011), 6.

10 See, for example, the website of the UK Border Agency (note 2 above), where it is stated that 'ILMs [Immigration Liaison Managers] have no legal powers abroad, so they cannot therefore: instruct an airline to deny boarding to a passenger. ILMs are only

able to give advice on whether a passenger is correctly documented. The final decision on whether or not to carry a passenger is solely a matter for the airline'. See also Brouwer and Kumin, 'Interception and Asylum', 10; Gammeltoft-Hansen, *Access to Asylum*, 126; Refugee Council, 'Remote Controls', 36.

11 Joint Action of 14 October 1996 adopted by the Council on the basis of Article K.3 of the Treaty on European Union providing for a common framework for the initiatives of the Member States concerning liaison officers, 96/602/JHA, OJ L 268, 19 October 1996.

12 Including a Joint position of the Council on pre-frontier assistance and training assignments of 1996 (96/622/JHA, OJ L 281, 31. October 1996) and a decision of the Schengen Convention's Executive Committee on coordinated deployment of document advisors of 1998 (SCH/Com-ex (98) 59 rev.). For further references see Sophie Scholten and Paul Minderhoud, 'Regulating Immigration Control: Carrier Sanctions in the Netherlands', *European Journal of Migration and Law* 10 (2008), 138 note 81.

13 See Scholten and Minderhoud, 'Regulating Immigration Control', 138–139. This lack of binding rules is reflected by International Air Transport Association, 'A Code of Conduct', published in 2002, seemingly in an attempt to fill this regulatory gap and to promote consistency between the various national approaches.

14 Article 1, Council Regulation (EC) No 377/2004 of 19 February 2004.

15 Council of the European Union (above, note Error! Bookmark not defined.).

16 Refugee Council, 'Remote Controls', 46.

17 Convention implementing the Schengen Agreement of 14 June 1985 between the Governments of the States of the Benelux Economic Union, the Federal Republic of Germany and the French Republic on the gradual abolition of checks at their common borders, OJ L 239, 22 September 2000.

18 Council Directive 2001/51/EC of 28 June 2001.

19 This obligation was included in the original proposal but later dropped on the basis of Germany's rejection. See Sianni, 'Interception Practices', 27.

20 European Council on Refugees and Exiles, 'Defending Refugees' Access', 28–29.

21 For further evidence concerning these three arguments see Refugee Council, 'Remote Controls', 45. Apart from producing major practical difficulties, tying reimbursement of fines to subsequent granting of protection status also raises serious concerns in terms of disclosure of confidential information about the traveller's status to the private carrier.

22 For this and the following three quotes see Refugee Council, 'Remote Controls', 46–47.

23 Cf. den Heijer, *Europe and Extraterritorial Asylum*, 45. See also International Air Transport Association, 'A Code of Conduct', section 2.3.

24 European Council on Refugees and Exiles, 'Defending Refugees' Access'; Brouwer and Kumin, 'Interception and Asylum'; Elspeth Guild, 'Moving the Borders of Europe', inaugural lecture given at University of Nijmegen, the Netherlands, 30 May 2001. See also Gammeltoft-Hansen, *Access to Asylum*, 169 note 46, for further evidence.

25 European Council on Refugees and Exiles, 'Defending Refugees' Access', 32; den Heijer, *Europe and Extraterritorial Asylum*, 178.

26 Gammeltoft-Hansen, *Access to Asylum*, 204.

27 UNHCR, UNHCR Position on Conventions Recently Concluded in Europe (Dublin and Schengen Conventions), 16 August 1991, 3 European Series 2, 385.

28 Gammeltoft-Hansen, *Access to Asylum*, 169–170.

29 Council of Europe and UNHCR, Proceedings: 'Round Table Process' on carriers' liability – Second expert meeting on carriers' liability, Topic B: Respect of the humanitarian dimension, Brussels, 24 June 2002, 3, quoted in Brouwer and Kumin, 'Interception and Asylum', 11.

30 UNHCR, Round Table on Carriers' Liability Related to Illegal Immigration, Brussels, 30 November 2001, www.iru.org/cms-filesystem-action?file=en_events_2001/Illegal 2001.pdf accessed 19 November 2014. See also Refugee Council, 'Remote Controls', 41; Sianni, 'Interception Practices', 28.

31 Gammeltoft-Hansen, *Access to Asylum*, 208.

32 The following section is solely concerned with instruments under international law. For an analysis under EU law, see den Heijer, *Europe and Extraterritorial Asylum*, chapter 5 and in particular 174–179, 198–199. Den Heijer basically suggests that ILOs are border guards in the sense of the Schengen Borders Code, which means that the procedural safeguards contained therein apply to their extraterritorial immgration control. He concludes that any other interpretation would lead to 'virtually complete and unchecked state power, which has the potential to displace the Union's substantive rules on legal migration and asylum'. See den Heijer, *Europe and Extraterritorial Asylum*, 203.

33 See, in particular, *Lopez Burgos v. Uruguay*, HRC Communication No. R 12/52, 6 June 1979, para. 12.3; for the ECtHR, see *Issa and others v. Turkey* App no 31821/96 (ECtHR, 16 November 2004) para. 71, *Solomou and others v. Turkey* App no 36832/97 (ECtHR, 24 June 2008) para. 45, *Isaak v. Turkey* App no 44587/98 (admissibility, ECtHR, 28 September 2006); for the Committee Against Torture, see Conclusions and Recommendations of the Committee against Torture concerning the second report of the United States of America, UN Doc. CAT/C/USA/CO/2 (2006) para. 15; for the ICJ, see *Application of the International Convention on the Elimination of all Forms of Racial Discrimination (Georgia v. Russian Federation)* (Order), ICJ Reports 2008, 15 October 2008, 353 at para. 149, where the Court finds that the CERD applies to the acts of Russian agents in Georgia, triggering positive obligations on Russia's part.

34 Jurisdiction has, therefore, been often understood in a primarily territorial sense, cf. *S.S. Lotus (France v. Turkey)* 1927 PCIJ (series A) No. 10, *Ilascu and others v. Moldova and Russia* App no 48787/99 (ECtHR, 8 July 2004), *Legal Consequences of the Construction of a Wall in the Occupied Palestinian Territory*, Advisory Opinion, ICJ Reports 2004 as well as the Northern Cyprus cases before the ECtHR, *Loizidou v. Turkey* App no 15318/89 (ECtHR, 23 March 1995) and *Cyprus v. Turkey* App no 25781/94 (ECtHR, 10 May 2001).

35 *S.S. Lotus (France v. Turkey)* 1927 PCIJ (series A) No. 10, paras 45, 165–167, 169.

36 Olivier De Schutter, 'Globalization and Jurisdiction: Lessons from the European Convention on Human Rights', in *Baltic Yearbook of International Law*, Vol. 6, ed. Carin Laurin (Leiden: Brill/Nijhoff, 2006), 191.

37 See, in particular the cases quoted above in notes 33, 37 and 42 (*Bankovic, Al-Skeini, Issa, Hirsi*, etc).

38 HRC, General Comment No. 31, CCPR/C/21/Rev.1/Add.13, 2004 para. 10; *Lopez Burgos* (above, note 32); CAT, Conclusions and recommendations (above, note 32) para. 15. See also Kees Wouters, *International Legal Standards for the Protection From Refoulement* (Antwerp: Intersentia, 2009), 370–372; Manfred Nowak, *UN Covenant on Civil and Political Rights: CCPR Commentary* (Kehl am Rhein: Engel, 2005), Article 2, Section IV, paras 27–30.

39 See e.g., UNHCR, Advisory Opinion on the Extraterritorial Application of Non-Refoulement Obligations under the 1951 Convention relating to the Status of Refugees and its 1967 Protocol (2007) paras 42–43; Volker Türk and Frances Nicholson, 'Refugee Protection in International Law: An Overall Perspective', in *Refugee Protection in International Law: UNHCR's Global Consultations on International Protection*, eds Erika Feller, Volker Türk, and Frances Nicholson, 3–45 (Cambridge: Cambridge University Press, 2003), 37–38; James Hathaway, *The Rights of Refugees under International Law* (Cambridge: Cambridge University Press, 2005), 64; Gammeltoft-Hansen, *Access to Asylum*, 81, 91–93. See also Article 31 (3) (c) of the Vienna Convention of the Law of Treaties.

40 For details see den Heijer, *Europe and Extraterritorial Asylum*, 19–28. See also Maarten den Heijer and Rick Lawson, 'Extraterritorial Human Rights and the Concept of "Jurisdiction"', in *Global Justice, State Duties: The Extraterritorial Scope of Economic, Social and Cultural Rights in International Law*, eds Malcolm Langford et al., 153–191 (Cambridge: Cambridge University Press, 2012); Marko Milanovic, 'From Compromise to Principle: Clarifying the Concept of State Jurisdiction in Human Rights Treaties', *Human Rights Law Review* 8 no. 3 (2008), 411.

41 See *Amuur v. France* App no 19776/92 (ECtHR, 25 June 1996) para. 43 where the European Court of Human Rights found that holding aliens in international zones is a restriction of liberty and must be in conformity with France's obligations under the Refugee Convention and the ECHR. That the French Minister of Interior had declared that aliens in these situations are 'not on French territory' (Official Gazette, 19 December 1991, 8256) was considered immaterial for this conclusion as '[d]espite its name, the international zone does not have extraterritorial status' (para. 52). See also Gammeltoft-Hansen (above, note 5) 115–120. For the case of 'Operation Relex', where Australia excised parts of its territory in order to deny 'entry' of boats, see Guy Goodwin-Gill and Jane McAdam, *The Refugee in International Law*, 3rd edn (Oxford: Oxford University Press, 2007), 270.
42 Cf. the case law cited above in note 33.
43 *Bankovic and others v. Belgium and others* App no 52207/99 (ECtHR, 12 December 2001), *Al-Skeini and others v. the UK* App no 55721/07 (ECtHR, 7 July 2011), *Issa* (above, note 32), *Öcalan v. Turkey* App no 46221/99 (ECtHR, 12 May 2005), *Medvedyev and others v. France* App no 3394/03 (ECtHR, 29 March 2010), *Al-Sadoon and Mufdhi v. UK* App no 61492/08 (ECtHR, 2 March 2010), *Pad and others v. Turkey* App no 60167/00 (ECtHR, 28 June 2007), *Solomou* (above, note 32), *Hirsi Jamaa and Others v. Italy*, App No. 27765/09 (ECtHR, 23 February 2012).
44 This is what the European Court of Human Rights has called the criterion of 'authority' or 'authority and control' over persons. See, in particular, *Illich Sánchez Ramirez v. France*, App no (ECtHR, 24 June 1996) and the cases of *Issa* and *Al-Skeini* (paras 123–124, 133–137, and the two concurring opinions of Judges Rozakis and Bonello) quoted above (in notes 32, 42).
45 Gammeltoft-Hansen, *Access to Asylum*, 149.
46 Helmut P. Aust, *Complicity and the Law of State Responsibility* (Cambridge: Cambridge University Press, 2011), 409.
47 This evolution is also reflected at the national level, with the UK Supreme Court's ruling in *Smith and others* being one of the most recent examples. This case concerned the question of whether British soldiers abroad are protected under the ECHR, in particular in territories that are *not* under UK control. In its decision, the UK Supreme Court found that the ECHR was applicable in such extraterritorial situations, thus discarding the requirement of effective territorial control. See *Smith and others v. The Ministry of Defence* (UKSC 41, 19 June 2013).
48 Elihu Lauterpacht and Daniel Bethlehem, 'The Scope and Content of the Principle of *Non-Refoulement*: Opinion', in *Refugee Protection in International Law: UNHCR's Global Consultations on International Protection*, ed. Erika Feller, Volker Türk and Frances Nicholson (Cambridge: Cambridge University Press, 2003), 67, 77–86. See also UNHCR (above, note Error! Bookmark not defined.) para. 24, Goodwin-Gill and McAdam, *The Refugee in International Law*, 248; Hathaway, *The Rights of Refugees Under International Law*, 315–317; Gregor Noll, 'Seeking Asylum at Embassies: A Right to Entry under International Law?', *International Journal of Refugee Law* 17 no. 3 (2005), 549 with further references.
49 See Concurring opinion of Judge Pinto de Albuquerque as annexed to the judgment in *Hirsi* (above, note 42).
50 Den Heijer, *Europe and Extraterritorial Asylum*, 289.
51 Den Heijer, *Europe and Extraterritorial Asylum*, 54.
52 Den Heijer, *Europe and Extraterritorial Asylum*, 54.
53 Den Heijer, *Europe and Extraterritorial Asylum*, 45–48; Gammeltoft-Hansen, *Access to Asylum*, 195–204.
54 Gammeltoft-Hansen, *Access to Asylum*, 207.
55 *Isaak v. Turkey* (above, note 32) para. 119.
56 *Ilascu*, para. 393.
57 Gammeltoft-Hansen, *Access to Asylum*, 202–203.
58 Discussed extensively in Sigrun Skogly, *Beyond National Borders: States' Human Rights Obligations in International Cooperation* (Antwerp: Intersentia, 2006), 83–98, 144–153.

59 For the following references see Gammeltoft-Hansen, *Access to Asylum*, 202–203.
60 Rick Lawson, 'Out of Control: State Responsibility and Human Rights: Will the ILC's Definition of the "Act of State" meet the Challenges of the 21st Century?', in *Human Rights, International Organisations and Foreign Policy: Essays in Honour of Peter Baehr*, eds Monique Castermans-Holleman, Fried van Hoof and Jacqueline Smith (The Hague: Kluwer, 1998), 111.
61 *Soering v. UK* App no 14038/88 (ECtHR, 7 July 1989).
62 *Legal Consequences of the Construction of a Wall in the Occupied Palestinian Territory* (above, note 34).
63 Den Heijer, *Europe and Extraterritorial Asylum*, 48.
64 Den Heijer, *Europe and Extraterritorial Asylum*, 48.
65 Thomas Gammeltoft-Hansen, 'The Externalisation of European Migration Control and The Reach of International Refugee Law', in, *The First Decade of EU Migration and Asylum Law*, eds Elspeth Guild and Paul Minderhoud (Leiden: Nijhoff, 2012); Noll, 'Seeking Asylum at Embassies', 569.
66 Gammeltoft-Hansen, *Access to Asylum*, 204.
67 Den Heijer, *Europe and Extraterritorial Asylum*, 58.
68 See ILC, Draft Articles on Responsibility of States for Internationally Wrongful Acts, with commentaries (2001), General commentary, para. 1.
69 Lauterpacht and Bethlehem, 'Scope and Content', 109–110.
70 This idea of a 'principal' and a 'subsidiary' protection responsibility appears, *inter alia*, in the European Commission's response to a question from the European Parliament (E-3228/2008, 9 June 2008) on the influence of ILOs on the number of asylum seekers in the EU.
71 Gammeltoft-Hansen, 'The Externalisation of European Migration Control', 21.
72 Cf. the commentary on Articles 5 and 6 in ILC (above, note 67).
73 For Article 8 see James Crawford, *The International Law Commission's Articles on State Responsibility: Introduction, Text and Commentaries* (Cambridge: Cambridge University Press, 2002), 110; James Crawford, *State Responsibility: The General Part* (Cambridge: Cambridge University Press, 2013), 144. For Article 16 ASR, see Aust, *Complicity*, 198–199, where the author lists various forms of support that could qualify as aid and assistance in the sense of Article 16 ASR, without requiring a formal basis between the acting and the complicit state. See also Gammeltoft-Hansen, *Access to Asylum*, 265.
74 This view is also supported by European Council on Refugees and Exiles, 'Defending Refugees' Access', 30; Gammeltoft-Hansen, *Access to Asylum*, 205; Refugee Council, 'Remote Controls', 48, 50.
75 See Refugee Council, 'Remote Controls', 35–49.
76 Refugee Council, 'Remote Controls', 36.
77 Refugee Council, 'Remote Controls', 44–45.
78 Scholten and Minderhoud, 'Regulation Immigration Control', 138.
79 For a detailed analysis see Aust, *Complicity*, chapter 5.
80 ILC (above, note 67), Article 16 para. 9.
81 Aust, *Complicity*, 267.
82 See, for example, ILC (above, note 67), commentary on article 16, para. 5, where it is held that '[t]here is no requirement that the aid or assistance should have been essential to the performance of the internationally wrongful act; it is sufficient if it contributed significantly to that act'.
83 Aust, *Complicity*, 210.
84 See Aust, *Complicity*, 232–237.
85 Aust, *Complicity*, 244–245, 249.
86 Crawford, *The International Law Commission's Articles on State Responsibility*, 13. We should also bear in mind that the intent requirement is problematic insofar, as it is hardly possible to identify a state's will (as precondition for intent). See Aust, *Complicity*, 241.
87 Den Heijer, *Europe and Extraterritorial Asylum*, 101–103.
88 See Aust, *Complicity*, 393–418.
89 Aust, *Complicity*, 397.

90   Aust, *Complicity*, 403.
91   Aust, *Complicity*, 417.
92   Aust, *Complicity*, 418.
93   Application of the Convention on the Prevention and Punishment of the Crime of Genocide (*Bosnia and Herzogovina v. Serbia and Montenegro*) Judgment (ICJ, 26 February 2007).
94   *Genocide* Case (above, note 92) para. 432.
95   See Andrea Gattini, 'Breach of the Obligation to Prevent and reparation Thereof in the ICJ's Genocide Convention Judgment', *European Journal of International Law* 18 no. 4 (2007), 669, 703.
96   For the ECtHR, see *Abdulaziz, Cabales and Balkandali v. the UK* (1985), Series A no. 94, para. 67 and *Boujlifa v. France* (1997) Reports of Judgments and Decisions 1997-VI, para. 42 and *Hirsi* (above, note 42) para. 113. For the Human Rights Committee, see *ICCPR General Comment No. 15: The position of aliens under the Covenant* (1986) para. 5.
97   See, for example, Emmerich de Vattel, *The Law of Nations, or Principles of the Law of Nature, Applied to the Conduct of Nations and Sovereigns* (London: T. & J.W. Johnson, 1883), book II, para. 94. Cf. also Goodwin-Gill and McAdam, *The Refugee in International Law*, 375; Bernard Ryan, 'Extraterritorial Immigration Control: What Role for Legal Guarantees?', in *Extraterritorial Immigration Control: Legal Challenges*, eds Bernard Ryan and Valsamis Mitsilegas, 3–38 (Leiden: Nijhoff, 2010); Wouters, *International Legal Standards for the Protection From Refoulement*, 569; Anja Klug and Tim Howe, 'The Concept of State Jurisdiction and the Applicability of the *Non-Refoulement* Principle to Extraterritorial Interception Measures', in *Extraterritorial Immigration Control: Legal Challenges*, eds Bernard Ryan and Valsamis Mitsilegas (Leiden: Nijhoff, 2010), 69.
98   Goodwin-Gill and McAdam, *The Refugee in International Law*, 388.
99   Violeta Moreno Lax, 'Must EU Borders have Doors for Refugees? On the Compatibility of Schengen Visas and Carriers' Sanctions with EU Member States' Obligations to Provide International Protection to Refugees', *European Journal of Migration and Law* 10 no. 3 (2008), 364.
100 Gammeltoft-Hansen, *Access to Asylum*, 234.
101 Thomas Gammeltoft-Hansen, 'Outsourcing Asylum: The Advent of Protection Lite', in *Europe in the World: EU Geopolitics and the Making of European Space*, ed. Luiza Bialasiewicz, 129–152 (Farnham: Ashgate, 2011), 148; Moreno Lax, 'Must EU Borders Have Doors for Refugees?', 334; Guy Goodwin-Gill, Submission on behalf of UNHCR to the Court of Appeal considering the Roma Rights Case, C1/2002/2183/QBACF, para. 29.iv) and v). For the interpretation of '*non-refoulement* as effectiveness' see Gammeltoft-Hansen, *Access to Asylum*, 96–99.
102 Wouters, *International Legal Standards*, 567–568. For an analysis of these practices' inconsistency with the obligation of states to interpret treaty obligations in 'good faith', see Goodwin-Gill and McAdam, *The Refugee in International Law*, 387–390.
103 Den Heijer, *Europe and Extraterritorial Asylum*, 285.
104 The summaries of these reports that are provided by the European Commission do not contain any details on the specific activities of ILOs and, in particular, no information on how their activities affect asylum seekers. For the most recent summary see European Commission, 'Commission Staff Working Document accompanying the document Communication from the Commission to the European Parliament and the Council, 4th Annual Report on Immigration and Asylum (2012)' COM(2013) 422 final, Brussels 16 July 2013, 55–57. For this problem of lack of information see also European Council on Refugees and Exiles, 'Defending Refugees' Access', 31; Refugee Council, 'Remote Controls', 36; Gammeltoft-Hansen, *Access to Asylum*, 170–171; den Heijer, *Europe and Extraterritorial Asylum*, 297.
105 Gammeltoft-Hansen, *Access to Asylum*, 170.
106 Den Heijer, *Europe and Extraterritorial Asylum*, 297.

107 Den Heijer, *Europe and Extraterritorial Asylum*, 297.
108 Den Heijer, *Europe and Extraterritorial Asylum*, 290–291; see also Gammeltoft-Hansen, *Access to Asylum*, 235, where the author lists various recommendations put forward by UNHCR, NGOs and scholars, such as the issuance of 'protection visas' by ILOs, clearer monitoring and reporting mechanisms, human rights trainings for private actors and the introduction of 'protected entry procedures'.
109 Hannah Arendt, *The Origins of Totalitarianism* (San Diego, CA: Harcourt, Brace, Jovanovich, 1968 [1951]), 177.

Bibliography

Arendt, Hannah. *The Origins of Totalitarianism*. San Diego, CA: Harcourt, Brace, Jovanovich, 1968 (First published 1951).

Aust, Helmut P. *Complicity and the Law of State Responsibility*. Cambridge: Cambridge University Press, 2011.

Brouwer, Andrew, and Judith Kumin. 'Interception and Asylum: When Migration Control and Human Rights Collide'. *Refuge* 21 no. 4 (2003): 6–24.

Crawford, James. *The International Law Commission's Articles on State Responsibility: Introduction, Text and Commentaries*. Cambridge: Cambridge University Press, 2002.

Crawford, James. *State Responsibility: The General Part*. Cambridge: Cambridge University Press, 2013.

De Boer, Tom. 'Closing Legal Black Holes: The Role of Extraterritorial Jurisdiction in Refugee Rights Protection'. *Journal of Refugee Studies* 28 no. 1 (2015): 118–134 (First published online October 9, 2014).

De Schutter, Olivier. 'Globalization and Jurisdiction: Lessons from the European Convention on Human Rights'. In *Baltic Yearbook of International Law*, Volume 6, edited by Carin Laurin. Leiden: Brill/Nijhoff, 2006.

de Vattel, Emmerich. *The Law of Nations, or Principles of the Law of Nature, Applied to the Conduct of Nations and Sovereigns*. London: T. & J.W. Johnson, 1883.

den Heijer, Maarten. *Europe and Extraterritorial Asylum*. Oxford: Hart, 2012.

den Heijer, Maarten, and Rick Lawson, 'Extraterritorial Human Rights and the Concept of "Jurisdiction"'. In *Global Justice, State Duties: The Extraterritorial Scope of Economic, Social and Cultural Rights in International Law*, edited by Malcolm Langford, Martin Scheinin, Wouter Vandenhole and Willem van Genugten, 153–191. Cambridge: Cambridge University Press, 2012.

European Council on Refugees and Exiles. 'Defending Refugees' Access to Protection in Europe'. Brussels: European Council on Refugees and Exiles, 2007.

Gammeltoft-Hansen, Thomas. *Access to Asylum: International Refugee Law and the Globalisation of Migration Control*. Cambridge: Cambridge University Press, 2011.

Gammeltoft-Hansen, Thomas. 'Outsourcing Asylum: The Advent of Protection Lite'. In *Europe in the World: EU Geopolitics and the Making of European Space*, edited by Luiza Bialasiewicz, 129–152. Farnham: Ashgate, 2011.

Gammeltoft-Hansen, Thomas. 'The Externalisation of European Migration Control and the Reach of International Refugee Law'. In *The First Decade of EU Migration and Asylum Law*, edited by Elspeth Guild and Paul Minderhoud. Leiden: Nijhoff, 2012.

Gattini, Andrea. 'Breach of the Obligation to Prevent and Reparation Thereof in the ICJ's Genocide Judgment'. *European Journal of International Law* 18 no. 4 (2007).

Goodwin-Gill, Guy S., and Jane McAdam. *The Refugee in International Law* (3rd edn). Oxford: Oxford University Press, 2007.

Guild, Elspeth. 'Moving the Borders of Europe'. Inaugural lecture given at University of Nijmegen, the Netherlands. 30 May 2001.

Guild, Elspeth, and Paul Minderhoud, (eds). *The First Decade of EU Migration and Asylum Law*. Leiden: Nijhoff, 2012.

Hathaway, James. *The Rights of Refugees under International Law*. Cambridge: Cambridge University Press, 2005.

International Air Transport Association. 'A Code of Conduct for Immigration Liaison Officers'. Montreal, Quebec: IATA Control Authorities Working Group, October 2002.

Klug, Anja and Tim Howe. 'The Concept of State Jurisdiction and the Applicability of the *Non-Refoulement* Principle to Extraterritorial Interception Measures'. In *Extraterritorial Immigration Control: Legal Challenges*, edited by Bernard Ryan and Valsamis Mitsilegas. Leiden: Nijhoff, 2010.

Lauterpacht, Elihu and Daniel Bethlehem. 'The Scope and Content of the Principle of *Non-Refoulement*: Opinion'. In *Refugee Protection in International Law: UNHCR's Global Consultations on International Protection*, edited by Erika Feller, Volker Türk, and Frances Nicholson. Cambridge: Cambridge University Press, 2003.

Lawson, Rick. 'Out of Control: State Responsibility and Human Rights: Will the ILC's Definition of the "Act of State" meet the Challenges of the 21st Century?' In *Human Rights, International Organisations and Foreign Policy: Essays in Honour of Peter Baehr*, edited by Monique Castermans-Holleman, Fried van Hoof and Jacqueline Smith. The Hague: Kluwer, 1998.

Milanovic, Marko. 'From Compromise to Principle: Clarifying the Concept of State Jurisdiction in Human Rights Treaties'. *Human Rights Law Review* 8 no. 3 (2008): 411–448.

Moreno Lax, Violeta. 'Must EU Borders have Doors for Refugees? On the Compatibility of Schengen Visas and Carriers' Sanctions with EU Member States' Obligations to Provide International Protection to Refugees'. *European Journal of Migration and Law* 10 no. 3 (2008): 315–364.

Nicholson, Eleanor T. 'Cutting Off the Flow: Extraterritorial Controls to Prevent Migration'. Berkeley, CA: University of California, Chief Justice Earl Warren Institute on Law and Social Policy, Berkeley Law School, 2011.

Noll, Gregor. 'Seeking Asylum at Embassies: A Right to Entry under International Law?' *International Journal of Refugee Law* 17 no. 3 (2005): 542–573.

Nowak, Manfred. *UN Covenant on Civil and Political Rights: CCPR Commentary*. Kehl am Rhein: Engel, 2005.

Refugee Council. 'Remote Controls: How UK Border Controls are Endangering the Lives of Refugees'. London: Refugee Council, 2008.

Ryan, Bernard. 'Extraterritorial Immigration Control: What Role for Legal Guarantees?'. In *Extraterritorial Immigration Control: Legal Challenges*, edited by Bernard Ryan and Valsamis Mitsilegas, 3–38. Leiden: Nijhoff, 2010.

Scholten, Sophie, and Paul Minderhoud. 'Regulating Immigration Control: Carrier Sanctions in the Netherlands'. *European Journal of Migration and Law* 10 (2008): 123–147.

Sianni, Areti. 'Interception Practices in Europe and Their Implications'. *Refugee Survey Quarterly* 21 no. 28 (2003).

Skogly, Sigrun. *Beyond National Borders: States' Human Rights Obligations in International Cooperation*. Antwerp: Intersentia, 2006.

Türk, Volker, and Frances Nicholson. 'Refugee Protection in International Law: An Overall Perspective'. In *Refugee Protection in International Law: UNHCR's Global Consultations on International Protection*, edited by Erika Feller, Volker Türk and Frances Nicholson, 3–45. Cambridge: Cambridge University Press, 2003.

Wouters, Kees. *International Legal Standards for the Protection from Refoulement*. Antwerp: Intersentia, 2009.

9

STATE RESPONSIBILITY AND MIGRATION CONTROL

Australia's international deterrence model

Nikolas Feith Tan

> International responsibility-sharing is the basis on which the whole global refugee
> system works. I hope that the Australian government will reconsider its approach.
>
> (António Guterres[1])

9.1 Introduction

Developed states are increasingly projecting migration control measures beyond their borders through cooperation with developing states, to prevent asylum-seekers from accessing their territory.[2] Such migration control arrangements are increasingly complex, often involving cooperation between states and non-state actors.[3] In the European context, the now-defunct Italy–Libya Treaty of Friendship, Partnership and Cooperation may be the most clear-cut example.[4] Recent developments in bilateral cooperation between Spain and Senegal and Mauritania,[5] for example, and the recent European Union and Turkey deal of 18 March 2016, suggest that cooperation-based migration control is on the rise.[6]

This chapter analyses the policies of Australia, a state that has led the way in preventing asylum-seeking arrivals over the past fifteen years.[7] Australia has sought to stem the flow of asylum-seekers arriving by boat by entering into a range of migration control arrangements with states in the region, such as Sri Lanka, Malaysia and Indonesia. Australia has also established offshore asylum processing agreements, under which asylum-seekers are transferred to Papua New Guinea and Nauru for processing. Most recently, Australia signed a deal with Cambodia to permanently resettle refugees in that country.[8] These policies significantly challenge the existing refugee and human rights protection regime, still largely tied to concepts of territoriality and single-state responsibility. On the other hand, measures to deter or prevent asylum-seekers' access are nothing new. Since the 1980s, developed states have taken steps to keep asylum-seekers from accessing their territory, jurisdiction and asylum procedures.[9] However, in the past these efforts were undertaken unilaterally by individual states. The defining feature of the relatively new migration control arrangements discussed in this chapter is the international cooperation component, whereby a state – in this case, Australia – undertakes extraterritorial measures in cooperation with another state – for example, Papua New Guinea – to prevent access to asylum in the first state. I term this form of state cooperation to prevent access to asylum 'cooperative non-entrée'.

The international element of cooperative non-entrée is significant, because it raises questions about the division of responsibility between states. At the level of general international law, State Responsibility is receiving increasing scholarly attention.[10] In such complex scenarios the attribution of responsibility to one state is often problematic, and not necessarily desirable.[11] Although such migration control policies challenge the reach of international law, extraterritorial human rights jurisdiction and the general international law doctrine of State Responsibility may fill this perceived gap in international human rights protection.[12] Whether these migration control measures neatly fit the definition of transnational law enforcement is not immediately apparent. A range of migration control policies do fall under the umbrella category of 'law enforcement', that is, action or activity compelling the observance of, or compliance with, the law. Measures to prevent the smuggling of persons under the Protocol against the Smuggling of Migrants by Land, Sea and Air[13] are often necessarily trans- or international in character, and are explicitly encouraged under the Protocol.[14]

One may argue that certain aspects of Australia's cooperation-based migration control arrangements are not law enforcement as such. For example, cooperation with third countries to detain asylum-seekers in remote camps appears more like the enforcement of deterrence policies than legal compliance. These policies aim to prevent asylum-seekers in boats from reaching Australian territory, or undertaking the journey in the first place. In fact, cooperation-based enforcement of migration control in the Pacific often seems to take place despite international legal norms, in pursuit of Australia's interests.

The structure of this chapter is as follows: the chapter first defines the phenomenon of cooperative non-entrée (Section 9.2), then outlines Australia's bilateral and multilateral cooperation arrangements with regional states to prevent access to asylum (Section 9.3). Next, the chapter raises the international legal questions raised by cooperative non-entrée, and offers avenues for establishing responsibility, namely extraterritorial human rights jurisdiction and complicity under the law of State Responsibility (Section 9.4). The chapter concludes that despite the extraterritorial and international character of its cooperative non-entrée regime, Australia is not beyond the reach of international law (Section 9.5).

9.2 The evolution of cooperative non-entrée

Hathaway first coined the term 'non-entrée' ('the refugee shall not access our community') in 1992 to refer to the 'array of legalized policies adopted by states to stymie access by refugees to their territories'.[15] Classical non-entrée may encompass actions by the territory of the receiving state, for example, readmission agreements and extraterritorial measures, such as pushbacks on the high seas. Vedsted-Hansen and Noll defined 'non-arrival' as extraterritorial migration control whereby the asylum-seeker is prevented from setting foot on the territory of the acting state, thereby 'operating as barriers for asylum-seekers to access a jurisdiction where they could seek protection'.[16] However, 'non-entrée' remains the predominant term used in the literature to refer to both territorial and extraterritorial measures, and is the term of art used in this chapter.

Existing scholarly work evaluates the spectrum of unilateral migration control measures undertaken by developed states over the past thirty years, including visa controls,[17] carrier sanctions,[18] establishment of so-called 'international zones',[19] excision of territory for the purposes of migration[20] and interdiction on the high seas.[21] However, little existing literature addresses cases of cooperative migration control, a phenomenon Gammeltoft-Hansen and Hathaway recently referred to as 'complex deterrence'.[22]

Cooperative non-entrée encompasses both bilateral and multilateral measures. Bilateral arrangements involve two states, for example, the Australia–Indonesia Regional Cooperation Model.[23] Multilateral measures involve more than two states, such as the Bali Conference on People Smuggling, Trafficking in Persons and Related Transnational Crime (the Bali Process), which brings together thirty-eight source, transit and asylum states throughout the region.[24]

The locus of cooperative non-entrée is outside the territory of the developed state, limited to measures carried out on the high seas or within the territories of cooperating states. Although at the conceptual level cooperative non-entrée may encompass migration control by air or land, for example, posting airline liaison officers,[25] this chapter confines itself to the methods by which Australia seeks to prevent asylum-seekers arriving by sea.

Cooperative non-entrée includes both formal and informal arrangements. Formal cooperation includes action under an international agreement between states, for example Australia's memoranda of understanding with Papua New Guinea and Nauru. Informal cooperation relates to actions forming part of a broader bilateral relationship, such as Australian assistance to Sri Lanka to prevent asylum-seeker boats leaving that country.[26]

Cooperative non-entrée may be conceptualised as extraterritorial measures undertaken by a developed state in cooperation with a developing state, to prevent access to asylum in the first state. Although cooperative non-entrée may be initiated by developing states in what has been termed 'mimicry',[27] in practice developed states are those that have the resources to carry out these measures. The chapter now turns to an account of Australian-led efforts in this field.

9.3 Australian-led cooperative non-entrée

To prevent access to asylum in its territory, Australia is part of six bilateral arrangements and the Bali Process, arrangements that form a highly developed migration control regime. Since the late 1990s, Australia has called on regional states to deter asylum-seekers attempting to access its territory, leading to the current policy of 'stopping the boats'. The control measures employed to achieve this include traditional unilateral measures – Australia has turned back at least twenty-three boats from Indonesia, Sri Lanka and Vietnam since 2013 – and more innovative, transnational measures in cooperation with regional states, the focus of this chapter. The rationales for these policies vary from the humanitarian desire to stop deaths at sea – an estimated 862 people lost their lives seeking asylum in Australia between 2008 and 2013[28] – to the desire to end the smuggling of persons in the region.[29] Simultaneously, Australia seeks to avoid jurisdiction over, and responsibility for, the individuals concerned, maintaining that Australia's exraterritorial policies do not incur international responsibility.[30] The following section maps Australia's cooperation agreements to prevent asylum-seekers from accessing its territory.

9.3.1 Sri Lanka

Sri Lanka is the only country of origin with which Australia cooperates to prevent asylum-seekers departing its shores, following a protracted civil war that came to an end in 2009. Although allegations of war crimes and crimes against humanity have been made against both sides of the conflict,[31] the state has remained relatively stable since the end of the war. In recent history, significant numbers of Sri Lankan asylum seekers have come to Australia by boat – between 2008–09 and 2011–12 no fewer than ninety per cent were found to be refugees.[32] However, since 2013, Australia's military-led migration control policy, Operation Sovereign Borders, has turned back boats from Sri Lanka in cooperation with local authorities.

Australia–Sri Lanka cooperation is informal, comprising a part of the broader bilateral relationship. However, so vital has cooperation in this area become that one observer calls it a 'preeminent' concern of the bilateral relationship.[33] According to a report of the Human Rights Law Centre:

> Since at least 2009 Australia has encouraged, facilitated and resourced Sri Lanka to stop its people leaving the country as part of Australian border control operations. The aim is to stop boats at their source before they can depart Sri Lanka.[34]

In line with this objective, Australian support to Sri Lankan authorities takes two main forms: funding, and gifts of equipment, and training or capacity building. The first category includes Australia's provision of AUD 2 million in funding to the Sri Lankan navy every year and, in 2013, the gift of two boats to the navy. Australia also provides surveillance, electronic and search and rescue equipment.[35] The second category consists of police, customs and defence personnel posted on the ground to train their Sri Lankan counterparts and assist in operations to intercept boats,[36] resulting in the detection of 67 vessels and the arrest by Sri Lankan authorities of 3,139 migrants seeking to leave the country in 2012 alone.[37]

Sri Lanka's status as a source country for refugees raises a different set of human rights and refugee law questions than does cooperation with transit countries in the region. Although a high proportion of asylum-seekers from Sri Lanka are refugees, until they depart that country they have no status under the 1951 Refugee Convention. Where asylum-seeker boats are intercepted outside Sri Lanka's territory, on the high seas, for example, the prohibition against refoulement may be invoked. Additionally, bilateral cooperation in this area may engage the right to leave, included in Article 12 of the International Covenant on Civil and Political Rights (ICCPR).[38]

9.3.2 Indonesia and Malaysia

Indonesia and Malaysia are key transit states in Southeast Asia, on a path between source countries in the Middle East and Asia (Nethery *et al.* 2012) (Nethery *et al.* 2013).[39] The archipelagic nature of Indonesia, coupled with high levels of corruption among immigration, border and police officials, make the prevention of irregular migration near-impossible. Despite ongoing efforts, 'Indonesian borders are still very porous and only partly policed'.[40] Although Indonesia is not a party to the Refugee Convention, it has historically tolerated the presence of irregular migrants, treating them with what Missbach terms 'benign neglect'.[41] Today around 14,000 asylum-seekers and refugees face a protracted wait with no prospect of resettlement in Indonesia.

Cooperation between Australia and Indonesia falls into three main categories: funding of immigration detention; gifts of equipment; training or capacity-building. Detention of asylum-seekers and refugees takes place under trilateral agreements among Australia, Indonesia and the International Organization for Migration (IOM). Since 2000, the Regional Cooperation Model (RCM), concluded by an exchange of letters,[42] provides for Australian funding of IOM-run detention centres.[43] Australia has actively encouraged Indonesia to detain asylum-seekers through a network extending to thirteen centres around the country, in what Nethery and Gordyn argue amounts to 'incentivised policy transfer'.[44]

The second form of cooperation between Australia and Indonesia relates to the funding and provision of technical equipment to prevent the departure of boats. In 2011, for example, the Australian Federal Police gave their Indonesian counterparts three new, high-speed patrol boats for the purpose of countering people-smuggling operations.[45] Third, Australia funds the Jakarta Centre for Law Enforcement Cooperation, where Australian police train their Indonesian counterparts to investigate and disrupt people-smuggling operations. Australia also stations customs and border protection officers in Indonesia, to 'coordinate efforts to prevent and disrupt maritime people smuggling'.[46]

In July 2011, the Australian government entered a non-binding political agreement with Malaysia to resettle 4,000 refugees in exchange for Malaysia accepting 800 asylum seekers intercepted at sea.[47] The cost of the refugees' transfer and settlement was borne by Australia. Like Indonesia, Malaysia is a transit country that has not signed the Refugee Convention, nor other key international human rights instruments such as the ICCPR, or the Convention against Torture (CAT).[48] There is no domestic legislation to regulate the status of refugees. Malaysia hosts almost 100,000 refugees and 55,000 asylum-seekers under the protection of United Nations High Commissioner for Refugees (UNHCR).[49]

The Malaysia arrangement was invalidated by Australia's High Court in the *M70* case, because there were inadequate legal guarantees that refugees in Malaysia would receive the protection required by the Australian Migration Act.[50] The *M70* judgement represents an important ruling that demonstrates that, as a matter of national law, Australia's power to carry out transnational law enforcement in the field of migration control is not unfettered. Instead, as Foster points out, such transnational arrangements 'can only be undertaken with a country that has legal obligations in respect of refugees'.[51] In the absence of a regional human rights treaty, the Australian High Court placed some meaningful limits on to the extent to which Australia may internationalise its obligations to asylum-seekers and refugees.

9.3.3 Nauru and Papua New Guinea

Moving from transit states to asylum processing states, Australia's cooperation with Nauru and Papua New Guinea dates back to the infamous Tampa incident in 2001. In August of that year, the Norwegian freight ship *MV Tampa* rescued 438 asylum-seekers on their way to Australia. The government refused to allow the ship to dock, requesting it return them to Indonesia.[52] Australia asked the microstate of Nauru, a former trust territory, to accept the asylum-seekers, prompting the 'Pacific Solution'. At the time, Nauru was not a signatory to the Refugee Convention. Under this policy, which lasted until 2008, asylum-seekers bound for Australia were intercepted and detained on Nauru while their protection claims were processed. Former Australian colony, Papua New Guinea, also agreed to house asylum-seekers under the policy. Both states rely on Australian development assistance.

In 2012, Australia resumed transferring asylum-seekers offshore, and entered into new deals with both Nauru (by then a party to the Refugee Convention) and Papua New Guinea in a move that largely recreates the Pacific Solution. Separate agreements re-established detention centres in both states to house and process the claims of asylum-seekers intercepted at sea by Australian border officials.[53] Australia selects who is to be transferred to the centres, and acknowledges that asylum-seekers are under its jurisdiction prior to being transferred.[54] According to the two agreements, Australia bears the costs of all elements of this cooperation, including funding and coordinating contractors at the centres,[55] and paying the Papua New Guinean police force for operations related to the detention centre.[56] These costs are significant: Australia pays Nauru a visa fee of AUD 1,000 (EUR 685, GBP 535) per month per person, for instance, amounting to AUD 29 (EUR 19.8, GBP 15.5) million between 2012 and 2015.[57]

Conditions at the offshore detention centres present grave human rights concerns. A 2015 report commissioned by the Australian government found evidence that on Nauru, asylum-seekers in detention, including children, had been sexually assaulted.[58] In October 2015, the Nauruan government announced that the facility would become an open centre with asylum-seekers free to come and go at all hours of the day.[59] In Papua New Guinea two asylum-seekers died – one killed by staff during a protest, and the other because of inadequate medical care.[60]

In an ambitious extension of the Pacific Solution, the current bilateral deals with Nauru and Papua New Guinea include the possibility of permanent resettlement for asylum-seekers identified as refugees.[61] The most recent statistics show that the vast majority of asylum-seekers are refugees.[62] Refugees in Nauru receive a 'settlement package' paid for by the Australian government, and are free to live in the Nauruan community.[63] In contrast, refugees in Papua New Guinea may only live in a transit centre, and cannot leave Manus Island, located in the remote north of the country.

9.3.4 Cambodia

In exchange for AUD 40 million in development assistance, Cambodia offers permanent resettlement to people identified as refugees on Nauru, under a memorandum of understanding (MoU) with Australia. Signed in 2014 and lasting for four years, the preamble to the agreement provides that Cambodia 'will provide safe and permanent settlement opportunities for Refugees from the Republic of Nauru, based on humanitarian spirit'.[64]

Under the MoU, only refugees who voluntarily accept an offer of resettlement will be transferred from Nauru to Cambodia, and, according to Article 9, Cambodia will treat refugees in accordance with its obligations under the Refugee Convention. As with Australia's cooperation with Nauru and Papua New Guinea, the arrangement is financed entirely by Australia, with the costs of 'settlement arrangements' added to the agreed-upon aid amount, according to the agreement.[65] Cambodia is a signatory to the Refugee Convention, but has little experience of protecting refugees, and only hosted eighty refugees and thirty-three asylum-seekers as of 30 June 2015.[66] Thus far, the deal has only resulted in five refugees being resettled from Nauru to Cambodia.

9.3.5 The Bali Process

At the multilateral level, Australia is co-chair of the Bali Process, a regional forum with a historical focus on migration control and border security.[67] Emerging from the Bangkok Declaration on Irregular Migration and Indonesia–Australia bilateral cooperation, the Process lapsed in 2003, only to be revived in 2009, following increasing numbers of asylum-seekers in Australia.[68] The Bali Process agenda has often been dominated by migration control, rather than human rights and refugee protection, framing refugees within a 'security/border control paradigm'.[69] In 2009, for example, the forum aimed for 'enhanced regional cooperation, including extradition of people smugglers and traffickers, [to] help dismantle criminal networks and reinforce regional efforts to counter the illegal trade in persons'.[70]

Although the Bali Process is the primary multilateral regional forum that addresses migration management in the region, it has been relatively inactive in recent years. Members did not meet at the ministerial level in 2014 or 2015, notwithstanding the Rohingya crisis that saw Bangladeshi and Rohingya asylum-seekers stranded at sea in the opening months of 2015.[71] A senior officials' meeting outcome statement from 6 May 2015 does not even mention the urgent situation in the Andaman Sea.[72] At the Bali Process ministerial meeting of 2016, members agreed to review the response to the crisis.

The Bali Process has been largely concerned with law enforcement cooperation in a region where human rights and refugee law are relatively weak. The Asia-Pacific hosts approximately one-third of the world's refugees, yet lacks a regional human rights instrument and court. Furthermore, within Southeast Asia only three states are party to the Refugee Convention. Against this backdrop, the Bali Process has served to employ transnational law enforcement for migration control ends, focusing on criminalisation and securitisation, with limited acknowledgement of asylum and refugee concerns.[73]

9.4 A challenge to the reach of refugee and human rights law

It is clear that cooperative non-entrée poses significant challenges to the application and efficacy of human rights and refugee law. Cooperation is effected on the high seas or the territory of third states in an attempt to avoid the reach of both domestic and international law.[74] Although Australia's cooperation arrangements give rise to a litany of human rights concerns, this chapter focuses on two possible violations of human rights and refugee law arising from Australia's obligations as a party to the Refugee Convention, ICCPR and CAT.[75] First, boat turn-backs raise concerns about direct or indirect violations of the principle of non-refoulement. When Australia sends back boats on the high seas in cooperation with Sri Lanka, or transit countries such as Indonesia, asylum-seekers may face persecution or onward return.[76] Non-refoulement is set out in Article 33 of the Refugee Convention and Article 3 CAT, and as a human rights law norm drawn from Article 7 ICCPR. The principle is widely accepted as customary in international law. Second, the conditions in offshore detention during asylum processing may amount to torture or other cruel, inhuman or degrading treatment or punishment under Articles 3 and 16 of CAT, or arbitrary detention in violation of Article 9(1) of the ICCPR. Currently, 1,469 men, women and children are detained in Nauru and Papua New Guinea.[77] In its last concluding observations on Australia, the Committee Against Torture found that the conditions of 'overcrowding, inadequate health care; and even allegations of sexual abuse and ill-treatment' on Nauru cause 'serious physical and mental pain and suffering'.[78]

This chapter now briefly explores international law norms that may apply in the context of cooperative non-entrée policies. The chapter considers two possibilities: extraterritorial jurisdiction under human rights and refugee law, and complicity under the law of State Responsibility.

9.4.1 Extraterritorial jurisdiction

Australia has certain human rights and refugee law obligations to all persons under its jurisdiction. Historically, jurisdiction is tied to territory in international law, but cooperative non-entrée arrangements challenge traditional territoriality both by physically removing the locus of activities outside sovereign territory and by involving a second sovereign state. Therefore, to establish jurisdiction, and thus international responsibility, in the context of cooperative non-entrée, Australia's treaty obligations must stretch beyond its territory to the high seas and the territory of other states.

The Refugee Convention has a rather complex gradation of rights based on the refugee's level of attachment to the host state.[79] A limited number of rights, including non-refoulement, accrue at the minimum level of attachment; that is, where a person is under the host state's jurisdiction. Under refugee law the territorial scope of the principle of non-refoulement is not settled law, as evidenced by the narrow interpretation of the principle undertaken by the American Supreme Court in the 1993 *Sale* case.[80] The Court found that the principle applied only after a refugee had entered the territory of a receiving state, stating that:

> . . . a treaty cannot impose uncontemplated extraterritorial obligations on those who ratify it through no more than its general humanitarian intent. Because the text of Article 33 cannot reasonably be read to say anything at all about a nation's actions toward aliens outside its own territory, it does not prohibit such actions.[81]

Subsequently, the UK House of Lords supported the US Supreme Court's interpretation in the *Prague Airport* case challenging the United Kingdom's pre-clearance checks of Roma at Prague airport.[82] Lord Bingham explicitly supported the decision in *Sale*.[83]

The exterritorial application of the non-refoulement principle has been expanded in the past decade. In light of key decisions of the European Court of Human Rights (ECtHR), such as *Hirsi Jamaa*,[84] there now appears to be consensus among refugee law scholars that the principle applies extraterritorially.[85] The UNHCR Advisory Opinion on this question concludes that 'the decisive criterion is not whether such persons are on the State's territory, but rather, whether they come within the effective control and authority of that State'.[86] The extraterritorial application of non-refoulement to refugee law is primarily based on the notion of complementarity between human rights law and refugee law.[87]

At the level of human rights law, Article 2(1) of the ICCPR requires Australia to respect and ensure the rights of 'all individuals within its territory and *subject to its jurisdiction*' (emphasis added). The Human Rights Committee has interpreted

Article 2 to require that states respect 'anyone *within the power or effective control* of that State Party, even if not situated within the territory' (emphasis added).[88] The Committee has further stated that Covenant rights extend 'to all individuals, regardless of nationality . . . such as asylum-seekers [and] refugees'.[89] It then follows that if individuals are not subject to Australia's jurisdiction when turned back on the high seas or when detained in Papua New Guinea or Nauru, Australia is not responsible for any violations of the Covenant.[90]

The CAT also applies extraterritorially to any territory under Australia's jurisdiction.[91] *JHA v. Spain* is especially relevant to the Pacific, as it involved Spanish authorities detaining asylum-seekers in Mauritania, pursuant to a bilateral agreement.[92] However, the Committee Against Torture found the applicant, a Spanish citizen and member of a human rights NGO (non-governmental organisation), lacked standing to bring the complaint. Notwithstanding, in *JHA v. Spain* the Committee recalled its General Comment 2, stating that:

> . . .the jurisdiction of a State party refers to any territory in which it exercises, directly or indirectly, in whole or in part, *de jure or de facto effective control*, in accordance with international law. In particular, it considers that such jurisdiction must also include situations where a State party exercises, directly or indirectly, de facto or de jure control over persons in detention.[93] (emphasis added)

Whether a State exercises a sufficient level of control to incur legal responsibility turns on the facts. Although the jurisprudence of the ECtHR is not binding in Australia, it offers influential guidance. In *Loizidou v. Turkey* the Court separately established extraterritorial jurisdiction under the European Convention on Human Rights (ECHR), based on a state party's control over an area outside its national territory.[94] In *Al Skeini* the Strasbourg court went further, finding that the ECHR applies extraterritorially, where a State 'exercises control and authority over an individual'.[95] Furthermore, in *Issa and Others v. Turkey*, the ECtHR found that state responsibility would be engaged 'where persons on the territory of another state but who are found to be under the former state's authority and control through its agents operating – whether lawfully or unlawfully'.[96]

This chapter proceeds on the basis that refugee and human rights law apply extraterritorially where Australia exercises effective control or authority. Furthermore, states cannot avoid responsibility under human rights treaties because of the existence of other bilateral agreements. In *Hirsi Jamaa*, Italian authorities pushed back Somali and Eritrean nationals to Tripoli under a bilateral arrangement with Libya. The ECtHR pointedly observed that:

> Italy cannot evade its own responsibility by relying on its obligations arising out of bilateral agreements with Libya. Even if it were to be assumed that those agreements made express provision for the return to Libya of migrants intercepted on the high seas, the Contracting States' responsibility continues

even after their having entered into treaty commitments subsequent to the entry into force of the Convention or its Protocols.[97]

In the present context, though Australia acknowledges the potential extra-territorial effect of the human rights treaties,[98] the government denies jurisdiction over the detention centres in Papua New Guinea and Nauru. The government states that involvement 'does not constitute the level of control required under international law to engage Australia's international human rights obligations extraterritorially'.[99] In the absence of a binding national or regional human rights instrument or monitoring body, testing Australia's responsibility is necessarily piecemeal. Notwithstanding this, it seems beyond question that Australia exercises a significant level of control over staffing, funding and operations at the Nauru and Papua New Guinea detention centres.[100]

The question of whether Australian influence over offshore detention centres amounts to the degree of 'effective control' required has attracted recent attention from human rights experts and judicial bodies. The Committee Against Torture's concluding observations on Australia support a finding of jurisdiction that:

> All persons who are under the effective control of the State party, because inter alia they were transferred by the State party to centres run with its finan-cial aid and with the involvement of private contractors of its choice, enjoy the same protection from torture and ill-treatment under the Convention.[101]

The recent High Court of Australia judgement in *M68* supports the contention that Australia participates in the detention of asylum-seekers on Nauru, though it does not authoritatively establish effective control.[102] Australian officials transferred a Bangladeshi asylum-seeker to Nauru under the bilateral agreement, where she was detained and filed an application for refugee status. Later, she was transferred to Australia for medical treatment while pregnant, where she applied to the High Court, requesting that it prohibit the Australian government from returning her to detention on Nauru, claiming that it was unconstitutional. She further claimed that the Australian government was responsible for her detention on Nauru.

Although the case failed on the basis of a 2015 amendment to migration legislation retrospectively authorising 'any action' in relation to offshore processing functions under the MoU, the judgement shows Australia's highest court's view of responsibility in offshore detention.[103] Keane J held that detention 'was effected by the Republic of Nauru, not by the Commonwealth',[104] a sentiment echoed by the majority of the bench. However, Nauruan responsibility for the detention centre does not rule out Australian responsibility as violations may engage the shared responsibility of multiple states.[105] In this vein, Gordon J stated that:

> It is evident from the terms of the MOU that it was intended that the Commonwealth would maintain a significant involvement in the outcome for each Transferee after their removal to Nauru, in the day-to-day operation

of processing activities and in overseeing the practical arrangements to implement the MOU.[106]

Bell J went further, stating that the Commonwealth of Australia 'funded the RPC [regional processing centre] and exercised effective control over the detention of the transferees' through contractual obligations imposed on private companies at the site.[107] An Australian Senate inquiry agreed, stating that:

> ... the degree of involvement by the Australian Government in the establishment, use, operation, and provision of total funding for the [Papua New Guinea] centre clearly satisfies the test of effective control in international law, and the government's ongoing refusal to concede this point displays a denial of Australia's international obligations.[108]

The question of Australia's extraterritorial jurisdiction over the detention centres in Nauru and Papua New Guinea remains open and requires further judicial attention. However, other aspects of Australia's cooperative non-entrée arrangements fall outside the scope of extraterritorial jurisdiction, for example funding, training or providing equipment for the purposes of migration control. In these cases, the requisite level of control is not reached, as the state has no control over persons or territory.

9.4.2 Complicity

At the level of general international law, the doctrine of State Responsibility provides secondary rules for establishing the responsibility of sovereign nations.[109] These principles are secondary to primary norms applicable to specialised branches of international law, such as human rights and refugee law.[110] The preeminent, though not exclusive, articulation of the law of State Responsibility is the International Law Commission's Articles on Responsibility of States for Internationally Wrongful Acts (ASR).

The law of State Responsibility may be invoked when a state or states violate a primary norm, in this context, refoulement or detention conditions contravening the CAT or ICCPR. There are two elements in establishing responsibility. The first is attribution: the act must be attributable to the state. The second is that the act must be a 'breach of an international obligation' in force for the State at the time of the breach.[111]

Elements of the ASR codify norms of customary international law.[112] Complicity is one such binding norm, as stated by the International Court of Justice in the *Genocide* Case.[113] The rule is expressed in Article 16:

> A State which aids or assists another State in the commission of an internationally wrongful act by the latter is internationally responsible for doing so if:

(a) that State does so with knowledge of the circumstances of the internationally wrongful act; and

(b) the act would be internationally wrongful if committed by that State.

Complicity as included in Article 16 relates to a subsidiary or derivative form of responsibility and, as such, does not cover attribution of the internationally wrongful act, as the assisting state does not itself carry out that act.[114] According to the Commentaries to the ASR, states providing aid to other states should not be held responsible for the diversion of such assistance to unlawful ends. Thus the aid and assistance must bear a 'close connection' and be 'clearly linked' to the subsequent internationally wrongful act.[115]

Complicity allows for the attribution of responsibility for acts that are not necessarily unlawful[116] and aid and assistance need not be 'essential to the performance of the internationally wrongful act', but it must contribute significantly to the act. The Commentaries to the ASR include 'financing of the activity in question' as an example of conduct meeting the requirements of Article 16.[117] As discussed above, all Australia's bilateral cooperative non-entrée arrangements include financing of various migration control functions. The law of complicity may hold Australia, 'the assisting state', internationally responsible for aiding or assisting 'the acting state' in the commission of an internationally wrongful act such as violating the principle of non-refoulement.

Turning to the elements contained in Article 16, complicity first requires that the assisting state have knowledge of the act. The level of knowledge required by Article 16 is subject to considerable debate.[118] The Commentaries to the ASR require that the aid or assistance be given 'with a view to' the commission of the wrongful act and that the act is in fact carried out.[119] As Aust points out, this seems to require a high level of knowledge approaching 'wrongful intent'.[120] Notwithstanding the significant financial and operational influence exercised by Australia in Nauru, for example, proving actual intent to violate CAT or the ICCPR may be problematic.

Other authors have argued for a lower knowledge requirement, requiring only 'constructive' knowledge on the part of the assisting State.[121] If one takes this broader view, establishing knowledge may become less onerous. Many of the cooperation measures outlined above are 'clearly linked' to subsequent breaches of international obligations, as referred to by the ASR Commentaries.[122] For example, Australian funding of the Indonesian detention infrastructure has taken place, notwithstanding the known risks of human rights violations in such settings.[123]

Article 16 also requires that an act must be 'wrongful had it been committed by the assisting State itself'.[124] The ASR Commentaries refer to obligations 'under treaties in force or under any other rules of international law that may be applicable'.[125] On the face of it, this element may also cause problems where the assisting and the acting state have different international legal obligations. For example, whereas Australia is bound by the principle of non-refoulement under Article 33 of the Refugee Convention, Indonesia is not a party. However, the two states do share human rights law non-refoulement obligations, as parties to the CAT and ICCPR.

Nollkaemper puts forward a relational theory of shared responsibility, homing in on the relationship between states carrying out a common purpose. Such an approach contemplates derivative responsibility for human rights violations, even where one state has territorial responsibility.[126] In applying this relational approach to Australia's cooperative non-entrée arrangements, it may be argued that Australia's conduct in funding, training and equipping the authorities of Indonesia and Sri Lanka is necessary for the prevention of asylum-seeker departures.[127] Similarly, Australia's conduct in transferring asylum-seekers, and funding and contracting detention centres on Nauru and Papua New Guinea, may be seen as aiding or assisting in detention in violation of human rights law. Indeed, in *M68* the Australian government 'concede[d] the causal connection between its conduct and the plaintiff's detention', and the Court found the state's involvement to be 'materially supportive, if not a necessary condition, of Nauru's physical capacity to detain the plaintiff'.[128]

9.5 Conclusion

This chapter has sought to carve out a definition of cooperative non-entrée: extraterritorial measures undertaken by a developed state in cooperation with a developing state, to prevent access to asylum in the first state. The transnational element of cooperative non-entrée raises questions about the division of responsibility between states for violations of human rights and refugee law. This chapter used the case of Australia to illustrate the architecture of perhaps the most developed cooperative non-entrée regime in the world, though the phenomenon is by no means confined to Australia. These issues are timely, in the context of Europe's response to the current refugee crisis.

This chapter has briefly identified three of the human rights and refugee law concerns to which cooperative non-entrée gives rise, namely non-refoulement, arbitrary detention and torture or other cruel, inhuman or degrading treatment or punishment. The chapter has put forward two possible avenues for holding states accountable. The ICCPR and CAT apply where Australia has 'effective control' over persons or territory in cooperating states, certainly arguable when it comes to the management and coordination of detention centres. However, this form of jurisdiction is unlikely to extend to include mere funding or the delivery of training or equipment in the context of migration control operations.

Complicity under the law of State Responsibility may hold Australia responsible for aiding and assisting another state to carry out international wrongful acts that violate human rights and refugee law in the course of cooperative non-entrée measures. Clearly, not all forms of cooperation will meet the threshold of complicity – where exactly this line is drawn requires further research and judicial attention. However, despite the extraterritorial and international character of its cooperative non-entrée regime, Australia is not beyond the reach of international law.

Notes

1 Former United Nations High Commissioner for Refugees, speaking with regard to Australia's agreement with Cambodia to resettle refugees on Nauru, 26 September 2014. This chapter draws on a paper presented at the Glasgow Human Rights Network graduate conference in May 2015 and a subsequent article, Nikolas Feith Tan, 'State responsibility for international cooperation on migration control: the case of Australia', *Oxford Monitor of Forced Migration* 5 no. 2 (2015): 8–19.

2 Thomas Gammeltoft-Hansen and James C. Hathaway, 'Non-Refoulement in a World of Cooperative Deterrence', *Columbia Journal of Transnational Law* 53 no. 2 (2014): 235–284.

3 Thomas Gammeltoft-Hansen, *Access to Asylum: International Refugee Law and the Globalisation of Migration Control* (Cambridge: Cambridge University Press, 2011).

4 Mariagiulia Giuffré, 'State Responsibility Beyond Borders: What Legal Basis for Italy's Push-Backs to Libya?', *International Journal of Refugee Law* 24 no. 4 (2012): 692–734.

5 European Union Agency for Fundamental Rights, *Fundamental Rights at Europe's Southern Sea Borders* (Vienna: European Union Agency for Fundamental Rights (FRA), 2012).

6 EU–Turkey statement, 18 March 2016, available at www.consilium.europa.eu/en/press/press-releases/2016/03/18-eu-turkey-statement/, accessed 7 April 2016.

7 Jane McAdam, 'Australia and Asylum Seekers', *International Journal of Refugee Law* 25 no. 3 (2013): 435–448.

8 The human rights and refugee law implications of this resettlement agreement are not dealt with in this chapter.

9 James C. Hathaway, 'The Emerging Politics of Non-Entrée', *Refugees* 91 (1992); Jens Vedsted-Hansen, 'Europe's Response to the Arrival of Asylum Seekers: Refugee Protection and Immigration Control', UNHCR Working paper No. 6 (Geneva: UNHCR Centre for Documentation and Research, May 1999).

10 André Nollkaemper and Ilias Plakokefalos, (eds), *Principles of Shared Responsibility in International Law: An Appraisal of the State of the Art* (Cambridge University Press, 2014), 1.

11 André Nollkaemper and Dov Jacobs, 'Shared Responsibility in International Law: a Conceptual Framework', *Michigan Journal of International Law* 34 no. 2 (2012): 359; André Nollkaemper', 'Shared Responsibility for Human Rights Violations: a Relational Account', in this volume.

12 Marko Milanovic, 'From Compromise to Principle: Clarifying the Concept of State Jurisdiction in Human Rights Treaties', *Human Rights Law Review* 8 no. 3 (2008): 411–448; Marko Milanovic, 'Extraterritoriality and Human Rights: Prospects and Challenges', in this volume; International Law Commission, Articles on Responsibility of States for Internationally Wrongful Acts, *Report of the ILC on the Work of Its 53rd Session*, UN Doc. A/56/10 (2001a).

13 UN General Assembly, Protocol against the Smuggling of Migrants by Land, Sea and Air, Supplementing the United Nations Convention against Transnational Organized Crime, 15 November 2000, available at www.refworld.org/docid/479dee062.html, accessed 22 February 2016.

14 See Arts. 2, 7, 11(6) and 14(1).

15 Hathaway, 'The Emerging Politics of Non-Entrée', 291; James C. Hathaway and Alexander Neve, 'Making International Refugee Law Relevant Again: A Proposal for Collectivized and Solution-Oriented Protection', *Harvard Human Rights Journal* 10 (1997): 120 fn 8.

16 Gregor Noll and Jens Vedsted-Hansen, 'Non-Communitarians: Refugee and Asylum Policies', in *The EU and Human rights*, eds Philip Alston, Mara Bustelo and James Heenan, 359–410 (Oxford: Oxford University Press, 1999), 382.

17 Vedsted-Hansen, 'Europe's Response to the Arrival of Asylum Seekers'.

18 Antonio Cruz, *Shifting Responsibility: Carriers' Liability in the Member States of the European Union and North America* (London: Trentham Books, 1995); Eleanor Taylor-Nicholson, *Cutting Off the Flow: Extraterritorial Controls to Prevent Migration* (Berkeley Law Issues Brief, 2011).

19 Hathaway and Neve, 'Making International Refugee Law Relevant Again', 122.

20 Tara Magner, 'A Less Than "Pacific" Solution for Asylum Seekers in Australia', *International Journal of Refugee Law* 16 no. 1 (2004): 53–90.

21 Stephen H. Legomsky, 'The USA and the Caribbean Interdiction Program', *International Journal of Refugee Law* 18 no. 3–4 (2006): 677–695; Jessica Howard, 'To Deter and Deny: Australia and the Interdiction of Asylum Seekers', *Refuge* 21 no. 4 (2003), 35.

22 Gammeltoft-Hansen and Hathaway, 'Non-Refoulement in a World of Cooperative Deterrence'.

23 Jesuit Refugee Service, *The Search: Protection Space in Malaysia, Thailand, Indonesia, Cambodia and the Philippines* (Bangkok: JRS Asia Pacific, 2012).

24 Itamar Mann, 'Dialectic of Transnationalism: Unauthorized Migration and Human Rights, 1993–2013', *Harvard International Law Journal* 54 no. 2 (2013): 315–391; Susan Kneebone, 'The Bali Process and Global Refugee Policy in the Asia-Pacific Region', *Journal of Refugee Studies* 27 no. 4 (2014): 596–618; Susan Kneebone, 'Comparative Regional Protection Frameworks for Refugees: Norms and Norm Entrepreneurs', *The International Journal of Human Rights* 20 no. 2 (2016): 153–172.

25 Maarten den Heijer, *Europe and Extraterritorial Asylum* (Oxford: Hart, 2012), 125–132.

26 Emily Howie, 'Asia-Pacific: Australian Border Control in Sri Lanka', *Alternative Law Journal* 39 no. 1 (2014): 52–53; Australian Minister for Foreign Affairs media release, 'Australia–Sri Lanka talks: four-point plan to fight people smuggling', 17 December 2012, available at http://foreignminister.gov.au/releases/2012/bc_mr_121217.html, accessed 20 April 2015.

27 Thomas Gammeltoft-Hansen, 'The Externalisation of European Migration Control and the Reach of International Refugee Law', in *The First Decade of EU Migration and Asylum Law*, eds Elspeth Guild and Paul Minderhoud, 273–298 (Leiden: Nijhoff, 2012).

28 Mary Anne Kenny and Sara Davies, 'FactCheck: Did 1200 Refugees Die at Sea under Labor?' *The Conversation*, 3 March 2015, available at https://theconversation.com/factcheck-have-more-than-1000-asylum-seekers-died-at-sea-under-labor-16221, accessed 17 February 2016; Australian Border Deaths Database, Border Crossing Observatory. Available at http://artsonline.monash.edu.au/thebordercrossingobservatory/publications/australian-border-deaths-database/, accessed 17 February 2016.

29 Antje Missbach and Frieda Sinanu, '"The Scum of the Earth"? Foreign People Smugglers and Their Local Counterparts in Indonesia', *Journal of Current Southeast Asian Affairs* 30 no. 4 (2012): 57–87.

30 With regard to the detention centres in Nauru and Papua New Guinea, the government has said: 'The consistent position taken by Australia is that while we are assisting PNG and Nauru in the management of the centres, this assistance does not constitute the level of control required under international law to engage Australia's international human rights obligations extraterritorially'. 'Australian Government's Response to Amnesty International reports arising from visits to Manus Offshore Processing Centre' in Legal and Constitutional Affairs References Committee, 'Incident at the Manus Island Detention Centre from 16 February to 18 February 2014' December 2014 para. 7.29.

31 Human Rights Law Centre, *Can't Flee, Can't Stay: Australia's Interception and Return of Sri Lankan Asylum Seekers* (Melbourne, VIC: Human Rights Law Centre, 2014), available at www.hrlc.org.au/wp-content/uploads/2014/03/HRLC_SriLanka_Report_11March2014.pdf, accessed 21 September 2015 3.

32 Refugee Council of Australia, 'Grant rates for asylum seekers in Australia 2011–2012', available at www.refugeecouncil.org.au/n/mr/131214_Asylum_Grant.pdf, accessed on 17 February 2016.

33 Emily Howie, 'Sri Lankan Boat Migration to Australia', *Economic & Political Weekly* 48 no. 35 (2013): 97.

34 Human Rights Law Centre, *Can't Flee, Can't Stay*.

35 Human Rights Law Centre, *Can't Flee, Can't Stay*, 3; Howie, 'Asia-Pacific: Australian border control in Sri Lanka', 52.

36 Howie, 'Asia-Pacific: Australian border control in Sri Lanka'.

37 Graeme Hugo and Lakshman Dissanayake, 'The Process of Sri Lankan Migration to Australia Focussing on Irregular Migrants Seeking Asylum', Irregular Migration Research Program Occasional Paper Series, Australian Government Department of Immigration and Border Protection (2014) 20.

38 For a detailed exploration of the right to leave in the context of European migration control efforts, see Nora Markard, 'The Right to Leave by Sea Legal Limits on EU Migration Control by Third Countries', paper presented at the European University Institute's seminar on Migration Control and Criminal Jurisdiction (Florence, Italy: 16 June 2015).

39 Amy Nethery, Brynna Rafferty-Brown and Savitri Taylor, 'Exporting Detention: Australia-Funded Immigration Detention in Indonesia', *Journal of Refugee Studies* 26 no. 1 (2013): 94.

40 Antje Missbach, 'Doors and Fences: Controlling Indonesia's Porous Borders and Policing Asylum Seekers', *Singapore Journal of Tropical Geography* 35 no. 2 (2014): 239.

41 Missbach and Sinanu, '"The Scum of the Earth"?', 66.

42 Mary Crock and Daniel Ghezelbash, 'Do Loose Lips Bring Ships? The Role of Policy, Politics and Human Rights in Managing Unauthorised Boat Arrivals', *Griffith Law Review* 19 no. 2 (2010): 238 270. The RCM is also referred to as the Regional Cooperation Agreement, see Nethery, Rafferty-Brown and Taylor, 'Exporting Detention', 95.

43 Australian Government, Department of Immigration and Border Protection, Annual Report 2013–2014, p. 149, available at www.border.gov.au/ReportsandPublications/Documents/annual-reports/DIBP_AR_2013-14.pdf, accessed 22 February 2016.

44 Amy Nethery and Carly Gordyn, 'Australia–Indonesia Cooperation on Asylum-Seekers: A Case of "Incentivised Policy Transfer"', *Australian Journal of International Affairs* 68 no. 2 (2014): 177–193.

45 Missbach, 'Doors and Fences', 233.

46 Harriet Spinks, Cat Barker and David Watt, 'Australian government spending on irregular maritime arrivals and counter-people smuggling activity', Parliamentary Library (Australia) 4 September 2013, table 8 p. 23.

47 Arrangement between the Government of Australia and the Government of Malaysia on Transfer and Resettlement (signed and entered into force 25 July 2011).

48 Opened for signature 19 December 1966, 999 UNTS 171 (entered into force 23 March 1976); opened for signature 10 December 1984, 1465 UNTS 85 (entered into force 26 June 1987),

49 UNHCR, Subregional operations profile – South-East Asia 2015, available at www.unhcr.org/pages/49e4884c6.html, accessed 17 February 2016.

50 *M70 v. Minister for Immigration and Citizenship*, 244 CLR 144 (2011).

51 For a thorough analysis of the Malaysia deal and subsequent high court decision, see Michelle Foster, 'The Implications of the Failed "Malaysian Solution": The Australian High Court and Refugee Responsibility Sharing at International Law', *Melbourne Journal of International Law* 13 no. 1 (2012): 422.

52 Andreas Schloenhardt, 'Deterrence, Detention and Denial: Asylum Seekers in Australia', *University of Queensland Law Journal* 22 no. 1 (2002): 54–73, 59.

53 Regional Resettlement Arrangement between Australia and Papua New Guinea 19 July 2013; Memorandum of Understanding between the Republic of Nauru and the Commonwealth of Australia, relating to the Transfer to and Assessment of Persons in Nauru, and Related Issues.

54 *Plaintiff M68/2015 v. Minister for Immigration and Border Protection (M68)* [2016] HCA 1 (3 February 2016).

55 Art. 9 of the Regional Resettlement Arrangement between Australia and Papua New Guinea and Art. 6 of the Memorandum of Understanding between the Republic of Nauru and the Commonwealth of Australia.

56 Legal and Constitutional Affairs References Committee, 'Incident at the Manus Island Detention Centre from 16 February to 18 February 2014' December 2014 para. 2.9.

57 Paul Farrell, 'Australia has paid Nauru $29m in visa fees to keep asylum seekers in detention', *The Guardian* 22 May 2015, available at www.theguardian.com/australia-news/2015/may/22/australia-has-paid-nauru-29m-in-visa-fees-to-keep-asylum-seekers-in-detention, accessed 22 February 2016.

58 Review into recent allegations relating to conditions and circumstances at the Regional Processing Centre in Nauru, Final Report, 20 March 2015.

59 Republic of Nauru, 'Regional processing – Open Centre', 2 October 2015, available at www.abc.net.au/news/2015-10-03/letter-from-republic-of-nauru-about-open-centre/6825366, accessed 18 February 2016.

60 Robert Cornell, *Review into the events of 16–18 February 2014 at the Manus Island regional processing centre*, Report to the Secretary of the Department of Immigration and Border Protection, 23 May 2014 67; Legal and Constitutional Affairs References Committee, para. 2.53.

61 Art. 5 of the Regional Resettlement Arrangement between Australia and Papua New Guinea and Art. 12 of the Memorandum of Understanding between the Republic of Nauru and the Commonwealth of Australia.

62 As of 30 September 2015, 563 people on Nauru had been found to be refugees (82 per cent), while 169 people in Papua New Guinea had been found to be refugees (94 per cent). Elibritt Karlsen, Australia's offshore processing of asylum seekers in Nauru and PNG: a quick guide to the statistics Parliamentary Library (Australia) Research Paper Series, 12 October 2015, 8–10.

63 Ibid., 9; Chris Kenny, 'Refugees long to be "anywhere but Nauru"', *The Australian* 24 October 2015, available at www.theaustralian.com.au/news/inquirer/refugees-long-to-be-anywhere-but-nauru/news-story/95c727c529918880696ed9a731777c34, accessed 18 February 2016.

64 Memorandum of Understanding between the Government of the Kingdom of Cambodia and the Government of Australia, Relating to the Settlement of Refugees in Cambodia 2014, available at http://dfat.gov.au/international-relations/themes/people-smuggling-trafficking/Documents/cambodia-australia-mou-and-operational-guidelines.pdf, accessed 21 April 2015.

65 Memorandum of Understanding between the Government of the Kingdom of Cambodia and the Government of Australia Art. 12.

66 Andrew & Renata Kaldor Centre for International Refugee Law, *Factsheet: Cambodia and Refugee Protection* (2014); UNHCR, 2015 UNHCR subregional operations profile – South-East Asia, available at www.unhcr.org/pages/49e487c66.html, accessed 22 February 2016.

67 Conference on People Smuggling, Trafficking in Persons and Related Transnational Crime, initiated in 2002.

68 Susan Kneebone, 'ASEAN and the Conceptualization of Refugee Protection', in *Regional Approaches to the Protection of Asylum Seekers: An International Legal Perspective*, ed. Ademola Abass and Francesca Ippolito, 295–323 (Farnham: Ashgate 2014), 309.

69 Kneebone, 'Comparative Regional Protection Frameworks for Refugees', 153–172; ibid.

70 Co-Chairs' Statement, 'Third Bali Regional Ministerial Conference on People Smuggling, Trafficking in Persons and Related Transnational Crime' (Bali, Indonesia. 14–15 April 2009); Kneebone, 'The Bali Process and Global Refugee Policy in the Asia-Pacific Region'.

71 See 'The Bali Process', available at www.baliprocess.net/ministerial-conferences-and-senior-officials-meetings, accessed 22 February 2016.

72 Bali Process ad hoc group senior officials meeting, Wellington, New Zealand, 6 May 2015, Co-chairs' statement. Available at www.baliprocess.net/files/Ad%20Hoc

%20Group/9th%20AHG%20SOM%20outcomes%20statement_150515_FINAL.pdf, accessed 22 February 2016.
73 Kneebone, 'The Bali Process and Global Refugee Policy in the Asia-Pacific Region', 596–618. The Bali Process discourse may, however, be shifting. The recently released Bali Declaration on People Smuggling, Trafficking in Persons and Related Transnational Crime affirms the importance of refugee protection and calls for strict respect for the principle of non-refoulement. Bali Declaration on People Smuggling, Trafficking in Persons and Related Transnational Crime, 23 March 2016. Available at http://kemlu.go.id/id/lembar-informasi/Pages/BALI-DECLARATION-ON-PEOPLE-SMUGGLING,-TRAFFICKING-IN-PERSONS,-AND-RELATED-TRANSNATIONAL-CRIME.aspx, accessed 7 April 2016.
74 Gammeltoft-Hansen and Hathaway, 'Non-Refoulement in a World of Cooperative Deterrence'.
75 Australia is also a party to the International Covenant on Economic, Social and Cultural Rights (ICESCR) and the Convention on the Rights of the Child (CRC). However this chapter confines itself to considering Australia's obligations to asylum seekers in the Refugee Convention, ICCPR and CAT.
76 Savitri Taylor and Brynna Rafferty-Brown, 'Difficult Journeys: Accessing Refugee Protection in Indonesia', *Monash University Law Review* 36 no. 3 (2010): 156.
77 Department of Immigration and Border Protection. 2015. 'Immigration Detention and Community Statistics Summary' 31 July, available at www.border.gov.au/Reportsand Publications/Documents/statistics/immigration-detention-statistics-30-nov-2015.pdf, accessed 21 September 2015.
78 Committee Against Torture, Concluding observations on the fourth and fifth periodic reports of Australia, 26 November 2014, para. 17.
79 James C. Hathaway, *The Rights of Refugees under International Law* (Cambridge: Cambridge University Press, 2005), 154.
80 *Sale, Acting Commissioner Immigration and Naturalization Service v. Haitian Center Council*, 113 S. Ct. 2549, 509 US 155 (1993), 21 June 1993.
81 *Sale, Acting Commissioner, Immigration and Naturalization Service, et al. v Haitian Centers Council, Inc, et al.*, 509 US 155, United States Supreme Court, 21 June 1993; Justice A. M. North, 'Extraterritorial Effect of Non-refoulement', speech delivered at the International Association of Refugee Law Judges World Conference, Bled, Slovenia, 7–9 September 2011.
82 *Regina v Immigration Officer at Prague Airport and Another, Ex parte European Roma Rights Centre and Others* [2004] UKHL 55, United Kingdom: House of Lords (Judicial Committee), 9 December 2004; North, 'Extraterritorial Effect of Non-refoulement'.
83 Lord Bingham at 70.
84 For example, see *Hirsi Jamaa and Others v. Italy*, application no 27765/09, 22 February 2012.
85 Gammeltoft-Hansen and Vedsted-Hansen, this volume; Tom de Boer, 'Closing Legal Black Holes: The Role of Extraterritorial Jurisdiction in Refugee Rights Protection', *Journal of Refugee Studies* 28 no. 1 (2015): 121.
86 UNHCR, 'Advisory Opinion on the Extraterritorial Application of Non-Refoulement Obligations under the 1951 Convention relating to the Status of Refugees and its 1967 Protocol', 26 January 2007, para. 43.
87 Justice A. M. North, 'Extraterritorial Effect of Non-refoulement'.
88 Human Rights Committee, General Comment No. 31 para. 10; Milanovic, 'From Compromise to Principle', 413; Manfred Nowak, *U.N. Covenant on Civil and Political Rights: CCPR Commentary*, 2nd edn (Kehl: Engel, 2005): 43–45.
89 Human Rights Committee, General Comment No. 31 para. 10.
90 Dominic McGoldrick, 'Extraterritorial Application of the International Covenant on Civil and Political Rights' in *Extraterritorial Application of Human Rights Treaties*, eds Fons Coomans and Menno T. Kamminga, 41–72 (Antwerp: Intersentia, 2004), 41–71, 47.

91 Milanovic, 'From Compromise to Principle', 414.
92 CAT/C/41/D/323/2007, UN Committee Against Torture (CAT), 21 November 2008 para. 2.10.
93 Committee Against Torture 2008 para. 8.2.
94 23 European Court of Human Rights 513, 18 December 1996.
95 *Al Skeini and Others v. the United Kingdom*, App no 55721/07, 7 July 2011 para. 137.
96 App 31821/96, [2004] European Convention on Human Rights 629, 16 November 2004 para. 71.
97 App no 27765/09, European Court of Human Rights, Grand Chamber, 23 February 2012 para. 129.
98 Parliamentary Joint Committee on Human Rights, 'Examination of Legislation in Accordance with the Human Rights (Parliamentary Scrutiny) Act 2011: Bills Introduced 9–12 December 2013; Legislative Instruments Received 23 November 2013–31 January 2014' (Second Report of the 44th Parliament, February 2014) para. 2.16.
99 Legal and Constitutional Affairs References Committee, 'Incident at the Manus Island Detention Centre from 16 February to 18 February 2014', December, Australian Senate Report, 2014 para. 7.29.
100 Ibid., para. 7.31.
101 Committee Against Torture 2014 para. 17.
102 *M68/2015 v Minister for Immigration and Border Protection* [2016] HCA 1, 3 February 2016.
103 Migration Amendment (Regional Processing Arrangements) Act 2015 (Cth).
104 *M68* para. 261.
105 Nollkaemper, 'Shared Responsbility'.
106 *M68* para. 291.
107 *M68* para. 93.
108 Legal and Constitutional Affairs References Committee para. 8.33.
109 See also Baxewanos, this volume.
110 Combacau, Jean, and Dennis Alland. ' "Primary" and "Secondary" Rules in the Law of State Responsibility Categorizing International Obligations', *Netherlands Yearbook of International Law* 16 (1985): 81–109.
111 International Law Commission 2001 34.
112 Robert McCorquodale and Penelope Simons, 'Responsibility Beyond Borders: State Responsibility for Extraterritorial Violations by Corporations of International Human Rights Law', *The Modern Law Review* 70 no. 4 (2007): 598–625.
113 Case Concerning the Application of the Convention on the Prevention and Punishment of the Crime of Genocide (*Bosnia and Herzegovina v. Serbia and Montenegro*). International Court of Justice. 26 February 2007 para. 173.
114 Giuffre, 'State Responsibility Beyond Borders', 725.
115 ASR Commentaries 65 para. 8.
116 Helmut, Aust, *Complicity and the Law of State Responsibility*, (Cambridge, 2011), 238.
117 ASR Commentaries 66 para. 1.
118 Aust 235–238.
119 ASR Commentaries 66 para. 5.
120 Aust 235.
121 Gammeltoft-Hansen and Hathaway, 'Non-refoulement in a world of cooperative deterrence', 258.
122 ASR Commentaries 66 para. 5.
123 Nethery, Rafferty-Brown and Taylor, 'Exporting Detention', 88; Human Rights Watch, *Barely Surviving: Detention, Abuse, and Neglect of Migrant Children in Indonesia* (New York: Human Rights Watch, 2013), 30.
124 United States Diplomatic and Consular Staff in Tehran case in International Law Commission 2001 66.

125 ICJ, United States Diplomatic and Consular Staff in Tehran, Judgment, ICJ Reports 1980, p. 29, para. 56. The formulation 'breach of an international obligation' In ASR Art. 2(b) is reflected in Art. 36(2)(c) of the ICJ Statute.
126 Nollkaemper, 'Shared Responsibility'.
127 Emily Howie and Pierre d'Argent, 'Reparation, Cessation, Assurances and Guarantees of Non-Repetition', in *Principles of Shared Responsibility in International Law: An Appraisal of the State of the Art*, eds André Nollkaemper and Ilias Plakokefalos (Cambridge: Cambridge University Press, 2014): 208–250.
128 *M68* para. 93.

Bibliography

Aust, Helmut. *Complicity and the Law of State Responsibility*. Cambridge: Cambridge University Press, 2011.

Australian Government. *Department of Immigration and Border Protection, Annual Report 2013–2014*. Available at www.border.gov.au/ReportsandPublications/Documents/annual-reports/DIBP_AR_2013-14.pdf. (p. 149).

Combacau, Jean, and Dennis Alland. ' "Primary" and "Secondary" Rules in the Law of State Responsibility Categorizing International Obligations'. *Netherlands Yearbook of International Law* 16 (1985): 81–109.

Committee Against Torture, 'Concluding observations on the fourth and fifth periodic reports of Australia', 26 November 2014, para. 17.

Cornell, Robert. *Review into the events of 16–18 February 2014 at the Manus Island regional processing centre*, Report to the Secretary of the Department of Immigration and Border Protection, 23 May 2014.

Crock, Mary, and Daniel Ghezelbash. 'Do Loose Lips Bring Ships?: The Role of Policy, Politics and Human Rights in Managing Unauthorised Boat Arrivals'. *Griffith Law Review* 19 no. 2 (2010): 238–287.

Cruz, Antonio. *Shifting Responsibility: Carriers' Liability in the Member States of the European Union and North America*. London: Trentham Books, 1995.

d'Argent, Pierre. 'Reparation, Cessation, Assurances and Guarantees of Non-Repetition'. In *Principles of Shared Responsibility in International Law: An Appraisal of the State of the Art*, edited by André Nollkæmper and Ilias Plakokefalos, 208–250. Cambridge: Cambridge University Press, 2014.

de Boer, Tom. 'Closing Legal Black Holes: The Role of Extraterritorial Jurisdiction in Refugee Rights Protection'. *Journal of Refugee Studies* 28 no. 1 (2015): 118–134.

den Heijer, Maarten. *Europe and Extraterritorial Asylum*. Oxford: Hart, 2012.

Department of Immigration and Border Protection. 'Immigration Detention and Community Statistics Summary', 31 July 2015.

European Union Agency for Fundamental Rights. *Fundamental Rights at Europe's Southern Sea Borders*. Vienna: European Union Agency for Fundamental Rights (FRA), 2012.

Foster, Michelle. 'The Implications of the Failed "Malaysian Solution": The Australian High Court and Refugee Responsibility Sharing at International Law'. *Melbourne Journal of International Law* 13 no. 1 (2012): 395–423.

Gammeltoft-Hansen, Thomas. *Access to Asylum: International Refugee Law and the Globalisation of Migration Control*. Cambridge: Cambridge University Press, 2011.

Gammeltoft-Hansen, Thomas. 'The Externalisation of European Migration Control and the Reach of International Refugee Law'. In *The First Decade of EU Migration and Asylum Law*, edited by Elspeth Guild and Paul Minderhoud, 273–298. Leiden: Nijhoff, 2012.

Gammeltoft-Hansen, Thomas, and James C. Hathaway. 'Non-Refoulement in a World of Cooperative Deterrence'. *Columbia Journal of Transnational Law* 53 no. 2 (2014): 235–284.

Giuffré, Mariagiulia. 'State Responsibility Beyond Borders: What Legal Basis for Italy's Push-backs to Libya?'. *International Journal of Refugee Law* 24 no. 4 (2012): 692–734.

Hathaway, James C. 'The Emerging Politics of Non-Entrée'. *Refugees* 91 (1992).

Hathaway, James C. *The Rights of Refugees under International Law*. Cambridge: Cambridge University Press, 2005.

Hathaway, James C., and Alexander Neve. 'Making International Refugee Law Relevant Again: A Proposal for Collectivized and Solution-Oriented Protection'. *Harvard Human Rights Journal* 10 (1997): 115–211.

Howard, Jessica. 'To Deter and Deny: Australia and the Interdiction of Asylum Seekers'. *Refuge* 21 no. 4 (2003): 35–50.

Howie, Emily. 'Sri Lankan Boat Migration to Australia'. *Economic & Political Weekly* 48 no. 35 (2013): 97–104.

Howie, Emily. 'Asia–Pacific: Australian Border Control in Sri Lanka'. *Alternative Law Journal* 39 no.1 (2014): 52–53.

Hugo, Graeme, and Lakshman Dissanayake. 'The Process of Sri Lankan Migration to Australia Focussing on Irregular Migrants Seeking Asylum'. Irregular Migration Research Programme Occasional Paper Series ACT: Australian Government Department of Immigration and Border Protection, November 2014.

Human Rights Law Centre. *Can't Flee, Can't Stay: Australia's Interception and Return of Sri Lankan Asylum Seekers*. Melbourne, VIC: Human Rights Law Centre, March 2014. Accessed 21 September, 2015: www.hrlc.org.au/wp-content/uploads/2014/03/HRLC_SriLanka_Report_11March2014.pdf.

Human Rights Watch. *Barely Surviving: Detention, Abuse, and Neglect of Migrant Children in Indonesia*. New York: Human Rights Watch, 2013.

Jesuit Refugee Service. *The Search: Protection Space in Malaysia, Thailand, Indonesia, Cambodia and the Philippines*. Bangkok: JRS Asia Pacific, 2012.

Karlsen, Elibritt, Australia's offshore processing of asylum seekers in Nauru and PNG: a quick guide to the statistics, Parliamentary Library (Australia) Research Paper Series, 12 October 2015.

Kneebone, Susan. 'ASEAN and the Conceptualization of Refugee Protection'. In *Regional Approaches to the Protection of Asylum Seekers: An International Legal Perspective*, edited by Ademola Abass and Francesca Ippolito, 295–323. Farnham: Ashgate, 2014.

Kneebone, Susan. 'The Bali Process and Global Refugee Policy in the Asia–Pacific Region'. *Journal of Refugee Studies* 27 no. 4 (2014): 596–618.

Kneebone, Susan. 'Comparative Regional Protection Frameworks for Refugees: Norms and Norm Entrepreneurs'. *The International Journal of Human Rights* 20 no. 2 (2016): 153–172.

Legomsky, Stephen H. 'The USA and the Caribbean Interdiction Program'. *International Journal of Refugee Law* 18 no. 3–4 (2006): 677–695.

McAdam, Jane. 'Australia and Asylum Seekers'. *International Journal of Refugee Law* 25 no. 3 (2013): 435–448.

McCorquodale, Robert, and Penelope Simons. 'Responsibility Beyond Borders: State Responsibility for Extraterritorial Violations by Corporations of International Human Rights Law'. *The Modern Law Review* 70 no. 4 (2007): 598–625.

McGoldrick, Dominic. 'Extraterritorial Application of the International Covenant on Civil and Political Rights'. In *Extraterritorial Application of Human Rights Treaties*, edited by Fons Coomans and Menno T. Kamminga, 41–72. Antwerp: Intersentia, 2004.

Magner, Tara. 'A Less Than "Pacific" Solution for Asylum Seekers in Australia'. *International Journal of Refugee Law* 16 no. 1 (2004): 53–90.

Mann, Itamar. 'Dialectic of Transnationalism: Unauthorized Migration and Human Rights, 1993–2013'. *Harvard International Law Journal* 54 no. 2 (2013): 315–391.

Markard, Nora. 'The Right to Leave by Sea Legal – Limits of EU Migration Control by Third Countries'. Paper presented at the European University Institute's seminar on Migration Control and Criminal Jurisdiction. Florence, Italy: 16 June 2015.

Milanovic, Marko. 'From Compromise to Principle: Clarifying the Concept of State Jurisdiction in Human Rights Treaties'. *Human Rights Law Review* 8 no. 3 (2008): 411–448.

Milanovic, Marko. 'Extraterritoriality and Human Rights: Prospects and Challenges'. In *Transnational Law Enforcement and Human Rights: the Dark Side of Globalisation*, edited by Thomas Gammeltoft-Hansen and Jens Vedsted-Hansen. London: Routledge, forthcoming in 2016.

Missbach, Antje. 'Doors and Fences: Controlling Indonesia's Porous Borders and Policing Asylum Seekers'. *Singapore Journal of Tropical Geography* 35 no. 2 (2014): 228–244.

Missbach, Antje, and Frieda Sinanu. '"The Scum of the Earth"?: Foreign People Smugglers and Their Local Counterparts in Indonesia'. *Journal of Current Southeast Asian Affairs* 30 no. 4 (2011): 57–87.

Nethery, Amy, and Carly Gordyn. 'Australia–Indonesia Cooperation on Asylum-Seekers: A Case of "Incentivised Policy Transfer"'. *Australian Journal of International Affairs* 68 no. 2 (2014): 177–193.

Nethery, Amy, Brynna Rafferty-Brown, and Savitri Taylor. 'Exporting Detention: Australia-funded Immigration Detention in Indonesia'. *Journal of Refugee Studies* 26 no. 1 (2013): 88–109.

Noll, Gregor, and Jens Vedsted-Hansen. 'Non-Communitarians: Refugee and Asylum Policies'. In *The EU and Human Rights*, edited by Philip Alston, Mara Bustelo and James Heenan, 359–410. Oxford: Oxford University Press, 1999.

Nollkaemper, André, and Dov Jacobs. 'Shared Responsibility in International Law: A Conceptual Framework'. *Michigan Journal of International Law* 34 no. 2 (2012): 359–438.

Nollkaemper, André, and Ilias Plakokefalos, (eds). *Principles of Shared Responsibility in International Law: An Appraisal of the State of the Art.* Cambridge: Cambridge University Press, 2014.

Nowak, Manfred. *U.N. Covenant on Civil and Political Rights: CCPR Commentary*, 2nd edition. Kehl: Engel, 2005.

Schloenhardt, Andreas. 'Deterrence, Detention and Denial: Asylum Seekers in Australia'. *University of Queensland Law Journal* 22 no. 1 (2002): 54–73.

Spinks, Harriet, Cat Barker and David Watt. *Australian Government Spending on Irregular Maritime Arrivals and Counter-People Smuggling Activity.* Parliamentary Library, Australia, 4 September 2013.

Tan, Nikolas Feith. 'State Responsibility for International Cooperation on Migration Control: the Case of Australia'. *Oxford Monitor of Forced Migration* 5 no. 2 (2015): 8–19.

Taylor, Savitri, and Brynna Rafferty-Brown. 'Difficult Journeys: Accessing Refugee Protection in Indonesia'. *Monash University Law Review* 36 no. 3 (2010): 138–161.

Taylor-Nicholson, Eleanor. *Cutting Off the Flow: Extraterritorial Controls to Prevent Migration. Issue Brief, the Chief Justice Earl Warren Institute on Law and Social Policy, University of California, Berkeley Law School, CA* (2011): 1–16.

Vedsted-Hansen, Jens. 'Europe's Response to the Arrival of Asylum Seekers: Refugee Protection and Immigration Control'. UNHCR Working Paper 6. Geneva: UNHCR Centre for Documentation and Research, May 1999.

10

MULTI-STAKEHOLDER OPERATIONS OF BORDER CONTROL COORDINATED AT THE EU LEVEL AND THE ALLOCATION OF INTERNATIONAL RESPONSIBILITIES

Maïté Fernandez

10.1 Introduction

In 2004, the Council of the European Union established a European Agency for the Management of Operational Cooperation at the External Borders of the member states of the European Union (Frontex).[1] It was mandated to improve 'the integrated management of the external borders'[2] and contribute 'to an efficient, high and uniform level of control on persons and surveillance'.[3] The creation of Frontex is often regarded as an important shift from traditional approaches to border management.[4] Whereas member states' cooperation in this field was initiated within an intergovernmental framework, it is now managed by 'a body of the Union'[5] with legal, administrative and financial autonomy.[6]

Beyond a move towards the 'Europeanisation' of immigration policies, the development of Frontex occurs against a general background of increasingly complex border controls. Since the 1980s, Western countries have developed strategies for delocalising and outsourcing these activities.[7] These models focus on stemming irregular immigration, and aim to extend states' regulatory capacities. On the one hand, interception measures are exported beyond the frontiers of states of destination, onto the high seas, international airports and third states' territories. On the other hand, states delegate their legal authority, or collaborate with other public and private actors to implement controls. The literature uses the term 'extraterritorialisation'[8] to designate these complementary phenomena that have deeply influenced the European Strategy for 'Integrated Borders Management' (IBM).[9] Indeed, Frontex coordinates common police and military patrols to intercept irregular migrants before or after they enter their country of destination without appropriate authorisation. These operations are called 'pilot projects, joint operations and rapid interventions',[10] which are different types of operational activities that we will categorise under the generic term of 'joint operations'. They involve a generalisation of pre-border controls, and bring together a complex set of actors, including several member states, Frontex, other EU agencies and third states.

These transformations raise specific issues in a field that is extremely sensitive to fundamental rights. Border management entails executive measures that may significantly impact migrants' legal status. 'Interception' encompasses all methods that 'prevent, interrupt or stop the movement of persons without the required documentation crossing international borders by land, air or sea, and making their way to the country of prospective destination'.[11] In Frontex's framework, border controls and surveillance activities involve identity checks and refusals of entry, searches, arrests and interceptions, escorting or conducting people out of the EU territory and/or towards the territory of third states, and sometimes handing over migrants to a third country.[12] All member states are all parties to core international treaties relating to human rights and international protection,[13] and EU secondary law regulating Frontex activities contains mandatory references to these texts.[14] Corresponding provisions of the EU Charter of Fundamental Rights bind member states and the EU agency.[15] Yet, Frontex-coordinated operations raise many concerns about respect for and protection of individual rights.[16] For instance, the *Hirsi Jamaa* judgement of the European Court of Human Rights[17] has brought to light practices violating the principle of non-refoulement that can occur during Frontex-coordinated operations.

In order to deter and sanction violations of human rights, effective legal remedies must be ensured in the context of EU external border management. However, processes of extraterritorialisation lead to a dilution of responsibilities. The present case study is symptomatic of this phenomenon. During joint operations coordinated by Frontex, potential violations of human rights lie in the acts and omissions of deployed border guards. In this regard, the multitude of intertwining executive competences generates important uncertainties. This is exacerbated by the fact that information about the actual chain of command is virtually non-existent. Given the position of irregular migrants, which often prevents them from accessing domestic courts, internal laws and principles governing states' civil liability will not be considered here. EU law will be analysed, since it determines the allocation of powers between EU bodies and member states. However, for now we suggest that EU secondary law does not offer a clear picture of operational arrangements, and risks preventing an accurate determination of legal responsibilities in case of human rights violations. Instead, we propose exploring joint operations in light of the law of international responsibility, for violations of international human rights law. More precisely, this paper will focus on the application of the concept of attribution to Frontex-coordinated operations, and consequences for the allocation of international responsibilities.

We aim to clarify the formal and practical allocation of executive powers during joint operations of migration control that are coordinated by the existing Frontex agency (Section 10.2), in order to draw preliminary conclusions concerning the imputability of wrongful conduct to one or several actors, and their international responsibility (Section 10.3). Such Frontex-coordinated operations should be analysed through a multiple-responsibilities analysis. This approach is necessary to frame judicial accountability that is consistent with the actual involvement and capacity of the multiple stakeholders to influence the direction of operations.

This contribution was written in June 2015. Yet, since then, the acceleration of irregular migration from the Middle East and the Horn of Africa to Europe and mass drownings of migrants in the Mediterranean Sea have encouraged EU member states and the Commission to reinforce EU policy on border management. Therefore, on the basis of a Commission proposal, the Council of the European Union and the Parliament have just adopted the regulation (EU) 2016/1624, transforming the Agency and its legal framework into a European Corps of Border and Coast Guards. Slowly the European Union is moving towards a clear, shared responsibility for these extended activities between the new European Border and Coastguard Agency, and the national authorities of member states. Therefore, the conclusions of this paper will surely help to analyse this new evolution of European law regarding operational cooperation at the external borders of the European Union.

10.2 Confronting law with practice: the allocation of executive powers during Frontex-coordinated joint operations

The choice to create a regulatory agency was no accident, constituting a politically preferable compromise in an area where member states were reluctant to relinquish their sovereign powers. This view is consistent with the fact that Frontex was not built as a European Border Police with discretionary powers. Instead, it constitutes a network of national border agencies under a 'central coordinating body'.[18] Its mission lies halfway between full supranationalisation and pure intergovernmentalism. Indeed, member states remain in charge of controlling their borders. As a result, the legal framework of Frontex-coordinated operations rests on two main assumptions. First, the external borders agency fulfils a limited role of coordination during joint operations of border control and surveillance. Second, each operation is implemented under the responsibility of the state(s) hosting the activities, in order to preserve member states' national prerogatives over their borders (Section 10.2.1).

EU law remains quite elusive regarding the precise allocation of competences during Frontex-coordinated operations. The lack of accurate legal provisions makes it difficult to get a clear picture of operational arrangements. Moreover, democratic and judicial follow-up is extremely limited, despite the most recent reform of Frontex regulations.[19] Frontex's activities inherited the historical opacity of the former third intergovernmental pillar.[20]

Information gathered through access requests for operational documentation and field investigations into the practical implementation of Frontex-coordinated operations question the basic assumptions of Frontex's legal framework. They do not seem consistent with either the agency's significant influence over operations owing to its expertise and privileged role in the organisational aspects, or with the important input and autonomy of participating member states required by the specificities and complexities of areas of intervention (Section 10.2.2).

10.2.1 The legal framework of joint operations under EU law

Frontex became operational on 1 May 2005, with headquarters in Warsaw, Poland. The agency's founding regulations have been amended twice since its creation. Frontex's capacities were strengthened considerably through an increased budget[21] and the development of its mandate. However, the Frontex Consolidated Regulation, which provides rules for the implementation of joint operations of border control and surveillance, limits the role of the agency to coordination, and places operations under the command of at least one host member state. Thus the allocation of executive powers during operations seems clearly defined, and presumably maintained by a restricted number of actors.

The agency and its limited mandate of operational coordination

Frontex was created as a 'first pillar agency', and is now a regulatory agency of the European Union. In EU law, the executive function naturally lies with member states, and the administrative execution of EU policies (material acts and individual decisions) has traditionally remained within the purview of member state authorities.[22] Nonetheless, the process of administrative implementation of EU law is far more diverse than a simple alternative between direct and indirect administration. According to Chiti, national and EU authorities cooperate through various solutions lying in 'a grey area of joint administration'.[23]

Among other possibilities, EU administrative governance may take the form of a 'regulatory agency' established through secondary law.[24] These bodies of the Union are part of an emergent European executive order,[25] even though the EU legal framework continues to ignore this institutional reality.[26] Each regulatory agency is based on a separate regulation, and granted legal, administrative and financial independence. In the meantime, the Meroni principle imposes strict limitations on the delegation of competence, and forbids agency empowerment with discretionary or legally binding powers.[27] Rijpma distinguishes 'executive action which has effects in law, i.e. which creates enforceable rights and obligations for third parties', and 'executive action which does not'.[28] According to the literature, most agencies have only 'instrumental powers',[29] which make reference to the second kind of power. Each agency performs very different functions, depending on the context of the action, but they usually provide only scientific and technical expertise, facilitate exchange of information and/or coordinate activities between national authorities.

According to Monar, this evolution is a persistent feature of governance in the Area of Freedom, Security and Justice (AFSJ). The sensitivity of the field has resulted in a distinct preference for 'lighter' modes of governance.[30] Agencies often imply a slight and controlled strengthening of the EU administration in areas where member states 'accepted the need for more uniform practising of EU legislation', while devising 'instruments that remain under their control instead of transferring more powers to the Commission'.[31] Agencies are independent and technocratic agents that incarnate 'apolitical European governance'[32] and have limited powers.

The formal design of Frontex fits well within the foregoing definition. First, all member states[33] are represented by the Management Board of Frontex,[34] whereas the European Commission has only two representatives. The Executive Director acts independently of any government or other bodies in the performance of his duties.[35] However, this Frontex agent is ultimately responsible before the Management Board,[36] which ensures member states' significant influence over strategic decisions. Second, the agency is limited to a role of facilitation and assistance. The agency fulfils a mission of 'technical support and expertise'.[37] It contributes to relevant research,[38] carries out risk analyses[39] and participates in the development of information sharing systems.[40] It also develops common codes of conduct and training for national border guards and members of European border guards teams[41] (EBGTs).[42] The most important part of Frontex's mandate is to

> facilitate and render more effective the application of existing and future Union measures relating to the management of external borders . . . by ensuring the coordination of the actions of the member states in the implementation of those measures. . . .[43]

Basically, Frontex supervises the implementation of collective operations of control and surveillance by member states, at their land, sea and air borders.

Despite being involved in, and present at, all stages of operations, Frontex is required to play the limited role of an 'orchestra conductor'.[44] Operations are always launched under the consent, the authority and the 'responsibility'[45] of member states, since they need a territory to depart from, as well as the human and technical means on which to rely. As a consequence, decision making and coercive powers, such as the option of carrying out controls, investigations or limiting personal liberty are supposedly left to national administrations. The underlying hypothesis is that the coordination of operational cooperation is a form of executive action that does not entail any legal effects for third parties.

The host member state and its exclusive executive competence

Joint operations are implemented by several member states. In practical terms, this means that member states contribute to operations by sending national human resources to serve within the EBGTs set up by Frontex, 'to be deployed during joint operations, pilot projects and rapid interventions'.[46] In accordance with a decision of the Frontex Management Board, concerning border guards profiles and numbers,[47] member states negotiate annual bilateral agreements with the agency, and establish their exact contribution to the teams.[48] Using the same mechanism of agreed contribution, national experts are seconded by member states second to the agency, which are then deployed within the EBGTs.[49] Home countries of border guards sent to serve during joint operations are called 'home member states'.[50] Similarly, member states contribute to the 'Technical Equipment Pool', and furnish assets such as vehicles, aircraft or vessels, which are managed by the agency. Member states' contributions are decided and made available at the request of the agency under the same rules as those governing EBGTs.[51]

Frontex prepares and organises the operational deployment of the EBGTs and technical equipment in the various theatres of operation.[52] Member states are bound to make their border guards available, 'unless they are faced with an exceptional situation substantially affecting the discharge of national tasks'.[53] For this reason, it has sometimes been said that the amended Frontex regulations create a mechanism of quasi-compulsory contribution from member states. This appears quite exaggerated, since member states first agree on the actual scope of their input, as described above.

Although several states participate, each joint operation is implemented under the authority of at least one 'host member state', that is the 'Member State in which a joint operation, a pilot project or a rapid intervention takes place or from which it is launched'.[54] This provision is fundamental, since it determines the rules of command of the EBGTs. During joint operations, these teams act under the specific status of 'guest officers', that is, 'officers of border guard services of member states other than the host Member State'.[55] Experts seconded to Frontex and deployed with the EBGTs have the same status; they are not Frontex staff.[56] In operational terms, this means that 'guest officers' can only act 'under instructions' and 'in the presence' of host authorities.[57] They are allowed to perform all tasks and exercise all powers for border checks and surveillance, including carrying weapons and using force when required, but only under the conditions outlined above. They must also respect the national laws of the host member state,[58] and are subject to its criminal legislation.[59] As a logical consequence, when addressing 'civil liability', the Frontex Consolidated Regulation states that the host state is responsible for any damage caused by guest officers.[60]

With a view to ensuring effective cooperation between the actors, an International Coordination Centre is systematically established in the host state. A host state official manages this structure and gives instructions to the EBGTs through it. There is also a Joint Coordination Board (JCB), which runs the tactical command of operations. It is usually comprised of host agents, home member states agents (National Officials or NOs) and Frontex agents. Regional and Local Coordination Centres are regularly deployed to complete the mission of the International Coordination Centre.

From a strict legal point of view, the host state is in charge of all border-related activities implemented within or from its territory, including border surveillance, processes of identification, acquisition of travel documents and returns of irregular migrants. Sending member states ensure only 'national contributions and deployments' they have agreed to. Similarly, Frontex agents are restricted to assisting operational coordination between guest and host officers, and making sure that all organisational aspects are implemented.[61] As specified in operational plans, the host member states remain responsible for 'conduct, lead, command and control of the overall border security measures strengthened by the joint operation'.

10.2.2 The uncertainties of the practical implementation of joint operations

Although amendments to the Frontex regulations have improved the transparency of the agency's activities, meaningful information about the actual implementation of joint operations remains quite limited. Operational plans are not public. When access is granted, part of the information remains undisclosed by virtue of the public interest provision under Article 4(1)(a) of Regulation no 1049/2001.[62] Yet, available information allows us to draw a clearer picture of practical arrangements.[63] Our understanding is that the actual chain of command seems less established than is foreseen in Frontex's legal framework, and leaves enough room for the various actors to be significantly involved in potential human rights violations.

Frontex's significant influence over joint operations

Frontex's role is particularly complex since there is no exact definition of what 'facilitation' or 'coordination' mean. Nevertheless, the agency seems able to influence decisions at many different levels of operational implementation. First, Frontex participates to a significant extent in the planning and initiation of joint operations. The agency evaluates and approves proposals made by member states. It may also initiate joint operations itself, 'in cooperation with the Member States concerned and in agreement with the host Member States'.[64] In any case, all operations are planned on the basis of risk analyses and a project recommendation conducted by the Risk Analysis Unit (RAU) of Frontex.[65] Additionally, Frontex can finance or co-finance joint operations and pilot projects,[66] which constitutes a strong incentive for member states to cooperate. Once the decision to launch a joint operation is taken, the relevant unit at Frontex Headquarters (Sea, Land or Air) elaborates the operational initiative. The operational plan is then agreed upon by the Frontex Executive Director and the host member state, with the input of all participating states.[67] In a documentary released on the television channel Arte 7+, about the management of borders in the European Union, a host member state officer stated explicitly that the relevant state's services followed the operational plan designed by the agency.[68] Thus even if Frontex cannot impose activities on a state's territory, it has the capacity to designate priorities of EU integrated border management. Second, Frontex agents seem present at every level of practical implementation. For each joint operation in which members of the EBGTs are deployed, at least one Frontex Coordinating Officer (FCO) is nominated[69] and deployed by the International Coordination Centre. In contrast to 'guest officers', they are agency staff members[70] who participate in operations to ensure the implementation of the operational plan and the synchronisation of member-state actions. We assume that the FCO participates directly in the tactical command of operations, since it sits at the JCB of operations within the International Coordination Centre. In this context, the FCO may communicate its views on the instructions of the host state, which has to take these opinions into consideration.[71] The FCO may also be authorised by the Executive Director of Frontex to assist in resolving any disagreement on the execution of the operational plan.[72] Finally, Frontex Consolidated Regulation states that the host state shall also give the FCO full access to EBGTs,[73] without clarifying what this provision actually means.

The vague description of the FCO's mission leaves the question of Frontex's concrete role on the operational ground quite open. The same conclusion applies to other Frontex staff, who seem to act as interfaces between member states and the agency, such as Frontex Operational Coordinators (FOCs), and Frontex Support Officers (FSOs). These functions are only briefly mentioned in operational plans, where it is not specified whether they refer to Frontex agents in the sense of Article 17(3) of the Frontex Consolidated Regulation. In the operational area of Poseidon and Attica, Frontex-coordinated operations in 2013, there were ten Frontex staff deployed on the ground. Although this number may seem marginal, it is likely that they were placed at the frontline of the operational decision-making process, owing to their expertise.

The growing presence of Frontex agents in the operational field makes it difficult to evaluate the extent of the agency's involvement, and to distinguish between instrumental and final powers. The roles and status of Frontex agents are defined in operational plans, and may change, depending on contexts of intervention. In this respect, it seems crucial to point out that Frontex has been analysed through the lens of 'experimentalist governance'.[74] Its scope of action is not fully pre-determined, which allows informal practices and a flexible extension of executive competence falling outside the agency's strict legal mandate.[75] Many academics and non-governmental organisations consider some of Frontex's legal attributions to be of a 'strong policy and operational nature going beyond mere technical support or assistance to the EU Member States'.[76] As illustrated by the role of Frontex FCOs, the literature confirms that EU agencies may play a decisive role in the implementation of EU law through strong recommendatory powers.[77] A significant 'zone of discretion'[78] may remain in practice.

The important autonomy and input of participating member states

In relation to participating member states, we find that they exercise a similar capacity to influence or intervene directly in the chain of command. Several examples lead to this conclusion.

In the context of joint operations implemented at sea, the input and the autonomy of participating countries seems quite important, contrary to what is suggested by the concept of the host state.[79] First, NOs of home member states participate in the JCB, which gives them influence over decisions. Furthermore, operational documentation shows that although the tactical command of operations is in the hands of the International Coordination Centre after consultation with the NOs, the operational command of aerial and naval assets remains with participating member states. Participating Member States deploy their NOs in the International Coordination Centre, in order to coordinate the actions of their national assets. This mission of coordination has to be done according to the legislation of their own country, and in cooperation with the International Coordination Centre Coordinator. Operational Plans also mention the presence of 'Commanding Officers' of aerial and maritime assets during operations.

The approach is similar in the regulation establishing rules for the surveillance of external sea borders. Although it endorses the mechanism of the 'host member state',[80] the margin of discretion left to home member states seems expansive. The EBGTs are organised in several 'participating units'[81] that receive 'instructions' from the host member state[82] when they implement coercive measures. However, Article 2(5) of this regulation specifies that participating units may be 'under the responsibility of the host Member State or of a participating Member State'. Combining these various aspects leads us to conclude that home member states regularly deploy vessels and aircraft together with a responsible officer and a team of national border guards. The national chain of command appears to remain at least partly in place.[83]

Beyond operational arrangements, the limited capacities of host state authorities challenge the exclusivity of the control they might exercise over patrols. Member states often request assistance from a Frontex-coordinated Joint Operation because of emergencies or disproportionate pressures at their borders. As a result, they are not always able to supervise operations as they should. For instance, during the implementation of the RABIT (Rapid Border Intervention Team) operation at the Greek–Turkish border in 2010,[84] experts from the EBGTs conducted screening interviews to determine the nationality of intercepted migrants. Empirical studies showed that many of these interviews did not occur in the presence of a Greek officer, as required by the Frontex regulation.[85] Additionally, since they lacked the means to conduct a second examination, Greek authorities used the foreign border guards' recommendations concerning the migrants' nationalities as decisive evaluations of needs for international protection. Thus they transformed guest officers' preliminary assessments into final administrative decisions.[86]

Available information shows that guest officers usually continue to report to their sending states during operations, which keeps them informed and gives them the opportunity to interfere with the chain of command.[87] Finally, the Frontex Consolidated Regulation provides for guest officers being subject to disciplinary measures by their 'home Member state'[88] during joint operations. Their remuneration is taken care of by their national authorities, and Frontex covers their deployment allowances. This information undoubtedly brings into question the exclusivity of control exercised by the host state over the EBGTs: home member states seem left with an important margin of discretion and control over their assets, and with a significant capacity to influence operations.

This outline, contrasting law and practice, is crucial to the reconstruction of international responsibilities. From this perspective, the International Court of Justice (ICJ) confirmed that it is sometimes necessary 'to look beyond legal status alone' and 'grasp the reality of the relationship between the person taking action and the State' (or the international organisation).[89] These legal and factual elements of the actual chain of command and allocation of executive powers during joint operations of border controls coordinated by Frontex are crucial. They will serve in the process of attribution of wrongful conduct to member states and/or the agency. Specifically, attribution appears problematic in situations involving a multiplicity of actors.

10.3 Drawing conclusions about international responsibility: multiple responsibilities for multi-stakeholder operations

In the context of multi-stakeholder operations, specific rules must be carefully considered before drawing conclusions concerning international responsibility. As set out in the International Law Commission (ILC) Draft Articles on State and International Organisations Responsibility,[90] conduct must both be attributable to a state/international organisation and be a breach of its international obligation to be characterised as an internationally wrongful act. 'Attribution' refers to the normative operation that establishes whether or not the conduct of a physical person may be characterised as an act of a state or of an international organisation according to international law.[91] This is central to the doctrine of international responsibility, since it is a prerequisite to the assessment of a specific act against an international subject's international obligations.[92]

The conduct of entities formally linked to an international subject are considered as its own,[93] a solution that remains applicable in cases where actions go beyond instructions.[94] However, when the relationship between the subject of international law and the acting entity is not well established by law, or when the apparent legal status of an entity is questionable, international law relies on the notion of control as the basis of a factual link between the subject and the acting entity.[95] Difficulties arise when more than one international subject participates in the conduct in question. Part of legal doctrine is that in principle, conduct is attributed to only one actor.[96] On the contrary, we espouse the theory formulated by Messineo, according to which multiple attribution constitutes the default rule under the law of international responsibility, and exclusive attribution amounts to a strictly regulated exception.[97]

In public debates, the question of responsibility regarding human rights violations committed during Frontex-coordinated operations is usually approached in exclusive terms. Several commentators accuse the agency arguing that it has a supervisory role over operational matters. Others consider that the rule of exclusive control foreseen by EU law prevails and automatically triggers the sole responsibility of the host state. Yet, the reality of operational arrangements shows that joint operations are not fully controlled by one actor. As a result, rules regulating exclusive attribution to one international subject cannot apply (Section 10.3.1). Therefore, the perspective of multiple attributions should prevail. However, if there is insufficient evidence to attribute the same wrongful conduct to several actors, Frontex-coordinated operations may still lead to multiple, indirect international responsibilities through positive obligations. This approach is necessary to embrace the entire scope of actors involved in the chain of actions leading to human rights violations (Section 10.3.2).

10.3.1 Frontex-coordinated operations in light of the concept of exclusive attribution

In the ASR (Articles on State Responsibility) Commentaries, the ILC states that the rules regulating the operation of attribution are 'cumulative'.[98] Therefore, different rules may apply to the same conduct, leading to multiple attributions. Nevertheless, one situation limits this possibility in cases where public organs are completely transferred to another international subject. This exception is formulated under Article 6 ASR and Article 7 ARIO (Articles on the Responsibility of International Organization), and 'prevent[s] multiple attribution of conduct from occurring if certain requisites are met'.[99] Frontex-coordinated operations do not seem to meet the criteria for exclusive attribution.

Exceptions in Article 6 ASR and Article 7 ARIO, and the nature of the control required

Article 6 ASR addresses situations where

> the conduct of an organ placed at the disposal of a State by another State shall be considered an act of the former State under international law if the organ is acting in the exercise of elements of the governmental authority of the State at whose disposal it is placed.[100]

Since it is designed to regulate 'limited and precise'[101] scenarios, the application of Article 6 is strictly circumscribed. The process of putting a state organ at the disposal of another state implies 'exclusive direction and control'[102] by the latter over the organ and its activities. This organ must act 'in the consent, under the authority of and for the purposes of the receiving State':[103]

> Not only must the organ be appointed to perform functions appertaining to the State at whose disposal it is placed, but in performing the functions entrusted to it by the beneficiary State, the organ must also act in conjunction with the machinery of that State and under its exclusive direction and control, rather than on instructions from the sending State.

The last sentence above insists on the exclusivity of control; indeed, Article 6 ASR does not apply to ordinary situations of interstate cooperation where organs maintain some 'autonomy'.[104] Confirming the exceptional nature of the rule, the ILC indicates that Article 6 covers a very specific situation of transferred responsibility, where the seconded entity may be equated with a state organ.

Article 7 ARIO expresses a rule equivalent to the foregoing, concerning organs transferred to international organisations:

> The conduct of an organ of a state or an organ or agent of an International Organisation that is placed at the disposal of another international organisation shall be considered under international law an act of the latter organisation if the organisation exercises effective control over that conduct.[105]

Although the ILC declares a similar approach to Article 6 ASR, the notion of control is formulated quite differently in the case of international organisations. Here, the concept of 'effective control' must clarify whether or not conduct is attributable to an international organisation or to member states when they implement operations jointly.[106] This notion has led to several contradictory interpretations.

In its Commentaries, the ILC suggests several occasions on which the notion of 'effective control' relates to the degree of factual/operational control over specific conduct. On the one hand, 'attribution of conduct to the contributing states is clearly linked with the retention of some powers by that State over its national contingent',[107] which means that there can be no exclusive attribution to an international organisation if its control over operations is not exclusive. On the other hand, this control must be demonstrated with regard to the specific conduct in question. Developments of the ICJ in *Bosnia and Herzégovina v. Serbia and Montenegro* on 'effective control' in relation to Article 8 ASR offer interesting insights. For the conduct of a specific individual to be attributable to a state,

> it must . . . be shown that 'effective control' was exercised, or that the State's instructions were given, in respect of each operation in which the alleged violations occurred, not generally in respect of the overall actions taken by the persons or groups of persons having committed the violations.[108]

In a contradiction of this approach of operational control on a case-by-case basis, the European Court of Human Rights attributed the conduct of the United Nations Interim Administration Mission in Kosovo (UNMIK) and the Kosovo Force (KFOR) to the United Nations, considering that the Security Council exercised 'ultimate authority and control'.[109] However, many authors demonstrated that this interpretation is ill-founded, since it refers to a remote notion of legal authorisation and completely undermines states' operational control during operations.[110]

Another understanding of the notion of 'effective control' may compete more successfully with the ILC's interpretation. Drawing on the drafting history of Article 6 ASR and Article 7 ARIO, Messineo states that the thresholds prompting their application should be interpreted similarly.[111] Two requirements would then need to be satisfied to eliminate the presumption of multiple attribution. First, an 'institutional link' ('functional link' in the words of the ILC[112]) must be established between the receiving state/international organisation and the transferred organ. The transferred organ exercises functions of the receiving state or international organisation under a 'general and ex ante control' of the receiving subject, a 'general requirement to obey orders'. Second, the original institutional link to the sending state should be temporarily severed in the sense of 'a lack of interference from the sending government'.[113] What matters is the reality of the transfer, that is, the exclusive control by the receiving state, not the degree of control exercised over specific conduct.[114]

In summary, the first view derived from the ILC Commentaries calls for an investigation of every specific event at issue,[115] to establish 'effective control'. This approach appears quite problematic because of the need to produce detailed evidence. The use of a different criteria for Article 7 ARIO is justified because no state organ is never actually fully transferred in the context of joint operations organised under the supervision of an international organisation.[116] This may explain why the process of attribution has to be based on the examination of every act, when no exclusive institutional link may actually exist. Conversely, the second view defended by Messineo searches for the existence of a more general institutional link between the receiving state or international organisation and the organ, which must be exclusive. What has to be proven is that the sending state/international organisation has no control over the conduct of the organ for the duration of the transfer.

Whatever the solution to the doctrinal debate under discussion here may be, one may make two concluding observations. First, there is little doubt that notions of 'exclusive direction and control' and 'effective control' rely on factual considerations. The ILC confirms that agreements on the distribution of responsibility between states and international organisations during operations are not conclusive in terms of attribution and responsibility under the general rules.[117] Second, regardless of the kind of control deemed necessary, the application of Article 6 ASR and Article 7 ARIO are conditional on the requirement of exclusivity. The transfer of attribution follows the transfer of the organ only if the original link with the sending state or international organisation has been temporarily severed.[118]

The inapplicability of exclusive attribution in the context of joint operations

Keeping all the above-mentioned conclusions in mind, we may now look at the specific question of Frontex-coordinated joint operations in light of the concept of attribution. First, can Frontex's competence in joint operations lead to exclusive attribution of wrongful conduct to the agency? There are several layers to this question. Although the status of EU agencies under international law is debated,[119] Frontex does not seem to enjoy international personality. The ILC Commentaries recall that an international organisation is 'established by a treaty or other instrument governed by international law'.[120] In contrast, Frontex was established by an instrument of EU secondary law, and is deprived of the capacity to conclude international treaties. Moreover, Frontex agents are EU officials to whom Staff Regulations of the European Union apply.[121] According to Boumghar, Frontex enjoys only independent legal personality within the European legal order as a body of the European Union.[122] Indeed, legal doctrine considers that regulatory agencies form part of the EU executive branch despite a lack of formal definition. In consequence, Frontex should be considered an organ (or agent) of the European Union, according to Article 6 ARIO,[123] which endorses a broad definition of the concept of international organisations' 'agent' or 'organ'.[124] Therefore, the agency's conduct should be attributable to the European Union.

Whose actions and omissions may be classified under the category of 'Frontex conduct'? The position of human resources deployed by the agency during joint operations is unquestionable. Not only do Frontex staff have the official status of European civil servants, but they also take instructions from, and report exclusively to the agency according to the Frontex regulations.[125] Wrongful conduct perpetrated by these individuals during Frontex-coordinated operations may be attributed to the European Union, under Article 6 ARIO. However, despite their presence on the operational field, and existing doubts as to the exact content of their mission, it is likely that the nature of Frontex's mandate limits the possibility of its agents committing unlawful actions. To our knowledge, the agency's agents do not interact directly with individuals, because they are not border guards.

The risk of wrongful conduct lies in the acts and omissions of the EBGTs, who implement executive measures directly affecting migrants. We know that Frontex staff participate actively in the planning and coordination of joint operations and the deployment of these teams. Given this important role, can conduct of the EBGTs be attributed to the agency? Answering positively to this question would imply that they are states' organs placed at the disposal of the European Union, a solution provided by Article 7 ARIO. However, both European law and known practices demonstrate that member states have significant (if not exclusive) authority over actions of the EBGTs. Therefore, if the agency's powers of planning and oversight can generate controversies about the influence exercised over the direction of operations, the condition of 'effective control' remains distant, regardless of the interpretation one prefers. More specifically, the necessary involvement of other actors in the command of the EBGTs prevents the fulfilment of the requirement of exclusivity. Without downplaying the European Union's share of responsibility for its participation in such operations, Frontex cannot be used as a scapegoat for member states to shift the blame when human rights violations occur.[126] The acts of the EBGTs cannot be attributed solely to Frontex.

We have already emphasised that Frontex-coordinated operations are implemented under the authority of one or several host states designated as responsible for all border-related activities initiated within or from its territory. The legal framework of Frontex-coordinated operations is based on the assumption that participating member states delegate their legal authority over human and technical resources to member states hosting operations. At first glance, this legal provision is a strong argument for attributing questionable acts solely to the host member state.[127] The question raised here is whether or not the EBGTs are state organs seconded to the host state according to Article 6 ASR. In this regard, our previous analysis of the chain of command during joint operations allows us to contradict the presumption of attribution to the host state. Indeed, the host state does not have the capacity to impose an exclusive direction on operations, even when they are exclusively deployed on its territory and member states appear to keep their autonomy and capacity to influence their human resources. Therefore, joint operations do not seem to meet the criterion of 'exclusive direction and control' set out by Article 6 ASR, in order for conduct of the EBGTs to be exclusively attributable to the host state. As a result, joint operations may hardly be said to be under the exclusive control of one actor, a situation that precludes the application of Article 6 ASR and Article 7 ARIO. However, this conclusion should preserve the possibility of attributing separately to each participant of these operations the acts of their own organs. It may even work in favour of the recognition of a multiple attribution situation and the establishment of multiple international responsibilities for wrongful acts during Frontex-coordinated operations.

10.3.2 A multiple responsibility analysis for Frontex-coordinated operations

In view of the international command structure during joint operations, it seems reasonable to argue that such multi-stakeholders operations should give rise to multiple responsibilities. Depending on the evidence available and following a case-by-case approach necessary for the study of such changing and flexible operational contexts, two hypotheses may apply. First, one could argue that wrongful conduct occurring during Frontex-coordinated operations is attributable to several actors simultaneously, prompting multiple 'direct' international responsibilities. Second, should multiple attribution be too complex to demonstrate, the concept of 'indirect' or 'derived' international responsibility should allow for judicial accountability of member states and the agency involvements in joint operations.

Multiple attribution and direct international responsibilities of member states and Frontex

According to den Heijer, although major international courts such as the European Court of Human Rights have already ruled on scenarios involving multiple responsibilities, there is a general consensus that 'international law on the distribution of responsibilities among multiple contributing actors is ill-developed'.[128] However, the law of international responsibility does recognise the possibility of invoking multiple responsibilities for the same wrongful conduct. Article 47 ASR 'deals with the situation where there is a plurality of responsible states in respect of the same wrongful act'. Article 48 ARIO addresses circumstances 'where an International Organisation and one or more states or other International Organisations are responsible for the same internationally wrongful act'. Regarding joint operations between states and/or international organisations, we earlier identified one of the main conditions for exclusive attribution as lying in the exclusivity of operational control exercised over specific acts or activities in general, depending on the interpretation chosen. This search for exclusive control and the restrictive nature of conditions regulating Article 6 ASR and Article 7 ARIO confirms the theory that exclusive attribution remains exceptional, although the question of multiple attributions may arise in all other situations.

Different situations in which states engage in joint conduct in breach of the same international obligation are relevant to our case study. For instance, a transferred organ can still partly act on the instructions of the sending state while implementing the orders of the receiving state. States and/or international organisations may also 'combine in carrying out together an internationally wrongful act', or 'act through a common organ which carries out the conduct in question'.[129] In all these circumstances, the different parties involved may be regarded as acting jointly in respect of the same wrongful conduct that may be imputable to them all at the same time. In our opinion, Frontex-coordinated operations require such a multiple attribution analysis.

Previous explanations confirm that participating member states can retain significant *de facto* autonomy during joint operations, just as Frontex has an important capacity to influence operational and strategic decisions. Host member states, participating member states and the agency, all contribute to the elaboration of operational plans. Similarly, they all participate more or less directly in the implementation of operations through an international structure (International Coordination Centre). Although the EBGTs are supposed to act under the orders of this common coordination unit and a host official, guest officers actually continue receiving instructions from, and reporting to, their sending state. In practice, these multi-stakeholder operations may very well turn out to be ordinary situations of international cooperation. Indeed, measures may either be considered as implemented jointly by multinational teams of border guards responding to common orders, or cooperatively among several international subjects that retain autonomy over their human and technical assets. Thus the acts of the EBGTs could be considered attributable to the agency, and to several participating member states at the same time.

The foregoing hypothesis necessitates further study and better access to information on the distribution of tasks during Frontex-coordinated operations, in order to demonstrate direct attributability of violations. In the absence of evidence clearly establishing the reality of control over operations and specific conduct, legal provisions might carry weight in the wrong direction. In particular, the presumption of responsibility falling on the host state might preclude the possibility of multiple attributions from being considered. Furthermore, a case-by-case approach could drag into the light situations where the involvement of actors other than the host state is too remote to lead to direct attribution. In this regard, the concept of 'jurisdiction', a threshold criterion for the application of human rights treaties, is often presented as a limit to states' international responsibility.[130] However, the author of this paper considers that human rights law has enough flexibility to cope with challenges raised by multi-stakeholders and extraterritorial controls. This question will not be discussed in detail in this paper, but human rights bodies and courts have adopted an evolutionary and pro-victim approach to the notion of jurisdiction that seems promising.[131]

When international courts are unwilling to take the path of multiple attribution, one thing remains certain:

> The rule of exclusive attribution does not necessarily preclude the lending State from incurring international responsibility for its own acts and omissions in relation to the conduct which is attributable to another State. . . . The lending State may still incur responsibilities for its own separate acts relating to the conduct of the lent organ.[132]

Indirect multiple responsibilities of all participants

The adaptability and the nature of human rights law offers ways to preserve the accountability of all the actors participating in joint operations. Even if their direct participation – with a scenario where wrongful conducts would be attributable to multiple actors at the same time – cannot be proven, 'indirect' or 'derived' multiple responsibilities may be applied in case of internationally wrongful acts.

The law of international responsibility includes notions of 'derived' or 'indirect' responsibility[133] in connection with the wrongful act of another state or international organisation. Article 16 ASR expresses this principle, according to which 'a State which aids or assists another State in the commission of an internationally wrongful act by the latter is internationally responsible for doing so'.[134] Article 14 ARIO extends this rule to international organisations.[135] This scenario may apply to Frontex-coordinated operations: Should the host state be considered 'the acting state' and hence primarily responsible, then Frontex and home member states would be 'assisting states' with a 'supporting role' only.[136] However, this provision contains a requirement of 'fault or wrongful intent', specifying that the assisting state or international organisation must have acted in full 'knowledge of the circumstances of the internationally wrongful act' and 'with a view to facilitating the commission of that act'. Therefore, this rule is difficult to apply.[137] In order to move beyond the 'wrongful intent' clause of Article 14 ASR and 16 ARIO, one has to search for grounds for responsibility under the notion of 'positive obligations'.

The particularity of human rights law has contributed to important developments for differentiating between responsibility for the acts of states' organs, and responsibility for indirect involvement in violations committed by forces that are not under direct state control. Negative obligations force states to 'respect' the rights of individuals under their jurisdiction, which means that their organs, agents and other persons or entities should not commit human rights violations that will be attributable to their state. However, there is an important difference between attribution and jurisdiction, although both concepts are based on similar evidence. The notion of jurisdiction is actually broader. Attribution relates to the control exercised over the authors of the conduct at issue. In contrast, jurisdiction refers more generally to the capacity for control (or even just influence) over victims of violations. As a consequence, all acts falling under a state's jurisdiction are not necessarily attributable to it under general public international law.

According to established case law, the European Court of Human Rights has defined positive obligations of states as their obligations to 'secure' and 'ensure' the rights of individuals under their jurisdiction, which means that they should prevent third actors whose acts are not attributable to them from committing human rights violations.[138] Other human rights bodies embrace this concept that human rights involve more demanding obligations than classic international law,[139] and the ICJ.[140] The theory of positive obligations seems to have the potential to transcend issues of attribution and jurisdiction, and places a general obligation of 'due diligence' on states and international organisations, where they have the capacity to 'prevent' violations of human rights by other actors. Despite few encouraging signs from international courts, these developments remain a matter of prospective thinking and *lex ferenda*.[141]

The specific nature of human rights already prohibits states from providing assistance to actors violating human rights. According to the European Court of Human Rights, when 'states cooperate . . . in an area where there might be implications as to the protection of fundamental rights . . .' they cannot be 'absolved of all responsibility vis-à-vis the Convention in the area concerned'.[142] Here, the Court refers to residual content of positive human rights obligations when states delegate their competences. As a result, when member states or Frontex participate indirectly in violations committed by a host member state during immigration regulation, even if they have no control over operations and provide only financial, human and/or technical support, their international responsibility may still be invoked.

In EU law, Frontex seems bound by an equivalent positive obligation to the one existing in the law of the European Convention of Human Rights. Its mission of coordination contains specific requirements. The most recent reform to the

Frontex regulation confirmed that ensuring respect for fundamental rights during joint operations constitutes an integral part of the agency's obligations.[143] Notably, the agency must set up a mechanism for suspending or terminating operations in case of violations of fundamental rights or international protection obligations. Hence, persevering in the facilitation of joint operations during which human rights violations occur, would be directly in breach of the agency's obligations under EU law.

10.4 Conclusion

Several commentators agree that border controls are currently implemented in Europe without adequate measures to ensure individuals' fundamental rights. The sharing of executive competences is partly responsible for this situation. It is aggravated by a lack of transparency, which constitutes a major obstacle to presenting evidence of violations in a context where identifying legal responsibilities is already difficult. Better understanding the allocation of executive powers during joint operations is a crucial step for reconstructing the legal responsibilities of the multiple stakeholders involved in Frontex-coordinated operations. Indeed, facts matter as much as legal provisions when it comes to the establishment of responsibilities under international human rights law. Neither Frontex nor the state hosting an operation may be the sole actor to bear liability in case of human rights violations. Maintaining this conclusion would not only undermine the objective of 'effectivity' underlying the theory of human rights, it would also amount to ignoring the practical reality of joint operations. Instead, it seems crucial to recall that states and/or international organisations involved in multi-stakeholder border control operations are not free of all responsibility, even when their participation is secondary.

Frontex-coordinated operations confirm the assumption that exclusive control is a rare exception during joint operations between states and international organisations. This observation underscores that a framework of multiple attribution is much more suitable to states and international organisations practices when they operate together. Wrongful acts committed in the course of Frontex-coordinated operations should lead to the establishment of multiple 'direct' responsibilities. This conclusion is applicable to scenarios of operations involving third states, which have not been discussed in this paper.[144] The most common type of partnership consists of the organisation of joint patrols on third-state territories under the coordination of Frontex.[145] In the context of maritime operations in third-country-territory seas and contiguous zones, member states' human and technical resources are deployed with a third state's officer stationed on European patrol boats. Despite the absence of clear legal provisions, observers note that the European Union and its member states consider the third state to be in charge of all measures of interception,[146] in order for the acts of patrols to be exclusively attributable to it, according to Article 6 ASR. However, available information supports the conclusion that member states' border guards act with a significant degree of independence, and that third states do not exercise sufficient effective control over joint patrols to be exclusively responsible.[147] In view of these practices, if multiple attribution remains contested as an established rule governing international responsibility, we can only wish for progressive development of international law in this direction. However, if evidence is insufficient to demonstrate the existence of multiple direct responsibilities, the analysis should focus on the remaining positive obligations. Indeed, the nature of the obligations at stake leaves plenty of opportunities for establishing multiple 'indirect' responsibilities of participants in Frontex-coordinated operations.

From a procedural perspective, this analysis of joint operations through the lens of human rights law and rules of international responsibility shows that EU secondary law does not provide effective and adequate remedies in the context of Frontex-coordinated operations. An individual cannot bring a complaint against one or several member states and the European Union directly before the Court of Justice of the European Union (CJEU).[148] He or she would be forced to make simultaneous claims within domestic jurisdictions and to the CJEU to obtain remedies.[149] Assuming that an individual complaint overcomes procedural barriers and reaches the CJEU, the risk is that the Court would probably respond to such a case in accordance with EU law and the rule of the host member state's exclusive responsibility. This would protect both participating member states[150] and Frontex[151] from liability.

The European Court of Human Rights does offer increased hope for adequate remedies. It frequently deals with multiple-responsibility scenarios, and has already considered that 'the Convention rights can be "divided and tailored" ', depending on the situation of an individual and the extent of a state's jurisdiction over him or her,[152] Thus in agreement with the *Bosphorus* case law, the Strasbourg Court could establish the responsibility of several participating member states, provided that they exercised discretion when implementing EU law. Frontex-coordinated operations certainly fall under this category of conduct. Conversely, if the acts reviewed were the strict result of a legal obligation coming from EU law, and

> as long as the relevant organisation is considered to protect fundamental rights, as regards both the substantive guarantees offered and the mechanisms controlling their observance, in a manner which can be considered at least equivalent to that for which the Convention provides,[153]

a request before the European Court of Human Rights would be inadmissible. The Court does not have jurisdiction over the acts of the EU and its bodies.

The accession of the European Union to the European Convention on Human Rights could have established the possibility of lodging a complaint against the European Union and member states simultaneously, as co-perpetrators of the same internationally wrongful act. Article 3 of the Draft Accession Agreement of the European Union to the European Convention on Human Rights, while recalling that acts and omissions of a member state's organ are attributable to that state,[154] also creates a 'co-respondent mechanism'.[155] This procedure provides that the

European Union or a member state could become a co-respondent to proceedings, either by accepting an invitation from the European Court of Human Rights, or by decision of the Court on a request of the Contracting Party. The respondent(s) and the co-respondent(s) should be found jointly responsible for a violation of the European Convention on Human Rights, unless the European Court of Human Rights decides that only one of them is responsible for that violation, based on their arguments and after hearing the position of the defendant. Participating states and the agency could all see responsibility invoked, independently or together with that of the host state, for having violated negative or positive obligations provided for in the Convention.

Unfortunately, the recent negative opinion of the CJEU regarding the compatibility of the Draft Accession Agreement with EU Treaties has postponed the accession for an indefinite period. Among other concerns, the CJEU considered that the co-respondent mechanism would require the European Court of Human Rights to assess the rules governing the division of powers between the European Union and its member states at the admissibility and the merits stage, thereby affecting the exclusive jurisdiction of the CJEU on these issues.[156] As long as the European Union has not ratified the European Convention on Human Rights, an individual complaint involving Frontex can only be assessed by the Luxembourg Court with all the difficulties that this procedure involves. Yet, the European Court of Human Rights will certainly not absolve member states of their participation in human rights violations during migration control if a claim reaches Strasbourg. A judgement might then force the European Union to better monitor operational practices, and clarify the allocation of responsibility during joint operations.

Notes

1 Council Regulation (EC) no. 2007/2004 of 26 October 2004 establishing a European Agency for the Management of Operational Cooperation at the External Borders of the Member States of the European Union, Official Journal of the European Union L349 ('Frontex 2004 Regulation'). Frontex 2004 Regulation was amended four times by Regulation (EC) no. 863/2007 of the European Parliament and of the Council of 11 July 2007, OJEU L199, Regulation (EU) no. 1168/2011 of the European Parliament and of the Council of 25 October 2011, OJEU L304, Regulation (EU) no. 1052/2013 of the European Parliament and of the Council of 22 October 2013, OJEU L295; and Regulation (EU) no. 656/2014 of European Parliament and of the Council of 15 May 2014, OJEU L189. The consolidated version, described as a documentation tool only, can be found online: http://eur-lex.europa.eu/legal-content/EN/TXT/?uri=CELEX%3A02004R2007–20140717&qid=1420550701883 ('Frontex Consolidated Regulation').
2 Frontex 2004 Regulation, Art. 1 §1.
3 Frontex 2004 Regulation, Art. 1 §2.
4 Jorrit Rijpma, 'Hybrid Agencification in the Area of Freedom, Security and Justice and its Inherent Tensions: the Case of Frontex', in *The Agency Phenomenon in the European Union: Emergence, Institutionalisation and Everyday Decision-Making*, eds Madalina Busuioc, Martijn Groenleer and Jarle Trondal, 84–102 (Manchester: Manchester University Press, 2012), 88; Andrew W. Neal, 'Securitization and Risk at the EU Border: The Origins of FRONTEX', *Journal of Common Market Studies* 47, no. 2 (2009), 343.

5 Frontex Consolidated Regulation, Recital (14) and Art. 15 §1. Frontex 2004 Regulation was based on Art. 62 §2 and Art. 66 TEC, falling under Title IV 'Visas, Asylum, Immigration and Other Policies related to the Free Movement of Persons'. Frontex Consolidated Regulation is based on equivalent provisions of Title V TFEU 'Area of Freedom, Security and Justice': Art. 74 and Art. 77 §2 (b) and (d).

6 The Agency is funded mainly by the EU budget. See Frontex Consolidated Regulation, Recital (14), Art. 29 and Art. 30. Also see Decision No 574/2007/EC of the European Parliament and of the Council of 23 May 2007 establishing the External Borders Fund for the period 2007 to 2013 as part of the General Programme 'Solidarity and Management of Migration Flows', OJEU L144, and Regulation (EU) no. 515/2014 of the European Parliament and of the Council of 16 April 2014 establishing, as part of the Internal Security Fund, the instrument for financial support for external borders and visa and repealing Decision No 574/2007/EC, OJEU L 150.

7 For further information, see Valsamis Mitsilegas, 'Extraterritorial Immigration Control in the 21st Century: The Individual and the State Transformed', in *Extraterritorial Immigration Control: Legal Challenges*, eds Bernard Ryan and Valsamis Mitsilegas, 39–68 (Leiden: Martinus Nijhoff Publishers, 2010).

8 Jorrit Rijpma and Marise Cremona, 'The Extra-Territorialisation of EU Migration Policies and the Rule of Law', *European University Institute Papers*, Law 2007/01.

9 Commission of the European Communities, 'Towards integrated management of the external borders of the member states of the European Union', COM (2002) 233 final, Brussels, 07.05.2002.

10 Frontex Consolidated Regulation, Art. 2 §1, (a).

11 United Nations High Commissioner for Refugees, 'Interception de demandeurs d'asile et de réfugiés: le cadre international et les recommandations en vue d'une approche globale', 9 June 2000, §10, 2.

12 Common rules for border checks and border surveillance: Regulation (EC) no. 562/2006 of the European Parliament and of the Council of 15 March 2006, establishing a Community Code on the rules governing the movement of persons across borders (Schengen Borders Code); Regulation no. 656/2014 of 15 May 2014, the European Parliament and of the Council establishing rules for the surveillance of the external sea borders in the context of operational cooperation coordinated by the European Agency for the Management of Operational Cooperation at the External Borders of the Member States of the European Union, OJEU L189 (henceforth 'Regulation establishing rules for the surveillance of the external sea borders').

13 International Covenant Relating to the Status of Refugees (CRSR), adopted in 1951, entered into force in 1954; International Covenant on Civil and Political Rights (ICCPR), adopted in 1966, entered into force in 1976; Convention against Torture and Other Cruel, Inhuman or Degrading Treatment or Punishment (UNCAT), adopted in 1984, entered into force in 1987; Convention for the Protection of Human Rights and Fundamental Freedoms as amended by its different Protocols (European Convention on Human Rights), adopted in 1950, entered into force in 1953.

14 Frontex Consolidated Regulation, Art. 2 §1a, Art. 1 §2; Schengen Borders Code, Art. 3a; Regulation establishing rules for the surveillance of the external sea borders, Arts. 3 and 4.

15 Charter of Fundamental Rights of the European Union, OJEU 2010/C82/02.

16 Substantive and procedural provisions of International and European Human Rights Law relevant to migration controls have been extensively discussed in the literature. For example, see Ruth Weinzierl, 'The Demands of Human and EU Fundamental Rights for the Protection of the European Union's External Borders' (Berlin: German Institute for Human Rights, July 2007); Andreas Fischer-Lescano, Tillmann Lohr and Timo Tohidipur, 'Border Controls at Sea: Requirements under International Human Rights and Refugee Law', *International Journal of Refugee Law* 21, no. 2 (2009); Anja Klug and Tim Howe, 'The Concept of State Jurisdiction and the Applicability of the Non-Refoulement Principle to Extraterritorial Interception Measures', in *Extraterritorial*

Immigration Control: Legal Challenges, eds Bernard Ryan and Valsamis Mitsilegas, 69–102 (Leiden: Martinus Nijhoff Publishers, 2010); Office of the UN High Commissioner for Human Rights, 'Report of the Special Rapporteur on the Human Rights of Migrants, François Crépeau: Regional study: Management of the External Borders of the European Union and its Impact on the Human Rights of Migrants', A/HRC/23/46 (Geneva: OHCHR/Human Rights Council, 24 April 2013); PACE (Parliamentary Assembly of the Council of Europe), 'Lives Lost in the Mediterranean Sea: Who is Responsible?' (Strasbourg: PACE Committee on Migration, Refugees and Displaced Persons, March 2012); Human Rights Watch, 'The EU's Dirty Hands: Frontex Involvement in Ill-Treatment of Migrant Detainees in Greece' (New York: Human Rights Watch, 2011); Human Rights Watch, 'Pushed Back, Pushed Around: Italy's Forced Return of Boat Migrants and Asylum Seekers, Libya's Mistreatment of Migrants and Asylum Seekers' (New York: Human Rights Watch, 2009); Council of Europe, 'The Right to Leave a Country' (Strasbourg: Council of Europe Commissioner for Human Rights, October 2013).

17   European Court of Human Rights, Grand Chamber, *Hirsi Jamaa and Others v. Italy*, (Judgment), Application no. 27765/09, 23 February 2012.

18   Jörg Monar, 'The Project of a European Border Guard: Origins, Models and Prospects in the Context of the EU's Integrated External Borders Management', in *Borders and Security Governance: Managing Borders in a Globalised World*, eds Marina Caparini and Otwin Marenin, 193–231 (Münster: LIT Verlag, 2006), 178.

19   Frontex Consolidated Regulation, Art. 3 §1a, Art. 14 §8 and Art. 20 §2 (b) and (c), Art. 25 §2, Art. 26 and Art. 33. See also Draft recommendation of the European Ombudsman in his self-initiated inquiry OI/5/2012/BEH-MHZ concerning the European Agency for the Management of Operational Cooperation at the External Borders of the Member States of the European Union (Frontex), 9 April 2013, 15.

20   Elspeth Guild *et al.*, 'Implementation of the EU Charter of Fundamental Rights and Impact on EU Home Affairs Agencies: Frontex, Europol and the European Asylum Support Office', Study for the Directorate General for Internal Policies (Luxembourg: European Parliament, 2011), 95.

21   Since 2005, the Agency's budget has increased from €6.3 million to €94 million in 2013, peaking at €118 million in 2011. For more details, see Frontex General Reports. Available online: www.frontex.europa.eu/about/governance-documents/.

22   Consolidated Version of the Treaty on European Union (TUE), OJEU C114/13, Art. 4 §3 and Consolidated Version of the Treaty on the Functioning of the European Union (TFEU), OJEU C115/47, Art. 291 §1 and §3. Exceptionally in cases where uniform action is necessary, the EU legislator is required to explicitly confer executive powers to the Commission or, in specific cases, to the Council. Direct administration is the exception, since the EU lacks necessary administrative services and coercive power. See Loïc Azoulai, 'Chapitre Introductif: Pour un Droit de l'Exécution de l'Union Européenne', in *L'Exécution du Droit de l'Union: Entre Mécanismes Communautaires et Droits Nationaux*, ed. Jacqueline Dutheil de la Rochère, 1–23 (Brussels: Bruylant, 2009); Jean Paul Jacqué, *Droit institutionnel de l'Union européenne* 7th edn, ed. Jacqueline Dutheil de la Rochère (Paris: Dalloz, 2012), 475.

23   Edoardo Chiti, 'Decentralisation and Integration into the Community Administrations: A New Perspective on European Agencies', *European Law Journal* 10, no. 4 (2004), 410.

24   For further reading about EU Agencies, see, among others, Madalina Busuioc, Martijn Groenleer and Jarle Trondal, eds, *The Agency Phenomenon in the European Union: Emergence, Institutionalisation and Everyday Decision-Making* (Manchester: Manchester University Press, 2012); Joël Molinier, ed., *Les Agences de l'Union Européenne* (Brussels: Bruylant, 2011); Edoardo Chiti, 'An Important Part of the EU's Institutional Machinery: Features, Problems and Perspectives of European agencies', *Common Market Law Review* 46 (2009), 1395–1442; Edoardo Chiti, 'The Administrative Implementation of European Union Law: A Taxonomy and its Implications', in

Legal Challenges in EU Administrative Law: Towards an Integrated Administration, eds Herwig C. H. Hofmann and Alexander H. Türk, 9–33 (Cheltenham: Edward Elgar, 2009); Berthold Rittberger and Arndt Wonka, 'Introduction: Agency Governance in the European Union', *Journal of European Public Policy* 18, no. 6 (2011), 780–789.

25 Busuioc, Groenleer and Trondal, *The Agency Phenomenon in the European Union*, 7.
26 Despite the Commission's wishes, EU agencies have no explicit definition in EU law. They were first based on Art. 308 EC, and later on specific policy provisions of the treaties. See Commission of the European Communities, Communication from the Commission. 'The operating framework for the European Regulatory Agencies', COM (2002)718 final, 11.12.2002; Commission of the European Communities, 'Draft interinstitutional agreement on the operating framework for the European Regulatory Agencies', COM(2005)59, 25.02.2005; Commission of the European Communities, 'Communication from the Commission to the European Parliament and the Council. European agencies: The way forward', COM (2008) 135 final, 11.03.2008; Joint Statement and Common Approach of the European Parliament, the Council of the EU and the European Commission on decentralised agencies, 19 July 2012.
27 CJEC, Case 9/56, Meroni and Co, *Industrie Metallurgiche SpA v. High Authority* [1958] ECR 133.
28 Jorrit Rijpma, 'EU Border Management after the Lisbon Treaty', *Croatian Yearbook of European Law & Policy* 5 (2009), 121–149.
29 Edoardo Chiti, 'European Agencies' Rulemaking: Powers, Procedures and Assessment', *European Law Journal* 19, no. 1 (2013), 93–110, Paul Craig, *EU Administrative Law* (Oxford: Oxford University Press, 2006), 143–190.
30 Monar, 'The Project of a European Border Guard: Origins, Models and Prospects in the Context of the EU's Integrated External Borders Management', 193–231.
31 Morten Egeberg and Jarle Trondal, 'EU-Level Agencies: New Executive Centre Formation or Vehicles for National Control?', *Journal of European Public Policy* 18, no. 6 (2011), 870; Rijpma, 'EU Border Management', 255–256; Renaud Dehousse, 'Delegation of Powers in the European Union: The Need for a Multi-Principals Model', *West European Politics* 31, no. 4 (2008), 796.
32 Michelle Everson, 'Agencies: the "Dark Hour" of the Executive?', in *Legal Challenges in EU Administrative Law: Towards an Integrated Administration*, eds Herwig C. H. Hofmann and Alexander H. Türk, 116–135 (Cheltenham: Edward Elgar, 2009).
33 All member states that are part of the Schengen area are represented. Ireland and the United Kingdom, exempted from the Schengen *acquis*, may however attend the Frontex Management Board as observers and request punctual participation in the agency's activities. Denmark has decided to participate in the development of the agency. Countries associated with the development of the Schengen *acquis* participate in the agency and enjoy limited voting power on the Frontex Management Board (Iceland, Norway, Switzerland, Liechtenstein). Frontex Consolidated Regulation, Art. 20 and 21.
34 The board controls the agency's function and makes strategic decisions. The management board adopts the agency's multiannual plan regarding future long-term strategy, votes on the agency's yearly programme of work, establishes procedures for taking decisions related to the operational tasks of the agency by the executive director, and adopts the general report of the agency for the previous year. Frontex Consolidated Regulation, Recital (15) and Art. 20, §2 (b), (c), (d) and (i).
35 Frontex Consolidated Regulation, Art. 25.
36 Frontex Consolidated Regulation, Art. 26 §2 and Art. 20 §2 (a) and (f).
37 Frontex 2004 Regulation, Art. 1 §3.
38 Frontex Consolidated Regulation, Art. 2 §1 (d).
39 Frontex Consolidated Regulation, Art. 2 §1 (c) and Art. 4.
40 Frontex Consolidated Regulation, Art. 2 §1 (h) and (i).

41 Frontex Consolidated Regulation, Art. 2 §1 (b) and Art. 5.

42 Frontex Consolidated Regulation, Art. 1a, §1a. Name introduced by the 2011 reform referring to all border guards deployed in any operational context.

43 Frontex Consolidated Regulation, Art. 1, §2.

44 Hélène Jorry, 'Une Agence Originale de l'Union: l'Agence Frontex', in *Les Agences de l'Union Européenne*, ed. Joël Molinier (Brussels: Bruylant, 2011), 172.

45 Frontex Consolidated Regulation, Recital (4) and Art. 1 §2.

46 Frontex Consolidated Regulation, Art. 2 §1 (ea).

47 Concerning joint operations and pilot projects, see Frontex Consolidated Regulation, Art. 3b, §1 and Art. 3 §1b. Concerning rapid interventions, see Frontex Consolidated Regulation, Art. 8b §2.

48 Frontex Consolidated Regulation Art. 3b §2.

49 Frontex Consolidated Regulation, Art. 3b §3.

50 Frontex Consolidated Regulation, Art. 1a, §2.

51 Frontex Consolidated Regulation, Art. 7 §2 and §3. In addition to the equipment provided by member states, Frontex Consolidated Regulation now allows the agency to acquire technical equipment itself or in co-ownership with member states, or to lease them. To our knowledge, it does not own any at this time. Frontex Consolidated Regulation, Art. 7 §1.

52 Concerning joint operations and pilot projects, see Frontex Consolidated Regulation, Art. 2 §1 (g), Art. 3 §1b, Art. 3b §2, Art. 8 §2 (c). Concerning Rapid Interventions, Art. 8a, Art. 8b §1, Art. 8d.

53 Frontex Consolidated Regulation, Art. 3b, §2, Art. 8b §1, Art. 8d §8.

54 Frontex Consolidated Regulation, Art. 1a, §2.

55 Frontex Consolidated Regulation, Art. 1a §6.

56 Frontex Consolidated Regulation, Art. 3b §3.

57 Frontex Consolidated Regulation, Art. 3c, §1 and Art. 10, §3.

58 Frontex Consolidated Regulation, Art. 10 §2.

59 Frontex Consolidated Regulation, Art. 10c.

60 Frontex Consolidated Regulation, Art. 10b.

61 Frontex Consolidated Regulation, Art. 3a, §3.

62 Regulation (EC) no. 1049/2001 of the European Parliament and of the Council of 30 May 2001 regarding public access to European Parliament, Council and Commission documents, L145/43.

63 Detailed information following about practical arrangements is extracted from: Joint Operation Poseidon Sea 2012, Operational Plan, Ref: 2012/SBS/02, on file with the author ('Operational Plan of JO Poseidon Sea 2012'); Joint Operation Poseidon Land 2012, Operational Plan, Ref: 2012/LBS/06, on file with the author ('Operational Plan of JO Poseidon Land 2012'); Joint Operation EPN Aeneas 2013, Ref: 2012/SBS/01, on file with the author ('Operational Plan of JO EPN AENEAS 2013'). See also: COWI, 'External evaluation of the European Agency for the Management of Operational Cooperation at the External Borders of the Member States of the European Union, Final Report', January 2009; Decision of the Management Board of 24 March 2006, 'Rules of Procedure for Taking Decisions related to the Operational Tasks of Frontex, European Agency for the Management of Operational Cooperation at the External Borders of the Member States of the European Union (Frontex)', described in Sergio Carrera, 'The EU Border Management Strategy: FRONTEX and the Challenges of Irregular Immigration in the Canary Islands', CEPS Working Document no. 261 (Brussels: Centre for European Policy Studies, March 2007), 13; Rijpma, 'Hybrid Agencification', 93–94.

64 Frontex Consolidated Regulation, Art. 3 §1.

65 Frontex Website, Section 'Intelligence', 'Risk analyses': www.frontex.europa.eu/ intelligence/risk-analysis.

66 Frontex Consolidated Regulation, Art. 3 §4.

67 Frontex Consolidated Regulation, Art. 3a §1.

68 'Les Secrets de la Forteresse Europe', documentary film broadcasted by ARTE TV, on October 17th, 2013. Available online at www.arte.tv/guide/fr/047330–000/les-secrets-de-la-forteresse-europe?autoplay=1#details-functions-share.
69 Frontex Consolidated Regulation, Art. 3a §3, Art. 3b §5, Art. 8g and Art. 17 §3.
70 Frontex Consolidated Regulation, Art. 17.
71 Frontex Consolidated Regulation, Art. 3c, §2 and §3.
72 Frontex Consolidated Regulation, Art. 8g §3.
73 Frontex Consolidated Regulation, Art. 3c §2 and §3.
74 Johannes Pollak and Peter Slominski, 'Experimentalist But Not Accountable Governance? The Role of Frontex in Managing the EU's External Borders', *West European Politics* 32, no. 5 (2009), 904–924; Charles F. Sabel and Jonathan Zeitlin, 'Learning from Difference: The New Architecture of Experimentalist Governance in the European Union', *European Law Journal* 14, no. 3 (2008), 271–327.
75 Guild *et al.*, 'Implementation of the EU Charter', 95.
76 Guild *et al.*, 'Implementation of the EU Charter', 12–13; Rijpma, 'Hybrid Agencification', 92.
77 Chiti, 'An Important Part of the EU's Institutional Machinery', 1405.
78 Deirdre Curtin, 'Delegation to EU Non-Majoritarian Agencies and Emerging Practices of Public Accountability', in *Regulation Through Agencies in the EU, A New Paradigm of European Governance*, eds Damien Gerardin, Rodolphe Muñoz and Nicolas Petit, 88–119 (Cheltenham: Edward Elgar, 2005), 92.
79 Operational Plan of JO EPN AENEAS 2013; Operational Plan of JO Poseidon Sea 2012.
80 Regulation establishing rules for the surveillance of the external sea borders, op. cit., Art. 2 (3).
81 Regulation establishing rules for the surveillance of the external sea borders, op. cit., Art. 2 (5).
82 Regulation establishing rules for the surveillance of the external sea borders, op. cit., Art. 6 §4, §5, §6, Art. 7 §4, §5, §6, §9, §11.
83 Benoit Grémare, 'L'Agence Frontex et la Marine Nationale: Essai d'une Frontière Maritime Européenne', Mémoire de Master 2 Droit Public, sous la direction de M. le Commissaire Général Jean-Louis Fillon, Année universitaire 2011–2012.
84 A RABIT operation was implemented between 11 November 2010 and 3 March 2011 on Greek demand. It was followed by Operation Poseidon Land, which became permanent.
85 Frontex Consolidated Regulation, Art. 3c, §1 and Art. 10, §3.
86 See Human Rights Watch, 'The EU's Dirty Hands'; and Paul McDonough and Evangelia Tsourdi, 'The "Other" Greek Crisis: Asylum and EU Solidarity', *Refugee Survey Quarterly* 31, no. 4 (2012), 67–100.
87 Human Rights Watch, 'The EU's Dirty Hands', 38–54.
88 Frontex Consolidated Regulation, Art. 3 §1a and Art. 3c §4.
89 ICJ, Case concerning application of the Convention on the prevention and punishment of the crime of genocide (*Bosnia and Herzégovina v. Serbia and Montenegro*), Judgment of 26 February 2007, § 392.
90 International Law Commission, Draft Articles on Responsibility of States for Internationally Wrongful Acts with commentaries, *Yearbook of the International Law Commission*, 2001, vol. II (ASR); International Law Commission, Draft Articles on the Responsibility of International Organisations, with commentaries, *Yearbook of the International Law Commission*, 2011, vol. II (ARIO). These texts were adopted by the ILC and submitted to the United Nations as part of the Commission's report on its sessions. They are not legally binding, however they reflect customary law and the progressive development of international law.
91 Luigi Condorelli and Claus Kress, 'The Rules of Attribution: General Considerations', in *The Law of International Responsibility*, eds James Crawford, Alain Pellet and Simon Olleson, 221–236 (Oxford: Oxford University Press, 2010).

92 Brigitte Stern, 'The Elements of an Internationally Wrongful Act', in *The Law of International Responsibility*, eds James Crawford, Alain Pellet and Simon Olleson, 193–220 (Oxford: Oxford University Press, 2010).

93 Art. 4 and 5 ASR; Art. 6 ARIO.

94 Art. 7 ASR; Art. 8 ARIO.

95 Ahmed Mahiou, 'La Responsabilité Internationale en Quête de Codification', in 'Le Droit International ou la Dialectique de la Rigueur et de la Flexibilité: Cours Général de Droit International (Volume 337)', Collected Courses of the Hague Academy of International Law (Leiden: Brill for The Hague Academy of International Law, 2016), 408.

96 For instance, see André Nollkæmper and Dov Jacobs, 'Shared Responsibility in International Law: A Conceptual Framework', *Michigan Journal of International Law* 34 (2013), 359–438.

97 Francesco Messineo, 'Attribution of Conduct', in *Principles of Shared Responsibility*, eds André Nollkæmper and Ilias Plakokefalos, 60–97 (Cambridge: Cambridge University Press, 2014).

98 Chapter II ASR, Commentaries (4) and (9).

99 Messineo, 'Attribution of Conduct', 26.

100 Art. 6 ASR. This principle was confirmed by the ICJ, *Bosnia and Herzégovina v. Serbia and Montenegro*, 2007, §389.

101 Art. 6 ASR, Commentary (1).

102 Art. 6 ASR, Commentary (2).

103 Ibid.

104 Art. 6 ASR, Commentary (4).

105 Art. 7 ARIO.

106 Art. 7 ARIO. The question of attributing conduct of state organs to international organisations has been considered mainly in relation to United Nations peacekeeping forces.

107 Art. 7 ARIO, Commentary (7).

108 On the controversy between the International Criminal Tribunal of Yugoslavia (ICTY) and the ICJ on this criterion, see explanations in ICJ, Military and Paramilitary Activities in and Against Nicaragua (*Nicaragua v. United States of America*), Judgment of 27 June 1986, §115, ICJ, *Bosnia and Herzégovina v. Serbia and Montenegro*, 2007, §396–407; also the explanations of Marko Milanovic, 'From Compromise to Principle: Clarifying the Concept of State Jurisdiction in Human Rights Treaties', *Human Rights Law Review* 8, no. 3 (2008), 436–441. This controversy falls beyond the scope of our analysis. In the *Bosnian* Case, the ICJ resolved the dispute by stating that there are two different tests regarding the attribution of individual conduct to states. The 'complete control' test operates at a first general level (§385–395); private 'persons, group of persons or entities' can exceptionally be considered as *de facto* organs of the state in case of a 'particularly great degree of state control' over the acting entity with no 'margin of independence' left. If this test is not satisfied, then the ICJ turns to the 'effective control' test (§396–400) where a specific operation or conduct of an organ that is neither a *de jure* or *de facto* organ must be conducted under the state's effective control in order to be attributed to the latter.

109 See in particular: European Court of Human Rights, Grand Chamber, *Behrami and Behrami v. France* and *Saramati v. France, Germany and Norway*, (Admissibility decision), no. 71412/01 and no. 78166/01, 2 may 2007, §133.

110 See Marko Milanovic and Tatjana Papic, 'As Bad as It Gets: The European Court of Human Rights' *Behrami* and *Saramati* Decision and General International Law', *International and Comparative Law Quarterly* 58 (2009), 283–286; Caitlin A. Bell, 'Reassessing Multiple Attribution: the International Law Commission and the *Behrami* and *Saramati* decision', *New York University Journal of International Law and Politics* 42 (2010), 501–548; Art. 7 ARIO, Commentary (10).

111 Messineo, 'Attribution of Conduct', 34–44.

112 Art. 7 ARIO, Commentary (4).
113 Messineo, 'Attribution of Conduct', 39.
114 Hence, the level of control required in order to equate an organ lent by a first state with an organ of a second state is similar to the level of control required in the complete control test developed in the *Bosnian Case* by the ICJ, in order this time to equate a non-state actor with an organ of the state. See note 110.
115 Bell, 'Reassessing Multiple Attribution', 523.
116 Art. 7 ARIO, Commentary (1).
117 Art. 7 ARIO, Commentary (3).
118 Messineo, 'Attribution of Conduct', 39.
119 For example, see Gregor Schusterschitz, 'European Agencies as Subjects of International Law', *International Organizations Law Review* 1 (2004): 163–188.
120 Art. 2 ASR.
121 Frontex Consolidated Regulation, Art. 17.
122 Mouloud Boumghar, 'La Licéité Internationale des Opérations Menées par Frontex', in *La Légalité de la Lutte Contre l'Immigration Irrégulière par l'Union Européenne*, ed. Laurence Dublin, 103–163 (Brussels: Bruylant, 2012).
123 Art. 6 ARIO and Commentaries: 'The conduct of an organ or agent of an International Organisation in the performance of functions of that organ or agent shall be considered an act of that organisation under International Law, whatever position the organ or agent holds in respect of the organisation'.
124 The ILC extends the International Court of Justice's definition in its advisory opinion on *Reparation for injuries suffered in the service of the United Nations* to all international organisations: 'any person who, whether a paid official or not, and whether permanently employed or not, has been charged by an organ of the organisation with carrying out, or helping to carry out, one of its functions – in short, any person through whom it acts'. It is the fact that a person or an entity has been conferred a mission by an international organisation that matters, rather than its official status or the rules of the organisation. This definition contrasts with the restricted scope of Art. 4 ASR which had to be complemented with further categories to cover all situations, such as Arts. 5 or 8 ASR.
125 Frontex Consolidated Regulation, Art. 17.
126 Sara Casella Colombeau, *et al.*, 'Agence FRONTEX: Quelles Garanties pour les Droits de l'Homme? Etude sur l'Agence Européenne aux Frontières Extérieures en Vue de la Refonte de Son Mandate' (Luxembourg: Les Verts/ALE, European Parliament, November 2010); Rijpma, 'EU Border Management', 262.
127 Boumghar, 'La Licéité Internationale des Opérations Menées par Frontex'.
128 Maarten den Heijer, 'Issues of Shared Responsibility before the European Court of Human Rights', SHARES Research Paper 06 (Amsterdam Centre for International Law: Research Project on Shared Responsibility in International Law, (2012–04)).
129 Art. 6 ASR, Commentary 4.
130 Indeed, the majority of human rights treaties use 'jurisdiction' to define their scope of application. See for instance: Art. 1 of the European Convention on Human Rights, Art. 2§1 of the ICCPR, Art. 2§1 of the CAT. Other human rights treaties present similar jurisdictional clauses, although their wordings are sometimes slightly different. When the conduct at issue does not fall under the state's jurisdiction, obligations deriving from human rights treaties do not apply and cannot trigger a breach of an international obligation. As a consequence, there can be no internationally wrongful act characterised, since one of the two core elements of international responsibility is missing.
131 On jurisdiction under human rights law and the extensive and evolving interpretation of the concept for encompassing all kind of authority, power, or control exercised over people or territories, whether lawful or unlawful, whether extraterritorial or not, see Milanovic, 'From Compromise to Principle', 434–436; Evelien Brouwer, 'Extraterritorial Migration Control and Human Rights: Preserving the Responsibility of the EU and its Member States', in *Extraterritorial Immigration Control: Legal Challenges*,

eds Bernard Ryan and Valsamis Mitsilegas, 195–224 (Leiden: Nijhoff, 2010), 217; Maarten den Heijer, *Europe and Extraterritorial Asylum* (Oxford: Hart, 2012), 44. Although this understanding is still controversial, a 'cause-and-effect' approach to jurisdiction is emerging in the case law of human rights bodies and in the literature in order to overcome the requirement of control over territories or people which is sometimes ill-equipped to respond to the ways in which states and international organisations may impact on the fundamental rights of persons. See, for instance, Klug and Howe, 'The Concept of State Jurisdiction', 88; Inter-American Commission of Human Rights, *Alejandre et al. v. Cuba*, Case 11.589, Report no. 86/99, September 29, 1999; European Court of Human Rights, *Drozd and Janousek v. France and Spain*, (Judgment) Appl no. 12747/87, 26 June 1992, § 91; European Court of Human Rights, *Xhavara and fifteen v. Italy and Albania*, (Admissibility decision), Application no. 39473/09, 11 January 2001.

132 Marteen den Heijer, 'Issues of Shared Responsibility before the European Court of Human Rights', op. cit., 2012–04, 23.

133 The literature refers to these situations with various different terms: 'indirect', 'dependent', 'derived' or 'accessory' responsibility. See den Heijer, 'Issues of Shared Responsibility before the European Court of Human Rights, op. cit., 2012–04, 26; Georg Nolte and Helmut Philipp Aust, 'Equivocal Helpers: Complicit States, Mixed Messages and International Law', *International and Comparative Law Quarterly* 58, no. 1 (2009), 1–30.

134 Art. 16 ASR.

135 Art. 14 ARIO.

136 Art. 16 ASR, Commentary (1).

137 Nolte and Aust, 'Equivocal Helpers', 13–15. See Art. 16 (a) ASR and Commentary (4); Art. 14 ARIO (a).

138 See European Court of Human Rights, Grand Chamber, *Ilascu and others v. Moldova and Russia* (Judgment), Appl. no. 48787.99, 8 July 2004. The ECtHR condemned Moldova for acts which were attributable to another state, but took place in a context where Moldova had sufficient jurisdiction left to take all measures in its power to guarantee the applicants' rights.

139 Among others, see, Human Rights Committee, *General Comment No. 31 [80], The Nature of the General Legal Obligation Imposed on States Parties to the Covenant*, CCPR/C/21/Rev.1/ADD., 26 May 2004, §8; Inter-American Court of Human Rights, *Velasquez-Rodriguez Case* Series C4 (1988), §172.

140 ICJ, *Bosnia and Herzégovina v. Serbia and Montenegro*, 2007, §413–429.

141 For case law and doctrinal developments on due diligence see ICJ, Case concerning Armed Activities on the territory of the Congo, *Democratic Republic of the Congo v. Uganda*, Judgment of 19 December 2005, §179; ICJ, *Bosnia and Herzégovina v. Serbia and Montenegro*, 2007, §430; ECtHR, *Manoilescu and Dobrescu v. Romania and Russia*, (Admissibility decision) Appl no. 60861/00, §101, 3 March 2005, 29; ECtHR, *Treska v. Albania and Italia*, (Admissibility decision) Appl no. 26937/04, 29 June 2006, 12–13; Concurring Opinion of Judge Bonello in ECtHR, Grand Chamber, *Al Skeini and others v. United Kingdom*, 7 July 2011, §11–13; den Heijer, 'Issues of Shared Responsibility before the European Court of Human Rights, op. cit., 2012–04, 11.

142 See among others: ECtHR, Grand Chamber, *M.S.S v. Belgium and Greece*, (Judgment) no. 30696/09, 21 January 2011, §342.

143 Frontex Consolidated Regulation, Art. 3 §1a. See also European Ombudsman, op. cit., 09.04.2013, 14 and Frontex Fundamental Rights strategy Endorsed by the Frontex Management Board on 31 March 2011, Point 13. Available online: http://frontex.europa.eu/assets/Publications/General/Frontex_Fundamental_Rights_Strategy.pdf

144 Frontex Consolidated Regulation, Art. 14. The agency facilitates cooperation between member states and third countries and can collaborate independently with the latter within the framework of working agreements.

145 The legal basis of Frontex-coordinated operations into third states' territorial seas is unclear. The last amendment to Frontex regulation added the possibility of including rules in bilateral agreements between member states and third states concerning the role of the agency and the exercise of executive powers by EGBT (Frontex Consolidated Regulation, Art. 14 §7). Prior to this reform, the Hera operations in Mauritania and Senegal were presumably based on this type of treaty with Spain, the host state. The agency can also cooperate with the authorities of third countries within the framework of working arrangements (WA) for matters strictly related to the management of operational cooperation (Frontex Consolidated Regulation, Art. 14 §2). Informal arrangements have been reported and seem frequently used for the implementation of these operations. See Efthymios Papastavridis, ' "Fortress Europe" and FRONTEX: Within or Without International Law', *Nordic Journal of International Law* 79 (2010), 75–111, at 98.

146 Den Heijer, 'Europe beyond its borders: Refugee and Human Rights Protection in Extraterritorial Immigration Control', in *Extraterritorial Immigration Control: Legal Challenges*, eds Bernard Ryan and Valsamis Mitsilegas (Leiden: Nijhoff, 2010), 91. See also Frontex website, 'HERA 2008 and NAUTILUS 2008 Statistics'. www.frontex.europa.eu/news/hera-2008-and-nautilus-2008-statistics-oP7kLN.

147 Weinzierl, 'The Demands of Human and EU Fundamental Rights'.

148 Guild *et al.*, 'Implementation of the EU Charter of Fundamental Rights and its Impact on EU Home Affairs Agencies', 86.

149 Under EU law, member states' responsibility for violations of EU law and compensation for damages to individuals falls under the competence of national courts. See CJCE, *Andrea Francovich and Danila Bonifaci and others v. Italian Republic*, C 6/90 and C-9/90, 19 November 1991. However, the CJEU could become aware of a case concerning Frontex-coordinated operations through different procedures such as a preliminary question brought to the Court by a national jurisdiction (Art. 267 TFEU), an action for failure against a member state brought to the Court by the Commission (Art. 358 TFEU), an action for annulment against an act of the agency (263, 265, 266 and 267 TFEU), and/or an action towards compensation for damages against the EU and its agency (Art. 268 and Art. 340 TFEU, Frontex Consolidated Regulation, Art. 19 §3 and §4).

150 The Luxembourg Court has identified conditions for state liability from breaches of EU Law in its judgment of 5 March 1996: CJEC, *Brasserie du Pecheur SA v. Germany* and *R. v. Secretary of State for Transport Ex p. Factortame Ltd (No. 3)*, C-46/93 and C-48/93, 5 March 1996. Among other conditions, the Court states that a direct link of causality must exist between the violation of EU law and the damage. This criterion might prove difficult to meet, given the formal attributions of participating member states.

151 See Guild *et al.*, 'Implementation of the EU Charter of Fundamental Rights and its Impact on EU Home Affairs Agencies', 82–85. As demonstrated by these authors, the nature of Frontex action makes it very difficult to prove in strict legal terms that an 'act' has been addressed by an agency directly to an individual, as required by admissibility criterion for the action for annulment. Similarly, the criteria identified by the CJEU for triggering the EU non-contractual liability, which are inspired by the Court's case law on state non-contractual liability, require also a 'direct causal link' between the violation and 'the damage sustained' by the individual. (See CJEC, *Bergaderm*, C 352/98 P, 2000, §. 42). The same authors remind us, however, that the EU liability could still be triggered for failing to exercise its supervisory power over member-state actions (CJCE, Société pour l'Exportation des Sucres, C-132/77, 1978, § 26–27).

152 ECtHR (GC), *Al Skeini and others v. United Kingdom* (Judgment), no. 55721/07, 7 July 2011, §137.

153 European Court of Human Rights (GC), *Bosphorus hava yollari Turizm ve ticaret anonim şirketi v. Ireland*, no. 45036/98, 30 June 2005.

154 Fifth negotiation meeting between the CDDH ad hoc negotiation group and the European Commission on the accession of the European Union to the European Convention on Human Rights, Final Report to the CDDH, Appendix I. Draft revised agreement on the accession of the European Union to the Convention for the Protection of Human Rights and Fundamental Freedoms, Strasbourg, 10 June 2013, Art. 1 §4 ('Draft revised agreement on the accession of the EU to the ECHR').
155 Draft revised agreement on the accession of the EU to the ECHR, Art. 3.
156 CJEU, Opinion 2/13 of the Court, 18 December 2014, §215–235.

Bibliography

Azoulai, Loïc. 'Chapitre Introductif: Pour un Droit de l'Exécution de l'Union Européenne'. In *L'Exécution du Droit de l'Union: Entre Mécanismes Communautaires et Droits Nationaux*, edited by Jacqueline Dutheil de la Rochère, 1–23. Brussels: Bruylant, 2009.

Bell, Caitlin A. 'Reassessing Multiple Attribution: The International Law Commission and the *Behrami* and *Saramati* decision'. *New York University Journal of International Law and Politics* 42 (2010): 501–548.

Boumghar, Mouloud. 'La Licéité Internationale des Opérations Menées par Frontex'. In *La Légalité de la Lutte Contre l'Immigration Irrégulière par l'Union Européenne*, edited by Laurence Dublin, 103–163. Brussels: Bruylant, 2012.

Brouwer, Evelien. 'Extraterritorial Migration Control and Human Rights: Preserving the Responsibility of the EU and its Member States'. In *Extraterritorial Immigration Control: Legal Challenges*, edited by Bernard Ryan and Valsamis Mitsilegas, 195–224. Leiden: Nijhoff, 2010.

Busuioc, Madalina, Martijn Groenleer and Jarle Trondal, (eds). *The Agency Phenomenon in the European Union: Emergence, Institutionalisation and Everyday Decision-making*. Manchester: Manchester University Press, 2012.

Carrera, Sergio. 'The EU Border Management Strategy: FRONTEX and the Challenges of Irregular Immigration in the Canary Islands'. CEPS Working Document no. 261. Brussels: Centre for European Policy Studies, March 2007.

Chiti, Edoardo. 'Decentralisation and Integration into the Community Administrations: A New Perspective on European Agencies'. *European Law Journal* 10 no. 4 (2004): 402–438.

Chiti, Edoardo. 'An Important Part of the EU's Institutional Machinery: Features, Problems and Perspectives of European Agencies'. *Common Market Law Review* 46 (2009): 1395–1442.

Chiti, Edoardo. 'The Administrative Implementation of European Union Law: A Taxonomy and its Implications'. In *Legal Challenges in EU Administrative Law: Towards an Integrated Administration*, edited by Herwig C. H. Hofmann and Alexander H. Türk, 9–33. Cheltenham: Edward Elgar, 2009.

Chiti, Edoardo. 'European Agencies' Rulemaking: Powers, Procedures and Assessment'. *European Law Journal* 19 no. 1 (2013): 93–110.

Colombeau, Sara Casella, Marie Charles, Olivier Clochard and Claire Rodier. 'Agence FRONTEX: Quelles Garanties pour les Droits de l'Homme? Etude sur l'Agence Européenne aux Frontières Extérieures en Vue de la Refonte de Son Mandate'. Luxembourg: Les Verts/ALE, European Parliament, November 2010.

Condorelli, Luigi, and Claus Kress. 'The Rules of Attribution: General Considerations'. In *The Law of International Responsibility*, edited by James Crawford, Alain Pellet and Simon Olleson, 221–236. Oxford: Oxford University Press, 2010.

Council of Europe. 'The Right to Leave a Country'. Strasbourg: Council of Europe Commissioner for Human Rights, October 2013.

Craig, Paul. *EU Administrative Law*. Oxford: Oxford University Press, 2006.

Curtin, Deirdre. 'Delegation to EU Non-Majoritarian Agencies and Emerging Practices of Public Accountability'. In *Regulation Through Agencies in the EU: A New Paradigm of European Governance*, edited by Damien Geradin, Rodolphe Muñoz and Nicolas Petit, 88–119. Cheltenham: Edward Elgar, 2005.

Dehousse, Renaud. 'Delegation of Powers in the European Union: The Need for a Multi-Principals Model'. *West European Politics* 31 no. 4 (2008): 789–805.

den Heijer, Maarten. *Europe and Extraterritorial Asylum*. Oxford: Hart, 2012.

den Heijer, 'Europe beyond its borders: Refugee and Human Rights Protection in Extra-territorial Immigration Control', in *Extraterritorial Immigration Control: Legal Challenges*, eds. Bernard Ryan and Valsamis Mitsilegas (Leiden: Nijhoff, 2010): 163-194

den Heijer, Maarten. 'Issues of Shared Responsibility before the European Court of Human Rights'. SHARES Research Paper 06. Amsterdam: Amsterdam Centre for International Law, Research Project on Shared Responsibility in International Law, 2012.

Egeberg, Morten, and Jarle Trondal. 'EU-Level Agencies: New Executive Centre Formation or Vehicles for National Control?'. *Journal of European Public Policy* 18 no. 6 (2011): 868–887.

Everson, Michelle. 'Agencies: the "Dark Hour" of the Executive?'. In *Legal Challenges in EU Administrative Law: Towards an Integrated Administration*, edited by Herwig C. H. Hofmann and Alexander H. Türk, 116–135. Cheltenham: Edward Elgar, 2009.

Fischer-Lescano, Andreas, Tillmann Lohr and Timo Tohidipur. 'Border Controls at Sea: Requirements under International Human Rights and Refugee Law'. *International Journal of Refugee Law* 21 no. 2 (2009): 256–296.

Grémare, Benoît. 'L'Agence Frontex et la Marine Nationale: Essai d'une Frontière Maritime Européenne', Mémoire de Master 2 Droit Public, sous la direction de M. le Commissaire Général Jean-Louis Fillon. Année universitaire 2011–2012.

Guild, Elspeth, Sergio Carrera, Leonhard den Hertog and Joanna Parkin. 'Implementation of the EU Charter of Fundamental Rights and its Impact on EU Home Affairs Agencies: Frontex, Europol and the European Asylum Support Office'. Study for the Directorate General for Internal Policies. Luxembourg: European Parliament, 2011.

Human Rights Watch. 'Pushed Back, Pushed Around: Italy's Forced Return of Boat Migrants and Asylum Seekers, Libya's Mistreatment of Migrants and Asylum Seekers'. New York: Human Rights Watch, 2009.

Human Rights Watch. 'The EU's Dirty Hands: Frontex Involvement in Ill-Treatment of Migrant Detainees in Greece'. New York: Human Rights Watch, 2011.

Jacqué, Jean Paul. *Droit institutionnel de l'Union européenne*, 7th edn, edited by Jacqueline Dutheil de la Rochère. Paris: Dalloz, 2012: 169–189.

Jorry, Hélène. 'Une Agence Originale de l'Union: l'Agence Frontex'. In *Les Agences de l'Union Européenne*, edited by Joël Molinier. Paris: Bruylant, 2011.

Klug, Anja, and Tim Howe. 'The Concept of State Jurisdiction and the Applicability of the *Non-Refoulement* Principle to Extraterritorial Interception Measures'. In *Extraterritorial Immigration Control: Legal Challenges*, edited by Bernard Ryan and Valsamis Mitsilegas, 69–102. Leiden: Martinus Nijhoff Publishers, 2010.

McDonough, Paul, and Evangelia Tsourdi. 'The "Other" Greek Crisis: Asylum and EU Solidarity'. *Refugee Survey Quarterly* 31 no. 4 (2012): 67–100.

Mahiou, Ahmed. 'La Responsabilité Internationale en Quête de Codification'. In 'Le Droit International ou la Dialectique de la Rigueur et de la Flexibilité: Cours Général de Droit International (Volume 337)'. Collected Courses of the Hague Academy of International Law. Leiden: Brill for The Hague Academy of International Law, 2016: 410–459.

Messineo, Francesco. 'Attribution of Conduct'. In *Principles of Shared Responsibility*, edited by André Nollkaemper and Ilias Plakokefalos, 60–97. Cambridge: Cambridge University Press, 2014.

Milanovic, Marko. 'From Compromise to Principle: Clarifying the Concept of State Jurisdiction in Human Rights Treaties'. *Human Rights Law Review* 8 no. 3 (2008): 411–448.

Milanovic, Marko, and Tatjana Papic. 'As Bad as It Gets: The European Court of Human Rights' *Behrami* and *Saramati* Decision and General International Law'. *International and Comparative Law Quarterly* 58 (2009): 267–296.

Mitsilegas, Valsamis. 'Extraterritorial Immigration Control in the 21st Century: The Individual and the State Transformed'. In *Extraterritorial Immigration Control: Legal Challenges*, edited by Bernard Ryan and Valsamis Mitsilegas, 39–68. Leiden: Martinus Nijhoff Publishers, 2010.

Molinier, Joël, (ed.). *Les Agences de l'Union Européene*. Brussels: Bruylant, 2011.

Monar, Jörg. 'The Project of a European Border Guard: Origins, Models and Prospects in the Context of the EU's Integrated External Borders Management'. In *Borders and Security Governance: Managing Borders in a Globalised World*, edited by Marina Caparini and Otwin Marenin, 193–231. Münster: LIT Verlag, 2006.

Neal, Andrew W. 'Securitization and Risk at the EU Border: The Origins of FRONTEX', *Journal of Common Market Studies* 47 no. 2 (2009): 333–356.

Nollkaemper, André, and Dov Jacobs. 'Shared Responsibility in International Law: A Conceptual Framework'. *Michigan Journal of International Law* 34 (2013): 359–438.

Nolte, Georg, and Helmut Philipp Aust. 'Equivocal Helpers: Complicit States, Mixed Messages and International Law'. *International and Comparative Law Quarterly* 58 no. 1 (2009): 1–30.

Office of the UN High Commissioner for Human Rights. 'Report of the Special Rapporteur on the Human Rights of Migrants, François Crépeau: Regional Study: Management of the External Borders of the European Union and its Impact on the Human Rights of Migrants'. A/HRC/23/46. Geneva: OHCHR/Human Rights Council, 24 April 2013.

PACE (Parliamentary Assembly of the Council of Europe). 'Lives lost in the Mediterranean Sea: Who is Responsible?'. Strasbourg: PACE Committee on Migration, Refugees and Displaced Persons, March 2012.

Papastavridis, Efthymios. ' "Fortress Europe" and FRONTEX: Within or Without International Law'. *Nordic Journal of International Law* 79 (2010): 75–111.

Pollak, Johannes, and Peter Slominski. 'Experimentalist But Not Accountable Governance? The Role of Frontex in Managing the EU's External Borders'. *West European Politics* 32 no. 5 (2009): 904–924.

Rijpma, Jorrit. 'EU Border Management after the Lisbon Treaty'. *Croatian Yearbook of European Law & Policy* 5 (2009): 121–149.

Rijpma, Jorrit. 'Hybrid Agencification in the Area of Freedom, Security and Justice and Its Inherent Tensions: The Case of Frontex'. In *The Agency Phenomenon in the European Union: Emergence, Institutionalisation and Everyday Decision-making*, edited by Madalina Busuioc, Martijn Groenleer and Jarle Trondal, 84–102. Manchester: Manchester University Press, 2012.

Rijpma, Jorrit, and Marise Cremona. 'The Extra-Territorialisation of EU Migration Policies and the Rule of Law'. *European University Institute Papers*, Law 2007/01.

Rittberger, Berthold, and Arndt Wonka. 'Introduction: Agency Governance in the European Union'. *Journal of European Public Policy* 18 no. 6 (2011): 780–789.

Sabel, Charles F., and Jonathan Zeitlin. 'Learning from Difference: The New Architecture of Experimentalist Governance in the European Union'. *European Law Journal* 14 no. 3 (2008): 271–327.

Schusterschitz, Gregor. 'European Agencies as Subjects of International Law'. *International Organizations Law Review* 1 (2004): 163–188.

'Les Secrets de la Forteresse Europe'. Documentary. ARTE TV, 17 October 2013. Available online at www.arte.tv/guide/fr/047330-000/les-secrets-de-la-forteresse-europe?autoplay =1#details-functions-share.

Stern, Brigitte. 'The Elements of an Internationally Wrongful Act'. In *The Law of International Responsibility*, edited by James Crawford, Alain Pellet and Simon Olleson, 193–220. Oxford: Oxford University Press, 2010.

Weinzierl, Ruth. 'The Demands of Human and EU Fundamental Rights for the Protection of the European Union's External Borders'. Berlin: German Institute for Human Rights, July 2007.

11

A 'BLIND SPOT' IN THE FRAMEWORK OF INTERNATIONAL RESPONSIBILITY?

Third-party responsibility for human rights violations: the case of Frontex

Melanie Fink[1]

11.1 Introduction

Within the areas of immigration, asylum and external border control, the EU and its member states have often been caught between two simultaneously unfolding processes – protecting human rights and tightening up immigration laws and external border controls. One of the areas increasingly subject to criticism in the human rights area is that of EU cooperation in the management of its external borders. Even though it is part of a more general trend towards international cooperation in migration control, the mutual assistance in this sphere between EU member states is remarkable in its extent and institutionalisation.

In 2004, the Agency for the Management of Operational Cooperation at the External Borders of the EU Member States (Frontex) was created. Its task is to ensure the coordination of the actions of member states in the implementation of Union measures relating to the management of external borders.[2] The agency provides technical expertise, facilitates the exchange of information and coordinates operational activities of member states.[3] Within this framework, Frontex also co-ordinates joint border control and surveillance operations in which financial and technical means as well as personnel are deployed by participating member states and Frontex to support a host member state in the control of their external borders.[4] One of the most recent Frontex-coordinated joint operations, for example, is named Triton and on 1 November 2014 started its activity in the Central Mediterranean in support of Italy's efforts to control its southern border.

In addition to Italian personnel and equipment, Triton relies on human and technical resources made available by at least nineteen participating states. The contributions include aircrafts, helicopters, vessels and guest officers for intelligence gathering and identification screening purposes.[5]

Apart from the challenges relating to reach, applicability and enforcement of human rights, these operations raise the question of how to allocate responsibility between the cooperating actors, in particular where allegations of human rights violations arise.[6] This, in turn, reflects a more general difficulty arising in the law of international responsibility when dealing with multi-actor situations – that is to say, instances where several actors are cooperating in or contributing to the realisation of a breach of international law.

The central aim of this contribution is to explore responsibility of 'third parties', understood as those states that merely contribute to a violation and are thus not the principal actors to whom the relevant conduct in breach of human rights is attributable. Attribution, as a precondition for responsibility, is binary. Hence there is no possibility of 'a bit of attribution' triggering 'a bit of responsibility'. Put simply, no attribution of the relevant conduct in breach of the law means no responsibility. Contributions to a wrong that remain below the threshold required to create an 'attribution link' thus seem to escape responsibility. The question therefore arises whether third parties operate within a 'blind spot' of the framework of international responsibility, making the primary actor the only bearer of the consequences following from the breach. For example, are states participating in a Frontex-coordinated joint operation released from responsibility for alleged human rights violations occurring during operations, if the relevant conduct is not attributable to them?

This chapter argues that the rules on attribution of conduct, coupled with the principle of independent responsibility, lead to a 'gap' in responsibility regarding those whose involvement falls short of creating an 'attribution link' (Section 11.2). Yet this does not absolve states from other forms of responsibility under international law when engaging in joint migration control or other forms of cooperation in regard to law enforcement functions. To make this argument, the chapter first sets out two forms of third-party responsibility: original third-party responsibility and derivative third-party responsibility (Section 11.3). Section 11.4 proceeds to analyse the circumstances under which these may fill the gap identified in Section 11.2. The case of Frontex-coordinated joint operations, focusing on participating states' responsibility under the European Convention of Human Rights, is used as an example to illustrate the application of these forms of responsibility. The chapter concludes that international law, and in particular international human rights law, offers mechanisms to hold third parties responsible for having played a role in breaches committed by other states or international organisations (Section 11.5). However, even though third parties by no means operate within a 'blind spot' of the law of international responsibility, implementation of such responsibility may prove difficult.

11.2 The need for third-party responsibility

International responsibility arises for every internationally wrongful act, defined as conduct attributable to a state or international organisation that is in breach of an international obligation.[7] The term 'attribution' is used to

> denote the legal operation having as its function to establish whether given conduct of a physical person . . . is to be characterised, from the point of view of international law, as an 'act of the state' (or the act of any other entity possessing international legal personality).[8]

A key role for the rules on attribution of conduct is thus to distinguish 'the "state sector" from the "non-state sector" for the purposes of responsibility'.[9]

The rules on attribution of conduct constitute an important element in the system of international responsibility, as states have to act through natural persons and 'attribution' provides for the required link between the individual actor and the legal entity.[10] The rules on attribution are based on the idea that a certain element of control by the state or international organisation over an individual or his or her actions renders them conduct of the 'controlling' legal entity from the perspective of international law.[11] The default rule is that organs of a state or international organisation act for the entity they are institutionally tied to.[12] Conduct of an organ of a state may additionally become attributable to a different state, when it is 'placed at the disposal' of the latter and acts 'in the exercise of elements of the governmental authority of the state at whose disposal it is placed'.[13] Where a state places its organs at the disposal of an international organisation that exercises 'effective control', its conduct becomes attributable to the international organisation.[14] Further, conduct which is *prima facie* private conduct may become attributable to an international legal entity where the persons or groups of persons act 'on the instructions of, or under the direction or control' of a state, or where a state or international organisation acknowledges and adopts the relevant conduct as its own.[15]

Since international responsibility is based on the principle that each state is (only) responsible for its own conduct, as a general rule, without attribution there can be no responsibility.[16] In this vein, the rules on attribution of conduct also function as a mechanism to allocate responsibility to the entity that has one of the above-mentioned 'attribution links' to the acting individual or his or her conduct, excluding responsibility for those who do not have such a link. Nothing, however, in principle, prevents a violation of international law from being attributed to more than one legal entity at the same time. A situation can arise where a single course of conduct is simultaneously attributable to several states and/or international organisations and is internationally wrongful for each of them.[17] If one course of conduct is simultaneously attributable to two or more entities, all of them are internationally responsible as 'co-authors'.[18]

The clearest illustration of attribution of conduct to a plurality of states is a situation where two or more distinct persons, acting on behalf of two or more different states, collaborate as co-perpetrators of a single wrongful act. In other words, multiple organs attributable to different actors may violate their respective home entities' international obligations through joint conduct. Two or more states may, for example, combine their troops and attack a third country in violation of the prohibition of the use of force. In such cases, the joint wrongful conduct engages the responsibility of each state. Another conceivable alternative of attribution of one wrong to several actors is the parallel application of two or more attribution rules with respect to one organ.[19] One person may simply 'wear two or more hats' at the same time and act on behalf of two or more entities. When states or international organisations avail themselves of a common organ (also 'joint organ'), its conduct 'cannot be considered otherwise than as an act of each of the states (or international organisations) whose common organ it is'.[20] An example is the *Certain Phosphate Lands in Nauru* case, where the International Court of Justice addressed an alleged failure to rehabilitate land from which phosphate was extracted in Nauru while this was placed under UN Trusteeship. The trusteeship was exercised by 'the Administering Authority', which did not have international legal personality distinct from those of its constituent states, and consisted of New Zealand, the United Kingdom and Australia. The Administering Authority was treated by the Court as a common organ of those three states and – though in the case at hand only Australia was sued – potentially attributable to all of them.[21] While a common organ can be formally established, even without a formal act one person may simply act in the name of two or more entities simultaneously, due to the parallel application of attribution rules with respect to a single course of conduct.[22]

Responsibility is assessed irrespective of whether or not other states or international organisations were involved in the wrongful act. This is commonly referred to as the principle of independent responsibility.[23] Even in cases of a single wrongful act committed by several actors, the principle of independent responsibility purports that each of them separately breached its obligations. Since international law is traditionally characterised as essentially bilateral in nature, the plurality of authors of the wrongful act is here reduced to as many independent bilateral relationships between the injured and the responsible parties as there are wrongdoers.[24] Rather than genuine cases of attribution to multiple states, these situations are multiple attributions to multiple states, the crucial difference being that the latter do not abandon the requirement of establishing the attribution link to every single state to be held responsible.

Accordingly, despite the possibility of multiple attribution of conduct where states cooperate, an 'attribution link' needs to be established with each of them if all are to be held responsible. International cooperation, however, goes far beyond situations where all involved actors can be considered 'co-authors' of an alleged breach, and includes more complex forms of interaction. The involvement may go as far as depriving the primary actor of any meaningful discretion, for example where conduct is determined by the internal law of an international organisation binding on the member states. Similarly, where another state or international organisation has *de facto* control over the actor's conduct, the latter may be constrained in its freedom to decide whether or not to commit an international wrong. At the other end of the spectrum, involvement may amount to little more than mere incitement or political support in relation to a breach of an international obligation. Most forms of participation of one international legal entity in the conduct of another, including financial or technical support, provision of information or logistic facilitation, are in between the two extremes of complete control and mere incitement. Save for in exceptional situations, such forms of involvement fall short of creating an 'attribution link'.[25]

This is evident in the implementation of Frontex-coordinated joint operations, where human rights violations are normally not attributable to all involved states at the same time.[26] On the one hand, if guest officers are considered to be 'put at the disposal' of the host state and are to exercise its 'governmental authority', their conduct – in line with Article 6 of the Articles on State Responsibility (ASR) – is attributable to the host state.[27] Since Article 6 ASR delimits 'two public sectors' from each other, it has been argued that its application breaks the link between the deployed personnel and their original home state.[28] In this vein, if Article 6 ASR is applicable, only the host state, not the participating states, is responsible for alleged human rights violations on the basis of attribution of the relevant conduct. On the other hand, if Article 6 ASR is not applicable and the conduct of deployed officers remains attributable to the officers' home member states, all participating states may incur responsibility for human rights violations during Frontex-coordinated joint operations, but only for the conduct of their own officers. Despite the lead role of the host member state in the operations, not all violations are attributable to it.

As this shows, conduct in violation of human rights can often not be attributed to all actors involved, and those states to which the wrongful conduct is not attributable seem to escape responsibility. In that light, it has been argued that the design of the legal relations between a wrongdoer and an injured state leaves virtually no 'room for the inclusion of third actors which may have also impacted upon the given legal relationship'.[29] The following sections discuss to what extent international law, despite its traditional bilateralist conception, is capable of accommodating responsibility of third parties.

11.3 Third-party responsibility

11.3.1 Forms of third-party responsibility

The variety of situations where third parties may incur responsibility for conduct closely related to the wrongful conduct of another state or international organisation can be divided into two categories.

The first category is concerned with cases where a third party breaches a provision prohibiting certain conduct in relation to acts by other states or international organisations, and thus incurs original responsibility for conduct attributable to it.

Where a specific obligation exists requiring a state or an international organisation to prevent internationally wrongful conduct, not to provide others with assistance in carrying it out, or to adopt any other specific attitude towards violations of international law of other states or international organisations, a violation of the obligation triggers responsibility. Responsibility in these cases arises simply because a breach of international law is attributed to the third party. This category is therefore governed by the principle of independent responsibility. Consequently each state or international organisation involved incurs 'original' responsibility, assessed independently of the wrongful conduct of other actors involved. Referring to third-party responsibility in these cases may be somewhat misleading, as the state or international organisation in question incurs responsibility for its own conduct in breach of international law. The term 'third party' is nevertheless used in order to underline that responsibility arises for conduct that is closely related to conduct of other states or international organisations.

The second category is concerned with responsibility derived from a wrong committed by another state or international organisation. International law provides for a set of rules dealing with responsibility of third parties for the involvement in an internationally wrongful act of other states or international organisations.[30] Such involvement can consist of aid or assistance in, or direction and control over, the commission of an internationally wrongful act or of coercion of another state or international organisation.[31] The underlying idea of this so-called derivative responsibility is that a contribution to a wrong ought to trigger legal consequences even though the actor has not engaged in conduct prohibited by a primary rule of international law. Hence the rules on derivative responsibility trigger responsibility for conduct that is so closely related to the wrongful conduct of another state or international organisation that incurring responsibility seems appropriate. Derived responsibility is therefore predicated upon the commission of an internationally wrongful act by another state, and is accordingly treated as an exception to the principle of independent responsibility.[32] Questions of derived responsibility can only arise as a result of the participation of a state or international organisation in the acts of another international legal person. Where a state's involvement in the acts of individuals or groups of individuals is at stake, this may raise questions of attributing those acts to the state, but no issue of derived responsibility arises.[33]

11.3.2 'Original' third-party responsibility

Even though international law exceptionally sets out primary obligations prohibiting the involvement of a state in the wrongful conduct of another, explicit requirements to prevent the occurrence of or otherwise react to a wrongful act are not very common.[34] Human rights bodies have been more willing than is customary in general international law to hold states responsible for human rights violations that are connected to abuse inflicted on individuals by others. Typically, they have applied the prohibition against refoulement or the doctrine of positive obligations to deal with these situations.[35] The prohibition against refoulement forbids the expulsion of an individual to another state where serious maltreatment would be inflicted upon the person.[36] Responsibility of the expelling state does not arise for the abuse inflicted on an individual by another state, but for the failure to protect an individual by expelling him or her despite the risk of maltreatment.[37]

More broadly, positive obligations require states, inter alia, to prevent human rights violations committed by others. Positive obligations originate in the need for protection of human rights against interference by private parties, but they equally require the protection of individuals from human rights violations by other states or international organisations.[38] In order to find responsibility on the basis of a breach of positive obligations, it is generally sufficient to establish that the state knew or ought to have known of the violation ('foreseeability'), but did not take reasonable steps available to it in order to prevent it.[39] States are accordingly under a due diligence obligation to take measures if they can reasonably be expected to do so. Positive obligations are therefore obligations of means, and a state does not incur responsibility if it proves that preventing the violation was impossible given the means available to it.[40]

Since this threshold is lower than what is required to create an 'attribution link', the doctrine of positive obligations may fill the gap that arises when conduct cannot be attributed to all the actors involved.[41] Whether a particular violation can be considered foreseeable for a state and whether reasonable measures would have been available to it depends on the particular role that a contributing state plays. In the context of Frontex-coordinated joint operations, for example, circumstances may arise where the states involved indeed have or ought to have knowledge of and means available to prevent a specific human rights violation, even when it is not attributable to them.

11.3.3 'Derivative' third-party responsibility

Derivative third-party responsibility covers three different scenarios: First, Article 16 ASR, Article 14 of the International Law Commission's Draft Articles on the Responsibility of International Organisations (henceforth ARIO) and Article 58 ARIO set out that aid or assistance rendered in the commission of a wrongful act triggers responsibility of the assisting state or international organisation. Second, Article 17 ASR, Article 15 ARIO and Article 59 ARIO concern direction and control exercised over the commission of an internationally wrongful act. Third, Article 18 ASR, Article 16 ARIO and Article 60 ARIO deal with coercion of another state or international organisation to commit an internationally wrongful act. Since what is being discussed in this chapter is the situation where a state *participates* in the act of another, rather than where a state *constrains* another state in its freedom to freely decide whether or not to commit an international wrong, the following discusses the provisions dealing with 'aid or assistance', also referred to as 'complicity'.[42]

It should be noted that unlike the attribution rules laid down in the International Law Commission's (ILC) Articles, which are to a large extent considered to reflect customary international law, the status of the prohibition of rendering aid or assistance remains disputed. Whereas the Special Rapporteurs initially leaned towards considering Article 16 ASR progressive development, the final commentaries to the Articles suggest a basis in customary international law.[43] Scholarly writings are divided on the issue, even though a majority of authors argue for a customary law basis of the provision.[44] In one of the rare cases where the prohibition on rendering aid or assistance in the commission of an internationally wrongful act has been addressed in international case-law, the International Court of Justice confirmed the customary nature of the principle underlying Article 16 ASR in the *Genocide Convention Case*.[45] This does not imply that the customary rule resembles Article 16 ASR in every detail; hence, a complete analysis of the prohibition on aid or assistance in the commission of an internationally wrongful act would require an analysis of state practice and *opinio iuris*. The following traces the meaning of Article 16 ASR, taking into account not only its wording and the ordinary meaning of the terms, but also the commentaries to and development of the provision.[46] As a thorough analysis of state practice and *opinio iuris* would go well beyond the scope of this section, the analysis takes as its starting point the assumption that Article 16 ASR reflects customary international law.

Article 16 ASR provides that:

> A state which aids or assists another state in the commission of an internationally wrongful act by the latter is internationally responsible for doing so if:
>
> (a) that state does so with knowledge of the circumstances of the internationally wrongful act; and
> (b) the act would be internationally wrongful if committed by that state.

Application of Article 16 rests upon three conditions. First, Article 16(b) sets out that the aiding state incurs responsibility only in case it is itself bound by the primary obligation breached. This is understood as a safeguard to prevent the rules on derivative responsibility from undermining the principle that obligations between two states create neither rights nor obligations for third parties. The second requirement is concerned with distinguishing conduct that is capable of triggering derivative responsibility from conduct that falls outside its scope. Assistance is required to reach a certain threshold and to show effects on the wrongful conduct that it facilitates.[47] This requirement is not explicitly addressed in the text of Article 16, but Special Rapporteur Crawford considered the use of the terms 'aid or assistance', accompanied by the commentaries, sufficient to make clear that a nexus between the wrongful act and the assistance rendered is to be established.[48] The commentaries to Article 16 explain in very general terms that 'the aid or assistance must be given with a view to facilitating the commission of the wrongful act, *and must actually do so*'.[49] Upon adoption of then Article 27 on first reading, the ILC suggested that the assistance rendered 'must have the effect of making it *materially* easier for the state receiving the aid or assistance in question to commit an internationally wrongful act'.[50] Yet there is no requirement 'that the aid or assistance should have been essential to the performance of the internationally wrongful act; it is sufficient if it contributed significantly to that act'.[51] The decisive element in distinguishing conduct capable of triggering derivative responsibility from other activities thus seems to be the impact, rather than the type, of assistance rendered. With respect to Frontex-coordinated joint operations, neither of the first two requirements for the application of Article 16 ASR will normally pose particular challenges. All participating states are contracting parties to the European Convention on Human Rights. A breach of the Convention by the host state is thus also internationally wrongful if committed by a participating state, fulfilling the Article 16(b) ASR requirement. Furthermore, the type and impact of the assistance given will usually be substantial enough to reach the threshold of Article 16 ASR.

The third and most controversial requirement is found in Article 16(a), setting out that the aiding state ought to have 'knowledge of the circumstances of the internationally wrongful act'. This suggests that responsibility arises if the aiding state is aware that its assistance will be used for the commission of a wrongful act. In its commentaries, however, the ILC seems to adopt a somewhat narrower approach. It points out that assistance must be given 'with a view to facilitating the commission of an internationally wrongful act'.[52] More explicitly, the ILC clarifies that a 'state is not responsible for aid or assistance under Article 16 unless the relevant state organ intended, by the aid or assistance given, to facilitate the occurrence of the wrongful conduct'.[53]

The nature of this requirement has given rise to divergent views. One position is either to regard intention as an additional limitation on derivative responsibility not contained in the wording of Article 16, or to narrow the meaning of 'knowledge' in Article 16(a) to 'intention' on the basis of the commentary or state practice.[54] Some authors, however, have questioned the usefulness of intent as a decisive criterion for complicity, or have pointed to the inherent difficulty in determining the state of mind of a state or an international organisation.[55] Apart from the fact that a state usually will not officially declare the purposes of its aid, it will often act through several officials who might not share the same state of mind.[56] In addition, the difficulties in proving that aid is given specifically for the illegal purpose have been advanced in opposition to an intention requirement.[57]

The knowledge requirement contained in the text of Article 16 seems to have developed in response to the wish to incorporate some form of intention as a 'subjective element'. Upon introducing the knowledge requirement into Article 16, which until then required that assistance 'is rendered for the commission of an internationally wrongful act', Special Rapporteur Crawford noted that 'the proposal in the text retains the element of intent, which can be demonstrated by proof of rendering aid or assistance with knowledge of the circumstances'.[58] This is in line with how Special Rapporteur Ago seems to have understood the requirement of intention:

The very idea of 'complicity' in the internationally wrongful act of another necessarily presupposes an intent to collaborate in the commission of an act of this kind, and hence, in the cases considered, knowledge of the specific purpose for which the state receiving certain supplies intends to use them.[59]

Thus it seems that the knowledge requirement may in itself be considered a manifestation of intention, without additionally requiring a volitional element.

Intention may therefore be established by demonstrating that the participating actor had knowledge of the specific circumstances. This means that the assisting state needs to be aware, first, of the commission of a wrongful act (as opposed to a general habit on the part of another state of breaching international law) and, second, of the fact that the assistance given is used for those purposes.[60] Assisting another actor while being aware that the assistance is used for an international wrong implies that the participating actor accepted the anticipated consequences.[61] States involved in Frontex-coordinated joint operations hence only incur derivative responsibility if they render their assistance in the knowledge of its use for a human rights violation.

11.4 Third-party responsibility: closing the gap?

11.4.1 Thresholds for responsibility

As the previous section shows, the provisions on 'aid or assistance' set a higher threshold for responsibility than positive obligations. Knowledge that is required for derivative third-party responsibility may be significantly more difficult to prove than the requirement that a third party 'ought to have knowledge', as required for original third-party responsibility. In addition, in many cases, at the moment when assistance is rendered, states may not have knowledge of its use for the commission of human rights violations. Using the example of Frontex-coordinated joint operations, it may even be the case that assistance is conditional upon human rights conformity.[62] It therefore seems difficult to argue that states contribute assets to Frontex-coordinated joint operations despite their full knowledge that this will be used by the host state in order to commit human rights violations. Clearly, however, it is normally at a later stage that states gain knowledge, after having rendered their contribution. In those cases, the question is whether they are under an obligation, upon gaining knowledge of a human rights violation, to withdraw the assistance rendered.

It is important in this context to note that the concepts of 'aid or assistance' on the one hand and positive obligations on the other have sometimes been differentiated along the lines of positive action and omissions. In the *Genocide Convention Case*, the International Court of Justice held that

complicity always requires that some positive action has been taken to furnish aid or assistance to the perpetrators of the genocide, while a violation of the obligation to prevent results from mere failure to adopt and implement suitable measures to prevent genocide from being committed. In other words, while complicity results from commission, violation of the obligation to prevent results from omission.[63]

The major difference between the concepts of 'aid or assistance' and positive obligation lies, indeed, in the role played by the third party in question. The former is an exception to the general rule that states are free to take either side in a conflict, insofar as it places limits on the possibility of supporting a perpetrator in the commission of a wrongful act. Yet there is generally no requirement to actively protect the victim, and it is normally legitimate for a state not to get involved at all. By contrast, the obligation to prevent human rights violations is aimed at protecting potential victims from unlawful interferences. This prohibits states from remaining inactive and requires their involvement on the side of the victim. Thus whereas the concept of derivative responsibility does not apply to a stranger to a dispute, states incur a duty to take preventive measures under the concept of positive obligations even without prior involvement.[64]

As a general rule, it can hence be said that 'doing nothing' is fine when assessed through the lens of derivative responsibility; accordingly, omissions usually do not trigger such responsibility. Under exceptional circumstances, however, where states cannot be considered strangers to a situation, they may be under an obligation to react to a wrongful act, failing which they incur derivative responsibility.[65] An example of such circumstances is the case of Frontex-coordinated joint operations. Owing to their institutional set-up, planning and design as 'joint operations' and the participating states' continued involvement therein, the latter cannot be considered 'strangers' to the operations. Consequently, participating states may, in principle, incur original or derivative responsibility for failure to withdraw assistance upon gaining knowledge of a human rights violation. In circumstances such as Frontex-coordinated joint operations, both original and derivative third-party responsibility may hence fill the gap in responsibility created when a human rights violation cannot be attributed to all actors involved.

11.4.2 The interplay between original and derivative third-party responsibility

Despite the lower threshold for original third-party responsibility, there is a major obstacle to its application. Human rights treaties are frequently characterised by a strict interpretation of their territorial applicability, an issue that can be well exemplified with the European Convention on Human Rights. According to Article 1 of the Convention, the high contracting parties owe their Convention obligations to those individuals who come within their 'jurisdiction'. Although as a rule any conduct by a high contracting party on its territory is subject to the Convention, the application of the Convention is more limited when states act extraterritorially. Although the question becomes more complex at a level of detail, it suffices to note here that state parties generally incur Convention obligations extraterritorially if they exercise either 'effective (overall) control' over a territory or 'authority and control' over individual victims. In the latter case, this can be achieved either by exercising physical power and control over the person in question (as with holding an individual in detention) or by exercising all or some of the public powers normally exercised by the government.[66]

As has been pointed out above, original third-party responsibility is governed by the principle of independent responsibility. Consequently, it is assessed independently of wrongful conduct by other actors involved. This also means that the applicability of the Convention has to be assessed for each state separately. Using the example of Frontex-coordinated joint operations, even where the alleged violations come within the jurisdiction of the host state, the Convention is not automatically applicable to all participating states operating on the territory of or in cooperation with the host state. Operations are extraterritorial from the viewpoint of the participating states even when they take place within the territory of the host state.

This may not pose an obstacle to the application of the Convention if all the deployed guest officers remain attributable to their original 'home states'. It can be argued that the Convention is applicable on the basis that the participating states are exercising public powers in the form of border control, thereby bringing the affected individuals within their jurisdiction.[67] However, if the officers of the participating states act in the name of the host states rather than in the name of their original 'home states', their authority is exercised in the name of the host state. It therefore seems that in this case the lack of control that impedes attribution of conduct also precludes extraterritorial application of the Convention to contributing states, and consequently of the obligation to take positive action to prevent a violation.

The precise relationship between responsibility based on attribution of conduct and the doctrine of positive obligations in the context of extraterritorial situations is indeed difficult to establish, since the European Court of Human Rights often seems to have struggled to clearly distinguish the two. It is unclear, for example, whether the Court in *Loizidou v. Turkey* attributed the Turkish Republic of Northern Cyprus (TRNC), operating in Cyprus, to Turkey or whether Turkey was held responsible because it had violated its positive obligations to prevent the TRNC from engaging in conduct contrary to the Convention.[68] Milanovic argues that much of the confusion stems from the use of the threshold of 'effective (overall) control' at different levels.[69] On the one hand, this threshold is relevant in the determination of whether acts by private parties are attributable to a state; on the other, the European Court of Human Rights uses notions of control in order to determine whether a situation falls under the 'jurisdiction' of a state within the meaning of Article 1 European Convention on Human Rights, which renders the Convention applicable. Whereas attribution is determined on the basis of control over the wrongful conduct, jurisdiction depends on control over a territory or over the victims of an alleged human rights violation. The European Court of Human

Rights has not always made it explicit whether a test of control was applied in order to determine the jurisdiction requirement or the attribution of the acts of private parties.

Nonetheless, in a number of cases the European Court of Human Rights has indicated its willingness to loosen the jurisdiction requirement in the context of positive obligations.[70] In *Manoilescu and Dobrescu v. Romania and Russia*, the Court held that 'even in the absence of effective control of a territory outside its border' the state may still incur positive obligations under the Convention.[71] This statement was repeated in the similar case, *Treska v. Italy and Albania*.[72] Both cases were eventually declared inadmissible. More importantly, the relevant statements were explicitly based on *Ilascu and Others v. Moldova and Russia*.[73] In that case, the Court held that Moldova incurred positive obligations with respect to Transnistria, an area within its own territory over which it had lost full effective control. This of course is quite different from saying that states have positive obligations with regard to any territory in the world, no matter whether they have jurisdiction over it or merely act there.[74] In addition, as these cases have not been relied upon since, the suggestion has been made that they be considered 'a mere slip of the tongue' rather than *carte blanche* to do away with the concept of jurisdiction altogether with respect to positive obligations.[75] Even if these are indications that the Court may loosen the requirements when positive obligations are at stake, the more cautious approach suggests that the strict interpretation of the territorial application of the European Convention on Human Rights poses a considerable challenge to responsibility of third parties under the Convention.

This leaves two options for finding contributing states responsible for a failure to prevent the host state's violations of the European Convention on Human Rights. The first is a more lenient interpretation of the jurisdiction requirement more generally; the second is a more general duty of states to secure Convention rights when they are capable of doing so, irrespective of whether the situation comes within their jurisdiction.[76] Paradoxically, though, in the light of the law as it stands, the lack of attribution of conduct to contributing states also prevents the incurring of positive obligations.

The strict interpretation of the concept of jurisdiction in Article 1 of the European Convention on Human Rights does not bar the application of derivative responsibility (as it does, by contrast, in the case of responsibility for the breach of positive obligations). As outlined in more detail above, the characteristic feature of derivative responsibility is its dependency on the wrongful act by another state. In other words, the aiding state incurs derivative responsibility only if the aid-receiving state breached its obligations in the first place. Conversely, with regard to the aiding state, wrongfulness as such is not necessary. Instead, it is required that the wrongful conduct by the aid-receiving state would be wrongful also if directly perpetrated by the aiding state. If all states incur the same human rights violations – as is the case with respect to Frontex-coordinated joint operations and obligations under the European Convention on Human Rights – this requirement is normally met. Since it is therefore enough to establish wrongfulness on the part of the aid-receiving state, the question of the Convention's applicability need only be assessed with respect to that state and does not rule out derivative responsibility on the part of other states for rendering aid or assistance. In light of the foregoing, the concept of aid or assistance may complement the doctrine of positive obligations with respect to third-party responsibility for human rights violations taking place under the jurisdiction of a contracting party to the European Convention on Human Rights but outside the territory of the assisting state.[77] Despite the ILC's statement that the provisions on aid or assistance also apply to human rights law, the concept has hardly ever been invoked by human rights bodies.[78] Similarly, the European Court of Human Rights has not, to date, explicitly relied on the concept of aid or assistance.[79] It thus seems to not have exploited the potential of this concept to fill in the gaps created by its strict interpretation of the territorial application of the Convention.

11.5 Conclusion

As a consequence of the traditionally bilateral nature of international law, the law of international responsibility struggles to accommodate the reality of two or more potential wrongdoers. Even where conduct may be attributable to multiple states – whether because the organs of several states cooperate in a breach of international law, or because the conduct of one organ is attributed to several states – the 'attribution link' has to be established with every single cooperating party. Each state's responsibility is thereby assessed irrespective of whether or not other actors were involved in the wrongful act. The complex forms of involvement of states in the acts of others, however, often remain below the threshold of attributability of the primary wrongful act. This raises the question whether third parties incur responsibility for having played a role in a breach of international law.

International law places limits on the involvement of third parties in wrongful acts by other states or by international organisations. These may result from a primary rule prohibiting certain conduct in relation to acts by other states or international organisations, or requiring positive action to prevent the breach. Whereas under general international law, primary rules governing third-party conduct are rare, human rights bodies have developed third-party responsibility in particular through the doctrine of positive obligations. Alternatively, third parties may derive responsibility from a wrongful act that they have not themselves committed, where they render aid or assistance facilitating its commission.

Generally speaking, positive obligations are more far-reaching in terms of the limits placed on third parties. Whereas under the doctrine of positive obligations states have to take all reasonable measures to prevent a foreseeable human rights violation, responsibility for aid or assistance requires a close link between the assistance rendered and the wrongful conduct, including proof that the participating actor had knowledge of the commission of a wrongful act and of the actual use of its assistance for those wrongful purposes. In addition, a 'hands off' approach fails to trigger derivative responsibility for states who are strangers to a dispute.

By contrast, positive obligations require a more active involvement on the side of the victim of unlawful interferences.

Even if third parties by no means operate within a 'blind spot' of the law of international responsibility, implementation of such responsibility can be difficult. As the European Convention on Human Rights example shows, strict interpretation of the extraterritorial reach of Convention obligations may complicate the application of the doctrine of positive obligations to multi-actor situations. Owing to the frequent lack of a clear distinction between the establishment of responsibility based on attribution of conduct and the doctrine of positive obligations in cases involving extraterritoriality, any conclusive analysis is difficult to make. However, a third party's lack of direct involvement in the human rights violation may at the same time place the situation outside its jurisdiction. By contrast, responsibility for rendering aid or assistance in the commission of an internationally wrongful act may be more readily applicable to multi-actor situations. Since the applicability of the Convention needs to be established only with respect to the primary actor, strict interpretation of the jurisdiction requirement does not bar derivative responsibility. In this context, the rules on aid or assistance may prove a useful complement to the doctrine of positive obligations, with respect to third-party responsibility for human rights violations taking place under the jurisdiction of a European Convention on Human Rights contracting party. To date, however, the European Court of Human Rights has not relied on these rules.

Notes

1   The author would like to thank Professor Gregor Noll and the editors for useful comments and suggestions on earlier drafts of this paper.
2   Council Regulation (EC) No 2007/2004 establishing a European Agency for the Management of Operational Cooperation at the External Borders of the Member States of the European Union (2004) OJ L349/1, amended by Regulation (EC) No 863/2007 ('Rabit Regulation') establishing a mechanism for the creation of Rapid Border Intervention Teams and amending Council Regulation (EC) No 2007/2004 as regards that mechanism and regulating the tasks and powers of guest officers (2007) OJ L199/30 and by Regulation (EU) No 1168/2011 amending Council Regulation (EC) No 2007/2004 establishing a European Agency for the Management of Operational Cooperation at the External Borders of the Member States of the European Union. This document is referred to hereafter as Frontex Regulation.
3   For a more detailed discussion of Frontex, see Jorrit J. Rijpma, 'Hybrid Agencification in the Area of Freedom, Security and Justice and its Inherent Tensions: The Case of Frontex', in *The Agency Phenomenon in the European Union*, eds Madalina Busuioc, Martijn Groenleer and Jarle Trondal, 84–102 (Manchester: Manchester University Press, 2012).
4   In particular, Articles 3–3c, Frontex Regulation.
5   Frontex, 'Operational Plan: Joint Operation EPN Triton 2014' (2014/SBS/09) 8, Annex 5 (on file with the author).
6   For many others, see Anneliese Baldaccini, 'Extraterritorial Border Controls in the EU: The Role of Frontex in Operations at Sea', in *Extraterritorial Immigration Control: Legal Challenges*, eds Bernard Ryan and Valsamis Mitsilegas, 225–251 (The Hague: Nijhoff, 2010), 233–236; *Implementation of the EU Charter of Fundamental Rights and its Impact on EU Home Affairs Agencies: Frontex, Europol and the European Asylum Support Office,*

study requested by the European Parliament's LIBE Committee (Luxembourg: European Parliament's Committee on Civil Liberties, Justice and Home Affairs (LIBE), 2011), 19, 83–87.

7   International Law Commission, 'Draft Articles on Responsibility of States for Internationally Wrongful Acts' YILC 2001, vol II, Part Two, Articles 1–2 (henceforth ASR); International Law Commission, 'Draft Articles on the Responsibility of International Organisations' YILC 2011, vol II, Part Two, art 3–4 (henceforth ARIO). In more detail, see Brigitte Stern, 'The Elements of an Internationally Wrongful Act', in *The Law of International Responsibility*, eds James Crawford, Alain Pellet and Simon Olleson (London: Open University Press, 2010); Chittharanjan F. Amerasinghe, 'The Essence of the Structure of International Responsibility', in *International Responsibility Today: Essays in Memory of Oscar Schachter*, ed. Maurizio Ragazzi, 1–6 (The Hague: Nijhoff, 2005).

8   Luigi Condorelli and Claus Kress, 'The Rules of Attribution: General Considerations', in *The Law of International Responsibility*, eds James Crawford, Alain Pellet and Simon Olleson, 221–236 (London: Open University Press, 2010), 221.

9   Special Rapporteur Crawford, First Report on State Responsibility, YILC 1998, vol II (1), 1, 33–34 (para. 154).

10 Jörn Griebel and Milan Plücken, 'New Developments Regarding the Rules of Attribution? The International Court of Justice's Decision in *Bosnia v. Serbia*', *Leiden Journal of International Law* 21 no. 3 (2008), 601, 602–603.

11 Christiane Ahlborn, 'To Share or Not to Share? The Allocation of Responsibility between International Organizations and their Member States' (Amsterdam: Amsterdam Centre for International Law, Research Project on Shared Responsibility in International Law, SHARES, 2013), SHARES Research Paper 28, 2013–26, 6.

12 ASR Article 4; ARIO Article 6.

13 ASR Article 6.

14 ARIO Article 7.

15 ASR Articles 8, 11; ARIO Article 9.

16 ASR Article 1, 'Every internationally wrongful act of a State entails the international responsibility of *that* State'. The same rule is contained in ARIO Article 3 in relation to international organisations.

17 ASR with commentaries, Article 47, para. 3.

18 For the following categorisation see also Christian Dominicé, 'Attribution of Conduct to Multiple States and the Implication of a State in the Act of Another State', in *The Law of International Responsibility*, eds James Crawford, Alain Pellet and Simon Olleson, 281–289 (Oxford: Oxford University Press, 2010), 282–283; similarly also Francesco Messineo, 'Multiple Attribution of Conduct' (Amsterdam: Amsterdam Centre for International Law, Research Project on Shared Responsibility in International Law, SHARES), SHARES Research Paper 2012–11, 10–23.

19 In more detail on common organs and a number of examples in this respect see Stefan Talmon, 'A Plurality of Responsible Actors: International Responsibility for Acts of the Coalition Provisional Authority in Iraq', in *The Iraq War and International Law*, eds Phil Shiner and Andrew Williams, 185–230 (Oxford: Hart Publishing, 2008), 198–204.

20 ASR Part I at first reading, International Law Commission, Report on its Thirty-Second Session, 190, para. 2; also pointing out the possibility of a common organ simultaneously attributable to several entities see Special Rapporteur Gaja, Second Report on Responsibility of International Organisations (UN Doc A/CN.4/541, 2004) 4, para. 6.

21 ICJ, *Case Concerning Certain Phosphate Lands in Nauru (Nauru v. Australia)*, Preliminary Objections, 26 June 1992, ICJ Reports 1992, 240; in more detail see Messineo, 'Multiple Attribution of Conduct', 10–21; see also André Nollkaemper, 'Issues of Shared Responsibility before the International Court of Justice' (Amsterdam: Amsterdam Centre for International Law, Research Project on Shared Responsibility in International Law, SHARES), SHARES No 2011–01.

22 Messineo distinguishes these cases, only using the 'joint organ category' for formally established joint organs. See Francesco Messineo, 'The Attribution of Conduct in Breach of Human Rights Obligations during Peace Support Operations under UN Auspices' (PhD diss., University of Cambridge, 2012), 193.

23 ASR with commentaries, chapter IV, para. 1.

24 In more detail see André Nollkaemper and Dov Jacobs, 'Shared Responsibility in International Law: A Concept Paper' (Amsterdam: Amsterdam Centre for International Law, Research Project on Shared Responsibility in International Law, SHARES), Research Paper No 2011–07. For the traditional characterisation of international law as 'bilateral' in nature see Bruno Simma, 'From Bilateralism to Community Interest in International Law', *Recueil des Cours de l'Académie de Droit International* 250 (1994), 217.

25 For a categorisation of different forms of cooperation in the context of migration control see Thomas Gammeltoft-Hansen and James C. Hathaway, 'Non-Refoulement in a World of Cooperative Deterrence', *Columbia Journal of Transnational Law* 53 no. 1 (2015), 235, 244–257.

26 In more detail on attribution during Frontex-coordinated joint operations, see Maïté Fernandez in this volume.

27 The parallel situation of Article 7 ARIO, which would make conduct during Frontex-coordinated joint operations attributable to the EU if 'effective control' on the part of Frontex can be proven, is not discussed here. In detail see Maïté Fernandez in this volume.

28 See for example Messineo, 'Multiple Attribution of Conduct', 26–44.

29 Helmut P. Aust, *Complicity and the Law of State Responsibility* (Cambridge: Cambridge University Press, 2011), 13; see also Bernhard Graefrath, 'Complicity in the Law of International Responsibility', *Revue Belge de Droit International* 29 (1996), 370, 372, who argues that a prohibition of assistance faces challenges as 'we still have a mainly bilateral structure of international law'.

30 ASR chapter IV; for the more specific obligations of third parties upon serious breaches of peremptory norms, see Annie Bird, 'Third State Responsibility for Human Rights Violations', *European Journal of International Law* 21 no. 4 (2011), 883.

31 ASR Articles 16–18.

32 Ibid., with commentaries, chapter IV, para. 8.

33 See for example Graefrath, 'Complicity in the Law of International Responsibility', 370.

34 Lea Brilmayer and Isaias Y. Tesfalidet, 'Third State Obligations and the Enforcement of International Law', *NYU Journal Of International Law And Politics* 44 (2011), 1, 6–7; an example is Article I of the 1948 Convention on the Prevention and Punishment of Genocide, which requires states to prevent others from committing the crime of genocide.

35 Christian Tams, 'The Abuse of Executive Powers: What Remedies?' in *Counterterrorism: Democracy's Challenge*, eds Andrea Bianchi and Alexis Keller, 313–334 (Oxford: Hart Publishing, 2008), 317–319; Maarten den Heijer, *Europe and Extraterritorial Asylum* (Oxford: Hart Publishing, 2012), 93.

36 United Nations Convention Relating to the Status of Refugees (28 July 1951) 189 UNTS 137 and United Nations Protocol Relating to the Status of Refugees (31 January 1967) 606 UNTS 297, art 33(1); in the context of human rights see in particular European Court of Human Rights, *Soering v. The United Kingdom*, 7 July 1989.

37 Monica Hakimi, 'State Bystander Responsibility', *European Journal of International Law* 21 (2010), 341, 343.

38 Dimitris Xenos, *The Positive Obligations of the State under the European Convention of Human Rights* (Abingdon: Routledge, 2012), 19; Hakimi, 'State Bystander Responsibility', 342.

39 Under certain circumstances, the European Court of Human Rights has additionally referred to the requirement of a causal link between the omission of positive measures and the wrongful event. In more detail see Benedetto Conforti, 'Exploring the Strasbourg Case-Law: Reflections on State Responsibility for the Breach of Positive

Obligations', in *Issues of State Responsibility before International Judicial Institutions*, eds Malgosia Fitzmaurice and Dan Sarooshi, 129–137 (Oxford: Hart Publishing, 2004), 132–135.

40   Vassilis P. Tzevelekos, 'Reconstructing the Effective Control Criterion in Extraterritorial Human Rights Breaches: Direct attribution of Wrongfulness, Due Diligence, and Concurrent Responsibility', *Michigan Journal of International Law* 36 no. 1 (2014), 129, 133. He hence speaks of a 'subjective obligation'.

41   Similarly pointing to the parallel functions, see Hakimi, 'State Bystander Responsibility', 347–349.

42   Already in his first more detailed discussion of derivative responsibility, Special Rapporteur Ago distinguished two conceptual categories of the '(i)mplication of a state in the internationally wrongful act of another state'. The overall proposition was to treat situations where a state *participates* in the act of another differently from those where a state *constrains* another state in its freedom to freely decide whether or not to commit an international wrong. See Special Rapporteur Ago, Seventh Report on State Responsibility, YILC 1978, vol I(1), 52–53. For a discussion of the various meanings of 'complicity' in international law see John Cerone, 'Re-examining International Responsibility: "Complicity" in the Context of Human Rights Violations', *ILSA Journal of International and Comparative Law* 14 (2008), 525.

43   Aust, *Complicity*, 97–98.

44   With extensive references to scholarly writings see Aust, ibid., 98–99, who – on the basis of a thorough analysis of state practice and *opinio iuris* – confirms that Article 16 ASR represents customary international law. See on page 191.

45   ICJ, Case Concerning the Application of the Convention on the Prevention and Punishment of the Crime of Genocide (*Bosnia and Herzegovina v. Serbia and Montenegro*), Judgment, 26 February 2007, ICJ Reports 2007, 43, para. 420. Hereafter referred to as ICJ *Genocide Convention Case*.

46   It should be noted here that even though the choice to draft the Articles in treaty form may induce the application of rules of interpretation inspired by the Vienna Convention on the Law of Treaties, these are unsuitable to give meaning to the ASR and the ARIO. The focus of the Vienna Convention on the ordinary meaning of the terms used rests on the basis that the language of a treaty reflects a final compromise reached by the contracting parties. This lends particular authority to the wording. In contrast, the ILC Articles represent the dominant view within the ILC, an expert body, meaning that minority views may not be reflected in the text. Since the wording of the Articles therefore does not have the same authority of the language of a treaty, the commentaries to and development of the Articles bear more weight than they do in relation to treaties, where preparatory works serve only as supplementary means of interpretation. In more detail, see David D. Caron, 'The ILC Articles on State Responsibility: The Paradoxical Relationship Between Form and Authority', *American Journal of International Law* 96 (2002), 857, 868–870.

47   See also James Crawford, *State Responsibility: The General Part* (Oxford: Oxford University Press, 2013), 405.

48   Special Rapporteur Crawford, Second Report on State Responsibility, Addendum, A/CN.4/498/Add.1, para. 180.

49   ASR with commentaries, Article 16, para. 3, emphasis added.

50   International Law Commission, Report on its Thirtieth Session, YILC 1978, vol II(2), 104.

51   ASR with commentaries, Article 16, para. 5; see also Crawford, *State Responsiility*, 403, arguing that 'the required standard would . . . appear to be one of substantial involvement on the part of the complicit state'.

52   ASR with commentaries, Article 16, para. 3, 5.

53   Ibid., with commentaries, Article 16, para. 5.

54   For the former see Crawford, *State Responsibility*, 406; for the latter see Aust, *Complicity*, 235–241.

55 For example Graefrath, 'Complicity in the Law of International Responsibility'; John Quigley, 'Complicity in International Law: A New Direction in the Law of State Responsibility', *British Yearbook of International Law* 57 (1986), 77; Kate Nahapetian, 'Confronting State Complicity in International Law', *UCLA Journal of International Law and Foreign Affairs* 7 (2002), 99.

56 Quigley, 'Complicity in International Law', 111.

57 Graefrath, 'Complicity in the Law of International Responsibility', 375.

58 At that time it was Article 27, Special Rapporteur Crawford, Second Report on State Responsibility, Addendum, A/CN.4/498/Add.1, para. 186, fn. 407.

59 Special Rapporteur Ago, Seventh Report on State Responsibility, YILC 1978, vol I(1), 58, para. 72.

60 See also Georg Nolte and Helmut P. Aust, 'Equivocal Helpers: Complicit States, Mixed Messages and International Law', *International and Comparative Law Quarterly* 58 (2009) 1, 14–15.

61 See also den Heijer, *Europe and Extraterritorial Asylum*, 75, citing the 'Grotian theory of *culpa*' in connection with state responsibility for acts of individuals. For *culpa*, knowledge is sufficient, because 'knowledge implies a concurrence of will'.

62 The Frontex Regulation contains numerous references regarding human rights compliance, see for example Article 3b(4), setting out that '[m]embers of the European Border Guard Teams shall, in the performance of their tasks and in the exercise of their powers, fully respect fundamental rights' or Article 10(2), requiring guest officers to observe fundamental rights. See also Article 9(1) Frontex Regulation regarding return cooperation, setting out: 'The Agency shall ensure that in its grant agreements with Member States any financial support is conditional upon the full respect for the Charter of Fundamental Rights'.

63 ICJ, *Genocide Convention Case*, para. 432; also arguing against the possibility of derivative responsibility being triggered by omissions see for example Andreas Felder, *Die Beihilfe im Recht der völkerrechtlichen Staatenverantwortlichkeit* (Zürich: Schulthess Verlag, 2007), 254–255; see also Crawford, *State Responsibility*, 405, who considers that 'the contribution must be in the form of a positive act: neither active incitement nor a mere omission will suffice to ground responsibility'.

64 For this conception of third-party responsibility see Brilmayer and Tesfalidet, 'Third State Obligations', 37–42.

65 See the examples given by Quigley, 'Complicity in International Law', 124–125 and Aust, *Complicity*, 229–230. It is, however, less far-reaching than Quigley, 'Complicity in International Law', 124–125, who argues: 'If a donor state supplies, for example, electrical apparatus and stipulates that it should not be used to administer torture, it should be liable for complicity if it learns that the apparatus is being used for torture yet takes no action to prevent continued wrongful use, when such action is available to it'.

66 For many others see European Court of Human Rights, *Al-Skeini and others v. the United Kingdom*, 7 July 2011 (GC); for a more detailed discussion of the Court's case-law on the extraterritorial application of the European Convention on Human Rights see Milanovic in this volume.

67 For a more detailed discussion see Gammeltoft-Hansen and Hathaway, 'Non-Refoulement in a World of Cooperative Deterrence', 266–272.

68 European Court of Human Rights, *Loizidou v. Turkey*, Preliminary Objections 23 March 1995, Merits 18 December 1996; in detail see Marko Milanovic, 'From Compromise to Principle: Clarifying the Concept of State Jurisdiction in Human Rights Treaties', *Human Rights Law Review* 8 no. 3 (2008), 411, 436–446; see also Hakimi, 'State Bystander Responsibility', 353–354; den Heijer, *Europe and Extraterritorial Asylum*, 70–71. A similar argument can be made in relation to European Court of Human Rights, *Ilascu and Others v. Moldova and Russia*, 8 July 2004: see Marko Milanovic, *Extraterritorial Application of Human Rights Treaties: Law, Principles, and Policy* (Oxford: Oxford University Press, 2011), in particular 140.

69 Milanovic, 'From Compromise to Principle', in particular 46.
70 See den Heijer, *Europe and Extraterritorial Asylum*, 45–48; Maarten den Heijer and Rick
    Lawson, 'Extraterritorial Human Rights and the Concept of "Jurisdiction"', in *Global
    Justice, State Duties: The Extraterritorial Scope of Economic, Social and Cultural Rights in
    International Law*, eds Malcolm Langford *et al.*, 153–192 (Cambridge: Cambridge
    University Press, 2013), 187–190.
71 European Court of Human Rights, *Manoilescu and Dobrescu v. Romania and Russia*,
    3 March 2005, para. 101.
72 European Court of Human Rights, *Treska v. Italy and Albania*, 29 June 2006.
73 European Court of Human Rights, *Ilascu* (n 67), the Court in *Manoilescu* (n 70) and
    Treska (n 71) more specifically cited para. 331.
74 For a more detailed discussion see Kjetil M. Larsen, *The Human Rights Treaty Obligations
    of Peacekeepers* (Cambridge: Cambridge University Press, 2012), 220–224.
75 Ibid., 224.
76 Developing an approach in this respect, Tzevelekos, 'Reconstructing the Effective
    Control Criterion'; see also Larsen, *Human Rights Treaty Obligations*, 224.
77 Arguing that the concept of aid or assistance may be better suited than the doctrine of
    positive obligations to determine a state's responsibility for its involvement in conduct
    of a primary actor contrary to the European Convention on Human Rights outside
    its territory, see den Heijer, *Europe and Extraterritorial Asylum*, 57–103, in particular 100,
    103.
78 ASR (n 6) with commentaries, Article 16, para. 9.
79 Maarten den Heijer, 'Issues of Shared Responsibility before the European Court
    of Human Rights' (2012) ACIL Research Paper No 2012–04 (SHARES Series),
    46–47.

Bibliography

Ahlborn, Christiane. 'To Share or Not to Share? The Allocation of Responsibility between
    International Organizations and their Member States'. Amsterdam: Amsterdam Centre
    for International Law, Research Project on Shared Responsibility in International Law,
    2013. SHARES Research Paper 2013–26.
Amerasinghe, Chittharanjan F. 'The Essence of the Structure of International Responsibility'.
    In *International Responsibility Today: Essays in Memory of Oscar Schachter*, edited by Maurizio
    Ragazzi, 1–6. Leiden: Martinus Nijhoff, 2005.
Aust, Helmut P. *Complicity and the Law of State Responsibility*. Cambridge: Cambridge
    University Press, 2011.
Baldaccini, Anneliese. 'Extraterritorial Border Controls in the EU: The Role of Frontex in
    Operations at Sea'. In *Extraterritorial Immigration Control: Legal Challenges*, edited by Bernard
    Ryan and Valsamis Mitsilegas, 225–251. Leiden: Martinus Nijhoff, 2010.
Bird, Annie. 'Third State Responsibility for Human Rights Violations'. *European Journal
    of International Law* 21 no. 4 (2011): 883–900.
Brilmayer, Lea, and Isaias Y. Tesfalidet. 'Third State Obligations and the Enforcement
    of International Law'. *NYU Journal of International Law and Politics* 44 (2011): 1–53.
Caron, David D. 'The ILC Articles on State Responsibility: The Paradoxical Relationship
    Between Form and Authority'. *The American Journal of International Law* 96 (2002): 857–873.
Cerone, John. 'Re-examining International Responsibility: "Complicity" in the Context of
    Human Rights Violations'. *ILSA Journal of International and Comparative Law* 14 (2008):
    525–534.
Condorelli, Luigi, and Claus Kress. 'The Rules of Attribution: General Considerations'.
    In *The Law of International Responsibility*, edited by James Crawford, Alain Pellet and Simon
    Olleson, 221–236. Oxford: Oxford University Press, 2010.

Conforti, Benedetto. 'Exploring the Strasbourg Case-Law: Reflections on State Responsibility for the Breach of Positive Obligations'. In *Issues of State Responsibility before International Judicial Institutions*, edited by Malgosia Fitzmaurice and Dan Sarooshi, 129–137. Oxford: Hart Publishing, 2004.

Crawford, James. *State Responsibility: The General Part.* Oxford: Oxford University Press, 2013.

den Heijer, Maarten. *Europe and Extraterritorial Asylum.* Oxford: Hart Publishing, 2012.

den Heijer, Maarten. 'Issues of Shared Responsibility before the European Court of Human Rights'. Amsterdam: Amsterdam Centre for International Law, Research Project on Shared Responsibility in International Law, 2012. SHARES Research Paper no. 2012–04.

den Heijer, Maarten and Rick Lawson. 'Extraterritorial Human Rights and the Concept of "Jurisdiction"'. In *Global Justice, State Duties: The Extraterritorial Scope of Economic, Social and Cultural Rights in International Law*, edited by Malcolm Langford, Wouter Vandenhole, Martin Sheinin and Willem van Genugten, 153–192. Cambridge: Cambridge University Press, 2013.

Dominicé, Christian. 'Attribution of Conduct to Multiple States and the Implication of a State in the Act of Another State'. In *The Law of International Responsibility*, edited by James Crawford, Alain Pellet and Simon Olleson, 281–289. Oxford: Oxford University Press, 2010.

Felder, Andreas. *Die Beihilfe im Recht der völkerrechtlichen Staatenverantwortlichkeit.* Zürich: Schulthess Verlag, 2007.

Frontex, 'Operational Plan: Joint Operation EPN Triton 2014'. (2014/SBS/09) 8, Annex 5 [on file with the author].

Gammeltoft-Hansen, Thomas, and James C. Hathaway. 'Non-Refoulement in a World of Cooperative Deterrence'. *Columbia Journal of Transnational Law* 53 no. 1 (2015): 235–284.

Graefrath, Bernhard. 'Complicity in the Law of International Responsibility'. *Revue Belge de Droit International* 29 (1996): 370–380.

Griebel, Jörn, and Milan Plücken. 'New Developments Regarding the Rules of Attribution? The International Court of Justice's Decision in *Bosnia v. Serbia*'. *Leiden Journal of International Law* 21 no. 3 (2008): 601–622.

Hakimi, Monica. 'State Bystander Responsibility'. *European Journal of International Law* 21 (2010): 341–385.

Implementation of the EU Charter of Fundamental Rights and its Impact on EU Home Affairs Agencies: Frontex, Europol and the European Asylum Support Office. Study requested by the European Parliament's LIBE committee. Luxembourg: European Parliament's Committee on Civil Liberties, Justice and Home Affairs (LIBE), 2011.

Larsen, Kjetil M. *The Human Rights Treaty Obligations of Peacekeepers.* Cambridge: Cambridge University Press, 2012.

Messineo, Francesco. 'The Attribution of Conduct in Breach of Human Rights Obligations during Peace Support Operations under UN Auspices'. PhD diss., University of Cambridge, 2012.

Messineo, Francesco. 'Multiple Attribution of Conduct'. Amsterdam: Amsterdam Centre for International Law, Research Project on Shared Responsibility in International Law, 2012. SHARES Research Paper no. 2012–11.

Milanovic, Marko. 'From Compromise to Principle: Clarifying the Concept of State Jurisdiction in Human Rights Treaties'. *Human Rights Law Review* 8 no. 3 (2008): 411–448.

Milanovic, Marko. *Extraterritorial Application of Human Rights Treaties: Law, Principles, and Policy.* Oxford: Oxford University Press, 2011.

Nahapetian, Kate. 'Confronting State Complicity in International Law'. *UCLA Journal of International Law and Foreign Affairs* 7 (2002): 99–127.

Nollkaemper, André. 'Issues of Shared Responsibility before the International Court of Justice'. Amsterdam: Amsterdam Centre for International Law, Research Project on Shared Responsibility in International Law, 2011. SHARES Research Paper no. 2011–01.

Nollkaemper, André, and Dov Jacobs. 'Shared Responsibility in International Law: A Concept Paper'. Amsterdam: Amsterdam Centre for International Law, Research Project on Shared Responsibility in International Law, 2011. SHARES Research Paper no. 2011–07.

Nolte, Georg, and Helmut P. Aust. 'Equivocal Helpers: Complicit States, Mixed Messages and International Law'. *International and Comparative Law Quarterly* 58 (2009): 1–30.

Quigley, John. 'Complicity in International Law: A New Direction in the Law of State Responsibility'. *British Yearbook of International Law* 57 (1986): 77–131.

Rijpma, Jorrit J. 'Hybrid Agencification in the Area of Freedom, Security and Justice and its Inherent Tensions: The Case of Frontex'. In *The Agency Phenomenon in the European Union*, edited by Madalina Busuioc, Martijn Groenleer and Jarle Trondal, 84–102. Manchester: Manchester University Press, 2012.

Simma, Bruno. 'From Bilateralism to Community Interest in International Law'. *Recueil des Cours de l'Académie de Droit International* 250 (1994): 217–384.

Stern, Brigitte. 'The Elements of an Internationally Wrongful Act'. In *The Law of International Responsibility*, edited by James Crawford, Alain Pellet and Simon Olleson, 193–220. Oxford: Oxford University Press, 2010.

Talmon, Stefan. 'A Plurality of Responsible Actors: International Responsibility for Acts of the Coalition Provisional Authority in Iraq'. In *The Iraq War and International Law*, edited by Phil Shiner and Andrew Williams, 185–230. Oxford: Hart Publishing, 2008.

Tams, Christian. 'The Abuse of Executive Powers: What Remedies?'. In *Counterterrorism: Democracy's Challenge*, edited by Andrea Bianchi and Alexis Keller, 313–334. Oxford: Hart Publishing, 2008.

Tzevelekos, Vassilis P. 'Reconstructing the Effective Control Criterion in Extraterritorial Human Rights Breaches: Direct Attribution of Wrongfulness, Due Diligence, and Concurrent Responsibility'. *Michigan Journal of International Law* 36 no. 1 (2014): 129–178.

Xenos, Dimitris. *The Positive Obligations of the State under the European Convention of Human Rights*. London/New York: Routledge, 2012.

12

THE LEGALITY OF FRONTEX OPERATION HERA-TYPE MIGRATION CONTROL PRACTICES IN LIGHT OF THE *HIRSI* JUDGEMENT

Niels W. Frenzen

12.1 Introduction

This chapter begins with a review of Frontex's first sea operation, which, according to Frontex, served as 'the foundation of all [subsequent] joint sea operations'.[1] Joint operation Hera, begun in 2006 in the Canary Islands, was also the first time that Frontex coordinated a joint operation with non-EU member states.[2] Hera was deployed soon after the creation of Frontex, and the experience acquired during Hera influenced the agency as it planned subsequent border control operations and programmes, including the creation of the European Patrols Network in 2007, and the European Border Surveillance System (EUROSUR) in 2013.[3] The lessons learned from Hera are likely to continue to have influence as Frontex and the European Union deploy maritime border control operations in the Central and Eastern Mediterranean and elsewhere, in response to shifting migration flown.

This chapter presents a case study of Spain and Frontex's migration control practices during the Hera operation, which succeeded in stopping most migrant boats. Hera is undoubtedly seen as a migration control success story, but to a large extent its success depended on the violation of migrant rights, including the violation of the non-refoulement obligation and the right to leave a country. This chapter reviews the migration control practices undertaken by Italy and Frontex in the Central Mediterranean in response to migrant boats departing from Libya during the period leading up to the 2011 Arab Spring, and before the European Court of Human Rights' 2012 *Hirsi* judgement.[4] This chapter considers the reasons why Italy and Frontex's migration control practices in the Central Mediterranean have not produced the same results as those achieved by Spain and Frontex in West Africa.

This chapter concludes with a discussion of whether the practices used in the Hera operation, or any replication of the practices elsewhere by EU member states, may legally continue in light of the *Hirsi* judgement.[5]

12.2 Spanish and Frontex practices in West Africa

12.2.1 Background

Between 2001 and 2005 an average of 7,300 migrants annually reached the Canary Islands from West Africa. In 2006 this number surged to over 30,000, and consisted primarily of migrants travelling from Mauritania and Senegal in ocean-going cayucos. Another 7,500 migrants sailed from Morocco and reached the Spanish mainland in the same year.[6]

Spain responded to the surge of immigrants by implementing a series of measures within the framework of its 2003 treaty with Mauritania on immigration matters, and by calling for assistance from the European Union and Frontex.[7] The Spanish measures included the provision of assistance and aid, initially to Mauritania

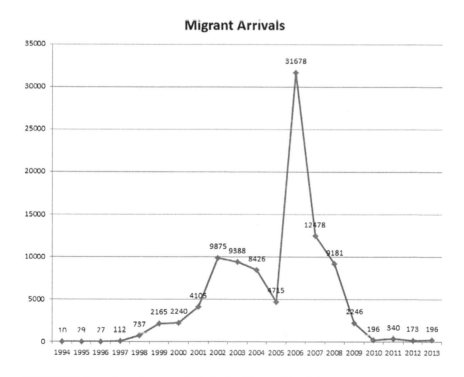

Migrant Arrivals

FIGURE 12.1 Irregular migrant arrivals in the Canary Islands by year.

Source: Data compiled from Interior Ministry, Government of Spain, 'Balance 2012 – Lucha contra la inmigración irregular', January 2013, p. 7; 'Balance 2013 – Lucha contra la inmigración irregular', April 2014, p. 7.

and then to Senegal, to facilitate better control of their borders and territorial waters, donations of vehicles, patrol boats and surveillance equipment, information sharing and, most significantly, deployment of joint maritime patrols. The goal of this assistance was to 'deter illegal immigrants' and 'intercept them before they [began] their journey to the Spanish coast'.[8]

As is discussed in more detail below, some of the measures taken by Spain within the framework of the bilateral agreements with Mauritania and Senegal implicated Spain's obligations under the European Convention on Human Rights and other international conventions. Although a state's obligations under the European Convention on Human Rights and other international human rights conventions arise only when a state exercises jurisdiction over a person, and although jurisdiction is typically territorial in nature, the European Court of Human Rights and other international tribunals recognise the existence of extraterritorial jurisdiction when a state exercises a sufficient level of effective control over a person.[9] And although the provision of financial assistance or vehicles by Spain to Mauritania or Senegal alone would not necessarily invoke Spanish jurisdiction, joint maritime patrols, especially if conducted with Spanish vessels under Spanish command, would present a situation of extraterritorial jurisdiction, even when the patrols were conducted within the territorial waters of West African states under the terms of bilateral agreements. The *Hirsi* judgement rejected Italy's claim that it could evade its non-refoulement and certain other responsibilities under the European Convention on Human Rights by relying on obligations arising from its bilateral migration agreements with Libya, which allowed for joint maritime patrols and provided for the return of intercepted migrants to Libya.[10]

The EU response to the Spanish request for assistance came in the form of operation Hera which consisted of maritime and aerial patrols by Spain and other EU member states, coordinated by Frontex. The maritime patrols were conducted in international waters and within the territorial waters of Mauritania and Senegal. Frontex took the position that Spain's bilateral migration agreements with Mauritania and Senegal authorised other EU member states operating as part of the Hera operation to be similarly deployed within the territorial waters of Mauritania and Senegal.[11] The Hera operation coincided with an almost complete halt to migrant boats successfully reaching the Canary Islands. Although migration routes are affected by factors other than migration control practices, it is reasonable to conclude that the Spanish and Frontex maritime patrols, coupled with the detention and expulsion of migrants from Mauritania and Senegal, were primarily responsible for the halt to the boats.

Since at least 2006, the Spanish Interior Ministry has released an annual report entitled 'Fight Against Illegal Immigration'.[12] For two years, 2006 and 2007, the Interior Ministry reported the numbers of migrants intercepted or detained as a result of various enforcement activities, including arrests within Mauritanian territory by Mauritanian authorities (though not in Senegal), interceptions by joint Spanish-Mauritanian and Spanish-Senegalese maritime patrols, and interceptions by Frontex vessels operating in the Hera operation.[13]

In one month, October 2006, 9,819 migrants were arrested in Mauritania and subsequently expelled from the country. In 2006, joint maritime patrols operating in 'waters near' Mauritania and Senegal intercepted 82 migrant boats resulting in the return of 5,384 migrants.[14] In addition to the more-than-5,000 migrants intercepted in 2006 by the joint patrols, 3,878 migrants in 57 boats were intercepted by the Hera operation by ships, aircraft or personnel provided by Italy, Portugal, France, Finland and Luxembourg.[15] In 2007, the Hera operation was responsible for the interception of 6,756 migrants in 77 boats. The Interior Ministry reports do not clearly specify where Frontex vessels were deployed, but Frontex's Director said that Frontex operated, at least some of the time, within the territorial waters of both Mauritania and Senegal:

> [Frontex] activities in [the Hera operational area] are based on the bilateral agreements between Spain and Mauritania and Spain and Senegal. That is the legal basis for us to have the possibility to have operational activities coordinated by Frontex in the territorial waters of these two aforementioned countries.[16]

After 2007, the Spanish Interior Ministry annual reports stopped providing information regarding the number of arrests within Mauritania or Senegal, or numbers intercepted by joint maritime patrols or Frontex patrols. Instead, the reports provide only the number of migrants who reached Spanish territory, and in so doing obscure the details of ongoing migration control practices in West Africa.

12.2.2 Hera's objectives

Frontex consistently maintained that one of Hera's important objectives was to save lives by discouraging migrants from embarking on dangerous sea voyages. Hera's objectives consisted primarily of stopping migrants from leaving land, and, when departures did occur, intercepting the migrant boats and returning them to their point of departure.[17] Hera's operation plan included the following objectives:

> Carry out the optimal maritime and aerial surveillance of the waters close to Mauritania and Senegal, with the authorisation of the Mauritanian and Senegalese authorities, carrying on board the EU vessels personnel from these countries that are the responsible [sic] of the operations and are the people that must send back the immigrants to the national authorities in the coast;
> Avoid the departure of the illegal immigrants towards the Canary Islands and in the case of departure, intercept the small boats and return the immigrants to the national authorities.[18]

12.2.3 Operation Hera: pre-departure arrests

Various practices were used by Frontex and Spain to prevent migrants from leaving West Africa. One practice consisted of arresting migrants within the territories of Mauritania and Senegal before they departed by sea. This practice, although effective as a migration control practice, was problematic for several reasons.

The right to leave a country applies whether or not the person seeking to depart a country is a national of that country. And although the right may be restricted under certain circumstances, including to protect national security or preserve public order, such restrictions must be limited in nature and must be provided for by law.[19] In its 2008 report on Mauritania, the UN Working Group on Arbitrary Detention, after noting Mauritania's agreements with 'Spain and the European Union to stem the tide of illegal migrants bound for the Canary Islands and to provide for the repatriation of migrants to their countries of origin', expressed concern over the arrests that were occurring, because at that time Mauritanian law did 'not criminalise attempts to leave the country illegally', and noted that this was 'often the reason given by the authorities for arresting foreigners heading for Europe'. The Working Group concluded that the arrests and detentions were occurring 'without any legal grounds'.[20]

Human rights organisations reported that Mauritanian security forces routinely and falsely accused foreign nationals of planning to leave Mauritania for Spain. Amnesty International reported that some migrant arrests were used by corrupt local authorities to extort money, and expressed the concern that such arbitrary arrests were 'one of the perverse effects of the pressure exerted by the EU on the Mauritanian government'.[21] In 2009, a United Nations High Commissioner for Refugees (UNHCR) protection officer described the pre-departure arrests of migrants to a US Embassy official as a ' "numbers game" for Mauritanian authorities. In order to keep Spanish cooperation and training flowing, [Mauritanian authorities] have to show high numbers of expulsions to underscore their efficiency in tackling the [migration] problem'.[22]

Even though Spain deployed its national police and Guardia Civil personnel within Mauritania and Senegal, it seems that arrests of migrants within Mauritania and Senegal were carried out largely, if not exclusively, by Mauritanian and Senegalese authorities. From the perspective of Spain and Frontex, such pre-departure arrests were an effective migration control practice because the migrants never reached EU territory, or otherwise came into direct contact with Spanish or Frontex patrols.[23]

In addition to financial and material support, Spain and Frontex conducted surveillance activities and provided the information gathered by these measures to Mauritania and Senegal for the purpose of intercepting migrants and migrant boats. The Hera operation included helicopter and airplane surveillance patrols that provided real-time information about migrant boats, and possibly about other activities showing preparation for boat departures. Frontex collaborated with the European Space Agency (ESA) within what is now known as the Copernicus framework (previously known as GMES – Global Monitoring Environment Security), and used information from ESA satellites for maritime border surveillance. In 2008, Amnesty International reported that Spanish officials would show satellite photos to Mauritanian authorities to demonstrate that migrants on board a particular migrant boat had departed from Mauritanian territory.[24]

12.2.4 Operation Hera – maritime patrols in territorial waters

When a migrant boat departed from Mauritania or Senegal, Hera relied on maritime patrols to intercept and turn back the boats. Hera's objective was to intercept the departing migrant boats as close to shore as possible. Although some of the migrants on board the boats were Mauritanian and Senegalese nationals, the large majority were nationals of countries other than Mauritania and Senegal.

Spain negotiated readmission agreements with Mauritania and Senegal, obligating both countries to accept the return of intercepted third country nationals. Spain secured agreements with both countries, addressing operational details under which Spanish vessels would conduct operations within the territorial waters of Mauritania and Senegal, and Frontex piggybacked on these agreements for the purpose of deploying other EU member state vessels within territorial waters. The details of these operational agreements have not been made public. It seems that an official from Mauritania or Senegal would be on board the EU vessel as a ship-rider, and that this official was at least nominally charged with a certain decision-making authority regarding intercepting and turning back migrant boats. What remains unclear is how genuine and extensive the Mauritanian or Senegalese ship-rider's authority was. A Frontex informational publication described the ship-rider relationship as follows:

> [. . .] European and African officials were at sea together on each other's vessels. Under this arrangement the authority for returning cayucos setting off from Africa rested with the Senegalese and Mauritanian officials involved in the Frontex operation. Colonel Eduardo Lobo, of the Spanish Guardia Civil, explained Frontex's relationship with the local officials: 'the Frontex members provide the platform and support them but they are the authority for intercepting and returning the boats'.[25]

As the Frontex document suggests, Mauritania and Senegal also conducted patrols using their own patrol vessels, including vessels provided for this purpose by Spain. And although a ship-rider agreement would typically not call for a Spanish official to be present on Mauritanian or Senegalese vessels while patrolling their own territorial waters, it seems that Spanish Guardia Civil officials were routinely present on Mauritanian vessels to advise on operations and provide training on vessel maintenance.[26] It may be that Spain considered its presence necessary to deter corruption.

Frontex documents refer to the practice of turning back migrant boats if the migrant boat was encountered within a 'certain distance' of the coast, but do not specify the distance.[27] According to statements made by the Meijers Committee, the agreements between Spain and Mauritania and Senegal authorised Spanish patrol boats to operate within a twenty-four-mile zone, that is, within the territorial waters and their contiguous zone.[28]

12.2.5 Operation Hera: turnbacks/pushbacks of migrant boats

During the Hera operation, various methods were used to intercept and turn back migrant boats within international waters, including the contiguous zone, and the territorial waters of Mauritania and Senegal. Although the frequency of specific tactics is not publicly known, it is clear that coercive tactics were used at times. Harsh tactics have been documented in past Frontex operations in the Mediterranean, where EU member-state patrol vessels boarded migrant boats and removed food, water and extra fuel in an effort to coerce the migrant boat to reverse course.[29] Frontex described the Hera operation as using interception tactics that would either 'convince' migrants to turn back or would 'escort' migrants back Senegal or Mauritania'.[30]

In addition to 'convincing' by ordering or otherwise pressuring a migrant boat to reverse course, or 'escorting' a migrant boat back to its point of departure, there are circumstances where migrants were removed from their boat and taken aboard the intercepting patrol vessel. Such actions may have been necessary to rescue migrants from a disabled or dangerous boat, or such actions may have been undertaken to compel the migrants to halt their journey.

12.2.6 Operation Hera: detention

A migrant detention centre in the northern Mauritanian city of Nouadhibou was opened in April 2006. The opening of the facility coincided with the launch of the Hera operation. According to Amnesty International, the agreement to open the detention facility was made during a March 2006 meeting between Spanish and Mauritanian officials, and Spain agreed to fund the construction and management of the detention centre.[31] A portion of its operational expenses was provided by the Spanish Red Cross. The facility was staffed by Mauritanian officials. The detention centre was used to detain those migrants intercepted at sea and those arrested before they departed. In 2008, the UN Working Group on Arbitrary Detention described conditions in the detention centre as 'appalling'.[32]

The detention centre was closed in 2010 owing to the dwindling numbers of migrants being detained; migrants are instead detained at a police facility in Nouadhibou.[33]

12.2.7 Operation Hera: expulsion and lack of access to international protection

Mauritania is a signatory to the Refugee Convention and Protocol, and has granted refugee status to a limited number of persons; however, as of 2016, Mauritania had not yet implemented a national system for considering asylum claims.[34]

The thousands of migrants intercepted during the Hera operation were not routinely provided with a formal opportunity to seek asylum or other forms of international protection. The UNHCR designated and funded a local non-governmental organisation (NGO) as an implementing partner for the purpose of making visits to the detention centre in Nouadhibou, but the UNHCR itself did not maintain a presence at the detention centre.[35]

According to the UNHCR, most of the intercepted migrants detained at the Nouadhibou detention centre prior to its closing in 2010 were not asylum seekers, but only a hundred or so asylum seekers were provided with a full-fledged refugee status determination (RSD) process after intervention by the UNHCR's local implementing partner.[36] In 2009, a UNHCR official informed a US Embassy official that although the UNHCR had been successful in stopping some expulsions of asylum-seekers, there were instances when Mauritanian authorities 'expelled refugees and asylum seekers without any regard to their status'. The UNHCR official attributed Mauritania's summary expulsion practices to the absence of a 'legal framework for migration issues' and to Mauritania's desire to ensure that Spanish cooperation and support would continue, which required the Mauritanians 'to show high numbers of expulsions to underscore their efficiency in tackling the [migration] problem'.[37]

It was necessary to expel intercepted migrants from Mauritania in order to make it more difficult for the affected migrants to renew efforts to depart from Mauritania by sea. Intercepted migrants were expelled to Mali or Senegal. Malians and other migrants believed to have entered Mauritania from Mali were sent across the border into Mali at the border town of Gogui. Other migrants were returned to Senegal, regardless of nationality or manner of entry into Mauritania.[38] The expulsions sometimes occurred fairly soon after interception at sea, or arrest. In 2009, the Deputy Chief of Mission at the Spanish Embassy in Mauritania informed a US official that arrested migrants were typically detained for forty-eight hours before being expelled from Mauritania.[39]

12.3 Italian, Frontex and EU military practices in the Mediterranean

Although the Canary Islands were the focal point for migratory pressure on the EU in 2006, in 2007 maritime migratory pressure shifted to the Central Mediterranean, with Italy and Malta receiving over 20,000 arrivals that year, and almost 40,000 in 2008. Frontex's response was the launch of the Nautilus operation, and an effort to engage with Libya.[40]

Frontex sent a technical mission to Libya in 2007 to ask Libya to take part in the Nautilus operation, and to explore the longer-term goal of 'engag[ing]' the Libyan authorities towards the gradual development of a sustained operational and technical cooperation with Frontex based on a working arrangement'.[41] As was the case with Spain, Italy had negotiated bilateral agreements with Libya and other North African countries, but none of the early agreements had a significant effect on the flow of boats. This began to change in 2007, when Italy and Libya signed several bilateral migration agreements that included provisions authorising the deployment of joint maritime patrols to conduct surveillance, and search and rescue operations in international waters and in Libyan territorial waters; Libya also agreed to accept the repatriation of intercepted migrants, including third-country nationals, who had departed from Libya.[42] The agreements provided for Italian control of the joint patrols in international waters, and Libyan control in Libyan territorial waters. Italy transferred at least six patrol vessels to Libya for the joint patrols. But unlike the situation with Mauritania and Senegal, neither Italy nor Frontex was able to base forces on Libyan territory or conduct sustained or effective maritime patrols in Libyan territorial waters.[43]

Italy's bilateral cooperation with Libya – as was Spain's cooperation with West African countries – was supported by EU policies that called for partnerships between EU member states and countries of origin and transit for the purpose of combating illegal migration. For example, the European Pact on Immigration and Asylum called for, *inter alia*, stepped up cooperation with countries of origin and transit in order to control illegal immigration,[44] and European Parliament Resolution No. 2006/2250 stressed the need for increased cooperation with Mediterranean countries with regard to the management of migration flows, and praised 'the fact that certain member States ha[d] signed cooperation agreements on immigration with various African countries . . .'[45]

Italy and Libya began joint maritime patrols in May 2009.[46] Prior to the institution of the joint patrols, migrants continued to be intercepted or rescued by Italian patrols in international waters. The intercepted migrants would be taken to Lampedusa or other Italian locations for processing. This changed in May 2009, when the agreement that authorised Italian vessels to return intercepted migrants, including migrants intercepted in international waters, directly to Libya took effect.

Italian officials conducted nine pushback operations in international waters involving 471 migrants of different nationalities.[47] All the intercepted migrants were returned to Libya, where they were detained. The maritime patrols that carried out the pushback operations were conducted by Italian vessels. Human Rights Watch reported that some of the Italian pushback operations were coordinated by Frontex.[48] The patrols and pushback operations had their intended effect, and the flow of boats leaving Libya was significantly reduced.[49] Although Libya is a party to the 1969 OAU (Organisation of African Unity) Convention Governing the Specific Aspects of Refugee Problems, it is not a signatory to the Refugee Convention or Protocol, and did not have a national system in place to consider claims for asylum.

The foregoing situation changed in early 2011, when the events of the Arab Spring overwhelmed the region. Italy unilaterally suspended its pushback operations and other provisions of the Libyan migration agreements during the 2011 Libyan revolution. In February 2012, the European Court of Human Rights issued its judgement in the *Hirsi* case, and concluded that Italy's summary transfer of migrants to Libya without considering their claims to international protection violated the prohibitions against non-refoulement and collective expulsion under Article 3 of the European Convention on Human Rights, and Article 4 of Protocol No. 4, respectively, and violated the right to an effective remedy under Article 13 of the European Convention on Human Rights.[50]

Significant migratory pressure in the Central Mediterranean resumed in 2013. In 2013, over 40,000 migrants crossed the Central Mediterranean and, after being rescued or intercepted, most were taken to Italy for processing. The flow of migrants over the summer of 2013 was comparable to that in the same period in 2011, during the height of the movement of boats during the Arab Spring.[51] A migrant boat accident near Lampedusa in October 2013 resulted in the deaths of 366 migrants.[52] Shortly after the Lampedusa disaster, Italy unilaterally deployed a large-scale naval search and rescue operation known as Operation Mare Nostrum.[53] The migrant flows in the Central Mediterranean more than doubled in 2014, and continued at a high rate in 2015, 'defying seasonal lows typical for the winter season, the most hazardous time to cross the Mediterranean Sea to Italy'.[54] Italy discontinued the Mare Nostrum operation in October 2014 after rescuing over 150,000 migrants.[55] In its place Frontex expanded joint operation Triton, a significantly smaller operation.[56]

The European Union sought to re-engage with North African countries in an effort to restrict migrant flows. The European Union attempted to engage with Libya, but the lack of a stable political and security climate made any engagement impossible.[57] In early 2015, Italy presented a proposal for the European Union to pursue the 'direct involvement of reliable third countries', specifically Egypt and Tunisia, to deploy maritime patrols to intercept or rescue migrants, and to disembark the migrants in Egypt or Tunisia, thereby preventing migrant boats from reaching Europe, and attempting to shift responsibility for protection from the European Union.[58]

The European Union launched a military operation, EUNAVFOR MED (European Union Naval Force Mediterranean), in June 2015, in response to increasing numbers of migrants leaving Libya,[59] and ongoing deaths at sea, including a boat accident off Libya in April 2015 that killed over 800 migrants.[60] The EUNAVFOR MED operation's initial phases were directed at disrupting human smuggling and trafficking activities, and rescuing migrants in international waters off Libya.[61] As of February 2016, over 10,000 migrants had been rescued and taken to Italy for processing.[62] A EUNAVFOR MED report issued after the first six months of its operations discussed the possible expansion of EU military operations to Libyan territorial waters, if and when there is a legal basis for doing so. According to the report, such an expansion would include Libyan 'cooperation in tackling the irregular migration issue', with the expectation that at a later point in time 'Libyan authorities could take the lead in patrolling and securing their territorial waters, with support being provided by EUNAVFOR MED'.[63]

Shortly after EUNAVFOR MED was launched in June 2015, migratory pressure on the European Union shifted drastically from the Central Mediterranean to the Eastern Mediterranean, specifically to the Aegean Sea. In 2015, migrant arrivals in Greece exceeded Italian arrivals for the first time, with over 850,000 migrants landing in Greece, compared to 150,000 reaching Italy.[64] Frontex responded by expanding its Aegean Sea operations with the Poseidon Rapid Intervention operation, and North Atlantic Treaty Organization (NATO) also deployed naval vessels in the Aegean Sea to monitor migrant boats.[65] As of March 2016, there was no evidence that vessels coordinated by Frontex or operating under NATO command in the Aegean Sea had returned migrants to Turkey, but there were indications from both NATO and NATO member-state defence ministers that NATO vessels would at some point return intercepted or rescued migrants to Turkey, and that Turkey would be willing to accept the migrants.[66]

12.4 Hera-type migration control practices and the *Hirsi* judgement

Frontex and EU member states have not been able to replicate the West African, Hera-type migration control practices in the Central Mediterranean. (This section of the chapter focuses primarily on efforts to replicate Hera-type practices in the Central Mediterranean, given the long-term efforts by the European Union in the area, and the newness of the situation in the Aegean.) There are several reasons for this. One is that Libya has not allowed Italy or Frontex to conduct joint maritime patrols or surveillance within Libyan territorial waters in the same manner and to the same extent as was the case with Mauritania and Senegal. Although prior to the events of the Arab Spring, Italy negotiated an agreement with Libya to conduct joint maritime patrols, the provisions of the confidential agreement seem to have required that any such joint patrols conducted within Libyan territorial waters be conducted under Libyan command; it is unlikely that the agreement authorised the use of Italian-only patrols within Libyan territorial waters.

The main legal impediment to any EU member state (or Council of Europe member state) attempting to replicate Hera-type practices is the 2012 *Hirsi* judgement.[67] Despite questions as to whether certain specific migration control practices used during the Hera operation are consistent with *Hirsi*, it seems likely that the European Union, EU member states and Frontex will, when possible, seek to engage with Libya and other North African countries in an effort to secure joint cooperation on migration matters, or to secure authorisation to deploy Frontex or EU member-state patrols within the territorial waters of North African states, with or without the participation of ship-riders. In the absence of legal impediments, such maritime patrols within the territorial waters of Libya or other North African states would probably be very effective. Indeed, regarding its first six months of operation, the EUNAVFOR MED report discussed the possible expansion of EU naval patrols and other military operations to Libyan territorial waters, and the enlistment of Libyan 'cooperation in tackling the irregular migration issue'.[68] Therefore, an important question is whether Hera-type migration control practices could be implemented, given the *Hirsi* judgement. What follows here is an effort to assess the extent to which Hera-type migration control practices are consistent with *Hirsi*. The first question in the analysis is one of jurisdiction. The protection of the European Convention on Human Rights and other human rights conventions will only be invoked if the actions in question occur within the jurisdiction of a state. Although jurisdiction is typically territorial in nature, the European Court of Human Rights and other international tribunals have recognised extraterritorial jurisdiction when a state exercises a sufficient level of effective control over a person. If a state does not exercise a sufficient level of effective control over a person through its actions, that state cannot be held responsible for enforcing or protecting the rights at issue.[69]

The various migration control practices used within a Hera operation present factually different scenarios of effective control. Certain practices, such as physically holding a migrant at a detention centre, or transferring an intercepted migrant from a migrant boat to an intercepting patrol ship, would clearly place the affected individual within the effective control of the relevant state. Other practices, such as surveilling a person on land, surveilling a boat at sea or encouraging a boat to divert its course or turn back by verbally warning of the dangers of a sea crossing, would, standing on their own, probably not yield a finding of effective control over a person.

The various practices used within Hera present factually different scenarios in terms of which state or combination of states acted to exercise effective control over a person during a given migration control practice. The different scenarios also vary according to the different human rights obligations that would apply to each state, for example, a European state bound by the European Convention on Human Rights, or a non-European state, not similarly bound.

The *Hirsi* case presented a straightforward, factual basis for the European Court of Human Rights to conclude that Italian authorities were exercising effective control over the intercepted migrants, and find that Italy's actions were subject to the European Convention on Human Rights. In *Hirsi*, Italian military ships intercepted a migrant boat in international waters, transferred the intercepted migrants to the Italian military ships, and transported the migrants to Libya, despite protests by the migrants. The European Court of Human Rights noted the established principle in international law that a vessel operating on the high seas is subject to the exclusive jurisdiction of the flag state, and the Italian military ships were therefore fully within Italian jurisdiction. The European Court of Human Rights determined that the *Hirsi* applicants were under 'the continuous and exclusive de jure and de facto control of the Italian authorities'.[70]

The *Hirsi* judgement does not address the question of whether there are circumstances other than the above-mentioned, under which a migrant boat could be intercepted in international waters without violating the European Convention on Human Rights; *Hirsi* simply stands for the important proposition that when a migrant boat is intercepted, the intercepted migrants cannot be summarily and forcibly returned without providing individualised screening and an adequate opportunity for the intercepted migrants to present a claim for asylum or other protection, among other requirements.

To the extent that interdiction activities similar to the *Hirsi* activities were carried out during the Hera operation by Spanish or Frontex vessels, for example, transferring intercepted migrants from the migrant boat to patrol vessels and summarily returning them to Mauritania or Senegal, or to the extent that similar activities might be conducted in the future, *Hirsi* makes clear that the European Convention on Human Rights' obligations of European states are invoked, and that such actions are prohibited.

As the nature of the interdiction activities at issue change, the jurisdictional analysis necessarily changes. For example, the Italian pushback practices at issue in *Hirsi* were not conducted by joint Italy–Libya patrols, and were initiated in international waters. Therefore, the question arises as to whether a pushback operation carried out by a joint Italy–Libya or joint Spain–Mauritania patrol would also result in the exercise of effective control over a migrant by the EU state, subject to the European Convention on Human Rights. One may advance different hypothetical situations that would strengthen or weaken an argument for effective control by a particular state. To what state does the vessel participating in a joint patrol belong? If the vessel is carrying a ship-rider, what actual command authority does the ship-rider possess? Is the patrol operating in international or territorial waters?

Putting aside the complications presented by joint patrols and the jurisdictional locations of such patrols, does the manner in which an EU patrol boat intercepts or orders a migrant boat to reverse course determine whether effective control exists? Rather than remove migrants from their boats and return them to their place of departure, what if an EU patrol boat were to simply give verbal advice or orders to reverse course? What if the EU patrol boat blocked the migrant boat, or fired warning shots? Frontex documents indicate that EU patrol vessels would try to 'convince' migrant boats to turn back, or would 'escort' migrant boats back to Mauritania or Senegal.[71] How would Frontex 'convince' a migrant boat to turn back? The more coercive and controlling the interception tactic is, the stronger the argument for finding effective control.

With regard to pre-departure arrests, detentions and summary expulsions conducted in conjunction with the Hera operation, although training and partial funding were provided by Spain and the European Union for these activities, the activities themselves were carried out by Mauritanian and Senegalese authorities. It is unlikely that the provision of partial funding for such practices by an EU state, standing on its own, would result in a finding of effective control by the EU state. But *Hirsi* emphasised that the determination of whether effective control exists 'must be determined with reference to the particular facts' of each case, and one may again consider different hypothetical situations. For example, what if the continued receipt of EU development assistance is made explicitly dependent on the detention and expulsion of migrants, does effective EU control exist? If the non-EU personnel involved in the arrests, detention and expulsion operations are trained and fully paid by an EU state, does effective control exist? If a detention centre's operation is funded by an EU state, or if EU officials are present to provide advice and guidance at the detention centre, does effective control result?

In 2008, the UN Committee Against Torture considered the *Marine I* case, where Spain detained a group of rescued migrants in Mauritania at a facility that was completely controlled by the Spanish; Spanish authorities deployed Spanish police to guard the migrants, paid for the detention facility, processed the detained migrants, and ultimately expelled most of the migrants from Mauritania. The Spanish action was authorised by Mauritania, pursuant to a diplomatic agreement. Given these facts, the UN Committee Against Torture found that Spain had maintained 'constant de facto control' over the migrants in Mauritania, who were therefore under Spanish jurisdiction for the purposes of the Convention against Torture (CAT).[72]

Even if it were clear that the provision of financial or technical assistance by an EU state to another state did not constitute an exercise of effective control by the EU state, the International Law Commission (ILC) Articles of State Responsibility (ASR) recognise that the EU state could still have responsibility, if the assistance facilitated the other state in violating the international obligations of that state. ASR Article 16 addresses those situations in which one state aids or assists another state in the commission of an internationally wrongful act. The relevant ILC commentary states that '[s]uch situations arise where a state voluntarily assists or aids another state in carrying out conduct which violates the international obligations of the latter, for example by knowingly providing an essential facility or financing the activity in question'.[73] The assisting state can only be responsible if it is 'aware of the circumstances making the conduct of the assisted State internationally wrongful', and if the assistance was 'given with a view to facilitating the commission of a wrongful act', and has actually done so.[74] An EU-funded migrant detention facility in another state and the subsequent expulsion of migrants in violation of the other state's non-refoulement obligations under the Refugee Convention, the CAT or the International Covenant on Civil and Political Rights (ICCPR) would fall within the actions addressed by Article 16.

The practical problem presented when seeking to analyse or challenge EU member-state assistive practices is establishing the nature of the specific migration control practice, including establishing the existence and details of the formal or informal agreements between the European Union, EU member states, Frontex, EUNAVFOR MED and the other non-EU states. This is difficult to accomplish, given the lack of transparency that exists in such matters. This secrecy serves to undermine democratic control by making it difficult, if not impossible, to monitor activities and promote the accountability of the European Union and EU member states. This lack of transparency is inconsistent with European Convention on Human Rights Article 10, which clearly includes the right to access to information.[75] The European Court of Human Rights has recognised the similarity between Article 10 and ICCPR Article 19, and has noted that the Human Rights Committee has interpreted Article 19 to embrace a right of access to government bodies.[76]

The lack of transparency and the secrecy associated with interdiction and other migration control practices interferes with the assessment of independent responsibility that might be incurred directly by Frontex as an international organisation.[77] The ILC Draft Articles on the Responsibility of International Organisations recognise situations where an international organisation would be responsible when an internationally wrongful act is committed, including situations where the international organisation exercises effective control over the organ of a state, where it aids or assists a state, or where it directs and controls a state.[78] Frontex's mandate is to coordinate border control activities that are carried out by individual EU member states. However, without access to the specific provisions that govern the joint operations and other activities coordinated by Frontex, the level and degree of control that Frontex exercises in regard to any particular operation where an internationally wrongful act might occur, for example, the refoulement of migrants on board an intercepted boat, cannot be ascertained. This lack of clarity not only shields Frontex from a determination of possible responsibility, but also acts to shield the individual EU member states that participate in the operation, by obscuring who is actually controlling the migration control practice at issue. Similar questions exist in regard to EU military operations conducted pursuant to EUNAVFOR MED.

12.5 Conclusion

The *Hirsi* judgement calls into question the legality of many Hera-type migration control practices, including the practices in which Spain and Frontex engaged, to intercept and turn back migrant boats off the West African coast. To the extent that such practices are ongoing or may be resumed, the practices must be changed to ensure that intercepted migrants are not subjected to collective expulsion or refoulement, and are provided with an opportunity to seek asylum and other forms of protection. In most cases this would mean that intercepted or rescued migrants would need to be brought to an appropriate location for processing, access to legal advice, and for consideration of any claims for asylum or other forms of protection.

The more complicated question of possible EU member state responsibility relates to the migration control activities carried out by Mauritania and Senegal, specifically, the pre-departure arrests, detentions and expulsions of migrants. To the extent that such practices are carried out independently by non-EU states, the European Convention on Human Rights and EU law are simply not implicated. But when an EU member state, Frontex or EUNAVFOR MED is in some way involved in the migration control activities carried out by a non-EU state, as was the case with the Hera operation, further analysis is required to assess the level of involvement, in order to determine whether the EU member state is engaged in the practice to such an extent that the EU member state might be found to be exercising effective control over the affected individuals, or whether state responsibility might otherwise be recognised under the ILC ASR. Given the lack of transparency when it comes to most bilateral migration agreements and operational plans, it is virtually impossible for an outsider to determine the level of involvement of an EU member state, Frontex or EUNAVFOR MED. Although a national or European court may at some point consider the question of the lack of transparency in this area, the European Union, EU member states, Frontex and EUNAVFOR MED should nonetheless take steps to ensure greater transparency in their activities.

Notes

1 Frontex, *Beyond the Frontiers: Frontex, the First Five Years* (2010) available at: http://frontex.europa.eu/assets/Publications/General/Beyond the Frontiers.pdf (accessed 1 October 2016), 37.
2 Ibid., 31.
3 See Sergio Carrera, 'The EU Border Management Strategy: FRONTEX and the Challenges of irregular Immigration in the Canary Islands', CEPS Working Document no. 261 (Brussels: Centre for European Policy Studies, 2007), 18–20 (review of the various early Frontex feasibility studies regarding Integrated Border Management).
4 *Hirsi Jamaa and Others v Italy* [GC], App No 27765/09, ECtHR (23 February 2012) (*Hirsi*).
5 Although the *Hirsi* judgement applies to the forty-seven Council of Europe member states, this chapter focuses on the border control practices of the EU, and the twenty-eight EU member states that belong to the Council of Europe.
6 The migratory pressure in the Canary Islands in 2006 followed the events of August and September 2005, when hundreds of migrants attempted to scale the border fences surrounding the Spanish enclaves of Ceuta and Melilla. The reinforced controls in Ceuta and Melilla probably had a displacement effect on the Canary Islands route. The migratory pressure on Ceuta and Melilla has resumed in recent years.
7 *Boletín Oficial del Estado* (4 August 2003) no. 185, 30,050.
8 Frontex Press Statement, 'Longest Frontex coordinated operation – Hera, the Canary Islands' (19 December 2006) available at: http://frontex.europa.eu/news/longest-frontex-coordinated-operation-hera-the-canary-islands-WpQlsc (accessed 1 October 2016) (Frontex press statement – Longest operation).
9 For example, see *Al Saadoon and Mufdhi v. UK*, App No 61498/08 (30 June 2009); *Medvedyev and Others v. France* [GC], App No 3394/03 (29 March 2010); *Al-Skeini and Others v. UK* [GC], App No 55721/07 (7 July 2011); *Jaloud v. Netherlands* [GC], App No 47708/08 (20 Nov. 2014); *Advisory Opinion Concerning Legal Consequences of the Construction of a Wall in the Occupied Palestinian Territory*, ICJ Gen. List 131 (9 July 2004); *J. H. A. et al. v. Spain*, Communication No 323/2007, UN Doc CAT/C/41/D/323/2007 (2008).
10 *Hirsi* (n 4) para. 129.
11 Frontex Director General Ilkka Laitinen's testimony before the European Union Committee, UK House of Lords, reproduced in the House of Lords publication, 'Frontex: The EU External Borders Agency – Report with Evidence' (5 March 2008) Appendix, Minutes of Evidence, 64, Q267 (UK House of Lords report).
12 The name of the report was changed to the 'Fight Against *Irregular* Immigration' in 2012.
13 Interior Ministry, Government of Spain, 'Balance de la lucha contra la inmigración ilegal en 2006 (21 Feb. 2007); 'Balance de la lucha contra la inmigración ilegal 2007' (Jan. 2008).
14 Senegal did not immediately agree to joint patrols. Although Senegal reportedly was willing to accept Senegalese nationals intercepted by the patrols, it was hesitant to agree to accept nationals of third countries. Senegal did finally agree to the joint patrols which began in late August or September 2006.
15 Patrol assets for the 2006 Hera I and II operation consisted of patrol boats provided by Spain, Italy, and Portugal and surveillance aircraft provided by Finland and Italy. Other countries provided immigration officers used to interview migrants. UK House of Lords report (n 11) 34.

16   UK House of Lords report (n 11) 64, Q267.
17   Frontex press statement – Longest Frontex coordinated operation – Hera, the Canary Islands (n 8) ('The main aim of this joint effort was to detect vessels setting off towards the Canary Islands and to divert them back to their point of departure thus reducing the number of lives lost at sea. . .'); Frontex Press Statement, 'A sequel of operation Hera just starting' (15 Feb. 2007) available at: http://frontex.europa.eu/news/a-sequel-of-operation-hera-just-starting-uy631h (accessed 1 October 2016) ('The aim of these patrols, carried out with Senegalese authorities, will be to stop migrants from leaving the shores on the long sea journey and thus reducing the danger of losses of human lives'.); Frontex Press Statement, 'Hera III operation' (13 April 2007) available at: http://frontex.europa.eu/news/hera-iii-operation-It9SH3 (accessed 1 October 2016) ('The aim of these patrols, carried out with Senegalese authorities, was to stop migrants from leaving the shores on the long sea journey and thus reducing the danger of losses of human lives').
18   UK House of Lords report (n 11) 167 (written evidence submitted by Meijers Committee).
19   UDHR, Art. 13.2; ICCPR, Art. 12.2; *African Charter on Human and Peoples' Rights*, Art. 12; ECHR Protocol No 4, Art. 2.2; see also Human Rights Committee, General Comment No 27, para. 11 (regarding restrictions on departures).
20   Report of the Working Group on Arbitrary Detention, Addendum, Mission to Mauritania, A/HRC/10/21/Add.2 (21 November 2008) para. 65 (Report of Working Group on Arbitrary Detention).
21   Amnesty International, 'Mauritania: "Nobody Wants to Have Anything to Do With Us", Arrests and Collective Expulsions of Migrants Denied Entry Into Europe' (Amnesty International Mauritania report: July 2008), 18–20; see also Migreurop, 'European Borders – Controls, Detention and Deportations, 2009–2010 Report', 22–23 (Migreurop report).
22   Confidential Cable, US Embassy Mauritania Nouakchott, 'Long Detention Periods and Poor Conditions at the "Mauritanian Guantanamo"' (8 June 2009) available at: wikileaks.org/plusd/cables/09NOUAKCHOTT379_a.html (accessed 1 October 2016) (US Embassy confidential cable).
23   Note, for example, that in 2006, in a single month, Mauritanian authorities arrested and expelled over 9,800 migrants who were suspected of preparing to depart by boat. This single month's total was roughly equivalent to the total number of migrants intercepted by maritime patrols in territorial and international waters over the course of the entire year. See Interior Ministry, Government of Spain, 'Balance de la lucha contra la inmigración ilegal en 2006' (21 Feb. 2007).
24   Amnesty International Mauritania report (n 21) 28; also see Carerra, 'The EU Border Management Strategy – Frontex and the Challenges of Irregular Immigration in the Canary Islands', (n3) 19.
25   Frontex, 'Beyond the Frontiers – Frontex: the First Five Years', (n1) 34.
26   Author's e-mail correspondence with Dr Stephan Duennwald, Centro de Estudos Internacionais, Lisbon (10–11 Nov. 2013).
27   Frontex Press Statement, 'Hera 2008 and NAUTILUS 2008 Statistics' (17 Feb. 2009) available at: http://frontex.europa.eu/news/hera-2008-and-nautilus-2008-statistics-oP7kLN (accessed 1 October 2016) (Frontex press statement – Hera 2008).
28   UK House of Lords report (n 11) 169, 171 (written evidence submitted by Meijers Committee).
29   M. Vella, 'Frontex, out of control?', *Malta Today on Sunday* (20 July 2008) (referencing 2008 documentary 'Krieg im Mittelmeer').
30   Frontex press statement – Hera 2008 (n 27).
31   Amnesty International Mauritania report (n 21) 22–23.
32   Report of Working Group on Arbitrary Detention (n 20) para. 67.
33   According to the UNHCR, the detention centre closed in 2010, however a researcher who conducted field work in Nouadhibou reported that the formal closing did not

occur until approximately May 2012. Author's e-mail correspondence with UNHCR Regional Bureau of the Middle East and North Africa (9 July 2014) and Dr Stephan Duennwald (n 26).

34 UNHCR Mauritania web page, available at: http://reporting.unhcr.org/mauritania (accessed 1 October 2016).

35 Author's e-mail correspondence with UNHCR Regional Bureau of the Middle East and North Africa (n 33).

36 Ibid.

37 US Embassy confidential cable (n 22).

38 Amnesty International Mauritania report (n 21) 24–25; see also Migreurop report (n 21) 23.

39 US Embassy confidential cable (n 22).

40 The Nautilus operation was briefly launched in October 2006, towards the end of high season for boat voyages, and resumed again in June 2007.

41 Frontex, Report of 'Frontex-Led EU Illegal Immigration Technical Mission to Libya, 28 May–5 June 2007', para. 10.1, available at: www.statewatch.org/news/2007/oct/eu-libya-frontex-report.pdf (accessed 1 October 2016).

42 *Hirsi* (n 4) paras 19–21.

43 On those occasions when joint maritime patrols on Libyan vessels were conducted, there is some evidence that Libyan authorities retained meaningful control of the patrol ship. See for example the incident in which a Libyan patrol boat with Italian observers on board fired on and damaged an Italian fishing vessel. BBC News, 'Libya Sorry for Shooting at Italian Fishing Boat' (patrol boat under Libyan command with Italian observers on board fired on Italian fishing boat) (14 Sept. 2010) available at: www.bbc.co.uk/news/world-europe-11307420 (accessed 1 October 2016). In the case of joint Spanish-Mauritanian or Spanish-Senegalese maritime patrols, it appears that Spanish officials exercised a greater degree of control over the patrols.

44 *Hirsi* (n 4) para. 94; European Pact on Immigration and Asylum, adopted by the Council of the EU on 24 Sept. 2008, para. II(e).

45 *Hirsi* (n 4) para. 94; EP Resolution No 2006/2250, paras 12, 24.

46 Frontex, 'Extract from the Annual Risk Analysis 2010' (March 2010), 18, available at: http://frontex.europa.eu/assets/Publications/Risk_Analysis/Annual_Risk_Analysis_2010.pdf (accessed 1 October 2016); also see 'Libya Sorry for Shooting at Italian Fishing Boat' (n 43).

47 *Hirsi* (n 4) paras 13–14, 38.

48 Human Rights Watch, 'Pushed Back, Pushed Around: Italy's forced return of Boat Migrants and Asylum Seekers, Libya's Mistreatment of Migrants and Asylum seekers' (New York: Human Rights Watch, 21 September 2009).

49 For example, see Frontex, 'Extract from the Annual Risk Analysis 2010', 18 (n 46).

50 *Hirsi* (n 4) paras 137, 158, 186, 207.

51 Frontex Press Statement, 'Update on Central Mediterranean Route' (4 Oct. 2013), available at: http://frontex.europa.eu/news/update-on-central-mediterranean-route-5wQPyW (accessed 1 October 2016).

52 See Tara Brian and Frank Laczko, 'Fatal Journeys: Tracking Lives Lost During Migration' (Geneva: International Organisation for Migration, 2014); also see IOM's Missing Migrants Project, available at: http://missingmigrants.iom.int (accessed 1 October 2016).

53 Italian Navy, Mare Nostrum Operation website, available at: www.marina.difesa.it/EN/operations/Pagine/MareNostrum.aspx (accessed 1 October 2016) (Mare Nostrum website).

54 Frontex Press Statements, 'Latest Trends at External Borders of the EU' (2 February 2015) available at: http://frontex.europa.eu/news/latest-trends-at-external-borders-of-the-eu-6Z3kpC (accessed 1 October 2016); 'Situational Update on Migratory Flows in February 2015' (24 March 2015) available at: http://frontex.europa.eu/news/situational-update-on-migratory-flows-in-february-2015-R7HeSD (accessed 1 October 2016).

55 Mare Nostrum website (n 53).
56 Frontex Press Statement, 'Frontex Expands its Joint Operation Triton' (26 May 2015) available at: http://frontex.europa.eu/news/frontex-expands-its-joint-operation-triton-udpbHP (accessed 1 October 2016).
57 The EU Border Assistance Mission (EUBAM) was deployed in Libya in May 2013 with the objective of supporting Libya in developing the capacity 'for enhancing the security of their land, sea and air borders'. Unsurprisingly, one of EUBAM's early priorities was a focus on training the Libyan Coast Guard, to enable it to engage in maritime border control, and search and rescue actions. EUBAM was forced to withdraw its personnel from Libya in August 2014 owing to the deterioration of the political and security situation in Libya.
58 See 'Non Paper on Possible Involvement of Third Countries in Maritime Surveillance and Search and Rescue' from the Italian delegation, presented to EC Justice and Home Affairs Council (12 March 2015) available at: www.statewatch.org/news/2015/mar/italian%20med.pdf (accessed 1 October 2016).
59 Migrant flows in the Central Mediterranean exceeded 170,000 in 2014. See the Frontex and IOM websites in general, for further data, available at: http://frontex.europa.eu/publications/ and http://migration.iom.int/europe/ (accessed 1 October 2016) (Frontex and IOM statistics).
60 Council Decision (CFSP) 2015/972 [19 May 2015] OJ L122/31 (regarding an EU military operation in the Southern Central Mediterranean); UNHCR Press Statement, 'UNHCR welcomes EU Mediterranean plans, but says more needs to be done' (21 April 2015) available at: www.unhcr.org/553623109.html (accessed 1 October 2016).
61 See European External Action Service (EEAS) EUNAVFOR MED website, available at: http://eeas.europa.eu/csdp/missions-and-operations/eunavfor-med/ (accessed 1 October 2016).
62 Ibid.
63 European External Action Service, 'EUNAVFOR MED Operation SOPHIA Six Monthly Report 22 June–31 December 2015' (27 January 2016) Doc No EEAS (2016) 126, Restricted available at: https://wikileaks.org/eu-military-refugees/EEAS/EEAS-2016-126.pdf (accessed 1 October 2016).
64 Frontex and IOM statistics (n 59).
65 Frontex Press Statement, 'Frontex Launches Rapid Operational Assistance in Greece' (29 December 2015) available at: http://frontex.europa.eu/news/frontex-launches-rapid-operational-assistance-in-greece-u3rqPy (accessed 1 October 2016); NATO Press Statement, 'NATO Secretary General welcomes expansion of NATO deployment in the Aegean Sea' (6 March 2016) available at: http://nato.int/cps/en/natohq/news_128833.htm?mode=pressrelease (accessed 1 October 2016).
66 See NATO Secretary General Jens Stoltenberg, 'NATO and Europe's refugee and migrant crisis' (26 February 2016) available at: www.nato.int/cps/en/natohq/opinions_128645.htm (accessed 1 October 2016); E. MacAskill and E. Graham-Harrison, 'Nato launches naval patrols to return migrants to Turkey', *The Guardian* (11 February 2016) available at: www.theguardian.com/world/2016/feb/11/nato-launches-naval-patrols-to-return-migrants-to-turkey (accessed 1 October 2016).
67 The Hera operation was never legally challenged. But some of Spain's migration control activities in Africa that occurred outside the Hera operation have been challenged. See *J. H. A. et al. v. Spain*, Communication no. 323/2007, UN Doc CAT/C/41/D/323/2007 (2008) (*JHA v. Spain*).
68 European External Action Service, 'EUNAVFOR MED Operation SOPHIA Six Monthly Report 22 June–31 December 2015' (n 63).
69 For further analysis of externalisation and jurisdictional questions, see Frank McNamara, 'Member State Responsibility for Migration Control within Third States – Externalisation Revisited', *European Journal of Migration and Law* 15 (2013): 319–355.
70 *Hirsi* (n 4) paras 76–78, 81.

71 Frontex press statement – Hera 2008 (n 27).
72 *JHA v. Spain* (n 67).
73 ILC ASR, Art. 16 Commentary, para. 1.
74 Ibid., paras 4, 5.
75 See *Youth Initiative for Human Rights v. Serbia*, App No 48135/06, ECtHR (25 June 2013) para. 20; *Társaság a Szabadságjogokért v. Hungary*, App No 37374/05, ECtHR (14 April 2009) para. 35.
76 Ibid., *Youth Initiative for Human Rights v. Serbia*, para. 13, citing to UN HRC General Comment 34, CCPR/C/GC/34 (12 Sept. 2011).
77 Frontex meets the definition of an international organisation under Art. 2(a), ILC Draft Articles on the Responsibility of International Organisations (2011).
78 Ibid., Arts 7, 14, 15.

Bibliography

Amnesty International. 'Mauritania: "Nobody Wants to Have Anything to Do With Us": Arrests and Collective Expulsions of Migrants Denied Entry Into Europe'. Report No. AFR 38/001/2008. 1 July 2008. London: Amnesty International, 2008.

Brian, Tara, and Frank Laczko. 'Fatal Journeys: Tracking Lives Lost During Migration'. Geneva: International Organisation for Migration, 2014.

Carrera, Sergio. 'The EU Border Management Strategy: FRONTEX and the Challenges of irregular Immigration in the Canary Islands'. CEPS Working Document No 261. Brussels: Centre for European Policy Studies, 2007.

Frontex. *Beyond the Frontiers: Frontex, the First Five Years*. Warsaw: Frontex, 2010. Available online at: http://frontex.europa.eu/assets/Publications/General/Beyond_the_Frontiers. pdf (accessed 1 October 2016).

House of Lords. 'Frontex: the EU External Borders Agency: Report with Evidence'. London: House of Lords European Union Committee, 5 March 2008.

Human Rights Watch. 'Pushed Back, Pushed Around: Italy's Forced Return of Boat Migrants and Asylum Seekers: Libya's Mistreatment of Migrants and Asylum seekers'. New York: Human Rights Watch, 2009.

McNamara, Frank. 'Member State Responsibility for Migration Control within Third States: Externalisation Revisited'. *European Journal of Migration and Law* 15 (2013) 319–355.

Migreurop. 'European Borders: Controls, Detention and Deportations'. 2009–2010 Report. Paris: Migreurop Observatoire des Frontières, 2010.

13

THE DARK SIDE OF GLOBALISATION

Do EU border controls contribute to death in the Mediterranean?

Elspeth Guild

13.1 Why are people dying in the Mediterranean Sea?

Concerns about the safety of people travelling in the Mediterranean Sea in small boats has grown since the early 1990s when all the countries of the southern Mediterranean were included in the European Union's visa black list.[1] The destination that is normally assumed, regarding people in unseaworthy little boats, is Europe. While there was much discussion of movement of people to the southern shores of Spain in the 1990s, now the debate is primarily about movement to Lampedusa and southern Italy, and in the eastern Mediterranean to Greece, primarily the islands.[2] The accuracy of estimates of deaths is problematic, not least as there has been little in-depth research on the subject. They range however from a few thousand to tens of thousands, and the time periods vary by decades. One large research project in Europe is currently trying to count the numbers of people who have drowned in the Mediterranean through an investigation of the death registries in southern European towns and municipalities.[3] Other interesting work is being carried out on practices for burial of bodies found in relation to irregular border crossings in Greece.[4] The subject is, however, for the moment, informed more by incidents that catch the attention and moral outrage of the media.

Nonetheless, the incidents and the political media attention have contributed to the use of the language of crisis, albeit a crisis now entering its third decade. A 2014 publication on the political construction of a crisis in the Mediterranean contributes enormously to our understanding of the salience of the matter.[5]

In the first week of October 2013, a boat carrying people from the southern shores of the Mediterranean towards the Italian island of Lampedusa foundered and sank, resulting in the deaths of about 300 persons and the rescue of about 160. Further horrific accidents took place throughout the autumn of 2014, leading to a variety of calls for action.[6] Responses from different actors within the European

Union have varied, though all have expressed sadness and condolences to those who lost loved ones in the disaster. *United Nations High Commissioner for Refugees* (UNHCR), the United Nation's refugee agency, immediately called for swift action by Italy to improve reception conditions for those arriving by sea. The focus was specifically on the conditions under which people, including asylum-seekers, are received in the country.

Pope Francis stated that the October 2013 incident was a 'day of tears', and denounced the 'savage' system that drives people to leave their homes for a better life, yet does not care when they die in the process. Focusing on the ethics of the international system that result in such deaths, the pope highlighted what is perhaps one of the least explored aspects of the deaths in the Mediterranean – why do the captains of the fishing boats and other vessels in the Mediterranean not rescue these people? This was a central issue in the Council of Europe parliamentary assembly's 2012 report on the responsibility to rescue, which also focused on the failure of NATO personnel to rescue people in a distressed small boat just before they were to take part in military action in Libya.[7] One of the less researched factors in this discussion is the role of EU anti-smuggling and trafficking legislation and the way it has been transposed into national law, which creates a presumption that a captain is committing the offence of smuggling or trafficking if he or she brings un-authorised people into harbours.[8] The consequence is criminal prosecution and confiscation of the individual's boat. While captains who prove that they were acting to rescue people from humanitarian motives may eventually be acquitted and their boats released, the process usually takes many years, during which their families have no source of income and the main breadwinner may be in pre-trial detention. Dr Tugba Basaran is one of the few researchers seriously examining this deterrent effect on humanitarianism.[9]

EU Commissioner Cecilia Malmström said:

> In the aftermath of the Lampedusa tragedy we heard solidarity expressions from all EU countries, but these will remain only empty words if they are not followed by concrete actions. I also call on North African countries, in particular Libya, to fight more effectively the criminals who put these people in unseaworthy vessels and organise these journeys of death.[10]

She placed the responsibility on North African governments to prevent people leaving their shores for the European Union. This creates a certain tension with the human right expressed in the Universal Declaration of Human Rights and the European Convention of Human Rights[11] that everyone has the right to leave the country in which he or she may be. In the same context, she claimed at an EU meeting in Luxembourg on 8 October 2013 that Frontex, the European Union's external border agency, needs greater funding. The annual Frontex budget had apparently decreased from €118 million in 2011 to €85 million in 2013. The focus is on the efficiency and management of the European Union's external borders, particularly in the Mediterranean. While she stressed the need for rescue and assistance of boats, the deployment of border guards for this purpose follows a very specific agenda – ensuring that rescue and assistance mean that people are returned to the North African states from which they departed, rather than being allowed to enter and seek refuge in the European Union. The sense of urgency about the state of affairs in the Mediterranean has been particularly acute since October 2013. The EU institutions determinedly looked at the states in North Africa and asked why they do not act as substitute border guards for the European Union so as to prevent people leaving their shores. According to *The Economist* of 12 October 2013, one reason among others why the boats are sailing is the political chaos in Libya since the toppling of the regime of Muammar Qaddafi by France and the United Kingdom. While Italy has a post-2011 arrangement with Tunisia to send its nationals back, it has none with Libya.

The lack of a readmission agreement between the European Union and Libya may not be so surprising, bearing in mind the current state of affairs in Libya. The news outlet *Daily Beast* reported on 11 September 2013 that on 19 August 2013, a group of gunmen attacked a convoy carrying the EU ambassador to Libya. The assault, outside the Corinthia Hotel in central Tripoli, was not far from Prime Minister Ali Zidan's main office. The gunmen robbed the EU delegation at gunpoint before shooting at passing cars. Police officers outside the hotel did not dare intervene, according to EU diplomats. It is not clear who was part of the EU delegation, or what they were doing in Libya. Accounts from people arriving in the European Union via Libya indicate that between criminal gangs who carry out kidnapping and extortion and Libyan border officials there is very little difference.[12] At the end of May 2013 the Council of the European Union authorised the opening of negotiations with Libya for an agreement on the status of the European Union integrated border management assistance mission in Libya (EUBAM Libya),[13] to be carried out in accordance with Libyan needs assess-ment on integrated border management, which the European Union undertook in 2012 and to which it allocated a budget of €30.3 million for the first twelve months.[14]

In the debate on the Mediterranean, one of the issues that arises regularly is that of technologies. Is there a technological fix to the movement of people across the Mediterranean from the south to the north (there is never any concern about the thousands of tourists, as they are called, who travel daily from the north shore of the Mediterranean to the southern shores in ferries)? The technological solution is just around the corner, according to many EU officials. In 2013 Eurosur, a Mediterranean surveillance and data-sharing system using satellite imagery and drones to monitor the high seas, including the North African coast, became operational.[15] One of the arguments in favour of creating the system was that it would assist in search and rescue at sea.[16] However, already by 14 May 2014, the deputy director of Frontex (which is responsible for Eurosur), Gil Aria Fernandez, stated: 'Unfortunately for the time-being, it [Eurosur] does not fulfil this [rescue] service.'[17]

In this chapter, I want to take a step back from the immediacy of the October 2013 events and debates. I will look at the issue of EU border controls from the perspectives of the technologies, new and old. There has been excellent academic research on border controls, and analysis of their meanings and effects. Didier Bigo and his colleagues have carried out a recent and extremely important study on the new technologies of border controls.[18] Bigo, Sergio Carrera and myself published a multidisciplinary analysis of EU border controls in 2013.[19] Anneliese Baldaccini has examined from a legal perspective exactly the issue of Frontex operations in the Mediterranean.[20] Ruben Zaiotti published a fascinating study on the cultures of EU border controls, looking at the sociology of these controls.[21] Nick Vaughan-Williams has taken the discussion into the field of international relations in his 2009 book on the theory of border controls.[22] Here I will build on this body of work, which crosses a variety of disciplines, to try to understand what is happening to border controls of the movement of persons in Europe, and why the results are so deadly. As Bigo and colleagues describe and discuss, the technologies available for border controls are increasing in both number and variety. Claims made on their behalf – often that, in some specific ways, they are 'smarter' than other technologies – abound. What has been less examined is what we can deduce about new and old border control technologies from the information that is available on movement of people into and out of the European Union. Most of the information we have about this comes from Frontex, which publishes both quarterly reports on EU border controls, with a wealth of information on the current situation, and annual reports on border controls. The information included in this chapter comes primarily from the Frontex 'Annual Risk Analysis 2014'.[23]

13.2 What happens at the European Union's external borders?

According to UNHCR estimates, in 2011, more than 1,500 people drowned or went missing while attempting to cross the Mediterranean to reach Europe.[24] The non-governmental organisation, Fortress Europe, estimates that between 1988 and 2013 approximately 19,142 persons have died trying to enter the European Union (though this figure includes all borders, land, sea and air).[25]

There is uncertainty about exactly how many people enter the European Union across its external borders each year. The European Union's Fundamental Rights Agency states that including EU citizens and third-country nationals, the number comes to about 300 million per year.[26] The latest Frontex Risk Analysis puts the figure at about 125 million people entering the European Union each year, which includes third-country nationals as well as EU citizens. The UN World Tourism Organisation put the figure of non-EU visitors to the Schengen area in 2011 at 275 million. All these estimates are rather general, for many reasons, but at least they represent a point of departure regarding the numbers of third-country nationals who enter the European Union each year. There is also a document published by the Council of the European Union on a data collection operation in one week in 2009, which provides information on exits and entries to the European Union over that period.[27]

According to the Council document, entries at sea borders probably account for about 500,000 per week. Assuming that, within a range of a few thousand persons, these figures are probably fairly representative, the arrival of a few hundred people across the Mediterranean seems rather minor. Indeed, according to Frontex, the total number of people who were found crossing into the European Union via sea borders (not all of them in the Mediterranean) irregularly in 2012 amounted to 23,254.[28] The precision of the number indicates that Frontex must be fairly confident about the accuracy of the figure. What one is encountering here is a problem of scale. The number of people entering and leaving the European Union in an authorised manner is so large, and the number of people dying in the Mediterranean because no one is able or willing to rescue them is comparatively so small, that it is hard to take in the distance. Further, the difference of scale is so large that it makes the crisis presented in parts of the press regarding the numbers of people arriving on the little boats seem very strange indeed. Christopher Chope MP of the Council of Europe's committee on migration was reported in the *Guardian Weekly* 11–17 October 2013 as saying, in reaction to the problem of the failure to rescue people in the Mediterranean, 'if traffickers think they can smuggle people in with impunity, that's the incentive for smuggling to increase'. If the European Union has no trouble admitting around 500,000 people a week on its sea borders, how can marginally over 60,000 a year constitute such a big problem?

The total population of the European Union is slightly over 508 million people. Of this population, 6.8 per cent are third-country nationals according to the European Union's statistical agency, Eurostat.[29] In 2013, according to Frontex, 128,902 people were refused admission to the European Union at its external borders. Only third-country nationals can be refused admission at the European Union's external borders; EU citizens have a right to enter the European Union, though entry can be limited to their member state of underlying citizenship. Assuming that well over 100 million third-country nationals enter the European Union each year, this means that the percentage of people refused entry at the external border is well below 1 per cent. Again according to Frontex, in 2013, 107,365 persons were detected attempting to cross the European Union's external borders other than at designated entry points. In comparison with the overall numbers, the figure is minute.

Why do people take the risk of boarding little boats in North Africa with the intention of coming to the European Union? Clearly they want to come to Europe, but they are not able to do so in accordance with the European Union's border control rules (I will discuss these below). As they cannot fulfil the border control rules to obtain visas and entry, they cannot get commercial carriers to sell them seats on normal scheduled transport means coming to the European Union.[30] The only transport businesses that will carry them are those that are under the wire of the official channels. What is the European Union's response to this unmet demand? I will examine this in the following sections.

13.3 Changing technologies at the EU external borders

A variety of border control technologies are deployed at the EU external border. The most traditional of the technologies is a manual check of the passport presented by an individual to a border guard at a designated border crossing point, and the manual stamping of that passport by a border guard with an entry stamp that includes the date of entry. All persons entering the European Union at an external border crossing point are obliged by EU law to present themselves to a border guard for this examination.[31] If they are on the Schengen visa black list,[32] then a condition of entry is that they have already received a Schengen visa or the equivalent before they arrive. Non-visa third-country nationals arriving at the European Union's external border and seeking entry, according to the Council's one-week count of third-country national entries and exits, account for 68.5 per cent of all third-country nationals entering the European Union. More than 100 countries are on the European Union's visa black list, accounting, according to Frontex, for about 80 per cent of the non-EU world's population. Non-visa nationals do not go through any additional identity control at the European Union's external borders over and above this manual check of their documents, unless the border guards have reason to carry out a more in-depth investigation. Thus it is non-visa nationals who are subject only to the oldest and most traditional border technology, which depends on the person's country of citizenship having issued him or her a passport that is accepted at the EU border as sufficient for entry.

However, these non-visa nationals may soon find themselves the objects of a new border technology system in the form of a Registered Traveller Programme (RTP). The Commission launched a proposal for the creation of such a system in 2013,[33] the objective of which is to change the fundamental principle of border control from one in which all nationals of a state are treated equally to what the Commission delicately calls a 'person-centric' approach, which means that the profile of the individual, rather than their citizenship, becomes the organising principle of the border control. The Commission describes the RTP as follows:

> In practice the RTP would work at the border the following way: A registered traveller would be issued a token in the form of a machine-readable card containing only a unique identifier (i.e. application number), which is swiped on arrival and departure at the border using an automated gate. The gate would read the token and the travel document (and visa sticker number, if applicable) and the fingerprints of the travellers, which would be compared to the ones stored in the Central Repository and other databases, including the Visa Information System (VIS) for visa holders. If all checks are successful, the traveller is able to pass through the automated gate. In case of any issue, the traveller would be assisted by a border guard.[34]

So any non-visa third-country national wishing to enjoy a facilitated entry at the European Union's external borders would have to provide a variety of personal data, including fingerprints, which will be held either in the Visa Information System (VIS; see below regarding visa nationals) or in a new database entitled the Central Repository; and these fingerprints, together with the passport, would constitute essential elements of entry at the external border. Databases of biometric information about individuals are one of the hallmarks of new border technologies. There is a substantial appetite for these databases in EU policies and laws regarding third-country nationals, which I will explain further below. What is central, however, to the use of biometric databases in external border controls of the European Union is that they partially replace the passport as the document that determines the identity of the individual. Instead of the individual's legal identity being a matter of negotiation between that person and his or her state of citizenship through the issue of a passport to him or her, the EU database makes an alternative claim to identifying the individual. No matter what the passport of the individual may say, the EU database containing the fingerprints of the individual enjoys an advantage: the capacity to tie the physical person with an inalienable part of his or her body – fingerprints. For instance, a person with dual nationality registers in the RTP with their fingerprints and their US passport. He or she then travels to the European Union on his or her valid Canadian passport. The EU database checks the person's fingerprints in the automated entry, and recognises the person as a US citizen (not a Canadian one). The automated entry system is likely to be uncomfortable with the outcome, but the problem is likely to be resolved so long as the person has both of his or her passports with him or her to show to a border guard sent to resolve the machine's confusion. But what has happened is that knowledge of the database as to who the person is has taken priority over the valid documentation issued to him or her by his or her country of citizenship.

For third-county nationals on the mandatory visa list, the passport issued to its citizens by their state is not sufficient for travel to the European Union. Those people must obtain a visa from an EU (Schengen)[35] consulate, through which process the person must provide substantial personal information (including about income and resources) as well as biometric data including fingerprints (unless the person is under 12 years of age[36] or physically unable to provide them).[37] This data, including information from sponsors in the European Union who may be EU citizens, is stored in a new EU database, the VIS, and is available to border guards and law enforcement authorities across the European Union. Thus these third-country nationals have a new identity created for them by the EU visa system. That identity is created while they are still in their country of origin. The value of that new EU-controlled identity (which is valid for 59 months – after that, the fingerprints need to be taken again)[38] is that it creates either the presumption that the person is admissible to the European Union (through any external border post) as a visitor for three months, if a visa is issued, or knowledge that an earlier application was refused for use in respect of any subsequent visa application. So, for example, if a dual Turkish/Lebanese national applies again for a visa using the Lebanese passport after refusal of such a request using his or her Turkish passport, the fingerprint record in the VIS is supposed to reveal the unique identity of the person.

Visas are not new,[39] even in the European Union. But their traditional role has been as a tool of foreign policy, a sanction against states between whom there is antagonism. Its development as an immigration tool in the European Union is a story that dates from about the mid-1980s.[40] The importance of visas as a foreign affairs tool re-emerges with the creation of no-visa lists in the European Union (and elsewhere), in particular following the Bosnian Wars of the 1990s.[41] During the post-Second World War period, the use of visas was primarily a foreign affairs tool indicating the state of relations between states, primarily between the West and the communist bloc. As the importance of the Iron Curtain began to lessen from the mid-1980s, leading to the big changes from 11 November 1989, the role of visas also began to change. Instead of being markers of relations between states, they were increasingly appropriated by interior ministries in pursuit of border and immigration control objectives. The Bosnian Wars played an important role for European states in this regard. As the numbers of persons fleeing the Balkan region increased, EU states gradually agreed to apply visa requirements to all the former Yugoslav republics (with the exception of Croatia).[42] Thus countries with close and friendly relations nonetheless introduced visa obligations on one another, not as a statement about their formal relations but to control unwanted migration.[43] This 'colonisation of visa regimes' by interior ministries has become surprisingly sophisticated, extending to include a wide range of foreign affairs instruments.[44]

The linking of visas with biometric databases is a much newer development. In the European Union it only begins with the creation of the VIS described above, made possible by the adoption of a measure in 2004, although the system only became operational on 11 October 2011.[45] According to the European Commission, the VIS consists of a central IT system combined with a communication infrastructure that links this central system to national systems. VIS connects EU (Schengen) consulates in non-EU countries and all external border-crossing points of Schengen states. It processes data and decisions relating to applications for short-stay visas to visit, or to transit through, the Schengen area. The system can perform biometric matching, primarily of fingerprints, for identification and verification purposes. The Schengen visa itself carries the fingerprints of the individual to whom it is issued. These fingerprints have been collected in the country of origin, then stored in the VIS (now managed by the European Union's IT agency, EU-LISA, based in Tallinn). When the person arrives at the EU external border, those fingerprints in the visa are checked against the VIS database to ensure that the person carrying the passport is the same person whose fingerprints were taken during the visa procedure. This checking process requires fingerprint machines to be available at EU external border posts (which was not universally the case in 2013). The system was still being rolled out by region in 2013. The choice of where to start rolling out the system was perhaps an indication of where in the world the European Union has least concerns. The first region to which it was applied was North Africa. The second region where collection and transmission of visa data to the VIS started for all visa applications was the Near East, with the exception of the occupied Palestinian territory, due to the serious technical difficulties (this has now been designated the eleventh region). The third was the Gulf region.[46] The next region consisted of West Africa, Central Africa, East Africa, Southern Africa, South America, Central Asia and South-East Asia.[47] The fourth and fifth regions, the rest of Africa, were rolled out in 2013.[48] On 14 May 2014 the rest of the Americas were rolled into the VIS system. The Commission estimates that roughly 2.4 million visa applications were introduced in VIS in 2012. That is some 16 per cent of total visa applications in that year. The objective of the VIS, again according to the Commission, is to tackle identity theft more effectively.[49]

The effect of the VIS is to bring into existence a large database with extensive personal information and biometric data in the form of fingerprints, a database that is available to consular officials, border guards and law enforcement agencies across the European Union. But the biometric information is only about third-country nationals who are on the mandatory visa list. The need for the VIS rests on the threat of identity fraud. The claim in favour of a need for biometric information in the form of fingerprints in order to combat identity theft in the crossing of the European Union's external borders needs to be examined in light of Frontex's information on the incidence of identity theft. According to Frontex in 2013, 9,804 incidents of people using false or fraudulent documents were detected in the whole of the European Union. Two-thirds of these documents were detected at airports.[50] The only single nationalities of persons detected using fraudulent documents that exceeded 1,000 were Albanians and Syrians. Syrians were most likely to be persons seeking to escape the civil war using someone else's passport. Considering the expense of setting up the VIS and its operation, the intrusion into the private lives of third-country nationals, not least with the collection of biometric data in the form of fingerprints, this is a dubious project. In 2012, 2.4 million sets of fingerprints were entered into the VIS and made available to all EU border and law enforcement agencies, yet EU border guards detected only 9,804 cases of document fraud in the following year, and many of those were in respect of people who do not need visas and whose details therefore are not in the VIS (i.e. Albanians and Serbian nationals). In light of this information, it is difficult to claim that the VIS is a border control technology. Yet for the moment, the EU agencies make no other claim regarding the reason for the VIS's existence.

13.4 Why are people refused admission at the European Union's external border?

The arguments in respect of the technologies, both new and old, for EU border controls on persons are based on the objective that unwanted people who do not fulfil the requirements for entry into the European Union should not be allowed to enter. The Schengen borders code spells out at Article 5 the requirements that people must fulfil in order to enter the EU Schengen area. People must show that:

(a) they are in possession of a valid travel document or documents authorising them to cross the border;

(b) they are in possession of a valid visa, if required except where they hold a valid residence permit;

(c) they justify the purpose and conditions of the intended stay, and they have sufficient means of subsistence, both for the duration of the intended stay and for the return to their country of origin or transit to a third country into which they are certain to be admitted, or are in a position to acquire such means lawfully;

(d) they are not persons for whom an alert has been issued in the Schengen Information System (SIS) for the purposes of refusing entry;

(e) they are not considered to be a threat to public policy, internal security, public health or the international relations of any of the member States, in particular where no alert has been issued in member states' national data bases for the purposes of refusing entry on the same grounds.

The Commission has proposed a new initiative: the creation of an electronic Entry–Exit system in order to have EU-wide record of entries and exits of travellers to and from the Schengen area, and thus a reliable means for member states to determine if a third-country national has exceeded his/her right to stay.[51] This will allow member states to know whether the people who have actually been admitted to the European Union do in fact fulfil the criteria of Article 5(1)(c) Schengen Borders Code (or not). But the Entry–Exit system will only be able to provide that information when the person leaves, so the record will be primarily historical. The Commission makes three main claims regarding the value of the proposed system. It will:

•   Calculate the authorised stay of each traveller; this includes at entry, in case of a traveller having visited the Schengen area frequently, to quickly and precisely calculate how many days there are left of the maximum of 90 days within 180 days; at exit, to verify that the traveller has respected the authorised stay; and within the territory, in relation to carrying out checks on third-country nationals to verify the legality of their stay.

•   Assist in the identification of any person who may not, or may no longer, fulfil the conditions for entry to, or stay on the territory of the member states; this concerns notably persons who are found during checks within the territory not in possession of their travel documents or any other means of identification.

•   To support the analysis of the entries and exits of third-country nationals; this includes notably getting a precise picture of travel flows at the external borders and the number of overstayers, for example by nationality of travellers.[52]

The Commission has proposed the allocation of €1.1 billion to develop the Entry–Exit system and the Registered Traveller Scheme. At the time of writing, the proposal was still before the European Parliament.[53]

According to Frontex, in 2013, 344,888 third-country nationals were treated as not fulfilling or no longer fulfilling their conditions of entry into the European

Union. The top five nationalities of those treated as overstayers were Syrians, Moroccans, Afghans, Albanians and Russians. They accounted for over one-quarter of all persons so treated. Of the 128,902 people refused entry at the European Union's external borders, the five top nationalities, accounting for almost 50 per cent of all refusals, were (in order of numerical importance) Russians, Ukrainians, Albanians, Serbians and Georgians. All these are nationals of countries neighbouring the European Union, and two – Albanian and Serbian nationals – are not required to obtain visas to enter the European Union (provided they have new-style biometric passports). In light of Frontex's information, it is not clear how either an Entry–Exit system or a Registered Traveller Scheme would substantially change the situation.

Turning to the reasons why third-country nationals are refused entry to the European Union, the five main reasons (leaving aside the category 'other'), according to Frontex, are as follows:

- No valid visa (or residence permit) – accounting for 50,054 refusals;
- No justification for the visit – accounting for 26,588 refusals;
- No or inadequate means of subsistence – accounting for 11,130 refusals;
- Entry on the Schengen Information System[54] as a person to be refused admission to the European Union – accounting for 10,817 refusals;
- No valid travel document – accounting for 9,001 refusals.

All of the main grounds for refusal, except the SIS entry, depend on traditional border control techniques – checking passports, visas and the reason for admission. Interestingly, only 3,077 persons were refused admission to the European Union on the basis that they were or were likely to be a specific security threat. The grounds for this refusal are public policy (which is usually related to criminality), internal security, public health, or the international relations of a member state. Most surprising of all is how banal the process is. The numbers are low given the size of the European Union and the probable volume of people entering and leaving the European Union; the reasons for the most part are mechanical (not the right documents, not enough money) or speculative on the part of the border guard (not the right reason to want to enter to the European Union). The information does not lead to an obvious and overwhelming need for overhaul, development or massive expenditure.

The last new technology that the European Union is rolling out as part of its external border controls agenda is Eurosur. This technology consists of a mix of satellite imaging and drones watching the European Union's external borders, with the objective of reducing the loss of lives at sea, reducing the number of irregular immigrants entering the European Union undetected, and increasing internal security by preventing cross-border crimes, such as trafficking in human beings and the smuggling of drugs.[55] For the system to work, cooperation with neighbouring third countries is essential, according to the Commission's Communication. According to the Commission's press release, the exchange of information in the framework of Eurosur will take the form of 'situational pictures', which can be described as graphical interfaces presenting data, information and intelligence:

> These situational pictures will be established at national and European level and will be structured in a similar way to facilitate the flow of information among them. In order to improve the capability of detecting small vessels, Frontex will also set up a service for the common application of surveillance tools, combining, among other things, satellite imagery with information derived from ship reporting systems.[56]

According to Frontex, Eurosur has three phases. The first is the rationalisation of surveillance systems among the Schengen states; the second is 'to improve surveillance at the EU level by introducing more advanced technologies and combining all the resultant data to form a coherent whole, available to its users 24 hours a day, seven days a week'; and the third involves creating a common information-sharing 'environment' for all member-state agencies affected. The cost estimates for Eurosur amount to €338 million for 2011–2020, according to the Commission.[57] This is indeed an expensive system, and one that uses technologies that are more commonly associated with military equipment than civilian ones. There is always the argument, and a very valid one too, that even one unnecessary death in the Mediterranean is beyond cost. But the question that arises is whether this enormously ambitious system will actually assist if the problem is a more mundane one. I have already cited the deputy director of Frontex, who only three months after the Eurosur programme went live questioned the capacity of the system (at least as it was at the time) to assist in any way to reduce loss of life at sea.

According to the *Guardian Weekly* 11–17 October 2013, in August 2013 the Italian authorities ordered two commercial ships to rescue a migrant boat, and then demanded that the captains transport the migrants back to Libya (where none of them wanted to go, and indeed from where they were in flight). One can well imagine the dilemma facing the captains, faced with a boat load of desperate people, terrified of being returned to Libya. Better satellite surveillance or drones will not resolve this ethical issue. Nor will it make the legal problem go away. State responsibility for people within its jurisdiction is not a geographical construct, as the European Court of Human Rights continues to advise its member states. It is a legal concept, which extends state responsibility to everyone who comes within the power of the state directly or indirectly, whether or not they are on the territory over which a state has formally declared state sovereignty.[58]

13.5 Conclusion

The debates about EU border controls since the second half of 2013 have been fierce. The continuing loss of life in the Mediterranean because of the failure to rescue people seeking to reach the European Union's southern borders fuelled much anguish on the subject; the language of crisis was deployed. While there is a general consensus that something needs to be done to diminish the loss of life, there are very different approaches to what that something must be. UNHCR has called for better reception facilities within the European Union; the Pope has called for humanity for those seeking a better life; the Commission has called for more responsible policing of North African borders, which would prevent people leaving in small boats. The backdrop to the debates is what kind of border controls the European Union should have.

There are two main frameworks around the border control issue in the European Union. The first is the traditional approach – passports, visas and checks carried out by border guards at the external frontiers. The second is the greater use of technology in the form of databases with biometric identifiers and electronic checks at external frontiers, and satellite images for border guards so that they can see who is approaching the borders, land or sea. I have examined the claims regarding border controls from the perspective of available knowledge about what happens at EU borders on the basis of the statistical information made available by the European Union's border agency, Frontex. What is particularly noticeable from the statistical information is the unclear articulation between the facts of EU border controls on persons and the claims and proposals for new technologies that emerge from EU institutions. The problem is one of scale. The numbers of third-country nationals entering the European Union per year (probably well over 100 million) and the population of the European Union (about 508 million) are of one order of magnitude. The numbers of persons drowning in the Mediterranean (about 1,500 in 2011), the numbers of persons refused admission to the European Union (under 130,000 in 2013), and even the numbers of persons treated as not fulfilling or no longer fulfilling their entry conditions to the European Union (under 350,000 in 2013), let alone those using false or fraudulent documents (just over 9,000 in 2013), are of a completely different order. In view of the tremendous disjunction between the two scales, measures adopted, which have a massive impact on the totality of people moving (such as large new databases with biometric information, Entry–Exit schemes that track everyone, satellite images and drones), in order to deal with issues that engage 0.1 per cent of that total are quite simply disproportionate. People need to be rescued in the Mediterranean – but the best way to do this is to encourage rather than discourage all those fishing boats, pleasure boats and other vessels travelling the Mediterranean from rescuing people. Massive collection, storage, use and transmission of sensitive personal data, including fingerprints, of people travelling is a very odd response to the problem of refusal of a small number of third-country nationals at the European Union's external borders, or the treatment of the EU population as overstayers.

Notes

1   Hein de Haas, 'The Myth of Invasion: The Inconvenient Realities of African Migration to Europe', *Third World Quarterly* 29 no. 7 (2008), 1305–1322.
2   Frontex Risk Analysis reports are available from 2010 and always focus on what they term 'routes' through the Mediterranean, available at: http://frontex.europa.eu/assets/Publications/Risk_Analysis/FRAN_Q1_2010.pdf. Visited 10 May 2014.

3   The Human Costs of Border Control (HSBC). www.rechten.vu.nl/en/research/top-research/vici-spijkerboer/sub-projects/index.asp. Visited 17 May 2014.

4   See e.g. Kim Rygiel, 'Geographies of Exclusion: Rethinking Citizenship from the Margin', paper presented at International Studies Association Annual Convention, Montreal, 16 March 2011. Available at: http://citation.allacademic.com/meta/p502935_index.html. Visited 10 May 2014.

5   Julien Jeandesboz and Polly Pallister-Wilkins, 'Crisis, Enforcement and Control at the EU Borders', in *Crisis and Migration: Critical Perspectives*, edited by Anna Lindley, 115–135 (London: Routledge, 2014), 115.

6   See for instance, 'Let Migrants Drown in the Mediterranean? Have We Lost our Humanity?', letter, *Guardian*, 28 October 2014. Available at: www.theguardian.com/world/2014/oct/28/let-migrants-drown-mediterranean-lost-sense-of-common-humanity. Visited 27 December 2014.

7   PACE (Parliamentary Assembly of the Council of Europe), 'Lives Lost in the Mediterranean Sea: Who is Responsible?' (Strasbourg: PACE Committee on Migration, Refugees and Displaced Persons, March 2012), available at: assembly.coe.int/CommitteeDocs/2012/20120329 mig RPT.EN.pdf.

8   Matilde Ventrella McCreight, 'Crimes of Assisting Illegal Immigration and Trafficking in Human Beings in Italian Law: Illegal Immigration between Administrative Infringement and Criminal Offence', in *Immigration and Criminal Law in the European Union: The Legal Measures and Social Consequences of Criminal Law in Member States on Trafficking and Smuggling in Human Beings*, eds Elspeth Guild and P. Paul E. Minderhoud, 141–168 (Leiden: Nijhoff, 2006).

9   See Tugba Basaran, research presentation at Recherche et enseignement en politique internationale, REPI (Brussels: Université Libre de Bruxelles, 27 April 2013). Also Tugba Basaran, 'The Saved and the Drowned: Governing Indifference in the Name of Security', *Security Dialogue* 46 no. 3 (2015), 205–220.

10 European Commission Press Release 11 October 2013, Memo 13/883.

11 Protocol 4 Article 2(2): 'Everyone shall be free to leave any country, including his own'.

12 See for instance Amnesty International, 'SOS Europe: Human Rights and Migration Control' (London: Amnesty International, June 2012), available at: www.amnesty.eu/content/assets/S_O_S_Europe_Report_Web_02.pdf. Visited 10 May 2014.

13 Press Release, Council meeting on Foreign Affairs 27–28 May 2013, Document number 9977/13.

14 Press Release, Council, 22 May 2013 Document number 9478/13.

15 Eurosur Goes Live. http://frontex.europa.eu/feature-stories/eurosur-goes-live-Z8ZM4f. Visited 4 June 2014.

16 EUROSUR: new tools to save migrants' lives at sea and fight cross-border crime. http://europa.eu/rapid/press-release_MEMO-13–578_en.htm. Visited 4 June 2014.

17 EU border surveillance system not helping to save lives. http://euobserver.com/justice/124136. Visited 4 June 2014.

18 Didier Bigo *et al.*, 'Justice and Home Affairs Databases and a Smart Borders System at EU External Borders: An Evaluation of Current and Forthcoming Proposals', CEPS Paper in Liberty and Security in Europe, No. 2 (Brussels: Centre for European Policy Studies, 2012).

19 Bigo, Didier, Sergio Carrera and Elspeth Guild, eds, *Foreigners, Refugees or Minorities? Rethinking People in the Context of Border Controls and Visas* (Farnham: Ashgate, 2013).

20 Anneliese Baldaccini, 'Extraterritorial Border Controls in the EU: The Role of Frontex in Operations at Sea', in *Extraterritorial Immigration Control: Legal Challenges*, eds Bernard Ryan and Valsamis Mitsilegas, 225–251 (Leiden: Nijhoff, 2010).

21 Ruben Zaiotti, *Cultures of Border Control: Schengen and the Evolution of European Frontiers* (Chicago, IL: University of Chicago Press, 2011).

22 Nick Vaughan-Williams, ed., *Border Politics: The Limits of Sovereign Power* (Edinburgh: Edinburgh University Press, 2009).

23 Frontex, 'Annual Risk Analysis 2014' (Warsaw: Frontex, May 2014), available at: http://frontex.europa.eu/assets/Publications/Risk_Analysis/Annual_Risk_Analysis_2014.pdf. Visited 4 June 2014.

24 UNHCR, available at: www.unhcr.org/4f27c01f9.html. Visited 13 October 2013.

25 Fortress Europe, available at: http://fortresseurope.blogspot.it/p/la-fortezza.html. Visited 13 October 2013.

26 EU Fundamental Rights Agency project, 'Treatment of Third-Country Nationals at the EU's External Borders: Surveying Border Checks at Selected Border Crossing Points' (Vienna: EU Fundamental Rights Agency), available at: http://fra.europa.eu/en/project/2011/treatment-third-country-nationals-eus-external-borders-surveying-border-checks-selected. Visited 27 December 2014.

27 Council Document 13267/09, 22 September 2009.

28 Frontex Annual Risk Analysis 2013, available at: http://frontex.europa.eu/assets/Publications/Risk_Analysis/Annual_Risk_Analysis_2013.pdf. Visited 27 December 2014.

29 Citizenship Statistics on Cross Border Activities, available at: http://epp.eurostat.ec.europa.eu/statistics_explained/index.php/EU_citizenship_-_statistics_on_cross-border_activities. Visited 28 December 2014.

30 Sophie Scholten and Paul Minderhoud, 'Regulating Immigration Control: Carrier Sanctions in the Netherlands', *European Journal of Migration and Law* 10 (2008), 123.

31 Article 7, Schengen Borders Code, Regulation 562/2006.

32 Regulation No 539/2001.

33 COM(2013)97.

34 COM(2013)97 p 3.

35 The Schengen countries which can issue Schengen visas valid for short stays of three months out of every six-month period in the Schengen area are all EU member states except Bulgaria, Croatia, Ireland, Romania and the United Kingdom, but including the non-EU states of Iceland, Liechtenstein, Norway and Switzerland: Carole Billet, 'Les Relations Extérieures des Agences ELSJ après le Traité de Lisbonne', paper presented at Colloque sur la Dimension Institutionnelle du Volet Externe de l'ELSJ, 4 March 2011. Available on open access at HAL SHS (Sciences de l'Homme et de la Société), available at: https://halshs.archives-ouvertes.fr/halshs-00642777.

36 Although according to the European Commission, it is having a study carried out to determine whether fingerprints from children younger than twelve can be reliable for database purposes. COM(2013)442, pp 7–8.

37 EU Visa Code, Regulation 810/2009 Article 13(7)(a) and (b).

38 EU Visa Code, Regulation 810/2009 Article 13(3).

39 Sarah Wolff, Nicole Wichmann and Gregory Mounier, eds, *The External Dimension of Justice and Home Affairs: A Different Security Agenda for the EU?* (London: Routledge, 2010).

40 Federica Infantino and Andrea Rea, 'La Mobilisation d'un Savoir Pratique Local: Attribution des Visas Schengen au Consulat Général de Belgique à Casablanca'. *Sociologies pratiques* 24 no. 1 (2012), 67–78; Mogens Hobolth, 'European Visa Cooperation: Interest Politics and Regional Imagined Communities', Europe in Question Series 34 (London: London School of Economics and Political Science, 2011).

41 See the EU External Action Service general comment, available at: http://eeas.europa.eu/cfsp/sanctions/docs/index_en.pdf#2.3 Visited 14 October 2013.

42 Sarah Collinson, 'Visa Requirements, Carrier Sanctions, "Safe Third Countries" and Readmission: The Development of an Asylum "Buffer Zone" in Europe', *Transactions of the Institute of British Geographers* 21, no. 1 (1996), 76–90; Grete Brochmann, 'Bosnian Refugees in the Scandinavian Countries: A Comparative Perspective on Immigration Control in the 1990s', *Journal of Ethnic and Migration Studies* 23 no. 4 (1997), 495–510.

43 Florian Trauner and Imke Kruse, 'EC Visa Facilitation and Readmission Agreements: A New Standard Eu Foreign Policy Tool', *European Journal of Migration and Law* 10 no. 4 (2008), 411.

44 Florian Trauner, 'The EU's Readmission Policy in the Neighbourhood: A Comparative View on the Southern Mediterranean and Eastern Europe', in *The EU, Migration and the Politics of Administrative Detention*, eds Michela Ceccorulli and Nicola Labanca (London: Routledge, 2014), 23.

45 European Commission, available at: http://ec.europa.eu/dgs/home-affairs/what-is-new/news/news/2011/20111011_en.htm. Visited 14 October 2013.

46 Commission Decision 30 November 2009, C(2009)8542.

47 Commission Decision 24 April 2012 C(2012)2505.

48 Commission Implementing Decision 2013/122/EU of 7 March 2013.

49 European Commission: An Open and Secure Europe: Making it Happen COM(2014)154 final.

50 Frontex Annual Risk Analysis 2013, available at: http://frontex.europa.eu/assets/ Publications/Risk_Analysis/Annual_Risk_Analysis_2013.pdf. Visited 27 December 2014.

51 European Commission Proposal for a Regulation Establishing an Entry/Exit System (EES) to Register Entry and Exit Data of Third Country Nationals Crossing the External Borders of the Member States of the European Union: COM(2013)95. By December 2014 it seemed increasingly unlikely that this proposal would seek the necessary approval of the European Parliament in order to become law.

52 Ibid.

53 Entry/Exit System (EES) to register entry and exit data of third country nationals, www.europarl.europa.eu/oeil/popups/ficheprocedure.do?reference=2013/ 0057 (COD)&l=en. Visited 4 June 2014.

54 Evelien Renate Brouwer, *Digital Borders and Real Rights: Effective remedies for Third-Country Nationals in the Schengen Information System*, Volume 15 in Immigration and Asylum Law and Policy in Europe series (Leiden: Brill, 2008).

55 European Commission proposal for a Regulation Establishing the European Border Surveillance System (Eurosur) COM(2011)873.

56 EUROSUR: 'connecting the dots' in border surveillance. http://europa.eu/rapid/ press-release_IP-11-1528_en.htm?locale=FR. Visited 15 October 2013.

57 EUROSUR: Providing authorities with tools needed to reinforce management of external borders and fight ctoss-border crime. http://europa.eu/rapid/press-release_ MEMO-11-896_en.htm?locale=FR. Visited 15 October 2013.

58 Thomas Gammeltoft-Hansen, *Access to Asylum: International Refugee Law and the Globalisation of Migration Control* (Cambridge: Cambridge University Press, 2011); Violeta Moreno-Lax, 'Access to Asylum: International Refugee Law and the Globalisation of Migration Control. Thomas Gammeltoft-Hansen', *Journal of Refugee Studies* 26 no. 2 (2013), 318–319.

Bibliography

Amnesty International. 'SOS Europe: Human Rights and Migration Control'. London: Amnesty International, June 2012. Available at www.amnestyusa.org/research/reports/ sos-europe-human-rights-and-migration-control. Accessed on 10 February 2015.

Baldaccini, Anneliese. 'Extraterritorial Border Controls in the EU: The Role of Frontex in Operations at Sea'. In *Extraterritorial Immigration Control: Legal Challenges*, edited by Bernard Ryan and Valsamis Mitsilegas, 225–251. Leiden: Nijhoff, 2010.

Basaran, Tugba. 'The Saved and the Drowned: Governing Indifference in the Name of Security'. *Security Dialogue* 46 no. 3 (2015): 205–220.

Bigo, Didier, Sergio Carrera and Elspeth Guild. *Foreigners, Refugees or Minorities? Rethinking People in the Context of Border Controls and Visas*. Farnham: Ashgate, 2013.

Bigo, Didier, Sergio Carrera, Ben Hayes, Nicholas Hernanz and Julien Jeandesboz. 'Justice and Home Affairs Databases and a Smart Borders System at EU External Borders: An Evaluation of Current and Forthcoming Proposals'. CEPS Paper in Liberty and Security in Europe No. 2. Brussels: Centre for European Policy Studies, 2012.

Billet, Carole. 'Les Relations Extérieures des Agences ELSJ après le Traité de Lisbonne [External relations of the ELSJ Agencies after the Lisbon Treaty]'. Conference paper given at Colloque sur la Dimension Institutionnelle du Volet Externe de l'ELSJ, 4 March 2011. Available on open access at HAL SHS (Sciences de l'Homme et de la Société): https://halshs.archives-ouvertes.fr/halshs-00642777.

Brochmann, Grete. 'Bosnian Refugees in the Scandinavian Countries: A Comparative Perspective on Immigration Control in the 1990s'. *Journal of Ethnic and Migration Studies* 23 no. 4 (1997): 495–510.

Brouwer, Evelien. *Digital Borders and Real Rights: Effective Remedies for Third-Country Nationals in the Schengen Information System* (Vol. 15 in 'Immigration and Asylum Law and Policy in Europe'). Leiden: Brill, 2008.

Collinson, Sarah. 'Visa Requirements, Carrier Sanctions, "Safe Third Countries" and Readmission: The Development of an Asylum "Buffer Zone" in Europe'. *Transactions of the Institute of British Geographers* 21 no. 1 (1996): 76–90.

de Haas, Hein. 'The Myth of Invasion: The Inconvenient Realities of African Migration to Europe'. *Third World Quarterly* 29 no. 7 (2008): 1305–1322.

Frontex. 'Annual Risk Analysis 2014'. Warsaw: Frontex, May 2014. Available at: http://frontex.europa.eu/assets/Publications/Risk_Analysis/Annual_Risk_Analysis_2014.pdf. Accessed on 4 June 2014.

Gammeltoft-Hansen, Thomas. *Access to Asylum: International Refugee Law and the Globalisation of Migration Control.* Cambridge: Cambridge University Press, 2011.

Hobolth, Mogens. 'European Visa Cooperation: Interest Politics and Regional Imagined Communities'. Europe in Question Series 34. London: London School of Economics and Political Science, 2011.

Infantino, Federica, and Andrea Rea. 'La Mobilisation d'un Savoir Pratique Local: Attribution des Visas Schengen au Consulat Général de Belgique à Casablanca'. *Sociologies pratiques* 24 no. 1 (2012).

Jeandesboz, Julien, and Polly Pallister-Wilkins. 'Crisis, Enforcement and Control at the EU Borders'. In *Crisis and Migration: Critical Perspectives*, edited by Anna Lindley, 115–135. London: Routledge, 2014.

McCreight, Matilde Ventrella. 'Crimes of Assisting Illegal Immigration and Trafficking in Human Beings in Italian Law: Illegal Immigration between Administrative Infringement and Criminal Offence'. In *Immigration and Criminal Law in the European Union: The Legal Measures and Social Consequences of Criminal Law in Member States on Trafficking and Smuggling in Human Beings* (Vol. 9 in 'Immigration and Asylum Law and Policy in Europe'), edited by Elspeth Guild and P. Paul E. Minderhoud, 141–168. Leiden: Nijhoff, 2006.

Moreno-Lax, Violeta. 'Access to Asylum: International Refugee Law and the Globalisation of Migration Control. Thomas Gammeltoft-Hansen'. *Journal of Refugee Studies* 26 no. 2 (2013): 318–319.

PACE (Parliamentary Assembly of the Council of Europe). 'Lives Lost in the Mediterranean Sea: Who is Responsible?'. Strasbourg: PACE Committee on Migration, Refugees and Displaced Persons, March 2012. Available at: assembly.coe.int/CommitteeDocs/2012/20120329 mig RPT.EN.pdf. Accessed on 15 February 2015.

Rygiel, Kim. 'Geographies of Exclusion: Rethinking Citizenship from the Margin'. Paper presented at International Studies Association Annual Convention, Montreal, 16 March 2011. Available at: http://citation.allacademic.com/meta/p502935_index.html.

Scholten, Sophie, and Paul Minderhoud. 'Regulating Immigration Control: Carrier Sanctions in the Netherlands'. *European Journal of Migration and Law* 10 (2008): 123–147.

Trauner, Florian. 'The EU's Readmission Policy in the Neighbourhood: A Comparative View on the Southern Mediterranean and Eastern Europe'. In *The EU, Migration and the Politics of Administrative Detention*, edited by Michela Ceccorulli and Nicola Labanca, 23–41. London: Routledge, 2014.

Trauner, Florian, and Imke Kruse. 'EC Visa Facilitation and Readmission Agreements: A New Standard EU Foreign Policy Tool'. *European Journal of Migration and Law* 10 no. 4 (2008): 411–438.

Vaughan-Williams, Nick (ed.). *Border Politics: The Limits of Sovereign Power*. Edinburgh: Edinburgh University Press, 2009.

Wolff, Sarah, Nicole Wichmann and Gregory Mounier (eds). *The External Dimension of Justice and Home Affairs: A Different Security Agenda for the EU?* London: Routledge, 2010.

Zaiotti, Ruben. *Cultures of Border Control: Schengen and the Evolution of European Frontiers*. Chicago, IL: University of Chicago Press, 2011.

14

'OUTSOURCING' PROTECTION AND THE TRANSNATIONAL RELEVANCE OF PROTECTION ELSEWHERE

The case of UNHCR

Julian M. Lehmann[1]

14.1 Introduction

Mechanisms to avoid processing claims for international protection abound. The EU Procedures Directive allows member states to reject applications for international protection under the concepts of 'safe third countries' and 'first countries of asylum', which challenge access to asylum by shifting responsibility to states with poor conditions for international protection. One future feature of such a shift could be the application of rules concerning protection elsewhere to asylum countries in which the United Nations High Commissioner for Refugees (UNHCR) takes on core tasks of refugee protection, including refugee status determination and running camps. This contribution enquires into whether international restrains the application of protection-elsewhere policies to countries in which refugee protection is shared by states and the UNHCR. It proposes to reaffirm the 1951 Convention as the basis for protection-elsewhere policies, because the Convention provides principled arguments against the provision of 'protection' by actors other than states.

This article first explores how norms on protection elsewhere fit within international refugee law and how they relate to the UNHCR taking on core protection tasks, then enquires whether the use of the concept of protection elsewhere to such country contexts.

14.2 Protection elsewhere and the transnational dimension of 'Outsourcing' to the UNHCR

14.2.1 International law and the proliferation of 'Protection Elsewhere'

Industrialised states have long created mechanisms designed to regulate responsibility for asylum applications.[2] They serve to relieve states of processing asylum applications, reduce so-called 'secondary movements' of refugees and to prevent situations in which no state accepts responsibility for processing an application (refugees 'in orbit'). Mostly, these rules are procedural in nature; they allow the rejection of applications for international protection when another state has already granted protection. In the European Union, in addition to the Dublin Regulation, regulating responsibility for handling asylum applications made in member states, the Procedures Directive allows member states to reject applications for protection where another, non-EU state could, or already has, granted protection.[3]

The lawfulness of rules on 'protection elsewhere' has been the subject of intense academic debate.[4] Rules on protection elsewhere are built on a gap for the allocation of responsibility for refugees inherent in the international legal regime on refugee protection. In particular, the 1951 Convention dissociates refugee status from asylum,[5] that is, permission to stay in the territory of the state of the refuge. Besides, the primary effort to remedy this gap, the negotiations on a convention on territorial asylum, failed.

Although in 1979 the UNHCR Executive Committee (EXCOM) cautioned that asylum should not be denied only because it could be sought by another state,[6] since then the UNHCR has carefully endorsed rules on protection elsewhere. Possibly, this was done for pragmatic reasons of policy, allowing the agency to shape the standards, to embrace their potentially beneficial effects on responsibility sharing,[7] and to avoid refugees 'in orbit'. Thus, the UNHCR has never questioned whether rules on protection elsewhere are, in principle, lawful under the 1951 Convention.[8] At least according to the predominant practice in Western countries of asylum, there is no individual entitlement to a particular country of asylum enshrined in the 1951 Convention.[9] Although the 1951 Convention does not explicitly provide for the creation of protection-elsewhere policies, international refugee law technically allows for the creation of arrangements for 'protection elsewhere'.[10]

Rules on protection elsewhere can shift responsibility for refugee protection to states closer to refugees' countries of origin – countries that are mostly less resourceful than the industrialised states of asylum, and that often already host higher numbers of refugees. For that reason, states closer to refugees' countries of origin often cooperate with non-state actors, including international organisations, to provide services to refugees.[11] Shifting responsibility closer to countries of origin means facing the reality that refugee 'protection' is no longer the monopoly of states.

14.2.2 The transnational dimension of 'Outsourcing' to the UNHCR

Of the various protection elsewhere mechanisms existing in EU law, EU states currently primarily apply the Dublin Regulation. In contrast, the Procedures Directive's concepts of 'safe third country' and 'first country of asylum' are seldom applied. Yet, there are reasons to believe that these latter rules will gain importance in the future. European Union and bilateral readmission agreements foresee that signatory states readmit third-country nationals who have transited through their territory, when they are staying irregularly in an EU member state.[12] Although readmission agreements do not provide the basis for a decision on the admissibility of asylum applications, they may be used to enforce the return of the safe third country/first country of asylum rules in the Procedures Directive.[13] The political appetite for the safe third country concept with respect to Turkey has been growing steadily during the 2015/2016 EU refugee crisis. At the time of writing it was still unclear whether individual EU states would classify Turkey as a safe third country.

One potential development could be the application of rules on 'protection elsewhere' to asylum countries in which the UNHCR is charged with core tasks of refugee protection. The UNHCR has gone from being a minor organisation with a specific legal focus to being the United Nation's largest humanitarian agency. Originally tasked with facilitating state obligations to refugees,[14] the agency now carries out many protection tasks itself, or supervises their implementation by deploying non-governmental organisations (NGOs). This includes the determination of refugee status, the provision of welfare, education and health services. For instance, between 2002 and 2012 the UNHCR conducted RSD in fifty to sixty-six countries per year.[15] The UNHCR's share of global applications was eleven per cent in 2011. Thus, the UNHCR remains the second largest RSD authority after South Africa.[16]

In the European region, there are several states in which the UNHCR still conducts RSD, including Algeria, Egypt, Morocco, Tunisia and Turkey (for non-Syrian refugees). All these states have entered into bilateral readmission agreements with several EU states. For instance, Greece has a bilateral readmission agreement with Turkey, although many third-country nationalities are still excluded.[17] In turn, Turkey has had a readmission agreement with the EU since 2014, which applies to third-country nationals as of 2016.[18]

Although the current scope of UNHCR activity may be a recent development, shared responses by states and international organisations have been common since the beginning of refugee protection.[19] This is also reflected in the 1951 Convention, which mentions international assistance and cooperation in the preamble,[20] and, in Article 35, enshrines the obligation of contracting states to cooperate with the UNHCR. While UNHCR support of states is frequent, it may raise issues of compliance with refugee law when a state has sufficient resources to discharge its obligations. Besides, shared refugee responses between states and the UNHCR also challenge the transnational application of the law – that is, the application of the law outside the country in which protection responsibilities are shared between states and the UNHCR. This becomes evident when analysing the various existing legal safeguards of protection-elsewhere policies.

14.3 'Outsourcing' and the safeguards of protection elsewhere

14.3.1 Non-refoulement under Article 33 of the 1951 Convention

There is widespread agreement that non-refoulement of refugees under Article 33 of the 1951 Convention circumscribes the primary safeguards for protection-else-where policies. There is also judicial authority that states that non-refoulement is subject to a state's jurisdiction, that is, also extraterritorially. Non-refoulement obligations apply both directly (to envisaged returns to the country of origin), and indirectly (to envisaged returns to a country that then expels the person to the country of origin).

It is clear that the UNHCR alone cannot guarantee non-refoulement, from either a legal or an actual perspective. Only states may be parties to the 1951 Convention, and only states have the necessary powers to implement the obligation of non-refoulement. Confronted with the question of whether it was duty-bound to assess the risks of persecution faced by witnesses who are applying for asylum, the International Criminal Court (ICC) in 2011 argued that respect for the principle of non-refoulement required control over territory:

> Admittedly, as an international organisation with a legal personality, the Court cannot disregard the customary rule of non-refoulement. However, since it does not possess any territory, it is unable to implement the principle within its ordinary meaning, and hence is unlikely to maintain long-term juris-diction over persons who are at risk of persecution or torture if they return to their country of origin. In the Chamber's view, only a State which posses-ses territory is actually able to apply the non-refoulement rule. Furthermore, the Court cannot employ the cooperation mechanisms provided for by the Statute in order to compel a State Party to receive onto its territory an individual invoking this rule. Moreover, it cannot prejudge, in lieu of the Host State, obligations placed on the latter under the non-refoulement principle.[21]

Obligations of non-refoulement incur derivative obligations, in particular relating to RSD. Thus, a precondition for a third country's compliance with non-refoulement is an accessible system of refugee status determination, in which the Convention's definition of 'refugee' is interpreted in good faith: Foster notes that the sending state must ascertain that the receiving state has an accessible RSD procedure with an independent review process, and that it 'respects "the true and autonomous meaning" of the definition of "refugee" in Article 1 of the Convention'.[22] Does the UNHCR's RSD satisfy this standard?

Academic research on UNHCR RSD standards is relatively dated. In a 1999 study, Alexander observed that the UNHCR's RSD procedures had been overtaken by the more generous standards of human rights law, and that they fell short of the standards the UNHCR promoted vis-à-vis governments.[23] Drawing thereon, Kagan analysed deficiencies in RSD in the Middle East, observing that the UNHCR did not provide specific written reasons for rejecting applications, that it withheld evidence and rejected most appeals without a rehearing.[24] Meanwhile, in 2005, the UNHCR issued procedural standards for its own RSD operations for the first time.[25] These standards, *inter alia*, affirm the right for legal representatives to accompany an applicant throughout the RSD process, foresee accelerated RSD for people with vulnerabilities, set minimum qualifications of RSD officers and interpreters and feature improved standards for the review process.[26]

Criticism of the above-described standards revolved around lacking institutional independence of the review process, or access to evidence on file.[27] A 2007 report on the UNHCR's RSD in Cambodia, Egypt, Hong Kong, Israel, Kenya, Lebanon, Thailand and Turkey observed significant improvement induced by UNHCR procedural standards.[28] Analysis of UNHCR compliance with its RSD standards in its Turkish office attested to the fact that the UNHCR complies with its own standards 'satisfactorily' in most cases.[29] However, it criticised long waiting times of up to 2 years for an initial decision, and the failure to systematically identify people with particular vulnerabilities. Because of limited state assistance and lack of access to the labour market, long waiting times had a 'devastating impact on refugee applicants'.[30] In sum, the UNHCR's RSD standards have significantly improved. Where state authorities respect the agency's status-determination decisions and grant residence pending and after status determination, non-refoulement obligations would not preclude return to a country in which the UNHCR carries out RSD.

14.3.2 Obligations of non-return other than Article 33

The safeguards refugee law requires for protection-elsewhere policies are still contested. Particularly controversial is whether there are obligations of non-return other than Article 33 of the 1951 Convention, which are applicable to these policies.

A potentially important challenge to protection-elsewhere policies is the entitlement of refugees while RSD is pending, as well as after the recognition of their status. From a factual perspective, this entitlement is particularly pertinent to states with defunct asylum systems, or in countries with UNHCR operations in camps. Both academic research and NGO reporting identify the problems pertaining to refugee camps.[31] In 2010, Amnesty International and Human Rights Watch (HRW) reported on the Dadaab refugee camps in Kenya. They reported overcrowding, insufficient allocation of water, high levels of theft and sexual violence, police inaction vis-à-vis reports of crime, recruitment of refugees for the Kenyan army, refugees' confinement to the camps and their imprisonment if they breach that rule.[32] Although the camps were not run by the UNHCR, the problems in the Dadaab camps exemplify common risks in refugee camps: physical security, nutrition and health, militarisation and economic immobilisation of refugees. Do such conditions preclude return, and thus narrow the application of protection-elsewhere policies?

From the perspective of international refugee law, additional safeguards for protection-elsewhere policies are interlinked with the structure of entitlement under the 1951 Convention. The Convention develops a framework of rights and obligations that depend on the refugee's level of attachment to the asylum state. Refugees acquire most rights once 'lawfully present' or 'lawfully staying' in the territory of an asylum state, but the most basic rights apply once refugees are under a state's jurisdiction.[33] However, where a Convention provision applies because of the relevant level of attachment, the scope of entitlement often remains contingent on the treatment of other foreigners in the same circumstances.[34]

The Michigan Guidelines on Protection Elsewhere, a non-binding, but authoritative expert paper compiled by international legal scholars, argue for a broad standard. The Guidelines take the view that 'protection elsewhere policies are compatible with the Convention so long as they ensure that refugees defined by Article 1 enjoy the rights set by Articles 2–34 of the [1951] Convention'. Consequently, although acknowledging that non-refoulement under Article 33 of the 1951 Convention is the most important constraint, the Guidelines take the view that all obligations under Articles 2–34 of the 1951 Convention, independent of the level of attachment they foresee, determine the lawfulness of return. The guidelines assert that before relying on protection-elsewhere policies, there must be a 'good faith empirical assessment by the state which proposes to effect the transfer ("sending state") that refugees defined by Article 1 will in practice enjoy the rights set by Articles 2–34 of the Convention in the receiving state'.[35] States must also '[. . .] afford the person transferred a meaningful legal and factual opportunity to make his or her claim to protection'. This is because refugee status is declaratory; thus refugees acquire rights once outside their countries of origin, rather than after a formal process of status determination.

Foster takes the view that the 1951 Convention rights that apply once a refugee is on the territory of an asylum state determine the lawfulness of return to country of asylum. Those rights include Articles 3, 4, 13, 16(1), 20, 22, 25, 27 and 31(1)–(2) (freedom of religion, right to property, access to courts, equality of access to rationing, right to education, administrative assistance, identity papers, freedom from fiscal charges, non-penalisation for illegal entry, no unnecessary constraints on freedom of movement, non-refoulement and consideration for naturalisation).[36] Additionally, Foster points out judicial authority that stipulates that sending states should not strip refugees of rights already acquired in a first country of asylum.[37]

A UNHCR-commissioned study argued that the complicity principle of international law[38] precludes a person's return to a state where it is known that the person's rights under international law will be violated.[39] Notably, this included all rights under the 1951 Convention (Articles 2–34), and under international and regional human rights instruments.[40] The study admitted that this widest conceivable scope would pose practical difficulties.[41] However, in order to keep the premises of the complicity principle intact, the study rejected narrowing the scope of rights precluding return.[42] Therefore, it proposed a set of criteria that include the advance consent of the receiving state to readmit and to provide a fair determination of refugee status, assurance that the third country will, in law and fact, respect the duty of non-refoulement and all other 1951 Convention rights, and respect international and regional human rights standards and access to durable solutions.

As far as the 1951 Convention is concerned, its framework of entitlement has made it relatively easy for states to adhere to a narrow understanding of the Convention. For such a narrow core of protection, Gammeltoft-Hansen coined the term *protection lite*, observing that:

> To the extent that protection responsibility is deflected or transferred to less developed States, or even to States with poor human rights records or underdeveloped asylum systems [. . .] this may effectively erode the quality of protection afforded [. . .]. The result is what could be termed 'protection lite', understood as the presence of formal protection, though with a lower certainty, scope and/or level of rights afforded. [. . .] [W]ithin a strict or restrictive reading, this may well fall within the operational flexibility made possible by the international legal framework. Indeed, the territorial principle of dividing responsibility and bestowing rights relative to the practices and situation of each particular country enshrined in the 1951 Refugee Convention is the very premise for this development.[43]

Indeed, the structure of the 1951 Convention and the 'protection gradient' to which it gives rise could be exploited to justify return to countries in which little more is secured than non-refoulement to the country of origin. Such 'protection lite' has sparked debate about what is 'effective protection' in third countries.

14.3.4 The UNHCR and the notion of 'Effective Protection'

The UNHCR has addressed restrictive protection-elsewhere policies by developing its own standards. In 1989, its EXCOM issued a conclusion on irregular secondary movement, stating that refugees who have moved to another state may be returned to another host state only if they are protected against refoulement, 'permitted to remain there and to be treated in *accordance with recognised basic human standards*'.[44] In 1996, the UNHCR elaborated additional criteria, and for the first time qualified the term *protection* as the relevant threshold for return. In an expert seminar on planned EU safe third-country legislation, the UNHCR stated that concepts of 'protection elsewhere' required the sending state to assess whether the receiving state has ratified and complied with international refugee instruments and regional human rights instruments, whether it permits the stay during the determination of asylum procedures, grants fair refugee status determination procedures and, following such procedures, grants '*effective and adequate protection*'.[45]

In 2002, the UNHCR organised an expert round-table talk to define criteria for 'effective protection'.[46] These criteria, known as the 'Lisbon Conclusions', necessitate that:

- there is no likelihood of persecution, of refoulement or of torture or other cruel and degrading treatment;
- there is no other real risk to the life of the person[s] concerned;
- there is a genuine prospect of an accessible durable solution in or from the asylum country, within a reasonable time frame;
- pending a durable solution, stay is permitted under conditions that protect against arbitrary expulsion and deprivation of liberty and that provides for adequate and dignified means of subsistence;
- the unity and integrity of the family is ensured; and
- the specific protection needs of the affected persons, including those deriving from age and gender, are able to be identified and respected.[47]

It is notable that these standards are mostly independent of the 1951 Convention, neither do they require a ratification of the 1951 Convention, nor are they predominantly modelled after the text of the Convention. Rather, some requirements resemble the language of international human rights law, in particular, the wording of 'arbitrary deprivation of liberty', whereas others derive from the mandate and activities of the UNHCR (durable solutions). The only exception is the first criterion, which broadly reflects the 1951 Convention's prohibition of refoulement. The notion of 'effective protection', apart from recourse to a 'durable solution', is not too different from the UNHCR's conception of the internal protection alternative (IPA). In fact, the UNHCR's proposed standards are less generous than those proposed by the UNHCR for the internal flight or relocation alternative (IFA/IRA). This is clear from the criteria laid down in the UNHCR's Guidelines on the concept, which require that there be neither persecution nor serious harm in the area of a proposed IPA, that stay is permitted and that the relocation would not be unduly harsh, including conditions above the level of subsistence, employment opportunities and healthcare.[48] Yet, because the IPA is associated with Article 1A(2) of the 1951 Convention, people who may be referred to such an alternative area of protection are not even refugees in the first place, in contrast to refugees referred to third countries.

Arguably, the UNHCR developed the notion of 'effective protection' out of a desire for a pragmatic set of standards on protection-elsewhere policies, allowing the agency to advocate for improvements without having to reject the use of such policies at all. This goal is understandable from a policy perspective, but may conflict with the UNHCR's supervisory function of the 1951 Convention. The UNHCR's definition of the notion of 'effective protection' is a 'slimmer, trimmer' version of the framework of Articles 2–34 of the 1951 Convention. Its definition of effective protection suggests that in pursuing protection-elsewhere policies, states may restrict the scope of rights under the 1951 Convention, and even fall short of the IPA. Indeed, the design of EU protection-elsewhere policies shows that such restriction is not just a theoretical possibility.

14.3.5 The EU Procedures Directive

The EU Procedures Directive contains a system of 'protection elsewhere' rules through the concepts Safe Third Country and First Country of Asylum. The 2005 Procedures Directive[49] in Article 25(2) provides that member states may consider an application for asylum as inadmissible if:

(a) another member state has granted refugee status;
(b) a country that is not a member state is considered as a first country of asylum for the applicant, pursuant to Article 26;
(c) a country that is not a member state is considered as a safe third country for the applicant, pursuant to Article 27;
(d) the applicant is allowed to remain in the member state concerned on some other grounds and as result of this he/she has been granted a status equivalent to the rights and benefits of the refugee status by virtue of Directive 2004/83/EC [. . .]

Importantly, in the past most of these provisions applied only to refugees, rather than to refugees and people with wider protection needs – that is, people falling under 'subsidiary protection' in EU jargon.[50] This changed under the Recast Procedures Directive, which applies the rules for 'protection elsewhere' to both refugees and people with wider protection needs.[51] Both the 2005 Procedures Directive and the Recast Procedures Directive contain provisions for the quality of protection in another state. Article 35 of the Recast Procedures Directive provides that a country may be considered a first country of asylum for an individual when:

(a) he or she has been recognised in that country as a refugee and he or she can still avail himself/herself of that protection; or
(b) he or she otherwise enjoys sufficient protection in that country, including benefiting from the principle of non-refoulement, provided that he or she will be readmitted to that country.

According to Article 35 of the Directive, in the individual assessment of 'sufficient protection', countries *may* take into account the criteria laid down in Article 38(1) on Safe Third Countries. These criteria include that:

- life and liberty are not threatened on account of race, religion, nationality, membership of a particular social group or political opinion;
- there is no risk of serious harm under the Qualification Directive;
- the principle of non-refoulement is respected;
- the prohibition of removal, in violation of the right to freedom from torture and cruel, inhuman or degrading treatment is respected;
- the possibility exists to request refugee status and, if found to be a refugee, to receive protection in accordance with the Geneva Convention.[52]

Although the Recast Procedures Directive did improve the individual criteria for the application, and for redress against Article 38 (see Article 38(2)), the substantive criteria for the safe third countries have remained almost the same as in Article 27 of the 2005 Procedures Directive. In fact, the only change to these substantive criteria relates to the absence of a real risk of serious harm, included in Article 38(1) of the Recast Directive.

Evidently, the EU standard poses a number of questions. What is 'sufficient protection' under Article 35? Why is an assessment of additional factors related to the quality of protection under Article 38 not mandatory? Why does Article 38 mention threats to life and liberty, rather than to the wider form of harm under the 1951 Convention's notion of 'being persecuted'? No jurisprudence of the member states has clarified the necessary criteria for the quality of protection.

The indirect reference to 'protection in accordance with the [1951] Geneva Convention' creates a curious contrast between the definition of a core of 'protection' (safety), on the one hand, and the full array of 1951 Convention rights and obligations circumscribing protection on the other. It resembles the political compromise that is apparent in the UNHCR's notion of 'effective protection'. Accordingly, the UNHCR did not initially criticise the substantive standards of Article 27 in its observations on the 2005 Directive.[53] However, the UNHCR did recommend using the term *effective protection* rather than *sufficient protection*, to make clear that 'the protection in the third country should be effective and available in practice', and recommended that clear benchmarks be elaborated '[. . .] in line with the standards outlined in the 1951 Convention and the Lisbon Conclusions on "effective protection"'.[54] Finally, the UNHCR argued that its activities in a country of asylum amount to a *prima facie* indication of lacking capacity by the host state of such operations.

> [. . .] the capacity of third states to provide effective protection in practice should be taken into consideration by Member States, particularly if the third state is already hosting large refugee populations. Countries where UNHCR is engaged in refugee status determination under its mandate should, in principle, not be considered first countries of asylum. UNHCR often undertakes such functions because the state has no capacity to conduct status determination or to provide effective protection. [. . .] The return of persons in need of international protection to such countries should [. . .] not be envisaged.[55]

EU law may be interpreted to allow precisely such return, if protection is narrowly conceived only as 'safety'. Could this change with the development of human rights law?

14.4 What future for 'Effective Protection'?

14.4.1 The European Court of Human Rights as a catalyst for broader standards on protection elsewhere

The emergence of the notion of 'effective protection' independent of the 1951 Convention was also spurred by the development of obligations of non-return under international human rights law, in particular by the European Court of Human Rights (ECtHR). The ECtHR has developed a corpus of jurisprudence on the relevance of humanitarian conditions to protection elsewhere.[56] Initially, this jurisprudence was concerned with transfers to signatory states of the European Convention on Human Rights. In the case of *M.S.S. v. Belgium and Greece*, the Court developed criteria for assigning responsibility in situations of serious deprivation or want incompatible with human dignity', under Article 3 of the Convention.[57] The applicant, an Afghan asylum-seeker, had lived for several months in extreme poverty without the possibility of meeting basic needs such as housing, food and hygiene, and was under threat of attack and robbery. Both the receiving state, Greece, and the sending state, Belgium, were found to be in violation of Article 3, because they had knowingly exposed the applicant to such conditions.[58]

In *Sufi and Elmi v. the United Kingdom*, the ECtHR also applied its *M.S.S.* decision to states that were not signatories of the Convention, notably to refugee camps in Kenya. Considering that it was impossible for the applicant to meet the most basic needs in such camps, that he would not be protected against ill-treatment, and that there was no prospect of improvement of the humanitarian situation in a reasonable time frame, the Court found that his removal would violate the United Kingdom's obligation under Article 3 of the European Convention on Human Rights.[59] Yet, the Court was quick to stress the extreme and exceptional nature of the conditions in refugee camps, and the fact that the humanitarian crisis was largely brought about by the actions of the parties to the conflict, in particular their refusal to allow humanitarian agencies to access and distribute aid. Thus in *S.H.H. v. the United Kingdom*, the Court came to a different finding in relation to Afghanistan, because Afghanistan had a functional central government that was in control of the place of return (Kabul), because remaining inadequacies were due to a lack of resources, rather than to deliberate actions or omissions, and because there Afghanistan retained 'a significant presence of international aid agencies'.[60]

Similar to the case of *Sufi and Elmi*, in the case of *Hirsi Jamaa and Others v. Italy*,[61] the ECtHR applied Article 3 of the Convention to an alleged safe third country. The Court held that the pushback of the applicants to Libya by the Italian Navy amounted to a violation of Article 3 of the European Convention on Human

Rights, because they faced detention in inhumane conditions, the risk of torture, poor hygiene conditions, lack of appropriate medical care, 'particularly precarious living conditions' and the risk of refoulement.[62]

In sum, jurisprudence by the ECtHR may hardly be seen as a catalyst for the development of standards for protection elsewhere. Although the European Convention on Human Rights' case law on the non-return of asylum-seekers outside the space of the European Convention on Human Rights is certainly a positive development, the fixation on Article 3 of the European Convention on Human Rights makes this case law a significantly narrower benchmark for 'effective' protection than the framework of 1951 Convention rights.

14.4.2 Reaffirming the 1951 Convention as a benchmark for protection elsewhere

It has become apparent that the 1951 Convention's dissociation of refugee status and asylum lies at the heart of states creating protection-elsewhere policies. Yet, the Convention also provides principled reasons against the provision of 'protection' by actors other than states. Its framework of rights and obligations may translate into safeguards against the application of protection elsewhere policies, where these rights are not being respected. If applied to protection-elsewhere policies, the 1951 Convention's rights framework would include the rights acquired by refugees in their sending states; thus all Convention entitlement that applies once a refugee is physically present and lawfully staying, that is, non-refoulement, freedom from arbitrary detention and penalisation for illegal entry, physical security, freedom of religion, freedom from deprivation (access to food and shelter, access to healthcare), property rights, family unity, education, self-employment, documentation of identity and status and judicial and administrative assistance.[63] It is true that Article 32 of the 1951 Convention only prohibits expulsion of refugees who are 'lawfully present' on a state's territory. States have interpreted the notion of 'lawful stay' rather restrictively, meaning that onward movement, even when refugee status in the first country of asylum is recognised, does not spark a lawful stay.[64] Yet, analysis of the drafting history reveals that the term *lawful stay* was conceived broadly; the term encompasses the authorisation to stay, pending application of asylum.[65]

Where the 1951 Convention determines the necessary safeguards for protection-elsewhere policies, they clearly exceed obligations of non-return for risks of inhumane or degrading treatment. In addition to the Michigan Guidelines, there is also some judicial support for such a view. In Denmark, the Refugee Board considered whether the Kurdish Autonomous Region could be deemed a 'first country of asylum' for an Iranian citizen. The applicants had been registered refugees with the UNHCR and lived in a refugee camp in the Suleimaniyah province, formerly supported by the UNHCR, but not run by the agency or one of its implementing partners at the time of the decision. The Refugee Board required as an 'absolute minimum' for first countries of asylum the protection against refoulement, the possibility of entering and staying legally and of security.[66]

However, it also referred to EXCOM Conclusion 58 (1989), in order to identify additional criteria for basic socioeconomic needs. In addition to non-refoulement and the legal conditions of stay, the socioeconomic rights of the applicant, including rights granted under the 1951 Convention, the Board considered access to housing, education, the possibility of moving within Kurdistan, access to medical care, permission to work in the private and public sectors and the right to own property.[67] The Refugee Board concluded that the applicant's living conditions were of such a nature that they violated basic humanitarian rights. Importantly, however, the Refugee Board found that 'the fact that UNHCR make asylum assessment and the applicant is required to stay in a designated place, managed by UNHCR' was insufficient in itself to disqualify Kurdistan as a first country of asylum.[68] This contrasts with a decision of the Dutch Council of State (*Raad van State*), which rejected the possibility of non-state actors providing protection in third countries. The Council of State seized on the question of whether the ICC, which in the past managed to find third countries for endangered witnesses, could be said to protect a person, rendering that person's claim for international protection inadmissible.[69] The Council discussed the basic premises of the 1951 Convention, stating that the 1951 Convention was to provide a backup for stripped protection in the home state, including rights that clearly exceeded non-refoulement.[70] It argued that, in principle, such protection may be guaranteed only by states. This was because international refugee law required more than a negative obligation to not expose refugees to a danger, namely, a positive obligation to grant a certain quality of protection.[71]

There may also be more fundamental reasons for casting doubt on applying protection-elsewhere policies to states in which the UNHCR runs the asylum system. The Convention provides for a set of rights and obligations that complement international human rights law.[72] Refugee law is backed by human rights law, to define the character of surrogate protection for a lack of protection in the country of origin. Since it is geared at vesting refugees with entitlement under international law, surrogate protection is *rights enfranchisement*. This implies *accountability for protection*, that is, liability for injuries arising from acts or omissions qualifying as breaches under international law.[73] A legal understanding of accountability, and in particular a rights-based one, focuses on legal or quasi-legal obligations for conduct, and to quasi-legal or legal remedies, including mechanisms to challenge decisions and misconduct, and pecuniary or non-pecuniary compensations for damages incurred.[74] It is relatively clear that the UNHCR is not legally accountable to the same extent as states. Although the legal framework for the legal responsibility of non-state actors has evolved considerably,[75] there are still many challenges to a legal regime on par with states' legal regimes. First, the test of 'effective control', which determines legal responsibility, has been the subject of considerable debate in the courts. For instance, the ECtHR treated the notion as a factual test that combines personal and territorial aspects in its jurisprudence on extraterritorial jurisdiction. Conduct was attributable when individuals were taken into custody, or when a state through the *effective control of the relevant territory and its inhabitants* abroad as a consequence of military occupation or through the consent, invitation or acquiescence of the Government of that territory, *exercises all or some of the public powers normally to be exercised by that Government.*[76]

Although most of the debate on attribution of conduct revolved around international peacekeeping operations, it is doubtful whether the criterion of effective control would apply to the UNHCR, even in situations of outsourcing. It is also unclear in which circumstances the UNHCR would bear responsibility. Given the effective control test, if responsibility were to be shared, it would be by countries that have outsourced to the UNHCR.[77] The International Law Commission's (ILC) Articles on State Responsibility[78] suggest that responsibility for a wrongful act under international law may be shared among several states, or between a state and an international organisation.[79] Also, the Draft articles on the responsibility of international organisations provide for an international organisation being responsible for aiding or assisting a state or another international organisation in committing a wrongful act where it does so with knowledge of the circumstances.[80] Jammyr argues that where the UNHCR fails to respect or protect customary law obligations, and the host state is willing but unable to give effect to its human rights obligations, responsibility for a violation of international human rights law is shared by the UNHCR and the state.[81] She argues that this contrasts with situations in which the state hosting UNHCR operations is simply unwilling to uphold its human rights obligtions. In such cases, responsibility for violations falls on the state alone.[82] However, there are open questions concerning how to determine the capacity and willingness of states to fulfil their human rights obligations.

In sum, if the 1951 Convention provides a yardstick for effective protection, the accountability then required raises issues of compliance, should protection-elsewhere policies be applied to countries in which the UNHCR takes on core protection tasks.

14.5 Conclusion

The safeguards of current EU protection-elsewhere policies and the UNHCR develop a notion of 'effective protection' independent of the 1951 Convention. Together with international and regional human rights law, this notion of 'effective protection' provides for the legality of protection-elsewhere policies. Yet, 'effective protection' so defined is far narrower than those obligations under the 1951 Convention, which apply once refugees are physically present on a state's territory. In turn, European human rights law currently remains fixated on violations of the rights to freedom from torture, or inhuman or degrading treatment as a safeguard against return. This focuses on the direst humanitarian conditions only, rather than on the rights refugees ought to enjoy under the 1951 Convention once they are lawfully on the territory.

The 1951 Convention is both a blessing and a curse to the development of protection-elsewhere policies: on the one hand, its dissociation of refugee status and asylum lies at the heart of states creating such policies; on the other hand, the Convention also provides principled reasons against the provision of 'protection' by actors other than states. The Convention's rights framework for refugees physically present/lawfully staying translates into safeguards against the application of protection-elsewhere policies where these rights are not respected. As the Convention provisions define the meaning of protection under the Convention, they also provide the test for the wording, 'receive protection in accordance with the Geneva Convention', in Article 38 of the EU Procedures Directive. This contribution does not argue that the UNHCR should refrain from, or is not legally entitled to, supporting asylum states, including by running RSD procedures or by running camps. Indeed, procedural standards for RSD by the UNHCR have improved significantly, and often the UNHCR's RSD may be better than those of states. Similarly, the agency is committed to assuring the best possible conditions in and outside of camps. Yet, although international law does allow for responsibility-sharing arrangements for refugees, it should preclude situations in which UNHCR operations are used to dilute state responsibilities.

Notes

1   The author is grateful for the comments by participants of the GLOTHRO Workshop 'Human Rights and the Dark Side of Globalisation: Transnational Law Enforcement and Migration Control', Copenhagen, 9–10 December 2013, especially to Ralph Wilde, Isabelle Swerissen, Thomas Gammeltoft-Hansen and Jens Vedsted-Hansen.
2   Michelle Foster, 'Protection Elsewhere: The Legal Implications of Requiring Refugees to Seek Protection in another State', *Michigan Journal of International Law* 28 no. 2 (2007), 223.
3   For an analysis of the emergence of various forms of 'protection elsewhere' rules, see Cathryn Costello, 'The Asylum Procedures Directive and the Proliferation of Safe Country Practices: Deterrence, Deflection and the Dismantling of International Protection?', *European Journal of Migration and Law* 7 no. 1 (2005), 35.
4   Foster (n. 1); Michelle Foster, 'Responsibility Sharing or Shifting?: "Safe" Third Countries and International Law', *Refuge* 25 no. 2 (2008), 64.
5   James C. Hathaway, 'A Reconsideration of the Underlying Premise of Refugee Law', *Harvard International Law Journal* 31 no. 1 (1990), 129, 166; Guy S. Goodwin-Gill and Jane McAdam, *The Refugee in International Law*, 3rd edn (Oxford: Oxford University Press, 2007), 355; Michelle Foster, 'Protection Elsewhere: The Legal Implications of Requiring Refugees to Seek Protection in another State', 226.
6   Conclusion No. 15 (XXX) – 1979.
7   As stated by the 'Michigan Guidelines on Protection Elsewhere', an authoritative document compiled by an international law scholar at an expert seminar, rules on protection elsewhere may lead to allocating responsibilities among states more fairly.
8   UN High Commissioner for Refugees (UNHCR), *UNHCR Position on Readmission Agreements, 'Protection Elsewhere' and Asylum Policy*, 1 August 1994, 3 European Series 2, 465, available at: www.refworld.org/docid/3ae6b31cb8.html [accessed 12 June 2014].
9   Examples include Australia's Migration Act (1958) section 36(3)–(5A); Directive 2013/32/EU of the European Parliament and the Council of 26 June 2013 on common procedures for granting and withdrawing international protection (recast) [2013]

OJ L180/60; Regulation (EU) No. 604/2013 of the European Parliament and of the Council of 26 June 2013 establishing the criteria and mechanisms for determining the Member State responsible for examining an application for international protection lodged in one of the Member States by a third-country national or a stateless person. For a list of case law, see James C. Hathaway and Michelle Foster, *The Law of Refugee Status* 2nd edn (Cambridge: Cambridge University Press, 2014), chapter 1, section 1.2.

10 This is acknowledged even in the otherwise extremely critical Michigan Guidelines on Protection Elsewhere.

11 Thomas Gammeltoft-Hansen, *Access to Asylum: International Refugee Law and the Globalisation of Migration Control* (Cambridge, Cambridge University Press, 2011); Thomas Gammeltoft-Hansen and Ninna Nyberg Sørensen, *The Migration Industry and the Commercialization of International Migration* (Abingdon: Routledge, 2012).

12 For instance, see Article 4 of the most recent readmission agreement of the EU with Turkey, Council Decision of 14 April 2014 on the conclusion of the Agreement between the European Union and the Republic of Turkey on the readmission of persons residing without authorisation, OJ L134/1.

13 Mariagiuila Giuffré, 'Readmission Agreements and Refugee Rights: From a Critique to a Proposal', *Refugee Survey Quarterly* 32 no. 3 (2013), 79.

14 See §8 of the Statute of the Office of the United Nations High Commissioner for Refugees, 14 December 1950, A/RES/428 (V).

15 See UNHCR Statistical Yearbooks 2002–2011; UNHCR Note on International Protection 2012.

16 Ibid.

17 Joanna Apap, Sergio Carrera and Kemal Kirişçi, 'Turkey in the European Area of Freedom, Security and Justice' CEPS EU–Turkey Working Papers No. 3 (Brussels: CEPS, 2004).

18 For an inventory of readmission agreements, see the data set compiled by the European University Institute, Robert Schuman Centre for Advanced Studies, available at: http://rsc.eui.eu/RDP/research/analyses/ra/ [accessed 12 June 2014].

19 See Alexander Betts, Gil Loescher and James Milner, The *United Nations High Commissioner for Refugess (UNHCR): The Politics and Practice of Refugee Protection*, 2nd edn (London: Routledge, 2012).

20 See recital 4, 'considering that the grant of asylum may place unduly heavy burdens on certain countries, and that a satisfactory solution of a problem of which the United Nations has recognised the international scope and nature cannot therefore be achieved without international cooperation [. . .]'.

21 ICC Trial Chamber II, Decision on an Amicus Curiae application and on the 'Requête tendant à obtenir présentations des témoins DRC-D02-P-03509, DRC-D02-P-0236, DRC-D02-P-0228 aux autorités néerlandaises aux fins d'asile' (Articles 68 and 93(7) of the Statute), June 2011, ICC-01/04-01/07-3003-tENG, para. 64.

22 Foster, 'Responsibility Sharing or Shifting?' (n. 3), 71.

23 Michael Alexander, 'Refugee status determination conducted by UNHCR', *International Journal of Refugee Law* 11 no. 2 (1999), 251.

24 Michael Kagan, 'The Beleaguered Gatekeeper: Protection Challenges Posed by UNHCR Refugee Status Determination', *International Journal of Refugee Law* 18 no. 1 (2006), 1.

25 Procedural Standards for Refugee Status Determination under UNHCR's Mandate, 1 September 2005, available at: www.refworld.org/pdfid/42d66dd84.pdf [accessed 18 November 2014].

26 Ibid.

27 Michael Kagan, 'UNHCR's RSD policy: Quick guide', available at: http://rsdwatch. wordpress.com/unhcrs-rsd-policy-a-guide/ [accessed 18 November 2014].

28 Michael Kagan (Asylum Access), No Margin for Error – Monitoring the Fairness of Refugee Status Determination Procedures at Selected UNHCR Field Offices in 2007 (Geneva: UNHCR RSD [Refugee Status Determination] Watch, 2008).

29 Helsinki Citizens' Assembly – Turkey, Refugee Advocacy and Support Program, An Evaluation of UNHCR Turkey's Compliance with UNHCR's RSD Procedural Standards, September 2007, available at: www.hyd.org.tr/staticfiles/files/hca_procedural_standards_report.doc [accessed 12 June 2014].

30 Ibid.

31 Harrel-Bond and Verdirame in the late 1990s conducted research in Uganda and Kenya, leading them to conclude that refugee camps were spaces 'beyond the rule of law' in which 'violations of the full catalogue of human rights' occurred – camps were unsafe, did not secure freedom of expression and of religion, and inhibited self-reliance. Guido Verdirame and Barbara Harrell-Bond, *Rights in Exile: Janus-Faced Humanitarianism* (Oxford: Berghahn, 2005), 16

32 Amnesty International, *Kenya: From Life Without Peace to Peace Without Life: The Treatment of Somali Refugees and Asylum-Seekers in Kenya*, 8 December 2010, AFR 32/015/2010, available at: www.refworld.org/docid/4cff404729.html [accessed 18 November 2014]; Human Rights Watch, *'Welcome to Kenya', Police Abuse of Somali Refugees*, 17 June 2010, ISBN: 1-56432-641-1, available at: www.refworld.org/docid/4c1b2b5b2.html [accessed 18 November 2014].

33 James C. Hathaway, *The Rights of Refugees under International Law* (Cambridge: Cambridge University Press, 2005), 154–190.

34 See Articles 13; 15; 17; 19; 21; 22; 26 of the 1951 Convention.

35 Also Hathaway, *The Rights of Refugees under International Law*, 332.

36 Foster, 'Protection Elsewhere: The Legal Implications of Requiring Refugees to Seek Protection in another State' (n. 1).

37 Foster, 'Responsibility Sharing or Shifting?' (n. 3), 67, pointing to the Federal Court of Australia's case of *NAGV v. Minister*.

38 Stephen H. Legomsky, 'Secondary Refugee Movements and the Return of Asylum Seekers to Third Countries: The Meaning of Effective Protection', *International Journal of Refugee Law* 15 no. 4 (2003), 567, 620. Legomsky drew on Article 16 of the Articles on State Responsibility on aid or assistance to the commitment of a wrongful act. For the complicity principle, see also Helmut Philipp Aust, *Complicity and the Law of State Responsibility* (Cambridge: Cambridge University Press. 2011).

39 Ibid., 620.

40 Ibid., 624.

41 Ibid., 642.

42 One option considered is to restrict the scope to provisions under the 1951 Convention, which cannot be subject to reservation.

43 Thomas Gammeltoft-Hansen, 'The Extraterritorialisation of Asylum and the Advent of "Protection Lite"', Danish Institute for International Studies Working Paper no. 2007/2.

44 EXCOM Conclusion No. 58 (XL) (1989), emphasis added.

45 UN High Commissioner for Refugees, *Considerations on the 'Safe Third Country' Concept* (1996), emphasis added.

46 UN High Commissioner for Refugees, Summary Conclusions on the Concept of 'Effective Protection' in the Context of Secondary Movements of Refugees and Asylum-Seekers (Lisbon Expert Roundtable, 9–10 December 2002), February 2003 (2003).

47 Erika Feller, 'Statement by Ms. Erika Feller, Director, Department of International Protection, at the fifty-fifth session of the Executive Committee of the High Commissioner's Programme, 7 October 2004', available at: www.unhcr.org/429d6f8e4.html [accessed 18 November 2014].

48 UN High Commissioner for Refugees, Guidelines on International Protection No. 4: 'Internal Flight or Relocation Alternative' Within the Context of Article 1A(2) of the 1951 Convention and/or 1967 Protocol Relating to the Status of Refugees, 23 July 2003, HCR/GIP/03/04 (2003).

49 Council Directive 2005/85/EC of 1 December 2005 on minimum standards for procedures by Member States granting and withdrawing refugee status [2005] OJ L326/13.

50 Article 15 of the Directive 2011/95/EU of the European Parliament and of the Council of 13 December 2011 on standards for the qualification of third-country nationals or stateless persons as beneficiaries of international protection, for a uniform status for refugees or for persons eligible for subsidiary protection and for the content of the protection granted (recast), OJ L337/9.

51 Article 32 (2) of the Directive 2013/32/EU (Procedures Directive).

52 Article 38 of the Procedures Directive, emphasis added.

53 UN High Commissioner for Refugees (UNHCR), UNHCR Provisional Comments on the Proposal for a Council Directive on Minimum Standards on Procedures in Member States for Granting and Withdrawing Refugee Status (Council Document 14203/04, Asile 64, of 9 November 2004), 10 February 2005, available at: www. refworld.org/docid/42492b302.html [accessed 18 November 2014], 34.

54 UN High Commissioner for Refugees, Improving Asylum Procedures – Comparative Analysis and Recommendations for Law and Practice, UNHCR research project on the application of key provisions of the Asylum Procedures Directive in selected Member States (2010), also Costello (n. 2) 58.

55 UNHCR Provisional Comments on the Proposal for an Asylum Procedures Directive, 34–35.

56 For a more detailed analysis, see Helene Lambert, ' "Safe Third Country" in the European Union: An Evolving Concept in International Law and Implications for the UK', *Journal of Immigration, Asylum and Nationality Law* 26 no. 4 (2012), 318.

57 *M.S.S. v. Belgium and Greece*, no. 30696/09, European Convention on Human Rights 2011, para. 253.

58 Ibid., para. 367.

59 *Sufi and Elmi v. the United Kingsom*, no(s) 8319/07; 11449/07 (ECtHR 28 June 2011).

60 *S.H.H. v. the United Kingdom*, no. 60367/10 (ECtHR 29 January 2013) para. 91.

61 *Hirsi Jamaa and Others v. Italy*, no. 27765/09, European Convention on Human Rights 2012.

62 Ibid., para. 125–126. For an analysis of *Hirsi Jamaa and Others v. Italy*, see also Cathryn Costello, 'Courting Access to Asylum in Europe: Recent Supranational Jurisprudence Explored', *Human Rights Law Review* 12 no. 2 (2012), 287.

63 Hathaway, *The Rights of Refugees under International Law*, 278.

64 Consider the example of the European Agreement on the Transfer of Responsibility for Refugees, Strasbourg, 16 October 1980, CETS No. 107.

65 Hathaway, *The Rights of Refugees under International Law*, 187.

66 Flygtningenævnet iran/2012/20.

67 Flygtningenævnet iran/2012/20, marking a significant development from an opposite decision in Iran/2011/15.

68 Flygtningenævnet iran/2012/20.

69 *Raad van State*, 12 November 2013, 201303197/2/V3 and 201303198/2/V3.

70 Ibid., 4.6.

71 Ibid., 1.12.

72 On this point, see Hathaway, *The Rights of Refugees under International Law*, 110. For an opposing view, Vincent Chetail, 'Are Refugee Rights Human Rights?: An Unorthodox Questioning of the Relations between Refugee Law and Human Rights Law', in *Migration and Human Rights*, ed. Ruth Rubio Marin, 19–72 (Oxford: Oxford University Press, 2011).

73 Compare International Law Association, Accountability of International Organisations, Berlin Conference, final report (2004).

74 See Article 2 of the ICCPR, according to which State Parties undertake:

(a) To ensure that any person whose rights or freedoms as herein recognised are violated shall have an effective remedy, notwithstanding that the violation has been committed by persons acting in an official capacity;

(b) To ensure that any person claiming such a remedy shall have his right thereto determined by competent judicial, administrative or legislative authorities, or by any other competent authority provided for by the legal system of the State and to develop the possibilities of judicial remedy;

(c) To ensure that the competent authorities shall enforce such remedies when granted.

75 Interpretation of the Agreement of 25 March 1951 between the WHO and Egypt Advisory Opinion, ICJ Reports 1980, 73. International Law Commission, Draft articles on the responsibility of international organisations, with commentaries, Adopted by the International Law Commission at its sixty-third session (A/66/10) (*Yearbook of the International Law Commission* II, Part Two, 2011), Article 1, 'The present draft articles also apply to the international responsibility of a State for an internationally wrongful act in connection with the conduct of an international organisation'.

76 *Al-Skeini v. UK.* no. 55721/07, European Convention on Human Rights 2011. For an extensive analysis on the issues around attribution of conduct, see Marko Milanovic, *Extraterritorial Application of Human Rights Treaties: Law, Principles, and Policy* (Oxford: Oxford University Press, 2013).

77 Ralph Wilde, 'Quis Custodiet Ipsos Custodes? Why and How UNHCR Governance of "Development" Refugee Camps Should be Subject to International Human Rights Law', *Yale Human Rights and Development Law Journal* 1 (1998), 107–128; Mark Pallis, 'The Operation of UNHCR's Accountability Mechanisms', *The New York University Journal of International Law and Politics* 37 no. 4 (2006), 869.

78 For the text of the Articles see *UN General Assembly, Fifty-sixth session (2001), Report of the International Law Commission, A/56/10* (2001). The articles were endorsed by the GA in UN GA Resolution 56/83 (12 December 2001).

79 See Article 19. 'This chapter is without prejudice to the international responsibility, under other provisions of these articles, of the State which commits the act in question, or of any other State'. According to the ILC, the article 'preserves the responsibility of the State which has committed the internationally wrongful act, albeit with the aid or assistance, under the direction and control or subject to the coercion of another State. It recognises that the attribution of international responsibility to an assisting, directing or coercing State does not preclude the responsibility of the assisted, directed or coerced State [. . .] [and] makes clear that the provisions of chapter IV are without prejudice to any other basis for establishing the responsibility of the assisting, directing or coercing State under any rule of international law defining particular conduct as wrongful'. See Draft articles on Responsibility of States for Internationally Wrongful Acts, with commentaries, 2001.

80 International Law Commission, Draft articles on the responsibility of international organisations, with commentaries, Adopted by the International Law Commission at its sixty-third session (A/66/10) (*Yearbook of the International Law Commission*, 2011, vol II, Part Two, 2011), Article 14.

81 Maja Janmyr, *Protecting Civilians in Refugee Camps: Unable and Unwilling States, UNHCR and International Responsibility* (Leiden: Martinus Nijhoff Publishers, 2014).

82 Ibid.

Bibliography

Alexander, Michael. 'Refugee Status Determination Conducted by UNHCR'. *International Journal of Refugee Law* 11 no. 2 (1999): 251–289.

Apap, Joanna, Sergio Carrera and Kemal Kirişci. 'Turkey in the European Area of Freedom, Security and Justice'. CEPS EU–Turkey Working Papers 3, August 2004. Brussels: Centre for European Policy Studies, 2004.

Aust, Helmut Philipp. *Complicity and the Law of State Responsibility*. Cambridge: Cambridge University Press, 2011.

Betts, Alexander, Gil Loescher and James Milner. *The United Nations High Commissioner for Refugees (UNHCR): The Politics and Practice of Refugee Protection*, 2nd edition. London: Routledge, 2012.

Chetail, Vincent. 'Are Refugee Rights Human Rights?: An Unorthodox Questioning of the Relations between Refugee Law and Human Rights Law'. In *Migration and Human Rights*, edited by Ruth Rubio Marin, 19–72. Oxford University Press, 2011.

Compare International Law Association, Accountability of International Organisations, Berlin Conference, final report (2004).

Costello, Cathryn. 'The Asylum Procedures Directive and the Proliferation of Safe Country Practices: Deterrence, Deflection and the Dismantling of International Protection?'. *European Journal of Migration and Law* 7 no. 1 (2005): 35–69.

Costello, Cathryn. 'Courting Access to Asylum in Europe: Recent Supranational Jurisprudence Explored'. *Human Rights Law Review* 12 no. 2 (2012): 287–339.

Foster, Michelle. 'Protection Elsewhere: The Legal Implications of Requiring Refugees to Seek Protection in another State'. *Michigan Journal of International Law* 28 no. 2 (2007): 223–286.

Foster, Michelle. 'Responsibility Sharing or Shifting?: "Safe" Third Countries and International Law'. *Refuge* 25 no. 2 (2008): 64–78.

Gammeltoft-Hansen, Thomas. 'The Extraterritorialisation of Asylum and the Advent of "Protection Lite"'. DIIS Working Paper 2007:2. Copenhagen: Danish Institute for International Studies, January 2007.

Gammeltoft-Hansen, Thomas. *Access to Asylum: International Refugee Law and the Globalisation of Migration Control*. Cambridge: Cambridge University Press, 2011.

Gammeltoft-Hansen, Thomas, and Ninna Nyberg Sørensen. *The Migration Industry and the Commercialization of International Migration*. Abingdon: Routledge, 2012.

Giuffré, Mariagiuila. 'Readmission Agreements and Refugee Rights: From a Critique to a Proposal'. *Refugee Survey Quarterly* 32 no. 3 (2013): 79–111.

Goodwin-Gill, Guy S., and Jane McAdam. *The Refugee in International Law*, 3rd edition. Oxford: Oxford University Press, 2007.

Hathaway, James C. 'A Reconsideration of the Underlying Premise of Refugee Law'. *Harvard International Law Journal* 31 no. 1 (1990): 129–182.

Hathaway, James C. *The Rights of Refugees under International Law*. Cambridge: Cambridge University Press, 2005.

Hathaway, James C., and Michelle Foster. *The Law of Refugee Status*, 2nd edition. Cambridge: Cambridge University Press, 2014.

Janmyr, Maja. *Protecting Civilians in Refugee Camps: Unable and Unwilling States, UNHCR and International Responsibility*. Leiden: Martinus Nijhoff Publishers, 2014.

Kagan, Michael. 'The Beleaguered Gatekeeper: Protection Challenges Posed by UNHCR Refugee Status Determination'. *International Journal of Refugee Law* 18 no. 1 (2006): 1–29.

Kagan, Michael. 'No Margin for Error – Monitoring the Fairness of Refugee Status Determination Procedures at Selected UNHCR Field Offices in 2007'. Geneva: UNHCR RSD [Refugee Status Determination] Watch, 2008.

'Kenya: From Life Without Peace to Peace Without Life: The Treatment of Somali Refugees and Asylum-Seekers in Kenya' London: Amnesty International, 2010. Accessed 18 November 2014. www.refworld.org/docid/4cff404729.html.

Lambert, Helene. ' "Safe Third Country" in the European Union: An Evolving Concept in International Law and Implications for the UK'. *Journal of Immigration, Asylum and Nationality Law* 26 no. 4 (2012): 318–336.

Legomsky, Stephen H. 'Secondary Refugee Movements and the Return of Asylum Seekers to Third Countries: The Meaning of Effective Protection'. *International Journal of Refugee Law* 15 no. 4 (2003): 567–677.

Milanovic, Marko. *Extraterritorial Application of Human Rights Treaties: Law, Principles, and Policy.* Oxford: Oxford University Press, 2013.

Pallis, Mark. 'The Operation of UNHCR's Accountability Mechanisms'. *The New York University Journal of International Law and Politics* 37 no. 4 (2006): 869–918.

Swerissen, Isabelle. 'Protection Without Allocation: The Gap in International Refugee Law'. Paper presented at the Danish Institute for Human Rights, Copenhagen, 10 December 2013.

UN High Commissioner for Refugees, Summary Conclusions on the Concept of 'Effective Protection' in the Context of Secondary Movements of Refugees and Asylum-Seekers (Lisbon Expert Roundtable, 9–10 December 2002), February 2003.

Verdirame, Guido, and Barabara Harrell-Bond. *Rights in Exile: Janus-Faced Humanitarianism.* Oxford: Berghahn, 2005.

'"*Welcome to Kenya*": *Police Abuse of Somali Refugees*'. New York: Human Rights Watch, 2010. Accessed 18 November 2014. www.refworld.org/docid/4c1b2b5b2.html.

Wilde, Ralph. 'Quis Custodiet Ipsos Custodes?: Why and How UNHCR Governance of "Development" Refugee Camps Should be Subject to International Human Rights Law'. *Yale Human Rights and Development Law Journal* 1 (1998): 107–128.

INDEX

access to asylum 14, 216–17, 228, 332
accountability 14, 110, 254, 307, 344–5;
  gap 38; judicial 240, 252
acquiescence 56, 84, 86, 345
actors 27–44, 239–41, 243–4, 247–8,
  252–6, 273, 275–8, 281–3; commercial
  4, 9; multiplicity of 27, 30, 68, 247;
  participating 35, 39, 281, 285; primary
  273, 275, 286; private 13, 202, 238;
  relevant 35–7; symmetrical 13, 115;
  third-state 194, 202–3, 205
administrative assistance 337, 343
admissibility 57, 206, 258, 334
admission refusals 318, 324, 326; reasons
  for 322–5
Aegean Sea 162, 171, 180, 303–4
Afghanistan 58, 60–1, 68, 342
AFSJ see Area of Freedom Security and
  Justice
aid 33, 178, 202–3, 226–7, 277–80,
  285–6, 295, 307–8; or assistance 10, 86,
  179, 278–9, 281–2; rendering 279–80,
  285–6
aiding states 39, 203, 279–80, 284
air borders 242
aircraft 140, 243, 246, 273, 297
airports 127, 194–5, 198–9, 205, 238,
  322
airspace 57, 68–9, 84, 109, 145
airstrikes 57, 83, 91
Albania 284
Albanians 322, 324

alleged human rights violations 9, 11, 14,
  60, 273, 276, 283
allocation of international responsibilities
  14, 238–9
Al-Skeini 10, 57–60, 84, 123, 224
Amnesty International 298, 300
anti-piracy operations *see* counter-
  piracy
applicable human rights law 121, 178
Arab Spring 294, 302–4
Area of Freedom Security and Justice
  (AFSJ) 242
Arendt Hannah 127
Argentina 102
ARIO *see* Articles on the Responsibility
  of International Organisations
armed conflict 12, 54, 59–61, 70
armed drones 12, 81–95
armed robbery at sea 140, 145
arrests 34, 121–2, 141, 145–6, 149–50,
  296–8, 301, 306; pre-departure 14,
  297–8, 306, 308
Articles on State Responsibility (ASR)
  29, 171–3, 201–5, 226–7, 248–50,
  252 6, 276, 278 80
Articles on the Responsibility of
  International Organisations (ARIO)
  31–2, 35, 169, 171, 178, 248–55, 278,
  308
ASR *see* Articles on State Responsibility
assignment of responsibility 14, 30, 34–7,
  43, 201, 258, 333, 342

 Taylor & Francis eBooks

Helping you to choose the right eBooks for your Library

Add Routledge titles to your library's digital collection today. Taylor and Francis ebooks contains over 50,000 titles in the Humanities, Social Sciences, Behavioural Sciences, Built Environment and Law.

Choose from a range of subject packages or create your own!

Benefits for you
- » Free MARC records
- » COUNTER-compliant usage statistics
- » Flexible purchase and pricing options
- » All titles DRM-free.

Benefits for your user
- » Off-site, anytime access via Athens or referring URL
- » Print or copy pages or chapters
- » Full content search
- » Bookmark, highlight and annotate text
- » Access to thousands of pages of quality research at the click of a button.

REQUEST YOUR **FREE** INSTITUTIONAL TRIAL TODAY

Free Trials Available
We offer free trials to qualifying academic, corporate and government customers.

eCollections – Choose from over 30 subject eCollections, including:

Archaeology	Language Learning
Architecture	Law
Asian Studies	Literature
Business & Management	Media & Communication
Classical Studies	Middle East Studies
Construction	Music
Creative & Media Arts	Philosophy
Criminology & Criminal Justice	Planning
Economics	Politics
Education	Psychology & Mental Health
Energy	Religion
Engineering	Security
English Language & Linguistics	Social Work
Environment & Sustainability	Sociology
Geography	Sport
Health Studies	Theatre & Performance
History	Tourism, Hospitality & Events

For more information, pricing enquiries or to order a free trial, please contact your local sales team: www.tandfebooks.com/page/sales

 Routledge
Taylor & Francis Group

The home of Routledge books

www.tandfebooks.com